D0207772

Technology and Society
under Lenin and Stalin

Studies of
the Russian Institute,
Columbia University

Technology and Society under Lenin and Stalin

Origins of the Soviet Technical Intelligentsia, 1917-1941

KENDALL E. BAILES

PRINCETON UNIVERSITY PRESS
Princeton, New Jersey

Copyright © 1978 by Princeton University Press

Published by Princeton University Press, Princeton, New Jersey
In the United Kingdom: Princeton University Press, Guildford, Surrey

All Rights Reserved

Library of Congress Cataloging in Publication Data will
be found on the last printed page of this book

The Russian Institute of Columbia University sponsors the *Studies of the
Russian Institute* in the belief that their publication contributes to scholarly
research and public understanding. In this way the Institute, while not
necessarily endorsing their conclusions, is pleased to make available the
results of some of the research conducted under its auspices. A list of the
Studies of the Russian Institute appears at the back of the book.

This book has been composed in Linotype Times Roman

Printed in the United States of America
by Princeton University Press, Princeton, New Jersey

Chapter Four first appeared in *The American Historical Review*, April, 1974,
under the title, "Stalin and Technocratic Thinking Among Soviet Engineers."
Used by permission.

Chapter Fourteen first appeared in *Technology and Culture*, January, 1976.
© 1976 by the Society for the History of Technology. Published by the
University of Chicago Press. Used by permission.

CONTENTS

CONTENTS

LIST OF ILLUSTRATIONS

To my family and friends,
whose love and faith
have been my greatest support

PREFACE

"Next to ingratitude," an American sage once wrote, "the most painful thing to bear is gratitude." Prefaces should be as short as possible, in the hope that neither an author's gratitude nor his ingratitude, if he has forgotten someone, will be too painful to bear. The present book began as a dissertation under the auspices of the Russian Institute and History Department at Columbia University. That initial work was a study of the technical intelligentsia in the years from 1928 to 1934, a pivotal time in its development. The critical comments of the dissertation committee (Loren Graham, director; Alexander Erlich, Leopold Haimson, John Hazard, and Marc Raeff) caused me to rethink my subsequent work considerably. The result represents a major change from the dissertation, both in the span of time covered and the scope of the questions asked.

In the intervening years a number of scholars and students have been involved in offering research assistance and suggestions. Particular thanks go to my colleagues in the Department of History at the University of California, Irvine, and to such far-flung scholars in the fields of Soviet studies and the history of technology as Harley Balzer, Alain Besançon, William Blackwell, James Brittain, Stephen F. Cohen, Sheila Fitzpatrick, Loren Graham, David Landes, Linda Lubrano, John P. McKay, Robert H. McNeal, Louis Siegelbaum, Peter and Susan Solomon, S. Frederick Starr, Charles Susskind, Robert Tucker, and Reginald Zelnik. In the Soviet Union, my advisor in the History Department at Moscow State University, V. Z. Drobizhev, and the scientific secretary at the Academy of Sciences' Institute for the History of Science and Technology, V. A. Volkov, were particularly helpful in steering me to the existing Soviet historical literature on this subject (both published and in unpublished dissertations). Although they will doubtless disagree with the interpretation presented here, their help was given in the best spirit of the U.S.-U.S.S.R. Cultural Exchange Agreement. I also wish to thank the International Research and Exchanges Board (IREX), which supported my travel to the U.S.S.R. in the summer and fall of 1973, as well as the Humanities' Institute of the University of California and the Regents of that institution, who supported this work at several crucial points. The Joint Committee on Soviet Studies of the American Council of Learned Societies and the Social Science Research Council provided a six-months' fellowship during 1975 during which I completed writing the book. The Kennan Institute

xi

for Advanced Russian Studies provided a short-term grant to check references at the Library of Congress in the final stages of the book's preparation. Not least among those whose help should be acknowledged are several students who assisted in the preparation of the computer study and checked references: Meredith Borton, Misha Norton, David Romagnolo, and J. C. Varada. The usual disclaimer, of course, is in order. None of the above share responsibility for the interpretation developed in this work, which is solely my own.

My typist, Natalie Korp, suffered through many a Russian footnote and my nearly illegible handwriting with remarkable élan. The staff of Princeton University Press, and in particular the social science editor, Sanford Thatcher, guided the manuscript through its crucial stages with a skill even Scylla and Charybdis would be forced to admire.

A final word of thanks goes to the numerous and usually anonymous librarians and archivists in the United States, Western Europe, and the Soviet Union whose patience and satisfaction in doing a difficult job well must usually remain their only reward. In this connection a word should be added about the sources used here. While Western historians are still denied access to Soviet archives in this area, there is an abundance of source material for writing a social history of the technical intelligentsia. This is particularly true when the focus is on controversies that were often debated in the pages of the Soviet press, not only in mass-circulation party and governmental periodicals, but also in the large number of specialized journals that catered to the interests of technologists.

These journals have been little utilized till now, and are especially rich for documenting the nature and outcome of major controversies involving the technostructure. I examined several dozen of them carefully for the years covered by this study. Beyond that, sources include collections of documents published by Soviet scholars, in addition to their historiography; a growing memoir literature by Soviet and Western participants in these events; the stenographic reports of party and trade union congresses and other official gatherings involving technical specialists; captured archives, such as that of the Smolensk party organization; several hundred interviews with American specialists employed in Soviet industry, some made in confidence during the 1930s by U.S. State Department officials, and others by a historian at Stanford University, H. H. Fisher; private archives of several such engineers, made available to the author by descendants; British diplomatic archives, which touch on some of these issues, as well as collections of materials by Soviet refugees who were members of the technical intelligentsia or or worked with them during this period. The materials of the Russian

Archive at Columbia University, the Harvard Project on the Soviet Social System, and the Hoover Institution at Stanford were especially rich in this respect. More than twenty-five Soviet dissertations, the most valuable written during the Khrushchev era, were made available to me while doing postgraduate research in the Soviet Union. Most of these dissertations remain unpublished, and many of them gave glimpses into archival and rare published sources hitherto unknown to me. The resources of the British Museum, the Bibliothèque Nationale, the Sovjets Institut in Helsinki, the Lenin Library, Fundamental Library of the Social Sciences (U.S.S.R. Academy of Sciences), the Russian State Historical Library, the Polytechnic Library, Gorky Library, and the Library of the Institute for the History of Science and Technology, all in Moscow, as well as the Ukrainian State Public Library in Kiev, were very useful.

All in all, the materials are rich enough to warrant the filling, at least in part, of a lacuna that has existed in Western historical literature. While many of the conclusions of this study must remain tentative until fuller access to Soviet archives is made available, the present effort will be considered a success if it raises important questions and elicits response and dialogue. Such a dialogue, it is hoped, will lead to a greater understanding of industrial societies and an increased awareness of their variety as well as their complexity.

Technology and Society
under Lenin and Stalin

INTRODUCTION

. . . things never cease from continually chang-
ing, at one time uniting through love, at
another dividing through strife.

Empedocles[1]

Friendship and enmity are close neighbors.

Russian proverb[2]

The recent history of the Soviet technostructure, or technical intelligentsia, as it is called in the U.S.S.R., reveals a paradox. Just as the Russian nobility staffed the upper levels of the Tsarist bureaucracy before 1917, and provided the core of the "critically-thinking" intelligentsia during the nineteenth century, since Stalin's death, the Soviet technical intelligentsia has emerged as the single largest element from which the ruling elite has been recruited, and has also been a large segment of the new, critically-minded intelligentsia, recent repressions of the latter notwithstanding. In the words of the Russian proverb quoted above, "Friendship and enmity are close neighbors"—an epigram that seems particularly applicable to the Soviet technostructure in its relations with the power structure. What was there in the social environment and history of this group that would help account for these apparently contradictory developments?

It was the existence of this paradoxical relationship of the technostructure to the Soviet power structure—becoming especially evident during the 1960s—that first attracted me to the history of this group. This occurred in the same period when John Kenneth Galbraith in *The New Industrial State* and others in the West were arguing that an emergent technostructure was becoming the key group in the management of modern industrial societies, an argument by no means universally accepted.[3] These developments raised a host of questions in my

---

[1] In G. S. Kirk and J. E. Raven, *The Presocratic Philosophers: A Critical History With a Selection of Texts*, Cambridge, England, 1962, p. 324.

[2] V. I. Dal', *Poslovitsy russkogo naroda*, Moscow, 1957, p. 774.

[3] J. K. Galbraith, *The New Industrial State*, Boston, 1967. For critiques of his notion of the technostructure, see Robert L. Heilbroner, "Capitalism Without Tears," the *New York Review of Books*, June 29, 1967; Michael Harrington, "Liberalism According to Galbraith," *Commentary*, October 1967; Paul M. Sweezy, "On the Theory of Monopoly Capitalism," *Monthly Review*, April 1972; Robert M. Solow, "The New Industrial State," *The Public Interest*, Fall 1967. I use the term "technostructure" here in a narrower sense than that of Galbraith

3

mind about the nature of Soviet society and its comparability with Western societies, for which no answers were readily available.

The remainder of this introductory essay will sketch the nature of the problem more clearly, highlight its significance, and set up a theoretical framework for its discussion, explaining the methodology used in seeking answers. The social history of the Soviet Union and comparative historical studies of Western and Communist societies are, in many respects, still in their infancy. The field of Soviet and Communist history has only recently begun to develop beyond the stage of political biography, intellectual and diplomatic history, and historical studies of the role of the Communist party, to the tasks of social history. The focus in such studies is on the process of change and continuity in the social structure—its dimensions and dynamics, and the interrelationship of major social groups in that process.[4]

An interpretation of Soviet society and, by extension, those societies of Eastern Europe and Asia that have borrowed heavily from Soviet experience, is incomplete without an understanding of the role played by the technical intelligentsia. This group is defined here as engineers, agronomists, technicians, and applied scientists, that is, scientists directly tied to material production. The focus in this study, however, will be primarily on those engineers with higher education, the most significant part of the technical intelligentsia, and a group that grew from around fifteen thousand at the time of the revolutions in 1917 to over a quarter million by the start of World War II.[5] Applied scientists, agronomists, technicians, and engineers without higher education will be considered primarily in their relationship to this core group. Graduate engineers proved to be the fastest growing professional group in Soviet society in this period, representing about eleven percent of the college-educated Russian population employed in the economy in 1914, and growing to

---

and include only those with a specialized knowledge of technology, not all those employed in industry who possess some specialized knowledge including knowledge of economics and management. (The terms "technical intelligentsia," "technostructure," and "technical specialist" are used interchangeably throughout this book. The term "technical elite," when used, refers to a smaller segment of the technostructure, distinguished by a higher level of education and/or greater power or status in Soviet society.)

[4] See, for example, Moshe Lewin, *Russian Peasants and Soviet Power: A Study of Collectivization*, New York, 1975; Sheila Fitzpatrick, ed., *Cultural Revolution in Russia 1928-1931*, Bloomington, Ind., 1977; Roger Pethybridge, *The Social Prelude to Stalinism*, New York, 1974; and Michael F. Hamm, ed., *The City in Russian History*, Lexington, Ky., 1976.

[5] *Sovetskaia istoricheskaia entsiklopediia*, vol. 6, p. 117. See also the trends documented in chap. 9 of this study and S. A. Fediukin, *Privlechenie*, pp. 39-40; Azrael, *Managerial Power*, p. 27 (see notes 6 and 7 below); and *Vysshee obrazovanie v SSSR*, Moscow, 1961, p. 43.

around thirty-two percent of Soviet citizens with higher education by 1941. Yet statistics on quantitative growth leave unanswered a host of questions about the social background and role of these engineers, including their class position, social consciousness, and cohesiveness as a group.

Soviet social theory and practice over the past half century have assigned a major place to this group in the process of social development, yet a systematic analysis of its origins and the role it has played in Soviet history has not yet been attempted either in Russian or in any of the major Western languages. The most that we have are fragments of its history for limited periods of time, for example in the works of such Soviet scholars as Fediukin, Grigoriants, Ulianovskaia, and Lutchenko. Though valuable, these works seem aimed primarily at justifying official Soviet policies toward this group.[6] Most of the Western studies that deal with some of the problems raised here are more concerned with the industrial managers than with the technical intelligentsia per se, though a number of them have also proven valuable.[7] The most recent volumes on the history of the Soviet Union by E. H. Carr and R. W. Davies, *Foundations of a Planned Economy*, devote several dozen pages to some of the questions discussed here, but for the limited period from 1926 to 1930.[8] In its focus and in some of its conclusions, the present study differs considerably from their treatment.

The present monograph, therefore, represents an initial effort at analyzing the origins and role of a central group within the Soviet technostructure in the period between the 1917 revolutions and the German invasion of 1941. Its focus is on social relations, not merely politics.

[6] S. A. Fediukin, *Privlechenie burzhuaznoi tekhnicheskoi intelligentsii k sotsialisticheskomu stroitel'stvu v SSSR*, Moscow, 1960; *Sovetskaia vlast' i burzhuaznye spetsialisty*, Moscow, 1965; *Velikii oktiabr' i intelligentsiia*, Moscow, 1972; A. K. Grigoriants, *Formirovanie i razvitie tekhnicheskoi intelligentsii Armenii 1920-1965*, Erevan, 1966; A. I. Lutchenko, "Rukovodstvo KPSS formirovaniem kadrov tekhnicheskoii intelligentsii (1926-1933 gg.)," *Voprosy istorii KPSS*, no. 2, 1966; V. A. Ulianovskaia, *Formirovanie nauchnoi intelligentsii v SSSR 1917-1937 gg.*, Moscow, 1966.

[7] See, for example, Jeremy R. Azrael, *Managerial Power and Soviet Politics*, Cambridge, Mass., 1966; Joseph R. Berliner, *Factory and Manager in the U.S.S.R.*, Cambridge, Mass., 1957; David Granick, *Management of the Industrial Firm in the U.S.S.R.*, New York, 1954, and *The Red Executive*, Garden City, N.Y., 1960; Barry Richman, *Management Development and Education in the Soviet Union*, East Lansing, Mich., 1967, and *Soviet Management*, Englewood Cliffs, N.J., 1965.

Another recent Western study, Antony C. Sutton, *Western Technology and Soviet Economic Development 1917-1945*, 2 vols., Stanford, 1968 and 1971, is a valuable contribution on a related topic, the transfer of technology and the efforts of foreign specialists in the U.S.S.R.

[8] Vols. 1 and 2, London, 1969 and 1970.

That is, it attempts to assess not only the political role of this group, but the significance of its social origins, education, role in the economy, and its relationship with other important groups in Soviet society in the process of social change. The study begins with a brief discussion of this group's origins prior to the 1917 revolutions, then analyzes its role and problems during the first decade of Soviet rule. The main body of the study relates to the expansion of its role during the rapid industrialization of the first Five-Year Plans, 1928-1941. It examines the fate of the old technostructure during the first Five-Year Plan, 1928-1933, and the attempts to replace it with a new group of young, "red specialists," in these years. Finally, it analyzes the three major areas of the technostructure's experience from 1928 to 1941: higher technical education, work in material production, and research and development. Each section contributes toward forming conclusions about the nature and role of this group in early Soviet society. The conclusion suggests reasons for its later significance and for its ambivalent position of friendship and enmity toward the Soviet power structure.

One result of this book, then, should be a better understanding of a social group, at least one portion of which has become—together with elements of the military, police, and other elites—one of the most influential in the Soviet Union. By 1966, one study shows, some 65% of the full members of the party's Central Committee had a higher technical education. A large proportion of these had some work experience as engineers and industrial managers, in addition to political work.[9] Individuals with such backgrounds included the three highest officeholders in the party and state: Brezhnev, Kosygin, and Podgorny. Actually, about eighty percent of the Politburo in the early 1970s could be numbered among those with a background in the technical intelligentsia. The degree to which this background has been important in the behavior of the ruling elite is a critical problem for Soviet history and one for which this study should provide much useful material.

The significance of the technical intelligentsia goes beyond their majority in the present ruling group of the Soviet Union, however. The term "intelligentsia" has a somewhat different meaning in Russian intellectual history from the one used here for the purpose of social history. That is, the prerevolutionary "intelligentsia" was frequently defined more narrowly, not as those engaged in intellectual pursuits or

---

[9] See Michael P. Gehlen and Michael McBride, "The Soviet Central Committee," *American Political Science Review*, 62, 1968, 1232-1237; George Fischer, *The Soviet System and Modern Society*, New York, 1968; Robert H. Donaldson, "The 1971 Soviet Central Committee, An Assessment of the New Elite," *World Politics*, 24, 1972, 391-394; *New York Times*, April 11, 1971; *Prominent Personalities in the USSR*, Metuchen, N.J., 1968, pp. 92, 307.

mental labor as such, but those "critically-thinking" individuals who were devoted to increasing human freedom and dignity. This is the sense in which the term was used by a number of writers, including the radical Peter Lavrov, one of the intellectual godfathers of Russian populism in the nineteenth century, and Ivanov-Razumnik, a cultural historian and revolutionary, who lived to survive a Soviet labor camp and write a memoir on the decline of this "critically-thinking intelligentsia" under Stalin.[10] In recent years there is again evidence of the revival of an intelligentsia in this meaning of the term, and members of the technostructure, albeit a small number, have been active in this respect.

It is interesting to note that the largest single group to protest actively the violation of civil liberties and human rights in the Soviet Union in the wake of the 1966 trial of Sinyavsky and Daniel was engineers and applied scientists, rather than members of the cultural intelligentsia.[11] (Members of the cultural intelligentsia, defined here as those with education and special knowledge concerned primarily with literature, criticism, law, the arts, etc., were predominant as leaders in the pre-1917 movements for revolution or reform.)

If a critically thinking, socially minded intelligentsia ever revives and grows within the Soviet Union, it may find a constituency among those with scientific and technical training and employment. We need to ask what there is in the background of the technostructure, or some of its elements, during its formative years before 1941 that would indicate a potential for revival—with a new social base—of the values of the critical intelligentsia found in the Russian culture of the nineteenth and early twentieth centuries.

Beyond that, the importance of technological issues and the interest devoted to them by Lenin and Stalin have not been given the attention they deserve from historians, including the many recent Western biographers of Lenin and Stalin. This study contends that Leninism and Stalinism cannot be fully understood without a study of the technical intelligentsia in this period, the role it played, and the significance attached by both Lenin and Stalin to technological controversies. One

[10] P. S. Squire, trans. *The Memoirs of Ivanov-Razumnik*, London, 1965. For Ivanov-Razumnik's definition of the intelligentsia, see his *Istoriia russkoi obshchestvennoi mysli*, St. Petersburg, 1914, vol. 1, pp. 1-10.

[11] Paul A. Smith, Jr., "Protest in Moscow," *Foreign Affairs*, October 1968, 157. Of some four hundred Soviet citizens who signed protest documents against the Ginsburg trial and the detention of the mathematician and philosopher, Yesenin-Volpin, almost all were professionals, and more than half were members of the scientific and technical intelligentsia. Engineers were one of the largest professional groups represented.

of the purposes of this work will be to illuminate the nature of the Lenin and Stalin periods from an angle previously neglected.

The interpretation developed here is that the Soviet technical intelligentsia was more active than previously thought in changing the social structure of the Soviet Union and the cultural values of its people in this period. Previous historiography, both Western and Soviet, has stressed the role of the Communist party, and individual leaders such as Lenin and Stalin, in the process of social change. Such views need to be revised to understand the complexity of that process and the active role played by the technical intelligentsia. This study will attempt to show how change proceeded through a combination of conflict and cooperation, both internally among various groups of the technostructure, and externally between the technical intelligentsia and other major social groups—the Communist party elite, industrial workers, the political police, the military, and industrial management.

Moreover, the aims of this study are not only historical but theoretical. That is, the monograph not only attempts to interpret a unique historical experience, it also aims at a more general applicability. Put briefly, it challenges the adequacy of two types of model most commonly used by Western social scientists to analyze and interpret Soviet politics and society—totalitarian and group conflict models. It develops an alternative way of understanding how Soviet society has functioned and changed, based in part on a synthesis of elements from totalitarian and conflict models, as well as factors neglected by these models. The alternative model focuses on the interaction of social forces, which the ancient Greek writer Empedocles, quoted in the epigraph above, identified as love and strife, or which a more modern author might prefer to call the forces of social cohesion, both voluntary and coercive, and the forces of social conflict.

The model developed here suggests that the evidence of this study, and perhaps Communist systems more generally, can be better understood by analyzing the interaction between the forces that tend to hold groups together for cohesive action and the forces of social conflict that tend toward their dissolution or transformation. Thus, I propose an interactional model that attempts to explain both change and continuity in terms of the constant tug-of-war between contradictory social forces —those of cohesion and those of conflict. The real problem for the historian of Soviet society, in my opinion, is to identify more precisely the composition of these forces and the particular nature of their interaction in any given historical process.

What seems abstract in the beginning, or, at most, the skeleton of a social theory, should begin to take on the flesh and blood of real people—particular individuals and groups working together and at cross purposes—in the pages that follow. Many historians and students of history tend to shun the abstractions of the social sciences in search of a more living reality embodied in complex people and events of the past. These, they feel, cannot be reduced to, or adequately explained by, the abstractions of social theory. For such readers, the present study also offers much of concrete human experience, including drama, folly, tragedy, and solid human achievements. While I hope that the theoretical portions of this study, which are the girders of its interpretation, will be found useful and interesting, much of the present book can be read and enjoyed without a particular interest in social theory. Readers with more concrete interests are offered, in addition to much new factual material, insights into the nature of Soviet society under Lenin and Stalin, a reinterpretation of a crucial era in the history of Soviet industrialization and, more generally, in the social history of technology.

For the theoretically minded, however, some further setting is required at this point, in order to understand the conceptual framework of the study. We need to look briefly at the main outlines of the totalitarian and conflict models and at how they have been used in Soviet studies, before suggesting how an alternative model can be used as an explanatory tool.

A recent, controversial article in an American historical journal suggested that the term "totalitarianism" is misleading and propagandistic, and should probably be discarded.[12] The authors of this article noted that the word "totalitarianism," although coined earlier, gained popularity in the United States as anti-Nazi propaganda during World War II, and later became an anti-Communist slogan in the Cold War. The word was often not given a careful definition and tended to slur crucial differences, for example, between German society under the Nazis and the U.S.S.R. under Stalin, as well as later differences among the various Communist systems that came into existence following World War II.[13]

Yet while "totalitarianism" may have been carelessly used at times in the mass media and by scholars, it stands for a definite concept that is not easily discarded by students of modern politics and social history. The concept of totalitarianism, for example, has been the most frequently used in creating models of how Soviet society functions and changes.[14] At the risk of oversimplifying a large body of theory, it can

[12] Les K. Adler and Thomas G. Patterson, " 'Red Fascism' and the Development of the Cold War," *American Historical Review*, April 1970, 1046-1064.

[13] Ibid., 1046-1049.

[14] See, for example, Carl J. Friedrich, ed., *Totalitarianism*, Cambridge, 1954; Carl Friedrich and Zbigniew Brzezinski, *Totalitarian Dictatorship and Autocracy*, Cambridge, Mass., 1956; Alex Inkeles and Raymond Bauer, *The Soviet Citizen:*

be said that totalitarianism describes primarily a set of methods of social organization and control, not the specific aims or results of those methods.

Briefly, totalitarianism can be defined as a system in which a single group seeks to monopolize all the levers of power in order to carry out rapid changes. Such a group seeks particularly to use modern technology and modern bureaucratic organization to achieve the total mobilization of a society for its goals. Its manifest goals are embodied in an ideology: an organized system of thought and values that serves as a guide not only to interpreting the world, but also, in the words of Marx, to changing it. In other words, the ideology provides a way of thinking that serves as a guide to action. Ideology unites a group of people into a political party that claims a monopoly of decision making and the power to implement decisions. Such a party is organized bureaucratically, from the local level in a chain of command to a small group, and sometimes to a single dictator at the top.

In seeking to achieve its goals, the totalitarian party tries to destroy or transform any intermediate sources of power or resistance to its goals, whether those sources are in the family unit, religious organizations, private economic organizations, or within the government itself. While dictatorships have existed from time immemorial, totalitarianism, according to this body of theory, is qualitatively different in that such systems monopolize modern technology and modern bureaucratic organization in the hands of a single group. That is, totalitarian systems seek to monopolize control of the means of persuasion (modern communications systems); the means of force (army, police, and the government overall); and the means of production and distribution (land, farms, factories, mines, trade, etc.).

Totalitarianism involves the use of modern bureaucratic organization throughout the society and economy. That is, the totalitarian party uses organizations with a highly complex division of labor, with written rules and regulations, and a hierarchy of slots for people with different functions and different levels of power within the system. Such officials are not subject to democratic recall or responsibility to the majority of citizens, but are responsible only to their superiors in a hierarchical chain of command. In a totalitarian state, so such models go, bureaucratic organizations run virtually everything. That is, they produce the

Daily Life in a Totalitarian Society, Cambridge, Mass., 1961; Alex Inkeles, *Social Change in Soviet Russia*, New York, 1971, especially pp. 65-85; Merle Fainsod, *How Russia is Ruled*, Cambridge, 1963; Hannah Arendt, *The Origins of Totalitarianism*, New York, 1966; and T. H. Rigby and L. G. Churchward, *Policy Making in the USSR 1953-1961: Two Views*, Melbourne, 1962.

bulk of all material goods in society, provide most services, and even seek to control youth organizations, the organization of the family unit, trade unions, religious organizations, and other social units outside the formal government.

In explaining the origins of such systems, theorists stress that totalitarianism is likely to arise in a society gripped by crisis, where the group that achieves power wants to make changes very quickly, for example, a defeated Germany in a depression, or an isolated Russia trying to pull itself out of the disastrous consequences of World War I, a civil war, and foreign intervention. Totalitarianism is also most likely to arise in a society with a weaker tradition of independent action, that is, societies with a strong tradition of autocratic rule, such as Imperial Germany and Tsarist Russia, where autonomous groups have been relatively weak vis-à-vis their governments. Groups likely to use totalitarian methods are those that put foremost value not on the individual human being or on personal liberty, but on some collective entity, such as the nation, the people, or the race, as in Nazi Germany, or the social class and its vanguard, the Communist party, in the Soviet Union. Such totalitarian groups put the strongest and most immediate emphasis on a kind of organic unity. Consensus, harmony, and unity in the achievement of particular goals are the aim of a totalitarian system, such theorists contend, and cooperation rather than conflict is viewed as the ultimate goal. Such groups emphasize human ability, the ability of human societies to plan and control their own fate, and human perfectability. Individuals may wither away and die, but the goal is for society, or part of society, to live on and perfect itself in some way.

Among Western specialists on the Soviet Union, the totalitarian model—along the lines set forth above—has come under increasing attack during the past several decades. Models based on group conflict—usually focusing on elite group conflict—have been the most common substitutes proposed by Western social scientists.[15] Most of the studies based on group-conflict models relate to the post-Stalin era, although their relevance for earlier Soviet history has been recognized. As one of the major writers on group conflict in Soviet society has put it:

> It was during the Khrushchev period that the visibility of conflict in Soviet politics became so great as to awaken serious dissatisfaction, among Western scholars, with the totalitarian model and to stimulate the use of group analysis. Retrospectively, it be-

[15] See, in particular, Churchward's essay in the book above (n. 14); H. Gordon Skilling, *Interest Groups in Soviet Politics*, Princeton, 1971, especially, pp. 3-46, 379-416; and Carl A. Linden, *Khrushchev and the Soviet Leadership 1957-1964*, Baltimore, 1966.

came evident that this approach was appropriate for any period of Soviet history, including the Stalinist phase, as well as for other Communist states. Even under Stalin, there was a sharp conflict of groups and tendencies, although in forms reflecting the more auto-cratic and terroristic nature of Soviet politics at that time and in a manner less easily observable.[16]

Such dissatisfied students of Soviet society have made several criti-cisms of totalitarian models. Such models describe more the intentions of the party in power, its aims, they claim, rather than the way the system actually functions. Beyond that, totalitarian models tell us little if anything about the conflicting values and material interests for which totalitarian methods may be used.

According to group-conflict theorists, a society such as the Soviet Union is far from harmonious; nor is all power monopolized by a single unified group. Behind the facade of formal unity and a single party, intense conflict often rages over disparate values, interests, and policies. The Soviet system is best understood, according to these writers, by an analysis of such conflicts and the groups involved in them. According to them, Soviet society functions and changes as a result of the give-and-take of interest groups in conflict: sometimes resolving their differences in a compromise, sometimes through the ascendancy of one or several groups in alliance against other groups. Such analysts admit that it is harder to document such group conflicts in Soviet society, because much of the conflict takes place behind closed doors, and is resolved in secret at the highest levels of the Communist party and Soviet govern-ment. Nonetheless, they claim that enough of such conflict reaches the public, through speeches and articles representing the conflicting groups in periodicals controlled by those groups, through memoirs and under-ground manuscripts (*samizdat*), and through the insights of non-Soviet observers that analysts can piece together much of the puzzle. Social change or stability occurs in part as a result of conflicts among such interest groups and the way they are resolved, not primarily through the total control of a single unified group.

Such theorists of Soviet society have focused primarily on conflicts over two issues: 1) the allocation of resources, that is, how much of the state's resources will be appropriated to each of the interest groups in Soviet society; and 2) the more general issue of access to power, that is, conflicts over access to power in the institutions that make and carry out policies in Soviet society. Groups that feel neglected in the allocation

16 Skilling, op. cit., p. 399.

of material resources and in access to power over policy making and implementation seek to enlarge their role, while groups already well entrenched in these respects either try to protect vested interests or widen their power and their proportion of allocated resources. This is the stuff of which Soviet politics is made, according to the group-conflict theorists, and an analysis of such conflict is the best way to understand why certain changes take place and others fail to occur in Soviet society. While these theorists often disagree about the particular configuration of groups, they all agree that social harmony—enforced or otherwise— is far from the norm in Soviet society.

In undertaking the present study, this author asked which of the two types of model could be the most useful in understanding Soviet society and politics under Lenin and Stalin. In the course of writing, an attempt was made to apply both kinds of model. Questions raised by each were found useful in analyzing the materials of this book, but neither by itself could fully account for, or integrate, the mass of evidence. Therefore, a new model gradually took shape, which attempts not only to synthesize elements from totalitarian and group-conflict models, but to add elements previously neglected. In the area of social cohesion, such elements include an emphasis not only on the coercive—or totalitarian— means of enforcing social cohesion, but also on the degree to which shared values and interests led at times to voluntary cohesion and initiative among some of the groups analyzed. In the area of social conflict, the neglected elements include conflict over differing cultural values and class conflict, in addition to bureaucratic and elite conflict, where most such studies have focused heretofore. Bureaucratic conflict, of course, cannot be neglected, since technical specialists worked within a bureaucratic context. Subgroups of the technostructure belonged to different bureaucratic interest groups that were sometimes at odds.

Interclass and intraclass conflicts (conflicts between classes and between strata within classes) are also important, since the technical intelligentsia—stratified by income, education, social background, and access to power and privileges—at times found itself in conflict among its subgroups, as well as with other strata and classes of Soviet society. The changing balance of conflict and cooperation with the industrial workers, for example, is a particularly important problem, which forms a major theme in this book, no less important than the relations of the technostructure with other Soviet elites.

It is appropriate at this point to state my understanding of class, and the class structure of Soviet society in this period. Without becoming involved in a detailed discussion of differing definitions of class, or controversies over the class structure of the Soviet Union I want to adopt the following framework for heuristic purposes in this study.[17] A class is understood as a major social group that differs from other groups in a broad cluster of traits, the most important of which are occupation, education, income, social consciousness, style of life, and access to power and privileges. While a large social class may itself be divided into a number of strata, reflecting among themselves lesser differences in such traits, they all share enough to make them distinct from other major social-economic groups. Although occupation is considered a crucial variable here, Marx's definition of class primarily in terms of relationship to the means of production seems to me too narrow. Some of Marx's distinctions, however, are extremely pertinent. As he expressed it, "In so far as millions of families live under economic conditions which separate their way of life, their interests, and their education from those of other classes and oppose them to others, they constitute a class."[18] Marx made the further distinction between a class *in itself* and *for itself*. A class in itself is a group that objectively differs from other groups in its relationship to the means of production, but has not developed the self-consciousness of its class position that impels it to act cohesively in its own interests.

Using the criteria of occupation, education, income, social consciousness, style of life, and access to power, I consider that Soviet society after 1917, and particularly with the liquidation of private-property-based classes (the NEP-men and private peasantry) after 1928, can be viewed as divided into three broad social-economic classes, *in themselves* if not *for themselves*: the nonmanual workers; the manual workers outside agriculture; and agricultural workers.[19] Each of these classes contained a number of strata and substrata, and it is these smaller groups where social cohesion and self-conscious pursuit of group interests were

[17] *Sovetskaia istoricheskaia entsiklopediia*, vol. 6, Moscow, 1965, p. 111. For Lenin's views of the intelligentsia, see *Polnoe sobranie sochineniia*, vol. 4, p. 209, vol. 5, p. 328, vol. 8, p. 309, vol. 14, p. 191, and vol. 7, p. 82. J. F. Stalin, *Problems of Leninism*, Moscow, 1953, pp. 702-703; see also *Politicheskii slovar'*, Moscow, 1958, p. 211. For an informative discussion of this question, see Ralf Dahrendorf, *Class and Class Conflict in Industrial Society*, Stanford, 1959, pp. 11, 41-48. For a discussion of recent controversies in the Soviet Union over whether the intelligentsia should be considered part of the working class or as a separate group, see the interesting monograph by S. L. Seniavskii, *Izmeneniia v sotsial' noi strukture sovetskogo obshchestva 1938-1970*, Institut istorii SSSR, Akademiia nauk SSSR, Moscow, 1973, pp. 3-144.

[18] Karl Marx, *The Eighteenth Brumaire of Louis Bonaparte*, New York, 1963, p. 124.

[19] For several intelligent recent discussions of the class structure of Soviet society, see Mervyn Matthews, *Class and Society in Soviet Russia*, London, 1972, and David Lane, *Politics and Society in the USSR*, New York, 1971, pp. 382-418.

likely to be greater. For this reason, they constitute a more meaningful unit of historical analysis than the three broad social classes posited above. For example, the nonmanual workers included not only the stratum of the ruling elite, who ran the Communist party and the Soviet government, but the cultural and scientific-technical intelligentsia, as well as all other white-collar employees.

The intelligentsia is defined here in the broadest sense as those professionals and semiprofessionals whose work generally required higher education, specialized secondary education, or equivalent experience.[20] These might be lawyers, physicians, economists, teachers, scientists, engineers, journalists, artists, and others. The Soviet technostructure—applied scientists, engineers, agronomists, and technicians—is defined as a substratum, within the stratum of the intelligentsia, which in turn forms part of a larger social class, the nonmanual workers.

A set of broadly similar occupations is what obviously binds the technostructure together for common consideration. Just as the nonmanual workers include all those who work primarily with their minds, rather than their hands, and possess the knowledge by which society is organized, so the technostructure includes all those who possess the specialized knowledge of technology necessary for material production. The second major criterion applied here in defining the focus for study is one of education. The focus is specifically on those members of the technostructure who received a formal higher education. One of my tasks in this monograph will be to assess how significant such traits as similarity of occupation and education were as binding forces, and beyond that, the degree to which the technostructure was bound together or divided by the other criteria of income, social consciousness, style of life, and access to power and privileges. I shall also consider the importance of social class background and ethnic and sexual variables. Answers to these questions will help us to determine, in the conclusion, the degree to which the Soviet technostructure, or at least a major element of it, can be considered a cohesive group, and the degree to which it must be considered simply a collection of professional and semiprofessional groups.

I intend to follow two approaches in finding answers for these questions; a case-study method, largely qualitative in nature, and a computer analysis of the social origins, composition, career patterns, and social status of approximately eleven hundred members of Soviet technical elites in this period. The computer analysis will be both quantitative and qualitative in form, and is developed in the conclusions and ap-

[20] See *Politicheskii slovar'*, Moscow, 1958, p. 211, and Seniavskii, op. cit., pp. 297-340.

pendix. The case studies, which compose the bulk of the monograph, are built around major policy controversies involving the technical intelligentsia in these years. Such controversies are especially revealing of group dynamics, and should provide some original insights into the ways the technical intelligentsia interacted with other elements of Soviet society and its own subgroups. The book will be organized around three major areas of experience: the changing political role of the technical intelligentsia and its significance; the social background, recruitment, and education of this group; and their work at different levels of the economy (on the production line, in factory management and higher industrial administration, and in research and development). The aim is not to be comprehensive, but to highlight some significant trends and general traits of the Soviet technostructure in this period, and particularly of its core group, the graduate engineers.

PART 1

The Early Years to 1928

1

BACKGROUND OF
THE RUSSIAN TECHNOSTRUCTURE:
FROM THE TSARIST ERA TO 1918

*Science and industry—these are my dreams.
They are everything today. . . .*[1]

Mendeleev

*To go into science means to endure pain.
There is no science without suffering.*[2]

Russian saying

A crisis often highlights features of a group that otherwise might be more difficult to define. Attitudes, interests, and behavior that, in normal times, seem habitual and almost unconscious become more focused when challenged by events. In early 1918 the technostructure in Russia, like the rest of society, was in crisis. In factories and mines all over Russia, committees of workers had seized control and were attempting to manage the enterprises. Uncooperative engineers were sometimes trundled away in wheelbarrows and dumped unceremoniously outside the gates by unfriendly workers, or even physically attacked and sometimes killed.[3] More cooperative engineers found themselves involved in endless meetings, forced to share powers they had earlier taken for granted, unable to stop the decline in industrial discipline and in production. In technical universities and institutes, classes were interrupted or closed down by political turmoil accompanied by severe shortages of fuel and food. In research laboratories, shortages of equipment and personnel made normal work impossible. In government bureaus, Baltic sailors, armed factory workers, bearded *muzhiks*, leather-jacketed students, and other representatives of the new government arrested or otherwise coerced civil servants, including government engineers, many of whom were striking to protest the Bolshevik takeover and the dismissal of the newly elected Constituent Assembly.

In this atmosphere, representatives of the All-Russian Union of Engineers (VSI), the trade union of the graduate engineers that had

[1] D. I. Mendeleev. *Arkhiv*, vol. 1, Leningrad, 1951, p. 36.
[2] V. Dal', *Poslovitsy russkogo naroda. Sbornik*, Moscow, 1957, p. 422.
[3] *Russkoe slovo*, no. 234, 1917.

formed less than a year before, gathered in Moscow to discuss the crisis. Their discussions and resolutions reveal an important segment of opinion among politically-conscious representatives of the technical intelligentsia, particularly among those based in the industries and technical schools of metropolitan areas or with strong ties to those areas. In order to understand how the technical intelligentsia fared under the Soviet system, we must look first at how their organized groups and individual members reacted to the events of the Russian revolution, i.e., what grievances, interests, and attitudes they revealed in this crisis. Then we will turn back briefly to the Tsarist era to look at their origins, structure, and consciously expressed interests. This should then provide a framework for understanding both the changes and the continuities later experienced by significant elements of the technical intelligentsia in the period between 1917 and 1941.

In early January 1918, seventy delegates of local units of VSI, mostly from the Moscow region, spent three days in discussing the crisis, their deliberations punctuated at times by machine gun and rifle fire, as Bolshevik and anti-Bolshevik forces clashed in the streets and public squares of the city. One member of the union, in fact, was killed demonstrating against the Bolsheviks. According to the transcript of the sessions:

> The Congress did not interrupt its work for a moment, even when on the second day of the Congress rifle and machine gun fire could be heard in the streets, a victim of which fell our co-member, Engineer Ratner, killed on Passion Square under a banner defending the Constituent Assembly.[4]

The meeting, which took place in Moscow, had been scheduled as a national congress of VSI, but because of transportation problems and the inability of many engineers to leave their posts, the chairman declared the sessions representative of the Moscow region only, although some delegates from other areas did attend. Since many of the delegates were prominent members of the technical intelligentsia, and the Moscow region at any rate contained one of the heaviest concentrations of technologists in the country, its deliberations are significant. Certain concerns stand out in the speeches and resolutions: the situation in industry was approaching anarchy, with a severe decline in production, destruction of the authority of technologists, rejection of such cherished incen-

---

[4] *Biulleteni moskovskogo oblastnogo biuro i moskovskogo otdeleniia vserossiiskogo soiuza inzhenerov*, no. 1, 1918, *Zaniatiia 1-ogo moskovskogo oblastnogo delgatskogo s''ezda, 4-6 ianvaria, 1918 g*, Moscow, 1918 p. 63. I found a copy of this rare transcript in the Lenin Library, Moscow.

tive methods as bonuses and piecework rates, etc.[5] Workers' control, in particular, was disturbing to members:

> . . . such a solution of the problem [of reorganizing the economy] is both technically and economically impermissible. The participation of knowledgeable technical forces in working out problems of reorganization is absolutely necessary to avoid all kinds of mistakes.[6]

What should be the role of the state in the economy and in solving the crisis? The congress strongly sympathized with a mixed economy. As the chairman, Professor Grinevetsky, a well-known heat technologist and rector of the Moscow Higher Technical School (comparable in prestige to MIT), expressed it, the state's role was one of regulation and active intervention when necessary, but it must also encourage private initiative, and protect labor from exploitation and other abuses. He was especially concerned that foreign capital, particularly German, might move in and take increasing advantage of the situation.[7] He proposed that supervision of the economy be in the hands of the most competent. Control groups for every industry should be set up, including representatives of capital, labor, and consumers, but in particular "the most competent technical and economic forces in the country, to whom must be given the leading and responsible positions."[8] These control organs could be effective, he stressed, only when backed up by state compulsion.

He was particularly critical of the Bolsheviks for their doctrinaire approach and lack of a clear economic program at this time, and he called for an end to the principle of a "one-sided class dictatorship."[9] The government, he stressed, must guarantee normal working conditions and the authority and safety of technical personnel. The Tactical Commission of VSI echoed Grinevetsky's concerns and blamed the ruin of industry on "pandering to the crowd and its crude instincts and destructive urges, as well as the proclamation of narrow class slogans and attempts to preserve authority among the masses."[10]

This commission concluded that "since politics and economics are closely intertwined, it is impossible not to interfere in politics." The resolutions passed by the Congress confirmed the strength of feeling that stood behind these opinions. The members of VSI were forbidden to participate in any organization that aided the "ruin of industry," including workers' directorates or commissions in plants that participated in workers' control. Members who did so would be expelled. If commissions of workers' organs took on the functions of engineers, engineers

---

[5] Ibid., pp. 27-30. [6] Ibid., p. 21. [7] Ibid., pp. 30-43.
[8] Ibid., p. 33. [9] Ibid., p. 36. [10] Ibid., p. 47.

should leave their jobs, and such plants should be boycotted by other engineers. At the same time, this Congress defined the interests of its members as differing from those of private entrepreneurs. Another prominent engineer, M. G. Evreinov, expressed the views of VSI's Tactical Commission:

> The majority recognized the impossibility of turning to the owners for a subsidy, even the smallest. If at a given moment, in the struggle to save industry, transport, etc., we find ourselves in agreement with the entrepreneurs, we should not forget that this has not always been so, nor will it be so in the future. The overwhelming majority of members in our union are people who sell their labor and are not entrepreneurs. The union of engineers has been created for the long haul, it has its own road to follow, and it is not necessary to become dependent either on organizations of entrepreneurs, nor on those of workers.[11]

While there was some disagreement on this subject, and the Congress voted to leave the decision of accepting loans from entrepreneurs up to individual members, the sense of the meeting was that members of the technical intelligentsia were a distinct group, with interests different from those of either labor or capital.

How representative of the technical intelligentsia as a whole were the views expressed at this Congress? That question cannot be answered with certainty, since we lack any data that would give a full spectrum of opinion for this group in 1918. At most we can say that the Moscow branch of VSI represented one of the most self-conscious elements of the technical intelligentsia and certainly one of the best organized. By October of 1918, this group, under the same leadership, had grown to some three thousand members, a considerable proportion of the approximately fifteen thousand engineers in the country with higher education, the group eligible for VSI membership.[12] Judging from other contemporary documents, including the national journal of VSI, the *Engineers' Herald* (*Vestnik inzhenerov* or *VI*), as well as from the memoirs of individual technologists, much of the opinion expressed at the January Congress was widely shared. In particular, the technical intelligentsia was oriented toward a strong government and government intervention in the economy, although it may have differed on the exact nature of that government and the degree of intervention. It feared

---

[11] Ibid., p. 60.
[12] *Vserossiiskii soiuz inzhenerov. Otchet' o zaniatiiakh 2-oi moskovskoi oblastnoi konferentsii, 18-21 oktiabria, 1918 g.*, Moskow, 1918, p. 45.

anarchy, it feared for the personal safety of its members on the job, and it favored clearly defined and strong powers for the technical intelligentsia in the economy. Workers' control, in particular, seems to have been anathema to most, if not all, technologists.

Attitudes differed, however, in regard to the Bolsheviks, representative democracy, including such institutions as the Constituent Assembly, and the engineer's right to use the strike and boycott as political weapons. It is difficult to judge numerically how significant splits on these questions may have been. At least some technologists, probably a minority, began to cooperate with the Bolshevilks from the beginning, for a variety of reasons. A few had ties with Lenin and the Bolsheviks dating from their student days, and some were active Bolsheviks. These included prominent engineers like L. K. Martens, Robert Klasson, the Krasin brothers, Gleb Krzhizhanovsky, Lev Karpov, P. A. Bogdanov, and others.[13] Yet it can be said with certainty that the active Bolsheviks among graduate engineers and applied scientists were a tiny minority.

A more sizable but less definable group comprised those who considered themselves apolitical, or felt it their duty to cooperate with whatever government was in power, no matter how much they differed personally with Bolshevik ideology. Among this group, those with military backgrounds and a history of loyal government service under the Tsars were sometimes prominent. Their opinions and reasons for cooperation are interesting, and reveal a connection between a military mentality and at least one segment of the technical intelligentsia. Here it is worth quoting from the memoirs of Lt. Gen. V. N. Ipatieff, a world-renowned chemical technologist and an officer in the Tsarist army who headed the Chemical Committee of the government in World War I. People like Ipatieff differed strongly with the leadership of VSI on the political role of the technical intelligentsia. The leadership of VSI was drawn heavily from among civilian engineers and the engineering professoriate, many of whom had a history of conflict with the Tsarist regime, going back several decades, and some of whom were strong liberals, supporters of the Constitutional Democratic party and the Provisional Government. Ipatieff and others like him, while scarcely admirers of the Romanovs, were more conservatively oriented. It was, in fact, their conservatism that impelled them to support the Bolsheviks,

---

[13] See the biographies of these engineers in *Biograficheskii slovar' deiatelei estestvoznaniia i tekhniki*, 2 vols., Moscow, 1958-1959, and the books of S. A. Fediukin, *Velikii oktiabr' i intelligentsiia*, Moscow, 1972, pp. 26-68, 143-172; *Sovetskaia vlast' i burzhuaznye spetsialisty*, Moscow, 1965; *Privlechenie burzhuaznoi tekhnicheskoi intelligentsii k sotsialisticheskomu stroitel'stvu v SSSR*, Moscow, 1960.

paradoxical as that may seem at first. The extent of conservative support for the Bolsheviks is surely a phenomenon that deserves more study than historians have given it.

One of the ironies of the Russian Revolution is that the Bolsheviks in 1917 and 1918 appealed not only to radicals, but to some who had worked loyally for the old regime. The following explanation seems to make sense of this apparent contradiction. The Bolsheviks were not the most radical group on the Russian left at the time. To Ipatieff and his kind, who felt that the right was thoroughly discredited and disorganized, the anarchists, Socialist Revolutionaries, anti-intellectual workers, and peasants seemed far more serious a threat to their deeply-held values of order, discipline, productive work, and hierarchical organization than the Bolsheviks, whom they may have disliked, but were willing to tolerate under the circumstances. Why? Ipatieff, publishing his memoirs in 1946 after fleeing Stalin's terror against the old specialists in 1930, gave some revealing answers, which other sources corroborate. While his explanation is self-serving, justifying to a Western readership why he worked loyally for the Bolsheviks between 1917 and 1930, it deserves notice:

> Whatever we may think of the ideals of the Bolsheviks, many of which experience proved to be purely "utopian," it must be admitted that the October Revolution, masterfully led by Lenin, saved the country from anarchy and at least temporarily preserved its intelligentsia and material wealth. . . . Many times I have maintained that but for the Bolsheviks in 1917 and 1918 I probably would have lost my life . . . if the Provisional Government had remained in power much longer the intelligentsia would have been the victims.[14]

Ipatieff may have disliked the Bolsheviks, at times intensely, but his fear of the prevailing breakdown and his dislike of other groups on the left were greater. His conduct went beyond neutrality. In contrast to VSI and similar groups, and such fellow members of the Russian Academy of Sciences as Pavlov and Vernadsky, Ipatieff refused to censure the Bolsheviks or to join a strike against them. According to his account, right after the October Revolution, in November and December of 1917,

[14] V. N. Ipatieff, *Life of a Chemist*, Stanford, 1946, pp. 256-257. Another conservative technologist with a military background and similar views was M. Bonch-Bruyevich (see his memoir *From Tsarist General to Red Army Commander*, Moscow, 1966). Besides being a technologist and Tsarist general, he was also a brother of one of Lenin's closest associates, Vladimir Bonch-Bruyevich.

Most of the staff of the Chemical Committee were opposed to the Bolshevik Revolution, and I was asked to call a meeting to discuss the possibility of calling a demonstration strike against Bolshevism, similar to those in other government offices. After full discussion, I spoke against the plan. The Chemical Committee, I argued, was composed of army men who had no right to stop their work in wartime. The government in power should be obeyed, and all responsibility for any action taken devolved on that government. I suppose that most of the staff disagreed with me, but my firm attitude and authority were too much for them to oppose. Our work went on, without a day lost. . . .[15]

At a meeting of the Academy of Sciences, of which Ipatieff was a full member, a protest against the Bolshevik takeover was proposed. "I argued that control of the state belonged to the group capable of setting up a strong government. . . . The autocracy of the Tsarist regime had dissatisfied many of us, yet we had continued to do our duty."[16] A motion censuring the Bolsheviks failed, to Ipatieff's satisfaction.

These two examples of how members of the technical intelligentsia reacted to the October Revolution are limited, but revealing of splits as well as common interests among members of this group. To understand the roots of such attitudes and the situation of the technical intelligentsia after 1917, we have to look briefly at this group in the last decades of Imperial Russia.

I will analyze trends among this group in the following areas: 1) social composition and education; 2) work in production and in research and development; and 3) professional organization and political role. One basis for differences among the technical intelligentsia can be found in differing social origins and in the different types of educational institutions that molded them. The Russian technical intelligentsia, in its origins, was a creation of the Russian state, one of the oldest groups being the Corps of Mining Engineers established by Catherine the Great in 1773 to manage state mines and metallurgical plants.[17] Similar bodies of trained state officials were set up in the early nineteenth century, e.g., schools for transport engineers, civil engineers, and forestry officials. The higher educational institutions that trained them were largely reserved for the children of the nobility, and often even for the children of those in a particular specialty, such as the officials of the Bureau of Mines. This created a corporate and caste-like mentality, a residue of

---

[15] *Life of a Chemist*, p. 259.   [16] Ibid., p. 260.

[17] V. P. Leikina-Svirskaia, *Intelligentsiia v Rossii v vtoroi polovine XIX veka*, Moscow, 1971, p. 107.

which remained strong in the years after 1917 and became an issue of some importance.[18]

Graduates of state technical schools in nineteenth-century Russia qualified automatically for certain ranks in the civil or military service, based on their level of success in school. They likewise earned certain privileges, if they did not already have them through their hereditary status, such as exemption from personal taxation and from corporal punishment. The elite technical schools, only a handful in number in the nineteenth century, produced people for positions largely with administrative and control functions.[19] Technical work directly in production was considered the province of the lower orders. During and after the reign of Nicholas I (1825-1855), a new series of so-called "practical" institutions was created to train production engineers for industry and communications. The St. Petersburg Technological Institute, which opened its doors in 1831, and the Moscow Technical School, founded in 1832, were originally intended to prepare technologists of the latter type. They were to recruit their students primarily from the under-privileged segments of society, especially in the cities.[20] The need for such institutions became more evident as the years went by. As an early graduate of one of the older, elite institutions expressed it, his school provided a good theoretical education, but he learned little that was practical. He acknowledged that he had not learned how to do anything with his "white and tender hands, even drafting!"[21] On an early job, he was amazed by the skills of an illiterate stonemason who helped him, and who did a better job of engineering, in the eyes of this Russian nobleman, than even the English engineers hired by the government to assist.[22]

After midcentury a greater trend toward democratization of students in technology began, even in the elite institutions, which became more open to commoners. Nevertheless, students of the elite institutions still felt themselves a group apart. As Sergei Timoshenko, a student at the Institute of the Ministry of Communications expressed it, they were required in the mid-1890s to wear a special uniform and were taught to salute fellow communications engineers on the street. They also wore distinctive uniforms, with their own insignia, as army officers did. This

[18] Ibid., pp. 107-109.
[19] Ibid. See also the section on technical education in William Blackwell, *The Beginnings of Russian Industrialization*, Princeton, 1968, pp. 328-387.
[20] For histories of these two schools, see *Tekhnologicheskii institut. Sto let, 1828-1928*, Leningrad, 1928, and V. I. Prokof'ev, *Moskovskoe vysshee tekhnicheskoe uchilishche*, Moscow, 1955.
[21] A. I. Del'vig, *Polveka russkoi zhizni, Vospominaniia 1820-1870*, vol. 1, Moscow, 1930, cited in Leikina, p. 109.
[22] Ibid.

sense of distinction was fostered by the difficulty of entering such institutes. There was intense competition in entrance exams, and the admissions system still favored the privileged and those with useful personal ties. Timoshenko's institute was one of the most selective in the country, with seven hundred qualified applicants for two hundred positions in the mid-1890s.[23] This intense competition was not unusual, even for the less prestigious technical institutes. In 1894 there were over twenty-six hundred qualified applicants for the seven existing government institutes of technology. Only six hundred were accepted.

Despite attempts to increase capacity, the demand of applicants continued to exceed the supply of places, down to the end of the Empire. In 1898, about twenty-five hundred students were accepted out of nearly forty-seven hundred qualified applicants, increasing the chances of acceptance somewhat. In this year, new polytechnics were established in Kiev and Warsaw, and, in 1902, in St. Petersburg. In 1899 a Mining Academy was established in Ekaterinoslav and in 1900 a Technological Institute in Tomsk. According to figures compiled by Nicholas Hans, the number of students in higher technical education increased some three times between 1899 and 1913, from 7,534 to 24,807.[24] Still, for a nation with a population ranging between one hundred twenty-five million and one hundred seventy million people during this period, such figures are unimpressive. Despite efforts to increase capacity, and to foster geographical distribution, a major grievance of the technical intelligentsia throughout the Imperial era was the limited governmental support for higher technical education coupled with the unbalanced geographical distribution of such schools. Most students who were lucky enough to find a place, crowded into the large cities, and often remained there after graduation, creating an even more severe shortage of trained technical talent in provincial areas. In 1897, thirty percent of graduate engineers lived in Moscow and St. Petersburg. They were often reluctant to leave for a career in some outlying area when the opportunities for lucrative work in higher education, production, or government service—as well as living amenities—were greatest in the major cities.[25] This pattern, established firmly by the end of the nineteenth century, remained a problem and became a major issue in the Soviet era.

[23] Sergei Timoshenko, *As I Remember*, Princeton, N.J., 1968, pp. 24-29. For other accounts by students of higher technical education in these years, see V. A. Rozentretter, *A. M. Terpigorev*, Moscow, 1965, pp. 12-22; D. N. Prianishnikov, *Moi vospominaniia*, Moscow, 1961, pp. 73-201; A. N. Krylov, *Moi vospominaniia*, Moscow, 1945, pp. 120-129.

[24] Leikina, 113-114; Nicholas Hans, *History of Russian Educational Policy, 1701-1917*, New York, 1964, pp. 239-240.

[25] *Sovetskaia istoricheskaia entsiklopediia*, vol. 6, Moscow, 1965, p. 115.

The popularity of careers in technology and the limited number of positions available in higher education were not the only problems in this area. Lack of financial aid and the poverty of student life served as further hurdles to many of those who did gain admittance. Economic problems and government repression of student life often impelled such students, no matter what their social background, toward a sympathy with radical politics. Such sympathy was strongest among the students of the newer institutions, the so-called "practical" institutes, but was common among most students in higher technical education. As early as the 1870s one could notice the difference between the privileged students of the university and older institutes, and such places as the Petersburg Technological Institute. According to the well-known radical writer V. G. Korolenko, in the 1870s "the student-technologists were easy to recognize on the street by their simple, cheap blouses, with belted sashes [peasant-style]. The usual appearance of this student crowd was democratic: many with long hair, wire-frame glasses and plaid scarfs."[26]

While the nonnoble students at such practical institutes stood to gain much after graduation—including the right to enter government service in civilian ranks at grades ten or twelve (fourteen was the lowest), and the legal status of "honored citizen," with its privileges—the road to a degree was long and arduous for many. The government, concerned with internal security, maintained a merciless surveillance of even such apparently harmless groups as school choirs, student library committees, and mutual aid societies for students from the same geographical area. The maintenance of an Inspectorate for such surveillance consumed a sizable part of the budget at a place like the Moscow Technical Institute (MTU) before 1905.[27] Only a minority of students lived in school dormitories, not so much because of overcrowding as from a desire to escape the eyes of informers placed there by the authorities to watch for "subversive activities." The government prohibited most student organizations, and was quick to expel the guilty or the merely suspect. Engineer Gubkin, later to be a major figure in Soviet technology, recalled that a report of political unreliability given him by an official in his school days for some satirical verses followed him through the remainder of his career in Imperial Russia.[28] Outlets for student energies, therefore, took the form of isolated academic work or illegal radical organizations. Timoshenko, struck later by the openness of student life in England and the amount of contact between students and teachers there, wrote of his own situation in the 1890s in St. Petersburg:

[26] Cited in Leikina, p. 116.
[27] Prokof'ev, pp. 79, 100-102; *Izvestiia MTU*, Moscow, 1899, p. 47.
[28] M. Lapidus, *Otkryvatel' podzemnykh tain*, Moscow, 1963, p. 47.

I recall my engineering school dormitory. Of all the students only five percent lived there, and those that did lived completely apart from one another. . . . There was no direct contact with the teachers either, except at examinations, and that, of course, had been the great defect in our own student life.[29]

Timoshenko noted that most of his fellow students, even at the elite Communications Institute, were on the left politically, divided between sympathizers of the Populists and the Marxists. Students at the Petersburg Technological Institute tended to be even more active politically. Lenin's first major revolutionary group in the early 1890s, the Union for the Emancipation of the Working Class, had a number of students from this Institute as members, including such later Bolsheviks as the Krasin brothers, and Gleb Krzhizhanovsky, who are important to this study.[30] The Moscow Technical Institute was a major organizing center for the 1905 uprising there, and some of its students were active participants. While student life became somewhat more open as a consequence of the 1905 revolution, the repressive atmosphere never entirely disappeared. It fostered a desire for student self-rule, which flowered briefly in 1905 and strongly for more than a decade after 1917. Although student political activities declined for some years after 1905, and student politics became more diverse—with a variety of groups allying themselves with political parties across the spectrum from right to left— sympathy for the left remained high.[31] Leftist and left liberal groups were the most prominent even after 1905. The economic conditions of students remained oppressive and influenced their attitudes strongly.

Data on the social background of students in higher technical education indicate that, although a large majority of such students were neither working class or peasant in background, they did not necessarily receive adequate financial support from home. Even children of the nobility, who attended such institutes far out of proportion to their numbers in society, were often impoverished or from families of declining economic status who wanted a promising profession for their children and lacked the ties or means for other careers.[32] Two surveys of

[29] Timoshenko, p. 126.

[30] G. M. Krzhizhanovskii, *Zhizn' i deiatel'nost'*, Moscow, 1974, pp. 8-12; Liubov' Krassina, *Leonid Krassin: His Life and Work*, London, 1929, pp. 24-30.

[31] See the section by Paul J. Novgorotsev in *Russian Schools and Universities in the World War*, New Haven, 1929, pp. 138-139, based on prerevolutionary studies and the student press. An interesting Soviet dissertation is Zoia S. Kruglova, "Studencheskoe dvizhenie v period novogo revoliutsionnogo podiema, 1910-1914," Moscow, 1965.

[32] See the article on this subject in *Vestnik Vospitaniia*, No. 10 (Oct.), 1914, cited in Novgorotsev, 141.

students, one published in 1909 and the other in 1911, indicate the subsistence level of most students. According to the 1911 study, only about eight out of one hundred of those surveyed were supported primarily by scholarships; another thirteen lived mainly by their own earnings, and fifty-one received most aid from relatives. Data for the remainder are lacking. Even though most were supported by relatives, some sixty percent of the students at the St. Petersburg Technological Institute lived on no more than 40 rubles a month, very little considering the cost of living in the capital.[33] The 1909 survey indicates that student budgets in Moscow averaged 25 rubles a month, considered the poverty level. On that amount, students could afford only one full meal a day and often ate only tea and bread for breakfast and supper.[34]

The 25-ruble figure is for the student body as a whole, including the more privileged and prosperous students of the university. Students of technology, drawn from a somewhat lower social-economic level, particularly in the "practical" institutes, probably fared even worse. Cases of students who worked, for example, as street car conductors in Moscow and who passed out on the job from hunger were not unknown. Given the financial hardships, as well as the dense course load, many students had to stretch the normal time in higher education, sometimes from the required four or five, to eight or nine years.[35] The overall percentage who never earned a degree is unknown. Given the economic circumstances it was probably not insignificant. Data from MTU show that one-third to one-half of those who entered this institute between 1891 and 1917 never finished a degree there.[36]

Nonetheless, the size of the technical intelligentsia continued to increase. By 1897, there were some twelve thousand graduate engineers alone, not counting applied scientists or technicians.[37] The number of such engineers had been counted only in the hundreds before 1861, and the size of this group continued to grow in the years prior to World War I. By 1914, Russia was producing most of its own graduate technologists, lessening its dependence on foreign engineers, a considerable achievement of the Tsarist educational system despite the problems discussed here. Their growth was matched by another group of the technical intelligentsia, the so-called "practicals" or "self-taught" (*praktiki* or *samouchki*), people who performed the work of technologists without having obtained a degree. By 1919, almost a third of the engi-

[33] A. Grodzinskii, "Material'nyi byt' studentov-tekhnologov," in M. V. Bernatsky, ed., *K kharakteristike sovremennogo studenchestva*, St. Petersburg, 1911, 49-59.
[34] *Studenchestvo v tsifrakh*, St. Petersburg, 1909, 29.
[35] Timoshenko, 113.   [36] Prokof'ev, 97.   [37] Leikina, 129-130.

neers employed in the economy were "practicals," a group whose significant and shaky status will be very important in the later pages of this study.

In addition to the political atmosphere and economic problems, many students were increasingly critical of their academic programs. Timoshenko was not alone, for example, in his criticisms of the engineering curriculum and teaching methods of his institute: "I am compelled to say that, owing to the unsatisfactory system of teaching, we left the Institute with no understanding of the most elementary things in mechanics."[38] He blamed this partly on the preoccupation of professors with their double function as teachers and as officials of the Ministry of Communications, which lead to a neglect of students. One may think this an exaggeration, given Timoshenko's own brilliant career later in Russia and the United States, but even so, it was not an uncommon complaint. The ratio of students to teachers was two to five times higher than in comparable schools in Germany as late as 1912.[39] As an engineering professor himself before the revolution, Timoshenko tried to correct some of the faults he had found in his own education, for example, by bringing theory and practice closer together. Yet the high student-teacher ratio and the large size of classes were structural problems that remained through this period.

Given such problems, young professors like Timoshenko concentrated on improving the quality of lectures, texts, and exercises:

> Another reason for our unsatisfactory training in mathematics and mechanics was the absence of any practical exercises. We listened to lectures, then we had tests, in which we had to show knowledge of what the lecturer had said. Problems were assigned too, but no one showed us how to solve these problems. Later on, when I myself was a professor at the Institute, that deficiency was eliminated, and we then had well-planned courses in mathematics and mechanics.[40]

Despite Timoshenko's own concern to bring theory and practice closer together, he himself never worked full time as a practicing engineer, but was recruited upon graduation directly into the teaching profession. This was the common pattern in Russian technical education, and may account for some of its deficiencies in this period. The trend had already begun, however, first in the practical institutions and then in the older elite institutes to bring theory and practice closer to-

[38] Timoshenko, 32.
[39] *Izvestiia MTU za 1912-1913 g.*, Vol. VIII, Moscow, 1913, 229.
[40] Ibid.

gether, a trend that was to develop, sometimes to extremes after 1928, before a balance was struck in subsequent years.

Another trend, more strongly felt among professors than students, was to adopt the polytechnic model of higher education, rather than the model of more specialized institutes in one area of technology. The first polytechnic was established in Riga, not by the government, but by private funds in 1862. The model was German, as was the language of instruction.[41] This model was reluctantly accepted by the Russian government only in the 1890s and only then because the polytechnics "were 'sold' to the State Council as a less expensive form of education, since during the first two years all students could take the same lectures and use the same labs."[41a] At the very least, the advocates of this model claimed, the polytechnic students were to save 20% in the cost of their educations by cutting a full year from their programs. (That is, the three polytechnics opened under the Ministry of Finance in this period were four-year schools, not five-year like the other technical institutes.) The most important organization of the Russian technical intelligentsia before 1917, the Russian Technical Society (RTO), strongly supported the polytechnic model from the 1860s on. Professors at the Moscow Technical School also waged a long battle to transform their institution into a polytechnic, which they finally accomplished only in April of 1918.[42] The reason for this trend among the engineering professoriate and other leading members of the technical intelligentsia who dominated the Russian Technical Society was their belief that a polytechnic education made students more flexible in their later careers and more creative. The polytechnic model required several years of general science and technology, and a heavy mathematics curriculum, before specialization in the final years of the course. Despite the way the polytechnics were first "sold" to the Tsarist government, in practice, such education tended to extend the degree program and was, therefore, often opposed by students, who were anxious to make a living, by government officials,

---

[41] Leikina, 114.

[41a] In a letter to the author from Harley Balzer, January 24, 1977. Balzer, a Ph.D. candidate in History at the University of Pennsylvania, is completing a dissertation entitled, "Educating Engineers and Entrepreneurs: Economic Politics and Technical Training in Tsarist Russia, 1877-1914."

[42] There is an excellent Soviet dissertation on the RTO in the Lenin Library, Moscow: N. G. Filippov, "Russkoe tekhnicheskoe obshchestvo, 1866-1905," Moscow State Historical-Archival Institute, Moscow, 1965. Filippov cites the RTO's 1883 project for polytechnic education in TsGIA, f. 90, op. 1, ed. khr. 610, ll. 21-30, p. 271, as well as the society's journal *Tekhnicheskoe obrazovanie* (1892-1916), Russia's major periodical in this field before the revolution. On the Moscow Technical School's struggle to become a polytechnic, see *Proekt razvitiia MTU v shkolu politekhnicheskogo tipa*, Moscow, 1915, 15, and Prokof'ev, 63-65.

who wanted less expensively educated specialists, and by industrialists, who in this period were more interested in engineers oriented toward production practice in one area of technology. The battle over this issue flared up again between 1917 and 1921, and in the years of the First Five-Year Plan, with major consequences.

Another issue of importance for many engineering professors, particularly in the civilian institutions, was the question of professional autonomy. The professors waged a long battle for self-rule, for elected deans and rectors, etc., a battle they temporarily won in the 1905 revolution, lost in the crackdown of 1911 by the Minister of Education, Kasso, and won again after the fall of the Romanovs, only to be challenged by Bolshevik centralization of higher education in later years.

A large number of engineering professors were fired in 1911, and this marked a watershed event in the history of this group, forging even stronger ties among those who suffered such discrimination, most of whom were liberal in their politics. For example, Timoshenko, who in 1911 was dean of a faculty at the Kiev Polytechnic, refused to enforce the Minister of Education's quota on Jewish students, or to expel those admitted over the quota. As a result in February, 1911 Timoshenko and two other deans at his institution were fired. In protest, all the professors on the left resigned. Their resignations were accepted, and the Kiev Polytechnic lost forty percent of its faculty. Similar events occurred at the Moscow Technical Institute and other institutions in 1911 over a variety of issues.

> Under the conditions then prevailing, dismissal from one's job had serious practical consequences. Nearly all schools and a large part of industry were government controlled, and no government institution could admit to its regular staff a dismissed professor.[43]

Timoshenko survived by means of some prize money, revenue from a textbook, consulting for the Russian Navy, which needed good engineers, and substitute teaching, which the government permitted. In 1913 he was forgiven and rehired in a regular teaching position. Nonetheless, for such professors, including many prominent scientists and engineers, the experience left a bitter aftertaste and intense dislike for centralized governmental control in the economy and education.[44]

The picture we are left with concerning major trends in this area before 1917 is one in which class distinctions were still important, though

[43] Timoshenko, 118. For a more general account of Kasso's 'cassation' of Russian higher education, see the article by P. B. Struve, *Russkaia Mysl'*, March, 1911. See also a recent Soviet dissertation V. P. Yakovlev, "Politika russkogo samoderzhaviia v universitetskom voprose, 1905-1911 gg.," Leningrad, 1971.

[44] Novgorotsev, pp. 147-153.

breaking down, and in which most technologists were recruited from the middle groups of Russian society, usually neither the richest nor the poorest. However, a trend toward further democratization of the student body was apparent by 1914. According to the figures compiled by Nicholas Hans and corroborated by other sources, both the universities and higher technical schools became more accessible in the period between 1880 and 1914. For example, the social composition of students in nine universities showed the following trend:

SOCIAL ORIGIN	1880	1914
Gentry and officials	46.6%	36.1%
Clergy	23.4	10.3
Merchants and honored citizens	14.3	14.8
Urban workers, craftsmen, small tradesmen, etc. (meshchanstvo)	12.3	24.3
Peasants	3.3	14.5

The student composition in higher technical schools tended to be even more democratic than in the universities by 1914, judging from figures available for the five higher technical institutes under the Ministry of Education:[45]

	1914
Gentry and officials	24.5%
Clergy	2.4
Merchants and honored citizens	19.1
Urban workers, craftsmen, small tradesmen (meshchanstvo)	31.6
Peasants	22.4

Another trend, given the limited number of such schools, was that old school ties proved important in an engineer's later career. One's alma

[45] Nicholas Hans, *History of Russian Educational Policy, 1701-1917*, New York, 1964, pp. 238-240. Hans's figures are drawn from official Russian sources and are based on legal estate categories. These can sometimes be misleading, since many urban residents, for example, were still listed on their passports as peasants, despite long-time residence in a town, and the category of *meshchanstvo* is a catch-all for many urban residents, including some industrial workers, lower-middle class elements, and more traditional craftsmen. Nonetheless, the general trend toward democratization and the more democratic nature of the higher technical schools by comparison with the universities seems clearly established.

mater forged bonds among alumni, and distinctions between alumni of differing schools. Several schools sought to foster a sense of professional community among their own alumni by forming technical societies to keep up old school ties, to aid those in need of jobs and money, and to further their later careers by upgrading their technical knowledge.

Distinctions among schools based on geography were also important; the better schools were considered to be those in Moscow, St. Petersburg, and, later Kiev, where the greatest concentration of technologists lived. Higher technical education in outlying areas was neglected, education in agronomy was especially limited, and secondary education for middle-level technicians in all branches of the economy was slighted. Women in technical careers were still a rarity, and women were not admitted to the established government technical institutes. These features gave the Russian technostructure a distinct profile in the years before 1917, and were to prove significant in the years after the October Revolution.

The poverty and repressiveness of student life contrasted with the possible rewards and rising status of graduate engineers in Imperial Russia. This gave the experience of young technologists two sharp edges: insecurity and the ambition of upward mobility. Their insecurity often pulled them to the left politically, and some found themselves caught between the urge for political activism, especially in a crisis, and the drive to excel professionally, especially in quieter times. At all times, Russian engineering students tended, on the one hand, to fear failure or expulsion, which meant slipping into the lower orders, and, on the other hand, to resent the privileged and often technically incompetent people who held so many of the commanding positions in Russian society before 1917. These feelings appear in almost all memoirs and biographies of technologists educated in this period, whether published in the West or the Soviet Union.[46] Although such feelings tended to make students critical of both the political order and many of their professors, they also divided the engineering professoriate; some teachers were content to hold stoutly to their hard-won privileges and established ways, unwilling to challenge the government, and another large segment felt compelled to work for further social change. The latter group sought the often contradictory goals of greater autonomy vis-à-vis the government, at the same time trying to increase their influence within the government and to gain greater financial support from the government for technical education. The seeds of many future conflicts between

---

[46] See not only Ipatieff and Timoshenko, but books by or about Bardin, Ioffe, Chaplygin, Gubkin, Terpigorev, Paton, and others listed in the bibliography. See also the accounts in L. I. Gumilevskii, *Russkie inzhenery*, Moscow, 1953.

students and professors in technology, and between the engineering professoriate and the Soviet government were sown in the late Imperial period in such areas as these.

What prospect faced the young technologist in late Imperial Russia after graduation? Although, prior to the 1890s, there had been an occasional oversupply of graduates, the trend in later years was toward an increasing number of opportunities and a rising social and economic status, due to the growth of Russian industry and the demand of the government for technical specialists. The growth was uneven, however, and the swings between feast and famine heightened a sense of insecurity. Increasing nationalism drove out a large number of foreign specialists, who had earlier been employed at high salaries, to go "to the lost country of the Tartars."[47] In 1897, for example, there was a greater proportion of foreign nationals among engineers than in any other Russian profession. But by 1914, foreign companies, mainly French, British, Belgian, German, and Swedish, which had invested some one-third of the capital in Russian industry, increasingly replaced foreign nationals with local technical personnel. Only a handful of foreign nationals remained in supervisory positions by the start of World War I. The increasing wave of strikes and industrial violence in the 1890s and during the revolution of 1905, as well as other difficulties of dealing with the Russian business environment, made such foreign investors see the wisdom of using Russian engineers, whatever doubt they may have had regarding their ability. The experience of one French-owned textile firm in May 1903, was not exceptional:

> The mills were stormed three times by the rioters in May 1903. The entire French and Belgian personnel fled for their lives. . . . After such an adventure there was no question of using foreigners to reform our top management. We needed Russians for our top personnel at any price, and above all a Russian managing director . . . after a series of extended Russian trips we have chosen Morganov, a Russian engineer who has been well recommended.[48]

Even such radical engineers as L. B. Krasin, one of the leaders of the military organization of the Bolsheviks during the 1905 revolution, in charge of their bomb-making efforts, was soon afterwards employed on excellent terms by the German electrical firm, Siemens-Schuckert, which helped him return to Russia in 1911 and avoid criminal prosecution by the Russian government for his revolutionary activities. In 1914,

---

[47] John P. McKay, *Pioneers for Profit: Foreign Entrepreneurship and Russian Industrialization, 1885-1913*, Chicago, 1970, p. 166.

[48] Ibid., pp. 194-196.

in fact, he was made manager of their St. Petersburg office, whence he was to have a prominent part in the Bolshevik revolution after 1917.[49]

Although most graduate Russian engineers in this period did not work directly in production but in government offices, business administration, and education, many enjoyed high pay and a growing demand for their services. A managing director, such as Morganov or Krasin, not only earned a high salary, but received bonuses based on profits or reductions in the costs of production. A chemical technologist like Ipatieff or a mechanical engineer like Timoshenko sometimes held several teaching jobs and received lucrative contracts from both government and private industry for consulting. In 1905, the minimum salary for a graduate engineer in the technical service of the state railways, the largest employer of technical specialists in this period, was 150 rubles a month, while lower-level technical personnel, such as draftsmen, earned only 25 rubles a month.[50] Most graduate engineers earned much more than 150 rubles a month. A chemical technologist, such as Ipatieff, earned 3000 rubles in one year alone from a single consulting contract with a private company, not to mention several teaching salaries and other sources of income.

While at the upper levels of the technical intelligentsia the rewards were great, for the bulk of the employed technical specialists a sense of insecurity was never entirely absent. A business downturn, a loss of government employment for political reasons, sickness, or accident, could mean real hardship, since unemployment insurance and most other forms of social security were largely unheard of until after the 1905 revolution, and even then, they remained minimal. Few graduate specialists went into business for themselves, so that they remained a group betwixt and between: far better off than workers and peasants, but still largely wage laborers with different interests from those of large-scale property owners in agriculture and industry.

In addition to a certain insecurity, graduate specialists faced other kinds of frustration as well. Not only were they often resented for their economic position and social status by workers and "practicals" (*praktiki*), they also faced a cultural gap between themselves and industrial workers, many of whom were only recently off the farm. Such peasant-workers brought many traditional attitudes with them to industry, including an aversion to industrial discipline, a tendency to work seasonally (they went to the countryside in the spring and summer), and curious beliefs. As a result, Russian labor productivity in

[49] Krassina, pp. 39-40. See also the interesting Soviet monograph on Krasin: B. Mogilevskii, *Nikitich*, Moscow, 1963.
[50] L. K. Erman, *Intelligentsiia v pervoi russkoi revoliutsii*, Moscow, 1966, p. 26.

industry remained well below that of the West, despite many large, modern plants in such industries as metallurgy and machine building.[51]

An incident related by Ipatieff in his work as a constultant to a metallurgical plant is indicative of the contradiction between the understanding of modern technology brought to industry by the graduate technologist, and the habits of workers who were still often close to the peasantry. When a blast furnace broke down and workers had trouble getting it back into production, Ipatieff relates, they would sometimes appeal to the saints for help, lowering a religious picture, or icon, into the furnace, not unlike the way peasants arranged religious processions with icons, praying for rain during a drought.[52]

Also frustrating to many technical specialists were the roadblocks to technological innovation and the limited opportunities for Russian inventors and others interested in research and development. Most Russian industrial firms did not have factory laboratories or industrial research institutes, a trend that was becoming strong in the West after 1900. Foreign firms relied mostly on foreign technology, where their expertise lay and where they had the greatest confidence, while Russian owned-and-operated firms were often run by self-taught or nontechnically trained entrepreneurs who had little understanding of the link between science and technology, or the dividends that could come from systematic support of innovation. The government, while giving some support to research and development, was extremely miserly in the view of the technostructure and often squelched promising projects through lack of foresight by decision-makers.

While the picture was perhaps not so bleak as that portrayed by Soviet historians, who wish to accentuate the contrast between Tsarist neglect of science and technology and generous Soviet support, there can be no doubt that major groups of the technical intelligentsia were very unhappy with the situation before 1917 and mounted a campaign to change it. This campaign was first spearheaded by the Russian Technical Society (RTO), founded in 1866, which took as one of its aims bringing science, technology, industry, and government into closer cooperation. Under the leadership of such people as the chemist Mendeleev; Count Kochubei, a military engineer and chemist; and F. N. Lvov, a Russian follower of Fourier who had earlier been imprisoned for his beliefs, the RTO tried to work as a lobby for the interests of the technical intelligentsia, and to stimulate support for Russian inventors and the application of their inventions in the economy.[53] Its work was

[51] McKay, pp. 242-267; see also Rozentretter, pp. 20-82; A. N. Krylov, *Moi vospominania*; and M. A. Pavlov, *Vospominaniia metallurga*, Moscow, 1945.
[52] Ipatieff, p. 74.   [53] Filippov, p. 70.

influential in acting as an organizing center for the technical intelligentsia, but far from successful in increasing the influence of this group in private industry and government, at least to the degree desired.

The government gave small subsidies to the RTO, and industrialists supported it somewhat, but the RTO still felt like an orphan in Russian society. Its leaders thought that by comparison with the millions of rubles appropriated for the Holy Synod or to maintain the Imperial Court, for example, the thousands given to the RTO were paltry. Nonetheless, some ten thousand persons became members of this society between 1866 and 1917, and the RTO was a pioneer in supporting Russian aviation, electrical technology, and wireless telegraphy (radio), as well as in promoting technical education and the popularization of technology. But attempts to interest the government and private industry in new areas of research and development were often dismissed as "fantasies" or treated with polite neglect.[54] As an Imperial naval officer wrote to the head of the Aviation Section of the RTO in 1905, ". . . how much pain and suffering has been caused by the lack of understanding by the military command of the goals, tasks, and applications of aviation . . . a rigid airship for observation was necessary at Port Arthur; that there was none—this is one of the crimes of the present military command."[55] (He was referring to the surprise attack by the Japanese on the Russian naval base at Port Arthur in 1904.) The RTO pointed out that in this respect, as in other aspects of technology, the Japanese were more far-sighted.

The early leaders of Russian aviation—Mozhaisky, Zhukovsky, Sikorsky, and others—were associated with, and helped by, the RTO, but with little or no encouragement from the government until after the Russo-Japanese War of 1904-1905.[56] Of course, such neglect of pioneering technology was not unusual among Western governments either, but Russian technologists felt that, given the weakness of private industry, Russian political leaders were even more backward. And, of course, if there was neglect in the military sector of technology, there was an even greater vacuum of support in civilian areas. Creative specialists interested in innovation, therefore, felt very much on their own in this period.

---

[54] TsGVIA, f. 401, op. 4/928, 1883 g., ed. khr. 34, 11. 4-10, cited in Filippov, p. 35.

[55] TsGVIA, f. 802, op. 3, ed. khr. 1060, ll. 111-115, cited in Filippov, pp. 217-218.

[56] TsGVIA, f. 90, op. 1, ed. khr. 497, l. 14, in Filippov, p. 217. For the later patronage of Russian aviation by Grand Duke Alexander, see the memoir of Elisabeth Baikalov-Latyshev concerning her father and uncle, the Lebedevs, who were early Russian aeronautical engineers (*Aerospace Historian*, forthcoming).

The experience of World War I seemed to many of these people a major opportunity to push for greater concrete support for research and development. The centers of research in Russian technology before the war were largely in three areas: the universities and higher technical schools, mostly the latter; governmental bodies, such as the Geology Committee (similar in function to the U.S. Geological Survey), which employed fewer than thirty specialists for the vast Russian Empire before 1917, and bodies of military technologists, such as the artillery specialists; and private inventors, Russian Edisons, like Tsiolkovsky, who built rockets and dreamed of interplanetary flight, but with much less support than Edison.

The Russian Academy of Sciences until 1915 was largely concerned with the "pure sciences" and theoretical studies, while industry did little in the way of systematic industrial research. A private foundation, the Ledentsov Society, endowed by a wealthy Russian industrialist in 1909 and in some respects analogous to such Western foundations as those of Carnegie and Rockefeller, provided grants free of government strings, but its resources were far more limited than those of Western analogs.[57]

Beneath this surface of outer weakness, however, an alliance was developing between natural scientists who were interested in technology, and elements among the engineers. This was natural, given the revolution in industry developing at this time, which was more directly science-based than the first industrial revolution, and emphasized applications of chemistry, electricity, thermodynamics, etc. in the economy.[58] This alliance pushed in several directions: to create more chairs in higher technical schools for the new disciplines and technologies; to create a series of specialized research institutes, which would bring together and coordinate the collective work of technologists interested in a single area, such as radiology, aviation, metallurgy, and others. In 1911-1912 this trend gained momentum through the leadership of, for example, P. N. Lebedev, a physicist, and Vernadsky, a geochemist, who were members of the Academy of Sciences but worked closely with elements of the engineering intelligentsia.[59]

They called for an end to the neglect of the applied sciences, and for the creation of a series of specialized institutes that would become the centers of such research in Russia. The work of the Soviet historian, Bastrakova, and the American historian of science, Loren Graham, has shown the important influence both of foreign models, especially Ger-

---

[57] M. S. Bastrakova, *Stanovlenie sovetskoi sistemy organizatsii nauki, 1917-1922*, Moscow, 1973, p. 30.
[58] David Landes, *Unbound Prometheus*, Cambridge, 1969, pp. 126, 235.
[59] Bastrakova, p. 38.

man, as well as the Russian milieu in the evolution of this trend.[60] This movement found a center of organization after 1915 in the Academy of Sciences. Under the leadership of Vernadsky, a Commission for the Study of Scientific-Productive Forces (KEPS) was established in the Academy to draw together scientists and engineers interested in applied research and development. By 1917, one hundred thirty-nine prominent scientists and technical specialists were working in this commission. They examined some twenty projects for specialized institutes, but none were realized until after 1917. Vernadsky outlined a major goal for KEPS: to make it a coordinating center for planning Russian applied science, while keeping the influence of the Academy of Sciences high.

An Academy member such as Vernadsky believed strongly in the role of this institution in planning and coordinating national research. This was an organizational pattern that had largely eroded in Western countries, where national academies had been overshadowed or displaced by higher educational institutions and industrial laboratories as centers of research by the early twentieth century. Vernadsky also hoped to use KEPS and the Academy as a lobby for increased government support for such activites, something that the government-supported Kaiser Wilhelm Society, formed in 1911, had been very successful doing in Germany. World War I was an opportune time for such an effort, Vernadsky believed, since it brought these groups closer together and showed those in power how important planning and support for applied science could be. At the same time, however, Vernadsky—a political liberal, and one of the founders and leaders of the Constitutional Democratic party in Russia—was concerned to achieve and protect the autonomy of scientists and technologists in running their own internal affairs.

How could this happen? In a report to KEPS in December, 1916, Vernadsky insisted that the government's role was simply to outline the broad areas of concern for technologists, provide the aid they needed, and then allow them self-rule in achieving results, without interfering in the details of their work: "The task is not the government organization of science," he wrote in this period, "but government aid for the scientific creativity of the nation."[61] This point of view was strong

[60] See the paper presented by Loren R. Graham, of the History Department, Columbia University, at the International Congress of Slavists in Banff, Canada, September, 1974, "The Formation of Soviet Research Institutes," pp. 1-6.

[61] Bastrakova, p. 56. See also Vladimir Vernadsky, *O blizhaishikh zadachakh KEPS*, Petrograd, 1916, and *Zadachi nauki v sviaze s gosudarstvennoi politikoi Rossii*, Petrograd, 1917, and Alexander Vucinich, *Science in Russian Culture*, vol. 2, Stanford, 1970, pp. 222-223, 413-415.

among the scientific-technical intelligentsia, and became an area of conflict not only between them and the Tsarist government, but later between the Soviet government and those with similar views. "Support without control," "autonomy with government aid," were popular slogans among that element of the scientific-technical intelligentsia that resented Tsarist repression and neglect over previous decades, including such abuses of government power as that of Kasso in 1911. The views of Vernadsky were close to those of many leaders of the technical intelligentsia, particularly those in the professional societies discussed below and in the higher technical schools, many of whom worked closely with KEPS. Such views were shared by the organizers of the All-Russian Union of Engineers, formed in May 1917 from among these elements.[62] KEPS, however, got little support from the government in World War I. In fact, it remained without a budget until after the fall of the Romanovs. None of the projects for specialized research institutes in technology were realized in the Tsarist period.[63]

Yet in other respects the experience of World War I led to greater emphasis by the government on planning and supporting applied research in vital military areas, through such organs as the Chemical Committee of the Chief Artillery Directorate (headed by General Ipatieff), the War Industry Committees, and other bodies. The War Industry Committees enlisted the aid of industrialists, labor leaders, technical specialists, and others in the war effort, with the technical intelligentsia making up a sizeable proportion of the membership.[64] This experience gave the Russian technostructure both a sense of its own indispensability and potential power, as well as a heightened feeling of frustration with the limitations placed on their influence by the non-technically trained in the power structure, and the contradictions of the social structure at all levels. It is not surprising, therefore, to find this group taking the offensive for its interests in World War I and afterwards, at times actively opposing decisions of the government in areas

[62] See *Vestnik inzhenerov*, nos. 1-2, 1917.

[63] Bastrakova, pp. 51-62.

[64] TsGVIA, f. 13251, opis' 1, d. 7, l. 67. A copy of this archival document was made for the author by a friend in Moscow. See also the following publications of the War Industry Committees: Tsentral'nyi voenno-promyshlennyi komitet (TsV-PK), *Spisok voenno-promyshlennykh komitetov*, Petrograd, 1917; *Deiatel'nost' oblastnykh i mestnykh voenno-promyshlennykh komitetov*, Petrograd, 1916; TsV-PK, *Organizatsiia*, Petrograd, 1915; TsV-PK, *Zhurnal*, nos. 2-6, 1915, 22, 1916; TsV-PK, *Otchety otdelov*, Petrograd, 1917; TsV-PK, Schetnyi otdel, *Doklad*, Petrograd, 1916. An interesting Soviet dissertation on this period is V. S. Daikin, "Russkaia burzhuaziia i tsarism v gody pervoi mirovoi voiny," Institut istorii SSSR, Leningrad, 1967. I found the publications and dissertation above in the Lenin Library, Moscow.

of their technical expertise.[65] Some of the later consequences of this experience will be seen as this study develops.

To sum up, by 1917 the Russian technical intelligentsia particularly its core group, the graduate engineers, while still small in size by comparison with the total population and limited in influence, began to grow, to organize itself internally, and to become increasingly self-conscious of its common interests as well as its internal divisions and conflicts. Its major organizing centers in this period were the higher educational institutions and the technical societies, which grew both in numbers and in size by 1917. Besides the newly formed KEPS, there were nine major technical societies. Their names, dates of origin, and membership are given below:[66]

	Initial Membership	Membership in 1914
Russian Technical Society, 1866	529	2000
Physical-Chemical Society, 1869	60	565
Polytechnical Society, 1879	75	306
Society of Technologists, 1884	56	904
Society of Civil Engineers, 1894	72	620
Electrical, 1900	81	526
Metallurgical, 1910	267	677
Mining Engineers, 1887	302	711
Hydraulic Engineers, 1893	12	211

The publications and conferences of these groups reveal much about the dynamics of the prerevolutionary technostructure, and we will have occasion to refer to them at points later in this study. An analysis of this environment, which will be made in greater depth in the following chapters, is an important key to understanding the social relations of the technical intelligentsia, both before and after 1914.

[65] Louis Siegelbaum of St. Antony's College, Oxford, is documenting such conflicts in a detailed study of the War Industry Committees.

[66] The figures are from an unpublished Soviet dissertation in the Lenin Library, Moscow: A. I. Kardash, "Organizatsiia nauchno-technicheskikh obshchestv v SSSR 1921-1929," Moscow, 1968, pp. 112-113. In addition to the Filippov dissertation on the Russian Technical Society, see the history of the Russian Physical-Chemical Society by V. V. Kozlov, *Ocherki istorii khimicheskikh obshchestv SSSR*, Moscow, 1958.

2

THE SOVIET TECHNOSTRUCTURE, 1918-1928

> *Workers without engineers are like soldiers without officers.*
>
> Russian engineer, 1917[1]

> *A communist who has not proved his ability to coordinate and modestly direct the work of the specialists, making a detailed study of the substance of the matter, is frequently harmful. We have a good many communists like that and I would give a dozen of them for a single bourgeois expert who has honestly studied his subject and is well informed.*
>
> Lenin, 1921[1]

In early 1918 the Bolsheviks actively began to court the technical intelligentsia in the hope of attracting their cooperation in the organization of a new society. The evidence below seeks to establish the ardor with which some of the leading Bolsheviks, with Lenin as chief matchmaker, wooed the technical intelligentsia in the early years of the Soviet system, and to show some of the results of that effort. In the years between 1918 and 1928 a match was struck between the Communist power structure and the prerevolutionary Russian technostructure, but the resulting relationship proved to be more a marriage of convenience than a love match. This chapter will analyze briefly the relations among the technostructure, the Communist power structure, and the industrial working class, focusing upon elements of conflict—social class and other interest group conflicts—as well as elements of cooperation that developed among these groups prior to 1928. This background will then provide a setting for the more detailed case studies to follow.[2]

As noted in the previous chapter, the technostructure was in a precarious position by 1918. Many of its members viewed with alarm the

---

[1] *Vestnik inzhenerov*, Feb. 1917, 126; Lenin, *Selected Works*, vol. 9, p. 299.

[2] Manfred Spaeth, a doctoral student at the Free University of Berlin, is doing a more detailed study of the Russian technical intelligentsia just before and after the 1917 revolutions.

economic chaos enveloping the country, some blamed the Bolsheviks, and most disagreed with the Bolshevik seizure of power, even though they disagreed among themselves on how to deal with the crisis. Some fled the centers to join anti-Bolshevik movements forming on the peripheries in 1918, or fled the country altogether, but the majority remained and, by late 1918, were working for the Soviet regime. Several censuses of specialists taken by Soviet government bureaus from 1918 to 1920 confirm this, and corroborate more scattered impressions from other sources.[3] During 1918, the strikes by technical specialists and other civil servants against the Bolshevik regime largely ceased, and the degree of cooperation rapidly increased. Why was this so?

The reasons involved both repression and positive incentives. Initiatives toward greater cooperation came from both sides: that is, the Bolsheviks made a number of conciliatory gestures to meet some of the demands and satisfy strong interests among the technical specialists, while also using repression against those who took up arms or conspired to overthrow the Soviets. At the same time, individual specialists and organizations of specialists, such as the All-Russian Union of Engineers (VSI) began to urge work and at least limited cooperation with the Bolsheviks. The second Moscow Congress of VSI, for example, which met in October 1918, contrasted considerably with the January meeting discussed in the previous chapter. Although the leadership remained the same, and class conflict between workers and technical specialists was still a prominent theme, the keynote was no longer boycott, but survival and the working out of a modus vivendi with the Bolsheviks. VSI asked to be recognized as a separate trade union by the Bolsheviks, a demand that was not to be met; but in a de facto sense, VSI played this role. There was a strong move within the organization to cease political opposition and concentrate on protecting the professional and economic interests of engineers. Reports from various parts of the country indicated that many members had been arrested in conflicts with other labor unions and industrial workers; the Congress gave a great deal of attention to the need to meet this situation.[4]

With the anti-Bolshevik uprisings and assassination attempts against Bolshevik leaders by a rival party, the Left Socialist Revolutionaries, during July and August 1918, a Red Terror had been launched against all opponents of the regime, and many technical specialists had been

---

[3] *Rabota nauchno-tekhnicheskikh uchrezhdenii Respubliki, 1918-1919 gg.* Moscow, 1919, pp. 56-64, and TsGAOR SSSR, f. 3429, op. 60, d. 527, ll. 31, 32, cited in Fediukin, *Velikii oktiabr'*, pp. 146, 164.

[4] *Vserossiiskii soiuz inzhenerov. Otchet' o zaniatiiakh 2-i Moskovskoi oblastnoi konferentsii, 18-21 okt., 1918 g.*, Moscow, 1918, pp. 4-45. A copy is in the Lenin Library, Moscow.

swept up in the resulting dragnets. VSI took the lead in gaining the release of these prisoners and protecting their interests, working with Lenin's secretary, N. P. Gorbunov, a young chemical engineer, and with the prominent Bolshevik engineer, then a government official, L. B. Krasin. Safe-conduct passes signed by Krasin, Gorbunov, or others were arranged by VSI and by the Supreme Council of the National Economy (*Vesenkha*), the new government body in charge of administering industry. These became essential to the safety of many *spetsy* (specialists) and brought an influx of new members to VSI and to work under the protection of *Vesenkha*.[5] VSI also pressed for the material interests of its members and was pleased when the government established, in the fall of 1918, a set of uniform pay scales for engineers in all government-controlled industries. Also through the efforts of VSI and *Vesenkha*, engineers were exempted from having their living quarters and personal property requisitioned by workers or government bureaus.[6]

The atmosphere of class war, which became a full-scale civil war by the fall of 1918, and the resulting physical dangers and material shortages were a strong incentive for technical specialists in areas controlled by the Bolsheviks to seek the protection of those in the new government who were well disposed toward them. Here personal ties were often important. Again and again in the memoirs of this period, one finds that technical specialists were helped by relatives, former students, or friends who had joined the new government. The old school tie was especially prominent. For example, Lenin's personal secretary, N. P. Gorbunov, who was also the secretary of the government's cabinet, the Council of Commissars (*Sovnarkom*), was the son of an engineer, and a 1917 graduate of the Petrograd Technological Institute. Krasin was a graduate of the same school and a prominent electrical engineer who had had many ties to other engineers before the revolution. Both of these men intervened in disputes between specialists and Communist activists or workers to protect the interests of the technical intelligentsia.[7] The memoirs of such later emigrés as Ipatieff and Timoshenko, contained kind words for a number of former students who, as Bolsheviks or Communist sympathizers, nevertheless helped their former teachers and specialists during these difficult times. As important as such links were, the technostructure had active protectors in two far more power-

---

[5] Ibid., p. 13; Ipatieff, p. 270.

[6] VSI, *Otchet'*, 13.

[7] Fediukin, pp. 107, 341-342; N. P. Gorbunov, *Petrogradskaia Pravda*, January 30, 1924; Bastrakova, pp. 85, 166; *Organizatsiia nauki v pervye gody Sovetskoi vlasti, 1917-1925. Sbornik dokumentov*, Leningrad, 1968, p. 91; N. P. Gorbunov, *Severnaia kommuna*, March 8, 1919, 3; E. I. Poliakova, "N. P. Gorbunov," in *Istoriia SSSR*, no. 5, 1968, p. 60.

ful figures, the best known radical writer of the period, Maxim Gorky, and the chief of state and party, Lenin himself.[8]

Lenin has been portrayed by at least one recent author as strongly antiintellectual, an *intelligent* whose dislike of fellow intellectuals was legendary.[9] In fact, Lenin's relationship with the intelligentsia was more complicated than that. He despised the dilettantism and lethargy that were traits of many prerevolutionary intellectuals among whom he had grown up. But Lenin remained a traditional Russian intellectual in other respects, and in the years after 1917 he defended many interests of the intelligentsia against attacks from antiintellectual workers and radicals on the far left—Communists, anarchists, and others—who set out to destroy much of the old culture and radically change the composition and institutions of the intelligentsia overnight. Lenin was especially well disposed toward intellectuals who sought knowledge as a guide to action, and this feature of his personality predisposed him to view favorably the scientific-technical intelligentsia. This same feature led him to dislike many members of the cultural intelligentsia and fellow radicals, whom he often considered mere babblers and do-nothings, especially, of course, when he disagreed with them. Lenin's intolerance toward many intellectuals whose views differed from his own has been much commented upon and well documented; it needs no further discussion here. This intolerance was only a part of the picture, however. With regard to the scientific-technical intelligentsia, one finds another side of his personality, a high degree of tolerance for members of this group and regard for some of their interests and welfare.

This was true even for many of those who disagreed openly with the Bolsheviks and occasionally even for those who had taken up arms against them, depending upon their prominence and usefulness to the government. While Lenin generally supported and justified the use of terror against active anti-Bolsheviks, including technical specialists, he also spared some, including such prominent opponents as Academician Vernadsky, a chemist and scientific administrator. After the fall of the anti-Bolshevik Volunteer Army, with whose members Vernadsky had active ties, he was arrested by the *Cheka* (Soviet secret police) and brought in a sealed train to Moscow. Lenin promptly released him and offered substantial support for his scientific work. Despite continued opposition to aspects of Bolshevik rule, Vernadsky remained to work in the Soviet Union, where he died in 1945 after a number of creative

[8] For Gorky's important role, see *Gor'kii i nauka. Stat'i, rechi, pis'ma, vospominaniia*, Moscow, 1964. For Lenin's role, see the notes below.

[9] This is the view developed by Adam Ulam in *The Bolsheviks*, New York, 1968, pp. 210ff.

accomplishments.[10] It was not unusual for someone in the uniform of the *Cheka* to show up at a Soviet technical bureau and hand over a rumpled, bearded prisoner, who turned out to be a technical specialist apprehended among anti-Bolshevik forces and spared from the usual execution meted out in such circumstances thanks to his technical qualifications.[11] While less prominent anti-Bolsheviks among the technical intelligentsia were sometimes imprisoned and executed during this period, Lenin's personal attitude toward the group as a whole was at times a conservative and protective influence. As he expressed it once to A. V. Lunacharsky, Commissar of Culture, "One must spare a great scientist or major specialist in whatever sphere, even if he is reactionary to the to the nth degree."[12]

Why was this so? It was not only a sign of Lenin's flexibility, his realistic attitude toward power, and his strong instincts regarding the survival of the Soviet regime, it was indicative of his high hopes for science and technology as pillars of the new society. This led to his respect for the groups that possessed the systematic knowledge without which these areas could never grow or prosper. In early 1918, Lenin and others in the Communist party set out to develop a policy toward the technical intelligentsia that mixed force with persuasion. Actually, Lenin had given a preview of this policy even before the Bolsheviks seized power. In a pamphlet written during September 1917, he noted:

> A proletarian government will say: we need more and more engineers, agronomists, technicians, scientifically educated specialists of every type. We will give all such workers responsible work to which they are accustomed. We will probably only gradually introduce equal pay for them, giving higher pay to such specialists during the transitional period, but we will surround them with workers' control and we will enforce the rule: "He who does not work, neither shall he eat."[13]

This was an accurate preview of what happened after the Bolshevik revolution, with the creation of a system of political commissars who oversaw the work of technical specialists in the economy and the military. The Soviet government also relied heavily for some years on

---

[10] See the manuscript memoirs of Nina Vernadskaia, in the Hoover Institution, Stanford; Vladimir Vernadskii, "The First Year of the Ukrainian Academy of Sciences," in *The Annals of the Ukrainian Academy of Arts & Sciences in the U.S.*, vol. 11, nos. 1 and 2, pp. 3-31. George V. Vernadskii, "Bratstvo 'Priutino' " *Novyi zhurnal*, Kniga 97, New York, 1969, pp. 228-231.

[11] O. Pisarzhevskii, *Stranitsy zhizni bol'shevika-uchenogo*, Moscow, 1960, p. 29.

[12] A. V. Lunacharskii, in *Revoliutsiia i kul'tura*, no. 1, 1927, p. 29.

[13] *Polnoe sobranie*, vol. 34, p. 312.

a collegial administration in which Communists, trade unionists, and old specialists worked collectively to manage the Soviet economy.

The first contacts between technical specialists and Bolsheviks began right after the revolution, and, by January of 1918, a Council of Experts had been established at the suggestion of L. B. Krasin in the *Vesenkha*. It was composed mostly of technical specialists who had worked in the old Central War Industry Committee under the Tsarist regime.[14] In January and February 1918, the Commissariat of Education (*Narkompros*) began talks with the Academy of Sciences. By spring, the Soviet government had agreed to subsidize the Academy, providing for the first time a budget for the Academy's commission of applied science, KEPS, formed in 1915 at the initiative of Vernadsky.[15] Despite the pas de deux between these two partners, however, both groups remained suspicious of each other and kept a polite distance.

Once the Treaty of Brest-Litovsk was signed in March 1918, and the war with Germany was concluded, Lenin turned greater attention to this question. His reasoning is revealing. For example, in his remarks of March 15, 1918, upon signing the treaty with Germany, which contained punitive terms for the Bolshevik regime, he noted ruefully:

> The war taught us much, not only that people suffered, but especially the fact that those who have the best technology, organization, discipline and the best machines emerge on top; it is this the war has taught us, and it is a good thing it has taught us. It is essential to learn that without machines, without discipline, it is impossible to live in modern society. It is necessary to master the highest technology or be crushed.[16]

It is no wonder, then, that Lenin looked fondly for the rest of his life on the work of defense intellectuals such as General Ipatieff, or that Ipatieff, despite his disagreements with much of Bolshevik ideology, personally liked and respected Lenin.[17] They had found common ground.

Although Lenin was preoccupied until 1921 with the civil war and the consolidation of power, he frequently intervened to protect the interests of old specialists and generally took their side in work disputes with nonspecialists. According to one recent Soviet historian with access to the archives of the Council of Commissars, over which Lenin presided, there was scarcely a meeting of this body in the years between

---

[14] Bastrakova, p. 164.

[15] AAN SSSR, f. 132, op. 1, ed. khr. 8, l. 23, published in *Organizatsiia nauki v pervye gody Sovetskoi vlasti*, pp. 174-175.

[16] *Polnoe sobranie*, vol. 26, p. 116.

[17] Ipatieff, p. 318. See also Lenin, *Polnoe*, vol. 53, pp. 125, 225-226.

1918 and 1922 that did not discuss the use of the so-called "bourgeois specialists." More than five percent of all official acts of the Soviet government in this period were concerned with scientific research alone, most of it applied research.[18] While this Soviet author may exaggerate in saying that the Soviet government was the first in the world to pay as much attention to scientific and technical policy as, for example, to economic or foreign policy, there is little doubt that Lenin personally showed a great interest in this area. And he worked hard to translate such interest into policy. For example, he and the Soviet government moved quickly several times to work out policies that went a long way, if not all the way, to meet the demands of technical specialists in several areas, among them, the reestablishment of labor discipline and the promotion of applied research and technical education.

By March of 1918 Lenin had moved to curb workers' control and the power of factory committees, a concern uppermost in the minds of most technical experts at this time. He also sought to change trade-union and Communist attitudes toward the use of progressive rates for piecework and other facets of "scientific management," the system worked out by the American engineer, F. W. Taylor, and generally opposed by radicals and trade unionists throughout the industrial world in this period.[19] In fact, much of Taylorism was adapted eventually to Soviet industry due to the efforts of Russian engineers working with Lenin, Gorbunov, and Alexei Gastev, who formed the Central Labor Institute, with Lenin's strong support, to develop such methods and promote a system of "social engineering," strongly embued with technocratic values.[20]

Such measures proved to be as popular among many industrial managers and engineers as they were unpopular among workers and Left Communists. Lenin justified his policy of "concessions with controls" over the technical intelligentsia by calling it a form of class warfare. In a war, as he put it, one must not refuse help from any quarter, even the most oblique. To weaken the opposition, therefore, "bourgeois specialists" should be attracted to serve in the Soviet regime in order to detach them from the bourgeoisie. They should not be compelled at the point of a gun to work, but should be treated with tact and respect,

[18] Bastrakova, pp. 75-79.

[19] For Lenin's unfavorable view of the Taylor system before World War I, see *Polnoe sobranie*, vol. 23, pp. 18-19, and vol. 24, pp. 369-371. For his change in views, see vol. 36, pp. 187-194. Russian engineers both before and after 1917, strongly urged the adoption of Taylorism. See *Vestnik inzhenerov*, Oct. 1915, 933-936; 1916, II, 553-564; 575-580; 585-595; June-July 1917, 265-272; 288-292, 302-308; Jan.-Feb. 1924, 3-4; and I. Rabchinskii, *O sisteme Teilora*, Moscow, 1921.

[20] On this subject see my article, "Alexei Gastev and the Controversy over Taylorism, 1918-1924, in the Soviet Union, 1920-1924" (*Soviet Studies*, July 1977).

and persuaded morally and materially to serve the Soviet system. Lenin developed these views most fully in a speech to the Eighth Congress of the Communist party, held in March 1919, in which he defended conciliatory policies toward the specialists against what he described as a great deal of disagreement and dissatisfaction over these policies in party ranks. He justified not only paying them salaries that were often five or six times higher than those of skilled workers and Communist activists—even of Lenin himself—but also creating attractive working conditions for them:

> We must immediately, without awaiting help from other countries, immediately increase the forces of production. To do this without the bourgeois specialists is impossible. This must be said once and for all. . . . We have a large stratum of these bourgeois physicians, engineers, agronomists and cooperative specialists, and when they see in practice that the proletariat attracts the wide masses more and more to help in their tasks, they will be convinced morally, and not simply politically severed from the bourgeoisie. Then our task will become easier. They will themselves be attracted to our *apparat* and make themselves a part of it.[21]

In December 1918 the Soviet government decreed compulsory labor service for all technical specialists, but, as Lenin explained to the Eighth Congress:

> It is impermissible to force an entire stratum to work with a club [over their heads]. This we have learned well from experience. We can compel them not to participate actively in counterrevolution, we can frighten them, so that they are afraid to extend a hand to a white-guard uprising. . . . But to force an entire stratum to work by such methods is impossible.[22]

Addressing skeptical or hostile comrades in the Communist movement and the trade unions, he warned that socialism and later communism could not be achieved without the help of this stratum. He ordered them "to learn humility and respect for the work of specialists in science and technology." Their proletarian overseers should "issue fewer commands, in fact, not command at all." Again, in 1921, Lenin warned such activists,

> If all our leading institutions, that is, the Communist Party, the Soviet government, and the trade unions do not cherish, like the

21 *Polnoe sobranie*, vol. 38, pp. 166-167.
22 Ibid.

apple of their eye, each specialist who is working conscientiously with a knowledge of his work and love for it, even if completely foreign to communism ideologically, then there can be no talk about any serious successes in building socialism.[23]

Lenin warned those activists who took a nihilistic or hostile attitude toward the achievements of bourgeois civilization, including the intellectuals who possessed the knowledge of these achievements:

It is necessary to grasp all the culture which capitalism has left and build socialism from it. It is necessary to grasp all the science, technology, and art. Without this, we will not be able to build life in a communist society. And this science, technology, art is in the hands and the heads of the specialists.[24]

Such sentiments, intended to counter the strongly anti-intellectual mood of the masses that had been released in the revolutionary storm of 1917, were gradually transformed into policies during the civil-war period, although often against strong opposition in the government and the party. Such policies became more effective only with the end of the civil war in 1921, and even then "specialist-baiting" remained a favorite sport among some Communists and workers, and an occupational hazard for old specialists. The class conflict between these groups was to be released with full fury—and with Stalin's connivance—again in 1928.

The sources of the post-1917 hostility to members of the technical intelligentsia were at least twofold: before 1917 most of the prominent technical specialists were known to be liberal and nationalistic in their politics, and the later antagonism was part of the general hostility toward those associated with the conduct of World War I and the February Revolution; prior to 1917 many members of the technical intelligentsia were doing sufficiently well to arouse envy among other members of society who, after 1917, were able to vent their anger in more explicit fashion.

During the civil war, policies were created to institutionalize Lenin's views toward the technical intelligentsia. With the onset of rationing in the harsh conditions of these years, specialists who worked for the Soviets were given preferential treatment. A system of five ration levels was set up for them, the highest being for those specialists with international reputations. Ipatieff, for example, who was in the highest category, was pleased with the results. During the civil war, he noted, "I was then receiving 40,000 rubles a month as director of the State

[23] Ibid., vol. 44, pp. 350-351.   [24] Ibid., vol. 38, p. 55.

Scientific Technical Institute; but forty pounds of flour cost above 2,000 rubles and some products were absolutely unobtainable. After the usual bureaucratic delay, my new 'ration salary' began to arrive regularly. Since meat, butter, sugar, and even some very good cheese were included among them, I was most thankful for these products, all of which were very expensive."[25] The mechanical engineer, Timoshenko, did less well during the Bolshevik occupation of Kiev in 1919, but at least his family did not starve. At the Kiev Polytechnic Institute,

> . . . the teachers elected a special committee for the procurement of food. It was headed by the energetic Prof. Paton. He succeeded in getting hold of a large quantity of wheat, of which my share amounted to a sack of grain. The wheat was still green, and had to be dried on the balcony. A cat was posted to keep away birds.[26]

A special relief organization for scientists and other scholars was set up in 1919 at Maxim Gorky's urging, but even then losses from disease and starvation were high. Seven of the forty-five members of the Russian Academy of Sciences died in these years of starvation. Two of the best-known energy experts in Russia, Profs. Kirsh and Grinevetsky, who were active opponents of the Bolsheviks, died in a typhus epidemic during 1919.[27]

Besides providing rations for those who worked loyally for the Soviets and trying to restore labor discipline among workers, the Soviet government after 1918 moved rapidly to transform into reality a number of proposals for new research institutes. These were generally proposals that had been formulated in earlier years under the Tsars but never realized. More than forty such institutes were created during the civil-war period, most in the applied sciences and technology. The majority remained very small in this period, averaging from twenty to twenty-five specialists. They were also poorly housed and poorly supplied, but the support of the government for these projects was generous under the circumstances. Psychologically, such gestures of support were very important, helping to neutralize the opposition of many specialists.[28] Many applied scientists and engineers who might otherwise have been tempted to join the Whites were occupied in organizing such institutes. Ipatieff, for example, received an invitation during the civil war, concealed in a loaf of bread brought by an agent of General Denikin, to

---

[25] Ipatieff, p. 297. [26] Timoshenko, p. 166.

[27] See their obituaries in *Vestnik inzhenerov*, no. 1, 1922.

[28] Bastrakova, p. 162. See also the collection of documents in *Organizatsiia nauki v pervye gody Sovetskoi vlasti*.

join the latter's White government, but he refused. He was fully occupied with his work for the Soviet government, including his directorship of a new research institute; besides, he was convinced that the Whites could not win.[29]

As one Soviet historian has recently noted, virtually all the institutes created during these years were based on projects initiated by the scientific-technical intelligentsia themselves. Although their demands for autonomy were not met, and such institutes were placed under the jurisdiction of Soviet organs and political commissars, the technical intelligentsia could not help but be impressed by the active interest of the government in their work. Financial support increased after the end of the civil war, and, according to one recent study by a British scholar, the commitment to research and development, most of it in applied science, was a higher proportion of the GNP than in Western European countries by the mid-to-late 1920s.[30] Of course, this did not necessarily mean the return on investment was as high in terms of discoveries and innovations, or that other difficulties were overcome, but this policy did prove highly attractive to a large element of the technical intelligentsia.

Some, however, were troubled by Soviet support. One agronomist, a prominent researcher and teacher, Prof. Dukelsky, sent a letter to Lenin, which was published in *Pravda* during 1919, accusing the Bolsheviks of trying to buy off the technical intelligentsia: "If you want to 'use' the specialists, then don't buy them, but learn to respect them as people, and not as temporarily useful inventory to you. . . ."[31]

Dukelsky's outspoken letter described the conditions under which he lived in the provincial city of Voronezh, conditions that were far from those Lenin had described or said he wanted for the technical intelligentsia:

> No doubt you are so cloistered in your Kremlin isolation that you don't see the life surrounding you. You haven't noted how many among the Russian specialists are not, it is true, government Communists, but real toilers, who obtained their special knowledge at the price of extremely hard work, not from the hands of capitalists and not for the goals of capitalism, but by prolonged struggle with the deadly conditions of student and academic life under the previous regime.[32]

[29] Ipatieff, p. 272.

[30] Robert A. Lewis, "Some Aspects of the Research and Development Effort of the Soviet Union, 1924-35," *Science Studies*, 2, 1972, 153-179. My thanks to a colleague, Karl Hufbauer, for pointing out this article to me.

[31] Dukelsky's letter and Lenin's reply were published in *Pravda*, March 28, 1919.

[32] Ibid.

Dukelsky considered his fellow specialists, whom Lenin had called "bourgeois," true proletarians serving their fellow human beings, while they were persecuted by

... these newly minted unconscientious Communists, made up of former lower middle class elements, village policemen, small-time civil servants, shopkeepers who in the provinces often compose a significant proportion of the "local powers." It is difficult to describe the full horror of the humiliations and sufferings caused at their hands. Constant, shameful denunciations and accusations, futile but extremely humiliating searches, threats of execution, requisitions and confiscations, meddling in the most intimate sides of personal life. (The head of a squad demanded that I, who am living in the school where I teach, that I absolutely must sleep in the same bed with my wife.) These are the circumstances in which many specialists of the higher schools work up to the present moment. And all these "petty bourgeois" [specialists] have not left their posts and have devotedly fulfilled their moral obligation to preserve, at the price of whatever sacrifices, their culture and knowledge for those who have insulted and humiliated them at the instigation of their leaders.[33]

Lenin replied immediately to this letter in *Pravda*, justifying some of the severe measures as necessary under the circumstances, but at the same time striking a conciliatory tone, agreeing with some of Dukelsky's complaints. Few specialists were as outspoken as Dukelsky in these years. Most specialists suffered more quietly, took the aid they were offered, even while they remained cautious or suspicious of the Bolsheviks. (Dukelsky, it is interesting to note, eventually not only praised Communist efforts for the technical intelligentsia publicly in 1934, but later joined the Communist party. He died, a much-decorated professor, in 1956.[34] Explaining the reasons behind such changes of position, which were not rare, is one of my purposes in this monograph.)

Few of the old specialists joined the Communist party until after 1928, but most became convinced in this period that they could live, at least for a time, with the Communists. Some even quarreled bitterly among themselves in their scramble for government research support and curried the favor of one or another Communist leader as part of the competition with their fellow specialists.[35]

During the civil war the favored areas of research were understandably those that served the immediate economic and military needs of

[33] Ibid.
[34] L. Genkin, *Pod'em*, no. 2, 1966.
[35] Ipatieff, pp. 414-415.

the state. The Central Aviation Institute (TsAGI), for example, created by a group of professors at the Moscow Higher Technical School in 1918, received a high priority on resources, as did automotive research and research on food and fuel resources. But even more peripheral areas got some endorsement and encouragement, with promises of more aid later. The Soviet government shared the technical intelligentsia's interest in bringing science and the economy closer together, and in creating institutes that would encourage collective research, i.e., research that often crossed older disciplinary lines and was problem-oriented and "practical."

Beyond that, planning and coordinating applied research and development had been a goal of many specialists, articulated by KEPS during World War I. It was a value the Communist party emphatically shared with leading elements of the technical intelligentsia. Such planning and coordination, however, remained largely a goal, not a reality, in this period.[36] Nonetheless, several governmental organs were created to begin this task. The Commissariat of Education established a Science Section (NO) shortly after the revolution, and charged it with coordinating all scientific research until the fall of 1918, but it was criticized by Lenin for its radicalism, and opposed by most technical specialists. Among other things, this institution failed to share its powers with nonparty specialists, lacking a council of experts to advise it. Its leaders wanted to dissolve the Academy of Sciences and to abolish the universities, which they saw correctly as centers of resistance to Bolshevism and which they wished to replace with more radical institutions. When Lenin's secretary, Gorbunov, learned of the plans being discussed for the Academy of Sciences, he appealed to his boss, who quickly scotched them.[37] As the Commissar of Education later recalled it, Lenin threatened, "If some brave fellow turns up in your establishment, jumps on the Academy and breaks a lot of china, then you will have to pay dearly for it."[38]

In August of 1918, at Gorbunov's initiative, a different body was created under the Supreme Council of the National Economy to plan and coordinate industrial research, and to attract scientists and engineers to work for Soviet industry. The Scientific-Technical Section (NTO) was given wide powers, which it promptly shared with the technical specialists themselves. Gorbunov, then twenty-six, was ap-

[36] I agree with Bastrakova's view on this question. See pp. 178-217 of her study.

[37] *V. I. Lenin i Akademiia nauk. Sbornik dokumentov*, Moscow, 1969, p. 61.

[38] *Novyi mir*, no. 10, 1925, 110, quoted in Sheila Fitzpatrick, *The Commissariat of Enlightenment*, Cambridge, Mass., 1970, pp. 72-73.

pointed its first head.[39] This body remained ineffectual in many respects, however, particularly in planning and coordinating applied research. Most industrial research was taken over by the separate branches of government industry and largely run by the Scientific Councils of these industries. Such councils were even more heavily dominated by the technical specialists, who achieved a good deal of de facto autonomy in their own areas. This was especially true since their faithful watchdogs, the political commissars, often knew little of science and technology and deferred to their expertise.[40]

Gorbunov was drawn off to political work in the Red Army during 1919-1920, and only in 1921 was NTO reorganized to strengthen its planning and coordination functions. Some Communists and specialists wanted to abolish NTO entirely, but Lenin disagreed and urged Ipatieff's appointment as its new head, with wide powers. In fact, by 1921 both NTO and *Vesenkha* were strongly under the influence of old specialists, some of them, to be sure, party members. The ruling board, or presidium, of *Vesenkha* had twelve members, of whom half were graduate technologists. At least three were old school chums from the Moscow Technical School.[41]

Ipatieff found the NTO in a sorry state and began to reassert and defend its original purposes. He felt particularly that a body like NTO was needed to concentrate on more long-range problems of "pure" research in technology. "An independent organization devoted to pure research, such as NTO, can accomplish much more than a group of trust-controlled laboratories which must concern themselves too much with routine problems,"[42] Ipatieff argued, and the Soviet government agreed. He was probably influenced by German models, with which he was most familiar, and which were very prominent in Russia at this time.[43]

After 1921, Ipatieff was even invited to join the Communist party, but refused for ideological reasons.[44] Few old engineers did join at this time, as already noted, and most continued to put a certain distance between themselves and the Communist party. Yet this does not mean

[39] On Gorbunov's role, see his very interesting letters to Lenin, TsGANKh, f. 3429, op. 60, ed. khr. 41, ll. 56-58, published for the first time in *Novyi mir*, no. 8, 1964, 278-279. Gorbunov reported on the effectiveness of the NTO in drawing specialists to cooperate with the Soviet government, and received Lenin's strong support in the effort.

[40] Bastrakova, pp. 181-217.   [41] Ipatieff, pp. 207-311.

[42] Ibid., p. 362.

[43] See Loren R. Graham, "The Formation of Soviet Research Institutes," paper delivered at World Congress of Slavists, Calgary, Canada, 1974.

[44] Ipatieff, p. 362.

that they simply became politically or professionally passive. In fact, a few of the more aggressive did join the Communist party, where they tended to act as a lobby for technological interests. For example, the prominent chemical engineer, S. D. Shein, a prerevolutionary manager of a large private chemical company and, in 1917 and 1918, one of the organizers of the Engineers' Union, VSI, joined the Communist party in 1918, but he was distrusted by trade unionists and many Communists, probably with some cause. Shein actively worked for the interests of the engineering profession within the party.[45] Until he was purged and imprisoned in 1930, Shein was prominent as an organizer and, later, the head of the new Soviet organization for engineers and technicians, VMBIT, as it was called.

The Soviet government refused to recognize VSI as a separate trade union for engineers, and, in 1919, it banned further conferences or publications during the duration of the civil war.[46] Instead, the Soviet government tried to bring workers and technical specialists closer together as members of the same branch industrial unions. After 1919, engineers were, however, allowed to organize "engineering-technical sections" (ITS) in such unions. This was a kind of subterfuge that many trade unionists opposed, since they correctly saw in such ITSs the trojan horse of a separate union for engineers. Engineers complained that many branch industrial unions refused to recognize ITSs or denied them any power. After the end of the civil war, however, in 1921, a nationwide "Inter-Bureau of Engineering Sections" (VMBIT) was allowed to hold a national congress. Five hundred seventy delegates, representing twenty-seven thousand engineering workers met in Moscow to pass resolutions in the interests of the technical intelligentsia.[47] Lenin defended their rights before the party in 1921. He called for the trade unions to safeguard the interests of engineers,

> . . . encouraging the best of them, defending and preserving their interests and so on. . . . On the shoulders of the trade unions rests the heaviest and most difficult task with regard to the specialists, of daily influencing the widest masses of workers to create correct relations on their part toward the specialists. Only such work can in reality give serious practical results.[48]

[45] Ibid., pp. 72, 262, 289, 301-313, 336, 350, 383, 433, 449-453, 487-496, 504. See also Shein's role in VSI, *Vestnik inzhenerov*, 1917-1918, and the discussion of his career in the following chapters.

[46] See the discussion in *Biulleten' VAI*, nos. 1-6, 1923, and in *Stenograficheskii otchet rabot I Vserossiiskogo s'ezda inzhenerov, chlenov profsoiuzov*, Moscow, 1923.

[47] Ibid.   [48] *Polnoe*, vol. 44, p. 351.

In 1923, the Soviet government moved to democratize this de facto Engineers' Union, VMBIT, opening its membership to both engineers and technicians, those with diplomas and without. As a consequence, by 1927, this union organization had grown from about twenty-seven thousand members to one hundred five thousand. Shein became its chairman. A survey conducted by the Central Trade Unions' Council in 1925 discovered, however, that most highly qualified graduate engineers avoided membership in VMBIT and joined the more exclusive All-Russian Association of Engineers (VAI), the successor organization to VSI.[49] Organized in 1919, VAI was recognized as a professional society, not a trade union. Although it requested the latter status again at this time, it was refused.[50] VAI was allowed to establish branches, nonetheless, and to publish a journal, with a circulation of around five thousand in the 1920s. It became the most important "nest" of old specialists who had opposed the Bolsheviks, and its fate will be an important part of the following chapters.

Despite some high-level support for their interests, old specialists remained in danger throughout this period. While the demands of such anarchist leaders as A. Y. Ge for mass repressions of the intelligentsia, including technical personnel, were rejected out of hand, and the Communist party supported Lenin's policy wholeheartedly in its resolutions and in the new party platform adopted in 1919, the struggle continued throughout the 1920s. Left Communist groups, like the Democratic Centralists and the Workers' Opposition, as well as adherents of the Proletarian Culture movement, believed that old specialists were being pampered and given too much power.[51] Alexander Shliapnikov, a former metallurgical worker and trade union official, openly attacked party policy in *Pravda*, accusing the party of "pandering to the specialists," and characterizing its slogan as "everything for the specialists."[52] The Democratic Centralists and Workers' Opposition made the old *spetsy* a prominent issue in their programs of 1920 and 1921. Most of these groups were for a genuine control of industry by the workers. They opposed Lenin's principle of one-man management, and called for the rapid preparation of new cadres of specialists, drawn from the workers

[49] TsGAOR SSSR, f. 5548, op. 4, d. 24, l. 5, cited in Fediukin, *Velikii oktiabr'*, p. 317.

[50] *Biulleten' VAI*, no. 6, 1923, 2-3.

[51] Fediukin, *Velikii oktiabr'*, pp. 80-83; Leonard Schapiro, *The Origin of the Communist Autocracy*, New York, 1965, pp. 130-147, 230-231, 221ff., and 290ff.; Robert V. Daniels, *The Conscience of the Revolution*, New York, 1969, pp. 109, 139; on the anarchists, see Paul Avrich, *Russian Anarchists*, Princeton, 1967, pp. 171-203.

[52] *Pravda*, March 27, 1919.

and peasants themselves, to replace the older groups of specialists. Lenin and his adherents regarded such a rapid transformation as unrealistic and were successful in maintaining their view as official policy.

Two political trials in 1921 and 1922 are significant in this respect, as they show how Lenin and the party leadership sought to enforce its policy. In order to placate antispecialist feeling and prevent the specialists from joining conspiratorial activities against the Soviet system, the authorities accused a group of specialists of active counterrevolution, tried them, and shot them in 1921. This was the well-publicized *Glavtop* case, in which a group of former Nobel engineers was accused of receiving money from that Swedish industrial firm to help restore the Nobel holdings in the Russian oil industry.[53] Ipatieff, in his memoirs, believed them innocent of any wrongdoing, basing his opinion on firsthand information from several specialist sources; but Lenin believed them guilty. Despite Gorbunov's intervention on their behalf, Lenin refused to take their part. The leader of the *Glavtop* group was Professor Tikhvinsky, a well-known chemical engineer who was shot by the *Cheka* in August 1921 after a widely publicized trial. Ipatieff, and at least one leading Communist, considered Tikhvinsky's execution a miscarriage of justice and a terrible waste of talent.[54] Lenin apparently saw it as a necessary act to discourage active counterrevolution.

Lenin did, however, intervene in several cases to gain the release of specialists whom he considered guilty of active counterrevolution, but whose youth or value to the Soviet regime tipped the scale in their favor.[55] Lenin also made major issues of the murder of technical specialists by workers and of the suicide of the engineer V. V. Oldenborger, who was hounded to death by worker and Communist zealots in 1921.[56] In a project on the role of the trade unions, written during December 1921 and January 1922, Lenin noted that the party's policy toward the

[53] For the official account of this trial, see *Izvestiia*, July 22-23, 1922. For an account from a different viewpoint, see Alexander Solzhenitsyn, *The Gulag Archipelago*, vol. 1, New York, 1973, pp. 334-336. Without more substantial evidence, it is difficult to judge if the *Glavtop* engineers were involved in active counterrevolutionary activities, or were innocent, as Ipatieff and Solzhenitsyn have asserted. For a recent Soviet account of early anti-Bolshevik groups, including some in which engineers were said to be involved, see D. L. Golinkov, *Krashenie antisovetskogo podpolia*, Moscow, 1975.

[54] Ipatieff, pp. 366ff.

[55] See, for example, the case of the young engineer, Nazvanov, for whom Krasin and Krzhizhanovsky intervened, and whom Lenin released, with the Politburo's agreement, to work under probation in *Gosplan*. (*Polnoe sobranie*, vol. 53, p. 255.) See also Lenin's intervention in the case of the Svirstroi hydroelectric engineers. (*Iz istorii VChK, Sbornik dokumentov*, p. 439.)

[56] N. V. Krylenko, *Za piat' let. 1918-1922. Obvinitel'nye rechi*, Moscow, 1923, pp. 438-444; Solzhenitsyn, *Gulag*, pp. 336-341; *Pravda*, Jan. 3, 1922.

specialists remained on paper, but was often not observed: "There are such facts as these, in the first place, the murder of engineers by workers in the socialized mines of the Urals and Donbass, and secondly, the suicide of the chief engineer of the Moscow Water Works, V. V. Oldenborger."[57] In a letter to the Politburo, Lenin called the latter case "a shocking affair: we must sound the alarum."[58] A show trial of the persons held responsible for Oldenborger's death received wide publicity in 1922, but it did not stop reports of specialist-baiting. In fact, the punishment meted out to Oldenborger's persecutors was very mild in contrast with the death sentences received by the *Glavtop* engineers. Soviet readers aware of the two trials no doubt drew their own conclusions. A recent Soviet historian believes specialist-baiting was not as widespread as one would judge from the Soviet press of this period, since the press gave considerable publicity to this issue; but one wonders.[59] The evidence suggests it remained a serious problem well into the 1930s and, in fact, became worse with Stalin's change of policy toward the technical intelligentsia in 1928.

Another area of conflict between the power structure and the technical intelligentsia in the years before 1928 was the field of higher technical education, an issue that came to a head in 1921 and 1922. During the civil war, higher technical institutes, like the universities, enjoyed a good deal of de facto autonomy.[60] The party and the state were preoccupied with the war, and professors had considerable leeway, despite the admission to higher education of everyone over the age of sixteen, and despite conflicts between students and professors over politics and academic issues. These will be explored at greater length in part 3. Here it is necessary only to sketch the outlines.

In 1921, the Commissariat of Education (*Narkompros*) worked out a new charter for higher education that deprived professors of a decisive voice in the appointment of deans and rectors. When, in 1921, *Narkompros* appointed its own candidate as rector of the Moscow Higher Technical School over the candidate of the professors' council, the issue exploded. Professors declared a strike, and Lenin was forced to intervene. The eventual compromise largely favored the professors. Although Lenin slapped their hands, describing the use of a strike as unacceptable, on the whole he sided with the professors. In a sharp

[57] Lenin, *Polnoe*, vol. 44, p. 350.

[58] Ibid., p. 354. The most severe sentence received by a defendant in this trial was a one-year imprisonment.

[59] Fediukin, *Velikii oktiabr'*, pp. 300-302.

[60] See the account in Fitzpatrick, pp. 157-163; Fediukin, op. cit., p. 323; James C. McClelland, "Bolshevik Approaches to Higher Education," *Slavic Review*, December 1971, 818-831.

exchange with the Communist official who had proposed the reformed charter, Lenin rebuked him and soon removed him from his job.[61] As the Commissar of Education, Lunacharsky, recalled the affair:

> During the confrontation of our party cells, who in a political sense were excellent, with the professoriate in higher education, whom Lenin always referred to as "bourgeois," he nevertheless, even during the harmful strikes by these professors, staunchly took their side. During my remarks to a meeting of the Central Committee, to the effect that the party cells were overflowing with hatred toward the bourgeois professoriate and involuntarily hindered the work of reconciliation and establishment of normal work with them, he replied, "Scholars are absolutely essential to us, we must fight the party cells to the hilt."[62]

As a result of these strikes a large number of professors in the humanities and social sciences were arrested and exiled from the country, yet the scientific-technical specialists involved were not punished. This major incident, in fact, must have seemed to them one more sign of the power their specialized knowledge gave them in the new Soviet state. A degree of de facto autonomy for higher technical education remained a reality until the purges of these institutions after 1928.

Why did Lenin twist arms to aid the engineering professoriate on this issue? In 1921 and 1922, with the advent of the New Economic Policy and the need to rebuild a shattered economy, the cooperation of the technical intelligentsia was more important than ever. Lenin placed high hopes, for example, on the new State Planning Commission (*Gosplan*), formed in 1921 at his initiative. In fact, he made explicit his desire that old specialists not only participate in this body, but dominate its work, under the supervision of such party members as Lenin's old comrade-in-arms, the electrical engineer, Krzhizhanovsky. One of the leaders of the academic strikes against the Bolsheviks became the vice chairman of *Gosplan*, and a number of prominent participants in these strikes

---

[61] *Pravda*, Feb. 21 and 27, March 1, 1921; TsPA IML, f. 17, op. 60, d. 224, ll. 10-11, 52-54; d. 234, l. 11, cited in an unpublished Soviet dissertation by T. M. Smirnova, "Reforma vysshei shkoly RSFSR 1917 g.-okt. 1922 g.," Moscow, 1968, pp. 230-231. This dissertation has a detailed account of the strikes at the Moscow Higher Technical School and other Soviet institutions of higher education in the period 1920-1922, with copious quotations from Soviet archival sources. See also the accounts in Fediukin, op. cit., pp. 325-329, and the article by E. M. Brusnikin, "Iz istorii bor'by KP za vuzovskuiu intelligentsiiu v 1917-1922 gg.," *Voprosy istorii KPSS*, no. 8, 1972, 90ff.

[62] Lunacharsky's account is from a document published for the first time in *Literaturnoe nasledstvo*, vol. 74, Moscow, 1965, p. 29.

headed sections of *Gosplan* or were members of its presidium, at Lenin's urging.[63]

Such a turn of events must have been a telltale sign to the technical intelligentsia. The old opponents of the Bolsheviks among the technostructure in 1917 and 1918 began to emerge from the woodwork in the years from 1921 to 1928, and often took an independent line. A congress of geologists and another of agronomists, held in 1921, called for professional autonomy, as did the congresses and publications of VAI in 1921-1923.[64] The prerevolutionary Physical-Chemical Society was bold enough in 1921 to intervene in behalf of the condemned Professor Tikhvinsky, although without effect. P. P. Pal'chinsky, a prominent mining engineer and former deputy minister in the Provisional Government overthrown by the Bolsheviks in 1917, reemerged in 1922 to head a section of the old Russian Technical Society. This organization was even allowed to publish a journal, *The Economist*, which took a mildly independent line until its closure in 1926.[65] In other words, the old technical intelligentsia emerged from the revolution and civil war with losses, but largely intact, still struggling for many of the professional interests and allied values that had concerned it during the Tsarist period. Its influence in the 1920s and later has generally been underestimated. In fact, in setting many of the goals of Soviet industrialization, including most of the major industrial projects of the period 1928-1941, the Communist party relied primarily on the ideas and expertise of the technical intelligentsia, which had begun to develop before the revolution and continued through the 1920s. The evidence for this point, and its significance, will be spelled out more fully in the Conclusions, which follows chapter 14. The degree of the Soviet debt to the technostructure in this respect has been obscured, due in part to the ambivalent political relations among the Communist party, the technical intelligentsia, and the working class.

Partly to placate opposition to the old technical specialists and to assure their political loyalty, the party appointed an increasing number of industrial managers from the ranks of workers and Communists, particularly with the ascendancy of the Stalinist *apparat* during Lenin's illness in 1923 and after his death in 1924. Of course, the pattern of such control had been established during the civil war, but it had not

[63] Lenin, *Polnoe*, vol. 44, p. 51; vol. 45, p. 349; Bastrakova, pp. 253-255.

[64] See the unpublished Soviet dissertation by N. A. Koroleva, "Opyt KPSS po perevospitaniiu staroi i podgotovke novoi intelligentsii," Moscow, 1968, p. 38; Fediukin, op. cit., p. 306.

[65] Koroleva, pp. 38ff.; Lenin, *Polnoe*, vol. 53, pp. 169, 410.

been followed consistently. From 1923 to 1924, a gradual consolidation of controls over the old specialists began, and, simultaneously, measures against their persecution were strengthened. Physical attacks on specialists, for example, were no longer treated as mere criminal assault, but judged much more severely, as "terrorist attacks."[66] Even during the civil war, by 1919, the *Cheka* had been forbidden to search or arrest *spetsy* simply because they were nonparty specialists.[67] In 1924, the head of the secret police, Felix Dzherzhinsky, also became head of *Vesenkha*, in charge of all large-scale government industry until his death in 1926. He proved to be a strong friend of specialist interests, to the pleasant surprise of someone like Ipatieff.[68] The same was true of the new head of state, Rykov, after the death of Lenin in 1924.[69] Dzherzhinsky brought many former secret police officers (*Chekists*) into *Vesenkha* to work side by side with the old specialists, which Ipatieff and others found generally to the advantage of the technical intelligentsia. Even though this meant a strengthening of controls over their work, it also often strengthened their hand in dealing with workers, trade union officials, and local party bosses.

The new industrial managers, or "Red Directors," as they were called, were almost invariably men without technical qualifications; in fact, often they had little formal higher education of any kind. A division of labor and an uneasy truce gradually developed between these managers and the old specialists. In most factories there were, in fact, two directors: the Communist manager, who fulfilled the role of political commissar and personnel director, and the technical director, who was generally an old specialist and handled the operational aspects of production. This system was eventually given de jure status, and the technical director acquired wide legal powers to make important production decisions.

The organization of personnel and the fulfillment of production goals in industry came to depend on the cooperation of these two groups. For largely political reasons during the first decade after the October Revolution, therefore, two largely separate groups developed at the top of Soviet industry, with different social and educational backgrounds and different career expectations under the Soviet system.

The Twelfth Party Congress in 1923 marked a watershed in the

[66] *Izvestiia*, Oct. 28, 1922.

[67] *Iz Istorii Vserossiiskoi chrezvychainoi komissii 1917-1921 gg. Sbornik dokumentov*, Moscow, 1958, p. 346.

[68] Ipatieff, p. 395; "Dokumenty F. E. Dzherzhinskogo po khoziastvennym voprosam 1922-1926 gg.," in *Istoricheskii arkhiv*, no. 2, 1960, 55; F. E. Dzerzhinskii, *Izbrannye proizvedeniia v dvykh tomakh*, vol. 2, Moscow, 1957, p. 157.

[69] *Izvestiia*, Dec. 4, 1924.

history of both groups. At this Congress, Stalin achieved greater control over the industrial managers when he obtained sanction for the Assignments Department (*uchraspredotdel*) of the party's secretariat to appoint the top industrial managers. Stalin largely controlled this apparatus and was quick to use the new power it acquired. At the time, this measure may have been aimed at the supporters of Trotsky, among whom were several prominent industrial managers, but it was to have wide repercussions for the old specialists as well.[70] After this shift in control, many of the old specialists found themselves demoted in the industrial hierarchy and forced to work under "Red Directors," whose qualifications for industrial management were lower than ever before, at least from the viewpoint of formal education. In 1922, seventy-three percent of the chief directors of the largest factories in the central industrial district, the region around Moscow, were still old specialists, but this percentage began to decline rapidly after 1923.[71]

The party's Assignments Department was given the power of appointment for eighteen hundred of the most important positions in industry.[72] Valerian Kuibyshev, at this time a secretary of the Central Committee and one of Stalin's appointees, carried out the original investigation that suggested this change. The special party commission he headed recommended a strengthened hand by the party in its control of industry, and the central organs of the party approved these recommendations in 1923.[73] In 1923 and 1924, the Assignments Department sent five hundred ninety-five persons, primarily Communist party stalwarts, to fill some of the highest positions in industry.[74]

While this new influx of Red Directors may have consolidated Stalin's potential control over Soviet industry, it also helped to widen the social gap between the managers and the old technostructure. A survey conducted in early 1928 showed that the educational level of factory managers continued to decline. Of some seven hundred seventy managers included in the survey, over seventy percent had only an elementary school education. The percentage of those with higher education declined from eleven percent in 1926 to nine percent in 1928.[75] The educational level varied inversely with the growth in the percentage of managers who were Communist party members. By 1928, approxi-

[70] Azrael, pp. 71-82.

[71] Fediukin, *Sovetskaia vlast' i burzhuaznye spetsialisty*, Moscow, 1965, p. 139.

[72] TsPA IML, f. 17, op. 168, ed. khr. 1, ll. 36-37, cited in V. Z. Drobizhev, *Glavnyi shtab sotsialisticheskoi promyshlennosti*, Moscow, 1966, p. 235.

[73] Ibid., pp. 238-239.

[74] TsPA IML, f. 17, op. 267, ed. khr. 101, l. 26, cited in the Drobizhev article in *Istoriia SSSR*, no. 4, 1961, p. 62.

[75] M. Vasil'ev, "O promkadrakh," in *Bol'shevik*, no. 8, 1928, 64.

mately eighty percent of all factory directors and higher industrial officials were Communist party members, and the proportion was a growing one. An increasing percentage of these was also being recruited from those of worker or peasant backgrounds, while the majority of specialists, even those new specialists educated after 1917, came from nonproletarian backgrounds.[76]

As the gap between these two groups increased, the danger of friction between them also increased, and this required frequent attention and mediation. Dzherzhinsky, as chairman of *Vesenkha*, sought to ameliorate feelings between these two groups. He was particularly conciliatory toward the old specialists, since, like Lenin, he considered their cooperation essential for the success of Soviet efforts. He obtained legislation in 1925 that condemned specialist-baiting in no uncertain terms. This legislation also raised the social status of the technical intelligentsia, and defined more clearly their rights within the industrial hierarchy.[77] His successor, Kuibyshev, who was transferred to *Vesenkha* from the party *apparat* in 1926, generally continued his predecessor's policy in this regard, at least until 1928. It must have seemed essential to managers such as Dzherzhinsky and Kuibyshev, concerned with the success of industry as their primary area of responsibility, to calm any troubled waters among specialists, Red Directors, and industrial workers.

But waters, once troubled, are easily stirred up again. In 1928, the party leadership was faced with a crisis that involved these groups. The leadership focused its attention once again on the relations among them. A debate began over policies that, once adopted, were to lessen the social and educational gap between the industrial managers and the technical intelligentsia, after an initial period of confusion and conflict.

[76] Ibid., p. 62.
[77] *Direktivy KPSS i Sovetskogo pravitel'stva po khoziastvennym voprosam*, vol. 1, 1917-1928, Moscow, 1957, pp. 552-553.

PART 2

The Old Specialists
and the Power Structure,
1928-1931

3

THE SHAKHTY AFFAIR

The White Queen: He's in prison now being punished; and the trial doesn't even begin till next Wednesday; and of course, the crime comes last of all.

Alice: But suppose he never commits the crime?

The White Queen: That would be all the better, wouldn't it?

Lewis Carroll,
Through the Looking Glass

Nineteen twenty-eight marked the beginning of a major attempt to change the social composition and behavior of the Soviet technostructure. This attempt had two aspects: pressure on the old technostructure, and an effort to create a large, new group of technical specialists, qualitatively different from the older groups. Part 2 will focus on the relations between the old specialists and the Soviet power structure in the years 1928-1931, the beginning of Stalin's "revolution from above," which was intended to transform Soviet society fundamentally. Many of the issues that had been important to the technostructure since before the revolution came into sharp focus in these years, particularly in the aftermath of the so-called "Shakhty affair" of 1928 and the terror practiced against a large segment of the old technostructure during the following three-year period.

A study of these years reveals the sharpening of class conflicts, as well as a series of conflicts that further involved the technostructure with such bureaucratic groups as the party apparatus, industrial management (*Vesenkha* in particular), the chief government inspectorate (*Rabkrin*), the political police (GPU), and other groups, too. Conflict over the role of the old specialists was a keynote of these years, to be replaced by greater attempts at forging bonds of cooperation between the old technostructure and the power structure after an official change of policy in June of 1931. But that is to run ahead of the story. How are we to explain Stalinist policies toward the old technical intelligentsia from 1928 to 1931?

During these years several spectacular show trials loom large, trials in which several thousand engineers were implicated, among them some of the most qualified and experienced specialists in industry.[1] They were accused of systematic sabotage of the economy in the interests of Western powers. Most of the men implicated were "old specialists," those who had received their higher education during the Tsarist period. Many of them had held responsible positions in capitalist industry, or in various Tsarist ministries and educational institutions.

The purpose of this section will be to interpret the meaning of these arrests and trials: the use made of them by Stalin and the somewhat different purpose to which they were put by various other Soviet leaders. In addition, the consequences of the terror on the political sympathies, social status, and work performance of the technical intelligentsia will be assessed.

Soviet policies toward the old specialists at this time included both the use of force—show trials and other forms of intimidation—and various other forms of persuasion, which primarily took the form of mass campaigns and professional organizations that attempted to enlist the support of specialists for Soviet policies. Of special interest in these years was the disbandment or reorganization of many of the professional societies of the old technical intelligentsia and the roles taken by the trade unions and by VARNITSO, a Marxist ideological organization that sought to enlist representatives of the scientific-technical intelligentsia as members.

The background of the Shakhty affair is still murky; the details are not well documented and they permit differing interpretations. All the evidence available strongly suggests, however, that the pressure for the show trial of the Shakhty engineers came from Stalin. Stalin may have been opposed originally by a number of prominent Soviet leaders, particularly Rykov, the head of the government, but the conclusion of the affair assuredly raised strong doubts and fears, not only among Stalin's new foes in the Politburo, such as Rykov, but also among some of Stalin's long-time political allies and closest supporters.

In the winter of 1927-1928, the Soviet leadership was involved in a crisis, the dimensions and consequences of which took shape only gradually over the following year. Grain deliveries from the peasants to

---

[1] The engineers arrested in these years apparently numbered between two thousand and seven thousand; two thousand is the number mentioned in the Industrial party trial of 1930, at the height of the terror against the old specialists (see chapter 4). A Western source with informants inside the Soviet Union, the Menshevik journal, *Sotsialisticheskii vestnik* (April 3, 1931, p. 19), gives the higher figure. Barring access to OGPU files, the true number is unknown, but most likely lies within this range.

the state took a sharp downturn, as the peasants withheld grain in a market situation unfavorable to them.[2] The so-called "grain crisis" threatened the food supply of the urban population and disrupted plans to sell grain abroad. Most important, it imperiled ambitious new investment projects as the regime set its sights on rapid industrialization after recovering from the economic devastation of the previous years. In January and February 1928, Stalin took matters into his own hands and reverted to the methods of the civil war, including forced requisitions from the peasantry. Rykov, by February, had become the rallying point for those opposed to Stalin's use of force against the peasants. Was there a connection between this crisis and the Shakhty affair, which broke in March? The evidence suggests there was: that the Shakhty affair may have been intended to discredit Stalin's opponents or, at the very least, to put them on the defensive, and to discourage any of Stalin's allies whose support may have been wavering.

The Shakhty affair was to become pivotal in the formation of the Soviet technical intelligentsia, the first in a series of show trials and arrests that were integral to Soviet industrial policy during the early years of rapid industrialization. Of course, show trials, as such, were not new to the Soviet scene; highly publicized court proceedings with strong political overtones were a standard device of the Soviet government throughout the period of the New Economic Policy. Lenin had approved and advocated show trials of political opponents, such as that of the Socialist Revolutionaries in 1922. He had also advocated show trials against private interests that violated economic laws under the NEP. A number of such trials were held in 1922 and 1923, designed to intimidate those in the nonsocialist sector of the economy who abused Soviet concessions to private enterprise.[3]

Several other show trials during this period involved engineers and other specialists, and workers and Communists accused of specialist-baiting. The trial of the former Nobel employees and those accused in the suicide of Engineer Oldenborger have already been discussed. In 1925, several engineers, former employees of foreign industrialists who had owned metallurgical firms in South Russia, were convicted of economic espionage.[4]

None of these earlier trials assumed the importance or received the publicity of the Shakhty trial of 1928. The earlier trials were concerned

---

[2] See M. Lewin, *Russian Peasants and Soviet Power: A Study of Collectivization,* New York, 1968, pp. 214-249.

[3] *Istoriia SSSR s drevneishikh vremen,* vol. 8, pp. 209-212; Lenin, *Polnoe sobranie sochinenii,* 5 ed., vol. 44, pp. 322-323; *Izvestiia,* July 22 and 23, 1922.

[4] *Pravda,* June 4-16, 1925.

in part with publicizing and enforcing existing policies toward political opponents or the economy in general, and involved the technical intelligentsia only rarely. The Shakhty trial became the focal point for a radical change in policy toward the technical intelligentsia; as such, it marked the start of a widespread campaign not only against elements among the old specialists who may have been hostile toward the Soviet system, but also against those who were politically indifferent or neutral.

Lenin, who was implacably against any organized opposition, had expressed tolerance toward individual specialists who worked conscientiously for Soviet institutions, despite holding political attitudes foreign to Communism. Stalin, however, as early as 1918, had established a record of active opposition and hostility to the widespread use of old specialists, whether Tsarist officers in the Red Army, or engineers who had worked for capitalist enterprises and were now employed in nationalized firms.[5]

During the course of the NEP, Stalin had been occupied with other matters, particularly with the struggle for power within his own party. He was concerned with the old specialists only to the extent they attempted to organize ideological propaganda outside the control of the party. Supported by his loyal *apparatchiki* within the secretariat, Emelian Yaroslavsky and Aleksandr Bubnov, Stalin led an attack against the "Change of Landmarks" movement (*smenovekhodstvo*). His attacks had widespread support among many Communist activists.[6] The "Landmarks" movement was based on a loosely organized trend of thought that began among Russian emigrés in Western Europe and Manchuria and soon gained great popularity among many intellectuals and old specialists within the Soviet Union.[7] The common thread that linked the members of this movement was a belief that intellectuals and specialists should cooperate with the Soviet system under the NEP, rather than

[5] I. Ya. Trifonov, "Iz istorii bor'by kommunisticheskoi partii protiv smenovekhodstvo," *Istoriia SSSR*, no. 3, 1959, p. 78; Leonard Schapiro, *The Origin of the Communist Autocracy*, New York, 1965, pp. 244ff.

[6] Fediukin, *Velikii oktiabr'*, pp. 248-276.

[7] A survey of two hundred thirty engineers, interviewed in Moscow in 1922, revealed that nearly half admitted active sympathy with the "Landmarks" movement, while only twenty-eight percent claimed active support of the Bolsheviks (*Pravda*, Sept. 3, 1922). If these results were typical, they indicate widespread support for the movement. The circulation of publications by representatives of the "Landmarks" movement ranged between two thousand to six thousand copies per issue. In a country where the intelligentsia who possessed a higher education, either scientific-technical or cultural, numbered around two hundred thousand, these circulation figures reflect an important, though probably limited, influence (A. E. Beilin, *Kadry spetsialistov SSSR*, Moscow, 1935, p. 58; Trifonov, pp. 78ff.). For background on this movement, see also S. V. Utechin, *Russian Political Thought*, New York, 1963, pp. 253-257; Robert C. Williams, " 'Changing Landmarks' in Russian Berlin 1922-1924," *Slavic Review*, December 1968, 581-584.

oppose it with force. They did so in the hope of gradually influencing Soviet policy in the direction of more democratic political forms and more liberal economic institutions.

While Lenin opposed the "Landmarks" ideology, he also opposed administrative measures against its representatives, considering the movement more advantageous than dangerous to Soviet objectives.[8] Between 1922 and 1926, representatives were even permitted to hold lectures and publish their books and journals. This movement was quite useful to the Soviet government, helping to divide its political opponents in the emigration, attracting skilled manpower back to the Soviet Union, and attempting to win over many old specialists to active cooperation.

Stalin's attitude to the movement was more hostile. He spoke against the movement at each party congress between 1923 and 1925. In general, he attempted at every opportunity to link his own opponents in the party leadership with the ideology of this trend.[9] In his countercampaign, Stalin was able to rely on the widespread public resentment of the old specialists, especially those employed in Soviet industry, who earned five to seven times more than skilled workers, and considerably more than unskilled workers.[10] Such workers were the groups whom the Bolsheviks courted as their chief political constituency within a country that remained more than eighty percent rural, peasant, and urban bourgeois.

Stalin could also count on the anti-intellectualism of many among the party rank-and-file, who may never have had the opportunity for formal higher education under the Tsarist system, or were expelled from universities and institutes for their political activities. The campaign against the "Landmarks" movement culminated in March 1926, when Stalin banned lectures by its representatives and suppressed its publications, such as *New Russia* in Moscow.[11]

According to one account, the Shakhty case began to develop late in 1927.[12] The following version comes from a source close to the moderate wing of the party, that headed by Rykov, Bukharin, and Tomsky. This was the wing that considered the policies of Lenin's last years still ap-

[8] Fediukin, *Velikii oktiabr'*, pp. 248-294.

[9] Trifonov, p. 71; Stalin, *Voprosy leninizma*, Moscow, 1926, p. 392; see also Stalin's speech at the Twelfth Party Congress in *XII s"ezd. Stenograficheskii otchet*, Moscow, 1924, p. 444.

[10] TsGAOR SSSR, f. 5548, op. 8, d. 64, l. 15, cited in Fediukin, *Velikii oktiabr'*, p. 296.

[11] Trifonov, pp. 79-80.

[12] Although this is possible, Stalin may not have supported the case until January or February of 1928. At any rate, in December 1927, Stalin praised the technical intelligentsia for their increasing support of Soviet policies; he reversed his public attitude toward this group only in the spring of 1928.

propriate, and was unwilling to make radical changes in them, at least not in the way that Stalin changed them.[13] While this version is apparently based on conversations in high party circles and cannot be substantiated in its details, it is consistent with the other evidence discussed below. Abdurakhman Avtorkhanov was a party member and a graduate student at the Institute of Red Professors in Moscow in 1928. He attended several private gatherings addressed by Rezhnikov, who was a member of the Central Committee and the Moscow Party Committee, and was a supporter of the moderates. The version below is attributed to Rezhnikov.[14]

According to this account, the case began at the initiative of the local OGPU chief in the Northern Caucasus District, Y. G. Yevdokimov. This is corroborated by the credit given to Yevdokimov at the Sixteenth Party Congress in 1930.[15] This secret police official was a noted *Chekist* of the civil-war era, who had been involved in the investigation and presentation of a number of political cases in that era.[16] Yevdokimov is also mentioned by another source as a crony of Stalin, who frequently accompanied him on vacations. As were others of Stalin's OGPU favorites, he was a man with an uncertain past. He was said to have been imprisoned as a common criminal, rather than a political prisoner in Tsarist times,[17] although this has not been substantiated. Late in 1927, Yevdokimov reported to Menzhinsky, the head of the OGPU at this

[13] A. G. Loewy, *Die Weltgeschichte ist das Weltgericht: Bucharin: Vision des Kommunismus*, Wien, 1969, pp. 343-377; Stephen F. Cohen, *Bukharin and the Bolshevik Revolution*, New York, 1973, pp. 243-336.

[14] Abdurakhman Avtorkhanov, *Stalin and the Soviet Communist Party: A Study in the Technology of Power*, New York, 1959, pp. 26-30. Stalin's strongest supporters of the next few years consistently gave him credit for initiating this case. See, for example, the speech of Kaganovich at the Sixteenth Party Congress in 1930, in which he praised Stalin's foresight in pursuing the prosecution of this case against Rykov's opposition to it in the Politburo. While Rykov became the chief whipping boy in this instance, the evidence below suggests that initially other key members of the Politburo, who later supported Stalin, were opposed to the affair. For Solzhenitsyn's account of this trial, see *Gulag Archipelago*, 1973, 373-376.

[15] *XVI S"ezd VKP(b). Stenograficheskii otchet*, Moscow, 1935, pp. 538ff.

[16] D. L. Golinkov, *Krushenie antisovetskovo podpol'ia v SSSR*, Moscow, 1975, pp. 327, 335, 489, 491, 593, 597.

[17] Alexander Orlov, *The Secret History of Stalin's Crimes*, London, 1954, p. 14. Despite the sensational title, this book of memoirs by a high police official, who defected to Western Europe during the purges of 1938, has proved to be generally reliable in the light of other evidence. For an evaluation of this source, see Robert Conquest, *The Great Terror*, New York, 1968, p. 570. Yevdokimov's role in the Shakhty affair was praised by Ordzhonikidze several years later, in a speech to the Sixteenth Party Congress in 1930 (see G. K. Ordzhonikidze, *Stat'i i rechi*, vol. 2, Moscow, 1957, p. 230).

time, the existence of a group of wreckers living in the town of Shakhty in the Northern Caucasus. According to the report, these engineers were in touch with the former owners of the coal mines there, who now lived abroad. Yevdokimov claimed to have evidence that these old specialists were part of a conspiracy to wreck the coal mines at the instigation of foreign interests.

When Menzhinsky demanded evidence, perhaps knowing the tendency of subordinates to build their careers on the basis of spectacular charges, Yevdokimov produced private letters from abroad addressed to some of the accused engineers, which the secret police had intercepted. Yevdokimov claimed that the letters were written in code, the key to which was in the possession of the old specialists. Menzhinsky denied his subordinate permission to arrest the engineers on the basis of such evidence, and gave him two weeks to decode the letters, or face the consequences of a false accusation. Yevdokimov, according to this account, then went to Stalin, who was the representative of the party's Central Committee on the governing board of the OGPU. Stalin gave Yevdokimov permission to adopt whatever measures were necessary, and several days later Yevdokimov arrested the engineers.

This action brought strong protests from Menzhinsky as well as Kuibyshev, who was chairman of the Council of the National Economy, and Rykov, chairman of the Council of People's Commissars (*Sovnarkom*) and, therefore, the official head of the Soviet government. When they suggested sending a special commission of the Central Committee and *Sovnarkom* to the Northern Caucasus to investigate the charges, Stalin opposed the proposal. A special session of the Politburo was called, at which Rykov, Kuibyshev, and Menzhinsky accused Stalin of exceeding his authority. According to the version related by Avtorkhanov, "Stalin countered by showing the Politburo a telegram from Yevdokimov in which the latter not only reported the existence of counterrevolutionary activities in Shakhty, but also hinted that the strings led to Moscow."[18] (One of the engineers later tried, Skorutto, was an important official of VSNKh in Moscow.[19] The threat that other high officials in VSNKh would be implicated was probably real.) Stalin's opponents backed down, and the party's general secretary then assumed direct supervision of the case. Detailed confessions were soon forthcoming from some of the imprisoned engineers, according to the sequence of events given in this version, and on March 7, 1928, five German nationals, specialists for German firms with contracts in the Soviet Union, were implicated in

[18] Avtorkhanov, p. 29.
[19] Carr and Davies, vol. 1, part 2, pp. 43-97.

the case and arrested. Overnight, the affair became an international incident. Soviet-German economic negotiations, underway since January, were disrupted, and an anti-Soviet furor was raised in the German press.[20]

On March 10, the affair became public in the Soviet Union with a front-page editorial in *Pravda* and an indictment of the engineers by the prosecutor general of the U.S.S.R. The announcement of this case in *Pravda* bears out, in part at least, the version given above.[21] Although certain unnamed "organs" of the OGPU were praised for uncovering the conspiracy, the secret police in general were criticized for delays in investigating the case. The Workers' and Peasants' Inspectorate was also blamed for dragging its feet, although neither Ordzhonikidze, its head, nor any other government or party leader was mentioned by name: "There can be no doubt that organs of the Peasants' and Workers' Inspectorate did not raise at the proper time the question of the shortcomings now revealed, while organs of the OGPU were undoubtedly dilatory in uncovering this most significant conspiracy."[22] The OGPU and Rabkrin were especially singled out for criticism, although managers, union officials, and party workers in general were criticized for lack of vigilance. This case, according to the *Pravda* editorial, showed how sabotage could continue undiscovered for five to six years "under the very noses of 'communist leaders.'" A statement such as this may have held special meaning for Ordzhonikidze, who, less than two years before, had served as the party's first secretary in the Northern Caucasus district, and then went to Moscow to head an agency with special responsibilities for uncovering such economic crimes and other failures.[23]

[20] Harvey Dyck, *Weimar Germany and Soviet Russia*, London, 1966, pp. 123-132.

[21] *Pravda*, March 10, 1928. Bukharin, soon to be a leader of the moderate opposition to Stalin, was then the most prominent member of the editorial board of *Pravda*, which was made up largely of his supporters. But Stalin and his allies were frequent contributors to the central newspaper of the party, a right that could scarcely be denied the general secretary. For example, an important unsigned editorial, which appeared three weeks before the announcement of the Shakhty case, in the issue of February 15, 1928, was written by Stalin, and foreshadowed his new position toward the peasants during the grain crisis of that winter. In its implications, this editorial was certainly directed against the point of view of Rykov and his supporters (Lewin, p. 235). While it is unknown who handled the treatment of the Shakhty affair for *Pravda*, it is possible that Stalin and Bukharin agreed on this issue at the time. As events developed, at any rate, it appears that *Pravda's* version was also Stalin's, as will be seen below.

[22] Ibid.

[23] V. S. Kirillov and A. Ya. Sverdlov, *Grigorii Konstantinovich Ordzhonikidze (Sergo), Biografiia*, Moscow, 1962, pp. 214-215. Stalin had other reasons to be at odds with his old comrade from the Caucasus during this period. Ordzhonikidze was considerably more conciliatory toward the Trotskyites than Stalin during

Only Stalin stood to gain politically from the way in which the case was presented, and, according to Avtorkhanov, he did, in fact, win prestige within the party. A confidential letter from the Central Committee was circularized among party members, praising Stalin for his vigilance, while tactfully avoiding "all mention of the government's efforts to 'sabotage' exposure of the Shakhty case."[24]

That other party leaders were alarmed by the case and its implications for the Soviet industrialization effort becomes apparent from a study of their speeches and articles in these months. The public statements of Rykov, Kuibyshev, and Ordzhonikidze at this time reflect a common element: though not denying the validity of the Shakhty arrests, they attempted to minimize the negative effects of this affair on the economy, and tried to convert the attendant publicity into channels useful to their own areas of responsibility. Their preoccupations were overwhelmingly economic. Stalin's approach and public emphasis was considerably different, focusing primarily on a political interpretation of the affair: the sharpening of the class struggle with "bourgeois" elements both at home and abroad, of which this case was a symptom in his view, and the need for greater political vigilance (*bditel'nost'*).

Kuibyshev was one of those most disturbed by the effect of this case on his own area of responsibility: industrial management. In 1918, Kuibyshev had been a member of the Left Communist groups that had originally opposed the use of old specialists in the army and economy, but over the years, he had changed his attitude toward many of these specialists.[25] As chairman of the Council of National Economy after 1926, he became a strong proponent of cooperation with the old specialists, attracting them to work in the Soviet economy and opposing any attempts by party or union officials to harass those who worked conscientiously and well. The Shakhty case threatened to destroy a relationship that had been carefully nurtured by Kuibyshev and his predecessor at *Vesenkha*, Felex Dzherzhinsky. Dzherzhinsky had often paid tribute to the work of the old specialists, protecting them from inter-

---

his showdown with that group in 1927. He had opposed the expulsion of Trotsky and his followers from the party. He also opposed Stalin's suggestion that Trotsky be brought to trial, rather than exiled (Daniels, pp. 319-320); see also Boris Souvarine, *Stalin*, New York, 1939, pp. 449, 452-453.

[24] Avtorkhanov, p. 30.

[25] Kuibyshev had found many of the directorates and sections of *Vesenkha* headed by old specialists. He worked well with such personnel, but he also asked the Central Committee's Department of Assignments (*uchraspredotdel*) to send him young "red specialists," such as recent graduates of the Institute of Red Professors, who were given high positions in Soviet industry at an early age. (G. B. Kuibysheva, p. 267.)

ference and in general striving to create a good working atmosphere for them.[26] In this respect, Kuibyshev continued the work of Dzherzhinsky after the latter's death in 1926.

The treatment Kuibyshev and *Vesenkha* gave to the Shakhty case differed considerably from that in *Pravda*. Even before the arrest of the Shakhty engineers was announced in *Pravda*, Kuibyshev published what may have been a veiled warning in the official newspaper of *Vesenkha*: "Every wrong assertion, every unjust accusation that has been exaggerated out of proportion creates a very difficult atmosphere for work, and such criticism already ceases to be constructive."[27] This statement was made in a speech delivered at a meeting of the country's highest industrial executives, held in the first week of March. Kuibyshev was speaking about the harmful effects of concentrating only on the failures and negative aspects of Soviet industry. He stressed that such failures were mainly due to inexperience, not criminal intent.

On the following day, the same newspaper carried a response by Kuibyshev to those in the Soviet Union who objected to the use of foreign specialists.[28] Kuibyshev censured those who met these foreign personnel with suspicion, or objected to the high salaries they were paid. He maintained that to invite these experts was the official policy of the party and government, and their work was extremely useful.

It is worth noting that these remarks were published on the same day that the five German specialists were arrested by the OGPU. Of course, Kuibyshev may not have known this at the time, although, as a member of the Politburo, he would likely have been informed beforehand of an action that affected his vital area of concern.[29]

---

[26] Felix Dzherzhinsky, *Izbrannye proizvedeniia*, Moscow, 1957, vol. 2, p. 214; Volkov (N. V. Valentinov), *Vospominaniia*, in the Archive of Russian History and Culture, Columbia University, 197-198, 218, 221, 232-233. In 1925, at Dzherzhinsky's instigation, the Central Committee of the party relieved the old specialists of some civil disabilities and generally boosted their status, defining their rights and responsibilities more clearly (see *KPSS i sovetskoe pravitel'stvo po khoziastvennym voprosam, Direktivy*, vol. 1, pp. 552-553).

[27] *TPG*, March 6, 1928.

[28] Ibid., March 7, 1928.

[29] It is known that on March 6 or before, the German ambassador, von Rantzau, paid a visit to the Soviet foreign minister, Chicherin, who opened the conversation by saying that he and Rantzau must cooperate to prevent a very disagreeable affair, about to break, from harming German-Soviet relations. Chicherin went on to explain that the OGPU was about to arrest five German specialists as they were delivering turbines to Soviet coal-mining firms, and Chicherin hoped that the effects of this on German-Soviet relations could be minimized. (Gustav Hilger and A. G. Meyer, *Incompatible Allies*, New York, 1953, pp. 217-218; Rantzau to Stresemann, March 6, 1928, and March 16, 1928, Archives of the German Foreign Ministry, 2860/D559468-70, 2860/D559755-6, cited in Dyck, pp. 129-130.) If Chicherin knew about the affair by March 6, it is even more

Kuibyshev continued in the same speech to say that *Vesenkha* had not yet had time to consider seriously the problem of filling the shortages in engineering and technical cadres. He noted that industry in Leningrad had only eleven engineers per thousand workers, in Moscow nine engineers per thousand, and in the Urals only four per thousand, a much lower proportion than in either Europe or America. This he considered one of the most important problems of the future, and he expressed the hope that *Vesenkha* would come to grips with it shortly, "in the next few weeks." He suggested that it be included as one of the vital elements of the First Five-Year Plan, then under discussion, and he noted that a preliminary attempt at planning such cadres had already been made in the industrial-financial plan for the current fiscal year. Much more emphasis, he noted, should be placed on the expanded education of new engineering cadres, especially those drawn from the working class. In these remarks, he foreshadowed an emphasis he was to give in his later remarks on the Shakhty case.

Unlike *Pravda*, which used banner headlines on the front page for the first announcement of the Shakhty case on March 10, the official organ of *Vsenkha* carried the announcement on page two, without editorial comment. Only the official statement of the prosecutor general was printed, together with a notice that the Central Trade Unions' Council, headed by Tomsky, had appointed a special commission to investigate the circumstances of the case and make recommendations concerning the involvement of the unions in this affair. The following day, the front page of the newspaper carried the notices of various professional organizations of engineering and technical workers, who had passed resolutions condemning the Shakhty engineers and pledging redoubled efforts in the cause of constructing Soviet industry. Again, no editorial comment was included, unlike the *Pravda* treatment. In the following days, the same restraint continued, although front-page editorials on other subjects were a regular feature.[30]

Especially noticeable, at this time, is the absence of the *Pravda* line that sabotage was one of the factors holding back the success of Soviet

---

unlikely that Kuibyshev, who far outranked him, was unaware of the impending arrests of foreign specialists when he made the speech cited above.

Another sign of concern within the Soviet government regarding the Shakhty case was relayed through the Lithuanian ambassador, who reported to the Germans that a Soviet foreign affairs official had complained to him of the "chauvinists" now forming Soviet policy (Archives of the German Foreign Ministry, 2860/D559935-9, cited in Dyck, p. 132).

[30] Kuibyshev was generally active in the editorial policy of the *Vesenkha* paper, *Torgovo-promyshlennaia gazeta*, and followed its coverage very closely, according to the Soviet journalist and historian, A. F. Khavin, who worked for the paper in these years (see his *U rulia industrii*, Moscow, 1968, pp. 79-81).

efforts at industrialization, and that this case marked a new form of class warfare by the "bourgeoisie." It was this line that Stalin developed, from the Shakhty case and subsequent affairs, as part of his doctrine that class struggle would intensify during the building of socialism, thereby justifying the wider use of police measures and terror.

On March 17, the *Vesenkha* newspaper carried on its front page a dispatch from Berlin about the interruption of German-Soviet economic talks, with long excerpts from German press sources about the cause of the disruption: the arrest of the five German specialists. Beneath this article was a shorter dispatch from TASS, the Soviet news agency, blaming the Germans for stopping the talks, and minimizing the arrests of these German nationals. Again, the paper carried no editorial comment. In the previous weeks, it had published a number of long, glowing articles about the usefulness of contracts being signed and carried out with foreign, and especially German, firms, for technical aid to Soviet industry.[31] Thus, the arrest of German specialists was bound to be a personal embarrassment to Kuibyshev and his newspaper.

On March 28, Kuibyshev met with a group of Moscow engineers and scientists and tried to calm their apprehension regarding the Shakhty affair: "It is necessary to declare at the start, with the fullest emphasis: the government will take all measures necessary to assure in connection with the Shakhty case that not a single innocent engineer will suffer."[32] At the same time, Kuibyshev vowed that those guilty would be tried and punished with the fullest severity of the law; he considered the number of such persons to be small. The trial would be given wide publicity, however: "The government, party and trade unions consider it obligatory to draw the necessary lessons from this trial." The focus of attention, Kuibyshev went on to explain, would include such questions as the need to overcome the extreme shortage of engineers, as well as the suspicion toward young engineers in industry and the conflict between generations of specialists. The cause of the latter problem he considered to be the "closed caste mentality" of many engineers, who were reluctant to share their privileged position. Added to this was the need to learn from foreign experience. The basic need, however, was to develop further the cooperation and dedication of existing engineers, as well as to create a new generation of dedicated "red specialists."

Not all the points Kuibyshev mentioned actually developed during

[31] Such an article was published as late as March 9, two days after the arrest of the German specialists. It included extensive favorable mention of the German Electric Corporation (AEG), which employed several of the arrested specialists. Possibly word of these arrests had not yet reached *TPG*, although this seems improbable, since even the German ambassador was informed prior to the arrests.

[32] *TPG*, March 29, 1928.

the trial: a favorable estimation of the value of foreign technical aid was most noticeably missing, apparently a result of the markedly different attitudes held by Kuibyshev and those officials in the police and prosecutor's office who actually conducted the trial. In other ways, as will be seen, however, the trial furthered Stalin's political purposes and many of the aims of Kuibyshev and *Vesenkha*, as well. It was to have wide consequences for conditions in industry.

In his speech to the Moscow engineers on March 28, Kuibyshev also had words of praise for the many distinguished specialists who were cooperating with the government. He maintained that the Shakhty case did not mark a radical, new policy toward the technical intelligentsia, a statement that was soon to prove untrue, however.

> Rumors by some elements in some places are being disseminated to the effect that the Soviets are preparing to change their attitude toward the specialists, are beginning to steer some kind of special course. I am fully authorized to declare in the most decisive fashion, in the name of the government and Central Committee of the party, that all the rumoring and whispering are slanders and inventions of those who wish to pick a quarrel between the Soviet power and the engineers.[33]

In retrospect, Kuibyshev seems to have protested too much, although he may have believed in the truth of his statement at the time. In actual fact, the Shakhty affair did mark the beginning of a radical, new set of policies toward the technical intelligentsia, and toward the older generation of graduate engineers in particular.

The alarm these arrests caused is also reflected in Rykov's public statements at the time. In a speech published in *Pravda* on March 11, 1928, he drew two conclusions from the affair. First, he berated everyone collectively for not uncovering the plot sooner: the party, the managers, and the trade unions. Second, he warned against letting the reaction over the affair develop into specialist-baiting: "Without a doubt, the existence of this conspiracy arouses extreme concern on all sides. But it would be unusually harmful and dangerous if the discovery of this conspiracy were to bring in its wake a development of specialist baiting."

Rykov mentioned the fears among engineers of such a development and expressed his belief that the workers were mature enough to prevent it, knowing that there is no technical progress without engineers. As for himself, he concluded that the affair emphasized the need to win over more specialists to active political support of Soviet efforts.

[33] *TPG*, March 29, 1928.

The Shakhty conspiracy had been uncovered by the OGPU, rather than by other specialists, because many specialists were still politically neutral and would not report such counterrevolutionary activities by their colleagues. The party needed to increase its efforts among the old specialists and to push forward with the education and training of new and politically more loyal engineering and technical cadres.

Ordzhonikidze stressed many of the same points in a speech to a class of new graduates in Moscow on March 26. He emphasized first that the Shakhty engineers were not typical of the mass of Soviet specialists, the majority of whom were working honestly to strengthen the economy and government. He also emphasized the need to educate more young "red specialists." To Rykov's points, he added several in which he had a vested interest: the vital importance of engineers and technicians in general for the success of Soviet efforts to rationalize the economy. His agency, *Rabkrin*, had a major responsibility in such efforts to improve the organization and technology of industry. He also stressed the need to learn from foreign experience in this area by sending Soviet experts abroad and by inviting foreign specialists to work in Soviet industry. Such efforts were now threatened by the arrest of the German engineers, although Ordzhonikidze did not explicitly make this point.[34]

Bukharin's attitude toward the Shakhty case in the weeks immediately after its announcement appears much more positive and less cautious than that of Rykov, Kuibyshev, and Ordzhonikidze. Bukharin's public remarks, for example, did not share the strong concern for the possible effects of this case on the old specialists and for the dangers of specialist-baiting and witch-hunting. There were probably several reasons for his attitude. Bukharin at this time was not directly concerned with the actual problems of industry or responsible for its management, as were Rykov, Kuibyshev, and Ordzhonikidze. He was rather a chief ideologist of the party and directly concerned with the Communist International. Also, because of his earlier attitude toward the old specialists, one of some suspicion, Bukharin may have been more willing to accept their guilt, especially if confessions had already been obtained from them by the OGPU.[35]

Bukharin was encumbered by his own past attitudes and public statements regarding the old specialists. Even if he had wanted to defend the accused engineers, he would have found it difficult to overcome the attitude he had long expressed about the old specialists. Although he

[34] Ordzhonikidze in *Pravda*, March 28, 1928.
[35] See Bukharin's April 13, 1928 speech to the Leningrad party organization, *Uroki khlebozagotovok, shakhtinskogo dela i partii*, 42-55.

had been opposed to the use of such specialists in 1918, he soon changed his mind and developed a rationale to justify their use by a proletarian regime. After 1918, he formed many ties with this group and was a staunch advocate of winning them over. At the same time, however, he was also on record as believing that some elements among the old specialists were not only hostile to the Soviet system but capable of wrecking activities, similar to those of which the Shakhty engineers were accused:

> We should be wrong, of course, to expect fidelity from these "experts," to expect from them devotion to Communism. It would be absurd to hope that such people, who are connected with the bourgeoisie by a thousand ties, will undergo a sudden transformation. But here the proletariat must act as a far-seeing employer. It needs the bourgeois experts, and it must compel them to work for it.
>
> We must employ the following methods. Economic considerations dictate our giving every possible encouragement to those who work well; we must not be stingy in the matter of their salaries. But towards any who prove to be counterrevolutionaries, who fight against the proletariat, who are traitors or saboteurs, we must be absolutely ruthless. The proletariat must prize those who serve it faithfully, and it knows how to prize them. But the workers cannot allow anyone to inflict an injury upon them unpunished, above all at such a time as this, when they have to suffer the pangs of hunger and a thousand additional evils.
>
> We must, therefore, exercise strict control, more particularly when we are dealing with experts from among the circles of the managers of great businesses, and from among those who were capitalists on the grand scale. Such persons will frequently attempt to serve their own side in secret.[36]

Bukharin's statement, particularly the last paragraph, sounds very like a description of the situation presented by the prosecutor in the Shakhty trial, even though it was written nearly ten years before. Bukharin's attitude toward the old specialists remained essentially unchanged between 1919 and the time of the Shakhty trial. His view helps to explain why he failed to raise any questions about it in public, even

[36] N. Bukharin and E. Preobrazhensky, *The ABC of Communism*, Ann Arbor, Mich., 1966, pp. 288-289. This book was first published in 1919. It was one of many similar, extensive statements on the use of the old specialists made by Bukharin between that year and 1928. See also, *Inprecor*, 8, no. 92, 1928, 1759-1760; *Revoliutsiia i kul'tura*, no. 2, Dec. 5, 1927, 5-10.

if he entertained any private doubts regarding the guilt of the engineers and Stalin's motives in this case. His inaction is all the easier to understand because many of the accused engineers had confessed in detail to the very crimes Bukharin was disposed to think them capable of committing.

Bukharin may not have been aware, however, of the use to which the Shakhty case would soon be put by Stalin. By the time of the Central Committee plenum, in April 1928, Bukharin had probably already joined Rykov and Tomsky in their opposition to Stalin's new course regarding the peasantry. Bukharin later dismissed Stalin's theory of increasing class struggle with advancing socialism, dubbing the theory "ignorant nonsense."[37] Stalin cited the Shakhty affair as major evidence to bolster this theory, which was used to justify the purge of all elements hostile to Stalin in the late 1920s and during the 1930s. It became a cornerstone of Stalinist political theory and practice.

Bukharin not only opposed the development of this theory after 1928, but later also opposed the way in which Stalin wished to change the composition of the technical intelligentsia by creating unusually high class and party quotas, thereby excluding many persons who had nonproletarian backgrounds. Yet Bukharin's position in these areas apparently developed only after the announcement of the Shakhty case in March 1928, for it was between March and June that the differences between the two men became apparent. By June, the break was complete.[38] Whether Stalin concealed his plans with regard to the Shakhty affair from Bukharin is unknown, but if so, this was probably one reason for the bitterness of the break between the two, especially if Bukharin had privately entertained doubts about the guilt of the arrested engineers.

Stalin withheld all public comment on the Shakhty case for more than a month after the *Pravda* announcement. His first statements on the affair were made public on April 13, 1928, two days after the end of the Central Committee plenum, which had discussed the Shakhty affair, but had focused on the developing crisis over food shortages and conflicts with the peasantry.

The minutes of the Central Committee sessions have not been published, but the resolutions passed reveal that Rykov, rather than Stalin, reported on the Shakhty affair. The resolutions concerning the case were

---

[37] Bukharin to Kamenev, *Sotsialisticheskii vestnik*, no. 6, 1929, 10.

[38] Lewin, pp. 294ff.; this is corroborated by the most recent Soviet study of the "right opposition," which refers to documents in central party archives; see F. M. Vaganov. *Pravyi uklon v VKP(b) i ego razgrom*, Moscow, 1970, pp. 139-140.

based, at least in part, on Rykov's report.[39] The politburo had appointed a "Special Commission to Develop Practical Measures for Liquidating the Faults Uncovered in Connection with the Shakhty Affair," and Rykov headed it. The other members of the Commission are not mentioned, but the resolutions developed from Rykov's report reveal a melding of viewpoints when compared with the different points emphasized in the individual public statements of Rykov, Kuibyshev, Ordzhonikidze, and Stalin. The resolutions, which were adopted unanimously according to the record, point to a compromise document. This document contained a number of elements that were to prove contradictory in practice and led to further clashes and divisions among members of the Politburo and Central Committee on industrial policy in general and policy toward the technical intelligentsia in particular.

The basic assumption of these resolutions was that the Shakhty engineers were guilty of the crimes for which they were imprisoned, even though the trial itself was not held until May and June. Since guilt was presumed, the document was concerned not so much with past acts of groups or individuals as with future policy toward the technical intelligentsia. The document offered guidelines in several distinct but interrelated areas: the role of the old specialists; policy toward the Red Directors, or managers; the recruitment and education of new specialists and managers; and working conditions and institutions in Soviet industry.

Concerning the old specialists, the Central Committee affirmed that this case represented the development of a "new form of bourgeois counterrevolution by a small group of specialists who had been especially privileged in the past." The vast majority of the technical intelligentsia were working honestly for the Soviet government, according to this document. The latter was a point Rykov, Kuibyshev, and Ordzhonikidze had been eager to emphasize from the beginning, while Stalin remained silent on the entire subject.

The resolutions of the Central Committee cited several faults of Soviet industry and recommended corrective measures. For example, new specialists were often met with suspicion on the part of older specialists, which prevented them from working effectively. The party must see to it that the new graduates of higher technical institutions gradually replaced the old specialists in positions of high responsibility. At the same time, the party should continue to attract honest specialists, whatever their background, and should struggle against any development of specialist-baiting. This resolution echoed the concern expressed publicly by Rykov, Kuibyshev, and Ordzhonikidze.

[39] *Pravda*, April 12, 1928.

The attraction of foreign specialists and foreign technical aid often proceeded without the "proper direction and control," according to these resolutions. Foreign specialists should continue to be hired for Soviet industry, but "with the proper control," and more Soviet specialists should be sent abroad for training. This resolution appears to have been a compromise between the leaders of *Vesenkha* and *Rabkrin*, who were eager to maintain these contacts with the West, and the OGPU, which was responsible for internal security and foreign intelligence, and frowned on too many uncontrolled contacts between foreign nationals and Soviet citizens.

According to the Central Committee, the trade union sections for engineering and technical personnel were often controlled by "bourgeois" specialists, and they considered this another serious fault of industry. Bureaucratic elements in the party and trade unions were to be removed in new elections and more suitable persons were to be elected to these posts. The Politburo was assigned the task of working out a project for this. At the same time, the trade unions were directed to intensify their work among the specialists and to look after their material and cultural needs. According to the resolutions, more emphasis should also be given to developing effective professional organizations of specialists. Technical propaganda should be encouraged through conferences and extensive publication efforts. The latter were measures that were to be effected within the next few years. The role of the trade union sections for the technical intelligentsia was soon to become a bone of contention between the Stalinists and their more moderate opponents. Some of the trade union leaders attempted to give legal assistance to specialists who were accused of "wrecking" or other crimes, only to be replaced by more pliable Stalinist officials.

With regard to the Red Directors, or managers, the Central Committee severely criticized their work on many counts and recommended corrective measures. Because of their own lack of technical qualifications, many managers placed blind faith in the old specialists and depended upon them in a variety of ways. "Up till now," according to the Central Committee, "very many managers have filled the role of a poor commissar in industry," signing papers and generally overseeing the work, but with little detailed knowledge of industrial processes. Such managers needed to raise their technical qualifications through special courses, particularly through the expansion of the special Industrial Academies (*promakademiia*) and correspondence courses. They also should be freed from dependence on their technical directors, usually old specialists, by a repeal of all legal and administrative restrictions on their powers to make decisions. Stalin was to emphasize this point particularly, although he was generally less critical of the managers than was the Central Committee as a whole. He attempted to increase the powers of the managers in the economy and to win their support by conciliation.

The guidelines discussed above were often vague, and they glossed over the basic conflicts of interest they embodied.[40] Events of the following few years were to make this apparent during a series of clashes between various interest groups. How these conflicts were resolved in practice, and how their resolution affected the technical specialists will form the basis of much of this study. For the sake of clarity, the various issues involved will be taken up topically in the chapters that follow.

In reporting the results of the April plenum to the party organization in Moscow, Stalin made his first public comment on the Shakhty case, two days following the adoption of the resolutions, and more than a month following announcement of the arrests. It is interesting to note which of the resolutions he chose to emphasize, and which he chose to ignore or gloss over. Stalin's approach toward the technical intelligentsia was to use both the carrot and the stick: encouragement for the industrial managers and for a new group of technical specialists to be recruited from those with working-class backgrounds and Communist party connections, together with a policy of intimidation of the old specialists. With regard to the latter group, Stalin gave full play to the conspiracy theory, which attributed many of the failures and problems of the Soviet economy to the class struggle and hostility from bourgeois elements:

> What is the class background of the Shakhty affair, where are its roots, and on what class basis could this economic counterrevolution arise?
>
> There are comrades who think the Shakhty affair accidental. They usually say: we were really caught napping this time; we didn't have our eyes open, but if we had not been yawning, we would not have had any Shakhty affair. That there was carelessness, and a good deal of it, there can be no doubt. But to explain everything by that is to miss the main point.
>
> . . .
>
> It would be stupid to assume that international capital will leave us in peace. No, comrades, that is not true. Classes exist, international capital exists, and it cannot calmly watch the development of the country which is building socialism. Formerly, interna-

[40] The resolutions of this plenum were published in *Pravda*, April 12, 1928.

tional capital thought of overthrowing the Soviet power by means of direct military intervention. The attempt failed. Now it is trying, and will try in the future, to weaken our economic power by means of invisible economic intervention, not always obvious but fairly serious, organizing sabotage, planning all kinds of "crises" in one branch of industry or another, and thus facilitating the possibility of future military intervention. It is all part and parcel of the class struggle of international capital against the Soviet power, and there can be no talk of any accidental happenings.[41]

Stalin had nothing to say at this time about the dangers of specialist-baiting. His attitude toward the old specialists was one of suspicion and contempt. He played down the criticisms that had been laid against the managers, for their faults, in his view, were not their own, but were caused by the situation in which they found themselves. He strongly criticized previous administrative measures at *Vesenkha*. These dated from 1926, when Dzherzhinsky was still its head, and, according to Stalin, gave "almost all rights to the technical director, leaving to the chief director the right to mediate conflicts, to 'represent,' and to play the balalaika." This situation, Stalin emphasized, made the Red Directors mere "tails," eager to be wagged by the bourgeois specialists.[42] Although the Red Directors had sometimes been judged incapable of learning enough technology to run industry by themselves, Stalin flattered them. According to him, there was nothing they were unable to do as Bolsheviks: "There are no such fortresses in the world which the toilers, the Bolsheviks cannot take." Stalin reminded the Red Directors of their superior status and tried to wean them away from dependence upon, and support of, the old specialists, one of the principal groups in Stalin's rapidly evolving demonology. In this, he went directly in the face of those governmental and industrial leaders, such as Rykov and Kuibyshev, who had worked hard to heal the conflicts between these two groups and make possible their close cooperation.

At the same time, Stalin held out a carrot, championing one of the favorite ideas of Kuibyshev and his staff. Stalin criticized the education of many young specialists, calling it too bookish and removed from production and practical needs. He advocated changes in their education

[41] Stalin, *Sochineniia*, Moscow, 1949, vol. 11, p. 53, as translated in Jane Degras, *Soviet Documents on Foreign Policy*, vol. 2, London, 1952, pp. 300-301.

[42] Stalin referred particularly to two measures of the Supreme Council of the National Economy, dating from 1926: the *Vesenkha* Circular No. 33 of March 29, 1926, "Ob organizatsii upravleniia promyshlennymi zavedeniiami," and, accompanying it, "Obshchee polozhenie o pravakh i obiazannostiakh tekhnicheskogo direktora zavoda v metallicheskoi i elektrotekhnicheskoi promyshlennosti." For the texts, see *TPG*, March 31, 1926.

that would let them use their learning in actual production work—a project close to the heart of Kuibyshev.

In his criticism of working conditions, Stalin also clearly favored industrial management over the trade unions. On the question of inadequate participation by workers in the administration of industry, he criticized the trade unions and party organizations for not doing more in this direction, failing to see that labor codes and safety regulations were enforced, and so on. The managers received no similar scolding from Stalin, although the Central Committee had blamed them as well for this situation.

Stalin ended his speech with a reminder of the dangerous situation created by capitalist encirclement and the resistance of "bourgeois elements" within the Soviet Union to the changes then taking place, both among the peasantry and in Soviet industry: "We have internal enemies. We have external enemies. We cannot forget this for one moment."[43]

In view of all the statements and speeches made by governmental and party leaders in March and April, the actual trial of the Shakhty engineers came almost as an anticlimax. The trial began on May 18, 1928, in the main hall of the former Club of the Nobility in Moscow, then the House of Trade Unions. The president of the court was a lawyer who became one of Stalin's most trusted officials, Andrei Y. Vyshinsky.[44] He was to reappear in virtually every important show trial thereafter, from the Industrial party trial of 1930 to the trials during the Great Purge of the later 1930s. The public prosecutor was Nikolai Krylenko, already well known for his role in the trial of the Socialist Revolutionaries in 1922 and for subsequent show trials.

Krylenko actually was no stranger to the technical intelligentsia. During the 1905 revolution he had been an engineering student at the Moscow Technical School (MTU), where he became one of the leaders of radical students in a dispute with the rector of that institution, Professor Konovalov. Expelled from the institute, Krylenko went on to become a prominent revolutionary, Bolshevik leader in 1917, and pub-

[43] *Pravda*, April 18, 1928. Stalin again singled out the managers for his protection in a speech on June 26, when he criticized those who were "persecuting" managers as a result of the Shakhty affair. Stalin issued no similar warning, however, against any specialist-baiting that may have arisen in connection with the aftermath of the Shakhty affair, as did Kuibyshev and others. (For Stalin's remarks against the persecution of managers, see *Pravda*, June 28, 1928.)

[44] From 1928 to 1931, while he was involved in the major show trials of engineers and economists, Vyshinsky was also head of the Chief Administration of Professional Education in the Russian Commissariat of Education. He helped to plan and supervise the changes in higher technical education discussed in part 3. Besides being a prominent lawyer, he was rector of Moscow University from 1925 to 1928 (*BSE*, vol. 9, 1951, p. 540).

lic prosecutor for the new Soviet regime.[45] At this trial, Krylenko made a striking, unscholarly appearance. In contrast to Vyshinsky's pince-nez and neatly trimmed mustache, Krylenko wore sporting clothes throughout the six-week trial—a hunting jacket, riding breeches, and puttees. According to some of those present, his shaved head fairly glistened under the klieg lights set up for movie cameras.[46]

It was clear that the trial had been arranged for maximum publicity. In addition to the movie cameras, nearly one hundred reporters, Soviet and foreign, were present. The remainder of the audience changed daily. More than one hundred thousand spectators—school children, Pioneers and Young Communists, workers, visiting delegations of peasants and others—had seen some of the proceedings by the end of the trial.

Fifty Russian mining engineers were in the dock with three German specialists, two of the Germans originally arrested having been released during the pretrial investigation. Since there were only eleven hundred mining engineers in the U.S.S.R. at this time, the trial was a serious blow to an entire industry.[47] Among the defendants were several who held high positions in Soviet industry, including Rabinovich, the head of the coal industry. A rich and successful engineer before the revolu-

[45] Ipatieff, pp. 144, 449, 563; L. K. Erman, *Intelligentsiia v pervoi russkoi revoliutsii*, Moscow, 1966, p. 148.

[46] The full transcript of the trial was not published, perhaps because of its length, perhaps because of certain incidents described below. The available record of the trial comes from the following sources: the extensive daily summaries and excerpts published by *Torgovo-promyshlennaia gazeta* (*TPG*), May 18-July 4, 1928, which agree in most details with the accounts of foreign correspondents, such as Eugene Lyons, *Assignment in Utopia*, London, 1938, p. 122. Walter Duranty, *The Curious Lottery*, New York, 1929, pp. 135-237. Selected documents were published as a book under the editorship of Nikolai Krylenko, *Ekonomicheskaia kontr-revoliutsiia v Donbasse; Itogi shakhtinskogo dela; Stat'i i dokumenty*, Moscow, 1928. *Pravda* also covered the trial extensively at the time, but comparing its coverage with that of *TPG* shows a greater tendency to editorialize, abstract, or omit details.

Current Soviet historiography reveals an interesting omission concerning the Shakhty case. The new, 12-volume history of the U.S.S.R. being published by the Academy of Sciences (*Istoriia SSSR s drevneishikh vremen*; volume 8 covers this period) entirely omits any discussion of the Shakhty trial or subsequent trials of engineers as "wreckers," such as the widely publicized Industrial party trial of 1930. Yet other recent Soviet historiography, especially studies of the Central Committee's Academy of Social Sciences, continue to emphasize the importance of these trials.

These latter works do not question the credibility of the Stalinist interpretation that they represented real justice for enemies and conspirators against the Soviet system. For this latter interpretation, see especially the studies of Trifonov, n. 5, and Fediukin and Drobizhev, listed in the bibliography.

[47] A. M. Terpigorev, *Vospominaniia gornogo inzhenera*, Moscow, 1956, p. 183. These eleven hundred engineers served an industry with a total of three hundred thirty thousand workers.

tion, he had been an active member of the War Industry Committee in World War I who had not shrunk from opposing Tsarist policies.[48] In 1920 Lenin had entrusted him with the task of restoring the Soviet coal industry. In short, his career was typical of those of many old specialists who had risen to prominence in the Soviet regime under Lenin's sponsorship, and who were to come under attack by the Stalinists after 1928.

The only evidence produced during the trial was the confessions of the accused—not all the defendants confessed—as well as statements of workers who had been their subordinates. Curiously, the intercepted letters, which had supposedly first aroused the suspicions of the secret police, were not produced, nor were any other documents submitted to support the indictment. Krylenko's accusations were unlikely to ease the fears of the technical intelligentsia concerning a new wave of specialist-baiting.

In his concluding speech, Krylenko summed up the indictment: the arrested engineers were accused of participating in a conspiracy, the directing center of which was located abroad and consisted of former capitalist owners of the mines, who had close ties to the agents of German firms and to Polish counterintelligence. This organization "had its supporters and active members among the higher technical directing personnel of the coal mining industry in Moscow" and had ties with similar organizations in other branches of industry.[49] The latter was an ominous statement that foreshadowed further arrests and show trials. The ultimate purpose of this conspiracy, according to Krylenko, was to aid the enemy in the intervention being prepared by the capitalist world. The acts of sabotage mentioned in the indictment were "irrational construction projects, unnecessary waste of capital, lowering the quality of production, raising the cost of production," wrecking mine shafts, sabotaging their ventilation systems, and so on. Because the engineers involved were among the most qualified specialists in industry, Krylenko quoted from the confession of one of them to the effect that "all engineers" believed that the Bolsheviks could not succeed economically. Another engineer had confessed that the technical intelligentsia by its very nature had been much closer to the capitalists than any other group of the intelligentsia and, therefore, was more prone to counterrevolution.

Krylenko also gave full rein to the resentment of workers toward their supervising engineers. He read from statements of workers who

[48] This is the contention of Louis Siegelbaum, St. Antony's College, Oxford, who is completing a study of the War Industry Committees, based in part on Soviet archives.

[49] Krylenko, p. 101.

accused some of these engineers of persecuting the men under their direction, of being "vampires of the working class," of having turned some workers over to the Tsarist secret police, and of brutality toward Red Army prisoners of the Whites during the civil war.

Unlike the decisions of the Central Committee plenum discussed above, Krylenko's case did not distinguish between a majority of loyal specialists and a few engineers accused of being wreckers. On the contrary, his target at times seemed to be the entire body of graduate engineers—those who held diplomas from universities or technical institutes —who were accused either of being careerists and politically indifferent, or of being actual criminals. In Krylenko's words, summing up the case for the prosecution,

> Such was the mood of the engineers, a mood which did not, of course, signify that the entire mass of engineers were counterrevolutionary, or that the entire mass of engineers were ready material for a counterrevolutionary organization. An analysis of the personal composition [of the accused] given above, shows that the best qualified engineers, who were closely tied economically with the capitalist world (former mine owners, stock holders, etc.) were the most counterrevolutionary group. But the middle and lower technical personnel are accustomed to them, accustomed to obeying them, and do not themselves still completely trust the Soviet power. All of this made the work of the counterrevolutionaries easier.[50]

Although the evidence presented to substantiate the charges was flimsy by legal standards, it did not always stand up to questioning even during the trial. Two of the three German defendants were especially uncooperative. Gustav Hilger, a German diplomatic official who attended all the sessions of the trial, reported one such incident. The German technician Mayer contradicted the allegation that he had sabotaged the turbines delivered by his firm. At that point, the presiding judge, Vyshinsky, who would take over from the prosecution at critical moments, presented Mayer with a confession he had signed. Mayer admitted that it was indeed his personal signature, but he added that he had signed the document only because he was exhausted from prolonged nightly interrogations. Furthermore, he had no idea at all of what he was signing, he claimed, since the paper was written in Russian and he was unfamiliar with the language.

Vyshinsky then asked Mayer to confirm that, if not he, at least the

[50] Krylenko, p. 109.

Russian defendant, Bashkin, had been engaged in sabotaging the turbines. Had not Bashkin inquired about the most suitable means of accomplishing this sort of sabotage?

Mayer, not knowing Russian, had not understood Bashkin's earlier confession in court, but once he understood Vyshinsky's question, he became agitated and declared that not one word of it was true. Bashkin, he stated, was the most conscientious engineer he had ever met in Russia; it had been Bashkin who had constantly been concerned about the fate of the turbines, which was why he had continually inquired how he could take the best possible care of them.

The proceedings came to life when Bashkin, sitting on the defendant's bench, heard Mayer speak. Bashkin sprang from his seat, shouting to the audience that Mayer's statement was true, and his own confession made earlier had been false. Vyshinsky at once announced a recess. Forty minutes later Bashkin reappeared and said that his original confession had been true.[51]

The American newspaper correspondent, Eugene Lyons, felt at the time that there was some truth behind the charges. He believed that most of the accused were probably guilty either of actual sabotage, or of apathy toward their work, but he also thought that the melodramatic international plot was largely "a figment of Soviet stagecraft." He reported another incident during the trial, in which a defendant changed his plea several times. This engineer, Skorutto, at first pleaded innocent, then changed his plea to guilty. His wife at this point cried out in the audience for him not to lie, that he was innocent. He retracted his confession, but before the end of the trial reaffirmed his guilt, at least for a portion of what he had formerly confessed.[52]

The most prominent of the defendants, Rabinovich, who had been head of the Soviet coal industry from 1920 until 1927 and had earned Lenin's confidence, refused to confess at all. In his final plea at the close of the trial, he again protested his presence there: "I am absolutely not guilty, I repent for nothing, I shall beg for nothing. I have behind me fifty years of complete trust, respect and honor, as the result of my public and private life. I have been open with everyone. To the extent of my strength, I served the cause of the proletariat, which has viewed me with full trust and helped create a good working atmosphere for me. My work was conscientious to the end. I knew nothing about sabotage;

[51] Gustav Hilger and A. G. Meyer, *Incompatible Allies*, New York, 1953, p. 219.
[52] Lyons, pp. 124-129. See also the accounts of this incident in *TPG* and *Pravda* for June 26, 1928.

there is no doubt that if I had known about it, I would have fulfilled my duty as a citizen."[53]

During the course of the trial, Rabinovich challenged Krylenko on a number of points. For example, when Krylenko tried to prove that one of the defendants was actually engaged in sabotage when he recommended the use of expensive equipment and American methods of mechanized labor rather than the manual labor then in use in Soviet mines, Rabinovich rose to defend his fellow engineer, and sought to prove the prosecutor technically ignorant. Charges of this kind—that expensive technical innovations were actually sabotage—recurred throughout the trial. Such charges undoubtedly were disturbing to industrial managers such as Kuibyshev, who, since August 1927, had headed a Commission of the Politburo to study how best to rationalize and mechanize all Soviet industry. Rabinovich and the defense lawyers in this trial finally won a point against accusations that made such rationalization proposals appear to be "sabotage." The court ordered all such questions referred to a commission of outside experts, headed by Professor Gubkin of the Moscow Mining Academy, one of Kuibyshev's most trusted consultants at *Vesenkha*.[54]

Although Krylenko demanded death sentences for twenty-two of the fifty-three defendants, the court was considerably less harsh in its final judgment. It decreed eleven death sentences, and six of these were commuted to life imprisonment. Thirty-eight of the defendants were sentenced to imprisonment for terms ranging from one to ten years.[55] Rabinovich received a six-year term. Four men were acquitted entirely, including two of the three Germans.

Although the prosecution achieved less than it had demanded, and the role of foreign specialists was partially exonerated, the outcome of the trial could scarcely have pleased those in the government responsible for industrial management. The door had been opened for harassment of technical personnel on political grounds, even for purely technical mistakes and shortcomings. Such harassment was, in fact, to increase during the next few years.

[53] This and all other final pleas of the defendants were published in *TPG*, July 4, 1928.

[54] *BSE*, vol. 13, p. 170.

[55] Gustav Hilger, on a German diplomatic mission to the Urals in 1932, reported encountering one of the convicted engineers, Bashkin, who was working in a new factory at Chelyabinsk. A Soviet colleague reported proudly that Bashkin was one of the best and most reliable engineers at the plant (Hilger, p. 220). Bashkin was still serving his term at the time.

4

THE INDUSTRIAL PARTY AFFAIR

Terror implies mostly useless cruelties, perpetrated by frightened people in order to reassure themselves.

Friedrich Engels

In the history of Communist societies, the leadership has devoted a good deal of attention to the recurring tension between "expert" and "red," that is, between the need for technical expertise and a certain unease with, and distrust of, technical and scientific groups by the regimes in power. An important theme in the early years of the Soviet system, this tension has reappeared in recent years.[1] In Communist Chinese society, in a different context and a somewhat different form, this conflict has also been apparent, and was a major theme during the Cultural Revolution of the late 1960s.[2] Why has such tension developed and how has it been dealt with in Communist societies? In the previous chapters, we have already begun to suggest some answers for Soviet society. But here, in the Industrial party affair of 1930, we will see many of the answers more clearly.

The whole affair seems puzzling when one considers that these arrests took place during the crucial years of the First Five-Year Plan, when the U.S.S.R. suffered from a severe shortage of technical talent. What possible purpose could such a reign of terror serve? If viewed solely from the standpoint of economics, it makes little sense, but when seen in a wider political context a clearer explanation emerges. Previous historiography has focused largely on the Industrial party trial itself, especially the dubious evidence and reasoning of the prosecution. This chapter develops an alternative approach to an interpretation of the case. By focusing on the background of the men implicated, it sug-

---

[1] See, for example, Nikolai Bukharin and Evgenii Preobrazhensky, *The ABC of Communism*, Ann Arbor, Mich., 1966; Loren R. Graham, *The Soviet Academy of Sciences and the Communist Party, 1927-1932*, Princeton, 1967; Albert Parry, *The New Class Divided*, New York, 1966; Zhores Medvedev, *The Medvedev Papers*, London, 1972; and Andrei Sakharov, *Progress, Coexistence and Intellectual Freedom*, New York, 1968.

[2] See, for example, the recent study by Stanley Karnow, *Mao and China: From Revolution to Revolution*, New York, 1972.

gests some new conclusions about the purpose of the trial itself and the wider implications of this affair for the history of Soviet society. It stresses the political rationality of the trial from Stalin's viewpoint, given the insecurity of his regime at the time and the existence of strong political passions in a country still emerging from the effects of World War I, two revolutions, and a prolonged civil war.

The Industrial party case was the high point of the terror against the old technical intelligentsia, and was the most widely publicized show trial in the Soviet Union before the purges of the late 1930s. It involved eight leading Soviet technologists whose positions convey some idea of their importance to the economy at the time: Leonid K. Ramzin, forty-three, director of the Thermal Technical Institute in Moscow, and a professor at the Moscow Higher Technical School; N. F. Charnovsky, sixty-two, professor of metallurgy at the Moscow Higher Technical School, and chairman of the Metallurgical Advisory Council of the Supreme Council of the National Economy (*Vesenkha*); I. A. Kalinnikov, fifty-six, vice-chairman of the production sector of the State Planning Commission (*Gosplan*), and a professor at the Military Aviation Academy; V. A. Larichev, forty-three, chairman of the fuel section of *Gosplan*; A. A. Fedotov, sixty-six, head of the Textile Research Institute, and an engineering professor; S. V. Kuprianov, fifty-nine, a technical director in the textile industry; K. V. Sitnin, fifty-two, an engineer of the All-Union Textile Syndicate; and V. I. Ochkin, thirty-nine, of the scientific-research section of *Vesenkha*, and scientific secretary of the Thermal Technical Institute under Ramzin.

The trial itself is discussed at length in the literature cited below, and requires only a brief summary here.[3] Suffice it to say that the men tried were accused of conspiring, together with some two thousand of their fellow engineers, to take over the government of the Soviet Union. They were allegedly aided by Western powers, Russian emigrés, and various dissident groups in the U.S.S.R. The guilt of the defendants, who were convicted of economic sabotage, does not stand up to careful scrutiny. As in the Shakhty case, the only evidence presented consisted of lengthy confessions by the defendants themselves and other arrested engineers who had been prisoners of the political police for some months prior

---

[3] See Roy A. Medvedev, *Let History Judge: The Origins and Consequences of Stalinism*, New York, 1971, pp. 110-139; and Robert Conquest, *The Great Terror: Stalin's Purge of the Thirties*, New York, 1968, pp. 549-556. Doubt regarding the validity of the verdict has been raised by a recent Soviet *samizdat* document, *Politicheskii dnevnik*, no. 43, April 1968, 60, as well as by the absence of any discussion of this trial in the most recent multivolume history of the U.S.S.R. published by the Academy of Sciences' Institute of History, *Istoriia SSSR s drevneishiki vremen do nashikh dnei*, Moscow, 1967, vol. 8.

to the trial. The testimony they offered was a bizarre mixture of fact and fiction. Some of it was truthful comment on their professional lives in the past and can be corroborated from earlier sources, although the relevance of such facts to the criminal charges was nebulous. Some of it was outright fiction, such as alleged meetings abroad with former Russian industrialists plotting a comeback. Two of the Russian emigrés named in testimony by the defendants had died long before the alleged meetings took place. As foreign newspapers were quick to point out, the defendants in their zeal for self-incrimination had even conjured up the shades of the dead. These facts have long been familiar to students of the trial. It is difficult not to agree with such studies that the evidence presented was contrived and at times ludicrous. A prime intention of the trial itself, judging by its emphasis on some of the actual economic problems that had developed between 1928 and 1930, was to divert the attention of an uncritical public from the mistakes of the Stalinist leadership during the First Five-Year Plan, and to find scapegoats among the engineers.

What has been missing from previous discussions of this affair, however, is a close look at its background. A careful analysis of the political context of the case suggests three other, interrelated reasons for the arrests of these particular men. First, the more prominent engineers implicated in the case shared certain technocratic tendencies and professional ties that linked them in a common outlook, which had been forged in their experiences during the Tsarist era and the first decade of Soviet rule. Second, this common outlook predisposed them to take strong stands regarding issues of professional policy with social implications, in opposition to the Stalinist leadership. Such positions included attempts on the part of some of these men in the late 1920s to oppose the Stalinist version of the First Five-Year Plan and affiliated changes in Soviet higher education. Third, their background and opposition to Stalinist plans suggest possible links to the moderates, the so-called "Right Opposition" in the Communist party—the last major anti-Stalinist group at the end of the 1920s, which also opposed key features of the First Five-Year Plan.

The Industrial party affair is viewed here, then, both as an attempt to find scapegoats, and also as a major effort to discredit pretensions among the technical intelligentsia for a greater political role in Soviet society. The Stalinist leadership sought to accomplish this by a general attack on the authority and sense of community of the Soviet technical intelligentsia. This attack focused particularly on one of the most prominent groups of engineers—the leaders of the organized engineering profession—in the Soviet economy at the time. These were the so-called "old specialists," or "bourgeois specialists," who had received their higher technical educations and begun their careers before the 1917 revolutions. They were the first important social group outside the Communist party to experience the Stalinist technique of show trials, widespread arrests, and social isolation.

The terror against the "bourgeois specialists" had actually begun with the Shakhty trial of 1928. In the months following that trial the arrests spread to "old specialists" in many other sectors of the economy. By 1930 the OGPU claimed to have found "wreckers" in the transportation, defense, chemical, shipbuilding, nonferrous metals, machine-building, textile, and food-processing industries.

A common pattern figured in most of the arrests of engineers in these years, as already noted above. Besides being related to the continuing general purge of Soviet institutions, arrests of engineers, in at least some of these cases, were preceded by failures to fulfill plans in particular branches of industry, or by serious industrial accidents. Newspaper articles usually blamed these failures on such causes as poor planning, lack of raw materials, lack of transportation facilities, and inexperienced cadres.[4] Investigations, involving *Rabkrin* and, eventually, the OGPU, invariably followed such breakdowns, and only then would it turn out that a group of wreckers had been at work causing failures, quietly gnawing at the scaffolding of Soviet industry like a colony of termites.[5]

In the Industrial party trial, the state's case pulled all these threads together. The state prosecutor, Nikolai Krylenko, portrayed the Industrial party defendants as leaders of a general conspiracy, which was said to include the Shakhty engineers and wreckers in the Commissariat of Agriculture (United Peasant party case), who were non-Communist agrarian specialists. The latter group was never brought to public trial, but another group of alleged wreckers, mostly economists from *Gosplan* and *Vesenkha*, was tried shortly after the Industrial party trial, in the Menshevik party case of March 1931. The state linked all these groups together as part of the same general "conspiracy," but the old graduate engineers bore the brunt of the attack. The Industrial party case be-

---

[4] This pattern can be clearly seen, for example, in the cases involving alleged wrecker groups in the textile industry and in the area of fuel supplies. A number of articles analyzing the failures of the textile industry appeared during February and March 1930 in *Za industrializatsiiu*. A wrecker group was disclosed in this industry only in the May 14 issue. Early articles on the difficulties of the fuel-supply industry, published April 10, June 27, October 30, 1929, and April 23, 1930, gave no hint of suspected wrecking activities in this area, yet engineers in this field, such as Ramzin, figured prominently in the Industrial party trial of November and December 1930 (see *Protsess 'Prompartii'*, pp. 304-311).

[5] Such a pattern is confirmed by Walter A. Rukeyser, *Working for the Soviets: An American Engineer in Russia*, London, 1932, pp. 177-188.

came the central focus of the terror against the old specialists, and warrants our closest attention.[6]

To gain some perspective on these events we must begin by looking at the technocratic trend of thought that had developed among a group of prominent Soviet engineers prior to 1930. We must neither exaggerate the number of engineers who adhered to this trend nor underestimate their influence. They had held some of the highest technical posts in Soviet planning, industrial administration, higher technical education, and research institutions, and they led the most important professional engineering organizations in the Soviet Union. Of the engineers implicated in the industrial party case, some of the most prominent had espoused this trend toward professional independence.

Technocracy as a concept has gained wide currency during the past half century. In its broadest sense, of course, it projects a society ruled by engineers. We use the term "technocratic trend" here, however, to mean any movement among technical specialists that urges them to develop a wider sense of social responsibility for the use of their technical knowledge, and particularly urges them to take important positions in forming policy. In other words, engineers should not be content as the technical executors of other men's policies; they should become politicians themselves. In particular, they should try to influence social policies by banding together in self-aware professional organizations to exert political pressure on the wider society. Engineers should not be satisfied with work in, and unquestioned loyalty to, such organizations as business corporations and government bureaus, which are run largely by people other than engineers.

The idea of a society in which engineers and other specialists would have important, even dominant, political responsibility can be traced at least as far back as the first half of the nineteenth century, in the discussions of such utopian socialists as Saint-Simon. The word "technocracy" and the ideas associated with it did not become common in Western social thought until the early twentieth century, however, when engineering emerged as a self-aware profession. The trend transcends national boundaries and exists, for example, in both the United States and the Soviet Union, having followed a roughly parallel development, although under vastly different social conditions. In both cases the technocratic trend produced uneven results in these years. In both cases the political ambitions of professional engineering groups lost out to

[6] *Za industrializatsiiu*, Nov. 27, 1930; for the campaign against nonconforming scientists, which corresponded in time with the terror against these other groups, and was part of the general process of Stalinization, see Loren R. Graham, *The Soviet Academy of Sciences and the Communist Party, 1927-1932*, Princeton, 1967.

those of broader organizations—such as the modern business corporation, the state, or political party—by the end of the 1930s. The way in which this trend failed, however, is unique to the history of each country. The development and fate of the technocratic tendency in the United States between the two world wars has been documented and interpreted in several recent studies.[7]

In the United States the technocratic trend was associated particularly with such developments as Progressivism, the conservation movement, and scientific management, the theory of industrial efficiency begun by the engineer F. W. Taylor. It reached its height just before and after World War I. A recent researcher has traced the origins of the word "technocracy" itself back to a group of writers who met in Greenwich Village during 1919 and 1920.[8] The most famous member of this group, Thorstein Veblen, promulgated the concept among the educated American public through his book, *The Engineers and the Price System*, published in 1921. Veblen proposed turning power over to "Soviets of Technicians," who would administer a planned economy outside the framework of the free market mechanism, a proposal obviously influenced by the Russian Revolution but not a carbon copy of that experience. Other members of this group included Stuart Chase, a writer, William H. Smyth, a mechanical engineer, and Howard Scott, a prime mover in the Technical Alliance, a technocratic research group that occupied quarters on the campus of Columbia University in the 1920s.[9] In 1932 Scott founded "Technocracy, Inc.," a social movement that proposed ending the depression by turning over all power to the engineers. "Technocracy, Inc." enjoyed a short-lived, if sensational, vogue during the year of its founding. The technocratic trend among American engineers, while generally less ambitious than the aims Scott proposed, has a complex and interesting history, documented in Edwin Layton's important study.

[7] See particularly Edwin T. Layton, Jr., *The Revolt of the Engineers: Social Responsibility and the American Engineering Profession*, Cleveland, 1971; Henry Elsner, Jr., *The Technocrats*, Syracuse, 1967; and Eugene Roger Wutke, "Technocracy: It Failed to Save the Nation," Ph.D. diss., University of Missouri, Kansas City, 1964.

[8] Wutke, "Technocracy," pp. 14-25. The word "technocracy" was apparently first used in print by the engineer William H. Smyth in a series of articles published during 1919. "Human Instincts in Reconstruction," *Industrial Management*, 57, 1919, 81-91; "Technocracy," ibid., 208-212; "Technocracy—Ways and Means to Gain Industrial Democracy," ibid., 385-389.

[9] Howard Scott and Stuart Chase made "technocracy" a household word through their writings and other activities. See, for instance, Chase's *Technocracy: An Interpretation*, New York, 1932.

The fate of the technocratic trend in early Soviet history is stormier and more significant for the history of that country, for it is closely linked with the rise of Stalinism. Its advocates in the Soviet Union did not simply fade into the relative obscurity of a Howard Scott after 1932. Some paid with their lives and others spent years in the kind of prison so vividly described in Solzhenitsyn's novel, *The First Circle*—prisons that, Solzhenitsyn notes, were first set up for the engineers arrested in the Industrial party affair.[10] The Russian language had no equivalent for the word "technocracy" in the 1920s, but the concept associated with it became well known in the Soviet Union during this period. This is probably no coincidence, although no evidence has been found of strong links between the trend as it developed in Russia and America.[11] The influence of World War I was probably crucial in both countries.

In the United States the machinery of government control over the economy was largely dismantled after 1918, but the idea remained and proved attractive to some as a cure for the economic ills of 1919 and 1920 and for the depression of the 1930s. In Russia the machinery of state economic control was not dismantled after World War I, but became the basis for Bolshevik control of the economy. Many of the same "experts" who had served the Tsarist state remained in prominent positions under the Bolsheviks, as we have already seen, and in the 1920s played important roles in Soviet industrial institutions during the New Economic Policy.

Discussion of the First Five-Year Plan and rapid, state-directed industrialization after 1926 promised to enhance the position and importance of the technical experts in government. The number of competent engineers with professional degrees was much smaller in Soviet Russia than in the United States; thus, their opportunities for greater political influence seemed promising. The success of rapid industrialization apparently depended to a large extent on their knowledge and rare skills. Many of the old specialists already had a distinct sense of community by 1926. The most important engineers were linked by many common ties. For example, the best known were generally graduates of a handful of institutes, such as the Moscow Higher Technical School, the Technological Institute, or the Polytechnic Institute in Leningrad, and were associated with the Technological Society in Leningrad, the

[10] Alexander Solzhenitsyn, *The First Circle*, Thomas P. Whitney, trans., New York, paperback, 1969, p. 72.

[11] Russian engineers were, however, at least aware of the existence of a similar trend in the United States by 1924, although by then the Russian trend was already well developed. *Vestnik inzhenerov*, nos. 1-2, 1924, 9-11.

Polytechnical Society in Moscow, or the Russian Technical Society. With all these factors to consider, therefore, it is not surprising to see the growth of a technocratic trend of thought among members of this community of engineers.

Attempts to develop such a movement emanated from several influential sources among the technical intelligentsia. The All-Russian Association of Engineers (VAI), successor of the Union of Engineers formed in May 1917, which had more than ten thousand members in the late 1920s, was one of these. In 1915 the Technological Society and the Polytechnic Society had begun to publish a journal for Russian engineers, aimed at providing a national forum for this professional group, uniting them in a way never previously undertaken.[12] The VAI had grown out of the joint efforts of these two societies, and their journal, *Vestnik inzhenerov*, later became the official organ of the engineers' association.[13]

During World War I the Academy of Sciences had begun to involve large numbers of engineers and technicians in the work of its newly formed Commission for the Study of Natural Productive Resources (KEPS), founded to aid in the war effort.[14] The establishment of the engineers' association increased the sense of cohesion of the small but growing group of professional engineers in Russia.

One of the prominent, early leaders of the engineers' association was P. I. Pal'chinsky, later considered the founder of the Industrial party, according to the prosecution in that case. (The transcript showed that Pal'chinsky had been arrested and shot prior to the trial itself.) Pal'chinsky had earned the enmity of the Bolsheviks for a variety of reasons. For example, during 1917 he had led a group of industrialists who tried to restore labor discipline in factories; he was a deputy minister of the Provisional Government; and he was among the defenders of the Winter Palace in October 1917, during the Bolshevik overthrow of the Provisional Government. In the 1920s he became an admirer of Herbert Hoover, who at the time was one of the leaders of the technocratic trend among American engineers. Pal'chinsky translated one of Hoover's engineering works into Russian and reported to Russian

[12] Ibid., no. 1, 1915.

[13] Ibid., no. 11, 1917, 26. Originally named the All-Russian Union of Engineers, the name was changed to "association" in 1919 when the Bolsheviks prohibited a separate "union" of engineers. Ibid., nos. 1-3, 1919, 34.

[14] See V. I. Vernadsky's memoirs in *The Annals of the Ukrainian Academy of Arts and Sciences in the U.S., Inc.*, vol. 11, nos. 1-2, 31-32, 1964-1968, 11-12; Vernadsky, "Ob izuchenii estestvennykh proizvoditelnykh sil Rossii," *Izvestiia Akademii nauk*, 6th ser., vol. 9, no. 8, 1915; A. Blok, *Obzor Nauchno-izdatel'skoi deiatelnosti, KEPS, 1915-20*, Petrograd, 1920; *Kratkii obzor deiatel'nosti postoiannoi kommissii po izuchenniiu estestvennykh proizvoditelnykh sil*, Petrograd, 1919.

engineers on Hoover's role as the first president of the Federated American Engineering Societies in 1920.[15]

The early relations between the Soviet government and most professional engineers had not been happy, as we have seen. The VAI journal was forced to suspend publication during most of the civil war, and the Bolsheviks prohibited any separate union of engineers. In the early 1920s, however, the engineers worked out a modus vivendi with the Bolsheviks. VAI resumed publication of its journal in 1922, but forswore support of any specific political party, including the Bolsheviks. The VAI journal, in 1922, defined its social role in the following way:

> So far as the guiding ideas and catchwords [of VAI] are concerned, the first of these is "apolitical"—being apolitical in the sense that the Association of Engineers does not adhere to the ideology or tactics of any political party. But this does not mean that the organized engineering community should not have its own opinion on political and economic questions and technical questions of wide social import. The Central Committee of VAI must have a definite opinion, a definite line of conduct and must defend it with energy, fearing neither reproaches of "counter-revolution" or of "extreme leftism."[16]

During most of the 1920s the association published its journal for some five thousand subscribers, and disseminated technical knowledge; rarely did the pages of the journal touch on broader social issues. Still, the group of men associated with VAI was clearly suspect in the eyes of the Soviet government and Communist party. For example, the "responsible editor" of the journal during most of the 1920s was Professor I. A. Kalinnikov, later one of the eight defendants in the Industrial party trial. Before 1922 Kalinnikov had been rector of the Moscow Higher Technical School. When the Soviet government changed the manner of choosing rectors and curbed the autonomy of higher education in 1922, Kalinnikov was replaced in that position. He then helped to lead a strike of professors there in protest. The strikers were attacked by name in the party and governmental press, which accused them of being active members of the outlawed Constitutional Democratic (*Kadet*) party, the liberals who earlier had been active in the Provisional Government.[17] (It has not been possible to confirm whether or not the strikers were

---

[15] *Vestnik inzhenerov*, nos. 1-2, 1924, 9-11; Ipatieff, pp. 249-250, 446-448, 580.
[16] *Vestnik inzhenerov*, nos. 1-3, 1922, 43.
[17] *Izvestiia*, Feb. 24, March 3, April 21, 1922; *Pravda*, Feb. 17, 21, 22, 1922. The other striking professors listed in these articles were all active members of VAI. See *Vestnik inzhenerov*, nos. 1-3, 1922.

active *Kadets*, although many had doubtless been sympathetic to that party in earlier years.)

One of those professors so attacked published a letter in *Izvestiia*, the government newspaper, denying that he had ever been a member of any political party,[18] but no such denial by Kalinnikov has been found in the Soviet press. That Kalinnikov was active in an outlawed political party in 1922, however, seems somewhat unlikely, whatever his former political sympathies had been. After the 1922 strike was discontinued Kalinnikov moved on to important positions as a professor at the Military Aviation Academy in Moscow and as vice-chairman of the production sector of the State Planning Commission. It seems unlikely that an active member of an illegal political party would hold responsible positions like these. Yet there can be little doubt that in official eyes, especially the distrustful eyes of Stalin, who had never liked the idea of employing bourgeois specialists, men with records like Kalinnikov's were suspect. What we know of Kalinnikov indicates that he was, at the very least, a man of independent mind and a non-Communist, a fact that will be made even clearer below. It is worthwhile noting in this connection that Stalin was one of three high party officials who were appointed in 1922 to investigate the academic strikes of professors in higher technical education. He was probably quite familiar, at least from this early date, with the personalities and attitudes of important engineering professors including Kalinnikov.[19]

As the "responsible editor" of the VAI journal, Kalinnikov sanctioned, during the spring of 1927, a small group of engineers that expressed a clear technocratic tendency. On May 5, 1927, a Circle on General Questions of Technology was formed, headed by the engineer, P. K. Engelmeier.[20] This group expressed as one of the reasons for its existence, "the need to work out a whole new world view, fully adapted to contemporary technical culture."[21] It was to begin by acquainting engineers with the history of technology and the lives of outstanding engineers and "industrialists" (*promyshlenniki*). The group would explore the relations of technology to science, art, economics, law, and ethics, and would aim at working out an overall philosophy based on

---

[18] *Izvestiia*, March 3, 1922.

[19] Stalin's role in the investigation of the 1922 academic strikes is mentioned in *Voprosy istorii KPSS*, no. 8, 1972, 90.

[20] Engelmeier had been an active member of VAI at least since early 1922, and was a contributor to various Soviet reference books on technology. *Vestnik inzhenerov*, nos. 1-3, 1922; I. F. Masanov, *Slovar' psevdonimov*, 4, Moscow, 1960, p. 541.

[21] *Vestnik inzhenerov*, no. 4, 1928, 231.

technology. No reference was made to the role of Marxism in this process, a fact that proved to be significant.

According to the first annual report of this group, it held twenty-one discussion sessions between May 5, 1927, and February 2, 1928. The average attendance was sixteen persons, scarcely a large following. The members included some prominent engineers, among them the chairman of the trade union organization for the Soviet technical intelligentsia (VMBIT), S. D. Shein, whose career has already been mentioned here. A chemical engineer by profession, educated before the revolution, Shein claimed to have taken part in the revolutionary movement prior to 1905,[22] but his record shows that he had also been a stockholder and manager of a capitalist-run plant before the Bolshevik Revolution. He was one of the few graduate engineers during the 1920s to be a Communist party member, but he had not become a member until after the 1917 revolutions. As a result of this uneven record many Old Bolsheviks, as well as non-Communists, distrusted him. Possessed of a somewhat cantankerous personality, he had made a number of powerful enemies over the years.[23] The engineering trade union, originally sponsored by VAI,[24] was a much larger organization than its parent, representing some one hundred fifty thousand engineers and technicians, the vast majority of the Soviet technical intelligentsia at the time. Shein, active in both organizations from their early days, was later cited as a major leader of the Industrial party, and was frequently mentioned in the transcript of the trial. (He failed to appear as a defendant, for reasons unknown, and disappeared after his arrest in 1930. Nothing is known of his fate.) The Engelmeier group had large ambitions, and forms an interesting chapter in the history of the Soviet technocratic tendency. The group expressed as its goal the hope of attracting large numbers of engineers in Moscow, establishing circles in other cities, and publishing reports and discussions in Soviet and foreign journals. Evidence on the extent of its success in this respect is lacking, but it was still functioning a year later.

The official journal of the engineering trade union, of which Shein was "responsible editor," published an article in January 1929 entitled "Is a Philosophy of Technology Necessary?" Engelmeier, its author, expressed the following line of thought:

Life itself has led our engineers to the necessity of uniting, not only along trade union lines, but on the basis, so to speak, of ideology,

[22] *Inzhenernyi trud*, no. 10, 1929, 290.
[23] V. Ipatieff, *The Life of a Chemist*, Stanford, 1946, pp. 309-310, 383.
[24] *Vestnik inzhenerov*, nos. 4-6, 1923, 43.

with the purpose of throwing objective light on various problems which arise under contemporary conditions of technical work. The first attempts, the first timid steps in this direction, were made in May 1927, in the womb of the All-Union Association of Engineers (VAI).

The Circle on General Problems of Technology, which outlines within very definite boundaries the extent of its work, occupied itself with exclusively scientific problems, which can widen the intellectual horizons of the members of the circle, and refrained from any kind of propaganda. For the near future, the circle has set itself the following tasks: to develop a program for the philosophy of technology; preliminary attempts to define the concept of "technology," the principles of contemporary technology, technology as a biological phenomenon, technology as an anthropological phenomenon, the role of technology in the history of culture, technology and the economy (economics), technology and art, technology and ethics, and other social factors . . . the construction of a philosophy of technology.[25]

This broad and intellectualized approach by a small circle of engineers may, in retrospect, seem somewhat impractical in its ambitions and rather harmless. The Engelmeier group at that stage may not even have been technocratic in the full sense of the word, since its published program did not cite a strong interest in political questions or a greater political role for engineers, unlike the later proposals of the Scientific-Technical Administration, discussed below. What they were able to express in print, under conditions of censorship and their own caution, may have been only part of their full program.

At any rate, the Stalinist leadership viewed the group somewhat differently, perhaps mindful that earlier opposition movements during the Tsarist era often had their origins in similar small "circles" of thinkers. The near totality of their interests, viewing virtually all branches of knowledge from the standpoint of technology, implied a challenge to Marxism as the reigning philosophy and, therefore, was a potential threat to the monopoly of a Marxist-Leninist party. Engelmeier had written nothing in his article about a possible role for Marxism in the plans of his group, and this fact was pointed out in a counter-article in the same issue by Vladimir Markov, the Stalinist writer, who a few months later was to link Bukharin with the pretensions of the technical intelligentsia. Markov did not deny the possibility of develop-

[25] *Inzhenernyi trud*, no. 2, 1929, 36-40.

ing a philosophy of technology, but he insisted that it must be based on dialectical materialism.[26]

Although the Engelmeier article said nothing about a political role for engineers, and stressed only that the technical intelligentsia unite on an ideological basis, as well as on trade union lines, Markov read between the lines and claimed to see the threat of political hegemony on the part of the engineers. He agreed that engineers should have more than just narrow technical interests. They should have a broad political conception of their work and a general world view, but he denied them the possibility of ever acquiring political hegemony. He did not consider them a class in the Marxist sense, but a small intermediary stratum serving whatever large social class was in power.

Clearer evidence of the importance of this trend and the possible dangers the Stalinists may have seen in it emanated from the Scientific-Technical Administration of the Supreme Council of the National Economy (*Vesenkha*), which managed most Soviet industry at this time. The Scientific-Technical Administration was the central government organ charged with overseeing the industrial laboratories and research institutes under *Vesenkha*, and helping to develop policies for researching and introducing new techniques in industry. Originally established in 1918, one of its first goals had been to attract non-Communist specialists for service in the Soviet economy.[27] We have already discussed the role of Lenin and his secretary, Gorbunov, in establishing this body.

In October 1929, more than a year before the Industrial party trial, the Scientific-Technical Administration had approved and published a series of proposals for reforms in its area of responsibility as part of a general effort to improve the structure of *Vesenkha*.[28] Although headed by a political commissar, V. D. Sverdlov, brother of a leading early Bolshevik, the Scientific-Technical Administration was largely run by old specialists. N. F. Charnovsky was a leading figure of its governing board, and S. D. Shein was its vice-chairman. The man in charge of its industrial research laboratories was V. I. Ochkin. All these men were later prominent in the Industrial party affair.[29]

The reform proposals called for upgrading the powers of the Scien-

[26] Ibid., 40.

[27] S. A. Fediukin, *Sovetskaia vlast'*, Moscow, 1965, p. 99.

[28] *Torgovo-promyshlennaia gazeta*, Oct. 12, 1929. On the role of this body, see also the documents published, many for the first time, in *Organizatsiia sovetskoi nauki v 1926-1932 gg.*, Moscow, 1974, pp. 264-305.

[29] *Izvestiia teplotekhnicheskogo instituta*, no. 3, 1929, 67; *Protsess "Prompartii,"* 43; *Inzhenernyi trud*, no. 1, 1930, 7.

tific-Technical Administration, and insisted that science should be placed at the center of all Soviet efforts in economic development, not only the natural sciences but economic disciplines such as industrial psychology and managerial science, as well. This group saw the country entering a period of technical revolution in which attention should be focused on methods of planning based on a correct understanding of technology and science. Accordingly, in its view, "the future belongs to managing-engineers and engineering-managers. Every active production worker (as part of a general rise in cultural levels) will more and more approximate this type."[30] The proposals also advocated raising the status of the Scientific-Technical Administration to equal that of the Planning-Economic Administration of *Vesenkha*. The work of *Vesenkha* would be divided between these two organs; by cooperating closely they would administer most of Soviet industry. The Scientific-Technical Administration would establish all policies regarding what technology should be used in various branches of industry. It would supervise all work in Soviet industry concerning inventions, standardization of parts and production methods, management science, and rationalization proposals. The Planning-Economic Administration would work out all plans and control figures for capital investment and production in industry. This proposal was doubtless very attractive to the specialists in an economy where, for several years, the technically competent had been challenged by the rise of the "Red Directors," Communist managers who were often technically illiterate, as we have already noted. For years Stalin had encouraged the trend for more Communists among the industrial managers, and had campaigned for an increase in their powers vis-à-vis the old specialists.[31]

The proposal to give more power to the specialists of the Scientific-Technical Administration elicited an immediate attack from the Stalinists, based in part on the ad hominem argument that these proposals originated among the old specialists and the moderate or so-called Right Opposition to Stalin. In an article by Markov, entitled "On the Pretensions of the Technical Intelligentsia and the Theses of the Scientific-Technical Administration," the attack was made clear:

> In the first place the collegium of the Scientific-Technical Administration is the mouthpiece of reactionary specialists who are almost invariably also the "old" specialists; and in the second place, [it speaks for] panic-stricken communists *who gleefully*

---

[30] *Torgovo-promyshlennaia gazeta*, Oct. 12, 1929.
[31] See K. E. Bailes, "Stalin and Revolution from Above: The Formation of the Soviet Technical Intelligentsia, 1928-1934," Ph.D. Diss., Columbia University, 1971, pp. 24-26, 58-60.

*find new landmarks in the ideology of the technical intelligentsia,
to whom, it seems, the future belongs.*[32]

According to Markov, some Communists were ideological captives of
the old specialists, and he included one of the leaders of the moderate
opposition, Bukharin, by name. Such elements, he asserted, dreamed of
giving the technical intelligentsia hegemony over the working class. The
proposal of the Scientific-Technical Administration, with its conception
that "the future belongs to the managing-engineers and the engineering-
managers," was said to reveal such a tendency. "Where [in all this] is
there an evaluation of the role of the proletariat and the Party in over-
coming capitalism?" Markov believed that the members of the Scientific-Technical Administration had assigned the workers to some distant
limbo: they would achieve an important role only in the future, when
they approached the cultural level and technical competence of the
engineers.

As a practical conclusion to his attack Markov said that elements
among the technical intelligentsia had become overweening and needed
to be brought down to earth. He claimed that during the previous spring
he had heard the head of the trade union sections for engineers and
technicians—the post held by Shein at this time—say in Moscow that
either the engineers' or the workers' organizations must administer industry; there could be no effective dual administration by both elements.
Markov believed that these remarks revealed a common opinion among
many engineers, including the newly minted specialists, to free themselves from the interference and control of various other groups: "Engineers (a very great many of them) dream of independence from
factory organizations and of achieving what would amount to a hegemony in factories and elsewhere: they are the stratum whose cutting
edge is the declaration of the Scientific-Technical Administration about
the master of the 'future.' "[33]

The author agreed that the engineers had some legitimate grievances,
but he insisted on the positive role of social controls over the engineers,
and in general he sniped away at what he considered the pretensions of
the technical intelligentsia: "The Soviet 'managing-engineer' and 'en-
gineering-manager' will be an element of the brilliant future, but only as
one part of the working class, strenuously conducting the struggle for
communism."[34] A month later, at a Central Committee plenum, one of
Stalin's closest associates, Lazar Kaganovich, added his name to the
attack and linked Bukharin in particular to the concept of a technocratic

[32] *Torgovo-promyshlennaia gazeta*, Oct. 26, 1929. Underlining in original.
[33] Ibid.   [34] Ibid.

order run by men with the dual skills of engineers and managers.[35] The extent to which opposition leaders like Bukharin may actually have shared such ideas is discussed below.

The prosecution's star defendant at the Industrial party trial was Prof. Leonid K. Ramzin, who had strong links to the technocratic trend. The Thermal Technical Institute he headed was named for two of the men most instrumental in creating the All-Russian Association of Engineers. These men, Professors Grinevetsky and Kirsh, both teachers at the Moscow Higher Technical School before dying of typhus during the civil war, had been prominent ideological opponents of the Bolsheviks.[36] Ramzin was their student and intellectual heir. He, too, had been an early opponent of the Bolsheviks, a fact not easily forgotten in a society where one's political biography was considered public property and subject to a ritual of periodic recital and confession. Like the other defendants in the trial, Ramzin had a "record," a political history that was a source of suspicion to a Stalinist leadership that had been hardened by its experiences in a civil war between ideological opponents. On Ramzin's record, for example, was the fact that he had written a pamphlet in 1918 stating that "the Bolsheviks have ruined the fuel industry and threatened Moscow with catastrophe." Ramzin's brochure was published by the Fuel Committee, a group headed by his mentor, Professor Kirsh. The Soviet scientific-technical intelligentsia was not allowed to forget this at the time of the Industrial party trial.[37] Ramzin was also an early leader of the engineers' association and was linked by ties of work and professional memberships to such men as Shein, Kalinnikov, and Osadchii.[38] Ramzin was prominent, therefore among the technical intelligentsia, and his appearance in the trial was bound to command the attention of Soviet engineers. This fact, plus his obviously more cooperative attitude in testifying against himself and his colleagues, may account for his featured role in the trial itself. Ramzin seems to have acquitted himself satisfactorily in the eyes of the state. The morning

[35] L. M. Kaganovich, "Problema kadrov," *Bolshevik*, nos. 23-24, 1929, 64.

[36] V. Grinevetsky, who was appointed rector of the Moscow Higher Technical School under Nicholas II in 1914, published a book just before his death in 1919 in which he maintained that Russian industry could not be revived without restoring capitalism and importing foreign investment. *Poslevoiennye perspektivy russkoi promyshlennosti*, Moscow, 1919; see also the obituaries of Grinevetsky and Kirsh in *Vestnik inzhenerov*, nos. 1-3, 1922.

[37] See the article in *Front nauki i tekhniki*, nos. 11-12, 1930, 32, a journal directed at this group.

[38] *Vestnik inzhenerov*, nos. 1-3, 1919, 35. Ramzin was one of the thirteen members of the governing council of VAI at this time. The board also included Professors K. V. Kirsh and I. A. Kalinnikov. Others listed in the same issue as active contributors to the journal were Engelmeier, Shein, and Charnovsky.

following the end of the trial, according to one memoir by a former Soviet technologist, Ramzin was seen in his office at the Moscow Higher Technical School, cleaning out his desk without apparent guard—scarcely the treatment one would expect for a dangerous state criminal.[39] He was allowed to continue his inventive work in prison, and he is the only defendant who is known to have been released later and rehabilitated. In 1943 he won a Stalin prize for his invention of a new technique in thermal technology and resumed his professorship in Moscow, which he held until his death in 1947.[40]

Given their independence of mind, the engineers associated with the technocratic trend, not surprisingly, figured prominently among the critics of the Stalinist First Five-Year Plan. For example, Kalinnikov, Charnovsky, Shein, Khrennikov, and Osadchii, all engineers accused of wrecking in the Industrial party trial, had been members of an industrial planning group in *Gosplan* that had opposed as unrealistic the Five-Year Plan officially adopted in 1929.[41]

It is possible to piece together some of the reasons for their opposition from scattered bits of evidence. Kalinnikov, the chairman of the industrial sector of *Gosplan*, was known to have favored a large role for private economic activity and investment in the First Five-Year Plan.[42] At a meeting of the presidium of *Gosplan* in December 1928, he doubted the capacity of industry to undertake the ambitious plans proposed for capital construction;[43] and at another meeting of *Gosplan* in February 1929, which was called to approve a final draft of the Five-Year Plan, Kalinnikov opposed the high targets suggested, "because we lack the time, the construction materials, and the basic technical resources."[44] Professor Osadchii, an important witness against his fellow

[39] M. M. Samygin, "Prompartiia," Columbia University Archive of Russian History and Culture, n.d. This typed memoir, judging by internal evidence, was probably written after 1956.

[40] V. A. Ulianovskaia, *Formirovanie nauchnoi intelligentsii v SSSR 1917-1937 gg.*, Moscow, 1966, p. 131. The Ramzin "once-through" boiler, for which much of the experimental work was done before Ramzin's arrest, is described extensively in Western technical literature of the late 1930s and early 1940s. According to a recent study, this invention was one of the handful of truly original Soviet inventions prior to 1945. See Antony Sutton, *Western Technology and Soviet Economic Development, 1930-1945*, Stanford, 1971, pp. 94-96, 329.

[41] *Torgovo-promyshlennaia gazeta*, Dec. 30, 1928. Kalinnikov and Charnovsky, as noted, were defendants at the trial; Osadchii was a prominent witness; Shein and Khrennikov disappeared after their arrests but were often mentioned as fellow "conspirators" in the transcript of the trial. Khrennikov reportedly died during the investigation.

[42] See his article in *Planovoe khoziaistvo*, no. 12, 1927, 80-107.

[43] *Pravda*, Dec. 30, 1928.

[44] "Stenogrammy rashirennykh zasedanii prezidiuma Gosplana," Feb. 5-12, 1929, in Arkhiv Gosplana SSSR, cited in I. Gladkov, "K istorii pervogo piatilet-

engineers at the trial itself, was also known for similar opposition. At the 1929 meeting of *Gosplan*, for example, he was quoted as commenting: "Speaking as an engineer, I think that to a great degree fellow engineers share my view. I must say in all good conscience that if I were told: sign this variant as the basic one, I would refuse."[45]

Several of the other defendants had opposed the changes in higher technical education, promoted by the Stalinists to speed up the preparation of engineering specialists and bring higher technical schools more directly under the control of industry. Four of the eight defendants in the Industrial party trial were engineering professors, and this was probably no coincidence. Some of their critical remarks had appeared earlier in the Soviet press; these articles were referred to in the trial proceedings.[46] One of the most prominent defendants, N. F. Charnovsky, for example, was especially well known for his opposition after 1928 to the changes in higher technical education, which are discussed in a later chapter. He had expressed his views in the Soviet press and had been attacked for them prior to his arrest as a wrecker.[47] A metallurgical engineer, who was a student in Moscow at this time, published his memoirs in the Soviet monthly *Novyi mir* a few years ago, and made an interesting reference to Charnovsky's views in this respect. The memoirist expressed general skepticism concerning the guilt of those accused in Stalin's show trials and purges, including the events between 1928 and 1931,[48] but he did recall the strong hostility among some groups, especially in education, to those with Communist connections or from working-class backgrounds.

He encountered this attitude by chance when he applied for an assistantship with Professor Charnovsky in the late 1920s. The memoirist, born to the family of an oil worker in the trans-Caucasus, and otherwise having impeccable proletarian credentials, appeared at his interview with Charnovsky wearing a Tsarist student uniform, which he had purchased secondhand and was in no sense a reflection of his political sympathies. His social background was unknown to Charnovsky, how-

---

nogo narodno-khoziaistvennogo plana," *Planovoe khoziaistvo*, no. 4, 1935, 136-137. The accuracy of Gladkov's account cannot be vouched for, but such quotations are consistent with the earlier published views of these men, and appear to be quoted directly from an archival transcript of the *Gosplan* discussions.

[45] Ibid.

[46] *Protsess "Pompartii*," pp. 199-200; *Za industrializatsiiu*, Nov. 28, 1930, Dec. 2, 1930.

[47] See his article in *Torgovo-promyshlennaia gazeta*, March 6, 1929; and the attack in *VARNITSO*, no. 4, 1929, 2.

[48] V. Emelianov, "O vremeni, o tovarishchakh, o sebe; zapiski inzhenera," *Novyi mir*, no. 1, 1967, 45.

ever, and the professor mistook his appearance as an expression of his social and political views. Charnovsky confided to the youth that he hoped to fill up his group of assistants with people personally congenial to him before the local party committee sent him some "comrades." Charnovsky's social views were clearly too independent for his own good at this time of tightening party controls over science and technology.

Professor Ramzin, the prosecution's lead witness at the Industrial party trial, may also have been involved in earlier opposition to aspects of the First Five-Year Plan. The Thermal Technical Institute, which he headed, had been at the center of Soviet efforts for electrification through the improvement and construction of steam power plants. There is some evidence that Ramzin and his associates opposed the emphasis on gigantic hydroelectric power plants in the First Five-Year Plan, such as the huge Dnieper Dam project, and advocated instead greater reliance on a network of smaller, steam plants. The advocates of "bigger means better" generally won the arguments during the First Five-Year Plan, and Ramzin's school of energeticists suffered at least a temporary eclipse.[49] As in the case of Lysenkoism in later years, arrest and imprisonment followed defeat in a struggle over a scientific-technical issue, although Ramzin did not share the bitter fate that would later befall many geneticists.

A possible link between the repression of leading engineers and the moderate opposition to Stalin has already been suggested several times in this chapter. Such Stalinists as Markov, a journalist, Kaganovich, a member of the Politburo, Krylenko, the state prosecutor, and eventually Stalin himself clearly sought to make a public link between engineers prominent in the Industrial party trial and the moderates. Was there, in fact, such a connection? The available evidence suggests that there was, but does not make clear the full nature of that connection. One prominent moderate leader, A. I. Rykov, who was head of state as chairman of the U.S.S.R. Council of Commissars until 1930, had been known since at least 1924 as a strong defender of those bourgeois specialists who worked loyally for the Soviet government. In 1924, at an All-Russian Congress of Engineers, he had even offered them a "bill of

---

[49] *Front nauki i tekhniki*, nos. 11-12, 1930, 34-35. Some idea of the importance of Ramzin's school can be gained from the reports of the Fourth All-Union Congress on Thermal Technology. *Izvestiia teplotekhnicheskogo instituta*, no. 6, 1928, 87-107. Ramzin was closely associated in this work with three other engineers implicated in the Industrial party trial—Osadchii, Ochkin, and Shein. Ochkin and Osadchii were elected vice-chairman and general secretary, respectively, of the Fourth Thermal Technical Congress. The controversy over energy policy will be discussed in a later chapter.

rights" against the attacks of Communist and worker zealots. In his speech at that congress he flatly asserted that "the specialist, the engineer, the man of science and technology must have full independence and freedom to express his opinion on matters of science and technology."[50] He went on to maintain that such specialists need not be subservient, "either to 'society' or to the 'administration.' "

Rykov also proved to be far more concerned than Stalin, at the time of the Shakhty case in 1928 and afterward, to protect those old specialists who had not already confessed to crimes from unfounded suspicions and specialist-baiting on the part of workers, managers, and Communist party activists.[51] While it is not known how close Bukharin's personal ties with technocratically-oriented old specialists may have been in these years, Bukharin apparently moved closer to members of the technical intelligentsia in the wake of the Shakhty affair. Not only did he oppose the Stalinist Five-Year Plan in 1928 and 1929, for some of the same reasons as engineers who were later arrested, but he also took some public positions in 1929 that were very close to those of technocratically-minded engineers.[52] Appointed chairman of the Scientific-Technical Administration of *Vesenkha* in June of 1929, to replace Sverdlov, he proved to be more active in the work of that body than his predecessor. For example, in an article published a few days after the reform proposal of the Scientific-Technical Administration, Bukharin expressed a similar position in print, and used some of the phrases from the reform proposal, including the phrase that Markov had found so offensive: "The future belongs to the managing-engineers and the engineering-managers."[53] Bukharin also strongly emphasized creating new cadres of scientists and technologists, and stressed the slogan of a "technical-economic revolution" as the first need of the Soviet Union, a position that echoed that of the Scientific-Technical Administration, and one that had been strongly attacked by Stalin's crony, Kaganovich.

The emphasis on encouraging original scientific and technical research was one to which Stalin's supporters took strong exception. The Stalinists at this time were playing down original research and theoretical studies generally, in both research institutes and higher technical

---

[50] *Izvestiia*, Dec. 4, 1924, quoted in E. H. Carr, *Socialism in One Country*, Baltimore, 1970, pp. 134-135.

[51] See *Pravda*, March 11, 1928; and Bailes, "Stalin and Revolution," pp. 22-84.

[52] *Pravda*, Sept. 30, 1928; Robert V. Daniels, *The Conscience of the Revolution*, New York, 1969, pp. 322-369; E. H. Carr and R. W. Davies, *Foundations of a Planned Economy*, vol. 1, pt. 2, London, 1969, pp. 843-897.

[53] See his appeal for more attention to scientific-technical research and expenditures in *Torgovo-promyshlennaia gazeta*, Oct. 15, 1929. See also his articles in *Pravda*, Jan. 20, and Dec. 15, 1929.

education, as we shall see in later chapters. In alliance with the Communist industrial managers of the Supreme Economic Council, Stalinist party officials emphasized the need to learn established techniques from the West and concentrate on work that was rapid and immediately practical. Bukharin, on the other hand, became a spokesman for those concerned with the importance of theory and scientific-technical creativity. These different positions were in character: Bukharin had been known since the civil war as a brilliant theoretician. Lenin, in his "testament" of 1922, had called Bukharin the party's "leading theoretician." Stalin and his associates, of course, had built their reputations as "practical" administrators.

Whether or not the moderates, as part of their opposition to Stalin, had formed a closer alliance with the old specialists, who had so long been suspect in the eyes of party members, is another matter. No evidence of closer links along these lines has been found. The main conclusion to be drawn from the evidence discussed above is that the positions of Rykov and Bukharin on certain issues dovetailed with positions expressed by leaders of the Soviet engineering profession who were later implicated in the Industrial party affair. Beyond the suggestiveness of such evidence, however, the only thing we can say with certainty is that the Stalinists claimed to see an alliance between the two groups and tried very hard to discredit it in the eyes of the Soviet public.

For Stalin, the moderate opposition, in league with elements of the technical intelligentsia, contained the seeds of a potentially dangerous threat. The moderates had resolved to unseat Stalin from the Politburo as early as July 1928, although their plan had been frustrated.[54] Along with leading engineers, they had openly opposed the variant of the First Five-Year Plan that he supported in 1928 and 1929. Even if the technocratic trend did not have a large number of adherents, it had a major potential with the growth of Soviet industry and the technical intelligentsia. Linked up with the moderate opposition, adherents of this trend may well have seemed threatening to the party officials and old revolutionaries around Stalin, who were not known for their theoretical or technical mastery. Acting on the analogy of the acorn and the oak, Stalin perhaps resolved to take prophylactic measures before the threat became more serious. He may have thought that some form of technocratic-moderate alliance would be a viable alternative to Stalinism, and would prove attractive not only to a relatively few old specialists and moderate oppositionists, but also to the mass of young specialists who might fall under the influence of those so oriented.

[54] Daniels, *Conscience of the Revolution*, pp. 322-323.

This could happen in several ways. A high respect for engineers had been fostered among the youth since the revolution. Fertile ground for technocratic attitudes had been prepared in both literature and education. To take one example, engineers had been the heroes of a number of novels popular among the young. These included the science fiction of H. G. Wells, A. A. Bogdanov (*Red Star* and *Engineer Menni*), and Alexis Tolstoy (*Aelita* and *The Hyperboloid of Engineer Garin*), which projected future societies where engineers would have crucial social and political roles.[55] Perhaps more important, institutions of higher technical education, higher organs of industrial administration and planning—such as *Vesenkha* and *Gosplan*—and important industrial research institutes might well have become focal points of technocratic opposition to Stalin. Stalinists probably feared that youth already oriented toward science and technology might fall under the influence of Stalin's opponents upon entering higher technical education and industry, as long as the old specialists held commanding positions in those areas. The transcript of the Industrial party trial support such a fear. One of the defendants, Professor Fedotov, claimed that the Industrial party had ordered engineering professors to organize student cells to support the moderate opposition.[56] His testimony may have been fabricated, but it supported a point that the Stalinists clearly wanted to make.[57]

The Industrial party case marked the culmination of the Stalinist campaign against a leading segment of the old technical intelligentsia. Although only eight men appeared as defendants in the trial, some two thousand were directly implicated in the alleged conspiracy, and the entire older generation of the technical intelligentsia was again put under suspicion by Krylenko, as he had done in the Shakhty trial two years before. He gave the reason for this in his summation of the case:

> The natural mistrust of the engineers by the Soviet power, the political and social control exercised over their work, deprived the engineers of that commanding position which they had occupied until the revolution; in addition to this, after the revolution living conditions, and the material situation of the best engineers had greatly deteriorated.[58]

[55] A. A. Bogdanov, *Krasnaia zvezda*, Moscow, 1918, and *Inzhener Menni; fantasticheskii roman*, Moscow, 1923; A. N. Tolstoy, *Aelita*, first published in *Krasnaia nov'*, Moscow, 1922-1923, and *Giperboloid Inzhenera Garina*, Moscow, 1927.

[56] *Wreckers on Trial. A Record of the Trial of the Industrial Party Held in Moscow*, November-December 1930, London, 1931, p. 95.

[57] See Stalin's speech in *Pravda*, April 18, 1928, and his *Sochineniia*, vol. 11, Moscow, 1954, pp. 63, 216.

[58] *Protsess "Prompartii,"* p. 11.

He linked the alleged plot to the political factionalism within the Communist party: "The increasingly heated struggle within the Communist Party aroused hopes for more successful results from counterrevolutionary acts on the part of those who counted on the weakening of the Communist Party by internal struggles."[59]

Stalin himself refrained from public comment on this affair until the summer of 1931, after the terror against the old intelligentsia had largely ceased, but then he offered some clues as to what his intentions may have been. Like Krylenko, he linked the "Right Opposition" within the Communist party to the Industrial party engineers. He singled out the most qualified sector of the technical intelligentsia as the main target of the repression, and he went on to express satisfaction with the results obtained from this campaign:

> The new situation had to create and did create new attitudes among the old technical intelligentsia. This explains the definite signs we have that a portion of this intelligentsia which earlier sympathized with the wreckers has now come over to the side of the Soviet government. . . . If at the height of sabotage our attitude to the old technical intelligentsia was expressed chiefly as a policy of repression, then now, when this intelligentsia is turning toward the Soviet government, our attitude toward it must be expressed chiefly in a policy of attraction and concern for it.[60]

The Industrial party affair and the related arrests of engineers continued to echo in the following years. Periodically, the Soviet public was reminded that the proper role of the technical intelligentsia was not a concern with major policy questions but with "following orders." For example, when H. G. Wells interviewed Stalin in 1934, and spoke of the creative potential of the technical intelligentsia as a political force shaping events, Stalin spoke at length of this group and dismissed its political ambitions. In Stalin's view the technical intelligentsia was only a small stratum, not a social-economic class; major historical changes, he asserted, are brought about only by classes. "The engineer, the organizer of production, does not work as he would like to but as he is ordered,

---

[59] Ibid. The link between the Industrial party engineers and the moderate opposition, which both Krylenko and later Stalin mentioned, may account for the inclusion of the three defendants in this trial who represented the textile industry: Professors Fedotov, Kuprianov, and Sitnin. The textile industry would have benefited from the emphasis that Bukharin, Rykov, and Tomsky wanted to give to light industry in the First Five-Year Plan. These three engineers, however, were not as prominent in the trial as the leaders of the organized engineering profession discussed in this chapter, who were the main targets of the trial.

[60] Stalin, *Sochineniia*, vol. 13, pp. 70-72.

in such a way as to serve the interests of his employers."[61] While acknowledging their economic function and expressing a concern for their well-being, Stalin reiterated his low regard for their political potential: "Of course, the assistance of the technical intelligentsia must be accepted and the latter, in turn, must be assisted. But it must not be thought that the technical intelligentsia can play an independent historical role."[62]

Stalin's views were echoed and expanded upon the following year in a lengthy article directed specifically at the technical intelligentsia.[63] The subject of the article was the technocratic trend among the engineers in the West, which had gained greater currency during the depression years. Like Stalin, the author of this article dismissed technologists as a "social stratum with no economic, political, or ideological independence." He reminded the Soviet technical intelligentsia that

> technocratic ideas once circulated among us in the USSR, among a group of the old engineering profession from the so-called "Industrial Party." . . . The Industrial Party served as a demagogical means for drawing engineers and technicians into sabotage, into a struggle against the Soviet power, in the same way as current ideas of technocracy [attempt to do so].

In conclusion, it should be emphasized that the conflict between "red" and "expert" in Communist societies may derive from varied factors and historical experiences. In addition to the unique and particular circumstances of such conflict, a more general source of tension may lie in an attitude toward specialization that is a part of Communist ideology. The ultimate goal is to eliminate occupational specialization, as a restriction on the development of human personality, even though over the short run the necessity for continued specialization may be recognized. Modern industry has, in fact, developed in the opposite direction, toward increasing specialization. The First Five-Year Plan not only marked a stage in Russia's first industrial revolution—that is, the development of railroads, metallurgy, mining, textiles, and so forth—but also marked the Soviet Union's fuller entry into the second industrial revolution, including the development of electrification, a chemical industry, and wide application of the internal combustion engine. All these industries require well trained and competent specialists for their proper functioning, the second cluster of industries even more than the first. Hos-

---

[61] *Wells-Stalin Talk, July 23, 1934*, London, 1934, p. 11.
[62] Ibid.
[63] S. Livshits, "Reaktsionnaia utopiia tekhnokratov," *Front nauki i tekhniki*, no. 4, 1935, 16-30.

tility toward technical specialists, as possessing a kind of "private property" in knowledge, was a strong attitude among Communist activists and workers in the 1920s. They resented the exclusiveness, high salaries, and other privileges of the technical elites. The Industrial party trial and related events could have done Stalin little political harm and may well have increased his popularity among the groups whose support he courted at this time—rank-and-file party officials and workers— whose resentment of the bourgeois specialists was legendary.[64] But Stalin and the Communist leadership had to transcend this attitude if industrial progress was to be made. The tension between hopes for a Communist future without specialization and the immediate demands of industry for more and better specialists required some kind of resolution at the start of the First Five-Year Plan.

Besides the Marxist attitude toward specialization, perhaps an even greater source of tension arose from another ideological factor. From the Marxist point of view the engineers and scientists represented a threat more dangerous than the capitalists themselves. If control over the means of production is the key to political power, then the historical role of the capitalists would come to a predetermined end with the abolition of private property. It was much more difficult to foresee the day when the technical intelligentsia might disappear as a unique and indispensable group. Did not the engineers and scientists represent a new stratum whose place in modern society seemed guaranteed indefinitely by the imperatives of industrialization? If their knowledge gave them control over the means of production, then what was to prevent the new technological elites from seizing political power in postcapitalist society? Viewed from this vantage point, the Industrial party affair and the related terror against an element of the old technostructure illuminate a real crisis in postrevolutionary Marxism. As the Soviet Union crossed the threshold of rapid industrialization, it became all the more urgent to define the relationship of the technical intelligentsia to the means of production and, by extension, to their political role in socialist society.

If specialists could not be dispensed with for a long time to come, what should their proper place be in a society on its way to communism? Stalin attempted to answer this question by a dual policy: the repression of the old specialists, particularly those who had been associated with technocratic tendencies; and the rapid promotion in the 1930s of a new group who combined the two categories, the so-called Red Experts, whose education and experience were intended to merge technical ex-

[64] See Bailes, "Stalin and Revolution," pp. 78-115; Carr and Davies, *Foundations*, pp. 574-590.

119

pertise and political loyalty.[65] The repression of the old technical intelligentsia was only one part, although a major one, of a more general aim: to bring the means of production and the social relations dependent upon them, under the fuller control of the Stalinist elite. Just as the independent peasantry were repressed in the same years in order to control the means of agricultural production, and the NEP-men, or small-scale manufacturers and tradesmen, were repressed to control another area of production and exchange, so the old technostructure in Stalin's eyes, required stricter control. One may well regard the means used as counterproductive and a form of surplus repression, but it is necessary to understand that the logic of Stalin's approach grew out of a Marxist-Leninist analysis of society and politics; it cannot be dismissed simply as a form of paranoia.

These changes were part of a more general pattern of Stalinist behavior, aimed both at political security and increased production. During the 1930s, Stalin had come to grips in a number of areas with long-range Communist hopes that seemed to conflict with the more immediate demands of modernization under Soviet conditions. Among other things, these hopes had revolved around the possibility of egalitarian wages, a withering away of the state, the abolition of the tight family unit, and the end of specialization in work roles. Stalin built his system around the antithesis of such hopes: a vast increase in the repressive machinery of the state, a tightening of family ties, a large increase in wage differentials, and a new emphasis on the need for technical specialization combined with political loyalty. The Stalinist dialectic moved in mysterious ways: Stalin postponed the realization of such hopes to the indefinite limbo of a future Communist society. In the stage of "building socialism" after 1928, such hopes were, in fact, to be replaced by their dialectical opposites.

If one of Stalin's primary aims in the Industrial party affair had been to discourage a technocratic trend among Soviet engineers and encourage political loyalty among the technical intelligentsia—as argued here —then he seems to have succeeded in one major respect. The public expression of technocratic tendencies outside the Communist party largely disappeared after the Industrial party case, and technical specialists, perforce, sought other channels of influence within the Communist party. Autonomous professional organizations, which the technocratically-minded had once favored, lost their autonomy. VAI, the Russian Technical Society, and other prerevolutionary professional societies of the technical intelligentsia were abolished or reorganized. As one recent

[65] See Bailes, "Stalin and Revolution," pp. 216-405; Carr and Davies, *Foundations*, pp. 590-597.

Soviet historian put it, reevaluating the role of such societies in a more favorable light, they were attacked not so much because of conscious wrecking or sabotage, but because they were believed to have outlived their usefulness to Soviet society. Citing archival sources unavailable to Western historians, this Soviet writer concludes that such autonomous organizations were dissolved or reorganized to break up what the power structure at the time perceived as the "caste-like" mentality of the old technostructure. The new Soviet technical societies that replaced them after 1930 were placed under tighter political controls, and were no longer restricted primarily to graduate technologists. They were thrown open to workers and others interested in technology, whether diploma-holders or not, in an attempt to bring the technical intelligentsia and the masses closer together and broaden the base of technical knowledge in Soviet society.[66] When viewed in the light of other, similar efforts during the First Five-Year Plan, the events discussed here begin to make more sense, whatever we may think of their effectiveness and overall consequences for Soviet society, which are discussed in the following chapter.

[66] A. I. Kardash, "Organizatsiia nauchno-tekhnicheskikh obshchestv v SSSR 1921-1941," Moscow, 1968, pp. 170-220, a dissertation on file in the Lenin Library, Moscow. Among other archives, Kardash cites documents concerned with the dissolution of the Russian Metallurgical Society, TsGAOR SSSR, MO, f. 695, op. I, d. 18. 31-32.

5

THE AFTERMATH OF THE SHAKHTY
AND INDUSTRIAL PARTY TRIALS

*The mistrust toward engineers and technicians
has brought forth numerous investigations and
various forms of control. It has even given rise
to a factory proverb: "While one person works,
five investigate."*[1]

The reaction of industrial managers and the technostructure itself to
the atmosphere created by the Shakhty and Industrial party affairs deserves some comment, particularly because it led to changes with major,
long-term effects. Contemporary observers reported both negative and
positive results. Opposition to some of the negative consequences developed among several interest groups. Such opposition was centered
especially in two groups: the highest officials and industrial managers
of *Vesenkha*, and representatives of the specialists themselves, particularly officials of the trade union sections that represented the technical
intelligentsia.

Neither of these groups publicly protested the trials per se or questioned the validity of the evidence or the vedicts, but their positions and
statements after the trials suggest doubts about arrests of wreckers in
general and the need to be especially careful in confirming the truth of
the charges.

That leaders of Soviet industrial management, such as Kuibyshev,
feared the economic effects of such affairs and spoke about the dangers
in a veiled way for months afterwards, there can be no doubt.[2] Kuiby-

---

[1] *Inzhenernyi trud* (IT), no. 10, 1929, 293.

[2] The pages of the official newspaper of the industrial managers were filled
with articles about the adverse effects of specialist-baiting after the Shakhty case
was disclosed. See, for example, the number of articles on this subject in just one
week, picked at random in this period: *TPG*, Jan. 4, Jan. 8, Jan. 10, and Jan. 11,
1929.

According to a recent study of the technical intelligentsia in the Armenian
S.S.R. at this time, based on archival sources, the Central Committee of the
Armenian party also viewed the growth of specialist-baiting with alarm, and discussed measures to alleviate the situation during several sessions held in 1928 and
1929. A highly motivated minority, Armenians were a disproportionately large
element among the technical intelligentsia in these years. Especially at the official
level, they held a high regard for their educated specialists, and no show trials of

shev's speeches in the year after the Shakhty trial repeatedly warned against the dangers of specialist-baiting. In July 1928, shortly after the conclusion of the Shakhty trial, he spoke out at a plenum of the *Vesenkha* presidium against false accusations and the bad work atmosphere they created.[3] Some workers were drawing the wrong conclusions from the Shakhty affair, he felt, and were attributing every technical failure to the sabotage of specialists. The theme arose again at a joint meeting of the Council of People's Commissars and the Council on Labor and Defense—the government's inner cabinet for economic affairs—which Kuibyshev addressed on March 5, 1929: "I would like to make clear that in the discussion of technical questions we will permit great ardor and fervor in disputes, but mutual suspicion must be excluded, because if this is permitted . . . then no technical disagreements are possible."[4]

A heated exchange that took place at the Sixteenth Party Conference in April 1929, between one of Kuibyshev's top industrial managers and officials of the Workers' and Peasants' Inspectorate (*Rabkrin*) illustrates the sharp conflict of interests that the Shakhty affair helped to focus. Although some of the discussion revolved around an investigation that had taken place just prior to the disclosure of the Shakhty case in early March of 1928, the issues discussed involved the situation existing in the spring of 1929.

S. P. Birman, the manager of the trust that controlled the southern steel mills (*Yugostal'*), took the floor following the official report of Rabkrin, to object vigorously to the number of investigations in his area and the way they were conducted. He noted that during an eight-month period of 1928, ending on October 1, some seven major investigations of *Yugostal'* were conducted, often covering the same ground as previous investigations.[5] In Birman's opinion, all of this consumed so much time on the part of managers and others in industry that it seriously disrupted work and endangered the fulfillment of plans.[6]

Birman claimed that, in principle, he was not opposed to investigations that were meant to check on the fulfillment of decrees and plans, but he was opposed to the great waste involved in the duplication of

---

engineers in Armenia occurred during these years, even though specialist-baiting apparently grew among the workers of that Republic in the atmosphere that followed the Shakhty affair (Arkhiv Armianskogo filiala IML pri TsK KPSS, f. 1, op. 11, d. 9, l. 5; op. 13, d. 17, l. 30, 33, 40, cited in A. K. Grigoriants, *Formirovanie i razvitie tekhnicheskoi intelligentsii Armenii* [*1920-1965*], Akademiia nauk Armianskoi SSR, Institut istorii, Erevan, 1966, pp. 119-123.)

[3] Khavin, *U rulia*, p. 71.
[4] Tsentral'nyi partiinyi arkhiv, Institut marksizma-leninizma, f. 71, op. 1, ed. khr. 606, l. 1, cited in Kuibysheva, p. 291.
[5] *Shestnadtsataia konferentsiia*, p. 494.
[6] Ibid., p. 496.

these efforts and also the "uncomradely" and disruptive way in which many were conducted. He felt that many of these inspectors were over-eager to uncover a crime:

> We sometimes encounter in this work a scarcely veiled sadistic approach on the part of individual inspectors. It is necessary to keep in mind, comrades, that neither Comrade Ordzhonikidze nor Comrade Yakovlev [an assistant of Ordzhonikidze, who gave the official report of *Rabkrin* at this Conference] are doing the investigating; but a type of apparat employee, an inspector who sometimes considers his chief service the uncovering of a crime. Some of these inspectors will stop at nothing in order to find a crime; they consider themselves unlucky, they consider their work unsuccessful if they do not disclose some kind of crime. (Voice: That is not so.) It is, comrades. This is a very frequent observation. I am far from saying that everyone approaches [the work] in this way, of course. And I certainly do not want to say that this is the official line of Rabkrin. But we see such an approach on the part of certain workers.[7]

Birman's remarks sparked a heated exchange on the floor. Representatives of *Rabkrin* and others asserted that some of the investigations in Birman's area had, in fact, helped to uncover criminal activities. As one of *Rabkrin*'s defenders noted:

> Well, it seems that the individual inspectors of Rabkrin aim at uncovering a crime at any price and if a crime is not found, then the inspectors consider their task unfulfilled. What does Comrade Birman want to say by this? Does he intend to say that the technical director of *Yugostal'*, removed from work after our investigation on account of his uneconomical use of imported equipment, was removed without cause and is imprisoned by the OGPU without cause? (Voice: "He was removed at the initiative of the GPU, not on your initiative." Yakovlev: "He was removed by Rabkrin.") Perhaps our fault lies in the fact that when we investigated the utilization of imported equipment in the factories of *Yugostal'*, we mentioned that if there were counterrevolutionaries in *Yugostal'* and if they did intend to harm Soviet power, then they must necessarily act as did the technical higher-ups of *Yugostal'* over the course of several years. So much we did say. But we furthermore said that we had no facts to confirm that there was indeed wrecking activity there. This is what we declared at a special

[7] Ibid., p. 497.

meeting of the Politburo where the question of the utilization of foreign equipment was analyzed. On the basis of our statement, it was considered possible to remove only the former technical director of *Yugostal'*, Svitsyn, from his post of administering technical activities. But we, not VSNKh, not *Yugostal'*, gave the correct characterization of Svitsyn's activity. We stated that the present activity of the technical director of *Yugostal'* was suggestive of conscious counterrevolutionary activity and from this we drew our own practical conclusion. If we can be accused of anything, then it is the fact that we did not say this with a loud voice, that we did not pose the question as it deserved to be posed. The GPU then decided on the basis of its own materials to arrest Svitsyn.[8]

This same observer went on to note that a whole nest of wreckers, consisting of the technical directors of factories under Birman, had been arrested and held by the OGPU. He read from the confessions of some of these engineers that they had acted as the conscious agents of the former capitalist owners of these plants.[9] The officials of *Rabkrin* went on to accuse Birman of virtual incompetence, since he had previously admitted turning over the major direction of *Yugostal'* to his technical director, the engineer Svitsyn, stating publicly that "Svitsyn was in reality the sole director of the trust."[10]

The representatives of *Rabkrin* also stated that the question involved was not simply the conduct of Birman, but a more general question of managers who blindly followed the advice of their specialists in everything, like the tail of a dog. Even more so, the question involved the problem of social controls over production and the best fulfillment of plans: "So far as the question concerns specialists, we know that they do not like control, they fight against control and quite understandably attempt to eliminate it."[11] Managers such as Birman strengthened the hand of such specialists who fought against the social control of *Rabkrin* and other agencies outside the economic apparatus. As another representative of *Rabkrin* noted, "Comrade Birman in his remarks states much that other comrades, who silently agree with him here, will not say."[12]

Yakovlev concluded the remarks of the *Rabkrin* officials in this discussion by agreeing that there were too many investigations and that

---

[8] Ibid., pp. 506-507. Svitsyn was removed from his post in February 1928, two weeks before public disclosure of the Shakhty affair. The date of his arrest is not given. However, it seems likely that, if not his arrest, then those of many other technical directors in *Yugostal'*, who were imprisoned as alleged accomplices of Svitsyn, took place after disclosure of the Shakhty case.

[9] Ibid., p. 508.   [10] Ibid., p. 556.   [11] Ibid., p. 559.   [12] Ibid., p. 569.

duplication should be eliminated; yet he reasserted the necessity of social controls over production, particularly while untrustworthy elements occupied important positions in industry. This would continue so long as "we do not have our own specialists; while they [the old specialists] deceive us at every step."[13]

The objections of the managers to such investigations and the interference by outside agencies in their work, were weakened by the widespread distrust of the old specialists in party circles, a distrust that Stalin was able to fan for his own partisan political purposes. Such protests as that of Birman above may have done little to prevent the continued arrests and prosecutions of highly qualified specialists in industry over the next year and a half, but they are indicative of an opposition among industrial managers that may eventually have helped to reverse the policy of terror against the old specialists, as will be seen below. Such opposition was diluted at the time, however, no doubt by the fear that managers themselves might have to share the responsibility for mistakes and problems in industry for which the old specialists received the blame.[14]

Even Kuibyshev, though he undoubtedly feared the economic disruption of such arrests and trials, changed his tone for a time at the height of the purges of Soviet economic institutions. By early 1930, he was running with the hounds. It must have become obvious by then that Stalin and the OGPU were not to be dissuaded from their campaign against the old specialists at that moment. That it was unwise and perhaps unsafe to oppose these efforts became increasingly apparent. It was in the interests of the industrial managers in such a situation to use the accused engineers as scapegoats. The arrests of old specialists served as a distraction, diverting the public from blaming industrial management for the mistakes and confusion that reigned in much of the economy at this time. Such arrests provided a ready explanation for the economic situation in the country—the widespread shortages and failures to meet production targets. Without such trials, the responsibility might have rested squarely on the shoulders of the industrial managers. In early 1930 Kuibyshev clearly sought to use the arrests in this way. He began one of several speeches on this subject at the time with the following remark: "The purpose of my address is to show the inseparable tie existing between the work of wreckers and our lack of fulfillment of economic and production plans."[15]

[13] Ibid., p. 574.

[14] Some managers openly shunned their technical personnel at this time, according to the journal of the engineering-technical union; see *IT*, no. 15, 1929, 445.

[15] *ZI*, Feb. 18, 1930. See also similar speeches by Kuibyshev published in this paper on Jan. 29, and Feb. 2 and 3, 1930.

In this and similar speeches, Kuibyshev made an abrupt about-face from his previous position, and publicly praised the OGPU for uncovering wreckers. He blamed the technical intelligentsia generally for not helping in these efforts to unmask their disloyal colleagues. It was probably no coincidence that Kuibyshev's change of tack occurred just before *Rabkrin* was scheduled to begin a massive purge of the *Vesenkha apparat* as part of the general purge of Soviet institutions called for by Stalin. It was more politic at this time for Kuibyshev to urge the technical intelligentsia to demonstrate their loyalty to the party than to encourage an undercurrent of opposition. Yet no sooner had *Rabkrin* completed its purge of *Vesenkha* than the newspaper of *Vesenkha* resumed publishing accounts of unjust arrests and the persecution of specialists; it was soon engaged in a polemic with state prosecutor Krylenko and his colleagues.[16] Kuibyshev was careful not to question the existence of wreckers per se, but to urge careful procedures in investigating specialists and others accused of such crimes.[17] Vesenkha's newspaper followed a parallel line, encouraging the technical intelligentsia by publishing frequent articles in praise of those specialists who proved especially loyal and hard working.

A somewhat similar evolution of views can be found among some representatives of the technical specialists themselves in these years. Not unexpectedly, however, they were more vociferous at first in expressing discontent with false accusations and the decline in morale and work performance, which they observed resulting from the atmosphere created both by the Shakhty affair and the further arrests of specialists during the next few years.

Much of this opposition was centered in the trade union sections of engineering and technical workers—the All-Union Intersectional Bureau of Engineers and Technicians, or as abbreviated, VMBIT. VMBIT considered one of its primary duties to represent the material and social interests of its members. Its sections were responsible for negotiating the collective agreements with management that defined the pay, functions, and general labor conditions for engineers and technicians.

As conditions changed after 1928, the ability of this organization to function in its former fashion also changed. Some of its leaders were especially vulnerable—for example, S. D. Shein, its chairman until 1930, whose earlier career has already been described. A former stockholder and manager of a capitalist-run plant before the Bolshevik revolution, he had not become a member of the Communist party until 1918. As a result, many old Bolsheviks distrusted the sincerity of his political views. Following the disclosure of the Shakhty affair, Shein attempted

---

[16] See, for example, *ZI*, April 18, June 4, and June 14, 1930.
[17] See his position on this question in *ZI*, June 21, 1930.

to walk a tight rope between various groups whose interests came into conflict in the wake of this affair. It became no easy task to fulfill his varied functions as party member, industrial manager, and representative of the technical intelligentsia. Not surprisingly, his attempts to balance these conflicting interests failed in the long run, and he was eventually arrested and implicated as a figure in the Industrial party trial of 1930.

But in 1928, Shein worked hard to roll with the punches. He was one of the "people's prosecutors" (*obshchestvennyi obvinitel'*) who appeared in the Shakhty trial to testify against the defendants in the name of Soviet society. He remained staunch in his affirmations of their guilt and frequently wrote and spoke in public on the subject.[18] At the same time, the pages of the professional journal he edited—the official organ of his union, *Engineering Labor*—were thrown open to discussions both of the harmful and constructive effects observed in the wake of the Shakhty trial. This discussion was bound to have a considerable impact on the technical intelligentsia. The union of which *Engineering Labor* was the official organ at this time counted one hundred fifty-two thousand members, a membership that included the majority of all who filled positions as engineers and technicians in Soviet industry, both diploma holders and *praktiki*.[19]

The editorial board of this journal took a clever position regarding the results of the Shakhty trial. It attempted to strike a balance between consequences that official party attitudes and policies marked as positive, and consequences that the technical intelligentsia found quite disturbing. An editorial published in January 1929, summed up the situation as it had appeared in the six months following the Shakhty trial:

> The criminal wrecking activities of the "Shakhty engineers" were condemned not only by the punitive hand of the Supreme Court but by all of Soviet society, and in the first instance by us. But this trial called to life an ambiguous set of phenomena, dialectically related to each other; in the first place, an anti-specialist atmosphere was strengthened among the workers. The latter phenomenon found expression in pogroms, hooligan attacks against individual

[18] See, for example, his book *Sud nad ekonomicheskoi kontr-revoliutsiei v Donbasse*, Moscow, 1928. Ipatieff (pp. 309-310, 383) somewhat unfairly accuses Shein of betraying the interests of the specialists and taking the side of the government and party at this period. The record shows that Shein's position was more complicated: he tried to defend the specialists in general against a campaign of harassment at the same time that he condemned those specialists who had confessed to sabotage or been convicted of it.

[19] *IT*, no. 7, 1929, 197.

representatives of the engineering-technical personnel. . . . In the second place, among a certain element of the engineers and technicians an atmosphere of passivity and indifference has appeared which could be characterized as an attempt to escape difficulties. Such moods have an influence both in lowering the productivity of labor, that is, they lessen the tempo of our growth, and in further strengthening the anti-specialist atmosphere among the mass of workers.[20]

This editorial struck an optimistic note at the end by affirming a conviction that the government was taking firm measures to squelch any manifestations of specialist-baiting. It referred specifically to a recent trial where a worker had been condemned for an act of violence against an engineer:

> The sentencing of Bykov showed that the Soviet power intends to dispense with any ceremonies regarding those who by their pogroms disrupt the normal relations between the engineering-technical forces and the mass of workers. This sentence proved that the Soviet power not only will not indulge [workers] in their anti-specialist escapades, but that it views the engineering-technical cadres as the *executors of the political desires of the working class*.[21]

According to this evidence, it was not only the representatives of the specialists who were concerned about specialist-baiting and attempts to curb it, but the state, too, that attempted to create strong sanctions against such random and independent attacks against specialists. The state sought to enforce its monopoly of whatever terror was practiced against specialists. While workers might participate in the official terror through denunciations and court testimony against accused specialists, as in the Shakhty case, the state attempted to crush any manifestations of independent initiative against engineers. Just as the state was nationalizing all industry and private trade, it intended to nationalize the practice of terror; although it may not always have succeeded, it condemned as "hooliganism" terrorist attacks by private individuals against the technical intelligentsia. The parties considered responsible for such actions were to be serevely punished when apprehended.[22]

Another article in this same journal, during April 1929, noted the growth of specialist-baiting and reminded the local engineering and tech-

---

[20] *IT*, no. 1, 1929, 2.   [21] Ibid.

[22] For other examples of such cases, including one involving the murder of an engineer by one of his workers, see *TPG*, Jan. 8, 1929, October 8, 1929, and October 10, 1929. See also *Inzhenernyi trud*, no. 15, 1929, 448.

nical sections of the unions that one of their prime responsibilities was to combat unjust accusations, providing legal help to members who found themselves in such trouble:

> Up to the disclosure of the Shakhty affair, legal help to members in engineering-technical sections was offered by union and sectional organizations, except in accident cases, and no doubts arose about the justice and advisability of such help. After disclosure of the Shakhty conspiracy, the situation sharply changed. Many union organizations began to view the offering of legal aid to engineering-technical workers who had been accused of dereliction of duty as some kind of harmful tendency.[23]

The article went on to note a recent improvement in the situation, with more legal help being offered to the accused by their unions. Many trials in such cases, however, still took place without expert commissions to advise the courts on technical questions. The problem, as many specialists saw it, was that they were often made the scapegoats for the mistakes of others, or held criminally liable for what were admittedly their own technical mistakes, not motivated by criminal intent. One specialist observed a large increase in investigations within factories, brought about by a growing distrust of the technical intelligentsia both by the workers and managers. He commented on the results of such investigations:

> Very often the reason for these investigations is, namely, the intention of an engineer to introduce new methods of work, which will make work easier and lower the cost of production. Mistakes in these circumstances are unavoidable. But at the same time, these mistakes—however small—cause gossip in the shop. In most cases, a commission is immediately formed to investigate the failure. No matter how favorable the outcome of this matter may be, it always leaves a heavy aftertaste in the mouth of a specialist and hinders him in further creative work.[24]

The results of such investigations created an atmosphere in which many specialists took every possible measure to avoid individual responsibility for decisions, and lost the desire to take the initiative in their work. At the fourth plenum of the Ukrainian engineering and technical workers, held in late 1928, one of its leaders took the optimistic

---

[23] *IT*, no. 8, 1929, 241ff. A similar view was developed in *Predpriiatie*, no. 3, 1929, 23-28. Published by *Pravda*, this was a journal read widely both by Red Directors and engineering and technical workers.

[24] *IT*, no. 10, 1929, 290.

view that this trend was not typical of the majority of specialists, but he noted an increase in this mood since the Shakhty affair:

Incidents of confusion noted among a certain part of the engineering-technical workers (this phenomenon has become more widespread since the Shakhty trial) find their outward manifestation in a distrust of the trade unions and their engineering-technical sections. It also leads to a weakening on their part of the direction of production and of their attention to fulfilling their legitimate obligations toward the workers. They seek ways of diluting their own responsibility and shifting it to various other individuals and organizations.[25]

One of the favorite ways to avoid individual responsibility among the technical intelligentsia was to create commissions to decide important questions, in the belief that there is safety in numbers. Commissions, like any kind of committee, however, usually involve long discussions and consequent delays in action. In an economy under intense pressure to fulfill high production goals, the formation of commissions to decide questions formerly decided by individuals led to delays many industrial managers considered intolerable. The managers, after all, were finally responsible for the fulfillment of production plans. As one industrial manager, a member of the presidium of *Vesenkha*, commented in the fall of 1929:

Much has been said in discussions about technical risks. The legal framework of technical risk-taking has been publicized many times. For mistakes resulting from taking technical risks we regularly call people to responsibility. As a result, a segment of the specialists have become very frightened and avoid acting at their own risk. Before deciding on any measure, this kind of specialist surrounds himself with dozens of commissions, so that in the event of a mishap, he can put the responsibility on them. We need to take decisive measures in this matter. It is high time that we began to bring to responsibility those that refuse to make independent decisions.[26]

Although this manager did not connect the extreme caution of the specialists with the atmosphere that developed after the Shakhty trial, representatives of the specialists themselves were bolder about making the connection. Such an attitude is apparent even in the Marxist ideological organization VARNITSO, which at this time was attempting to rally

[25] *IT*, no. 1, 1929, 7.
[26] I. A. Kraval' in *TPG*, October 9, 1929.

members of the scientific-technical intelligentsia around the party and government.

Begun in 1927 by a small group of party members and fellow travellers among the scientists and engineers who held high positions in Soviet industry, education, and research institutes, the organization also fulfilled the role of a lobby for the interests of these groups within the party and Soviet society. There was clearly an ambivalent attitude among such specialists toward the atmosphere created by the arrests and trials of specialists. For example, in the April 1929 issue of this association's journal, a report from the Donbass region, the area in which Shakhty was located, noted some unpleasant traces of that affair:

> The first of these is a mistrust of technical personnel. This mistrust reaches deep and it is necessary to have strong nerves in order to calmly take into consideration the mood of the workers which has arisen since the Shakhty affair, to overcome in oneself this mistrust and go on working.
>
> Of course, all of this has worsened the atmosphere of work, made the activity of the engineer more difficult and consequently that of the manager and party activist who depend on the engineer. As a result, in the course of 1928, labor discipline has fallen, technical personnel have lost their authority, and very difficult living conditions have been created for the families of engineers.[27]

This observer further confirmed the effect that this atmosphere had had on the initiative of the technical intelligentsia and their willingness to take on responsibility. He compared the situation to a soccer match, with everyone trying to pass the ball: "Everyone is afraid of everyone else, no one trusts anyone, sabotage is seen in every mistake, no one dares to give a final answer."[28]

Another favorite device for spreading the responsibility for technical decisions at this time was the use of foreign consultants. As one American engineer wrote to his employer in 1931: "As consultants on design, they simply failed to use us; the main desire was to get us to use their designs and thus take the responsibility off their hands. This dividing of responsibility is the only thing that keeps a Russian engineer out of prison."[29]

---

[27] *VARNITSO*, no. 1, April 15, 1929. [28] Ibid.

[29] Mr. L. H. Garaux, in Berlin, to Mr. Archer Wheeler, New York City, July 19, 1931. Mr. Garaux was a mining engineer employed by Mr. Wheeler to work as a consultant to Soviet industry. A copy of this letter was given to George S. Messersmith, American Consul General in Berlin, who transmitted it to The Secretary of State, July 22, 1931 (State Department Decimal File, The National Archives, 861.5017/310). This use of foreign specialists as a device for spreading

It is not easy to measure the overall effect of this atmosphere on industrial production and the introduction of technical innovations in Soviet industry. In the area of creative work, especially new inventions, the available evidence, which will be analyzed in chapter 13, suggests that the terror had a harmful effect. While the fear of arrest may not be the best incentive, particularly for taking risks and for doing creative work of high quality, it was not necessarily a depressant, either, especially for ordinary, repetitive work. It may even have stimulated concentration on this kind of work, while doubtless feeding strong resentments as well. Such stimulation of work, of course, is likely to be stronger when fear is combined with other incentives, such as higher pay and social status. These incentives increased in Soviet industry only in 1931. In June of 1931 Soviet policy toward the technical intelligentsia in general began to change and the use of terror aimed particularly at this group declined. But even before 1931 the effects on production had lessened somewhat probably because of the wide-scale recruitment of foreign industrial specialists. After 1928, the recruitment of such specialists was stepped up and by 1930, some seven thousand were working in Soviet industry, although with varying degrees of effectiveness.[30] It is obvious that so many highly qualified foreign engineers and technicians were likely to be of considerable help in these times, even when language barriers and resentment limited their effectiveness somewhat. After 1933, as young Soviet specialists graduated in large numbers, most of these foreign specialists were gradually sent home.

Between 1928 and 1931, however, fear predominated among the specialists, especially those who were older and better qualified. Although the specialists were reacting to a genuine threat, their fear may also have contained an element of hysteria, caused at least in part by injured pride, a result not only of the arrests and trials, but also of many small incidents and attacks on their social status and their superior living conditions.

An example of this is contained in an article published in January 1929 in *Engineering Labor*. The author believed the majority of workers to be on the side of the specialists and not guilty of harrassing them.

---

responsibility and protecting Soviet engineers in case something went wrong is confirmed by another American specialist at this period, Mr. Jacob Stiriss, who worked for the State Electrical Trust in Moscow (see the report of an interview with him in the dispatch of John L. Bouchal, American Consul, Helsingfors, Finland, May 11, 1932, to The Secretary of State, State Department Decimal File, NA, 861.5017).

[30] N. P. Sharapov, "Ob uchastii inostrannykh rabochikh i spetsialistov v sotsialisticheskom stroitel'stve na Urale (1930-1934 gg.)," *Voprosy istorii KPSS*, no. 3, 1966, 71-72.

Still, he went on to state that in some areas, particularly more backward parts of the Soviet Union, even responsible officials and organizations permitted violations of the privacy and dignity of specialists. The author described one such incident in highly emotional terms:

> In the scandalous affair reported below, the guilty parties are not unthinking workers. No, they are parties invested with the trust of the working class, responsible workers and even organizations. . . . In an organized, intentional, public, and pre-meditated way, they slandered the character of a man from the podium of a workers' club, libeled his family life, insulted him in front of his colleagues and subordinates, destroying his authority at work. We demand an investigation of this affair.[31]

Here is the incident that so disturbed the writer: the local drama group in an outlying factory town had written and performed a play that obviously ridiculed the chief engineer of the local mine administration. The play used events from his life that were clearly recognizable, and fabricated episodes that were slanderous, according to this account. The engineer was portrayed as an alcoholic whose wife was the mistress of another man, as scornful of the men who worked under him, and as a man who lived a vulgarly rich life on the sweat of the proletariat. According to one line of dialogue, the character portraying the engineer commented: "I don't like to watch movies at the workers' clubs, there is always such a stench of cabbage soup which no perfume is able to hide."[32]

The author of this article considered the affair an impermissible violation of privacy and truth. He noted that the chief engineer, having incurred the jealousy and suspicion of young hooligans as a result of the play, had later been forced to resign.

VARNITSO noted other events that struck at the pride and social status of the technical intelligentsia at this time. An article that connected such incidents directly with the general atmosphere of specialist-baiting noted:

> For example, at one mine the wife of the chief mechanic, standing in a bread line with the wives of workers was shoved out of line with the comment, "There is no room here for a 'bourgeois' "; no one came to her defense. At school the children of engineers have suffered a series of blows to their pride.[33]

[31] *IT*, no. 1, 1929, 5–6. Apparently this was no isolated incident at the time. A report from another area complained that the villain in a local political skit was dressed in the uniform of an engineer (see *TPG*, Jan. 11, 1929).

[32] *IT*, no. 1, 1929, 5–6. [33] *VARNITSO*, no. 1, 1929, 9.

In other places, temporary control commissions—investigative bodies composed primarily of workers—attempted to take away the apartments of specialists and lower their pay.[34] According to a report made to the Central Committee of the Armenian Communist party in 1929, workers were then likelier to express their resentments at certain privileges the technical intelligentsia enjoyed than they had been prior to 1928. For example, in one factory meeting in that Republic, a worker boldly asked an engineer in front of the entire assembly: "Why do you have two rooms? Why do you travel first class?"[35] In those years of scarcity, workers and their families frequently doubled up in a single room or lived in crowded barracks and traveled by third class or boxcars. After 1928, workers felt bold enough to speak out against the privileges enjoyed by a group under general attack by the party and state.

The situation apparently became so serious late in 1928 that Molotov, one of Stalin's closest associates in the Politburo, spoke out publicly against specialist-baiting, a gesture Stalin personally was not to make until June 1931. Molotov's remarks gave some rather feeble and backhanded support to the technical intelligentsia, but he began with a comment critical of them as a group:

> It is especially necessary to comment on the necessity for raising labor discipline among engineering-technical personnel. In this area, matters are far from satisfactory. On the other hand, there is clearly not a sufficient struggle against specialist baiting, nor against direct hooligan attacks on engineering-technical personnel. . . . With regard to these facts it is necessary to underline the obligation of creating such a moral attitude among workers which would make impossible the presence in factories of hooligans and those who disrupt production.[36]

The Central Council of Trade Unions approached the problem somewhat differently. It noted a general decline of labor discipline in factories, not just among engineering and technical personnel. It blamed this decline on the weakening of the authority of the technical intelligentsia, among other factors, and called for immediate measures to strengthen that authority. The engineering and technical workers needed to know what their rights and powers were in order to use their authority fully and have it respected.[37] Widespread measures to defend and raise the authority of the technical intelligentsia were not taken until 1931.

---

[34] *IT*, no. 1, 1929, 8.

[35] Arkhiv Armianskogo filiala IML pri TsK KPSS, f. 1, op. 13, d. 17, l. 30, cited in Grigoriants, p. 122.

[36] *IT*, no. 8, 1929, 252.   [37] *IT*, no. 6, 1929, 191.

At the time of this statement, the trade unions themselves were under attack by the Stalinists. In the following months, many of the established trade union leaders, such as Tomský, who were allied with the moderate opposition to Stalin and were determined to defend the material interests of the workers they represented, were ousted.

Those specialists who commented in print on the existence of specialist-baiting at this time, were careful to balance their critical comments with some positive evaluation of the results of these trials of engineers. The April 1928 party plenum had recommended a strong effort to change some of the attitudes of the technical intelligentsia, especially the mentality that considered their position superior to that of workers, and considered the technical intelligentsia a closed caste. The engineering and technical sections of the unions, as well as VARNITSO, led the way in attempting to change attitudes among specialists. In the spring of 1929, for example, the Fourth All-Union Congress of VMBIT resolved to do away with all outward symbols of a "closed-caste mentality." Although epaulets and various insignia of rank had been discarded by the Red Army in an early stage of the revolution, engineers still wore uniforms that were similar to those of the Tsarist period and were symbols of professional rank.

For example, engineers had been entitled to wear service caps with an insignia consisting of a wrench crossed with a hammer. The engineering and technical sections resolved to do away with such signs, which set them apart from the working class. (Such measures were only temporarily successful, however. By the end of World War II, even more ornate uniforms for engineers had become the vogue.)[38] For a time at least, this seemed to help erase one of the visible barriers between them and the working class.

More important, from the standpoint of working relationships, however, were the efforts of VMBIT to encourage the specialists to tutor workers in technical study groups and to give more attention to inventions and improvements worked out by the proletariat. An article in *Engineering Labor* also noted that "there is no doubt that technical personnel have become more attentive toward the mass of workers: instances in which collective work agreements and the code of labor laws have been violated by the engineering-technical personnel have become much rarer."[39]

In many factories, according to this article, the technical intelligentsia had begun to include workers in their consultations on plant conditions,

---

[38] See, for example, the photograph of A. M. Terpigorev on the frontispiece of his autobiography.

[39] *IT*, no. 1, 1929, 11. See also no. 4, 1930, 103.

Fig. 1. A cartoon from a Soviet engineering journal of 1930 that satirizes the attachment of engineers to the external symbols of their status, in this case the cap with the insignia of the engineering profession. The worshipful engineer is exclaiming "They want to separate us." (*Smithsonian Institution.*)

and were more concerned about plant safety and the living and working conditions of the proletariat in general. Of course, some of this may have been wishful thinking or propaganda on the part of their trade union representatives to demonstrate the good behavior of the technical intelligentsia, but, in general, it is a human tendency to try to disarm the hostility of fellow workers and ease even normal frictions and strains. It seems even likelier that in the situation described here many specialists would increasingly exert themselves to win the sympathy of workers. In some instances, however, as the author of this article complained, specialists went too far and became lax in exerting their authority, giving in to illegal demands by workers. Such a tendency, he argued, had the end result of lowering labor discipline and harming the interests of production.

Beyond measures to encourage a rapprochement between specialists and workers on the factory level, VMBIT and VARNITSO worked hard to recruit members of the technical intelligentsia into the Communist party and to whip up enthusiasm for party policies among them. In the course of 1930, some thirty-five hundred engineers and technicians joined the party.[40] This seems insignificant when compared with the overall party membership of some one million, but this fact marks a turning point both for the technical intelligentsia and for the party.

In 1928, fewer than one thousand members of the technical intelligentsia belonged to the party, and most of them were among the least qualified; only one hundred thirty-eight were engineers, compared with seven hundred fifty-one technicians. Special recruitment of these groups, especially the most highly educated, was a change of great importance, for it led eventually to a Communist party leadership in which a majority of the top officials possessed dual skills: higher technical education and experience, combined with a career in political work.[41] This was to be a new development in a party that had formerly been recruited heavily from the student radicals and disaffected intellectuals of Tsarist times—most often members of the cultural intelligentsia—as well as from skilled and unskilled workers.

Between 1927 and the end of 1929, the growth in party membership among the technical intelligentsia was faster among those with higher technical education than those with lesser qualifications, although their percentage of membership in the party was still the lowest among the technical intelligentsia overall.[42] The rapid growth in the number of

[40] *IT*, no. 11, 1930, 321.

[41] George Fischer, *The Soviet System and Modern Society*, New York, 1968, pp. 19-46, 92-95.

[42] *IT*, no. 11, 1930, 321.

party members who had higher technical educations may be explained in part as a rush by many members of this group to prove their political loyalty and attempt to insure themselves against arbitrary arrest and interference by party and police authorities.

The attempt to increase Communist influence among the technical intelligentsia is also indicated by the membership rolls of VARNITSO. This organization, one avowed purpose of which was political indoctrination of the scientific-technical intelligentsia, grew from one thousand members in 1929 to three thousand in 1930.[43] This number rose to eleven thousand by the end of 1932. Members of this organization were promised freedom from secret police interference in their work in return for participation, but one of the conditions was the acceptance of party discipline.[44] It was a hard bargain for many specialists, but one that must have seemed increasingly attractive to those who valued their work above all else, when they saw the fate that befell many of their colleagues at the hands of the OGPU. A few, such as Ipatieff, who were able to emigrate, went to Western Europe or the United States,[45] but the vast majority had little choice at this point, hoping eventually to increase their influence within Soviet institutions to the point where they could create a more favorable atmosphere for themselves.

The campaign to win over the technical intelligentsia to the party climaxed in 1930, the same year that the terror against this group also reached its height, in the events leading up to the Industrial party trial. The two processes, coercion and persuasion, were undoubtedly connected, although details concerning the personalities and the discussions involved in forming and fulfilling these policies are not available.

The most visible leaders in the movement to demonstrate the political loyalty of the scientific-technical intelligentsia were a few Communist party members in VARNITSO and VMBIT: S. D. Shein, who was a leader in both organizations until his arrest in 1930; and Professors A. N. Bakh, B. I. Zabarsky, and others among the founders of VARNITSO, who were applied scientists with high professional reputa-

---

[43] *VARNITSO*, no. 2, 1929, 2; L. M. Zak, "Sozdanie i deiatel'nost' 'VARNITSO' v 1927-1932 gg.," *Istoriia SSSR*, no. 6, 1958, 104-105.

[44] Zak, *Istoriia*, 107; Ipatieff, p. 451.

[45] Two members of the Academy of Sciences who had held high posts in Soviet industry, Ipatieff and Chichibabin, emigrated at this time in fear of their lives. In the defense industry, where Ipatieff had spent a good part of his career, ten former Tsarist generals and twenty-one former colonels were arrested during this period. At least five of the accused specialists had been students of Ipatieff at the Tsarist Artillery Academy. The OGPU dealt more perfunctorily with this group than with many other accused wreckers. When their arrests were announced on October 23, 1929, the announcement stated that they had already been shot by the secret police. (*TPG*, Oct. 23, 1929; Ipatieff, pp. 485-486; Graham, pp. 150-151.)

tions, and who remained prominent throughout these years, escaping the fate of the Shakhty and Industrial party engineers.

In addition to encouraging party membership among the technical intelligentsia, leaders of VARNITSO and VMBIT helped to mobilize the engineering-technical intelligentsia for a series of mass public demonstrations held early in 1930—a favorite device for influencing public opinion. In January, some thirteen thousand Leningrad engineers and technicians, it was reported, took part in a public demonstration, shouting such slogans as "Down with the political neutrality of engineers." In Moscow on February 5, thirty thousand engineers and technicians joined some two hundred thousand Young Communists to demonstrate for the fulfillment of the Five-Year plan in four years. *Engineering Labor* noted these events as the first public demonstrations in which the technical intelligentsia participated as an organized group, supporting Soviet policies. The journal remarked that such demonstrations signified that the technical intelligentsia had cut its ties with the past.[46]

Perhaps so, but much of the evidence in the remainder of this study tends to suggest another conclusion: that the technostructure did not become passive followers of the party line; it had merely changed its tactics. Many of its members tried increasingly to exert influence on policy within the party itself, abandoning the earlier struggle to influence public policy through autonomous professional societies and independent trade unions.

One younger specialist heard such opinions expressed frequently among members of the technical intelligentsia in the 1930s. As he remembered one graduate engineer, the director of a new automotive plant, express it, "Bureaucrats have arisen from the workers and peasants. This is a uniformly harmful phenomenon with which one must struggle, using the methods of technical progress. Engineers, physicians, scientists—people of concrete knowledge—must move into governing posts. . . ."[47] The first step in such a move would be to change the composition of the ruling party itself, bringing in as members ever larger numbers of technical specialists. Such a change was to have major consequences not only for the technical intelligentsia itself, but for the Communist party and Soviet society.

[46] *IT*, no. 3, 1930, 66.
[47] Memoirs of M. M. Samygin, Columbia University Archive of Russian History and Culture, pp. 3-4.

6

OLD SPECIALISTS AND NEW PATRONS:
THE END OF TERROR

In her memoirs of Soviet life in the 1920s and 1930s, Nadezhda Mandelstam, wife of the Soviet poet, discusses an aspect of Soviet behavior little commented upon elsewhere. The wife of an important party official once asked her during conversation: "Whom do you go to see?" The questioner wondered who among the party leadership was the patron of the Mandelstams. When she passed this on to her husband, the poet assured his wife, "Everyone goes to see someone. There's no other way. We go to see Nikolai Ivanovich [Bukharin]."[1] Nadezhda Mandelstam called this informal institution "transmission belts," the manner in which members of the intelligentsia and others who had little or no power sought to cut red tape and attain influence, privileges, or other help by finding a patron among the power elite of the Communist party. The "transmission belt," as an institution of Soviet society, figured critically in the social relations of the technical intelligentsia during this period. Sometimes difficult to document, it has received little systematic study from historians and social scientists. Yet informal relations, including informal channels of communication to the centers of power, may be as important, sometimes more important, to understanding a series of events as more formal relations, and this is particularly true where the formal institutions and channels no longer function effectively. This was the situation in which many of the technical intelligentsia found themselves right after the October Revolution, and again after 1928, when some of its formal institutions—professional societies and trade unions—were dissolved or disregarded and put under official suspicion.

We have already seen how crucial were the roles of Gorbunov, Lenin's secretary, of L. B. Krasin, and of Lenin himself as patrons of technical specialists in the early years of the Soviet system. After Lenin's death, two men in the Politburo particularly filled that function: Rykov, the head of state, and Felix Dzherzhinsky, head of the secret police and head of industrial management (*Vesenkha*) shortly before his death in 1926. Some technical specialists continued to look to Rykov for help during the terror after 1928, but Rykov's influence waned after his

[1] *Hope Against Hope: A Memoir*, New York, 1970, pp. 112-118.

141

forced recantation as a leader of the moderate opposition to Stalin in 1929. Although Rykov remained the head of government until replaced by Stalin's crony, Molotov, early in 1931, he warned the technical specialists publicly in February 1930 that they could no longer count on his help as a patron, although, in fact, he did try to help some of them.

In a long speech to members of the technical intelligentsia, he told them, in effect, that they must demonstrate their loyalty to the Soviet system by intense work, and that they could not depend on his help to stop the arrests: "Together with others, I have continually received complaints that arrests are taking place among the technical personnel and that they make work very difficult. Numerous engineers and technicians, so they say, are afraid they will be arrested for one thing or another; and they have therefore lost the will to work. We did not accept their complaints, however, but rather gave just the opposite advice to the OGPU: arrest everyone who is unmasked as a wrecker."[2]

Rykov went on in the same speech to state that he had, in fact, intervened in some cases and convinced the OGPU not to arrest certain engineers accused of wrecking. He urged the police instead simply to keep suspects under surveillance. Rykov mentioned by name a half dozen such specialists. "We did this, of course, not because we want to give them freedom of action to continue wrecking but because we do not number them among the most active. We think there is a chance for their rehabilitation."[3] In essence, Rykov was telling the technical intelligentsia to work harder and grumble less or face continued terror.

One may well ask if the technostructure abandoned "transmission belts" to attain protection and other help after the fall of Rykov and Bukharin. Evidence from the early 1930s indicates that it did not. In fact, because older, formal institutions were blocked, informal relations became even more important to the technical intelligentsia, a conclusion suggested by the evidence of this chapter and even more so by that of chapters 7 and 11.

We can see clearly how formal channels of communication came to be blocked during 1930 in the fate of VMBIT, the trade union sections for technical specialists. With the arrest of S. D. Shein, the head of VMBIT, and an important spokesman for the technostructure within the Communist party, the position of the organization as a defender of the rights of specialists was greatly weakened for the time being. The January 1930 issue of *Engineering Labor*, the official organ of VMBIT, furnished an early hint that Shein was in trouble when it dropped his name from the masthead, although it still listed him as chairman of

[2] *ZI*, Feb. 21, 1930.   [3] Ibid.

VMBIT.[4] With this issue, one can also note a change in editorial policy. Calls for heightened vigilance against class enemies took a more prominent place; the journal, which had previously conducted a discussion concerning the complaints of specialists about the atmosphere of specialist-baiting, began to criticize such complaints; eventually it dropped all discussion of such questions for nearly a year. The reason for such passivity is probably the following.

By June 1930, the general purge of Soviet institutions had reached the officials of the engineering and technical sections. A brigade of factory workers had begun an investigation of VMBIT to see how well this union "had rallied engineering-technical workers around the policies of the party."[5] After this time, all mention of Shein disappeared from the pages of the journal, not to reappear until the discussion of his arrest in connection with the Industrial party case. The new head of VMBIT, V. V. Prokof'ev, later minimized Shein's importance in the organization, and stated that he had always been a figurehead and never a real power in the organization.[6] To offset this allegation, Prokof'ev's accusation that Shein used his position in the union to spread discontent among the technical intelligentsia and to recruit new conspirators, implies that he had at least some influence there:

> His basic task [as a member of the Industrial party] was propaganda and agitation of anti-Soviet attitudes in engineering circles, the exaggeration of discontent with arrests, indicating the injustice of these arrests, influencing the Five-Year plan, pointing to the annihilation of the pre-revolutionary engineers, and so on. His activity also extended to the careful recruitment of members of the Industrial Party among the broad mass of engineers.[7]

In August 1930, *Engineering Labor* published a letter from a specialist complaining about the frequent trials of specialists in cases that did not warrant such severe treatment.[8] The letter writer had carefully qualified his complaint, limiting it to those instances of technical mistakes, especially those involving young specialists, where no ulterior motive was suspected. He did not bring up the delicate question of how ulterior motives could be detected in such instances, and he omitted any direct references to wrecking or sabotage. His letter was simply a plea for greater caution in making specialists liable for technical mistakes, pointing to a government decree that had been issued to prevent such instances. In presenting his case, however, he had indicated that

---

[4] *IT*, no. 1, 1930, 7. I have been unable to discover Shein's fate after his arrest.
[5] *IT*, no. 11, 1930, 343. [6] *IT*, nos. 22-23, 1930, 667.
[7] *IT*, nos. 22-23, 1930, 670. [8] *IT*, no. 15, 1930, 476.

prosecution by local administrations in such cases led to apathy and a passive attitude toward work on the part of many specialists. The editors of the journal attacked him for this: "The author is mistaken in the general way he poses the problem. He considers that individual instances in which specialists have been incorrectly called to responsibility can affect their activity at work, can give rise to a tendency for them to become sullen in their administrative and technical work."[9] The editors condemned this attitude as untrue and apolitical, and an aspersion on the good name of the majority of the technical intelligentsia, even though for months previously they had filled their journal with reports of low morale and a tendency to evade responsibility, brought about by the arrests and trials of specialists. The letter and the editorial comments attached to it ended all questioning of arrests and trials of specialists and, in fact, any mention of specialist-baiting in the journal for months to come.

Can we conclude from this that the entire technostructure became inert and passive in the face of continued arrests and disruptions of their work? It seems unlikely that all of them did, particularly in light of what we know about their earlier history, both in the Tsarist era and the first decade of Soviet rule. Rather, informal relations and the establishment of new "transmission belts" became even more important. Our hypothesis in this chapter and the next, with supporting evidence, is that active members of the old technostructure, who were not arrested and continued to work in Soviet institutions, turned to other party leaders for influence before the formal change of policy Stalin announced in June 1931.

A prime figure in that respect was Sergo Ordzhonikidze, a recent appointee to the Politburo. After the Sixteenth Party Congress in August 1930, there had been a shakeup in Soviet industry. Ordzhonikidze, then head of the Workers' and Peasants' Inspectorate, had severely criticized *Vesenkha*, headed by Kuibyshev, for the failures of industry. Kuibyshev was then appointed head of *Gosplan*, formally in charge of all economic planning, and Ordzhonikidze was transferred to *Vesenkha* in November 1930, becoming a full member of the Politburo in December.[10] As head of the most important sectors of Soviet industry during the remainder of the First Five-Year Plan, Ordzhonikidze no doubt found his interests changing. From being the economy's chief inspector and watchdog, he now found himself responsible for fulfilling the enormous targets set for the First Five-Year Plan, targets that he

[9] Ibid.
[10] See I. M. Dubinski-Mukhadze, *Ordzhonikidze*, Moscow, 1963, and V. S. Kirillov and A. Ya. Sverdlov, *Ordzhonikidze*, Moscow, 1962.

FIG. 2. Sergo Ordzhonikidze, the Commissar of Heavy Industry, with the workers, engineers, and managers of the Gorky Automotive Works, inspecting the 100,000th auto produced there, in 1935. The factory had been built in the early 1930s under a technical aid contract with the Ford Motor Co. Once an intimate of Stalin, Ordzhonikidze died by his own hand in February 1937, a victim of harassment by Stalin and the NKVD.

himself had earlier supported in alliance with Stalin. Ordzhonikidze, a former paramedic and revolutionary, had little formal education and no training in industrial technology, but he had a quick mind and a quicker temper, and he was a man of direct action. He prided himself on getting things done, and was quick to use coercion if necessary. That fact had gotten him into trouble with Lenin in the early 1920s when he had beaten up some Georgian Communist leaders who had resisted more centralized party control after their nation had been conquered by the Red Army. Generally known as an ally of Stalin in earlier years, after 1930 their paths began to diverge. As the head of the most important sectors of Soviet industry, Ordzhonikidze became heavily dependent on the technostructure for achieving results in his new area of responsibility. It would have been entirely in character for him to fight for those whose help he needed to attain results, and it would have been entirely in character for those old specialists who remained under his jurisdiction to turn to him for protection and help in achieving their own aims, first among which in early 1931 would have been an end to terror against the old technostructure and the restoration of their authority in the economy. The weight of the evidence available suggests that this was what happened, although Ordzhonikidze moved cautiously at first, and more boldly only when Stalin himself finally put his weight behind a change of policy in June 1931. Such a conclusion must remain tentative until archival documents become available to scholars, since we know nothing about the internal discussions of this question in the Politburo, Central Committee or the inner councils of industrial management (*Vesenkha*). The evidence that is available leads us to conclude that public pressure for change came first from Ordzhonikidze and party leaders concerned with industry in the first half of 1931. Ordzhonikidze, not Stalin or Stalin's closest allies in the party apparatus, became one of the new patrons of the old specialists. A pattern was being repeated in which the old specialists sought influence through important party members who were directly concerned with the economy.[11]

Slightly more than one month after the conclusion of the Industrial party trial, Ordzhonikidze called together more than seven hundred top

---

[11] A good memoir account of how Ordzhonikidze acted as a patron of the technical intelligentsia in conflicts with party and police officials can be found in Kravchenko (especially pp. 197, 237). Ordzhonikidze's role as a patron of the technical intelligentsia in conflicts over planning targets in metallurgy, for example, is corroborated by a recent Soviet source containing the memoirs of engineers and managers active in the 1930s: *Byli industrial'nye*, Moscow, 1973, pp. 9-18, 190-195. On the way in which managers sometimes protected technical specialists, see also, The Harvard Project on the Soviet Social System, Interviews # 480, 4; 26, 9-14, Widener Library, Harvard University.

industrial managers and technical personnel for the first national conference on the problems of socialized industry.[12] The problems they faced were extremely serious, involving lags and breakdowns of major proportions, especially in the coal industry, metallurgy, and transportation, three of the areas that were among the hardest hit by the arrests of the previous three years. No one at this conference, however, directly connected the problems of industry with the terror against the old specialists, but by analyzing and comparing the speeches of Ordzhonikidze and Stalin at this conference, and the resolutions it produced, based on Ordzhonikidze's report, we can see important differences of emphasis.

Ordzhonikidze addressed the Congress three times, and warned each time that old specialists who worked honestly and well were to be respected and not molested. While Ordzhonikidze did not neglect to warn against wreckers, in his opening speech he reminded his audience, "It would be completely incorrect if we turned our class hatred, which wreckers had fully deserved, without proof on the remaining, honest segment of the technical intelligentsia."[13] He gave even greater emphasis to the specialists in his concluding speech, noting how few experienced engineers there were in industry. "Without technical direction, there is no direction," was the first point he emphasized, and he warned against industrial managers who sought scapegoats for every problem. "I have already mentioned that the place for wreckers is in the OGPU, but there must be an attentive attitude toward those engineers who work honestly with us. Without this, they are forced to work in an atmosphere poisoned by the likes of Ramzin, Charnovsky, and other bastards. It is, therefore, all the more necessary to be attentive toward the others. (applause)"[14]

The first resolution passed by the conference echoed Ordzhonikidze's concern. It called for a strengthening of technical direction in industry and singled out the key role of the specialists in this area: "The role and significance of technical cadres is growing. The creation of new cadres of engineers and technicians, composed of people from the working class, is attaining a decisive significance. At the same time, all necessary conditions must be created for the work of all old specialists who

[12] Two-thirds of the nearly seven hundred fifty delegates were listed as administrative-technical personnel, fourteen percent as engineers, and twelve percent as shock-workers. The remainder were representatives of factory and party organizations. (*Za industrializatsiiu*, Feb. 1, 1931). For an account of this industrial conference, see *Za industrializatsiiu* (hereafter *ZI*) for February 1931, and the transcript, published as *Pervaia vsesoiuznaia konferentsiia rabotnikov sotsialisticheskoi promyshlennosti: Stenograficheskii otchet*, Moscow, 1931.

[13] *ZI*, Jan. 30, 1931.　　　　　　　　[14] *ZI*, Feb. 9, 1931.

have definitely placed themselves in the ranks of the builders of Soviet industry."[15]

Thus, while Ordzhonikidze did not publicly question the existence of wrecking or the outcomes of the Shakhty and Industrial party trials, he was concerned with the fate of the old specialists who remained untainted by such arrests. Stalin and his ally, Molotov, who also addressed this conference, showed no similar concern. In fact, they completely ignored the question of creating good working conditions for the remaining old specialists, and they gave a somewhat different analysis of the problems of industry.[16] Stalin criticized, although not by name, those who called for a slowdown in the tempo of growth, and stressed that Bolsheviks themselves must master technology and quit relying on others. Referring to a story from the famous nineteenth-century writer, Saltykov-Shchedrin, about a bureaucrat who believed it was not necessary to study science, but only to sign papers, Stalin excoriated those Communists who considered a knowledge of technology too difficult for them. The Shakhty case had been the first warning about the effects of this attitude, he noted, and the Industrial party case was the second warning. "It is time that Bolsheviks became specialists," Stalin emphasized, and added, "There are no fortresses which Bolsheviks cannot storm."[17]

Ordzhonikidze certainly had no disagreement with Stalin on the latter point. Stalin's words on the need for Communists to master technology were used by Ordzhonikidze and others in industry during the following years to bolster their case for more attention to technological issues and technical education. There was no open disagreement or confrontation between Stalin and Ordzhonikidze at this conference, only a difference in emphasis. But this difference seems, in the light of what happened subsequently, significant of underlying tension between their two positions. Such differences were to lead to a series of conflicts in following years, and eventually to a break between the two men, the death by suicide of Ordzhonikidze, and a massive purging of his followers in Soviet industry in 1937 and 1938, a theme developed in chapter 11.

A careful reading of the industrial newspaper, *For Industrialization*, published under Ordzhonikidze's direction during the first six months of 1931, reveals additional evidence along these lines. While Ordzhonikidze and the journalists who worked for him occasionally condemned the "right" or moderate opposition as well as wreckers among the old specialists, the newspaper also featured many articles and accomplishments of old specialists and of former oppositionists who had recanted.

[15] *ZI*, Feb. 20, 1931. [16] *ZI*, Feb. 5, 1931.
[17] Ibid.

For example, in the first half of 1931 Bukharin's name appeared prominently, without criticism or editorial comment, on two long articles concerning his new area of responsibility as head of industrial research under Ordzhonikidze.[18] Articles by or about such prominent old specialists as A. F. Ioffe, who was close to the party boss of Leningrad, Kirov, and such famous old engineers as Vedeneev, Graftio, Krzhizhanovsky, et al., helped to create a more favorable image for the old technostructure, as did the newspaper's supplement, *New Technology*, which appeared once or twice weekly.[19]

In the wake of the February conference, a campaign began in the pages of this newspaper to promote new technology and technical risk-taking in industry. The well-known industrial journalist, A. Khavin, and others were sent into the field to analyze the lags in industry. Curiously enough, the area singled out at first for greatest attention was the Shakhty mining district. Beginning right after the conference, on February 23, a feature appeared on page one, written by a mining engineer, who claimed that for two years now a technical revolution in coal mining had been held back in this region by the fear and neglect of technology displayed by local managers. One of the managers attacked in this article replied on March 13, defending himself against the charge that after the Shakhty trial he had held back technical progress in that area, failing to apply a major new invention worked out by technical specialists. An editorial note attached to this letter again attacked him, reiterating the charge. Such articles, including a page-one editorial, continued into June, at times blaming the technical conservatism and passivity of both specialists and managers. These articles seem especially significant, since the reader will recall that one of the charges made by the public prosecutor during the Shakhty trial of 1928 was that recommendations for expensive technical innovations, including the use of American methods of mechanized labor, rather than manual labor, were actually a form of sabotage. This was a charge that had seriously concerned *Vesenkha* at the time. The articles of 1931 may have been concerned with showing some of the results of such charges: technical conservatism and apathy toward innovations at work and new mechanical inventions.[20]

In June, the newspaper began to connect the problem directly with an atmosphere of specialist-baiting and the destruction of the authority of engineering and technical workers.[21] The reason for this bolder em-

[18] *ZI*, Jan. 9, 1931, June 25, 1931.
[19] See, for example, *ZI*, Jan. 4, 1931, Feb. 26, 1931, March 16, 1931, and subsequent issues.
[20] For example, *ZI*, March 18, 1931, March 19, 1931, and June 4, 1931.
[21] *ZI*, June 27, 1931.

phasis in June, which had been missing from the Soviet press for more than a year, will be discussed below.

In the spring of 1931 Khavin and other journalists working for this paper also investigated the metallurgical and chemical industries and found a similar problem: lack of technical direction. Visiting the metallurgical plants of the Donbass during March, Khavin wrote: "The plants must work in extremely difficult conditions. It is thus especially important to have authoritative technical direction, technical advice. Does ferrous metallurgy have such direction? To this question, the plant workers reply crisply, 'No, We have no technical direction.' "[22] The year 1930, he noted, was especially bad in this respect, resulting in accidents and lags in production. On March 20, Khavin devoted an article to the problems of technical specialists. He noted that there were almost no old engineers left in the factories of the south that he had visited. Most specialists were twenty-eight to thirty years of age, fresh from school, with little theoretical knowledge, and little experience. Most were dependent on old workers (*mastera*) who were experienced in their jobs, but lacked a mastery of theory.

This theme was repeated frequently in the spring and early summer, an article in early June noting, "Accidents and interruptions are the barometers of technical direction."[23] We are told by another source, the recent work of a Soviet historian, which is based on archival documents, that by 1931 one-half of all the engineering and technical workers in the Donbass, one of the largest industrial regions in the U.S.S.R. had been arrested. It is no wonder then that top industrial management was concerned to reverse the policy of repression and trim the powers of the OGPU in industry.[24] A few days later, another article on page one analyzed the lags in metallurgy, the area in which we are told that Stalin and Ordzhonikidze had clashed at this time. "The disruption in technical direction is the cause of the lag in metallurgy," the article stated flatly.[25]

What does such evidence add up to? It does not prove that Ordzhonikidze and Stalin clashed over the continuance of arrests among the old specialists, or that Ordzhonikidze and his allies forced an end to such terror, but it does indicate, at the very least, that pressure for a change in this area came most strongly and most consistently during the first half of 1931 from the leaders of industry and not from Stalin and his closest associates. The campaign by industrial management to

[22] *ZI*, March 17, 1931.   [23] *ZI*, June 3, 1931.
[24] TsGAOR, f. 5548, op. 8, ed. khr. 5, l. 134; TsPA IML, f. 85, op. 28, ed. khr. 8, l. 38, cited in Brodskii, pp. 72-73.
[25] *ZI*, June 6, 1931.

restore the authority and prestige of the technical intelligentsia, including both old and new specialists, was a major element in an attempt to solve the problems encountered in fulfilling the First Five-Year Plan. While Ordzhonikidze shared Stalin's concern to prod Communists into mastering technology, he and others who worked for him were also concerned with restoring the authority and improving the working conditions of the remaining old specialists, in an atmosphere soured by the Shakhty, Industrial party and Menshevik trial, the last major show trial of old specialists, mostly economists, which took place in March 1931.[26]

Interestingly enough, the reversal of policy in June came first not from Stalin, but from the party's Central Committee, although this fact remained secret. Stalin became the first to announce the change publicly several weeks later. In the second week of June 1931, the Central Committee met and endorsed a set of secret guidelines that marked a radical departure from the events of the previous three years. The transcript of this Central Committee plenum has never been published; thus, we can only speculate on what differences of opinion may have been expressed there, or in the Politburo sessions that usually preceded such a plenum. A secret document, issued on June 10 by the Central Committee, has come to light, however. It was a circular about the technical intelligentsia sent to all party organizations in the country and it was later found among the documents in the Smolensk party archive, captured during World War II. This document reveals that the Central Committee went a long way toward meeting the concerns expressed by Ordzhonikidze and those working for him during the first half of 1931.[27]

This decree ordered the managers and administrators of all Soviet institutions to "enhance the authority of the engineering and technical personnel" and declared that it was especially necessary to "support young specialists, insuring their further growth during their work."[28] The decree also instructed managers to widen the practice of appointing members of the technical intelligentsia "to the position of heads of

[26] For an account of this trial, see the author's dissertation, pp. 169-172.

[27] A copy of this decree was found in the Archive of the Smolensk party organization, captured by the Germans in 1941 and, in turn, by the Americans at the end of World War II (see Merle Fainsod, *Smolensk under Soviet Rule*, Vintage edition, New York, 1958, pp. 318-320). This decree was preceded by a circular of the Commissariat of Justice, dated May 22, 1931, and signed by Vyshinsky. It scolded the employees of this Commissariat for unfounded prosecutions and careless arrests of specialists and managers, which disrupted industrial production (*Sovetskaia iustitsiia*, no. 16, 1931, 15). This may indicate that the Politburo had already begun to change policy in this area before the Central Committee circular in June.

[28] Fainsod, *Smolensk*, p. 319.

shops, heads of construction, heads of technical and like divisions and other leading positions." A variety of measures was prescribed for increasing the living standards of engineering and technical personnel. Their status was to be enhanced by praise and material rewards for good work: "The leaders of enterprises and institutions must in every way encourage specialists to display inventiveness in their work, skillful leadership, energy and initiative through rewarding them with premiums, writing in the press about their achievements, and in especially outstanding cases, nominating engineering-technical workers for rewards."[29]

That many specialists had been sentenced to forced labor for technical mistakes and other shortcomings of the economy was implied by the emphasis this decree gave to curbing the legal actions inflicted upon members of the technical intelligentsia. They were no longer to be criminally liable simply for unsatisfactory results in their work. Administrators were directed to "offer to the engineering and technical personnel the opportunity to display broad initiative in the rationalization and improvement of the processes of production—unsatisfactory results are to be subject to technical and economic analysis by leaders of factories and units alone." The independent power of the police in the economy was to be curbed. The decree prohibited "the organs of the militia [the regular police force], the criminal investigative department, and the procuracy to interfere in the productive life of the factory and to investigate production matters without special permission from the director of the enterprises or higher organs."

The Central Committee also forbade "the party organizations to change, correct, or delay the operative orders of the directors of the factories" and considered inexpedient "the presence of official representatives of the OGPU in the enterprises." Although later evidence shows that this last stricture did not become the rule—the secret police generally retained their representatives in factories, while party organizations continued to interfere in the work of the factory directors—this decree did herald an important change in the status of the technical intelligentsia.

Even those specialists who had been sentenced to forced labor for their mistakes were to have their cases reviewed, implying that some specialists may have been harshly or even unjustly punished. Administrators were ordered to "review the cases of those specialists tried and sentenced to forced labor for defects which they allowed in work and for blunders and violation of labor legislation. With regard to sentenced specialists who have proven by their work devotion to the cause of social-

[29] Ibid.

ist construction, annul the sentence, eliminating entries from their work papers."[30]

This decree did nothing directly to connect these changes with the show trials and arrests of engineers for wrecking. But in his comments a few weeks later, Stalin made the connection clearer. Speaking at a conference of industrial managers in Moscow, Stalin reviewed the party's policy toward the old specialists for the previous several years and the reasons now for reversing it:

> Some two years ago a situation developed in which the most qualified section of the old technical intelligentsia was infected with the illness of wrecking. More than that, wrecking became something of a fashion. Some practiced it, others covered up for the wreckers, yet others wavered between the wreckers and the Soviet power. Of course, the majority of the old technical intelligentsia continued to work more or less loyally. But the question here is not about the majority, but about the most qualified part of the technical intelligentsia.
>
> . . .
>
> If even some old Bolsheviks from the right wing deviationists could not withstand this "infection" and were drawn away from the party at this time, then it is not surprising that a particular section of the old technical intelligentsia, never savoring Bolshevism, likewise, with God's help, wavered.
>
> It is understandable that as things stood then, the Soviet power could practice only one policy toward the old technical intelligentsia—the repression of active wreckers, neutralizing those who were uncommitted and attracting those who were loyal.
>
> Such was the situation a year or two ago.
>
> Can we say that we now face the same situation? No, we cannot. On the contrary, we now have an entirely different situation. To begin with, we have fought and successfully overcome the capitalist elements of city and countryside. Of course, the old intelligentsia will not rejoice in this. . . .
>
> In addition, for six years intervention seemed likely, and not once was intervention attempted. It is time to confess that our sagacious bourgeois intelligentsia was simply leading us by the nose. I do not even mention the fact that the conduct of the active wreckers in the well-publicized trial in Moscow [Industrial party] must have and in fact has deglamorized the idea of sabotage.

[30] Ibid.

It is understandable that these new circumstances could not remain without effect on our old technical intelligentsia. The new situation had to create and did create new attitudes among the old technical intelligentsia. This explains the definite signs we have that a portion of this intelligentsia which earlier sympathized with the wreckers has now come over to the side of the Soviet power. The fact that not only this stratum of the old intelligentsia, but even some of yesterday's wreckers are beginning to work in many plants and factories side by side with the working class—this fact without doubt demonstrates that a change has already begun among the old technical intelligentsia.[31]

Beyond the reasons given above, the question remains why Stalin publicly sanctioned such a reversal in 1931, when he had remained silent regarding specialist-baiting and related problems during the three years following the Shakhty trial. There are probably several reasons for this, in addition to the pressure exerted by Ordzhonikidze and others directly concerned with industry. By the middle of 1931, the technical intelligentsia no longer represented a strong political threat to his position in the party. Stalin's opponents in the so-called Right Opposition, such as Bukharin, Tomsky, and Rykov had lost their struggle to oust him from the Politburo, and had themselves been ousted from their positions at the pinnacle of various hierarchies. The old specialists, who had held considerable influence in the Soviet system, while at the same time nursing some grievances against the system, no longer could so easily line up with the moderate opposition, providing the necessary skills for running the economy without the Stalinists. By 1931, they had been humiliated and put under tighter party and police controls. According to available records, many, if not all, eventually resumed work in their professions, often as prisoner specialists under the supervision of the OGPU.[32]

---

[31] I. V. Stalin, *Sochineniia*, vol. 13, pp. 70-72.

[32] Allan Monkhouse, *Moscow 1911-1933*, Boston, 1934, p. 265; John Scott, *Behind the Urals*, Boston, 1942, p. 89; Hilger, pp. 246-247; Anton Ciliga, *Au Pays de Mensonge Déconcernant*, Paris, 1950, pp. 109-111. Several articles appeared in *Za industrializatsiiu* on Jan. 6, 1933, praising four engineers who had been implicated in the Industrial party case and had subsequently worked in the Economic Section of the OGPU as prisoner specialists. They had designed and built a type of blooming mill (manufacturing steel ingots) that had previously been imported from abroad, thus saving the Soviet government millions of rubles. These articles, which had the sponsorship of Ordzhonikidze, Commissar of Heavy Industry at the time, served as a form of rehabilitation for such prisoner specialists. Their original guilt was not called into question, but they were now said to have been won over to loyal support of the Soviets by their work as prisoner specialists, and their professional reputations were given a renewed boost.

Also by 1931, the first waves of young "red specialists" were completing their educations and going into industry. Recruited from the ranks of party members and industrial workers, they were to replace the "bourgeois specialists" in responsible positions, in Stalin's view. They were part of a massive new emphasis on higher technical education, and their presence would soon obscure the small number of old specialists, some of whom were approaching retirement age. For these young specialists to work effectively, the authority of the technical intelligentsia as a whole needed a large boost.

Stalin had little to fear from the mass of new technical talent. The majority knew to whom they owed their rise from obscurity. It was Stalin and his apparatus who favored recruiting as many students as possible from the industrial workers and who insisted on a quota system that gave them preference in admissions to higher technical education, as we shall see in the following chapter. It was the Stalinists who had commandeered thousands of young Communists to become engineers, giving them higher stipends and privileges not enjoyed by other students. These new "red specialists" were people who had grown up largely under Soviet conditions; few had worked in capitalist industry, and many were accustomed to accepting party discipline. They seemed to promise a more loyal and subservient technical intelligentsia for the immediate future.

Stalin was quick to clarify that the change of policy toward the technical intelligentsia did not mean that the danger of sabotage from this group had passed. In June 1931, he said: "There are and will be wreckers as long as we have classes and as long as we are encircled by capitalism." He now considered such saboteurs largely isolated from any wide public support, however. As a result, they would be forced to go even deeper underground. But for the first time in this period, Stalin put his full public support behind a statement condemning specialist-baiting:

> If at the height of sabotage our attitude to the old technical intelligentsia was expressed chiefly as a policy of repression, then now, when this intelligentsia is turning toward the Soviet power, our attitude toward it must be expressed chiefly in a policy of attraction and concern for it. It would be incorrect and undialectical to continue the old policy in new and changed conditions. It would be stupid and unwise now to view virtually every specialist and engineer of the old school as a criminal and saboteur to be caught. "Specialist baiting" always has been considered by us and remains a harmful and shameful phenomenon.[33]

[33] *Sochineniia*, vol. 13, pp. 70-72.

The trade union organization of the technical intelligentsia was quick to read the signals from Stalin's speech and the change in policy by the Central Committee. VMBIT had only lately condemned its ousted leader, S. D. Shein, for stirring up discontent regarding the arrest of engineers. It now began to discuss and condemn specialist-baiting for the first time in many months.[34]

Only a few months before, the trade union leadership insisted that VMBIT should concentrate its work on the struggle to unmask wreckers and should fight against "blind worship of scientific and technical authorities," making its prime task an increase in production. Now the emphasis shifted back somewhat to an older position. Once again a basic task of these trade union organizations was the protection of the technical intelligentsia from unjust accusations: "A prime function of an official of the engineering-technical sections is the preliminary investigation of any case involving accusations of an engineering-technical worker, in order to prevent instances of unfounded prosecutions. The participation of an official representative of the engineering-technical sections in the discussion of such affairs is therefore especially valuable."[35] The presidium of VMBIT, referring to Stalin's June speech, resolved to wage an energetic struggle against every "kind of distortion and exaggeration on the part of managerial investigators and judicial organs in instances involving the legal liability of engineering-technical workers."[36]

It remains to ask what actual effect such decrees, speeches, and resolutions had on the legal position and status of the technical intelligentsia. The special form of terror directed particularly at the old specialists from 1928 until 1931 largely ceased. The balance began to swing from an emphasis on conflict between a major element of the technostructure and other groups in Soviet society to an emphasis on positive incentives to attract the technical specialists, old and new, toward greater cooperation in building a new society. Although conflict by no means disappeared, the authority, pay, career prospects, and general status of the technical intelligentsia as a whole increased greatly after 1931. The situation faced by the mass of new "red specialists" who came into the Soviet economy from higher education in the 1930s was considerably different from that faced by their predecessors. Who were these new specialists and what attitudes and experiences did they bring with them from their years as students? The following chapter will attempt to answer these questions.

[34] *IT*, no. 19-20, 1931, 438, 439; no. 30, 1931, 722-723.
[35] Ibid., no. 30, 1931, 722-723.
[36] Ibid.

PART 3

The New Specialists: Recruitment and Education, 1928-1941

7

CULTURAL REVOLUTION AND THE CREATION OF A NEW TECHNICAL INTELLIGENTSIA, 1928-1933

Education is a weapon, whose effect depends on who holds it in his hands and at whom it is aimed.

Stalin

There is a certain minimum of general scientific culture which an engineer must master and which we cannot dispense with. We must not lower the theoretical studies of our engineers, otherwise we will be defeated . . . in that economic struggle we are conducting with the bourgeois world.

Lunacharsky

Fundamental to an understanding of the Soviet Union in the years from 1928 to 1933 is a controversy over the creation of a new technical intelligentsia. The issues involved are interesting for their own sake, but this controversy has implications that go beyond the immediate context of Soviet society in upheaval during the First Five-Year Plan. They touch on a more general question: the relationship between science, technology, and higher education in an industrializing society, particularly under a socialist system. This chapter deals with the specifics of this controversy and some of the more general implications of these events.

The launching of the First Soviet Five-Year Plan made the expansion of technical education a necessity, yet the existing educational system was not producing the required numbers of competent people. Although this was a period of great faith in technology, there was no immediate consensus on how technical knowledge was to be acquired by a wider segment of the population. The policy disputes over this question involved the higher organs of the Communist party and conflicting institutional interests in the Soviet government and the engineering profession. Underlying these disputes were differences in cultural values and social interests that divided not only the upper

159

levels of the party and government, but a variety of other groups within Soviet society. The issues were complicated because the existing technical intelligentsia, whose cooperation was necessary for a solution to this problem, was considered "bourgeois" by many proletarian and Communist party activists and was widely distrusted. The issue of "class war," therefore, became involved, as it did in so many other areas of the cultural revolution during these years, and made the question of creating a new technical intelligentsia a highly charged issue.

Before turning to the conflicting institutional and group interests involved, we should note a basic clash of cultural values in Soviet education at the beginning of this period, namely that between the proponents of what I will call here "socialist humanism" and the advocates of more immediate specialization in science and technology. This conflict is somewhat analogous to the difference between the "liberal arts" tradition in the West and the advocates of greater vocational and technical training.

The tradition of socialist humanism in Soviet education was most widely articulated during the 1920s by Anatol Lunacharsky, Commissar of Education from 1917 to 1929. Lunacharsky placed a high value on the development of human personality through a broadly based education that would liberate people from the fetters of narrow specialization. If anything, he leaned more toward the arts and humanities in education than science and technology.[1] This approach, never unchallenged after 1917, was increasingly questioned in the cultural revolution after 1928. Not least among the challengers was Stalin. His words on the subject were turned into slogans and repeated in a litany familiar to any reader of the Soviet press in these years: "Technology in the period of reconstruction decides everything," "Bolsheviks must master technology," etc.[2] Many of Stalin's opponents within the

[1] For Lunacharsky's views on education see the following: *Problemy narodnogo obrazovaniia*, Moscow, 1923; *Prosveshchenie v sovetskoi rossii*, Moscow, 1924; *Osnovy prosvetitel'noi politiki sovetskoi vlasti*, Moscow, 1924; *A. V. Lunacharskii o narodnom obrazovanii*, Moscow, 1958. For his biography and early role in the Soviet government, see Sheila Fitzpatrick, *The Commissariat of Enlightenment*, Cambridge, Mass., 1970, and for his intellectual background and views of culture, see K. E. Bailes, "Sur la 'Theorie des Valeurs' de A. V. Lunacarskij," *Cahiers du Monde Russe et Soviétique*, vol. 8, no. 2, pp. 223-243.

The first version of this chapter was presented as a paper at a conference on "Cultural Revolution in Soviet Russia," sponsored by the ACLS and held at the Russian Institute, Columbia University, November 1974. My thanks to Professor Sheila Fitzpatrick, the organizer of that conference, and Professor Loren R. Graham for their many useful comments and criticisms. For the other papers presented there, see Sheila Fitzpatrick, ed., *Cultural Revolution in Soviet Russia, 1928-1931*, Bloomington, Indiana, 1977.

[2] For a fuller collection of Stalin's remarks on this subject, see I. V. Stalin, *O tekhnike: podbor vazhneishikh vyderzhek*, Moscow, 1931.

party, such as Bukharin, shared his concern for expanding technical knowledge in the cultural revolution. Bukharin, for example, wrote in 1931: "The problem of the cultural revolution turns out to be a problem of technical culture. . . . We have got to understand that the whole of our culture must be much less 'literary and humanistic' in the old sense of the term, and in a certain sense become much more 'technical.' "[3]

If such disparate leaders as Stalin and Bukharin agreed on the enhanced importance of technical education, however, there was little agreement on the specifics of how to create a new technical intelligentsia. Even among the proponents of more vocational, technically oriented education, therefore, a clash of social and institutional interests surfaced. We will examine several key areas of disagreement in these next pages: who should administer higher technical education—economic managers, student organizations, professional educators; who should become technical specialists, i.e., what criteria should be used to select people for higher technical education; what kind of technical education should they receive, a narrow specialization or a broader polytechnic and scientific background.

The debate over these questions can be divided into two major periods. A series of radical changes was debated and adopted between 1928 and 1929 and then was largely reversed in 1932 and 1933. One of the mysteries of the cultural revolution in this period concerns this reversal in the early 1930s. Did the switch to milder policies indicate a retroactive victory by the earlier opponents of the more radical line, many of them anti-Stalinist, or was such reversal the reflection of a more general problem of industrial society, a lesson learned in the trial-and-error process of industrialization and cultural revolution, and endorsed fully by Stalin? Some answers to these complex questions will be suggested.[4]

The beginning of this controversy was shaped especially by the Shakhty case of 1928 and its aftermath. In early April 1928, the party's Central Committee met to discuss the Shakhty affair. Beyond the more general purpose that the Shakhty affair served in Stalin's scheme of things, it opened a major debate over the creation of a new technical

[3] N. Bukharin, *Socialist Reconstruction and the Struggle for Technique*, Moscow, 1932, pp. 14-19.

[4] After turning up new evidence and rethinking this topic, I am proposing a revision of my own earlier ideas (as stated in my dissertation), as well as some of the views put forward by Sheila Fitzpatrick in her recent article, "Cultural Revolution in Russia, 1928-32," *Journal of Contemporary History*, January 1974, 33-52, and by James McClellan, in the paper he delivered to the Pacific Coast Branch of the American Historical Association in 1975, "Stalin's Changing Educational Goals: Proletarianizing the Student Body," pp. 5, 15, and 23.

intelligentsia. This debate first crystallized around three issues: institutional control of higher technical education; proletarianization of the student body; and narrow specialization of the curriculum.

Although a number of resolutions on the Shakhty affair were passed at the April plenum of the Central Committee, a sharp disagreement first developed over the question of institutional control. Stalin, in a surprise move, put forward a resolution to turn over control of all higher technical education to the Supreme Council of the Economy (*Vesenkha*), that is, to the industrial managers. Rykov, who headed the Politburo commission appointed just before this plenum to draw practical conclusions from the Shakhty affair, opposed the move. He defended the Commissariat of Education (*Narkompros*), which controlled most higher technical education at this time. Although the actual transcript of this plenum has not been made public, apparently Stalin failed to rally the necessary support, according to a contemporary report in the Trotsky archive at Harvard, which is consistent with what happened subsequently.[5] Stalin's resolution was defeated by two-thirds of those voting, with some abstentions. This defeat led to a struggle in the ensuing months not only over the administrative control of higher technical education, but more substantively over its content and quality. The issue was vital: what kind of person would the new Soviet specialist be? *Narkompros* and *Vesenkha* represented very different positions on this question.

At this time, the Central Committee passed a rather watery resolution, stating that *Vesenkha* should exercise more control over the selection of students to higher technical schools, assuring the predominance of those who were workers by social origin. Details of how this was to be done remained vague, however, and control over higher technical education was left for the time being to *Narkompros*. A major debate over this question developed in the press between April and July of 1928, when the Central Committee again took up the question. That the issue was opened for wide debate would, of itself, seem to indicate that the party apparatus was gathering information and wanted additional points of view.[6] It is interesting to compare the various positions expressed publicly by important groups and individuals and the actual changes eventually adopted. In this way, we can gain a clearer idea of the alignment of forces at this time.

[5] Trotsky's letter to leading supporters, undated, but, according to internal evidence, written sometime early in June 1928 (Trotsky Archive, Houghton Library, Harvard University, T 1588).

[6] See the calendar of Politburo activities published in *TPG*, April 12, 1928. See also A. I. Lutchenko, "Rukovodtsvo KPSS formirovaniem kadrov tekhnicheskoi intelligentsii (1926-1933 gg.)," in *Voprosy istorii KPSS*, no. 2, 1966, 31.

The Politburo members, Rykov and Bukharin, supported creating a Soviet technical intelligentsia through the established channels of *Narkompros*. They urged not a change in administrative controls, but large new appropriations to the established institutions of education up and down the line—in elementary, secondary, and higher education. As Rykov pointed out, a more balanced investment policy between material production and education was the real requirement: "The chief obstacle in the final analysis, is our technical and cultural backwardness, which cannot be abolished in the course of a year or two. In order to overcome it, we need huge disbursements for cultural-educational work, for the development of our higher educational institutions and special scientific establishments."[7] Stalin, Kuibyshev, and higher industrial management gave their greatest attention to higher technical education, disappointing the moderates who sought measures that would go to the root of cultural backwardness.

Two days following the end of the plenum, Stalin made his first public comment on the Shakhty case and its implications. His comments, though calling for more technically literate Communist managers, were very critical of higher technical education, describing recent graduates as too bookish and cut off from production and practical needs.[8] Only a month later, at the Congress of Young Communists held in May, did Stalin add his public voice to the chorus of Soviet leaders who—in connection with the Shakhty affair—called for the creation of a new technical intelligentsia. In contrast to Rykov, he maintained, "We must train *at a high speed* new cadres of experts, drawn from the working class, Communists, and members of the Young Communist League."[9] Stalin thus put himself at the head of those who wanted a rapid proletarianization and politicization of the students in such schools.

What was the position of the technical intelligentsia on such questions? There was no general agreement. A number of the older engineers prominent in *Gosplan* and higher technical education in 1928 and 1929 rallied to the defense of *Narkompros* and the position represented by its Chief Administration for Professional Education (*Glavprofobr*).[10] This included an opposition to class quotas, entrance rather to be based

---

[7] *Torgovo-promyshlennaia gazeta* (*TPG*), April 20, 1928.

[8] I. V. Stalin, *Collected Works*, vol. 11, Moscow, 1954, p. 63.

[9] Ibid., p. 80.

[10] Particularly striking evidence of this is the book published by *Glavprofobr* (probably in early 1928), containing the answers of forty-five outstanding specialists and managers, most of them engineers, to a questionnaire circulated by *Narkompros* on the general theme: "What Kind of Engineer Must Our Higher Technical Schools Prepare?" (*Kakogo inzhenera dolzhny gotovit' nashi vtuzy: otzyvy deiateli promyshlennosti, nauki, i tekhniki*, I. I. Khodorovskii, ed., Moscow, 1928.)

on talent through competitive examinations, and an emphasis on poly-technic education rather than shortcuts based on narrow specialization.[11] Other members of the technical intelligentsia, including a few who were party members or fellow travellers, leaned toward the more radical line, but they were probably a minority of prominent engineering professors, as things turned out.

The trade union for the technical intelligentsia (VMBIT) criticized many engineering professors for neglecting their students in order to do industrial consulting. Although it called for closer ties between higher technical education and industry, it largely sidestepped the controversial questions of class quotas and administrative control at this time.[12] The union did take a clear stand on one issue: technical education, in its view, should not become narrowly specialized, but should prepare two types of engineers: those of high qualifications and those of more nar-row, practical orientation (*ispolniteli*).

Strongest support among elements of the technical intelligentsia for more radical policies at this time came from the fledgling, Marxist pro-fessional organization for scientists and engineers (VARNITSO), al-though even here there seems to have been disagreement among its members.[13] In 1928, this organization supported the more radical

[11] See also K. E. Bailes, "Stalin and Revolution from Above: The Formation of the Soviet Technical Intelligentsia, 1928-1934," Ph.D. diss., Columbia University, 1971, pp. 346-356, 376.

[12] *TPG*, May 8, 1928.

[13] Begun a year earlier by a small group of party members and supporters among scientists, engineers, and other members of the intelligentsia who held high positions in industry, education, and research, the organization had a twofold purpose: winning over the specialists to a Marxist outlook and to cooperation with the party and government in building socialism, and, at the same time, serving as a lobby for their own interests within the Soviet system. For example, its leadership contained a number of prominent chemists, and it was particularly active in pro-moting the development of a chemical industry. The government responded favor-ably to a petition signed by some of its leaders in March 1928, and appointed a Committee for Chemicalization, headed by a Politburo member and composed of prominent VARNITSO members to supervise such development (German Tru-kans, *Ian Rudzutak*, Moscow, 1963; V. S. Lelchuk, "Deiatel'nost komiteta po khi-mizatsii, 1928-34," *Istoriia SSSR*, no. 3, 1958, 201-203).

In 1928, VARNITSO still had fewer than a thousand members, although they included many prominent scholars of Marxism, as well as applied scientists and some engineers. An idea of its activities can be gained from the transcript of its first national conference, held just after the Central Committee plenum in April 1928. One of its founders, Zbarsky, a chemical technologist, maintained that a fundamental task of the organization was to attract the intelligentsia away from those hostile toward the Soviet system. The Communist party had not been suf-ficiently active in attracting and helping specialists, he maintained, partly because such a small percentage of the party membership came from the intelligentsia. (In 1927, ninety-one percent of all party members had only a primary education or less. Only eight-tenths of one percent had a higher education, according to T. H.

position, with apparent reservations by some of its members, however. In the 1930s it became a forum for critics of the radical line.

The transcript and resolutions of the April 1928 conference of this organization, and its later publications show that VARNITSO tried to act as a pressure group on the left wing of the intelligentsia, as well as representing to the government and party interests of the intelligentsia considered vital by its members.

The report on higher technical education at this conference was given by O. Y. Shmidt. A 1913 graduate of Kiev University in mathematics, and a member of the party since 1918, Shmidt leaned toward the radical line. He had been in charge of higher technical education (*Glavprofobr*) at *Narkompros* during the civil war, when he had favored shortening the education of engineers to a three-year course, instead of the five years required by a polytechnic curriculum. He also had favored attracting far greater numbers of proletarians, introducing mandatory study of Marxism, and ending the autonomy of higher education. As head of a commission established in 1920 to develop the first Soviet charters for higher education, he was at the center of controversy. Thanks to the resistance of much of the professoriate, led by a number of engineers at the Moscow Higher Technical School, the charter developed by Shmidt's commission was eventually revised in a compromise that Lenin and other high party leaders insisted upon.[14] Shmidt admitted in 1928 that most of what he had advocated earlier had yet to be realized.

In his report to VARNITSO at this time, Shmidt reiterated much of his earlier program. His remarks shed interesting light on the thinking of the more radical members of the intelligentsia. Preferential quotas for proletarians were essential, he maintained, and gave an interesting rationale:

Rigby: *Communist Party Membership in the USSR, 1917-1967*, Princeton, 1968, 401.) In Zbarsky's view, VARNITSO could help here by attracting more specialists to active cooperation and to party membership. (*Biulleten' VARNITSO*, no. 2, 1928, *Stenograficheskii otchet I Vsesoiuznoi Konferentsii, 26-28 April 1928, 67*). As Prof. Zavadovsky, another founding member, put it, members of VARNITSO must accept the hegemony of the party, but reserve the right to criticize: "We must not simply be bureaucrats and civil servants without the right to speak out about mistakes." (Ibid.) Engineer Stuikhel agreed that VARNITSO should criticize poor organization and mistakes made in the process of industrialization. (Ibid., pp. 112-113). Such remarks brought a caveat from a party *apparatchik* in attendance, who warned that VARNITSO must not become a political party for the intelligentsia (*Biulleten' VARNITSO*, no. 1, 1928, 34).

[14] TsGA RSFSR, f. 2306, op. 1, d. 596, l. 25; op. 2, d. 1777, ll. 15, cited in T. M. Smirnova, "Reforma vysshei shkoly RSFSR, 1917-1922 gg.," diss. in Lenin Library, Moscow, pp. 110, 206. For a general discussion of these events see the same source, pp. 205-276; see also Shmidt's article in *Pravda*, Feb. 21, 1921, outlining the proposed changes.

There exists an opinion that entrance to higher education must not be based on representatives of this or that class, but on those who are most able. Since only a small percent of Soviet youth can enter higher education, we must make all classes equal and find a way of selecting the most talented. When we heard this from representatives of the intelligentsia who are hostile to class quotas, we did not believe it but felt that beneath this argument lay a desire to make access to higher education more difficult for the children of workers, especially since the kind of entrance exams employed require a quick intellectual grasp of the bookish type.[15]

According to Shmidt, children of the proletariat were best adapted for careers in technology, since "they have a more concrete form of thinking, useful in engineering, than bourgeois intellectuals with two ancient languages."[16] Furthermore, he maintained, the proletariat displayed more determination in mastering technical knowledge and more enthusiasm for the task. He acknowledged that some, even in VARNITSO, doubted the wisdom of such a policy, pointing to the abuses and fraud practiced when such preferential policies had been followed prior to 1926. Care would have to be taken to prevent others from posing as children of workers, he noted.

On the question of narrow specialization versus polytechnic education, Shmidt indicated that he leaned toward shortening the course and adding more actual production practice in industry as part of the curriculum, although "it must be decided whether we need one or two types of engineers."[17] His doubts in this regard are significant in light of what later happened.

Many leading specialists, he noted, opposed production practice (practice work) as part of the curriculum, believing that higher technical schools should give a general theoretical preparation, leaving actual production experience to the first several years of an engineer's work career. Dragging out a young person's time in school, Shmidt felt, was just another way in which those already established in engineering slowed down entrance into the profession. They reasoned as follows, he postulated: "We had to study for so many years, then let the new ones also study for so many years, so that access to our privileged caste will be made more difficult."[18] VARNITSO went on record to endorse Shmidt's recommendations in most respects. For example, the conference called on its members to support preferential class quotas for the proletariat, an increase in political education, and closer ties of higher

---

[15] *Biulleten' VARNITSO*, no. 2, 1928, 120-121.
[16] Ibid., 119.   [17] Ibid., 121-122.   [18] Ibid., 122.

education with industry, warning, however, against purely formal ties, "of the administrative type, from above." The Conference ducked the direct question of *Narkompros* control versus a transfer to the industrial managers of *Vesenkha*.[19] It also ducked the question of polytechnic education versus a narrower specialization. These omissions are probably significant, given the change in position by this organization in the early 1930s.

Other organizations were to deal with the latter two questions more directly in 1928. One of the most important youth organizations at this time was the Union of Proletarian Students (*Soiuz proletarskikh studentov*). Similar to the trade unions, it acted as a lobby for the interests of students from working class backgrounds. The Central Bureau of this organization held a plenum in April 1928, in which it criticized the average length of study in engineering courses and many other aspects of higher technical education.[20] These included the absence of close ties with production, and a curriculum that lagged far behind the latest advances in technology and the needs of the Soviet economy. In its resolutions, this organization called for a restructuring of the higher technical schools that would put them under the control of the trade unions, of which this organization was a part, as well as *Vesenkha*. Each higher technical school should be attached to the economic organ that employed its graduates. This change, in the opinion of the Central Bureau, would help to coordinate curriculum planning and provide students more opportunities for practice work in their areas of specialization.[21] Considering that proletarian students played an important, even a key, role in the governance of universities and institutes at this time, their alliance with Stalin and *Vesenkha* on this question is significant, although their desire to share in the administration of higher technical education eventually proved incompatible with the Stalinist program.

In the spring of 1928 the management of *Vesenkha* developed the line that control by industry was necessary to fill the manpower needs of industry. The official newspaper of *Vesenkha* became the forum for a number of articles on the subject. In May, for example, a report appeared concerning the views of professors and students at the Moscow Higher Technical School (MVTU). This was the MIT of the Soviet Union, with some six thousand students at the time. According to the article, the majority of students and professors wanted the institution transferred to the control of *Vesenkha*. A minority preferred to stay under *Narkompros*, fearing that the industrial managers would mass produce only narrow specialists.[22] The source of this report and the exact figures for

[19] Ibid., 202-204.   [20] *TPG*, April 27, 1928.   [21] Ibid.
[22] *TPG*, May 15, 1928.

those taking sides are not given. One may doubt its accuracy, especially when one considers that many of the professors at MVTU had been at the center of efforts in 1918 through 1922 to resist changes similar to those represented by *Vesenkha* in 1928. This article does again suggest, however, that the technical intelligentsia, including the engineering professoriate, was divided on this question in 1928.

One reason some engineering professors favored the administrative change was financial. This was the reason, for example, given by the dean of the Electromechanical Faculty of MVTU, who in supporting the transfer, recalled favorably that Ministries had supported their own educational institutions generously under the Tsars![23] Butiagin, the vice rector of MVTU, reported that in the current academic year his school had received only forty-three percent of its budget requests. In the previous four years only eleven percent of the funds requested for replacing outworn laboratory equipment had been granted. Students were often forced to prolong their studies for seven years or more because of inadequate financial aid. (In fact, other figures show that only a small minority of all Soviet engineering students completed the five-year course in the alloted time.[24] Faculty salaries were so low that some two-thirds held three other jobs, teaching or consulting for industry.)[25]

The views of *Vesenkha* were further developed in a series of articles and speeches by members of its presidium during May and June.[26] They encouraged students in higher technical schools (*vtuzy*) to speak out about the faults of the educators. According to an assistant of Kuibyshev, a Politburo member and head of *Vesenkha*, who was responsible for manpower development, all *vtuzy* should be directly attached to the largest factories or enterprises for which they provided specialists, echoing the proposal of the Union of Proletarian Students. He advocated that these higher schools, like industry, should be open year round and that the maximum course of study should not exceed five years in practice. To make this a reality, adequate stipends would be provided students, and the cost of technical education generally would be underwritten from the budget for capital investment in industry.

Lunacharsky and his colleagues at *Narkompros* were quick to re-

[23] Ibid.

[24] According to a recent Soviet dissertation, citing an archival source, almost ninety-two percent of all students at MVTU before 1929 took seven or more years to complete the five-year course (MPA, f. 158, op. 1, ed. khr. 42, 1. 158, cited in S. F. Klishin, "Moskovskaia partiinaia organizatsiia v bor'be za podgotovku inzhenerno-tekhnicheskikh kadrov, 1928-1937 gg.," diss. in Lenin Library, Moscow, 1967, p. 44).

[25] *TPG*, May 15, 1928.

[26] See, e.g., *TPG*, June 16, 1928; *Pravda*, June 21, 1928.

spond to the barrage of criticism.[27] In his conciliatory way, Lunacharsky granted the validity of many of the criticisms, but pleaded inadequate financial support from the government. He agreed that more proletarian students must be attracted and that technical education must be brought closer to industry, but he neatly sidestepped the question of class quotas and opposed the transfer of *vtuzy* to the industrial managers. (In 1929, after class quotas had been adopted, Lunacharsky wrote to Stalin to protest vigorously the exclusion of nonproletarian students and professors from higher education.)[28]

The basic problem, Lunacharsky maintained, was not the question of control, but of greater support for all education. Industry tended to concentrate on only one aspect—higher technical education—to the neglect of more general cultural and educational tasks. Concerning current budgets for education, he noted, "It is as if, discovering that it is possible to live with four fingers, they have decided to cut off the 'extra' finger."[29]

The reason for *Narkompros'* opposition to many of the changes proposed was based on the need for quality education, according to Lunacharsky: "There is a certain minimum of general scientific culture which an engineer must master and which we cannot dispense with. We must not lower the theoretical studies of our engineers, otherwise we will be defeated . . . in that economic struggle we are conducting with the bourgeois world."[30] Lunacharsky and other opponents of the radical line, however, were overruled by the policy changes adopted at this time. The July plenum marked the beginning of a series of new policies.

A great deal of detail has been related above, to give the reader some idea of the spectrum of opinion expressed publicly in 1928 on issues involving the creation of a new technical intelligentsia. It is interesting to see which of these positions were adopted, and their results. Despite the opposition of Rykov, who opposed class quotas, high preferential quotas for proletarians were adopted.[31] Rykov preferred the more neutral term "Soviet specialists" to "new red specialists," bringing to the July plenum a whole pocketful of quotations from Lenin to support his

---

[27] *A. V. Lunacharskii o narodnom obrazovanii*, Moscow, 1958, p. 431.

[28] S. A. Fediukin, *Sovetskaia vlast' i burzhuaznye spetsialisty*, Moscow, 1965, p. 144; TsPA IML, f. 142, op. 1, ed. khr. 42, l. 40, cited in L. I. Brodskii, "Ideino-politicheskoe vospitanie tekhnicheskikh spetsialistov dorevoliutsiionnoi shkoly v gody pervoi piatiletki," *Trudy Leningradskogo politekhnicheskogo instituta, Obshchestvennye nauki*, no. 261, 72; TsPA IML, f. 142, op. 1, d. 465, l. 64, cited in S. A. Fediukin *Velikii oktiabr' i intelligentsiia*, Moscow, 1973, pp. 392-393.

[29] *Narodnoe prosveshchenie*, no. 5, 1928, 5; see also the report of Lunacharsky's assistant, Khodorovsky, the head of *Glavprofobr*, in the same issue, pp. 64ff.

[30] *Lunacharskii o narodnom obrazovanii*, p. 438; *Pravda*, June 27, 1928.

[31] *Rabochaia Moskva*, July 17, 1928.

point, according to one source hostile to Rykov.[32] This seems plausible given Rykov's history as a patron of the old technical intelligentsia, continuing a policy of which Lenin had been a major initiator.[33]

On the question of administrative control, at this time, the July plenum transferred only six higher technical schools and five technicums to *Vesenkha*, but the process was accelerated in 1929, when Stalin's loyal supporter Kaganovich criticized *Narkompros* at the November plenum of the Central Committee for its penchant to produce "artists and ballet dancers."[34] By 1930, all of higher technical education had been transferred to economic organs. The reason can probably be found in Stalin's own attitude toward this question.

Stalin was blunt in his remarks just after the July 1928, plenum, revealing some of his own motivations: "The facts have shown that Narkompros has not been able to cope with this task [of educating a new technical intelligentsia]. We have no reason to assume that Narkompros, left to its own devices and with few ties to production, with its inertness and conservatism, will be able to cope with this task in the near future."[35]

At the time of the Sixteenth Party Congress in 1930, Stalin noted the earlier opposition of some elements to transferring only a few *vtuzy* to the control of economic managers. By then all had been transferred, Stalin noted, "And nothing [terrible] has happened. We are still alive."[36] Others were having doubts, however, including some important industrial managers.

Stalin's position on higher technical education in these years was probably colored as much by who controlled it and its results as by any careful consideration of its content or methodology. In other words, he was primarily concerned with ends rather than means, although he did have certain general attitudes toward the means that were to have important consequences between 1928 and 1932—particularly a general concern for speed, practicality, and the creation of "Bolshevik specialists" in technology. Beyond these general attitudes, however, there is no evidence that he had thought deeply about many of the issues discussed above. His views were, not surprisingly, influenced primarily by political considerations. In general, *Narkompros* was a bastion of people whom Stalin had long distrusted or disliked, and he had no desire to give aid

[32] G. K. Ordzhonikidze, *Stat'i i rechi*, Moscow, 1957, vol. 2, p. 231; see also TsPA IML, f. 17, op. 2, ed. khr. 3354, l. 79, cited in Lutchenko, p. 331; *Bol'shevik*, no. 23-24, December 31, 1929, 70; and V. V. Ukraintsev, *KPSS—organizator revoliutsionnogo preobrazovaniia vysshei shkoly*, Moscow, 1963, p. 151.

[33] See K. E. Bailes, "The Politics of Technology," *American Historical Review*, April 1974, 462.

[34] *Bol'shevik*, December 31, 1929, 56.

[35] *Sochineniia*, vol. 11, p. 216.   [36] *Prokof'ev*, p. 317.

or comfort to an institution allied with his new opponents in the Politburo, Rykov and Bukharin. As he later summed up his philosophy of
education in a remark to H. G. Wells, "Education is a weapon, whose
effect depends on who holds it in his hands and at whom it is aimed."[37]
Before loading that weapon, Stalin clearly intended to have firmer control on the trigger. After the July plenum, Stalin's crony, A. Y. Vyshinsky, was placed in charge of technical education at *Narkompros* (as
head of *Glavprofobr*), an organ that theoretically retained control over
curriculum and methodology until the changes of 1932, although this
arrangement proved unworkable in practice.[38] Lunacharsky resigned in
1929, after protesting many of the changes, and a Stalinist official,
Bubnov, former head of the Political Administration in the army and a
member of the party secretariat, succeeded him.[39]

With *Narkompros* emasculated, Stalin was willing to allow greater
appropriations to higher technical education and widespread experimentation, but there is little indication that he gave that area very much
personal attention. (There was not even a section of the party secretariat concerned primarily with education, science, and technology until
1935). Most of the internal changes in the *vtuzy* were carried out by the
industrial managers and the students themselves, at least until 1930.
Student power is an interesting issue in this connection, since the proletarian student organization had supported the radical position: class
quotas, a shorter course, narrower specialization, more practice work,
and a transfer of technical education to the control of *Vesenkha* and the
trade unions, of which this organization formed a part.

During the 1920s, student power had loomed large in the administration of Soviet higher education. Students, who were often civil war
veterans and party activists—older than the normal undergraduate before the revolution—not only shared in the administration of higher
education, their representatives from the proletarian student organization, Young Communists, and party cells commonly had the deciding
voice in how faculties were run. In 1930, however, student power was
ended, despite the opposition of the proletarian student organization at
its 1929 congress.[40]

[37] Interview of July 23, 1934 in Stalin, *Sochineniia*, vol. 1 (XIV), Robert H.
McNeal, ed., Stanford, Calif., 1967, p. 67.

[38] It is interesting to note that the former head of *Glavprofobr*, Khodorovsky,
eventually went to work for Ordzhonikidze, as did so many former oppositionists
and old specialists whom Ordzhonikidze seems to have protected. After 1930,
Khodorovsky was an official of *Glavtuz*, the industrial organ in charge of technical
education for *Vesenkha* and its successor, the Commissariat of Heavy Industry.

[39] Fediukin, *Sovetskaia vlast'*, p. 144.

[40] *Rezoliutsiia III vsesoiuznogo s"ezda proletarskogo studenchestva*, Moscow,
1929, p. 43.

Student activism had risen sharply with the onset of cultural revolution in 1928. As an official of *Vesenkha* noted in the fall of 1929, "It is no secret that the burden of the reform of thè higher technical school has rested on the shoulders of our students. Students organized uninterrupted practice work in production, re-examined the curriculum, conducted the reselection of professors. How much time have they left for academic work?"[41] The Assignments Department (*orgraspredotdel*) of the party's Central Committee conducted an investigation of student power in Moscow and Leningrad during January 1930, and found widespread abuses. For example, according to the student representative of the Chemical Faculty of the Leningrad Technological Institute, one of the country's leading higher technical schools: "The dean, in actual fact, drops in once a week. At meetings of the dean's office, the assistant dean takes no initiative and all questions are decided by agreement with the student representative. The latter is occupied with the entire direction of the faculty, for example, the hiring and firing of teachers, drawing up the schedule of classes and so forth."[42] Students played a major role in this period in the nationwide campaign for the reselection of professors, in which many older teachers were, for a time at least, excluded from teaching. They also frequently harassed professors with whom they disagreed. (A parallel to the radicalism of the student activists can be found in the activities of belligerent young Communist groups, such as those of the literary organization RAPP.)

But radical student activism came under increasing criticism, both from party and industrial spokesmen and the professors themselves, who were evidently not wholly intimidated by the student offensive.[43] At the Third Congress of Scientific Workers, held early in 1929, this trade union, which represented the professoriate, called for an end to student power.[44] Such professors apparently hoped for the support of the industrial managers and the party on this issue, and they proved correct in this expectation. Kaganovich, Stalin's loyal supporter in the Politburo, told the November 1929 plenum of the Central Committee that "order, in higher technical schools as in factories, must be strict," and went on to suggest changes in the way *vtuzy* were administered. Students should be freed from the administrative tasks they had assumed in higher education. These tasks should, in his view, be taken over by the rectors and deans, who would no longer be elected, but appointed

[41] *Nauchnyi rabotnik*, no. 4, 1929, 51ff; *ZI*, Jan. 25, 1930; Jan. 26, 1930.
[42] Ibid.   [43] *TPG*, Oct. 18, 1929.
[44] IMELS, f. 17, op. 8, d. 24, 1. 57, cited in V. E. Vovk, "Deiatel'nost' KPSS po podgotovke rukovodiashchikh khoziastvennykh i inzhenerno-teknicheskikh kadrov dlia promyshlennosti v gody sozdaniia fundamènta sotsialisticheskoi ekonomiki 1926-1932 gg.," diss., 1970, in Lenin Library, Moscow, p. 122.

by higher authority. Following Kaganovich's suggestion, the Central Committee resolved "to concentrate all administrative-pedagogical functions in the administrative organ of the higher technical schools, freeing the student organizations from these."[45]

In January 1930, the leadership of the Union of Proletarian Students was called in by the Central Trade Union Council, to which it was subordinate, and told to restructure its organization and make it oriented more toward "raising the class consciousness" of its members and less toward being administrators in higher education.[46] Student activists were firmly sent back to their studies and out of administration—a step conducive to the tightening of educational discipline and to the happiness of many professors. In return, the students got a higher level of financial support and were expected to study hard, joining the Komsomol and later the party.[47]

This change amounted to a minor revolution in Soviet higher technical education, and is significant for an understanding of the reversal of the radical line in 1932 and 1933. Since the student organizations, especially the proletarian and party activists among them, had provided much of the support for the radical line, and played an important role in carrying it out, their removal from power was a necessary, if not sufficient, condition for the reversal of that line. The sufficient condition, of course, was support for such reversal among the professoriate and particularly among industrial management. It also required at least neutrality, if not active support, among significant elements of the party leadership in the Politburo and Central Committee.

This leads us then to the changes of 1932 and 1933. What was changed, why did these changes occur, and who in fact initiated and supported them? These are difficult questions. The answers given here are tentative, but they should prove helpful in interpreting the turnabout.

The changes in higher technical education seem to be part of a pattern that dates at least from the spring of 1931 and the Seventeenth Party Conference in January and February of 1932. This pattern was marked by a general retreat from the cultural radicalism of the previous three years. The reversal was marked by a deemphasis and then an abolition of class quotas that favored the proletariat in higher technical education, a retreat from very narrow specialization, and a strong reemphasis on scientific theory and the polytechnic approach. If class warfare and "Bolshevik tempo" (i.e., speed) had been the dominant slogans of the

[45] *KPSS v rezoliutsiiakh*, part 2, p. 518.
[46] *Za industrializatsiiu* (hereafter *ZI*), Jan. 25, 1930; Jan. 26, 1930.
[47] *Sobranie zakonov i rasporiazhenii*, no. 47, Sept. 16, 1930, art. 488; no. 26, May 3, 1931, art. 206.

period 1928 to 1931, the changes after 1931 seem to be associated with the slogans of quality and cooperation: quality of work, quality of education, and a new cooperation among social groups, as long as they were united in "building socialism"—in other words, a partial return to the atmosphere of civil peace of the NEP period. One must emphasize a *partial* return, since Stalin and Molotov warned that any sign of renewed "wrecking by class hostile elements" would be severely repressed. Soviet periodicals after the spring of 1931 and the end of the last major show trial of that period (the "Menshevik party affair"), show the switch in emphasis, putting more stress on the catchword of quality.

What was the source of these changes? Stalin and his closest associates endorsed and perhaps even initiated some of them, but not all. Those they approved, they endorsed in their own way. Other authors have pointed to the existence of a moderate bloc in the Politburo and Central Committee, led by Ordzhonikidze and Kirov, that emerged in 1933 and 1934 and was responsible for a Second Five-Year Plan focused on somewhat lower growth rates and higher standards of quality. This bloc, according to some recent writers, served as a brake on Stalin's repressive policies until the purges of the later 1930s.[48]

The research for this study has led me to a similar conclusion, with one important difference. The emergence of a more moderate group can be dated as early as the spring of 1931, with its center of gravity among the industrial managers, headed by Ordzhonikidze, Commissar of Heavy Industry, and supported by his close friend in the Politburo, Kirov, party secretary of the heavily industrialized Leningrad region. In order to carry more moderate policies, of course, they needed, and apparently gained, support from some of the seven other members of the Politburo.[49]

Until more information is available regarding policy alignments

[48] See, for example, Leonard Schapiro, *The Communist Party of the Soviet Union*, New York, Vintage ed., 1964, pp. 392-398; Robert Conquest, *The Great Terror*, New York, 1968, pp. 27-42; Stephen F. Cohen, *Bukharin and the Bolshevik Revolution*, New York, 1973, pp. 337-358.

[49] The most likely candidates, judging from limited evidence, would have been Jan Rudzutak, V. I. Chubar, Stanislas Kossior, Vladimir Kuibyshev, and possibly Mikhail Kalinin on some issues. On Rudzutak and Kalinin, see below. On the others, see, for example, recent Soviet biographies: V. Z. Drobizhev and N. Dumiova, *V. Ya. Chubar*, Moscow, 1963; Pohrebinsky, *S. V. Kosior*, Kyiv, 1963; Anatolii I. Melchin, *Stanislav Kosior*, Moscow, 1964; Kuibyshev's role is not entirely clear. He was closely associated with the ever increasing Stalinist targets for industry, but, according to his later biographers, by the early 1930s he was pointing out to the Central Committee that the material means to realize such high production goals were not always boosted proportionately, and that this jeopardized their fulfillment (TsGANKh, f. 4372, op. 28, ed. khr. 16, l. 111), cited in G. B. Kuibysheva, et al., *V. V. Kuibyshev: Biografiia*, Moscow, 1966, pp. 305-306.

among the top party leadership, we must be content with only shreds of evidence and hints of the reasons for changes. The policy changes themselves are part of the record, however, and it is interesting to look at the evidence available for what preceded these changes, what discussion surrounded them, and the differing emphasis given them by staunch Stalinists, the "moderate" leadership postulated here, and elements of the technical intelligentsia who directly commented on them.

What reasons can we find for the development of more moderate views among elements of the Politburo, views closer to those expressed by Rykov, Bukharin, Lunacharsky, and some of the "old specialists" in 1928 and 1929? Basically, the earlier moderates had emphasized quality, a slower pace, more balanced growth, i.e., balanced between agriculture and industry, between consumer and heavy industry, between investment in material production and in all levels of education. The disasters of collectivization and the bottlenecks of industrialization in subsequent years may have been enough to turn some allies of Stalin into moderates. Actually, Ordzhonikidze, Kirov, and Kuibyshev had doubts about aspects of Stalinist policies as early as 1928, in the wake of the Shakhty affair and its aftermath. But having doubts and translating those doubts into strong pressure for change are two different things. Did such an evolution take place? I think it did, and that it can be dated at least from the spring of 1931.

We are told by recent Soviet sources that Kirov was appalled by the decline in the quality of production during this period, and by the witch hunt against many of the old specialists, some of whom he and the Leningrad party committee protected.[50] An unpublished Soviet memoir, cited by Medvedev, relates how Stalin and Ordzhonikidze also clashed over the failure of the iron and steel industry to reach impossibly high targets in this period. In February and again in June of 1931 Ordzhonikidze called together his top industrial managers to discuss the problems of industrialization. Among important conclusions reached at these meetings were those stressing the need for improvement in the technical direction of industry, greater industrial discipline, and a rapid increase in the technical knowledge of specialists and workers, many of whom were fresh off the farm. To achieve these ends, the powers and prestige of the technical intelligentsia would need to be increased and greater stress would have to be placed on the quality of technical education for

[50] See, for example, Brodskii, p. 73, citing a party archival source (TsPA IML, f. 17, op. 21, ed. khr. 2628, ll. 49-50); a recent Soviet doctoral dissertation, M. A. Akopov, "Partiinaia i gosudarstvennaia deiatel'nost' S. I. Kirova, 1926-1934 gg.," Lenin Library, Moscow, 1967, vol. 2, p. 37, citing an archive of the Kirov Museum in Leningrad (Rechi, 1928 g., t. 10, kn. 1, 117); and a volume of recent memoirs about Kirov, Nash mironych, Leningrad, 1967, p. 112.

specialists and on technical training for workers on the job.[51] This, in fact, is what we see from the spring of 1931 on.

In his June 23, 1931 speech on the technical intelligentsia, Stalin did not publicly lend his authority to stress the quality of higher technical education. In fact, his conception of the new technical intelligentsia reveals a rather different twist. The Commissariat of Heavy Industry, harped away at the theme that industrial managers (the vast majority of whom had only an elementary education or less in these years) and *praktiki* (promoted workers who occupied engineering positions without higher engineering degrees) must study on the job to raise their qualifications and acquire engineering diplomas. Stalin in contrast emphasized that the new technical intelligentsia would be recruited from two distinct groups: those "passing through our higher schools" and workers in production who would be promoted to higher posts.

Stalin's conception envisioned two distinct segments in the new technical intelligentsia: those with diplomas and those with production experience but not necessarily diplomas.[52] This, in fact, was the prevailing situation in 1928, and the rapid growth of industry accelerated it in the First Five-Year Plan. Due to the disproportion of investments in capital construction for industry, as opposed to investment in technical education, higher technical schools could not meet the demands for new technical personnel. The proportion of *praktiki* was actually greater in 1933, amounting to more than half of all industrial specialists, than it had been in 1928.[53] Stalin's views turned a necessity into a virtue. His recurring anti-intellectualism and his awareness that the *praktiki* were a key part of his support, were probably the reasons. Stalin, who had portrayed himself as a *praktik* among the party leadership, had a natural affinity with such men in industry, as well as a long-time preju-

[51] Roy Medvedev, *Let History Judge*, New York, Vintage ed., 1971, pp. 154-155. For an account of these two industrial conferences, see the paper *Za industrializatsiiu (ZI)* for February and June of 1931; proceedings of the February conference are also reported in *Pervaia vsesoiuznaia konferentsiia rabotnikov sotsialisticheskoi promyshlennosti; Stenograficheskii otchet*, Moscow, 1931.

[52] For some unexplained reason, Stalin's speech of June 23 was not published until nearly two weeks later (*Pravda*, July 5, 1931).

[53] On Oct. 1, 1927, only thirty-nine percent of the technical intelligentsia in industry were *praktiki*. By the beginning of 1934, fifty-four percent of the technical intelligentsia in the largest economic commissariat, Heavy Industry, were *praktiki* (*Za promyshlennye kadry*, no. 2, 1934, 39). In 1930, e.g., graduates of technical schools met only one-third of the demand for new engineering and technical personnel (TsGANKh, f. 3429, op. 79, ed. khr. 47, l. 8, cited in Vovk, p. 72). According to another recent Soviet dissertation, in the spring of 1934, Ordzhonikidze, troubled by this situation, decreed that all managers and *praktiki* had to reach a certain minimum of technical knowledge and pass examinations given by special certifying commissions (Klishin, p. 120, citing TsGANKh, f. 4372, op. 32, ed. khr. 760, l. 12).

dice against formal, academic education and the old intelligentsia.[54] Given the much higher proportion of *praktiki* who were party members than those with formal education among the technical specialists, it is hard to suppress the thought that many *praktiki* sought in party membership protection for their jobs and precarious status, and that among party leaders, Stalin was their chief protector.

It is from another direction, that of the Politburo members Ordzhonikidze, Kirov, and the manpower authorities in industry, that we must seek an explanation for renewed emphasis on quality in higher technical education and a downgrading of class and political elements in such education. The question of class quotas, as already noted, was one of the most sensitive issues in these years, and the Commissariat of Heavy Industry handled it delicately. Its officials in charge of higher technical education noted a sharp decline in the preparation of entering students for the academic year 1930-1931, but they did not publicly connect it with the high quota for "proletarian students" adopted in that year and the exclusion of many qualified students from other social groups. However, in 1932, Heavy Industry and then the government, changed the criteria for scholarship aid from a class basis to academic performance exclusively. Academic performance was to be judged solely on the evaluations of instructors.[55]

Privately, Ordzhonikidze was even franker about his concern for the consequences of class quotas. Calling together a group of engineering professors in November of 1932, he asked them:

Is it true that professors are reluctant to probe in depth the knowledge of students, giving them credit on the basis of their proletarian origins?

The head of this delegation replied: Yes, there is an element of truth in that.

Then you must understand, once and for all, that we need not simply engineers with diplomas, but good engineers. You must demand real, not superficial knowledge from your students.[56]

[54] It is interesting to note in this connection, from a 1930 survey of specialists, the reverse correlation between educational attainments and party membership:

	Party members	Nonmembers
Higher education	6.9%	93.1%
Secondary education	11.1	88.9
Praktiki with special education	27.7	72.3
Praktiki without special education	38.5	61.5

(Data relate to May 1, 1930, *Narodnoe khoziastvo SSSR: Statisticheskii spravochnik*, Moscow, 1932, pp. 492-493.)

[55] *Sobranie zakonov i rasporiazhenii*, July 19, 1932, Otdel I, no. 54.
[56] *ZPK*, nos. 3-4, 1937, 8.

In 1932, the Commissariat of Heavy Industry and then other Commissariats changed the rules for entry into their higher technical institutes. Quotas for proletarians remained high, but if an insufficient number of such applicants could meet the entrance requirements, then institutes would be filled with other students who could. All applicants, by these new rules, had to pass difficult entrance examinations in a series of academic subjects. Only then would preference be given to those of proletarian origin. "As a rule, those failing even one exam cannot enter secondary professional schools or higher schools."[57]

The emphasis on extreme practicality and neglect of scientific theory and polytechnic studies also proved less than workable in the years from 1928 to 1931. During these years a major struggle developed over curricular questions. By 1932, the Commissariat of Heavy Industry convinced the government to put more stress on academic preparation, particularly general science and technology. One reason, suggested by the author of a recent Soviet dissertation, who cites some interesting statistics to make his point, was that engineering institutes were not following the instructions of higher authorities.[58] Despite a vast proliferation

---

[57] *Programmy priemnykh ispytanii*, Moscow, 1932, p. 3; Klishin, pp. 121-122. Although the desire for quality was undoubtedly a major factor in the shift away from class origin (such quotas were abolished entirely in 1935, and entrance legally based on academic qualifications), the reasons probably go beyond that factor. Class quotas were difficult to administer and encouraged widespread fraud on the part of applicants and duplicity on the part of committees, which in each *vuz* actually made the decision to admit. While recent Soviet historians claim class quotas were deemphasized and eventually abolished only after they had accomplished their purpose of attracting a flood of new proletarian students, Soviet sources contemporary with these events suggest less positive reasons (see McClellan, p. 23). Who, after all, was a proletarian? There was never a clear definition; students from other backgrounds often tried to appear as genuine workers by spending a year or two in industry and acquiring a proletarian credential from their union. This could then be attached to an application form. (This practice was called "earning yourself a proletarian stage," according to one refugee source: Harvard Project on the Soviet Social System, Interview 64, Widener Library.) Less legally, nonproletarian applicants simply concealed their social origin or used forged documents (see my dissertation, pp. 293-298). When uncovered, such students were usually expelled, at best. The whole process tended to sour the atmosphere in higher education, exacerbating class divisions, and encouraging dishonesty on the one hand and a witch hunt by proletarian students and authorities on the other.

[58] A. I. Ocharkov, "Bor'ba KPSS za sozdaniiu inzhenerno-tekhnicheskikh kadrov tiazheloi promyshlennosti, 1928-1933 gg.," 1965 diss., Lenin Library, Moscow, pp. 200-201. The figures he cites show the gap between the highly specialized model curriculum of 1931 and the actual curricula of *vtuzy* in heavy industry during the academic year 1931-1932. Almost all *vtuzy* under Heavy Industry in 1931-1932 spent more time on general science and general technology, and less time on a particular specialty than had been established in the model curriculum of *Glavtuz* in 1931. These data are based on the following documents: *Tipovye uchebno-proizvodstvennye plany industrialnykh-tekhnicheskikh vuzov*, Moscow, 1931, p. 12, and *Novye kadry tiazheloi promyshlennosti*, Moscow, 1934, p. 57.

of narrow specialties and a model curriculum established by the organ in charge of most higher industrial schools (*Glavtuz*), which emphasized extreme specialization, most higher technical education under its jurisdiction did not follow the model curriculum to the letter, and continued to give somewhat greater emphasis to general science and technology. Although they had been forced to make concessions in this area, engineering professors did so reluctantly and slowly.

While the resistance of a large part of the engineering professoriate was undoubtedly a key element, it seems clear from reading the Soviet press for 1932 and 1933 that industrial management and the government had also become convinced that the success of their work depended on a change of policy in this area. The resistance of engineering professors alone would not have been sufficient, given their weakness in years when many of their most noted members were removed and arrested for such resistance, but their point of view was felt strongly and proved influential. Curricula had to be approved by industrial managers, who, by 1932, headed the majority of engineering institutes. Few of them at this time were engineers themselves, and they could scarcely have run these institutions without the cooperation of the specialists.

Let us look at how these changes developed and the reasons given for them at the time. A hint that change was in the air can be seen in the December 1931, article of Professor Lapirov-Skoblo, reporting on the Fourth Congress of Scientific Workers (the trade union that represented the professoriate as well as research workers).[59] Skoblo, a construction engineer and government administrator, was an important representative of the old technical intelligentsia. In the 1920s he was closely associated with the industrial research institutions of *Vesenkha*, and in 1928 he had supported the program of Lunacharsky and *Narkompros* in higher technical education.[60]

In reporting on the deliberations of this December 1931, Congress,

[59] *Izvestiia*, December 5, 1931.

[60] See his contribution to Khodorovsky, ed., *Kakogo inzhenera*, pp. 109-110. Along with Bakh, Zbarsky, and a number of engineers who were repressed from 1928 to 1931, Lapirov-Skoblo was a member of the collegium of the Scientific Technical Administration (NTU) of *Vesenkha*, the institution that Bukharin headed from mid-1929. Skoblo was one of its most active members, judging from a new collection of Soviet documents. He was also an active member of the Union of Scientific Workers. His principal areas of concern, reflected in these documents, was the expansion of industrial research institutions and the preparation of a new generation of qualified research workers. (Akademiia nauk SSSR. Institut istorii estestvoznaniia i tekhniki. Leningradskoe otdelenie. Arkhiv. *Organizatsiia sovetskoi nauki v 1926-1932 gg. Sbornik dokumentov*, Leningrad, 1974, pp. 4, 8, 41, 87, 140, 267-268, 273-274, 284-288, 297-301, 304, 359, 360, 367, and 368. See also *III Vsesoiuznyi s"ezd nauchnykh rabotnikov. Sputnik delegata s"ezda*, Moscow, 1929, pp. 120-140, and the journal of this trade union, *Nauchnyi rabotnik*, no. 1, 1929, 39ff.)

he noted that "along with the many successes of higher education" delegates discussed a number of problem areas. There was a lack of direction in curriculum and methodology. There were serious problems with the definition of technical specialities, the organization of practice work, and the introduction of better teaching methods. His article was very cautious and simply pointed out the problems without proposing remedies in print.[61] Change was in the air, however, and it is significant that Skoblo singled out areas around which much of the earlier controversy had revolved and with which the government decree of September 1932 soon dealt when it began to reverse the radical line.

A more active discussion of such questions was set in motion by the Seventeenth Party Conference of January 1932. According to the transcript of this Conference, Ordzhonikidze took the initiative in raising the question of higher technical education. Stalin was strangely silent, unlike him at major party gatherings. Not a single remark of his is recorded in the transcript, although he was listed as a delegate. Ordzhonikidze reported first and set the tone for the conference. After talking of the many accomplishments of industry, he spoke of the difficulties, particularly with meeting high targets in such areas as fuel production and metals.[62] "The difficulties we have experienced in mastering newly opened plants," he emphasized, "arise first of all from an insufficient number of cadres."[63] While noting other reasons as well, he returned to the subject of technical cadres and especially their preparation:

> I have already noted that the problem of preparing cadres is for us one of the most essential. Cadres limit us more than anything else. This year up to three million people in industry will be studying. The quality of [their] preparation—that is the fundamental question, since young engineers and technicians must be trained to conduct work in plants using the latest technology and the most complex technical processes.[64]

Ordzhonikidze indicated that the quality of new graduates was not always up to snuff, referring to a report of his assistant, Mezhlauk. The latter had visited a large foundry in the summer of 1931 and had reported that most of the responsible posts were held by young engi-

---

[61] *Izvestiia*, Dec. 5, 1931.

[62] The yearly 1931 plan was not fulfilled, and production actually fell in some areas, such as coal production in the Donbass during July and August 1931 (*Semnadtsataia konferentsiia VKP(b). Biulleten, no. 2. Tol'ko dlia chlenov VPK(b)*, Moscow, 1932, 10-11). I have used this serialized transcript from the Nicolaevsky collection at the Hoover Institution, Stanford, since it seems to be closer to the actual events than other transcripts.

[63] Ibid., p. 17.   [64] Ibid., p. 52.

neers, fresh out of school. "These are excellent lads, enthusiasts, who in a year, two, three, will become excellent engineers. But today they are learning, and their education is very hard on the machinery."[65]

While all the resolutions of this conference taken together bear the earmarks of a compromise between the Stalinist emphasis on quantitative growth and the moderates' concern for quality, the resolution on higher technical education echoed most sharply the remarks of Ordzhonikidze, Bukharin, Ioffe, and other participants at the Congress:

> The quantitative growth of technical cadres in the Soviet Union must in no way diminish the significance of the problem of their scientific qualifications, or of their corresponding obligation to assimilate all the basic achievements of world science and technology. Solving the problem of technical cadres is the most important element in a Bolshevik solution to the task of cultural revolution and the successful construction of socialism.[66]

With this general statement on the record, a vigorous discussion of changes in higher technical education began in the press. Significant differences between the Stalinists, writing in *Pravda*, and other groups in their own journals, can be discerned. For example, a series of articles in the government newspaper *Izvestiia* bore down hard on the need to raise the quality of teaching and the scientific-technical knowledge of new cadres. These articles emphasized defects and areas for change: "We must admit that young specialists are often insufficiently prepared for independent and rapid solution of tasks required by modern science and technology."[67] Focusing on the same problems pointed out by Professor Lapirov-Skoblo, these articles began to suggest solutions. The lack of overall direction in curriculum and methodology and in defining specialties should be remedied by turning over such duties to an overall supervising body. The Stalinist line on higher technical education at this time showed a significant difference of emphasis. Stalin himself remained publicly silent during this debate of 1932, but a major two-part article by his loyal tool in the party secretariat, Yezhov, appeared in *Pravda* in late March.[68] Whereas the critics gave a passing nod to achievements attained, Yezhov took the other tack: a nod to the problems, while defending the substance of the policies of 1928-1931. Yezhov echoed the need for higher quality (he could scarcely avoid doing so, now that the Seventeenth Party Congress was on record in that

[65] Ibid., p. 31.
[66] *KPSS v rezoliutsiiakh i resheniiakh*, vol. 5, Moscow, 1971, p. 39.
[67] *Izvestiia*, April 5, 1932. See also Feb. 18 and March 7.
[68] *Pravda*, March 17 and 20, 1932.

respect), but his actual proposals were incompatible with most changes favored by the "moderates." He said nothing about setting up a new organ for overall coordination of higher technical education, one of the measures soon to be adopted. (An opponent of Stalin was soon assigned to head that body.) He pointed with pride to the dissolution of large universities, replaced by specialized higher technical institutions subordinate to the corresponding branch of production.[69] "Our higher educational institutions have been transformed into a form of factory, fulfilling the orders of the economy for the preparation of those specialists necessary to it," he noted in praising the earlier changes. He also praised the changes attempted in curriculum, especially the three-year or four-year course for completing a degree, another policy soon to be reversed with a renewed emphasis on a five-year engineering course. Forty to fifty percent of the time was now spent on practice work in a student's specialty, Yezhov noted, and "the opposition of reactionary professors to this has been ended." However, one wonders if such opposition ended, since the amount of time devoted to practice work was, in fact, gradually trimmed back in the following few years. Yezhov also emphasized the creation of *proletarian* specialists, and noted the accomplishments of the quota system in raising the proportion of such students to as high as eighty-two percent in some entering classes. Turning to certain problems for which he blamed industry (singling out the Commissariat of Heavy Industry by name), as well as the administrators of higher technical schools and their teaching staffs, Yezhov criticized the insufficient *quantity* of engineers for key sectors, and suggested an even greater acceleration by concentrating only on those disciplines "which have a direct relationship to production." Better prepared students should be allowed to skip the lower courses, and more specialists should be prepared on the job, while working full time.

On the key question of the role of theoretical studies, Yezhov echoed the common concern for better coordination of theory and practice work, but nowhere in his articles did he note a need for *more* general

[69] Yezhov, in these articles, ignored a party decree of April 1931, that condemned such dissolutions and emphasized the importance of universities. According to a recent Soviet source: "The struggle against hairbrained schemes and experimentation in the system of university education began in 1931. In April, the Central Committee adopted a decree 'On the Function of Universities,' in which it asserted the leading role of universities in the general system of higher education in the USSR, and put an end to talk concerning the liquidation of university education." (Ukraintsev, p. 220.) Judging by Yezhov's views in 1932, however, such talk continued. I have been unable to locate a copy of this decree, and assume it to have been a confidential instruction from the party. The existence of such a decree is significant in that it indicates a struggle over higher education among the party leadership as early as April 1931.

science, mathematics, and polytechnic studies. In fact, his proposals still echoed the narrow utilitarian concerns of the previous three years: "The center of gravity for producing new proletarian *spetsy* must shift to factories, state farms," etc., he emphasized. Those theoretical disciplines must be mastered that allow someone, "working in production to represent to himself not only the narrow process of his own lathe, but the process of production as a whole, and to conceive theoretically his own everyday practice. (For example, a metallist working on a lathe, should study disciplines such as the resistance of materials, estimates, the construction of lathes, etc.)"[70] This was scarcely what prominent engineering professors had in mind when they spoke of a broader theoretical preparation, one that would make newly minted engineers more adaptable and technically creative. In sum Yezhov's position represented a counterattack against critics of the radical line. It seems likely that Yezhov was not speaking just for himself, but that he represented the position of Stalinist officials in the party secretariat and, most probably, of Stalin himself.

In contrast to this position, what many engineering professors wanted was a renewed emphasis on scientific theory, a broad polytechnic approach, and the selection of students according to academic qualifications, not social origins. This point of view had been articulately represented by Jan Shpilrein, an engineering professor in Moscow, during the controversies of 1928-1931. In the summer of 1932, he returned to the attack. Among the technical intelligentsia Shpilrein generally supported the party as a fellow traveller. He was a delegate to the first Conference of VARNITSO in 1928 and remained active in that organization in 1932, choosing its journal to express his views. While VARNITSO had supported much of the radical position in 1928, its members had apparently disagreed on some questions. By 1932 opponents of the radical line in this organization, such as Shpilrein and Ioffe, had come to the forefront. Although a fellow traveller in politics, Shpilrein was much more traditional in his view of academic issues, a fact pointed out as early as 1929 by the more radical engineering educator, Kagan-Shabshai, who bitterly attacked Shpilrein as a "reactionary" and "saboteur" who hid his actions "under the flag of the left"; while opposing practice work and a shorter engineering course.[71]

Probably protected by his membership in VARNITSO, Shpilrein escaped arrest in these years (only to perish during the purges of the later 1930s).[72] Overstating the case, Shpilrein's 1932 article noted that freeing teachers from administrative work in education had "also freed

---

[70] *Pravda*, March 20, 1932.   [71] *TPG*, October 6, 1929.
[72] Medvedev, p. 226.

them from influence on higher education."[73] The result had been new engineers of poorer quality. They were especially weak in theory and, therefore, "lacked independence and were often helpless to solve new tasks." Theoretical studies had often been driven out entirely, or such subjects as math and physics were taught only in the "narrowest way." Shpilrein rejected the idea of creating two kinds of engineers: narrow specialists and polytechnicians. He wanted a renewed stress on polytechnic education for all engineers. "We need engineers who can grow with the growth of technology."[74] An end to experiments in group study (the so-called laboratory-brigade method) and the reinstitution of lectures by highly qualified teachers who were also advanced researchers, reinforced by stiff individual examinations, was part of his solution to the problem of declining quality in higher technical education.

The government decree of the next month went a long way to meet the demands of educators like Shpilrein. It was signed by Kalinin, the head of state, and passed without comment or endorsement by Stalin, Molotov, and other members of the party's secretariat, unlike other important documents on higher technical education both before and after.[75] The decree brought higher technical education much closer to the position argued by *Narkompros* and the moderates in 1928 and 1929 than to that of the Stalinists and their allies.

The decree set up a new coordinating body, the Committee on Higher Technical Schools, headed by Gleb Krzhizhanovsky, who had been ousted as *Gosplan* head by Stalin in 1930, and had since worked under Ordzhonikidze in industry. It reiterated many of the criticisms of higher technical education just discussed, especially the insufficient attention to quality and theory: "Some of our *vtuzy* and *vuzy* have been graduating specialists whose qualifications are on the level of technicians and not engineers."[76] While it opted, as distinct from Shpilrein's position, for a continuation of two kinds of specialists—narrow and broad—it stressed that the "introduction of new technology" requires a higher theoretical level "for all kinds of engineers." It opposed the proliferation of increasingly narrow specializations and a growing number of tiny institutes to produce them. Practice work, a favorite plank of the radicals, was to remain an obligatory feature of Soviet higher technical education, but it "must be tied to and subordinate to" a period of relevant theoretical study in higher technical schools.

Quality would also be improved by reemphasizing lectures and work

---

[73] *Front nauki i tekhniki*, nos. 7-8, 1932, 101-105.

[74] Ibid., p. 104.

[75] *Sobranie zakonov*, Otdel I, 1932, no. 68, art. 409.

[76] *Izvestiia*, Sept. 20, 1932.

sessions with assistants, supervised by the professor, immediately following lectures. The laboratory-brigade method was made optional, and individual grading of students by their teachers became obligatory. In all, while this decree reflected some concerns shared by Stalinists and "moderates" alike, its provisions leaned heavily toward measures stressed by the latter.

The role of Krzhizhanovsky was critical in carrying out the changes decreed for higher technical education in 1932. One of the few old Bolsheviks who was also a graduate engineer, Krzhizhanovsky had largely severed personal and professional relations with Stalin by this time. According to his biographer and private secretary, even before leaving *Gosplan* in 1930, Krzhizhanovsky had received his reports back from Stalin with such written comments as "professorly impotence," and "It is necessary to introduce into *Gosplan* people who work on the principle of reporting results."[77] As Krzhizhanovsky commented to his secretary in 1931, "It seems we are too intellectual and discuss things too much. People of another stamp are wanted now, people with a narrow kind of mind who can only report, 'Your order has been fulfilled. Are there any other orders?' "[78] His biographer claims that Krzhizhanovsky, a Central Committee member until 1939, was put under police surveillance in these years. Though he escaped arrest and imprisonment, many of his closest associates among the old specialists in *Gosplan* before 1930 did not, and a number of them figured prominently in the show trials of that period.[79] As head of the Chief Energy Administration (*Glavenergo*) under Ordzhonikidze from 1930 to 1932, Krzhizhanovsky drew up a plan for electrification in the Second Five-Year Plan. Stalin and Molotov ignored the plan and refused even to acknowledge the inquiries of Krzhizhanovsky about its fate.[80]

This was scarcely an auspicious beginning for the head of the new State Committee on Higher Technical Schools. Yet Krzhizhanovsky proceeded to carry out most of the changes called for in the government decree of 1932, until his removal and the abolition of his Committee in 1936. Noting, in sharp contrast to Yezhov's articles, that a serious mistake had been made in giving primary attention to numerical expansion and not quality, he proceeded to revamp the curriculum of higher technical schools in 1933 and 1934. His committee radically reduced the number of specialties, lengthened the course of formal study,

---

[77] I. N. Flakserman. *G. M. Krzhizhanovskii*, Moscow, 1964, p. 245.
[78] Ibid.
[79] See K. E. Bailes, "The Politics of Technology: Stalin and Technocratic Thinking Among Soviet Engineers," *American Historical Review*, April 1974, 445-469.
[80] "Krzhizhanovsky," in *Liudy russkoi nauki*, vol. 4 (*Tekhnika*), Moscow, 1964.

and established faculties of general science and general technology for the first two years of such schools.[81] It seems particularly significant in this respect that not only was more time devoted to general science and general technology, it was increased at the expense of hours devoted to Marxism-Leninism. In 1934, this committee reduced the number of hours devoted to political studies from three hundred fifty in the previous year to two hundred thirty.[82] This, again, was in contrast to views in 1932 advocated by Stalinists such as Yezhov.[83] Beyond that, class preferences in admissions were to be given after *all* entrance exams had been passed, thus confirming the change introduced earlier by the economic commissariats.

If these changes had their source in a coalition of industrial management, Politburo "moderates," and elements of the scientific-technical intelligentsia, as argued here, then the informed reader may wonder why most of the changes remained and were even extended in later years, after the "moderates" and most of the industrial managers associated with Ordzhonikidze had been destroyed or silenced by Stalin during the purges of the later 1930s. While the neglect of political education was severely criticized by Stalinists in 1935, Stalin and Molotov gave their imprimatur to most of the changes in 1935 and 1936. In exchange for greater Stalinist control and a renewed emphasis on political education, which was made at that time, the positions favored by an important segment of the most experienced technical specialists became an accepted part of Soviet cultural practice. This acceptance should not be surprising to most students of Stalin's career. It was part of his modus operandi, after all, sometimes to adopt criticism, while at the same time trying to destroy the critics.

But the question remains why a line, later judged counterproductive, was followed for three years, from 1928 to 1931. The following explanation seems to make sense: many people in a transitional society, such as the Soviet Union in this period, were impatient for change. Convinced of the benefits of technology, they often did not see the usefulness of more abstract thought, and felt hindered by established academic methods. They wanted action, not abstraction, failing to perceive the long-range connection, between, for example, the theoretical sciences and actions that might ultimately benefit society. The *praktiki*, the proletarian student organizations, many industrial managers, and Stalinist *apparatchiki* at first were a formidable phalanx in opposition to the more established scientific-technical educators, a significant portion of whom saw a need for emphasis on scientific theory and general

---

[81] *Izvestiia*, Dec. 18, 1932; Klishin, p. 191-195; Ukraintsev, pp. 224-226.
[82] *Biulleten VK VTO*, no. 16, 1934, 16.
[83] Ibid., no. 4, 1933, 12.

technology, for the selection of students according to academic criteria, and for a share in the administration of higher technical education.

Because of the overwhelming emphasis put on rapid industrialization and the widespread distrust of the existing technical intelligentsia, therefore, a series of radical experiments in higher technical education was first tried and then found wanting. In the trial-and-error process of centrally-administered industrialization, such experiments came to be judged as counterproductive to the economic goals of the First Five-Year Plan. This outcome had the ironic result of justifying the views of many members of the old technical intelligentsia, who had opposed such changes. After 1932 and 1933, higher technical education once again came under the sway of more conventional methods of the established academic traditions in technology.

The years of experimentation left their traces primarily in a somewhat greater emphasis than before on specialization and on more practical ties between the economy and higher technical education, particularly in the amount of time spent by students in practice work. Still, it left shaken, but not fundamentally changed, a deeply ingrained academic conservatism that has continued to the present.[84] It led, among other things, to a decline in the percentage of students from proletarian and peasant backgrounds, and to a reemphasis on academic learning and hierarchical structure in higher technical education.[85] This outcome was far removed from the goals of the radical experimenters of 1928-1931, who wished to open opportunities more widely to proletarians and to a greater student voice in their educations. It was also far removed from the earlier ideal of socialist humanism, with its emphasis on general education and the creation of people with a well-rounded understanding of both the humanities and the sciences. The practice of cultural revolution in this area from 1928 to 1933 ultimately helped to entrench the vocational-technical approach to higher education in the Soviet Union, although not so narrowly as first attempted. Perhaps as significant, however, it served to discredit radical experimentation in a more egalitarian direction. Only the future can demonstrate the wider consequences of this experience for the Soviet Union and show not only what was gained, but also what was lost as a result. An evaluation of the effects of this outcome on the quality and role of the new technical specialists in Soviet society after 1933 will be dealt with in the following chapters.

[84] On trends in Soviet higher technical education during the 1950s and 1960s, see A. G. Korol, *Soviet Education for Science and Technology*, Cambridge, Mass., 1957, and Barry M. Richman, *Management Development and Education in the Soviet Union*, East Lansing, Michigan, 1967.

[85] See, for example, Klishin, pp. 129-130; Mervyn Matthews, "Soviet Students—Some Sociological Perspectives," *Soviet Studies*, January 1975, 86-93.

8

RECRUITMENT OF
THE NEW TECHNOSTRUCTURE:
CLASS, SEX, AND ETHNIC ORIGINS, 1928-1941

Soviet records concerning the early Five-Year Plans are rich in statistics on the social composition of the student body in higher technical education. We must use these statistics with some caution, however, for we have no way of carefully evaluating how accurate they are, and we can only compare and analyze them for internal coherence. They tell us more about what the party and government attempted to do in their recruitment policies, or what they wished the general population to think they were doing, than they tell about the actual composition of the new technical specialists who finished higher education in these years. Even at that, the statistics available reveal a considerable disproportion between the social composition of the student body in this area and that of the population as a whole. Since the official statistics probably tend, if anything, to underrate such disproportions, which official policies were pledged to overcome, we can conclude that recruitment policies adopted in these years were far from successful in several crucial respects discussed below.

It is probably significant that the statistics we have from the numerous surveys published in handbooks and articles during this period are all for the social composition of *entering* students, or of the student body as a whole during this period. No statistics have ever been published showing the breakdown by class origins, sex, ethnic and political background for actual graduates, those who received diplomas as technical specialists in this period. The absence of the latter figures is especially significant, since we know from the official statistics that the dropout rate was very high, as much as two-thirds of all such students in the First Five-Year Plan (1928-1933) and about forty-five percent of such students between 1934 and 1941.[1]

The conclusion one tends to draw from such figures is that the disproportions regarding the student body discussed below may have been even greater among the actual graduates of higher technical education,

---

[1] Calculated by Nicholas De Witt on the basis of official Soviet figures for entering students and for graduations in these years (*Educational and Professional Employment in the USSR*, p. 342).

and the party and government were not particularly eager to publicize them. For example, certain nationalities and graduates from certain social class backgrounds—such as the intelligentsia and other white collar employees—may have been more preponderant—out of proportion to their representation in the general population—than the authorities cared to reveal. Otherwise, how can one explain the plethora of statistics on entering students and the student body as a whole, and the nearly complete absence of any figures on the social composition of graduates? For graduates, all we have are aggregate figures, by branch of education, but without breakdowns for sex, class, political, or ethnic background. (Nor in most instances do we have any such official figures for technical specialists actually employed in the economy during these years, which could be used for comparison.) If some other explanation can account for this absence, then we hope Soviet scholars will be forthcoming with the evidence, and make it available to other scholars.

One reason for the reticence of Soviet authorities on this subject may be the degree of controversy that surrounded admissions policies for higher education. Since access to higher education was much sought after in Soviet society during this period, it became the subject of special attention from the authorities, and from such interest groups as non-Russian nationalities, technical specialists, etc. In the first two decades of Soviet rule, tension developed over contradictory notions of how students should be selected for higher education. The struggle was basically between those who wanted to widen educational opportunities for elements not privileged under the former regime, particularly workers, peasants, women, and ethnic minorities, and those who wished to base entrance to higher education primarily on academic criteria, regardless of social origin. The latter group wished to make entrance examinations and school records the primary criteria for admission to higher education, while the former generally supported the use of preferential quotas that favored those from underprivileged backgrounds. The struggle over this issue was fought intermittently between 1918 and 1935, and was eventually won by those who emphasized academic criteria, for reasons we have already examined in chapter 7. In this chapter, we need to examine how this struggle affected the actual recruitment of the new technical intelligentsia in the years of its greatest expansion, 1928 to 1941. We will analyze four features of this group in particular: its social class composition, sexual and ethnic origins, and political ties.

One of the early moves of the new Soviet regime in 1918 had been to throw open the doors of higher education to anyone sixteen years old or older, regardless of sex, social origin, or previous educational background. Entrance examinations and secondary school diplomas were not required. This situation led to the creation of remedial schools, called Workers' Faculties (*rabfaks*), in higher educational institutions in order to prepare less qualified students to benefit from the regular courses of instruction. With the beginning of the New Economic Policy in 1921, access to higher education was somewhat restricted. Academic criteria were used, but preference was given to political activists and workers and peasants, through a quota system.[2]

Between 1922 and 1926, the selection of students for higher education in the Soviet Union had been based in part on a system that gave preference to those with special recommendations from such Soviet institutions as the trade unions, the party, and the Red Army. In a sense this was a reflection of a similar situation under Tsarist rule, only with different preferences. Various kinds of discriminatory measures and quotas had been a standard feature of the Russian educational system during the nineteenth century. The Tsarist higher educational system, while it varied with time and place, had given preference to the children of the nobility and clergy for admission to the universities, while encouraging trade school and technical education for the children of the middle and lower classes, putting restrictive quotas on such ethnic groups as the Jews, and barring women for long periods from much of higher education. Higher technical education, while not exclusively reserved to the middle and lower classes, had tended to recruit its students to a greater degree from less privileged social groups, as we have seen.[3]

In the last years of Tsarist rule, however, competitive examinations were beginning to replace the quota system as the principal method of selection, although the level of tuition fees and availability of scholarships were still indirect ways of limiting the proportion of students from the working class and the peasantry. Russian higher education in the years before World War I was becoming more democratic in the social composition of its student body, even while remaining authoritarian and repressive in its administration.

The Soviet system, as it existed between 1922 and 1926, was an attempt to turn the tables on those groups that had been more privileged

[2] Sheila Fitzpatrick, *The Commissariat of Enlightenment*; D. K. Konchalovsky, "Sovetskie vuzy i studenchestvo," *Novyi zhurnal*, no. 90, 215; *Sovetskaia intelligentsia*, Moscow, 1968, pp. 170-175; on these quotas and their actual results, which differed considerably from the intended results, see James C. McClellan, "Bolshevik Approaches to Higher Education," in *Slavic Review*, December 1971, 830-831.

[3] Nicholas Hans, *History of Russian Educational Policy (1701-1917)*, London, 1931, pp. 71-74; Robert Byrnes *Pobedonostsev: His Life and Thought*, Bloomington, Ind., 1968, pp. 245-248.

under Tsarist rule. Yet, regarding the quality of higher education many professors considered this system regressive, a turning away from a system that had been moving rapidly from class and ethnic preferences to admission based on academic merit, regardless of social origin.[4]

Students from the working class and the peasantry were, by and large, less well-prepared academically than those from the urban middle classes, clergy, and former nobility. A system that gave strong preference in all forms of higher education to the former groups, while limiting or excluding those with better preparation, was thought by the academic establishment to lower the quality of higher education. Recognizing this fact, and the strong opposition of most of the professoriate, the quota system had been replaced in 1926 by a system based on academic merit—the secondary school record of applicants and the results of competitive examinations.[5]

In addition to a danger of lowering the quality of higher education, a chief difficulty with a system of class preferences lay in defining the terms "worker," "working class," and "proletarian." These were categories with rather slippery definitions in Soviet parlance. The difficulty of determining who was a real "worker" was especially sensitive because so many of the party elite, who claimed to represent the interests of the industrial working class in the early years of Soviet rule, were not workers by social origin. In many cases they had no experience at all in industrial production.

Lenin, who came from the upper middle class, considered anyone a "worker" or "proletarian" who identified himself with the interests of the industrial proletariat and adopted their way of life, no matter what his social origin. Lenin, in fact, maintained that it was possible for a genuine industrial worker not to be a "proletarian" if his outlook was that of the petty bourgeoisie—that is, focused on his own narrow material interests. In Lenin's sense, then, someone from the middle class or even the aristocracy could be more proletarian than an actual industrial worker, if he had the correct psychological outlook.[6]

The question of definition, therefore, was a confusing one, and the adoption of any quota system in higher education that gave preferential treatment to members of the "industrial working class" or "proletar-

---

[4] Beilin, *Kadry spetsialistov*, p. 62; Stephen P. Timoshenko, "The Development of Engineering Education in Russia," *Russian Review*, July 1956, 177-181.

[5] V. V. Ukraintsev, *KPSS-organizator revoliutsionnogo preobrazovaniia vysskei shkoly*, Moscow, 1963, p. 188.

[6] *Ocherki po istoriografii sovetskogo obshchestva*, Akademiia obshchestvennykh nauk pri TsK KPSS, Moscow, 1965, p. 255; Drobizhev, *Glavnyi shtab*, pp. 55-56; Lenin, *Sochineniia*, 4th ed., vol. 33, p. 229; *Leninskii sbornik*, 36, p. 249.

ians" was bound to be fraught with difficulties. A careful, legal definition had never been worked out, a fact that made any quota system based on this criterion difficult to administer. This alone was considered sufficient grounds for abolishing the class system of admissions as it existed in the Soviet Union until 1926.

The question of a class system in Soviet higher education was reopened in 1928 by Stalin's insistence on paying particular attention to the recruitment of new specialists from those of working class origins and those with connections in the Communist party. Politically, this was an adroit suggestion that may well have increased Stalin's popularity with the constituency his *apparat* most strongly courted—the industrial workers and rank-and-file party members. In a society where professional education was receiving higher value as industrialization increased, the pressure for admission to higher technical education intensified. Anyone who could promise a competitive edge in admissions to a particular group was likely to increase his standing with that group.[7]

Judging by the Soviet press in these years, the problem of administering an admissions policy based on class origins was never fully solved. This was especially true, since the quotas for those from industrial and working class backgrounds were set so high that other groups were severely limited in their access to higher education, especially for industrial professions. The temptation to find loopholes or to cover up one's social background was great, and it was increased by the continuing lack of sharp definition. Who was to be considered working class in origin, only those whose fathers had been industrial workers, together with those who had themselves been factory workers at some time in their past, or simply those who could claim an identification with the interests of this group? The question eventually came down to one of self-definition, although documentary proof might be required in questionable cases.

The method of selection by social origin, which was finally adopted by the party and government in July 1928, differed somewhat from the system that had existed until 1926. Under the earlier system, workers and peasants were grouped together for special preference in all types of higher education. The system adopted in July 1928 singled out industrial workers and higher industrial education for special attention. Even before a quota system was reinstated for higher industrial education, these schools contained the largest proportion of students from the working class when compared to other Soviet institutions. Approximately forty percent of the students in these schools claimed a working

[7] Stalin elaborated on the political motivation behind these class quotas in his remarks of June 23, 1931 (*Sochineniia*, vol. 13, p. 66).

class origin in 1928. (Other categories at this time included peasants, employees, specialists, or the children of these groups.)[8]

Workers and the children of workers, as might be expected, were far more attracted to these institutions than to those training teachers, doctors, or agronomists, for example, but an interesting factor to note was the general attraction of careers in industrial technology among all groups. This may be partly attributable to the barrage of propaganda that emphasized the importance of the industrialization effort, but a more personal reason, at least after 1931, was probably the large differentials in pay, privileges, and opportunities for advancement when compared to other fields.[9] These factors, taken together, created enormous pressure for admission to higher education in industrial technology. Admission to such institutions, therefore, would have been competitive under the best of circumstances in these years. A quota system based on social origin made entrance especially difficult for those from nonworking class backgrounds, no matter how able they were academically.

The quota system established for higher industrial education at the July 1928 plenum of the Central Committee required that sixty-five percent of those admitted must be from a working class background.[10] This quota was raised to seventy percent more than a year later, at the November 1929 plenum of the Central Committee.[11] This was almost double the proportion of such students actually enrolled in these institutions prior to July 1928. While the number of those enrolled was also allowed to increase, the increase in class size alone was not sufficient to accommodate all qualified applicants of nonproletarian background.

Doubtless many well-qualified applicants were thereby excluded from this kind of higher education, but a closer examination of the situation reveals that the quotas were far from effective.

While standards and entrance requirements were established centrally by the government, based on the guidelines of the party, they were administered locally in each institution by an entrance commission composed of students, faculty, and administrators.[12] This decentralized system of acceptance led to considerable flexibility and some confusion. Local commissions, as well as the central directing organs, could make exceptions to the rules. Even when exceptions were not made, applicants who were turned down in a particular year were often accom-

---

[8] *Kul'turnoe stroitel'stvo v SSSR 1930-1934*, Moscow, 1935, p. 8; Drobizhev, *Glavnyi shtab*, p. 259.

[9] Scott, p. 49.   [10] *Direktivy KPSS*, vol. II, p. 848.

[11] *KPSS v rezoliutsiiakh*, pt. 2, p. 518; *Izvestiia TsK*, no. 25, 1929, 29; *PS*, no. 15, 1930, 21-27; no. 5, 1931, 62-63.

[12] *Krasnoe studenchestvo* (hereafter *KS*), no. 2, 1928, 26.

modated by permitting them to become "auditors" with the right to attend classes, use the library, and generally to follow a course of instruction in the hope of eventually becoming regular students.[13] Although the percentage of workers accepted varied from year to year, and actually met the quota of seventy percent in 1929-1930, in the following year it slipped to below sixty-two percent, and never again rose much over sixty-two percent before the quota system based on social origin was abolished permanently in 1935.[14]

Despite the exceptions often made for nonproletarian applicants, the limited number of places open in higher industrial education and the system of high quotas for one particular social group often led to abuses. Attempts by applicants to falsify their social background in the hope of being admitted to these institutions under the quota for industrial workers were fairly common. The Soviet press in these years was filled with examples where such falsification had been uncovered, often with serious consequences for the offenders.

Complaints that many students from nonproletarian backgrounds were slipping into higher education under false pretenses came especially from proletarian students and their backers. The Central Bureau of the Proletarian Students Union, passed a resolution early in 1929 to "exclude from higher education all persons who cover up their actual social origin and use false documents when applying."[15] This same article discussed several instances in which students who had falsified their background or participated, for example, in activities sponsored by religious organizations while receiving state scholarships had been expelled and even brought to trial in some instances.

According to another article on the same subject, "In 1928, a marked pressure was observed on the part of the small-time urban bourgeoisie, white-collar workers and groups socially foreign to the proletariat. Having no hope in the general scheme of things of entering higher education, this element resorts to the method of 'petty larceny.' They convert themselves into workers, fabricate false documents with the aim of hiding their real social origin, making use of 'recommendations' and other tricks."[16]

Another article on the same subject published at this time maintained that some nonproletarian students received help from local authorities in covering up their past:

> Numerous facts from higher educational life testify to the fact that a foreign element is slipping in through all the cracks. Even in

[13] *KS*, no. 15, 1929, 18-19; no. 16, 1929, 60.
[14] *Kul'turnoe stroitel'stvo v SSSR 1930-1934*, p. 8.
[15] *KS*, no. 13, 1929, 4.   [16] *KS*, no. 15, 1929, 6.

the workers' faculties [*rabfaks*, or secondary schools preparing workers for higher education] we have recently seen the expulsion of many children of *kulaks*, rich land owners, and priests who had come to the *rabfaks* with official documents from local authorities testifying to their "lowly origins."[17]

The proletarian students, through their representatives on admissions committees, were cautioned to be on the outlook for such fabrications and urged to bring all those falsifying their records to responsibility through the courts. Proletarian students were also urged to oppose the institution of "auditors" and "candidates," which provided a loophole for nonproletarian elements to study in higher educational institutions without being formally admitted. While the complaints that quotas were not rigidly observed continued to appear in the student press,[18] there is also evidence of strong opposition to indiscriminate exclusions and expulsion of nonproletarian students.[19]

Much of this opposition came from the Commissariat of Education (*Narkompros*), which in several instances reversed local decisions to exclude nonproletarian applicants. It also came from *Vesenkha*, which was especially solicitous for the children of specialists, many of whom were denied admittance because of the increased quotas for workers. Special exceptions were made to reverse these decisions and assure the entry of more students whose parents were specialists, treating them on a par with those from the working class.[20] This would seem to be another example of how the technical intelligentsia used "influence," working through industrial management to protect their interests in these years.

Even the proletarian student press cautioned its readers against abuses of the party's policy for raising the proportion of students from the working class. Some local party cells and proletarian students were criticized for creating a purge atmosphere in higher education. A purge was not called for, students were warned, only vigilance against those who falsified their past: "It is entirely wrong to drive out of higher education *every* son of a former white officer, every person from another social group if he did not hide his social origin when applying and if, once admitted, he draws constantly closer to us. It is idiotic to exclude someone from higher education because his mother has been a scientific worker since 1912, his sister is married to an engineer, and his father, while still living, was a priest."[21]

17 Ibid., no. 18, 1929, 8.
18 Ibid., no. 16, 1929, 60; see also the controversy over this question in *Komsomolskaia pravda*, May 14, May 15, May 17, and May 21, 1929.
19 See, for example, *Nauchnyi rabotnik*, December 1928, 42-43.
20 *KS*, no. 11, 1929, 57; no. 18, 34; *TPG*, Oct. 3, 1929, 4.
21 *KS*, no. 17, 1929, 4.

Although exceptions were often made for those from white-collar backgrounds, due to their high level of preparation, the quota system nevertheless decreased the proportion of these groups. It also had a deleterious effect on the proportion of students coming directly into these schools from the peasantry.[22] In a country where the peasantry had constituted more than eighty percent of the population in 1926, this quota system made entry into an industrial specialty more difficult for most peasants than it had been before.[23] Instead of increasing social mobility into these occupations, the quota system actually created a hindrance to such rapid mobility for the mass of the population, unlike the earlier quota system that had existed prior to 1926. Careers in agronomy, medicine, and teaching, however, became more readily available to the peasant masses who had managed to acquire a secondary education. Higher education in these fields was greatly expanded after 1928, and lacked the high quotas for industrial workers that existed in the industrial schools.

The effect of this system was to create a greater continuity between past background and experience and the future career of an individual seeking higher education. Thus, a peasant was far likelier to be studying agronomy, while an industrial worker would find his way into engineering school far easier than it had been prior to 1928. Higher professional education became more readily available than ever before in Russian and Soviet experience, but social compulsion was also greatly increased. Free choice of future occupation became more limited, as individuals found themselves increasingly channeled by the system into a field and a destiny not necessarily of their own choosing.

The Soviet government abolished class preferences in 1935, and ceased to publish data on the social origins of students in higher technical education after the late 1930s. The social origins of students in this area show that those claiming working class origin rose to almost sixty-five percent in 1933 and 1934 and then declined to forty-four percent in 1938 and 1939, only slightly above the figure for 1928 (thirty-eight percent). By 1938, fifty-three percent of the engineering students were from nonworking class or peasant origins.[24] The latter

[22] Drobizhev, *Glavnyi shtab*, p. 259.

[23] Sometimes the yearly quotas for entering students included agricultural laborers (*batraky*) in the same preferential group with industrial workers, but the number of such poor peasants who had completed secondary school and could pass the entrance exams was very small. The mass of the peasantry was not included in the preferential quotas for higher industrial education (see *Sobranie zakonov i rasporiazhenii*, June 26, 1930, no. 35, art. 284).

[24] *Sotsialisticheskoe stroitel'stvo SSSR*, Moscow, 1934, p. 411; *Sotsialisticheskoe stroitel'stvo SSSR 1933-38*, Moscow, 1939, p. 126.

figure is particularly striking because nonworking classes and peasants made up less than ten percent of the overall Soviet population at this time. By the 1950s, when data on this subject were again published, children of the intelligentsia had a marked advantage over others in admission to higher education, a situation that has continued to the present day.[25]

In addition to raising the proportion of students from working-class backgrounds in higher technical education, the period from 1928 to 1935 was marked by a large-scale effort to recruit Communist party activists as students for these schools. While such recruitment did not become a subject of *public* controversy among Soviet leaders, it is interesting to note that spokesmen such as Rykov, Lunacharsky, and even Bukharin—who was a strong advocate of more students from proletarian backgrounds—omitted discussion of it in their articles and speeches. Considering party membership a criterion for special recruitment in these schools was a point stressed by Stalin, Molotov, and Kaganovich in their public statements on technical education.[26] Such a policy was to give the party *apparat* another powerful tool, along with the control of jobs, for dispensing patronage in Soviet society.

In 1928, before the beginning of an effort to flood higher technical education with party members, only one hundred thirty-eight engineers in all of Soviet industry were party members.[27] A special survey taken by the Central Committee a year later among nine thousand specialists revealed a small but growing percentage of party members among this group. The survey showed that over fifty-six percent of those included had received their higher education after the October Revolution, and of this group only about seven percent were party members. This was a very small percentage compared to the industrial managers, few of whom had a higher education, but over seventy percent of whom were party members.[28] Of the specialists in this survey who had received their higher education before the revolution, even fewer, just over two percent, claimed party membership.[29]

In order to change this situation, the Central Committee at its plenum in July 1928 called for the recruitment of party "thousands." The party was charged with enlisting one thousand of its members as students in higher technical education.[30] Such students were to be assured of

---

[25] On this subject, see the excellent article by Mervyn Matthews, "Soviet Students—Some Sociological Perspectives," *Soviet Studies*, January 1975, 86-108.
[26] *Sochineniia*, vol. 11 (English trans.), p. 63; vol. 11 (Russian), p. 215; Molotov in *KS*, Oct. 1928, 21. Kaganovich in *Bolshevik*, no. 23-24, Dec. 31, 1929, 63ff.
[27] *KS*, no. 1, 1928, 21.   [28] *Bol'shevik*, no. 8, 1928, 62.
[29] *Bol'shevik*, no. 23-24, 1929, 63.   [30] *Direktivy KPSS*, vol. 1, p. 849.

financial support and given any special preparation that might be required. The system was expanded considerably at the November 1929 plenum of the Central Committee. At that time the party was given the goal of recruiting two thousand of its members for higher technical education in the academic year 1930 to 1931, and three thousand in the following academic year. These students were assured of higher stipends than the average.[31]

In practice, the party thousands received privileged treatment, including higher monetary incentives for study. Yet they were also subject to special hazards, such as party purges, and special assignments to social and political activities that were time-consuming and often unpleasant, such as helping to enforce collectivization in the villages.[32] The practice of recruiting party thousands for higher technical education, added to other methods of increasing party influence and membership in these institutions, had an appreciable effect on the proportion of students who became subject to party discipline, especially in the higher schools of industrial technology. In 1928, thirty-eight percent of the students in these schools were already either party or Komsomol members, and this percentage grew to over fifty-eight percent by 1931. This was considerably higher than the percentage of students with party ties in other areas of higher education. For example, in medical schools the proportion was only twenty-two percent in 1928, and grew to thirty-five percent in 1931.[33] The majority of those recruited for the party thousands came from the working class, and were enlisted by local party committees or by the Central Control Commission of the party. They were recruited from party members who had five to ten years of production experience to their credit, and especially from those with records of social activism and a strong interest in technical questions, including the rationalization of production where they worked.[34] Most of those selected as a result of these criteria were likely to be older than the average student—with a high proportion between twenty-five and thirty—and more likely to be leaders than many of the younger students.

The process of selection, and the feeling of pride and elite status that accompanied membership in a party thousand has been described by a member of the Soviet technical intelligentsia who resided in the West after World War II. Despite his later disillusionment with the Soviet system, his selection by the party to enter an engineering institute re-

---

[31] *KPSS v rezoliutsiiakh*, pt. 2, p. 519; *Izvestiia TsK*, no. 4, 1929, 12; *PS*, no. 15, 1930, 24-27.
[32] See chapter 10.
[33] *Kul'turnoe stroitel'stvo v SSSR 1930-1934*, p. 9.
[34] Lutchenko, p. 34; *KS*, no. 16, 1929, 14.

mained a highlight of his life. He had been a skilled worker in metallurgy prior to his recruitment as a student:

> In 1930, a group representing the Central Control Commission of the party arrived to investigate the activities and personnel at our plant. I was summoned to the director's office. Behind the vast mahogany desk and its forest of telephones, in the director's chair, now sat a stranger whom I recognized from pictures as Arkady Rosengoltz, one of the most important Moscow leaders and a prominent member of the Central Committee.[35]

Rosengoltz congratulated him on his interest in the technical improvement of production and his public-spirited articles in the local press, and asked the young worker to describe his background:

> I gave him a brief sketch of my life. My childhood in a revolutionary family. The work on the commune. The period in the coal mines and how I joined the Komsomols. My service in the Red Army. My job in this plant and how I entered the party. How many times I would have to tell that story! This unreeling of one's private biography is almost a ritual in Soviet society, to be performed verbally and in questionnaires on the slightest provocation.[36]

After hearing the account of his life, Rosengoltz proposed sending him to a technical institute, on condition that he repay the party by giving it his best efforts. It was an offer difficult for any party member to refuse, especially a young man from the working class, whose father had never risen above the level of a foreman:

> My parents and brother were joyful at the turn of events. Mother, in particular, had never reconciled herself to my remaining a foreman like her husband. In her heart she worried because the revolution had interrupted my education. Now, though belatedly, I was to prepare myself for a career as an engineer and she was thrilled by the idea. Even my father seemed thoroughly happy.
>
> "My son will be an engineer," I heard him say to cronies one evening around the family samovar. There was pride in his tone.
>
> I devoted several months to cramming for the entrance examination. Special pre-Institute courses were made available to the fortunate young men selected for the "thousands," those chosen

---

[35] Victor Kravchenko, *I Chose Freedom*, New York, 1946, p. 56.
[36] Ibid.

to be the new Soviet intelligentsia. Then, early in 1931, I matriculated in the Technological Institute in Kharkov.[37]

According to the Soviet press at the time, not all those chosen for the party thousands were well prepared to enter the educational process again after long absences from school:

> The difficulties of comrades entering studies in this manner are, of course, great. Their general educational background—even with a secondary education—is not great, since there has already been a lapse of some years since they were in school, years when all of their time was absorbed by lively organizational work ordinarily allowing no time for study.[38]

At the same time, the Soviet press claimed that these students were highly motivated, and with the help of special courses and tutoring by teachers who were often also party members, very few became dropouts.[39] One might question whether their success was due as much to their academic abilites as to their political credentials and the fear of professors to give bad marks to students in whom the party had placed its hopes. But the thousands doubtless did possess an esprit de corps and sense of their own elite status that may have increased their motivation.

The system of party thousands was discontinued after the early 1930s, and the percentage of students who were full party members also declined as the student body became younger after 1933. A high incidence of Komsomol and party influence among students of technology was assured in other ways, however, by the use, for example, of letters of recommendation from party officials as part of the application procedure. The proportion of such students who were Komsomol or party members throughout these years generally averaged fifty percent or greater, a fact that encouraged the Stalinists to hope that the new technical intelligentsia would remain under the strong influence of the party machinery.[40]

The process described above was, however, a two-way street. While the technical intelligentsia became politicized in favor of the Communist party, the Communist party became in part "technocratized" by an infusion of new members who combined political background with technical skills. The party and technical elites in Soviet society never

---

[37] Ibid., p. 58. [38] KS, no. 2, 1928, 13.
[39] KS, no. 11, 1928, 41.
[40] See S. F. Klishin, "Moskovskaia partiinaia organizatsiia v bor'be za podgotovku inzhenerno-tekhnicheskikh kadrov 1928-1937 g.," diss., Leningrad, 1967, pp. 227ff.; Lutchenko, pp. 41-42.

merged entirely, but this system of overlapping and interlocking elites marked a profound social change from the situation in 1928.

While the social origin and party ties of students in higher technical education was a matter of great concern to party leaders, there is less evidence of a similar concern on their part for sexual or ethnic balance. Discussion of women's issues, which had been so prominent in the early years after the revolution, became much less so in the Five-Year Plans.

The *Zhenotdel*, the special women's section of the Communist party, was disbanded in 1929, and special women's organizations largely ceased to exist, or became passive. Nonetheless, the proportion of women studying technology increased dramatically, more in response to the needs of the economy than to any visible pressure by women's groups. However, the percentage of women in higher industrial education lagged behind those in other sectors of higher education, despite the major gains recorded.

The proportion of women in higher technical education (excluding agronomy) in 1914-1915 was a little over one percent.[41] By 1928, it had grown an additional thirteen percent but remained less in such elite institutions as the Moscow Higher Technical School (MVTU), where it was slightly more than six percent, and the Moscow Mining Academy, where it remained under four percent. Just as the party and government sought to correct other disproportions with quotas in this period, the party sought to meet this situation with a quota for women students. On February 22, 1929, the Central Committee decreed that at least twenty percent of all students in higher technical education must be women. Money was appropriated by local party organizations to establish preparatory courses for women in such institutes as MVTU.[42] Even at that, the quotas for women in the technical schools of industry were not met during the First Five-Year Plan, according to official Soviet figures, although no discussion of the reasons for this has been found in Soviet sources.[43]

Heavy industry lagged even further behind the average for industry overall (Table 8.1), and in early 1934, the Commissar of Heavy Industry, Ordzhonikidze, established a special quota of twenty to twenty-five percent women in the *vtuzy* of this branch.[44] The percentage of women in higher technical education approached their percentage in the

[41] *SSSR i zarubezhnye strany*, Moscow, 1970, p. 217.

[42] TsPA IML, f. 17, op. 20, ed. khr. 209, l. 34; ed. khr. 208, l. 121, cited in Klishin's diss., pp. 142-143; *Moskva v tsifrakh*, Moscow, 1934, p. 226; *Novye kadry tiazheloi promyshlennosti 1930-1933*, Moscow, 1934, pp. 132-133.

[43] De Witt, *Education*, p. 654.

[44] *Za promyshlennye kadry (ZPK)*, no. 5-6, 1934, p. 73.

TABLE 8.1. WOMEN IN HIGHER EDUCATION, 1928-1932

Year	Engineering Schools (Industry)	Agricultural Schools
1928	14.3%	18.4%
1929	15.6	20.4
1930	15.5	25.4
1931	17.7	28.1
1932	19.8	30.6

work force, about forty-three percent, only in 1940 (Table 8.2), and then only because a large number of male students were being drafted into the army.[45] Although women entering technical professions made genuine gains in this period, by 1941 they constituted only fifteen percent of all engineers with higher education employed in the economy, despite their having represented more than twenty percent of all technical students between 1928 and 1941, when the vast majority of technical specialists were educated.[46] This leads one to conclude that the

TABLE 8.2. WOMEN IN HIGHER EDUCATION, 1933-1940

Year	Industrial	Agricultural	All Higher Education
1933	22.4%	32.1%	36.5%
1934	23.3	31.8	38.0
1935	25.6	30.2	39.5
1936	26.6	29.3	41.0
1937	28.0	30.2	43.1
1940	40.3	46.1	58.0

dropout rate among women students, those who never received an engineering diploma, must have been higher than for men. This is a reasonable assumption given the economic and social pressures for women to marry and help support their families in these years, and the extra burden of housework and child rearing many of them were forced to assume in an era of economic hardship. Soviet sources, however, do not discuss the reasons for dropout rates, or who actually dropped out.

Regarding a policy toward nationalities, the speeches of major leaders in party and government and the policy statements of the Central Committee largely ignored the question of ethnic balance in higher technical

45 De Witt, *Education*, p. 654.
46 Ibid.; *Vysshee obrazovanie v SSSR*, Moscow, 1961, pp. 52-53.

schools. On a lower level—in the Council of Nationalities, a chamber of the government's Central Executive Committee, but a rather powerless body in the scheme of things—there was a strong concern for preferential quotas in higher education for industrially backward minorities. This effort apparently had little backing in the real power centers of Soviet society. The effort to establish preferential quotas for minority nationalities was an attempt to eliminate a serious imbalance in the ethnic composition of higher education, which was especially apparent in higher technical schools. In part, this imbalance may have been increased by the quota system for proletarian students and the recruitment of party thousands for study in higher industrial education. The policy of political and class preferences in education created an inherent advantage for certain nationalities who had stronger representation in the party and were more industrialized.

Industrialization in the Soviet Union prior to 1928 was unevenly distributed geographically and ethnically. Industry, especially heavy industry, which was so strongly favored after 1928, was concentrated in regions of central and northwestern Russia, the Urals, the southeastern Ukraine, and the Caucasus. The majority of industrial workers were Russian, Jewish, and Caucasians—mostly Armenian, Georgian, and Azeri—by nationality. With regard to party membership, several of these groups were overrepresented, when contrasted with their proportion of total population. This was especially true for those of Russian and Jewish background, as well as those who were Armenian and Georgian by nationality.[47] Quotas strongly favoring those with party ties and some background as industrial workers, therefore, affected the ethnic composition of the student body as well.

While it would be an oversimplification to attribute the ethnic imbalance of the student body in higher industrial education solely to this factor, it was one of considerable importance. Policy-makers wanted to relate higher education closely to the past experience and background of students. Therefore, students from less industrialized groups who entered higher education would be more likely to find themselves in agricultural, teaching, or medical institutes than in industrial higher education. In a more general sense, the imbalance was due to large differences in cultural levels and attitudes toward modern, secular education among various ethnic groups in Soviet society. Thus, while the disproportion between the more industrialized nationalties and those

---

[47] *Natsional'naia politika VKP(b) v tsifrakh* (Kommunisticheskaia akademiia, Kommissiia po izucheniiu natsional'nogo voprosa, Moscow, 1930), Table 1, p. 137, Table 19, pp. 126-128; see also Alec Nove, "History, Hierarchy and Nationalities," in *Soviet Studies*, July 1969, pp. 71-92.

less industrialized was greatest in technical education, it also existed in higher education as a whole.

Official Soviet figures for the ethnic composition of students in higher education between 1928 and 1936, when such statistics largely disappeared, show the disproportion quite clearly when compared to the distribution of various nationalities in the overall population; see Table 8.3.

TABLE 8.3. COMPOSITION OF STUDENTS
IN HIGHER EDUCATION, BY NATIONALITY

Nationality	% of Total Population	% of Students in Higher Education			% of Total Population
	1926[a]	1929[b]	1933[b]	1935[b]	1939[c]
Russians	52.1	56.1	56.0	54.4	58.4
Ukrainians	21.2	14.6	15.5	14.3	16.6
Belorussians	3.2	2.9	2.7	3.0	3.1
Kazakhs	2.7	0.2	0.3	0.4	1.8
Uzbeks	2.7	0.3	0.9	0.5	2.9
Tatars	2.0	0.8	1.4	1.3	2.5
Jews	1.8	13.5	12.2	13.3	1.8
Georgians	1.2	2.4	2.7	3.5	1.3
Turks	1.2	1.1	1.5	1.3	1.3
Armenians	1.1	2.0	2.0	2.3	1.3
Germans	0.8	0.5	0.5	0.7	0.8
Chuvash	0.8	0.5	0.5	0.5	0.8
Tadjik	0.7	0.05	0.1	0.1	0.7
Bashkir	0.5	0.1	0.2	0.2	0.5
Polish	0.5	0.6	0.8	0.7	0.4
Turkmen	0.5	0.05	0.1	0.1	0.5

[a] *Sotsialisticheskoe stroitel'stvo SSSR. Statisticheskii ezhegodnik* (Tsentral'noe upravlenie narodnogo khoziastvennogo ucheta Gosplana SSSR, Moscow, 1934), p. 411. The census figures here are taken from the two all-union censuses of December 1926, and January 1939, which included breakdowns of the ethnic composition of the entire population. The ethnic composition was altered in the early 1930s. The famine of 1932 and 1933 struck the Ukrainian population with special devastation. An estimated three and a half million Ukrainian peasants died in this famine (Conquest, p. 23). Therefore, the percentages for different nationalities in the 1926 census are more applicable in this comparison to the figures for the student body in 1929; the breakdown in the census of 1939 applies more to the student enrollments in 1933 and 1935.

[b] *Socialist Construction in the USSR* (Central Administration of Economic and Social Statistics of the State Planning Commission of the U.S.S.R., Moscow, 1936),

From the data in Table 8.3, we can see that students of three nationalities—Russian, Ukrainian, and Jewish—accounted for eighty to eighty-five percent of all those enrolled in Soviet higher education during these years. Those who were ethnically Russian, the majority of the Soviet population, held a share as students in higher education that was close to their share of the total population, with a slight tendency to decline by the mid-1930s, a variation that does not seem to have been significant, however. Partly, this slight decline was an indication that less industrialized and urbanized minorities were beginning to catch up in a period of wide educational opportunities. Besides this, the system of class preferences was abolished in 1935, which may partially account for the drop in proportion registered by Russian students in that year.

Although the Ukrainians were the second largest ethnic group in Soviet society, and among students in higher education, they never seem to have sent their young people into higher education proportionate to their population. In part, this may be due to the somewhat lower level of urbanization and industrialization among the Ukrainians than among the Russians, Jews, and Armenians, for example. It may also have resulted partly from special circumstances in these years, since the Ukraine suffered heavily from collectivization, the famine of 1932-1933, and local purges, including the suppression of Ukrainian cultural autonomy.

Nationalities that achieved a higher percentage of students in higher education than their proportion of the population were Jews, Armenians, Georgians, Azeris, and Poles, all ethnic groups with a comparatively high degree of urbanization and industrialization. The Central Asian nationalities—Kazakhs, Uzbeks, and Tadjiks, for example—still largely rural and premodern, were the least represented in higher education, although they generally improved their proportions in these years.

It is interesting, then, to compare these conclusions for Soviet higher

---

p. 457. Only the major ethnic groups in Soviet society are included here, so that the total of these percentages is less than one hundred.

Unfortunately, Soviet statistical collections often provide little or no detailed discussion of the categories and methodology used. The basic trends reflected in the figures above, and the possible explanations for them discussed here are corroborated by other sets of Soviet figures for this period, discussed later in this section.

e Kul'turnoe stroitel'stvo SSSR. Statisticheskii sbornik (Tsentral'noe upravlenie narodno-khoziastvennogo ucheta Gosplana SSSR, Moscow, 1940), p. 8. Although these figures from the 1939 census apparently reflect the changes brought about as a result of the collectivization and famine of 1932 and 1933, especially the mass starvation of Ukrainian peasants, which altered the ethnic composition of the Soviet population, they may not have reflected the full extent of the changes and should be used with caution.

education overall with the ethnic composition of students specializing in industrial technology. Here the data are somewhat more scattered and generally less complete. Of the two sets of figures in Table 8.4, those for 1927-1928 are more complete, since they include all students enrolled in higher industrial education at that time. The other figures are only for the entering class in the fall of 1934, in those institutions of

TABLE 8.4. COMPOSITION OF STUDENTS
IN HIGHER INDUSTRIAL EDUCATION, BY NATIONALITY

Nationality	1927-1928[a]	1934[b]
Russians	64.5%	58.0%
Jews	16.7	17.6
Ukrainians	7.3	13.6
Belorussians	1.7	1.9
Armenians	3.5	1.6
Georgians	.7	1.5
Tatars	.4	.8
Turks	.9	.7
Poles	.7	.7
Germans	.5	.4
Chuvash	.2	.4
Uzbek	.02	.2
Kazakh	.01	.2
Bashkir	.03	.1
Tadjik	—	.03
Turkmen	.05	.02

[a] *Natsional'naia politika VPK(b) v tsifrakh*, Table 15, pp. 290-294. Based on a school census of 15/XII 1927.

[b] These figures include all students enrolled in institutions under all-union jurisdiction. Most students seeking specialties in heavy industry and the larger sectors of light industry would be included in these figures. Institutions under the jurisdiction of the various republics generally concentrated on training cadres for smaller, local industry, agriculture, and medicine, as well as local education and culture (*Kul'turnoe stroitel'stvo SSSR 1930-1934*, p. 59).

industrial technology that were subordinate to the central industrial commissariats in Moscow.

Comparing these figures shows a trend in most higher industrial education for the proportion of Russians, Armenians, Turks, and Turkmen to decrease somewhat, while the proportion of Ukrainians, Georgians, Jews, Tatars, and most of the Central Asian nationalities increased. The declines for Armenians, Turks, and Turkmen were probably offset somewhat by the opening of new technical schools under the local jurisdiction of their own Republics.[48] The enrollments for such locally administered schools would not be reflected in the figures for 1934. While the proportion of Russians undoubtedly did fall somewhat in these years, as other nationalities industrialized and sent more of their members into higher industrial education, Russians remained by far the largest group numerically, and their actual numbers increased greatly with the large increases in the enrollments of these schools.

Also interesting, for comparative purposes, is the comprehensive breakdown by ethnic groups for the student body in different kinds of higher education (Table 8.5). Such figures are available for the entering

TABLE 8.5. COMPOSITION OF STUDENTS IN VARIOUS BRANCHES OF HIGHER EDUCATION, BY NATIONALITY

Nationality	All Higher Education %	Heavy Industry %	Other Industry %	Transport %	Soc.-Econ. %	Agriculture %	Education %	Medicine %
Russians	53.8	57.7	54.3	55.2	55.6	61.0	45.5	57.1
Ukrainians	20.8	16.3	19.0	16.5	11.8	19.2	30.4	18.4
Jews	12.0	12.8	15.6	15.1	10.1	5.0	10.2	13.7
Belorussians	1.6	1.8	1.5	3.3	2.1	1.7	1.0	.8
Tatars	1.6	1.1	1.0	.6	2.4	2.0	2.2	1.9
Armenians[a]	1.0	1.1	1.2	2.0	1.2	1.6	.5	.6
Germans	.9	.3	.2	.5	.4	2.0	1.5	.9
Poles	.8	.5	.3	.7	.3	.5	1.4	.9
Kazakh	.6	.7	.1	.3	1.0	.5	.6	.8
Georgians[a]	.5	.3	.4	2.2	.2	1.1	.1	.2
Uzbeks[a]	.4	.5	.3	.3	3.5	.4	.0	.0
Bashkirs	.3	.1	.1	.1	.4	.4	.5	.7
Turks[a]	.3	.5	.5	.9	.1	.1	.0	.1
Tadjiks[a]	.1	.2	.0	.0	.3	.1	.0	—
Turkmen[a]	.0	.1	—	.0	.2	.1	.0	—

[a] The percentages in this table are based on data for 80,252 students accepted for institutions of higher education under Union and Republic jurisdiction, except for institutions under the jurisdiction of the Georgian SSR, Armenian SSR, Azerbaidzhan SSR, Uzbek SSR, Tadjik SSR, and the Turkman SSR. The lack of data from local higher education in these Republics would slightly lower the percentages here for the predominant nationalities of these Republics, particularly for those going into more locally oriented professions, such as teaching and medicine, for example, where most institutions were under Republic jurisdiction. The figures above are most reliable for those going into industry and transport, since most higher education for these specialists was under Union jurisdiction.

[48] See, for example, Grigoriants, pp. 128-179.

class in the fall of 1933, and include higher educational institutions under both Union and Republic jurisdiction.[49]

With the possible exception of the nationalities mentioned in the footnote, Table 8.5 may be taken as an indication of the ethnic composition in different areas of Soviet higher education at this time. These figures show that Russian and Jewish students were even more preponderant in industrial higher education than in most other areas, with the exception—for the Russians—of medicine and agriculture. When we look at the figures for industrial higher education in Tables 8.4 and 8.5, for the entering classes in 1933 and 1934, a pattern similar to that in Table 8.3 for higher education overall emerges, although the disproportions in higher industrial education are even greater than in higher education overall, when compared to the ethnic composition of the general Soviet population. Approximately fifty-eight percent of the students in higher industrial education were Russian, fourteen to sixteen percent Ukrainian, and between thirteen and seventeen percent were Jewish.

Data from 1936 (Table 8.6), the last year for which such information was found for students in the technical institutes of heavy industry, the largest sector in these years, corroborate the trends discussed above.[50]

The decline for most of the Turkic minorities—such as the Uzbeks, Tatars, Tadjiks, etc.—and the Ukrainians between 1933 and 1936 probably reflects the abolition of ethnic quotas for them in 1934, and the construction of more local technical institutes in their own republics, institutes that would not have come under the system of heavy industry. This probably explains also the increase in representation between 1933 and 1936 for the more urban and industrialized ethnic groups such as the Russians, Jews and Armenians. While these changes by no means indicate a denial of educational opportunities for the Turkic and Ukrainian minorities, they do have important implications for the ethnic composition of technical cadres in heavy industry during this period. This is especially important, since heavy industry was to remain for decades the most prestigious sector of the economy and a major avenue of upward social mobility, particularly into the political elite.

While the proportion of Russians in higher technical education was somewhat higher than their proportion of the overall population, the educational achievement of those of Jewish background in all fields of

[49] *Podgotovka kadrov v SSSR* (Tsentral'noe upravlenie narodno-khoziastvennogo ucheta Gosplana SSSR. Sektor ucheta kadrov, kul'tury i nauki, Moscow, 1934), p. 28.

[50] D. Petrovskii, ed., *Kadry tiazheloi promyshlennosti v tsifrakh*, Moscow, 1936, p. 36.

TABLE 8.6. COMPOSITION OF STUDENTS IN HIGHER SCHOOLS
OF HEAVY INDUSTRY, BY NATIONALITY

Nationality	% of Total Population	% of Students		
	1939	1929-1930	1933	1936
Russians	58.4	66.36	57.70	59.66
Ukrainians	16.6	8.72	16.30	11.30
Belorussians	3.1	1.76	1.80	1.62
Kazakhs	1.8	—	0.70	—
Uzbeks	2.9	—	0.50	0.12
Tatars	2.5	0.50	1.10	0.82
Jews	1.8	15.18	12.80	17.20
Georgians	1.3	0.28	0.30	2.40
Azeri (Turks)	1.3	—	0.50	—
Armenians	1.3	1.66	1.10	2.00
Germans	0.8	0.51	0.30	0.45
Chuvash	0.8	—	—	—
Tadjik	0.7	—	0.20	0.02
Bashkir	0.5	0.03	0.10	0.08
Polish	0.4	0.65	0.50	0.63
Turkmen	0.5	—	0.10	0.02

higher education was remarkable and deserves some comment here. This ethnic group was the most highly urbanized in Soviet society,[51] and this fact may partially explain their achievement in education. Together with a long scholarly tradition and experience in industrial and commercial occupations, those of Jewish background were often better adapted to the Russian language and culture than other minority groups. They had a strong predilection for education and a degree of identification—especially among many Jewish youth—with the social and economic changes in the Soviet Union in these years.[52]

Scattered throughout the urban areas of the Soviet Union, the majority of Jewish youth knew the Russian language well, and had assimilated Russian culture to a high degree. Although there were many trends in Russian Jewry, the youth especially lacked much of the cultural and linguistic particularism of various other nationalities. In short, many Jewish young people were among the most assimilated to Russian

[51] John A. Armstrong, "The Ethnic Scene in the Soviet Union," in Erich Goldhagen, ed., Ethnic Minorities in the Soviet Union, New York, 1968, pp. 9-10.
[52] Salo W. Baron, The Russian Jew under Tsars and Soviets, New York, 1964, pp. 81-83, 90-117, 254-259, 268, 348.

culture of all Soviet minorities. For them, especially those living in non-Russian Republics, careers in industrial technology were particularly attractive, for they were keys to the mainstream of Soviet society and offered the most geographic mobility.

Data on the Armenians in higher industrial education during these years are more sketchy, but the figures available suggest that they, too, were strongly attracted to such careers, far out of proportion to their numbers in the general population. For example, in 1928, three and one-half percent of the students in this form of higher education were Armenians, contrasted with their proportion of about just over one percent of the population. In 1928, higher industrial education was more popular among Armenian youth than any other form of higher education except education in the arts.[53] Industrial education apparently retained a high level of popularity among Armenians during the period covered by this study. Though the proportion of Armenian students may have declined somewhat in these years, it continued to be larger than their proportion of the general population.

Some of the same reasons that help to explain the high motivation of Jewish students in higher industrial education also pertain to the Armenians. Although the Armenians had their own historical region within the Soviet Union, one of the Soviet Republics, unlike the Jews, the land there was agriculturally poor. There was a large diaspora of Armenians who had sought a living in other parts of the USSR. Like the Jews, the Armenians had a long history of Near Eastern civilization and a learned tradition—in their case the links were Christian and Byzantine. They likewise had a history of persecution, which may have increased their motivation to succeed under changed circumstances, where opportunities once closed were now opened. Perhaps of equal or greater importance, with respect to their attraction to careers in industrial technology, was their higher degree of urbanization than many other Soviet minorities.[54] Whatever the reasons for their high motivation, the Armenians occupied a strong position among the smaller minorities by their high degree of representation among the technical intelligentsia in Soviet industry.[55]

The situation of Ukrainians was considerably different. In the Ukraine, Stalin had fought a prolonged struggle with Ukrainian cultural

[53] *Natsional'naia politika*, p. 293.

[54] Mary Kilbourne Matossian, *The Impact of Soviet Policies in Armenia*, Leiden, Holland, 1962, p. 133. For historical background on the Armenians, see Vahan M. Kurkjian, *A History of Armenia*, New York, 1958; Sarkis Atamian, *The Armenian Community*, New York, 1955; and H. Thorossian, *Histoire d l'Armenie*, Paris, 1957.

[55] Grigoriants, pp. 180-206; *Natsional'naia politika v tsifrakh*, p. 293.

nationalism during most of the 1920s. He early set himself against the centripetal forces of minority nationalism. In 1928, however, he temporarily compromised with the Ukrainian nationalists by withdrawing from the Ukraine Kaganovich and others considered to be advocates of Russification.[56] This was probably an attempt to gain Ukrainian support in his struggle with the Moscow-centered Right Opposition. The Ukrainian Communists who replaced the Russifiers between 1928 and 1932, including Mikola Skrypnyk, the Ukrainian Commissar of Education, set about to make the Ukrainian language and culture predominant within that republic. It was an effort that should have attracted more Ukrainian youth to an interest in education, since the lingua franca was now to be their own mother tongue. In many instances it probably had that effect, but these policies were administered in a high-handed fashion. Rather than being implemented gradually—beginning at the primary school level in education and working up slowly—Ukrainization proceeded at a forced pace. Many officials and teachers who could not cope with the Ukrainian language lost their jobs. In 1932, taking advantage of the ferment caused by these policies, Stalin began to reverse them, and he purged the Ukrainian party of "bourgeois nationalists," as Skrypnyk and his followers were then labelled. Skrypnyk committed suicide, while a Russification as arbitrary as the phenomenon it replaced became the order of the day in education and public life. Use of the Russian language resumed a prominent place in the Ukraine.[57] These changes foreshadowed Stalin's general crackdown on minority nationalism in 1934.[58]

Apparently some Ukrainians, especially members of the technical intelligentsia and students in higher technical education, were happy about Russification. For example, Victor Kravchenko, whose native language was Ukrainian and who was personally impressed by Skrypnyk's honesty and talents, was an engineering student in Kharkov at the time. He considered the policy of Ukrainization, as implemented in technical education, a fiasco:

> Another dimension of confusion was added to our life in the Institute soon after I entered by an order that all instruction and examinations be conducted in the Ukrainian language, not Russian. The order applied to all schools and institutions. It was Moscow's supreme concession to the nationalist yearnings of the largest, non-Russian Soviet Republic.

[56] Ivan Dzyuba, *Internationalism or Russification? A Study in the Soviet Nationalities Problem*, London, 1968, pp. 127-131. Dzyuba, a Ukrainian Communist, desired more autonomy for the Ukrainian SSR.

[57] Hryhory Kostiuk, *Stalinist Rule in the Ukraine*, New York, 1960, pp. 38-42.

[58] Schapiro, p. 476; *XVII S"ezd. Stenograficheskii otchet*, pp. 31-32.

In theory, we Ukrainians in the student body should have been pleased. In practice, we were as distressed by the innovation as the non-Ukrainian minority. Even those, who like myself had spoken Ukrainian from childhood, were not accustomed to its use as a medium of study. Several of our best professors were utterly demoralized by the linguistic switch-over. Worst of all, our local tongue simply had not caught up with modern knowledge; its vocabulary was unsuited to the purposes of electro-technology, chemistry, aerodynamics, physics and most other sciences.[59] Most Ukrainian higher technical education reverted to the use of Russian, therefore, after 1932. Although the proportion of Ukrainian students in technology gradually increased in the later 1930s, linguistic Russification became the order of the day.

The Central Asian nationalities provide another contrast. Perhaps the greatest cultural gains in this period among the less modernized minorities, especially the Central Asian nationalities, were made in elementary education and the reduction of illiteracy.[60] Although some gains were also made by these groups in higher education, progress was slow and hampered by special features. In the academic year 1927-1928, only three institutions of higher education existed in the largest Republic of Central Asia, the Uzbek SSR. By 1933-1934 there were twenty-seven such institutions and three times as many students. Only a third of these students were Uzbeks by nationality, however; the remainder were generally Slavic, Jewish, or Caucasians.

A similar situation could be found in all the Central Asian Republics: although many new institutions of higher education were constructed in all these areas, fewer than half their students came from the predominant ethnic group in the area.[61] Within these Republics, the largest minorities were attracted less to higher education for industry than to other professions, such as teaching, medicine, and agriculture. Some of the reasons for this have already been mentioned—the high level of illiteracy and the need to concentrate first on basic education, as well as the traditional culture and rural economy of these areas. Great attention to public health, agronomy, and basic education was required before industrialization could gain momentum.

---

[59] Kravchenko, p. 63. For a confirmation of the difficulties this linguistic policy caused and the attitudes of many students and professors of technology in the Ukraine, see also *Biulleten' VARNITSO*, no. 2, 1928, 127; see also a recent Soviet dissertation in Ukrainian: M. M. Polishchyk, "Borot'ba komunistichnoi partii ukraini za otvoreniia i vikhovanii inzhenerno-tekhnichnyikh kadriv (1928-1932 rr)," Kiev, 1971, pp. 62, 151.

[60] *Kul'turnoe stroitel'stvo SSSR 1930-1934*, pp. 20-24, 26.

[61] Beilin, *Kadry*, pp. 301-310; *Vysshee obrazovanie v SSSR. Statisticheskii sbornik, Moscow*, 1961, pp. 106-108.

Other reasons for the slower development of higher industrial education among these peoples—as distinct from other forms of higher education—are given in the press of the period. One writer, for example, called for more attention to the use of the local language in industrial schools, a practice that he admitted was being held back by the lack of qualified teachers.[62] The reversal in 1933 of a similar policy for use of the local language in the Ukraine has already been noted. In general, these languages were not well adapted to the teaching of technical subjects, lacking the necessary vocabulary, and little came of contemporary attempts to develop and use them for technical subjects. At the same time, many students from these Central Asian minorities were ill prepared to use Russian on a formal level, and their weak knowledge of this language proved a barrier to higher education, especially in technical subjects.[63] Unlike the Ukrainians, whose mother tongue was closer to Russian, the Central Asian nationalities found language a greater barrier to entering the technical intelligentsia. For this reason, among others, a large proportion of students from such minorities were more likely to enter teaching institutes—where their native language could be readily used—than institutes for industrial technology.

As early as 1931 special quotas for underrepresented minorities were established in most higher technical schools. Although the quotas were sometimes as high as a quarter of the places available in higher industrial education, they were to a degree window dressing, and often remained unfilled for lack of qualified applicants. When they were filled, explosive tensions sometimes resulted, as in the instance discussed below. The economic commissariats that actually administered and financed most higher technical education at this period were criticized for giving little attention to this problem.[64] Basically, however, it was not a problem that could be solved quickly by such crash measures as high preferential quotas.[65]

Despite petitions by the Council of Nationalities of the Supreme Soviet, and a special conference on the subject, the proportion of students from Central Asian and other, less modernized, minorities remained a small—though growing—percentage of all students in higher industrial education.

To sum up, then, high-level officials gave little attention to the ethnic composition of the new technical intelligentsia. Stalin and the highest party members virtually ignored the question. Although the party elite

[62] *Revoliutsiia i natsional'nost'*, no. 3, 1933, 90.
[63] *Revoliutsiia i natsional'nost'*, no. 4, 1934, 59.
[64] *Revoliutsiia i natsional'nost'*, no. 4, 1934, 59.
[65] Nationality quotas were abolished in higher education during 1934. In 1933, only 1026 of 5678 places reserved in these quotas were actually used and this was cited as the basic reason for their abolishment (*ZPK*, no. 10, 1934, 9).

was largely Great Russian—with a higher proportion than their percentage of the general population—a number of party members were themselves from ethnic minorities, including Stalin. Groups, such as the Caucasians and Jews, that had large numbers of assimilated, Russian-speaking members more than held their own within the party, at least until the purges of 1936 to 1938.

Such minorities in the ruling group may, in fact, have been happy to divert attention from ethnic differences in order to avoid attracting attention to their own high positions in a country with a history of ethnic antagonisms. Since the major ethnic group, the Great Russians, were also overrepresented, they had no strong incentive to stir up resentment among such minorities as the Ukrainians and the Central Asian nationalities, who were underrepresented in the party and in higher technical education. When these factors are added to their Marxist point of view, it is not surprising that most party leaders preferred to speak in terms of class rather than racial or ethnic categories.

What effect did such policies have on traditional ethnic conflicts? Some memoirs of students who attended higher technical schools in the 1930s refer to the relative lack of tension among different ethnic groups. The emigré Nikolai Ivanov, a student of structural engineering in Moscow, who entered an institute in 1935 and was graduated in 1940, mentioned that in his immediate group of student friends were two Armenians, two Jews, a Ukrainian, a Belorussian, a Tartar, a German, and several Russians: "I can attest that no hostility of any sort nor any sort of difference was ever shown by reason of nationality."[66] Ivanov, a post-World War II emigré, living in the West, was critical of many other aspects of Soviet society in the 1930s. His views on this subject were seconded by another Soviet emigré, a woman engineer who finished her education in the Ukraine during 1933.[67] Despite this testimony, ethnic tensions were not entirely absent, as indicated by the conflict over the use of the Ukrainian language in technology and a significant incident documented in a recent Soviet dissertation.

According to the dissertation, a conflict broke out in 1931 at the Moscow Energy Institute, one of the country's leading technical schools, occasioned by the influx of students from Central Asia and the Caucasus. This was the first year in which large ethnic quotas were established in higher technical education, and, by January 1931, twenty-five percent of the students at this institute were minorities from these two

[66] Nikolai Ivanov, "Higher Technical Training in the USSR," a memoir in the Archive of Russian History and Culture, Columbia University, n.d.

[67] Taped interview with Mrs. Rose Jermain, Feb. 13, 1970. A copy is in my possession.

areas. Many of them claimed they were rudely insulted by academic authorities and denied their stipends for about four months. When the issue came before the local party committee, according to a later investigation, the party committee at the institute failed to take a position "condemning Great Russian chauvinism."[68] The Moscow regional party committee eventually took up the issue, condemned the party authorities at the institute and recommended their replacement, denouncing both "Great Russian chauvinism" and "local nationalism"—a formula that became standard in these years when dealing with ethnic tensions between Russians and non-Russians.[69] The writer of this Soviet dissertation notes that tensions over nationality in Moscow, where some ninety percent of the population was Great Russian, decreased appreciably after 1933, when ethnic quotas were abolished and the percentage of minorities studying in Moscow declined as higher schools were built in their own localities.[70]

The relationship among ethnic groups in Soviet higher education during these years deserves further exploration, especially since it has implications for the work roles of newly graduated technologists. It would be surprising if some ethnic conflicts did not develop between the technostructure and ordinary workers in parts of the Soviet Union where these years marked an influx of new industrial workers from ethnic groups still underrepresented among the technical intelligentsia. As we will see in part 4, there is evidence that some tensions did develop, and ways had to be found to cope with them on the job. Differences in language, customs, and level of education led to such conflicts, for which students were poorly prepared by an education that slighted the humanities and human sciences, including ethnic studies, and overwhelmingly emphasized technical subjects. The nature and quality of this education forms the theme of chapter 9.

[68] Klishin diss., pp. 132-135, citing archival source, MPA, f. 63, op. 1, ed. khr. 404, l. 79; see also *Pravda*, Jan. 17, 1931, and the student newspaper, *Proletarii na uchebe*, Feb. 7 and March 5, 1931. The latter source is in the Lenin Library, Moscow.

[69] Ibid.

[70] Klishin, p. 135.

9

THE EDUCATIONAL EXPERIENCE:
QUANTITY AND QUALITY, 1928-1941

What happened to students once they were enrolled in higher technical education? This study has already focused on some critical policy conflicts and the recruitment of students into technical education, seeking insights into the relationship between industrialization, higher technical education, and Stalinism. It is appropriate now to shift the focus to an analysis of critical trends in the quantity and quality of such education during the first three Five-Year Plans, the years from 1928 to 1941. Among other things, such an analysis develops a setting for interpreting the relationship between the technical intelligentsia and the changing social structure of the Soviet Union in these years. Education played a very important role in this process. Not least important were the effects of the purges on Soviet higher technical education and on the social position of its graduates. The massive social upheaval of the later 1930s would scarcely have been possible in the way it occurred without the education of large numbers of new technical specialists. This is especially so since they were used to fill the places of many who disappeared in the purges. Solzhenitsyn, Conquest, Medvedev, and others have focused on the victims of the purges and some of the reasons behind Stalin's ruthlessness in these years, filling many gaps in our knowledge.[1] Their interpretations are incomplete, however, without an understanding of the developments treated here.

What current historiography of Soviet society lacks is a clearer analysis of the link between the purges and other social processes of the 1930s, a crucial element of which was the education of a new technical intelligentsia. For a more satisfactory understanding we need to examine not only the victims of the purges, but their replacements, among whom were the new technical specialists who had emerged from higher education. We will note particularly the quality of education received and the nature of the faculty-student experience, as a key to understanding the attitudes and behavior of this segment of the Soviet technical intelligentsia, including its relationship to the Stalinist power structure. This is especially important because higher technical schools formed one of

[1] Robert Conquest, *The Great Terror: Stalin's Purge of the Thirties*, New York, 1968; Roy A. Medvedev, *Let History Judge: The Origins and Consequences of Stalinism*, New York, 1971; Alexander Solzhenitsyn, *The Gulag Archipelago*, vol. 1, New York, 1973, vol. 2, 1974.

three major environments for the technical intelligentsia, the others being research institutes and production units, which will be examined in subsequent chapters.

First we must provide a brief comparative framework for understanding the environment of Soviet higher technical education. There are a variety of ways in which modern societies have attempted to prepare technical specialists to serve their needs. The particular approach adopted and the alternative methods rejected may reveal a great deal about a society, its cultural values, class structure, and social dynamics. For example, formal higher education for engineers was a rather late development in Great Britain and the United States. In the nineteenth century most engineers were prepared on the job through a kind of apprenticeship. A formal degree did not become mandatory for most engineers and other technical specialists in these countries until well into the twentieth century.[2] This condition reflected a variety of factors, including the empiricism of important elements of the population and prejudices against theoretical studies and lengthy formal education. These factors declined only gradually with the centralization of economic power and the scientific-technical revolution of the late nineteenth and early twentieth centuries.[3]

French and German practice reveals a somewhat contrasting experience, with an earlier reliance on formal education for technical specialists, a reflection probably of an earlier centralization and bureaucratic control of education, and of the greater role of the state in economic development.[4] In fact, the growth of formal technical education seems clearly a function of bureaucratic centralization in such societies, as sociologists and historians have already observed.[5]

[2] See, for example, Gordon W. Roderick and Michael D. Stephens, *Scientific and Technical Education in Nineteenth Century England*, New York, 1972; Monte Calvert, *The Mechanical Engineer in America 1830-1910*, Baltimore, 1967; W. H. G. Armytage, *A Social History of Engineering*, London, 1961, pp. 108ff, 149-52, 185ff.

[3] See Peter William Musgrave, *Technical Change, the Labor Force and Education. A Study of the British and German Iron and Steel Industries 1860-1964*, Oxford, 1967.

[4] Frederick B. Artz, *The Development of Technical Education in France, 1500-1850*, Cambridge, Mass., 1966; William E. Wickenden, *A Comparative Study of Engineering Education in the United States and in Europe*, New York, 1929; W. Lexis, *A General View of the History and Organization of Public Education in the German Empire*, Berlin, 1904; Peter Lundgreen, *Bildung und Wirtschaftswachstum im Industrialisierungsprozess des 19. Jahrhunderts*, Berlin, 1973; *Techniker in Preussen*, Berlin, 1975; J. P. Callot, *Histoire de l'Ecole Polytechnique*, Paris, 1958.

[5] In addition to the works in n. 4, see Peter Blau, *Bureaucracy in Modern Society*, New York, 1971; Henry Jacoby, *The Bureaucratization of the World*, Berkeley, 1973; Peter Lundgreen, "Industrialization and the Educational Formation of Manpower in Germany," *Journal of Social History*, Fall, 1975, 64-80.

Given this framework, we need to examine more carefully the particulars of Communist experience in this area. In the Soviet Union in the 1920s and 1930s, both formal and informal methods of preparing technical specialists coexisted. It comes as no surprise, however, to find that the increasing centralization of political and economic power during the 1930s was accompanied by an enormous growth in higher technical education. By 1941, the formal path leading to a diploma was the one followed by those who sought highest prestige, pay, and career prospects. Although the proportion of *praktiki*, who had no degrees and had been trained on the job, remained high well into the 1950s and 1960s, the trend was toward their eventual replacement in the most responsible positions by specialists with formal higher education.

It is worth noting that the Communist Chinese, after lauding and following the Soviet model of formal technical education during the 1950s, returned to the concept of on-the-job training outside formal degree programs during the cultural revolution of the 1960s, closing down for some years most of their separate higher technical institutes and universities. This was in reaction to what some Chinese leaders, chief among them Mao Tse-tung, saw as the connection between bureaucracy, class inequality, and the formal educational systems of both the West and the Soviet Union. In the Chinese attempt to decentralize economic and political power, they attacked the educational system that prepared specialists for places in a bureaucratic system.[6] I do not intend, in this monograph, to explore the reasons for such differences in depth, but to show that they exist, and that we must take them into account when placing Soviet experience in context. We need to ask not only what were the underlying reasons for Soviet preferences and practices in this area, but what were the results of Soviet experience in the period from 1928 to 1941. Some answers to these questions can then provide a comparatively solid empirical base and a useful theoretical framework for later comparative studies of such questions.

QUANTITATIVE TRENDS

The Soviet technical intelligentsia with higher education grew impressively during the years from 1928 to 1941. According to census figures, the total number of engineers with higher education employed in all branches of the national economy grew from 47,000 in 1928 to 289,900 in 1941, more than a sixfold increase, and the highest growth rate of any professional area.[7] The total of agrarian specialists (agronomists, veteri-

[6] Theodore Hsi-en Chen, *The Maoist Educational Revolution*, New York, 1974, pp. 24-36, 137-186; Stanley Karnow, *Mao and China*, New York, 1972.

[7] *Vysshee obrazovanie v SSSR. Statisticheskii sbornik*, Moscow, 1961, p. 52.

narians, foresters, etc.) with higher education grew from 28,000 to 69,600 in the same period, slightly more than a twofold increase. By 1941, graduate engineers alone made up 31.9% of all specialists with higher education employed in the national economy, up from 20.2% in 1928. (The relative weight of agrarian specialists with higher education, however, fell from 12% to 7.7% in the same period, a reflection of the overwhelming importance attached to industrialization and the relative neglect of agriculture.) Overall, the growth in numbers and relative weight of the technical intelligentsia with higher education was very significant. The technostructure (including agrarian specialists) had represented only 18% of those with higher education employed in the national economy in 1914. By 1941, they represented 39.6%, bringing about a major shift in balance among the educated groups of Soviet society.[8]

We must not underestimate the achievement represented by this expansion of technical education and availability of opportunities to a wider segment of the Soviet population. Nevertheless, a closer look at the statistical side shows the unevenness of such growth, a fact that must be taken into account when explaining many of the problems encountered.

As Tables 9.1 through 9.4 show, higher technical education over-

TABLE 9.1. ENROLLMENTS
IN HIGHER TECHNICAL EDUCATION[a]

Year	Industry, Transport, and Communications Specialities	Agricultural Specialities	Total
1928	52,300	26,900	79,200
1931	197,300	57,500	254,800
1932	233,400	62,200	295,600
1933	188,300	54,200	242,500
1937	170,500	53,300	223,800
1940(R)[b]	176,800	45,700	222,500
1940(A)[c]	204,600	52,100	256,700

[a] De Witt, pp. 636-637.
[b] R = regular, full-time students in both day and evening classes.
[c] A = all students in a degree program, including correspondence courses. Correspondence students were a small part of the total before 1940, and were generally not included in overall statistics, since correspondence courses could not lead to a degree in the alloted time, prior to the reorganization of this branch of education in 1938-1939. The change was probably an attempt to compensate for the slower growth in full-time enrollments.

[8] Ibid., p. 52. Percentages computed by the author.

expanded during the First Five-Year Plan in a rush to meet the demands of the economy. The most rapid growth took place during the years 1928 to 1932, and was followed by cutbacks and retrenchment from 1933 to 1937, and a much slower resumption of growth in the years just prior to World War II. The drop in enrollments after 1932 can be attributed largely to reduced acceptances, as the advocates of more attention to quality won their case in the policy debates already discussed.[9]

TABLE 9.2. GROWTH IN ENROLLMENTS
FOR INDUSTRIAL HIGHER EDUCATION, INCLUDING INDUSTRIAL,
TRANSPORT, AND COMMUNICATIONS SPECIALTIES[a]

$$\frac{1932}{1928} = 446\% \quad \frac{1937}{1928} = 326\% \quad \frac{1940(R)}{1928} = 338\% \quad \frac{1940(A)}{1928} = 391\%$$

[a] De Witt, pp. 640-641. Percentages computed by the author. All of De Witt's figures have been verified by means of *Kul'turnoe stroitel'stvo SSSR, 1928-38*, Moscow, 1940.

TABLE 9.3. GROWTH IN ENROLLMENTS
FOR ALL HIGHER TECHNICAL EDUCATION,
USING 1928 AS BASE YEAR[a]

$$\frac{1932}{1928} = 373\% \quad \frac{1937}{1928} = 283\% \quad \frac{1940(R)}{1928} = 281\% \quad \frac{1940(A)}{1928} = 324\%$$

[a] *Sobranie zakonov*, Otdel I, Sept. 25, 1932, no. 68, art. 409.

TABLE 9.4. ACCEPTANCES IN
HIGHER TECHNICAL EDUCATION

Year	Industry, Transport, and Communications Institute	Agricultural Institutes	Total
1928	16,800	5,400	22,200
1931	88,600	28,400	117,000
1933	55,800	19,200	75,000
1937	40,000	13,200	53,200
1940(R)	41,100	9,200	50,300

[9] De Witt, pp. 636-637.

QUALITY

Given these quantitative trends, the critical question becomes one of quality. How good an education did these newly minted technical specialists receive? Here our answers must be more tentative. Nonetheless, a good deal of evidence exists to indicate the unevenness of the experience in these years, and the difficulty of generalizing for the entire period. Therefore, we should begin by discussing trends during each of three distinct periods: the years of radical experimentation from 1928 to 1932; the years of transition to a more centralized system from 1933 to 1937; and the years in which a more defined and hierarchical system came to completion, 1938 to 1941. Table 9.5 shows how many new specialists were graduated in each period.[10] (The high proportion of graduates in the years from 1933 to 1937 reflects the high acceptance rate of the period four years earlier, as well as a decline in dropout rates, as we shall see below.)

TABLE 9.5

	Graduates with Industrial Specialties	Graduates with Agricultural Specialties
1928-32	67,700 (23.3%)	30,600 (29.6%)
1933-37	134,400 (46.1%)	41,600 (40.2%)
1938-40	89,000 (30.6%)	31,200 (30.2%)
Totals	291,100 (100%)	103,400 (100%)

What can we say about the quality of the education received by graduates in each of these periods? Quality is difficult to measure in any circumstances; the difficulty is compounded when the evidence is not as complete as a scholar would wish. As there were no standardized comprehensive examinations for graduates during these years, no good basis of comparison exists, and our answer to this question must be based on other kinds of evidence: the subjective evaluations of contemporaries, and more objective, though indirect, kinds of statistical evidence, such as student-teacher ratios, dropout rates, curricula, etc. The following discussion uses both kinds of evidence and analyzes the quality of the educational experience particularly in the following areas:

[10] Ibid., pp. 640-641. Percentages computed by the author. All De Witt's figures have been verified with *Kul'turnoe stroitel'stvo SSSR, 1928-38*, Moscow, 1940.

the teaching staff and administration of higher technical education; teaching methods; curricula; the relationship between teaching and research.

1928-1932

According to overwhelming evidence, the quality of higher technical education dropped dramatically during the First Five-Year Plan. Since much of the evidence for these years has already been discussed in chapter 7, I will reiterate only a general summary of trends, and follow with a more detailed analysis of the evidence.

The decline in the quality of higher technical education during the First Five-Year Plan is indicated by both the subjective views of many contemporaries—in the accounts of many Soviet technical specialists and industrial managers themselves—and in the major governmental and party decrees on this question issued between 1932 and 1936. Statistical and other evidence related to the teaching staff corroborate a decline during this period.

The period from 1928 to 1932 was an era of reorganization and class war in higher technical education. Teaching staffs were under attack from proletarian students below and many government and party officials above during the first several years, and their resources were strained to the breaking point. Higher technical education overexpanded, but the increases in facilities and teaching staffs did not keep pace with the growth in enrollments. The result was lessened contact between students and teachers, which led to lower requirements, abbreviated courses, and independent study by brigades of students.

The administration of higher technical education was turned over largely to economic managers, who were to supervise the training of specialists for their particular branch of industry. Most of these managers were not drawn from the professoriate and did not have higher technical educations themselves. The decentralization of such education was an attempt to draw higher education and the economy closer together, but, in terms of quality, it was judged largely a failure by 1932. Economic managers, in fact, neglected their supervisory role, and, in their rush to meet high production goals, often assigned higher technical education a low priority when allocating resources. Narrow utilitarian interests took over, and, in many cases, specialized secondary schools were simply upgraded without the concomitant changes in staff and curricula; their graduates were considered engineers merely to fill the shortage of production specialists. By 1932, in the view of the government, ". . . higher technical schools and institutes frequently have graduated specialists with the qualifications of a technician rather than an engineer."[11] The overwhelming emphasis was to graduate narrow production specialists who could carry out routine jobs in the economy, rather than a variety of specialists, at least some of whom were adapted to a variety of jobs and were creative in their work. If the trend in Soviet higher technical education before 1928 had been to overemphasize the broad specialist, the pendulum during the following four years swung too far to the other extreme.

As already stated in chapter 7, after the policy debates of 1932, higher technical education began to revert to a more traditional system. If there was widespread agreement on the decline in quality technical education from 1928 to 1932, which seems corroborated by our evidence, we need to evaluate what effects the changes of the following years had on quality.

1933-1937

The dissatisfaction with the results of the First Five-Year Plan led to a recentralization of higher technical education in the years after 1932. Higher technical institutes remained attached to particular branches of the economy, but control over curriculum and, later, over the conditions of work and the qualifications of the teaching staff passed to a central government body. This was a centralization in which the teaching staff reasserted its role, however, and shared some powers with government and party officials. Increasingly, deans, directors of institutes, and officials of the central government body concerned with higher technical education came from the professoriate itself.

Student influence on the administration of higher education largely evaporated as student energies were channeled into subordinate roles and "cheerleading" functions, such as the organization of socialist competition and propaganda for the party's general line. Student enrollments decreased appreciably by comparison with the earlier period, and most students had completed their secondary educations. The student body also became much younger in composition as fewer "practicals," civil war veterans, and party activists entered higher technical education.

These changes brought several consequences. The atmosphere of class war diminished, except for the period of the purges in 1937-1938. Many smaller and weaker institutes, particularly in provincial areas, were closed or merged to form larger institutions, and the few new institutions were mainly polytechnics. The lecture method was reemphasized, as were discussions and laboratories supervised more closely

---

[11] *Sobranie zakonov*, Otdel I, Sept. 25, 1932, no. 68, art. 409.

by teaching staff.[12] Independent work by student brigades became optional, and individual grades, assigned by the teaching staff, replaced collective grading. The size of the teaching staff stabilized, so that student-teacher ratios improved by comparison with the previous period.

The statistical indicators in certain key respects suggest that the quality of higher technical education improved during the Second Five-Year Plan, although one cannot say with certainty if it reached or surpassed the levels before 1928. Student-teacher ratios (Table 9.6) show some trends, as teaching staffs stabilized and enrollments dropped considerably.[13]

TABLE 9.6. NUMBER OF STUDENTS PER TEACHER
IN SOVIET HIGHER EDUCATION

Year	Industrial	Agricultural	All Higher Education
1914	18.9	12.7	19.1
1927-1928	10.6	9.1	10.2
1932-1933	39.5	18.8	15.7
1937-1938	17.9	10.8	12.6

The qualifications of teachers seem to have changed little in this period. The effort to train new cadres of teachers through advanced study met little success because a large percentage of graduate students either dropped out to take jobs in other areas of the economy, or were so overburdened with administrative tasks that their graduate work extended well beyond the expected three-year course.[14] Only the qualifications of directors of technical institutes began to improve dramatically. For example, most directors of the higher technical schools of heavy industry who lacked engineering degrees had been removed by the fall of 1935. By that time, eighty-six percent of all directors of such institutes had a higher technical education, and they were also expected to have

[12] For discussion of changes in this area, see the article by G. Malis in *Front nauki i tekhniki*, no. 4, 1934, and the replies in no. 7, 1934, 109-111, and no. 10-11, 54-59.

[13] Only full-time students and full-time teaching staffs are included. Calculated from figures in E. V. Chutkerashvili, *Razvitie vysshego obrazovaniia v SSSR*, Moscow, 1961, 14, 40, 156, 163; A. Sinetskii, *Professorsko-prepodavatel'skie kadry vysshei shkoly SSSR*, Moscow, 1950, 61, 108; *Vysshee obrazovanie v SSSR*, Moscow, 1961, 79-81.

[14] *Za industrializatsiiu*, January 6, 1937. See also the reports of A. F. Sukhanov and S. V. Kaftanov, in *Vysshaia shkola*, no. 6-7, 1938, and the resolutions of the First All-Union Congress on Higher Education, pp. 143-146.

some production experience in the appropriate area of technology, as a way of guaranteeing closer ties to industry.[15]

The years of the purges, 1937 and 1938, were difficult ones in this part of Soviet life, as in others. Students and teachers were arrested, although statistics on such arrests have not been released, and are unavailable for meaningful comparisons with other spheres of Soviet society. The available evidence suggests, however, that directors of institutes and teachers of social-economic and political subjects were harder hit than teachers of technical subjects. In fact, evidence from later sources suggests that specialists trained prior to 1928 continued to dominate Soviet higher technical education, in a numerical sense, throughout the 1930s.[16]

The purges were aimed more at former oppositionists within the Communist party and their families and close associates, so that others were apparently not severely affected. We should not neglect to add, however, that many may have suffered through association with prominent purge victims. Some, with close ties to old Bolsheviks, were killed. Trotsky's son, Sedov, an engineer teaching at the Moscow Aviation Institute, was arrested and died, as did the head of higher technical education for heavy industry, Petrovsky, himself an old Bolshevik.[17] The directors of more than a dozen higher technical institutes were named in the press during this period as "enemies of the people" and were arrested.[18] Prominent engineering professors appear, on the whole, to have weathered the storm with far less trouble than in 1928 to 1931, when arrests were aimed more directly at them. In fact, many of the teachers of technical subjects found their prestige and influence enhanced after 1937, and their ideas largely vindicated in practice, as a more structured and traditional system of education emerged from the rubble of these years.

This process had begun to take hold in 1933, and came to completion after the purges. Between 1933 and 1937 the standard engineering course was once again lengthened to five years, the first two years given to general science, mathematics, and polytechnic studies, and the final years permitting increasing specialization.[19] Specialties were no longer as narrow as they had been in the previous period: by 1934, in

[15] Klishin, p. 115; *Za promyshlennye kadry*, no. 11, 1935, 7; *Biulleten' VKVSh*, no. 1, 1936, 9.

[16] Sinetskii, pp. 61ff.

[17] *Za promyshlennye kadry*, no. 2, 1937, 4-5; *ZI*, March 21, March 27, and October 6, 1937.

[18] Ibid., no. 5, 1937, 3-5.

[19] TsGAOR, f. 7297, op. 7, d. 150, l. 1, cited in Ukraintsev, p. 224.

heavy industry, for example, a number of specialties had been combined so that one hundred eighty-four specialties replaced the three hundred eighty-eight available earlier.[20] By the fall of 1936, the higher schools of heavy industry had fifty-six specialties, and a similar trend was taking place in higher agricultural education.[21]

The dropout rate, too, suggests an improvement in higher technical education. It declined from an average of more than seventy students for every hundred admitted in 1928-1932, to an average of forty to forty-five per hundred in 1933-1937.[22] Given the stiffer academic standards of the Second Five-Year Plan, this decline corroborates the other evidence of improvement during this period. Various reasons, besides the lower student-teacher ratio, account for this decline.

Entering students were better prepared; by 1937-1938, the majority had completed secondary education, whereas, in 1932, only some sixteen percent had completed secondary school.[23] General economic conditions also improved considerably after the terrible hardships of the First Five-Year Plan and the famine of 1932 and 1933 brought about by the collectivization of agriculture. While enrollments declined, material support from the government for higher technical education more than tripled from 1933 to 1937.[24] Some of this support was used to increase scholarship aid for needy students, who might otherwise have dropped out, and to improve the physical plant and equipment.[25]

Along with increased support came increased control, however, as the party and government sought to correct the deficiencies they found. Centralization and standarization of curricula and other conditions became the order of the day in higher technical education, as in most other areas of Soviet life. Control over curricula was centralized in 1933 under the All-Union Committee on Higher Technical Schools, headed by Krzhizhanovsky, an old Bolshevik and an electrical engineer.

The model curriculum approved for heavy industry by Krzhizhanovsky's committee in 1935 (Table 9.7) shows very well the trend during the Second Five-Year Plan, compared with the model curriculum for heavy industry of 1931.[26]

[20] Ibid., p. 226.

[21] TsPA IML pri TsK KPSS, f. 77, op. ed. khr. 602, ll. 2-3, cited in Ukraintsev, p. 226. For more extensive discussions of these changes, see *Za promyshlennye kadry*, 1933-1937, and *Biulleten' VKVSh*, 1933-1936.

[22] De Witt, pp. 342-344.

[23] *Industriia*, Aug. 15, 1937, Sept. 9, 1939; *Kul'turnoe stroitel'stvo SSSR 1930-1934*, Moscow, 1935, p. 96.

[24] Ukraintsev, pp. 218-219.

[25] TsGAOR, f. 8060, op. 1, d. 1, l. 21, cited in Ukraintsev, p. 235; Bashevoi, 160-170; *Kul'turnoe stroitel'stvo SSSR, 1930-1934*, p. 68.

[26] *Front nauki i tekhniki*, no. 5-6, 1935, 102. That this was the trend for all higher technical education, not just in heavy industry, is confirmed by Ukraintsev, p. 225.

TABLE 9.7. CURRICULA FOR SCHOOLS
OF HEAVY INDUSTRY

	1931	1935
General science, math, and general engineering	26.5[a]	48.9[a]
Specialized engineering	44	45.7
Other	29.5	5.4

[a] Percentage of classroom hours.

Table 9.7 shows that the reemphasis of general science and technology took place not at the expense of specialized engineering studies, but at the expense of other studies, particularly social-economic and political education. (Discussions in the Soviet press of the time corroborate this finding.) The number of hours devoted to the latter subjects declined precipitously between 1933 and 1937. In machine-building institutes, for example, the number of hours devoted to dialectical materialism declined from ninety in 1934 to seventy in 1937; classroom time for the study of political economy plummeted from two hundred nine to seventy; never excessive in context, the hours allocated to Leninism also declined somewhat, from sixty-nine in 1934 to sixty-four in 1937.[27]

Such declines were typical throughout higher technical education, as other sources have attested.[28] This trend may well have improved the technical qualifications of the specialists who graduated during this period, but it assuredly did nothing to improve the attitudes of Stalinist officials in the party. In 1935, the party apparatus moved to further centralize supervision by the party's secretariat. In May 1935, the Central Committee established a special commission on higher education that conducted a detailed investigation, leading to new legislation and further centralization.[29] In the fall of 1935, the Central Committee also established for the first time a permanent section of its secretariat to supervise education. This section had corresponding subdivisions in party organizations down to the local level.[30]

As a consequence of this centralized supervision by the party, political education was again emphasized after 1937. Stalinist officials used the purges to focus attention on the faults of technical education as they

[27] *Vysshaia shkola*, no. 5, 1938.
[28] Klishin, pp. 191-194; *Biulleten' VKVTO*, no. 16, 1934, 16; *Za promyshlennye kadry*, no. 6, 1937, 30.
[29] Ukraintsev, pp. 218-226. This investigation led to the major decree of 1936: *Sobranie zakonov*, no. 34, 1936, art. 308.
[30] *Partiinoe stroitel'stvo*, no. 11, 1935, 45.

saw them, and this brought renewed emphasis on political education. Many students and teachers had earlier dismissed such courses as "Communist religious education" (*kommunisticheskoe bogoslovie*), comparing them to required courses in the Russian Orthodox religion before the 1917 revolutions.[31]

This increased emphasis came only after Krzhizhanovsky had been removed as head of higher technical education in 1936 and his committee had been replaced by one more closely controlled by party officials. Another obstacle to change vanished when Ordzhonikidze, Commissar of Heavy Industry, died in early 1937.[32] Ordzhonikidze had shared Krzhizhanovsky's approach. The purge of industrial officials who had been associated with these men fully opened the way to major changes.

The situation in technical education was an important motive of Stalin in the purges, a fact that has not been previously recognized in the historical literature on Stalinism. Stalin developed this theme in his speech of March 3, 1937, which launched the massive purge of Soviet cadres: "The old slogan about mastering technology we must now supplement with a new slogan about mastering Bolshevism, about the political education of cadres and the liquidation of our political apathy."[33]

Too exclusive a concentration on economic tasks and successes, he maintained, had led some of the leaders of the economy astray and caused them to neglect the role of the party and its ideology. Stalin's concern was followed by a barrage of similar articles in the press, in which the reasons for the party's concern were made clearer.[34] Of particular concern was the nature of the student body: students were much younger now and were increasingly drawn from the children of the intelligentsia. During the First Five-Year Plan, a large proportion of the students had been from working-class and Communist backgrounds, and many were veterans of the civil war, but by 1937 most entering students in higher technical education were between seventeen and nineteen years old, and nearly half, in some cases more than half, were children of the intelligentsia. The director of one Moscow technical institute noted in July 1937 that only five to six percent of the students entering his in-

[31] *Biulleten' VARNITSO*, no. 2, 1928, 128.

[32] See the last chapter in I. M. Dubinski-Mukhadze, *Ordzhonikidze*, Moscow, 1963. The second edition of this book, published in 1967, omits entirely the account of Ordzhonikidze's quarrel with Stalin and his death. See also the account in Roy Medvedev, *Let History Judge*.

[33] *Za industrializatsiiu*, March 29, 1937.

[34] See, for example, the editorial in *Pravda*, "Inzhenery-Bol'sheviki," April 7, 1937; *Za promyshlennye kadry*, no. 6, 1937, 30-31; *Industriia*, July 3, 1937, July 27, 1937, August 12, 1937, September 30, 1937; *Pravda*, January 15, 1938; *Pod znamenem marksizma*, no. 3, 1938.

stitute were party members, contrasted with twenty-five percent four years earlier. "The influence of the party on non-party students and professors is weak," he noted, adding, "Professors can have tremendous influence on the attitudes of students."[35] This was particularly disturbing, since only about twenty percent of the teaching staffs in technology were party members and those educated before the revolution still dominated the upper ranks of the faculty. If such students were soon to replace many of those arrested in the purges, then Stalin could scarcely afford a student population dangerously exposed to non-Stalinist influences.

What is particularly interesting here is what Stalin and party officials did not say. For whatever reasons, they did not propose a return to the system of class quotas and party thousands, which they had favored for some years before 1935, as a means of controlling the political orientation of the new technical intelligentsia. The unworkability of that system, including the widespread resistance to it, had probably been too apparent to propose a return. Rather, they settled for a stronger influence on the curriculum, and a combination of party and police controls, as we shall see in the pages that follow.

1938-1941

The purges inaugurated a new era in higher technical education. Stalin's *Short Course*, giving his own version of the party's history and ideology, became a required textbook in the fall of 1938.[36] Stalin and the party apparatus were concerned to increase the level of political education among students. As a result, the time devoted to political subjects increased, but the time devoted to technical studies did not decrease. Most schools lengthened the overall course and had a stiff and rigid curriculum that, in many respects, exceeded that of leading Western schools of technology, such as MIT. Decreases came primarily in the amount of emphasis put on practice work. What practice work remained as part of the curriculum was more closely supervised by educational and economic officials.

Student-teacher ratios improved, and the formal qualifications of teachers were raised considerably. Graduate degrees were reinstituted in 1937, and periodic checking and upgrading of credentials was reemphasized. The rights and responsibilities of teaching personnel were more clearly defined in writing, and administrative controls over their time increased. Independent study by students in brigades disappeared altogether; lectures, followed by supervised activities in small groups, became the standard teaching method. All in all, academic discipline was tightened considerably, and bureaucratic centralization increased.

[35] *Industriia*, July 3, 1937.   [36] Ibid., September 9, 1939.

In line with more pronounced emphasis on graduate study and formal degrees, the research function of higher technical education also became an important factor to keep faculty abreast of advances in their fields. After 1937, teachers were expected to spend about half their time in research related to their fields, a function that had largely been ignored after 1928, when research had become centered in separate institutes often isolated from education, and teachers had devoted all their time trying to cope with huge enrollments.

It seems reasonable to conclude that by 1941 the Soviet Union had laid the basis for a system of higher technical education that produced specialists competent in their fields of specialization, but neither unusually creative nor likely to show initiative in their work. One should also add that the whole thrust of Soviet policy and practice in these years was toward the assimilation of Western technology and expansion of production, not toward creative breakthroughs in new technology. Hence, it should not be surprising that higher technical education was oriented toward the former outcome, not the latter. Even in this respect, however, serious problems remained in assimilating the latest Western technology.

The data available do not permit detailed comparisons with the quality of technical education in the West, but, certainly in a formal sense, by 1941 Soviet students of technology devoted as much, in some cases more, time to general science, mathematics, and technology than their peers in the West, and far more time to specialized engineering studies and practice work, areas of experience that Western technologists generally picked up only after receiving their degrees. In other respects, particularly in the study of the humanities and social sciences, and also in some areas of general science such as agricultural biology, however, Soviet courses were more intellectually limited than those in the West.[37] Among the serious problems that remained by 1941 was a greater isolation from contact with technical fields in the West than had existed in Tsarist times. This was a result of the purges and spy mania of these years, as well as the government's drive for economic self-sufficiency.

Political controls over higher technical education were much tighter than they had been before 1928, and professional autonomy and job security for teaching staffs, in the fullest sense, remained a distant dream, although the prestige and power of the faculty increased in contrast with

[37] On the situation in agricultural biology and education, see Zhores Medvedev, *The Rise and Fall of T. D. Lysenko*, New York, 1971, pp. 3-102; David Joravsky, *The Lysenko Affair*, Cambridge, Mass., 1970, pp. 1-134. The best study of controversies over scientific theories in the U.S.S.R. is Loren R. Graham, *Science and Philosophy in the Soviet Union*, New York, 1972.

the years 1928 to 1932. Such controls bred caution, and affected the daring with which creative changes in higher technical education were sought.[38] Controls were the price the academic establishment paid for increased material support from the party and government and some share in the governance of their institutions. The result was clearly a compromise forged in the conflicts of the preceding years, and one that left important problems unresolved.

The evidence for this summary of trends can be found in a closer analysis of the data below. For example, student-teacher ratios (Table 9.8) improved somewhat by comparison with 1914, but only in agricultural institutes did they improve over those of 1927-1928.[39] In other technical institutes, as well as higher education overall, these ratios still fell short of the levels at the beginning of the First Five-Year Plan.

TABLE 9.8. STUDENT-TEACHER RATIOS

Year	Industrial	Agricultural	All Higher Education
1914	18.9	12.7	19.1
1927-1928	10.6	9.1	10.2
1932-1933	39.5	18.8	15.7
1937-1938	17.9	10.8	12.6
1940-1941	14.3	8.3	11.5

The quality of the faculty improved, thanks to a major effort begun in late 1937. Working conditions were regularized, and pay was increased as an incentive to improve quality. It is probably no coincidence that these changes took place during the height of the purges in the fall of 1937. Considerable increases in pay were probably intended to calm the unrest the purges may have caused in higher education. Faculty were offered more status and a somewhat larger role in influencing curricula and other conditions of higher schools. Their rights were spelled out more clearly, but more was also expected from them. The first step in this direction was the reestablishment of graduate degrees, which had been abolished in the spirit of egalitarianism after the 1917 revolutions: the degree of *kandidat* was awarded after a three-year course of graduate study, and the much more exalted degree of *doctor*

[38] Bashevoi, p. 89.
[39] E. V. Chutkerashvili, *Razvitie vysshego obrazovaniia v SSSR*, Moscow, 1961, pp. 14, 40, 156, 163; A. Sinetskii, *Professorsko-prepodavatel'skie kadry vysshei shkoly SSSR*, Moscow, 1950, pp. 61, 108; *Vysshee obrazovanie v SSSR*, Moscow, 1961, pp. 79-81.

of science could be earned after further distinguished work in a scholar's career.[40] The latter degree could be granted only by a limited number of schools, and only with the approval of the Higher Qualifications Commission (VAK), a body centralized in the Committee of Higher Schools in Moscow. The Committee of Higher Schools also retained the final voice on the appointment of professors, heads of departments, deans, and directors throughout the Soviet Union.[41]

The initiative in nominating candidates for such degrees and positions, however, belonged to the schools themselves. Only those with academic experience were allowed to hold administrative positions, including those of director, in higher technical education.[42] The highest positions in the Committee of Higher Schools were also held by former academics, who were generally party members. For example, after 1937 the section on higher industrial education of this Committee was held by S. Plotkin, an engineer and former director of the Moscow Chemical-Technical Institute.[43] His boss was S. V. Kaftanov, an engineer who, at the age of thirty-two, enjoyed an even more meteoric rise, from assistant research director of a Moscow chemical institute in 1936, to head of the All-Union Committee on Higher Schools after 1937.[44] Such rapid social mobility was not atypical for young technical specialists who enjoyed Stalin's patronage at this time.

In line with Stalin's antiegalitarianism, which had already greatly increased differentials in pay and status in industry, pay differentials were also greatly increased in higher education, by some twenty-five to thirty percent in one year.[45] Prior to the decree of November 11, 1937, academics had been paid by the hour, and rates were comparatively low. The 1937 decree established new scales, as outlined in Table 9.9.[46]

Considering that the average pay of graduate engineers at lower levels in the economy was about 600 rubles per month, this scale tended to put the teachers of higher education more on a par with graduate specialists in production and economic administration.[47] The purpose of

[40] *Sobranie zakonov*, no. 21, 1937, 172.

[41] See the report of S. V. Kaftanov in *Vysshaia shkola*, no. 6-7, 1938.

[42] Ibid.; *Industriia*, November 12, 1936; *Sobranie zakonov*, no. 41, art. 237, p. 558.

[43] See Plotkin's remarks in *Vysshaia shkola*, no. 6-7, 1938.

[44] See "Kaftanov, S. V.," in *Prominent Personalities in the USSR*, Metuchen, New Jersey, 1968. Kaftanov was Minister of Education after World War II, Deputy Minister of Culture, and Chairman of the State Committee on Radio and Television. In 1968, he was a professor and rector of the Mendeleev Chemical-Technical Institute in Moscow.

[45] See report of S. V. Kaftanov in *Vysshaia shkola*, no. 6-7, 1938.

[46] *Industriia*, November 12, 1937.

[47] Nikolai Ivanov, "Higher Technical Training in the USSR," memoir in the Columbia University Archive of Russian History and Culture, p. 24.

TABLE 9.9. PAY SCALES
IN HIGHER EDUCATION AFTER 1937[a]

	Teaching Experience in Years		
	0-5	*5-10*	*10+*
Professor, department head	1100	1300	1500
Professor with doctorate	1000	1150	1300
without doctorate	800	900	1000
Dotsent with *kandidat* degree	700	800	900
without *kandidat* degree	600	700	700
Assistant and instructor (*Prepodavatel'*)			
with *kandidat* degree	600	700	800
without *kandidat* degree	500	600	600

[a] All figures are in rubles per month.

the new scale was to attract more able people into teaching, which had been seriously neglected in the allocation of resources.

Teachers were forbidden, after 1937, from holding more than one full-time slot (*shtat*) in higher education, and they were supposed to spend at lease five to six hours per day, six days a week, in the institution where they worked full time. At least half that time was to be spent teaching, in lectures, seminars, or consultations with students. The other half was to be spent in research, and research plans closely related to one's area of specialization were required of all faculty. Since research in higher technical institutes had been largely an afterthought following the changes of 1928, the renewed emphasis on graduate degrees and research plans was intended to firmly reestablish what had been a major function of higher schools in the Tsarist era and prior to 1928.[48]

Sources from this period complained that, as a result of the neglect of the research function, instruction often tended to lag behind the latest advances in world technology and the actual practices of the Soviet economy. Lectures and texts, teachers were advised, should reflect the best Western techniques, especially American, and for this purpose foreign language training, which had often been rudimentary, was held to be especially important.[49] While complaints about neglect of research and advanced technology in teaching continued in the press over the following three years, the ideal swung back to that of prerev-

[48] *Vysshaia shkola*, no. 6-7, 1938, 143-146.
[49] *Za promyshlennye kadry*, no. 1, 1937, 9; *Industriia*, February 2, 1937; September 30, 1937; *Vysshaia shkola*, no. 6-7, 1938, 143-146.

olutionary days. As two scientists educated before the revolution, one a member of the Academy of Sciences, expressed it in 1939, the goal should be to raise the level of all specialists, not just teachers in higher education, to the level of scientists, through research and earning higher degrees deriving from their productive work.[50]

That this was not simply the pipe dream of a few scientists is indicated by the remarks of the Soviet premier, Molotov, to the Eighteenth Party Congress in 1939. Molotov stated that a chief cultural goal of the Third Five-Year Plan should be to raise the level of all industrial workers to that of engineering-technical workers.[51] The scientists' goal, therefore, was a logical extension of Molotov's remarks. This goal was curiously reminiscent of that enunciated by Bukharin and some prominent old specialists in 1928, already referred to in a previous chapter. That this aim has become an important element in Soviet cultural thought is affirmed by Roy Medvedev, in his recent critique of Soviet society. Medvedev, quoting Soviet studies, sees this rise of Soviet workers to the level of the intelligentsia as the route to a more egalitarian society over the long run.[52] While one may question its ultimate validity as a solution to industrial society's inequality, the idea is clearly a major theme in Soviet thought and one key to Soviet social practice, both recently and in the past.[53]

Although that goal was utopian in the conditions that prevailed prior to 1941, considerable efforts were made to improve the quality of new Soviet specialists. The assumption that closer student-faculty contact was essential to sound education, and that the situation in this regard had been far from ideal prior to 1937, was made explicit in the comments on these changes. As Engineer Zhil'nikov, director of the Moscow Mining Institute, put it: prior to the decree of November 1937 most teachers in higher technical education had held two or more jobs because of financial need, and were rarely available, scurrying from one institute to another.

Working in one school, teachers will have free time every day which they can use to raise their qualifications, to improve their

[50] *Sovetskaia nauka*, no. 4, 1939, 145ff. The article was written by Academician Fersman, a geologist, and Prof. N. N. Sheftel.

[51] *Industriia*, March 17, 1939.

[52] Roy Medvedev, *On Socialist Democracy*, New York, 1975, pp. 301-309.

[53] While these aims could scarcely have been realized before 1941, the trend in this direction grew in subsequent years, as emphasized by two recent Soviet publications: D. M. Gvishiani, ed., *Nauchno-tekhnicheskaia revoliutsiia i izmenenie struktury nauchnykh kadrov SSSR*, Moscow, 1973; and S. L. Seniavskii, *Izmeneniia v sotsial'noi strukture sovetskogo obshchestva 1938-1970*, Moscow, 1973, pp. 297-340. Gvishiani, it should be noted, is the deputy chairman of the State Committee on Science and Technology and is also the son-in-law of Premier Kosygin.

research work. In addition, professors can get better acquainted with students and this is most important. They will have the opportunity to discover the best, most talented comrades, to direct the creative thought of students, to check on and consult them in their work.[54]

Complaints about the quality of teaching declined in the years from 1938 to 1941. Although the situation remained far from ideal, most comments reflected improvement, if not satisfaction with every aspect. A number of reforms were also introduced into the curricula. Among the major complaints of educators and students prior to 1937 were the disruptive effects of constant changes in the curricula. During 1938 to 1940, curricula were stabilized in most schools, and remained fairly constant until the late 1950s.[55] The influence of students on these new courses of study was apparently negligible, but the role of faculty increased. Between 1933 and 1937, curricula were established and changed centrally by the officials of various Commissariats and the Committee of Higher Technical Schools. The Committee of Higher Schools, which replaced the latter body after 1936, resolved to establish new curricula only after consultation with faculties, a resolution strongly endorsed by Molotov as head of state.[56] When there were controversies among the faculty in a particular specialty, conferences of educators were called to discuss the curricula, and afterwards legislation was formulated to institute changes.[57] While the Committee of Higher Schools had the final say, the authority of these new curricula was enhanced no doubt as a result of the consultation involved. The practice of consultation was not always followed, however, as evidence from 1940 indicates.

A long letter appeared in *Pravda* in July 1940, signed by more than ten professors and administrators in higher technical education, including the director of the Bauman Institute, the successor to the famous Moscow Higher Technical School. Complaining of faults in higher technical education, the signers noted:

> Worst of all is the fact that the curricula often originate without the knowledge of the higher technical schools, without any participation by them in this matter. For example, the Bauman Institute —one of the oldest higher technical schools—in preceding years was always consulted on the reworking of curricula, but this year it received a considerable number already prepared. . . . The fol-

[54] *Industriia*, November 26, 1937.
[55] De Witt, p. 289; *Vysshaia shkola*, no. 2, 1938; no. 5, 1938, 39ff.
[56] *Industriia*, May 20, 1938.   [57] See n. 65 below.

lowing testifies to the fact that the Committee on Higher Schools ignores the opinion of the higher technical schools: in the Committee there are a series of expert commissions, composed of the best representatives of science and technology. The Commission on Machine Building this past winter examined various curricula, as part of its business. However, when the matter concerned a major and fundamental re-examination of all curricula [in machine building], for some reason the expert commission was left out of this most important task.[58]

The writers of the letter were particularly concerned that such a bureaucratic handling of curricula questions was designed to bypass educators and lead once again to a narrowing of the curricula, an indication that the struggle between educational ideals and bureaucratic realities continued throughout this period:

> The fastest development and application of technology in the industry of the Soviet Union demands from the specialist a very solid and many-sided preparation. The engineer must not only head up technical work in the enterprise, but move technology forward, creating new machines and apparatuses, perfecting methods of scientific investigation. For this he must be a specialist of broad profile. However once again, for unknown reasons, the cultivation has begun of narrowly defined profiles of specialists, close to that [taught] in technicums [secondary schools]. Objectively, lowering the level of general engineering preparation will lead precisely to such a result.[59]

This letter was more alarmist than it needed to be. The situation did not revert to the narrow specialties of the First Five-Year Plan, and was probably only a temporary response to the acceleration of industry as it retooled for war production. But vigilance proved to be the eternal price of influence on the part of educators, and they continued their struggle against the narrowly utilitarian demands of government administrators and industrial managers, whom they feared would cut them out of an influence on the curricula they were required to teach.

Among the curricular problems with which educators wrestled after 1937, several took priority. In the period from 1933 to 1937, complaints were rife that curricula were overloaded with too many subjects, sometimes taught out of logical sequence, and poorly coordinated.[60]

---

[58] *Pravda*, July 12, 1940. [59] Ibid.

[60] See Kaftanov's report in *Vysshaia shkola*, no. 6-7, 1938, and resolutions of the All-Union Congress, pp. 143-146; *Industriia*, July 27, 1937; "O nedostatok uchebnykh planov," *Vysshaia shkola*, no. 12, 1937, 90-94.

Sometimes, for example, a course in applied mechanics might be taught before the necessary mathematics course. Students were often overloaded with eight to nine courses a term, too many to assimilate properly. The ideal was set at five to six courses per term, and educators sought to coordinate better the first two years of general studies with later specialized courses in technology. While detailed information on curricula for all branches of technology has not been found, two sample curricula from this period can be compared with the model curriculum of heavy industry from 1935 to suggest some trends (Table 9.10).[61]

TABLE 9.10. COMPARISON OF CURRICULA IN HEAVY INDUSTRY[a]

	1935	1938[b]	1938-1941[c]
General science, math, and general technology	48.9	63.2	47.5
Specialized engineering	45.7	22.4	38.2
Other	5.4	14.4[d]	14.3[e]

[a] All figures are given in the percentage of hours devoted to each category.

[b] Chemical engineering curriculum in technology of silicates, published in *Tsement*, no. 10, 1938, 6, and analyzed in De Witt, *Soviet Professional Manpower*, pp. 319-320.

[c] Mechanical engineering curriculum with specialty in agricultural machinery maintenance, abstracted from J. Budanow, *Technical Institutes in the USSR*, Research Project on the USSR, no. 26, 1952, pp. 16, 19, 22, 24, 27, in De Witt, *Soviet Professional Manpower*, pp. 321-322.

[d] Includes 8.1% devoted to political economy, dialectical and historical materialism, and Leninism, and 6.3% devoted to physical education and military training.

[e] Eight percent devoted to the political subjects in note *d*, and 6.3% to physical education and military training.

The figures for 1938 in the table are the most reliable, since the figures for 1938 to 1941 are based on a later refugee report by a former student in Soviet higher technical education. While it is risky to generalize from limited information, it seems likely that the time devoted to general science and technology, at the very least, stabilized by comparison with the period from 1933 to 1937, and probably increased in some instances, as indicated by the 1938 figures. An increase in the proportion of time devoted to general science and technology and to political education was a goal of the Committee on Higher Schools in 1938, and was endorsed in the resolutions of the First All-Union Con-

[61] See sources for n. 26.

ference on Higher Education, attended by some eight hundred representatives of higher schools in May 1938.[62]

It is interesting to note, as De Witt has done, that in most cases the actual number of hours devoted to mathematics, general science and technology, and specialized engineering was considerably higher than comparable curricula at MIT in the early 1950s. Soviet curricula by 1938 appear to have been longer overall, and more oriented to science and technology.[63] While by 1938 the Soviet institutions spent more hours on subjects classified as "other," MIT allotted a slightly larger proportion of its curriculum to these categories; its courses in the humanities and social sciences were, of course, quite different in content and purpose.

From the data above, we can conclude that Soviet engineers by 1941 were more highly and rigidly schooled, and received more general scientific-technical education, as well as more specialized education, than engineers in similar fields who graduated from MIT in the early 1950s. De Witt's conclusions concerning Soviet higher technical education in the 1950s, based on a variety of data, seem valid for the late 1930s as well: "Specialization in the Soviet curriculum is achieved not in place of, but rather in addition to, basic engineering training."[64] What De Witt does not indicate, however, is the reason for this development. Sources from the late 1930s suggest that it resulted from a compromise between the desires of industrial managers for specialists trained in a particular branch of production, and the bulk of technical educators, who preferred a more broadly educated specialist. This is spelled out in the debates over curricula in chemical, agricultural, mining, and metallurgical education between 1938 and 1940.[65] The solutions reflected the interests of both sides. Students, who might have opposed lengthier curricula, as they had in the 1920s, no longer had a voice in such matters.

In addition to carrying a heavy course load in specialized subjects during the last three years of a technical course, students still spent a considerable amount of time in "practice work." The amount of practice work declined in this period, however, and attempts were made to regularize it and make the experience more meaningful. If between 1928 and 1931 up to forty to fifty percent of a student's overall time in higher technical education was spent in "practice work" at a production enterprise, by 1938 to 1941 it had declined to some ten to twenty per-

[62] *Vysshaia shkola*, no. 6-7, 1938, 143-146.

[63] De Witt, *Education*, pp. 726-730.

[64] Ibid., pp. 286-287.

[65] See *Industriia*, May 16, 20, 28, 29, and June 3, 1940; *Sovetskaia Nauka*, no. 2, 1940, 128-137, nos. 3-4, 145-156; no. 5, 1940, 124-132; *Kauchuk i rezin*, no. 5, 1938, 6-9; Nov. 12, 1938, 6-7; *Sobranie zakonov*, no. 30, 1940, art. 724, p. 1001.

cent.[66] Evidence indicates that the problem of integrating this experience with classroom instruction improved though it was never completely solved.

The problems in this area were addressed once again in 1937 and 1938, and many of the complaints familiar from earlier years were repeated. A series of letters from students published by the newspaper *Industriia* in November 1937, for example, suggested the frequent ineffectiveness of this form of education.[67] The blame for this situation was laid on the apathy of students, teachers, and industrial managers alike. Some students simply used this time as a holiday and occupied themselves having a good time and getting receipts and vouchers for tickets, living expenses, etc. One student of mining indicated that "many students don't even consider it necessary to go down into the mine." It was all the easier to get away with this "since the reports about one's production practice are not always verified. In the institute these reports are usually only scanned briefly."[68]

In order to make students, faculty, and industrial managers more responsible for results in this area, the government passed a new law on practice work in late March 1938.[69] Students were to be given grades for their practice work, and were to be accompanied to the site by a faculty member, who could use the time to familiarize himself with current production practices in his specialty. Economic enterprises were to assign special technical personnel to supervise students in groups of not more than ten, after approval of their work plans by their academic advisors. Such technical supervisors were to be freed from other work or paid ten to thirty percent extra for such activity.[70] In actual practice, this ideal was not always followed, but students were made more aware of what they were supposed to learn. Practice work came to be broken up into three periods generally, ranging from eight to twelve weeks during each of three summers. The first period, usually at the end of the freshman year, required students to familiarize themselves with the overall production process in a plant. After the second year, they were expected to work with particular machines in their specialization. Just before the start of their diploma project in the fifth year, they were required to work as an assistant to the head of the shop where they were likely to work after graduation.[71]

[66] De Witt, *Soviet Professional Manpower*, p. 322; *Vysshaia shkola*, no. 2, 1938.
[67] *Industriia*, Nov. 12, 1937; see also the issue for Feb. 2, 1937.
[68] Ibid.
[69] *Vysshaia shkola*, no. 5, 1938, 102ff.
[70] Ibid.
[71] Kaftanov report, *Vysshaia shkola*, no. 6-7, 1938; Ivanov memoir, Columbia University Archive, pp. 40-42; Ukraintsev, p. 225.

Supervision, strict grading, conformity to rules, and discipline keynoted the new era as the government sought to improve the quality of new specialists. Not only was practice work tightened up, but the last vestige of independent study disappeared in 1938. The one free day a week reserved for such study during the regular academic year was abolished; students were expected to spend at least six hours per day, six days a week doing supervised work at their schools.[72] Graduates from this period indicate that this was indeed the practice. As the new head of the Committee on Higher Schools, S. Kaftanov, noted, at the May 1938 conference of educators, student discipline was still poor and many students did not complete their work on time. He warned: "The government gives the student everything: free tuition, dormitories, textbooks, a scholarship and it demands firm discipline in higher educational institutions. *Firm discipline is one of the elements educating students, forcing them to be organized.*"[73] Students who skipped classes, or read newspapers or slept in class were generally reprimanded, and if they repeated their offenses, they were called to the dean and eventually suspended or expelled. Students were also generally expelled if they received failing marks in two courses.[74]

Other problems remained to plague Soviet educators and serve as a brake on the quality of higher technical education. Good textbooks, informed by the latest advances in technology, were very scarce. Quotas for their production were consistently underfulfilled.[75] Foreign language competence remained at a low level, cutting young Soviet technologists off from Western advances. This deficiency was especially serious since travel abroad, which had been common during the Tsarist era and still existed in the early 1930s, became very rare after 1937. At this time most remaining foreign technologists were expelled from the country, and some Soviet technologists who had studied abroad found themselves under suspicion and sometimes under arrest.[76]

A major gap in quality also remained between the higher technical schools of the three major cities—Moscow, Leningrad, and Kiev—and those in the provinces. As late as 1933, almost seventy-five percent of all Soviet students in industrial higher education (industry, transport, and communications) were centered in these three cities, and the best teachers and facilities were found there.[77] This situation was little

---

[72] Kaftanov report, cited above.
[73] Ibid.   [74] Ivanov memoir, p. 40.
[75] *Industriia*, June 12, 1939; June 5, 1939.
[76] See the experiences of Alexander Gramp, a transport engineer who earned a master's degree at Purdue in the early 1930s and was arrested after his return to the U.S.S.R. in 1937: *Komsomol'skaia Pravda*, Nov. 15, 1964.
[77] Klishin, p. 177.

different from that of Tsarist times, even though the Soviet government had established many new institutes in parts of the country that had had none prior to the revolution. After 1933 the proportion of students in the three metropolitan areas dropped. Provincial institutions struggled to attract the best students and teachers, an effort that met only limited success before the start of World War II. In 1938, the government provided monetary incentives of ten to thirty percent above scale to teachers in provincial technical institutes.[78] Instruction in the Russian language became more common in non-Russian areas, and Russian became a required language for all students.[79] These measures were no doubt designed both to make such schools more attractive to teachers whose culture was Russian, and to make the scientific-technical literature in Russian accessible to young technologists of other cultural backgrounds. But it also reflected the resurgent Russian nationalism of the purge years, when condemnations of local nationalism were no longer balanced by equal condemnations of Great Russian chauvinism. Local nationalism became equated with "bourgeois nationalism," and advocates of local languages in higher technical schools flirted with danger. As a result, minority graduates of such schools during the Third Five-Year Plan were likely to undergo a process of Russification more intense than their predecessors a few years earlier. The situation in this respect came to resemble, if not fully duplicate, that existing in the higher technical schools of Tsarist Russia.

Finally, the network of higher technical schools was never able in this period to meet the demands of the economy for new specialists. In most specialties there were two, three, or more jobs for every graduate; even the expansion of correspondence courses after 1938 did not solve the problem.[80] The ultimate brake on growth, of course, was the support of the government. Although the number of graduate students preparing to be teachers of technology nearly doubled between 1937 and 1941, and the government increased its material support to levels far above those of the Tsarist government, the imbalance between the support given to the expansion of material production and the support given to higher technical education remained. This, of course, was no accident and ultimately reflected Stalin's approach to development. While Stalin's

---

[78] *Industriia*, April 14, 1938; Kaftanov report; *Vysshaia shkola*, no. 6-7, 1938. See also the confidential Kaftanov memorandum, TsGANKh, f. 8875, op. 38, d. 143, ll. 141-148, published for the first time in *Industrializatsiia SSSR 1938-1941*, p. 243.

[79] *Vysshaia shkola*, no. 6-7, 1938, 143-146; *Spravochnik dlia postupaiushikh v vuzy i vtuzy*, Moscow, 1940.

[80] *Industriia*, June 3, 1940; September 9, 1939; Kaftanov memorandum cited in n. 78 above. See also the recently published document, TsGANKh, f. 8243, op. 4, d. 544, ll. 1-3, 6-9, 11-13, in *Industrializatsiia SSSR 1938-1941*, p. 232.

attitude to higher education had evolved since 1928, his remarks between 1934 and 1938 indicate a lingering prejudice against formal
higher education and a bias toward the "practical," productive sector of
the economy. As he put it to a group of metallurgists in December 1934:

> We had too few technically educated people [in 1928]. We were
> faced with the dilemma: either to start training people in technical
> schools and postpone the production and mass exploitation of
> machines for ten years until technically educated cadres were
> trained in the schools, or to proceed immediately to make ma-
> chines and to develop their exploitation on a mass scale in our
> national economy so that people could be taught to master tech-
> nique, so that cadres could be trained in the process of making and
> exploiting machines. We chose the second path. We were fully
> aware that this would inevitably entail cost and overexpenditure
> due to the shortage of technically trained personnel capable of
> handling the machines, but we willingly resigned ourselves to this.
> True, lots of machines were damaged during this period, but on
> the other hand we gained the most precious thing—time, and we
> created what is the most valuable in national economy—cadres.
> . . . What in Europe took decades to do, we succeeded in doing,
> in the rough and in the main, in the course of three or four years.
> . . . This is the basis of the rapid industrialization of our country.[81]

In his short remarks to the Conference on Higher Education during
May 1938, Stalin spoke out against the "closed monopolists of science."
He reminded the learned delegates, most of whom had degrees and
years of experience as educators, not to overlook the talents and innovative ability of "simple, practical people," those without formal education.[82] While he may simply have been playing to the crowd, arousing
the populist instincts of the "little people" without formal higher education, who still constituted over ninety percent of the population, such
attitudes no doubt affected the development of higher technical education throughout this period. Stalin by 1938 was firmly in charge of Soviet
policy. While he had apparently compromised with the established engineering professoriate and had come to accept the need for formal
education of higher quality, his instincts still occasionally tugged him in
the other direction. At least some of the problems of higher technical
education can be attributed to the lower priority Stalin attached to such
education compared to other areas of Soviet investment, such as the
growth of heavy industry.

[81] *Lenin and Stalin on Labour*, Moscow, 1940, p. 563.
[82] *Vysshaia shkola*, no. 5, 1938, 258.

To sum up, on the basis of the evidence discussed here, the quality of technical education received by Soviet graduates throughout this period was far from satisfactory, and was viewed as such by most contemporary Soviet observers who were familiar with this area. Whether by 1941 Soviet higher technical education was inferior to, on a par with, or superior to that of general Western practice is more difficult to say. Without considerably more research on a comparative basis, we cannot answer that question with certainty. We can only affirm that higher technical education in the U.S.S.R. was different and improving in quality by 1941, though still plagued by many deficiencies.[83] These differences and deficiencies proved important in shaping the way young technical specialists approached their later work, as we shall see in subsequent chapters. With these conclusions, our case concerning quality must rest, and we can turn to a closer analysis of the student experience and its influence on the attitudes of the new technostructure.

[83] For a careful analysis of these deficiencies, see the article by a Soviet engineering professor, I. G. Sherbakov, *Sovetskaia nauka*, no. 4, 1939, 149-152.

10

THE EDUCATIONAL EXPERIENCE:
STUDENT LIFE AND ATTITUDES, 1928-1941

> *How do you expect a person to be vigorous at work when he has been conditioned to be passive in the face of oppression, even in defense of his own person?*
>
> Nikolai Chernyshevsky, 1859

> *Students lack the self-discipline for individual work . . . our knowledge is limited to what we hear in lectures. But this is very little for an engineer.*
>
> Soviet student, 1937

> *Students avoided political conversations like the plague.*
>
> Soviet student, 1935-1940

The student environment in Tsarist Russia was important both for the development of the revolutionary movement and for the origins of professions in the Russian Empire. Before 1917, the halls, classrooms, and student quarters of higher technical education were filled not only with talk of technical studies, but with the arguments and rhetoric of social change, revolutionary and otherwise. Students in technical schools were active in a variety of revolutionary and reformist movements.

As students in higher technical education before 1917 had been a volatile and dynamic element in Russian society, and had provided part of the nucleus for revolutionary movements and other forms of social change, then what happened to student life after the revolution? In particular, what happened to the student milieu during the massive expansion of higher technical education after 1928? Were these students in this area as revolutionary as many of their predecessors?

In this chapter I contend that students in higher technical education were no longer revolutionary in the same way. Although they continued to be agents of rapid social change, their role gradually changed from that of active initiators of this process, to that of more passive participants, whose activity was increasingly directed and channeled from above. Their social role and expectations were formed in a very different

244

environment from that of Tsarist students. How and why did this transformation take place and what were some of its consequences? For an understanding of these differences we must look more closely at the student milieu in the years between 1928 and 1941. This chapter will do so by examining the following critical areas: material conditions of students; social conditions and divisions among the student body; and political conditions. The evidence below points to two conclusions. The change in the student environment can be attributed to both positive and negative factors: on the positive side, the Soviet system, at least until 1940, provided more aid and incentives to students than the Tsarist system, and attempted in a more organized way to direct the energies of students into channels acceptable to the government; on the negative side, police controls and repression were greatly strengthened by comparison with the Tsarist era and proved more effective.

MATERIAL CONDITIONS

Before the changes of 1928, the Moscow Higher Technical School, one of the largest in the country with some six thousand students, reported that only six percent of its students received a stipend of fifty-two rubles or more a month, the minimum required to live in Moscow at this time. Forty-eight percent of the student body received half that amount, and the remainder, some forty-six percent, received nothing. As a result, most students were forced to earn funds to complete their education and the majority required seven years or more to finish a five-year course.[1] While detailed data are lacking for other technical schools before 1928, the matter of financial aid seems to have been only slightly better than before the revolution. The major improvement before 1928 came not in scholarship aid, but in the abolition of tuition fees and the greater availability of places in higher technical education.

The large influx of new students to Soviet higher education after 1928 created many problems, not the least of which concerned financial support. Many of these students were chosen from among those who had already begun careers as skilled workers or employees in state firms. Many of these older students were married and had families to support. The government greatly increased its financial support in order to speed students through their courses as soon as possible; but even so, such stipends were often barely sufficient to cover minimum living expenses.

As a result of the shortage of specialists and the financial needs of students, another form of support became widespread in technical education for a time after 1928, especially among students in their last two

[1] *TPG*, May 15, 1928.

years of study. Under the "contract system" a student would agree to work for a particular plant or firm for a given number of years, in return for financial support during his years of study. The amounts of these stipends from individual plants varied widely from place to place, but were often more generous than state scholarships. Competition among state firms for young specialists became so intense after 1928 that some students began to break their contracts with one firm in order to accept a better offer elsewhere. Better terms might include either more money or a shorter work obligation after graduation.

No penalties were imposed against those who broke contracts in this way, and one journalist complained of the "self-seeking" and "wheeler-dealer" tendencies that were developing among many young specialists.[2] Many managers came to prefer a uniform system of financial aid and compulsory job assignment after graduation. Such a system was established through the People's Commissariat of Labor and the various branches of industry in 1930.[3] This system greatly increased the dependence of students on the government, by comparison with Tsarist times, since one's job assignment and career were more than ever controlled from above; and nonconformity could have serious consequences for a student's future. The increasing differentials in pay and living standards in Soviet society after 1931 became another powerful form of social control for shaping the attitudes of students. Whereas between 1928 and 1931, industrial workers had often been as well off materially as technical specialists, the situation became sharply reversed in subsequent years. The fear of falling back into the working class, or even worse, the peasantry at the bottom of Soviet society, increased the incentive to study and to conform to the government's wishes.

John Scott, an American working in the industrial center of Magnitogorsk in the Urals in 1933, commented that wage differentials helped greatly to overcome "the traditional sluggishness of the Russian peasantry" and "stimulated the intellectual curiosity of the people." But, it might be added, such wage differentials also increased the government's control over students seeking entrance to a technical profession. Such students were not likely to risk jeopardizing their future by political nonconformity. Material incentives, plus the virtual absence of unemployment and the assurance of a job in the field one had studied, opened wide opportunities to the ambitious:

> The two together were so potent that they created a student body in the Magnitogorsk night schools of 1933 willing to work eight,

---

[2] *KS*, no. 8, 1928, 8.

[3] An attempt was made by statute in the fall of 1930 (see *Sobranie zakonov*, September 16, 1930, no. 47, art. 488).

ten, even twelve hours on the job under severest conditions, and then come to school at night, sometimes on an empty stomach, and, sitting on a backless wooden bench in a room so cold that you could see your breath a yard ahead of you, study mathematics for four hours straight.[4]

Night school students, such as these, had little energy left to think about anything else. Even for full-time students, however, conditions in higher technical schools came increasingly to resemble factory discipline, and left little time or energy for students who may have been oppositionally minded.

During the 1930s, scholarship aid increased substantially and alleviated what had been a major grievance before 1917; nevertheless some qualifying remarks are pertinent. The figures show that by 1934, an average of nearly seventy percent of all students in industrial higher education were receiving state scholarships.[5] The figures for those in agronomy were slightly higher.[6] By 1936, eighty-two percent of all students in higher education were receiving stipends, which ranged from 55 rubles to 135 rubles per month, depending on the year of study and grade average.[7] By 1938, almost ninety percent of all students received stipends.[8] This was a considerable improvement over Tsarist times. The average monthly Soviet wage in 1937 was 253 rubles, however, and, during times of shortage, particularly during the first several years of a course of study when stipends were lowest, a student could scarcely subsist on scholarship funds alone. During the famine of 1933 and 1934, many students from poorer and less well-connected families were forced to drop out of higher technical education. The situation was particularly severe in the Ukraine, which was struck hardest by the famine. There, according to one archival source, students were spending an average of 72 rubles a month for food alone in 1933, a time when their stipends ranged from 55 to 90 rubles per month.[9] Since more than one-quarter of all students in industrial higher education were studying in the Ukraine at this time, one can see the considerable impact of these conditions.

Corruption among the trusts that operated student cafeterias worsened the situation. According to the same source, these trusts raised food prices while decreasing the portions. Meat meant for four hundred sixty

[4] John Scott, *Behind the Urals*, Boston, 1942, p. 49.

[5] *Kul'turnoe stroitel'stvo 1930-1934*, Moscow, 1935, p. 68.

[6] Ibid.

[7] TsGAOR, f. 8060, op. 1, d. 1, l. 21, cited in Ukraintsev, p. 235.

[8] S. V. Kaftanov, report in *Vysshaia shkola*, no. 6-7, 1938.

[9] PAIIP TsK KP (Ukr.), op. 1, ed. khr. 1072, l. 282, cited in Bashevoi diss., p. 160.

portions was stretched to make five hundred eighty, and soup meant for one hundred fifty portions was watered to provide two hundred thirty. To deal with the situation a commission of the Ukrainian Communist party was appointed, and conditions improved somewhat after 1934. The quality of food increased, student discounts for the public baths, transportation, and movies were introduced, and living space increased slightly, practices that became standard throughout the Soviet Union.[10] After 1934, married students were allotted land for their own garden plots, and at least one school, the large Kiev Industrial Institute (formerly the Polytechnic) began to raise its own food. By 1935, this institute had nine head of horned cattle, three hundred pigs and over a thousand acres to provide food for its own students![11]

Material conditions in higher technical education, and in Soviet society as a whole, reached nadir in 1933. While conditions were never more than spartan by Western standards throughout this period, the government was more responsive to student hardships than during Tsarist times, and this fact no doubt served to quell student unrest somewhat. But it also strengthened a dependence upon the authorities and a form of social control that had been far weaker before 1917.

In 1937, at the height of the purges, student scholarships again increased dramatically, an act hailed in headlines as evidence of Stalin's concern for students in higher education. At the same time that teacher salaries were increased, stipends were raised from a range of 55 to 135 rubles per month to a range of 130 to 200 rubles per month. Students in Moscow and Leningrad were given a cost-of-living supplement of ten rubles additional per month.[12] Then in 1939, a small number of "Stalin scholarships" for the best students were introduced, providing monthly sums of 500 rubles, not far below the average salary of young engineers in industry.[13] With these positive incentives, aimed at improving material conditions for the nation's future elites, more negative forms of social control also appeared. Directors of institutes had the right to deprive students of stipends if their grade averages fell below a certain level or if they ran into political trouble.

Other changes in the system of financial aid had important implications for social conditions in higher technical education. At first based largely on financial need, the system of student aid was changed in 1932

---

[10] Ibid., pp. 154-159; H. G. Friese, "Student Life in a Soviet University," in George Kline, ed., Soviet Education, New York, 1957, p. 68.

[11] PAIIP, TsK KP (Ukr.), op. 1, ed. khr. 1079, l. 20, cited in Bashevoi, p. 153.

[12] ZI, Nov. 12, 1937.

[13] Ivanov memoir, Columbia University Archive of Russian History and Culture, p. 26.

to one based on the quality of academic work, as determined by the teaching staff and administration.[14] This was already a glimmer of a return to recognizing the importance of academic merit in higher education, a recognition that led to the abolition of class quotas for admission in 1935. It was a hint, too, that a lessening of educational opportunities was in store for financially needy students, whose academic preparation and performance may not have been as high as those from more privileged backgrounds. A further step in this direction occurred in 1940 when tuition fees were reinstated for higher education, and scholarships were abolished for students who earned fewer than three grades of "excellent" and two grades of "good" in their work.[15] While the system of granting stipends on the basis of academic merit alone may have hurt those needy students whose performance lagged, it no doubt acted as a strong incentive to improvement, and this was clearly the effect that government leaders sought. In addition to that effect, lawmakers hoped to attract students into those professions with the greatest shortage of specialists by offering higher stipends in these areas, just as wage differentials in the economy were used to stimulate output and attract workers to areas with shortages.[16]

Despite the increase in financial support, the student's lot was difficult in these years, since many basic consumer goods were rationed or in very short supply because of the high rate of investment in capital goods. The student press was filled with complaints about dormitories where students were cramped four, five, and more into a small room where cockroaches and bedbugs often had a prior claim on living space. In Moscow, domitory space was so short some students were forced to bed down, temporarily at least, on dissecting tables and in the aisles of the library.[17] Poor sanitary conditions led to a high rate of illness and absenteeism, and the Young Communists and student organizations organized periodic campaigns to improve the situation.[18] Programs of obligatory physical education and military training became more prominent. The student press urged students to form voluntary communes to improve their living conditions. In Tomsk, a Russian Orthodox convent was turned over to the students, and its buildings soon housed a thousand people attending various institutes in the area, while the chapel was converted into a student club.[19]

[14] *Sobranie zakonov*, July 19, 1932, Otdel I, no. 54.

[15] See the decree of October 2, 1940 in *ZI*.

[16] *Sobranie zakonov*, September 16, 1930, no. 47, art. 488; July 19, 1932, Otdel I, no. 54.

[17] *KS*, no. 3-4, 1928, 16.

[18] Ibid., no. 10, 1929, 23, 36; *ZPK*, no. 7, 1934, 559-561.

[19] Ibid., no. 9, 1929, 18.

Primitive as conditions may have been, they did not necessarily seem so to many students accustomed to poverty. Some of the students in these years came from backgrounds where they had never learned how to use a fork and spoon, or such amenities as a toothbrush.[20] One student in a Kharkov Aeronautical Institute described the student situation in these years:

Along with thousands of other students from various Kharkov institutes, I lived in the vast beehive of a dormitory on Pushkin Avenue called *Gigant*, the Giant. Here we were packed four, five, or more in a room, numb with cold in winter and grilled by summer heat.

Often, in that winter of 1930-31, the Gigant was so cold that the water in our washbasin was frozen. We picked up stray pieces of wood, fence slats, broken furniture, old newspapers to feed the tiny iron stove in our room, with its crazy, many-jointed chimney stuck out of a window. Thus we lived, studied, argued and dreamed of our country's industrialized future while fighting frost and hunger here and now.[21]

In spite of the hardships, this author—writing as an emigré in the West after World War II—continued to view his student years with a good deal of nostalgia. Optimism and hope for the future characterized many of the students:

In the morning we did calisthenics in our narrow room to take the edge off the frost. Then we would eat in the Gigant dining room. The standard breakfast was a small bowl of porridge, a piece of black bread and tea without sugar or lemon. Hiking to the Institute, chilled to the bone and still hungry, however, we were by no means a sorrowful lot. We were full of talk and plans—about the Institute, the Gigant, the party and ourselves.[22]

Spartan living conditions alone did not lead to the kind of unrest common before 1917, partly because material conditions among students seemed better by comparison with their former situation and certainly by comparison with the surrounding conditions of the 1930s. The more active concern and control of the government and party helped to short-circuit the growth of active antigovernment movements

[20] Emelianov memoirs in *Novyi mir*, no. 1, 1967, 8ff.
[21] Kravchenko, p. 61. This was considered one of the best dormitories in the U.S.S.R. (See *ZPK*, no. 4, 1934, 54-56.)
[22] Ibid.

among the students. Students were considered a privileged element in society, and had a higher status to protect than their predecessors.[23]

The evidence presented here suggests that material conditions, massive propaganda about the need to work for a better future and repay the state for one's education, combined with a fear of losing scholarship aid and military deferments, served to channel student energies in other directions.

SOCIAL CONDITIONS

Material conditions were not the only factors that accounted for changes in the student milieu. During the First Five-Year Plan, the party and government sought to exploit social divisions among the students, and the resulting atmosphere of class war served as a lightning rod, diverting many students into a form of activism that did not threaten the established powers.

There were sharp divisions among various groups of the student body in these years, and little mingling socially between the proletarian element and those whose parents were members of the intelligentsia. In Moscow, an observer also noted a division between the Muscovites and students from the provinces. The Muscovites tended to look down upon the provincials, especially the peasants and urban poor who often came to Moscow wearing felt leggings and little more than the homespun clothes on their backs. Students from poorer backgrounds sometimes envied the children of the well-to-do, and the government sought to exploit these differences through the Proletarian Student Union, until its dissolution in 1934. Many of the activities of this organization have already been discussed in prior chapters, but we need to look further at how its members viewed these differences. A 1929 article in the Union's journal *Red Students* is very revealing in this respect. A student, who had grown up in a state orphanage and was attending a Moscow institute on scholarship, wrote: "The most closely-knit group, not surprisingly, are our local 'gentry' (children of the specialists and the intelligentsia). At lectures, they occupy several benches, always sitting together, and during breaks, their group is always filled with boisterous conversation and laughter. They avoid everyone else, never strike up a conversation, and when addressed—if they answer at all— then it is in a coldly polite tone." She noticed that the girls in this group were always well-dressed with good shoes, and exuding a fragrance of

[23] Friese, pp. 74-77. This view is confirmed by Nikolai Ivanov, "The Training of Soviet Engineers," in Kline, pp. 182-184.

powder and perfume. While envious of such students, the same observer also criticized the proletarian students and "practicals"—the older group with work experience and families back in the provinces. She considered most of them too narrow in their interests and motivations: "I was reminded involuntarily of Ostrovsky [the nineteenth century playwright who portrayed the manners and morals of traders and merchants], of merchants who were petty tyrants and their slippery shop assistants who would tolerate everything, knuckle under and—once having crawled to the top—acted the very same way," that is, by emulating their tyrannical masters.[24]

Although an editorial note to this article cautioned that its tone was too pessimistic, it was published for "purposes of discussion," and its final judgment on the motives of many students was harsh: "It is very difficult to work in the atmosphere of higher education; here people work not in order to help society, not out of an interest in their work, but almost exclusively from ambition, a desire to get ahead, a desire to join the party."[25]

This view was subjective and personal, yet there is little doubt that the party and government sought to make private motives of ambition in higher education serve the state interest, rather than allowing these same ambitions to threaten the authorities. After 1932, the atmosphere of class war in education diminished, although the social divisions remained. Student energies were increasingly taken up by a more rigid curriculum, which by 1938 consumed six hours a day, six days a week in supervised instruction. In addition the government sought to project student hostilities outward, toward a common enemy: capitalist encirclement and the growing fascist threat abroad. Military training was required, and even physical education became militarized. Learning to toss grenades and fire small caliber weapons and rifles was a standard part of higher education. While the Tsarist government might justifiably have feared that such skills would be turned against it, the Soviet government managed to prevent any outbreaks of student unrest, filling up the student schedule with controlled activities.[26]

POLITICAL CONDITIONS

A final key to the success of controlling students must be sought in the political conditions of higher technical education. Where the Tsarist government had relied largely on repression to quell student unrest, the

[24] KS, no. 8, 1929, 11ff.   [25] Ibid.

[26] For some idea of these activities and the demands made upon students, see the Soviet journal, Sovetskoe studenchestvo, 1934-1938.

Soviet government combined a much stricter and more severe repression with attempts to co-opt revolutionary energies and control them through student organizations. The Tsarist government had outlawed most student organizations, but the Soviet government and party sought to enlist as many students as possible into officially approved organizations. Between 1928 and 1934 there were three major political organizations on campuses: the Union of Proletarian Students, the Young Communists (Komsomol) and the Communist party. These organizations were most active in the years from 1928 to 1933. After 1934, with the deemphasis on class criteria in higher education, the Proletarian Student Union was disbanded, leaving only the Komsomol and regular party organizations. Their relative role also changed (Table 10.1). Be-

TABLE 10.1. COMPOSITION OF STUDENTS
ENTERING HIGHER TECHNICAL EDUCATION

Year	Heavy Industry	Communications	Agriculture
	CP Members & Candidates		
1931	26.0%	35.3%	22.4%
1932	21.0	37.9	21.5
1933	15.0	16.8	15.3
1934	8.6	9.0	6.0
1935	6.7	6.3	6.1
	Komsomol Members & Candidates		
1931	25.7%	18.2%	33.7%
1932	30.7	30.5	38.4
1933	41.8	42.8	35.7
1934	45.1	46.5	36.4
1935	46.1	49.7	37.9

tween 1929 and 1933 the percentage of students in the higher schools of heavy industry, for example, who were members of either the party or Komsomol ranged from seventy-one percent down to fifty-six percent.[27] After 1933, party membership declined sharply among students, as they became younger, and the Komsomol became the primary student organization. (The minimum age for party membership was twenty-six, and after 1933 most students were younger.)[28]

Between 1936 and 1941 about half the students in higher technical

[27] Chutkerashvili, p. 23.
[28] Kul'turnoe stroitel'stvo SSSR 1935, Moscow, 1936, p. 76.

education felt obliged to join the Komsomol, although its activity in educational administration during the 1920s was curbed in the 1930s, and it grew more passive, serving largely to transmit party propaganda and directives and to urge students to do better in their school work. "By the end of the 1930s Komsomol members were complaining more and more frequently that they had only duties and no privileges or rights," according to one former student.[29]

Nonetheless, students learned that their career prospects would be affected favorably by membership. Although nonparty students generally did better academically, that fact could scarcely compensate for failure to participate in the Komsomol and, preferably, to join the party in their student years or shortly thereafter. When a majority of the students in a given class, group, or course were Komsomol members, it was rather difficult for the others not to join. Nonmembers were frequently cross-examined as to why they had not joined; their "social origins" were examined, etc.[30]

Membership in the Komsomol or Communist party proved to be a potent form of political control over the student body. The admission procedure gives some idea of the atmosphere these organizations created:

> The mechanism of admission to the Komsomol was fairly complicated. Each candidate had to write out a short autobiography and then submit to a detailed oral questioning. He was asked such questions as "What did your father do before 1917? What did your father or older brother do during the Revolution? What are they doing now? Are any of your relatives living abroad or under arrest? Do you write to them?"[31]

Friends of the candidate and Komsomol members who had endorsed the membership application were questioned as well. Once a member, students were sometimes rebuked for spending too much time on partying, sports, or romances, to the neglect of their work, and for being untidy, or otherwise departing from accepted norms. "You should be ashamed of the example you're setting," was a not infrequent comment from Komsomol officers to nonconforming members.[32]

Full party membership among students in higher technical education fell to as little as three to five percent in the later thirties.[33] Party members enjoyed special status, but bore even heavier responsibilities

---

[29] Friese, p. 75.

[30] Ibid. See also the Ivanov article in Kline, pp. 180-183, and *Komsomolskaia pravda*, for the period from 1933 to 1941.

[31] Friese, p. 73.   [32] Ibid., pp. 73-77.

[33] *Industriia*, July 3, 1937; August 15, 1937; Ivanov in Kline, p. 180.

than Komsomol members. In the early 1930s, students who belonged to the Communist party were frequently called upon to perform special missions that might take them away from their studies for long periods. For example, many of these students were mobilized for work in the villages, requisitioning grain from the peasants, and enforcing collectivization. They could also be called up at any time to aid a local factory in production work or to perform a variety of party tasks related to propaganda and other political and social work. The most disruptive of these political obligations ceased after the early 1930s, but the drain on the time of students who were party members remained heavy and probably helps to account for their poorer academic performance, confirmed by contemporary Soviet sources.[34]

The advantages of party membership for one's future career and current living conditions were great, but so were the risks. In the years between 1929 and 1941, there were three general purges of party members that affected students in higher technical education. These students were subject to a degree of discipline and political control from above even greater than that of the student body at large and quite unlike anything known in Tsarist times. Although before 1917 students may have joined a variety of political parties, none were so tightly disciplined by or closely tied to the ruling powers in Russian society. To have joined the Communist party and to have been purged was to live in an atmosphere of ostracism and closed doors reminiscent of a Kafka novel, and this introduced into higher technical education an external element that was basically new.

The purge among student Communists in higher technical education has been described by several sources, and is worth recounting to show one means used to enforce political conformity among this element of the student population. At every university and institute a special purge commission, composed of two or three trusted party members, would conduct a public examination of every party member in that institution. Sometime before this public hearing, a special box was set up where any individual could submit comments about a particular party member. The Special Department [secret police] and local purge commission would examine these signed or anonymous statements and include them in each member's dossier, to be used as evidence and a basis for cross-examination. At the public examination, "the commission members sat behind a red-draped table on a platform decorated with portraits of

---

[34] *ZPK*, no. 2, 1937, 10. See also the party decree of August 7, 1933, seeking to reduce the burden of social obligations placed on Komsomol members and the interference of such duties with academic work: *Spravochnik partiinogo rabotnika*, Vypusk, 8, 871-872, Moscow, 1934.

Politburo members and slogans; a bust of Stalin, banked with flowers, held the most prominent position."[35] Each member handed his party card to the commission chairman and related an outline of his life. "It was a political and spiritual strip act—an outline of his origins, his career, his interests, with confession of sins, near-sins and mistakes as the chief purpose. It was always better to bring up errors yourself, if you suspected that they were known to the Commission; 'concealing' anything from the party compounded the gravity of the crime concealed."[36]

If there was no serious evidence against a member—if he had been honest in his autobiography, and any denunciations against him could be disproven—the commission would give him its stamp of approval and return his party card. If there were serious grounds against him, such as an association with some anti-Stalinist opposition group, a bourgeois background, or a variety of other factors—not all of which might be apparent in the formal reasons given—a member might be deprived of his card. It was possible to appeal such decisions to higher party organs, but the process could take months. In the meantime, a former party member often found himself treated like an unperson.

Finally, we must mention police controls in higher technical education, since these proved to be highly effective and influential in forming student attitudes, and were increasingly relied upon as the more active role of student political organizations was curbed after 1933. Political surveillance of the student body took on an added intensity. Kravchenko described the situation as he experienced it in the Kharkov Aeronautics Institute during the early 1930s:

> There was at the Institute, as in every Soviet industrial undertaking or government bureau, a Special Department connected with the G.P.U. It was headed by a Comrade Lebed. No one could enter its office, except in a state of terror when summoned for questioning. Few of us knew what went on behind the grated little window in the steel door. At the same time few of us were so naive that we did not realize that every student had his own dossier in the Special Department, where his every word and act, where the very accent of his behavior was recorded.

[35] Kravchenko, pp. 132ff.

[36] Ibid. While Kravchenko is describing the purge that he experienced in 1933 at the Dniepropetrovsk Metallurgical Institute, the procedure was similar to that outlined for the 1929 party purge in *Krasnoe studenchestvo*, no. 14, 1929, 4. Another description of the purge procedure, as experienced by an aeronautical engineer in this period is given by A. S. Yakovlev in his autobiography (*Tsel' zhizni*, Moscow, 1966, pp. 5-6); it confirms the two accounts above in many of their details.

The files on "Personal Cases" contained information about the student's or teacher's private life, his relatives, his political past. It contained, above all, the reports and denunciations by secret agents deployed through every class and dormitory and by volunteer informers currying favor with officialdom or moved by grudges and rancor.[37]

According to a former Soviet woman engineer, who graduated from the Odessa Polytechnic Institute in 1933, arrests of students and professors were frequent. Sometimes a student would awaken to find entire classes cancelled because so many of the teachers and students had been arrested the previous night.[38]

The illegal "student circle" had been an institution of Tsarist student life. Like-minded students organized small groups to discuss political ideas and trends and, frequently, to become more active politically. Stalin and other old Bolsheviks had grown up participating in such circles, and were, therefore, very well aware of their potential for revolutionary action. Did such opposition "circles" exist in higher technical education during the 1930s? Kravchenko was aware of one such group in 1935, but it failed to develop, and its leader committed suicide in the wake of the Kirov assassination and the repression of oppositionists that followed swiftly.[39] While scattered groups may have continued to exist, it seems more likely that they were small and isolated, and quickly repressed. Most students were unaware of any underground opposition groups. As Nikolai Ivanov, a student of engineering in Moscow between 1935 and 1940 expressed it: "I cannot report any student plots or conspiracies directed against the regime; so far as I know there were none, because of the utter hopelessness of such attempts and the extraordinary risk attendant upon their failure."[40] It seems much more likely that passivity and avoidance of unapproved political activities became the norm by the late 1930s if not before. Whereas in Tsarist times students had met and circulated oppositional literature, sometimes even operated illegal printing presses, the barriers to such activity had become enormous by the 1930s. Ivanov noted that in the late 1930s it was even forbidden for students to have a private typewriter. A central typing office was maintained by the Institute. Papers and manuscripts submitted to it for typing were read and censored by the Special Section of the NKVD in his institute, which kept a file on every student and

[37] Kravchenko, p. 75. For a similar account of the way political controls affected students, see Konchalovsky, pp. 215ff.

[38] Interview by the author with Mrs. Rose Jermain, Feb. 13, 1970.

[39] Kravchenko, pp. 167-171.   [40] See Kline, p. 184.

teacher.[41] While such Special Sections obviously had an analogy in the Inspectorates maintained for student surveillance by the Tsarist government, the control of the NKVD, with its network of secret informers among the student body and staff, was tighter and more effective than that of its predecessors. The result was a level of conformity to higher authority unknown in later Tsarist times. Such conformity, however, was not inconsistent with a degree of disillusionment and growth of oppositional attitudes, if not oppositional activity. Both Kravchenko and Ivanov began to experience a degree of disillusionment and internal criticism of the regime during their student years. Kravchenko was especially troubled by the violence of collectivization, in which he participated as a party member, and the effects of the subsequent famine that he and his family witnessed at first hand in the Ukraine. His conscience was also troubled by the privileges and closed life of the political elite, with which he became familiar during several student romances.[42] Ivanov's view of the regime was affected by his first contact with the forced labor system of the NKVD:

> All of us—especially the students in hydraulic engineering construction—when we undertook our first practical work, had a chance to observe conditions at a large construction project (the hydroelectric power station at Rybinsk) which was being built by inmates of concentration camps under NKVD supervision. This experience opened the eyes of many students, changing their attitude from one of approval or indifference to one of condemnation of Soviet policies. Nevertheless, the relatively good treatment accorded students caused many of them to try to find excuses and justifications for the criminal acts of the Politburo.[43]

Thus, while the student experience of the 1930s was not conducive to active student protest or political initiative, it sometimes left a residue of doubt; it raised questions in the minds of some students concerning the gap between the words and deeds of the regime.

What can we say, by way of summing up, about the effects the educational experience had on the attitudes and behavior of the new Soviet technical intelligentsia? Young people who had grown up during a world war, two revolutions, civil war, famine, and poverty, often experienced quite intensely the sense of growth and the wide opportunities for education and professional advancement. Whatever their immediate

[41] Ivanov memoir in Columbia Archive, pp. 43ff.
[42] Kravchenko, pp. 68-73, 91-131, 148-166.
[43] Ivanov in Kline, p. 184.

hardships, these opportunities gave them a general basis for optimism about the future of the Soviet Union and their own futures.

Despite some exceptions, optimism seems to have prevailed among the new technical intelligentsia in the years covered by this study. It was inculcated by their educations and much of what they saw around them. Even the horrors of collectivization, the famine and terror, could be explained away as necessities of the day and no cause for despair about the future. As a group, the new technical intelligentsia were assured by their skills of a place in the future and were conditioned by their privileged position to view themselves as an elite, with the possibility of access to party and managerial positions. While, as individuals, their positions may still have been insecure and vulnerable—they saw the power wielded by Stalin over the old specialists, and they themselves were often manipulated and moved around like chessmen—as a group, they shared a community of interest that combined material advantages with limited but growing status in society. The terror and the suffering of individuals were factors they were generally conditioned to disregard, although certainly not all were able to.

Soviet higher technical education in this period tended to mold people more likely to think in terms of the manipulation of things than in terms of human needs and psychology. The technical specialists were accustomed to think about the production of material objects. The human element was largely ignored as a formal part of their professional education. Courses in management and industrial psychology were largely nonexistent in these schools, and courses in Marxism and Leninism, which replaced the humanities and empirical social science to a large degree, taught unequestioning acceptance of certain values and the actions of the ruling party.

During the 1930s, it was easy to transfer attitudes acquired in the manipulation of things to the human sphere, treating people as objects, rather than to think independently in terms of individuals and human groups with highly complex attitudes and needs, the kind of thinking fostered by critical studies in the humanities and social sciences. Force and manipulation were among the methods used to master the natural world of inanimate objects. Without a countervailing trend of thought in their educations or elsewhere in society, it was relatively easy for technical specialists to view these methods as natural ones in the human sphere as well. The values and goals of society, and the reliance on force to achieve these goals, came from higher authority and were to be accepted, not questioned.

Whereas in the 1920s, students in higher technical education had more actively shaped their own educations, by the early 1930s, students were conditioned to view self-initiative as something less than desirable, even harmful in attaining a quality education. One of the major failures of Soviet technical education in this period was its inability to combine quality and student initiative. After the early 1930s the assumption that hierarchy, rigid authority, and student passivity were necessary to raise the quality of higher technical education was never strongly questioned in public Soviet discussions of this area, a fact not surprising in light of the increasingly authoritarian tone of Soviet society. Yet this assumption seems questionable.

As the evidence discussed in these chapters suggests, many other factors help to account for the decline in quality between 1928 and 1932: higher student-teacher ratios, intimidation of the teaching staffs, insufficient material resources, poor preparation of entering students, etc. Certainly the ideas of shared power, mutual help, collective work, and responsibility for one's education, which had been prevalent in the 1920s, were not necessarily harmful in attaining a quality education. Yet such ideas were publicly discredited and blamed in part for the chaotic situation in this area before 1932; as we have seen, the pendulum swung to the opposite extreme in later years. The result, by the late 1930s, suggests that students were better prepared in scientific and technical subjects, but often lacked initiative and social cohesion. Not a few tried to get by with a minimum of work, and were unlikely to be as creative in their future professional roles as they might have been in a different atmosphere.

Reports were frequent in the Soviet press during the later 1930s of student passivity, trying to avoid compulsory lectures by falsifying attendance records, paying little attention in class, doing only the required minimum, even hiring other students to do homework or the important diploma project in the final year of a technical course.[44] The excitement of shared learning that one senses in accounts from the First Five-Year Plan gives way in later years to a sense of routine, of duty fulfilled, of individual competition for grades and future jobs, but often not much else. One can scarcely suppress the thought that the centralization and more rigid authoritarianism of Soviet technical edu-

[44] See, for example, the articles in *ZPK*, no. 1, 1937, 7-9; *Industriia*, Jan. 6, 1937, Feb. 2, 1937, Nov. 12, 1937; *Pravda*, January 15, 1938; article by Glauberman in *Vysshaia shkola*, no. 1, 1938; no. 3, 1938, pp. 56ff. See also the journal *Sovetskoe studenchestvo* and the following student newspapers for these years: *Industrial'nyi* (Leningrad Industrial Institute, formerly the Polytechnic); *Nash put'* (Leningrad Transportation Institute); *Za kadry verfiam* (Leningrad Naval Architecture Institute); *Na uchebe* (Moscow's Bauman Institute of Mechanical Engineering, formerly the Moscow Higher Technical School).

cation in later years, together with the neglect of the humanities and empirical social sciences, took its toll in the attitudes of students toward their education and future social roles.

This is not to say that an education that tended to condition the technical intelligentsia in such attitudes was wholly successful, but it did create a danger of such rigidity and one-sidedness. Fortunately, human beings are often not as narrow as their formal educations. Once disciplined to think methodically and solve problems in one area, they may be sufficiently flexible to concentrate independent thought and actions on other problems. The experience of working after graduation with large, organized groups of people may have helped some members of the new technical intelligentsia break out of the mold of unquestioned values, inculcated by their educations, and methods inappropriate in dealing with human beings. For this purpose as well as others, it will be useful to examine working conditions in the Soviet economy and to investigate their general influence on the social relations of the technical intelligentsia. Part 4 will attempt to determine how effective this group proved at both routine and creative work, and what role and status they achieved in Soviet society after graduation.

The Technical Intelligentsia at Work, 1928-1941

11

THE PRODUCTION SPECIALIST
AND THE POLITICS OF PLANNING

*It is in the interests of us, the engineers, that
the director be powerful in the Party. We look
to the director to promote our interests, the interests of the plant,*

Soviet production specialist[1]

The role of the production specialist was probably the most difficult
and risky of any filled by members of the technical intelligentsia. As
one Soviet specialist active in these years put it, the production engineer
had to be "able to walk a tightrope without an umbrella."[2] Work at the
production level subjected technical specialists to intense pressures, for
which their educations had only partially and often poorly prepared
them. Such work changed the lives and careers of many young specialists, drove some to drink or to prison and many others to seek a more
prestigious or less dangerous role in higher economic administration,
party work, research, or teaching—the other major alternatives for graduates of Soviet higher technical education.

One of the major reasons for this situation can be found in the way
the planning system under Stalin functioned between 1928 and 1941,
and the pattern of conflicts and alliances it fostered. The present chapter
will analyze the political struggle over plan *formulation* in the 1930s, the
environment this created for production specialists, and the tendency for
closer alliances with industrial managers that this system fostered. Chapter 12 will analyze the major kinds of conflict that the system of plan
fulfillment, and other factors, created for production specialists. It will
deal particularly with the way such conditions led many graduates from
Soviet higher technical education to avoid production work or flee from
it as quickly as possible, with major consequences for Soviet society.

Before 1928, Soviet politics was largely concerned with consolidating
political power within the country and the Communist party and re-
building a shattered economy; after 1928, however, it increasingly ad-

[1] Harvard Project on the Soviet Social System, Interview no. 384, B 2 Schedule,
p. 20, copy on deposit at the Widener Library, Harvard University.
[2] Ibid., Interview no. 65, p. 8.

dressed itself to planning economic growth, allocating resources, and distributing power within the system of planned economy. Since industrial growth received the highest priority, the politics of formulating industrial plans and the bureaucratic context in which they were carried out had a crucial effect on the work of production specialists. The planning process and organization of Soviet industry have been well detailed elsewhere, and will not be repeated here.[3] Yet, the politics of industrial planning, particularly for heavy industry as the most important sector, has not been well understood. This subject forms a necessary context for understanding the role of production specialists and their relations with industrial management.

During the years from 1928 to 1941 generally between one-half and one-third of all graduates of higher technical schools were employed in direct production work. Therefore, it is essential to analyze the work environment for specialists in this area.[4] The focus here will be on levels from the rank-and-file production engineer without administrative duties up to and including chief engineers and technical directors of plants and mines. A case study of the work of agronomists would be useful, but is not attempted here because a far smaller proportion of agronomists worked directly in agricultural production. Production specialists in industry were the largest segment and received the most attention from the authorities and the press. They, therefore, tended to set the pace for others.

It is in the matrix of social relations at the production level in industry that the consciousness of a crucial element of the technical intelligentsia developed. The focus in this and the next chapter will be on the social relations of production specialists with the following groups: industrial managers; party, police, and trade union officials; industrial workers; and fellow specialists, in particular, the large number of "practicals" (*praktiki*) without formal technical education.

Although a large literature exists on industrial management in the Soviet Union during this period, no published study has specifically examined the work relations of the technical intelligentsia at the produc-

---

[3] See, for example, A. Baykov, *The Development of the Soviet Economic System*, Cambridge, 1947; Abram Bergson, *The Economics of Soviet Planning*, New Haven, 1964; Maurice Dobb, *Soviet Economic Development*, London, 1948; Peter Diaconoff, "Gosplan and the Politics of Soviet Planning, 1929-1932," Ph.D. diss., Indiana University, 1973.

[4] *Industrializatsiia SSSR 1938-1941*, Moscow, 1973, p. 270; I. Lyashnikov, *Podgotovka spetsialistov promyshlennosti SSSR*, Moscow, 1954, pp. 79-80; A. Beilin, *Kadry spetsialistov SSSR*, Moscow, 1935, p. 188; *Podgotovka kadrov v SSSR, 1927-31*, Moscow, 1933, p. 14; *Itogi vypolneniia pervogo piatiletnego plana razvitiia narodnogo khoziastva SSSR*, Moscow, 1935, p. 215.

tion level, or tried to interpret the broader implications of this experience.[5] Previous works have generally emphasized the economic side of the planning process and the organization of production. A great deal of new material on Soviet industry before 1941, including the role of production specialists, has become available in recent years, and the political importance of the subject has also become more apparent with an analysis of the ruling elite of the post-Khrushchev era. These developments make it both possible and important to assess the role of production specialists in the light of new knowledge.

It is widely known that in the 1960s and early 1970s some two-thirds of the ruling elite of Soviet society, members of the Politburo and Central Committee, had higher technical educations, a proportion that has tended to increase in recent years. The degree of their early involvement in production work has not so far been carefully analyzed. Using Soviet biographical data published between 1958 and 1965, I analyzed the careers of one hundred twenty-six members of the Central Committee and Politburo who had higher technical educations.[6] I learned that all had begun their professional careers in the two decades before 1941. Ninety-nine of them (seventy-eight and one-half percent) had some direct experience as production specialists during the years this monograph covers. Of these, the large majority, eighty out of ninety-nine, had spent some time as production engineers in industry. The remaining nineteen had direct production experience in agriculture. The years spent as production specialists averaged over eight and a half for the overall group, although for those who reached the highest level, the Politburo, the average dropped to less than five years, still long enough to be an important formative stage in their careers, along with the years spent in higher technical schools. No Politburo member spent more than eight years directly as a production engineer in industry, although more than half of the Central Committee members surveyed spent eight or more years, some much longer, in such work.

These data suggest that direct experience in production, beginning before World War II, was an important stage in the early careers of the Soviet ruling elite. Statistics often raise more questions than they answer, however. In this case, we must ask if there are any clues from a

[5] G. Bienstock, S. M. Schwartz, and A. Yugov, *Management in Russian Industry and Agriculture*, Ithaca, 1944; David Granick, *Management of the Industrial Firm in the USSR*, New York, 1954; J. S. Berliner, *Factory and Manager in the USSR*, Cambridge, Mass., 1957.

[6] The biographical data for these conclusions were drawn from *Deputaty soveta soiuza i soveta natsionalnosti*, Moscow, 1959, 1965; and *Prominent Personalities in the USSR*, Metuchen, N.J.

qualitative study of the production environment to account for the eventual rise of men from this group to numerical dominance in the ruling elite.

On this question, the evidence presented below is suggestive, if not conclusive. There was no clearcut indication by 1941 that men with higher technical educations and production experience might later come to prominence as the single largest group in the party and state leadership. In fact, the evidence below suggests that they were far from being the most numerous element promoted to head party, police, and government posts in the wake of the purges from 1936 to 1938. The largest group among the new cadres appear to have been Stakhanovites, and other promoted workers and party rank-and-file, generally young people under the age of forty, who lacked the combination of higher technical educations, production work, and party affiliation that has increasingly characterized the post-Stalin and post-Khrushchev elites. Why, then, did those with higher technical educations emerge as the single largest element in later years? Despite, or perhaps because of, the nature of the planning system and other difficulties at the production level, a certain cohesiveness of outlook and experience developed among them. This, together with their indispensable knowledge, made such men more useful to the regime over the long run than other elements that were promoted immediately after the purges. This was particularly so, because of the nature of the tasks that faced the Soviet Union in preparing for World War II, in the war itself, and in the economic reconstruction and competition with the West after World War II. A conclusive answer to this question must await further studies of this group carried beyond 1941, but certain traits that developed from their experience before the German invasion probably helped provide the competitive edge. The reasons for this outcome are suggested, in part, by the kinds of conflicts and alliances experienced at the production level in the years before World War II.

In this and the following chapters, I contend, on the basis of the available evidence—contemporary, archival, and memoir in nature—that certain kinds of conflict became endemic at the production level, and that alliances developed that had far-reaching consequences for the role and status of the technical intelligentsia as a whole, including the ambitious young party engineer. Although the relationship with industrial managers remained ambivalent throughout this period, the closest alliances of production specialists were with managers, a point I have already discussed in earlier chapters concerning the political trials of the old specialists and conflicts over higher technical education. This point will be developed in a different, corroborative context here. Industrial managers tried to protect specialists with whom they had developed good working relations and to build teams of such people to take with them when they were transferred. Promotions of production specialists into the ranks of industrial management also became more frequent from the early 1930s on, a process that continued during and after the purges of 1936 to 1938. These two groups began to merge, although never fully during this period. (Kosygin, to take one example, rose from shop foreman to plant director and finally Commissar of the textile industry before World War II. His case was not unusual, as a study of the career patterns of major industrial managers corroborates.[7]) One result was that production ties as well as old school ties became increasingly important in career patterns.[8]

Industrial managers and production specialists tended to form alliances because of shared interests. Both managers and specialists were responsible for the fulfillment of planning targets set by the party and government. They were rewarded primarily for such fulfillment, particularly for quantitative output. Therefore, managers and specialists needed each other to survive and prosper. The result was a form of symbiosis, which biologists define as "the living together of two dissimilar organisms, especially if the association is mutually beneficial."[9] Analogies from biology can be misleading, of course, and we must not neglect elements of friction that could also develop between these two groups, the sources of which will be discussed in chapter 12. But the force of mutual need often overrode whatever friction existed. Both groups wanted targets they considered realistic. Both needed the authority and the resources to meet such targets. Production specialists needed the managers to exert influence within the system, first of all to obtain realistic targets for production, and secondly, to obtain the materials and labor to fulfill the targets received. Managers needed the specialists for the information to formulate realistic plans and for their technical and organizational skills at the production level in fulfilling plans. Such plans, once adopted, had the force of law in Soviet society after 1928, and managers were ultimately held responsible for their fulfillment. Of course, if the plans were not fulfilled, they could always try to find scapegoats, and at such times managers—particularly the older ones

[7] Ibid.

[8] An interesting example of how production and old school ties can link careers can be found in the biographies of Tevosian, Emelianov, and Brezhnev—the former two are outstanding metallurgical engineers, industrial managers, and government officials, and Brezhnev, of course, is a metallurgical engineer and party official. See Emelianov references in note 74 below and Ashot Azumanian, *Taina bulata*, Moscow, 1967.

[9] *Webster's Third New International Dictionary of the English Language*, Springfield, Mass., 1965.

who were often technically illiterate and very different in background from the old specialists—might try to find such scapegoats among the specialists, a situation already discussed in an earlier chapter. Both centrifugal and centripetal forces were at work in these relationships, but over the course of time the centripetal forces drawing these two groups together tended to become stronger, especially as their backgrounds and expectations became more similar.

These relationships are important not only for understanding the role of production specialists, but because they permit a broader, more informed view of Soviet history during this period. Evidence suggests that there is a common thread running through the politics of the period from 1928 to 1941, and it concerns the process of planning. An understanding of the political side of this process provides, for example, a link between the trials of engineers from 1928 to 1930, and the purges of 1936 to 1938. Of course, both series of events were aimed at destroying Stalin's real or potential opponents, although the purges were much broader in scope and not focused specifically on the technical intelligentsia. Still, our analysis needs to go much deeper than this. Whereas several historians have provided evidence that Stalin was far from an unchallenged dictator well beyond 1929, no one has yet analyzed the centrality of the planning process as a focus of conflict between Stalinists and more moderate elements in the party leadership. One of the primary reasons Stalin had opponents in these years can be found in differences over planning goals and the way such plans were carried out. We have already seen how this was true in the case of the Industrial party trial, by looking at the background of its defendants, and their opposition to elements of the First Five-Year Plan. The way in which the policy of repression against the old technical intelligentsia was ended and a new policy of reconciliation was adopted in 1931 also provides evidence for this view, in chapter 6. The politics of higher technical education fits this pattern, as we have seen in chapter 7. What needs to be recognized is that many of the political events of this period, including the purges are linked together by conflicts over the planning process. Both the terror against the old specialists and the purges were also aimed at asserting the dominance of the political machine in the planning process —the personal, party, and police apparatuses headed by Stalin—over the economic and educational bureaucracies. And both periods of terror were aimed, in part, at breaking up potentially threatening alliances of managers and technical specialists. Such alliances had a tendency to reassert themselves at every opportunity, forming a powerful coalition of interests within the Soviet system that periodically challenged the political apparatus.

A central thrust of the purges, although certainly not the only one, was aimed at practices followed by Ordzhonikidze, the Commissar of Heavy Industry, and the industrial managers around him. Together with their technical specialists, this element challenged Stalinist goals and seemed a threat to Stalinist political dominance, beginning in the early 1930s. This challenge was part of a pattern that grew out of the nature of the Soviet economic system and the roles of these groups. It showed a tendency to grow stronger, not weaker, as the system developed and as industry grew larger. The challenge of Ordzhonikidze and his allies in the 1930s was more serious, for example, than the rather feeble attempts by old specialists and by the Bukharin-Rykov opposition to influence the planning process and make it conform to goals they considered realistic in the years 1928 and 1929.[10] The old specialists and the moderate "Right Opposition" had failed in their attempts. Ordzhonikidze and his allies succeeded to a surprising degree, until the purges of the later 1930s and the formulation of the Third Five-Year Plan, which went into effect in 1938. The degree to which this tendency grew stronger in later years falls beyond the scope of this study and awaits a definitive answer. It would seem useful for future researchers to see where this line of reasoning leads them, particularly when investigating the Voznesensky affair of 1949 and the emergence of a powerful managerial machine under Kosygin and other former technical specialists in the political leadership during the later 1950s and 1960s.[11]

Ordzhonikidze, an old Bolshevik and former paramedic, generally known as a crony of Stalin's until 1930, was appointed to head industry in the fall of that year.[12] He replaced Kuibyshev, after industrial management was severely criticized for failures in fulfilling the enormous goals of the First Five-Year Plan. Ordzhonikidze, in fact, had been one of industry's severest critics. His report to the Sixteenth Party Congress in the summer of 1930 probably was a major factor in Kuibyshev's transfer from *Vesenkha*, the operational organ for state-controlled industry, to head of *Gosplan*, where his primary duties involved plan formulation, not plan fulfillment.[13] Ordzhonikidze, until his own transfer in late 1930, was head of the Workers' and Peasants' Inspectorate (*Rabkrin*), where one of his major duties had been investigating the

---

[10] See chapter 4 above, and Stephen F. Cohen, *Bukharin and the Bolshevik Revolution*, New York, 1973.

[11] *Khrushchev Remembers*, New York, Bantam ed., 1970, pp. 261-273.

[12] I. Dubinskii-Mukhadze, *Ordzhonikidze*, Moscow, 1967, pp. 288ff.; *Po puti chrezvychainogo komissara*, Rostov na donu, 1970; Zinovii I. Fazin, *Tovarishch Sergo*, Moscow, 1970; V. S. Kirillov and A. Ya. Sverdlov, *Grigorii Konstantinovich Ordzhonikidze (Sergo). Biografiia*, Moscow, 1962, pp. 254-256.

[13] *XVI S"ezd VKP(b). Stenograficheskii otchet*, Moscow, 1934, pp. 300-329.

problems of industry. It was in that capacity that he severely criticized *Vesenkha*. Afterwards, he received an opportunity to put his muscle where his mouth was, so to speak. As head of *Vesenkha* and then as Commissar of Heavy Industry, after the reorganization of industry in 1932, he became the most important industrial manager in the country until his suicide in February of 1937. In the process of changing jobs, his interests and viewpoint also changed. From being an advocate of high Stalinist goals, he soon began to act as a brake upon them, once fulfillment was his direct responsibility. In doing so, he found the advice and cooperation of technical specialists indispensable. Several memoirs and studies indicate the nature of this relationship.

For example, a memoir by a metallurgical engineer, A. S. Tochinsky, provides a significant glimpse into the planning process, consistent with the other evidence from these years.[14] According to this source, Tochinsky was called to Moscow in the summer of 1931 to discuss before the collegium of Heavy Industry the extremely poor performance of the southern metallurgical industry in meeting its production targets. Tochinsky had met Ordzhonikidze in 1918 during the civil war in the Caucasus, when he had organized production to aid the Bolsheviks at Ordzhonikidze's request. Meeting again in 1931, Ordzhonikidze invited him privately to the Commissar's office. The conversation reported below is a later reconstruction by this engineer, but it is consistent with what we know of Ordzhonikidze's behavior in these years.

Ordzhonikidze began by urging Tochinsky to speak frankly. "You are non-party; I am already a long-time Communist. The party has placed me in a most important post, and we have lost the first battle [in achieving high targets]. Today, in the collegium, this was again confirmed, although even before it had become evident. It seems that there is something we have not yet learned. What is it? You are a specialist, this must be more evident to you. Tell me what it is, only straight out, frankly. Is it possible that the plan is not realistic?"

Tochinsky answered that the present psychological atmosphere did not facilitate success: "I am non-party, but I know well that the Bolsheviks above all are realists, that they act out of realistic possibilities, and any kind of utopianism (*manilovshchina*) is foreign to them."

Ordzhonikidze asked where this specialist had uncovered utopianism.

"In the tasks, the plans, which are given to the factories. They are not realistic, because the conditions for their fulfillment have not been created. . . . Plans are given to factories not on the basis of a survey

---

[14] I. S. Peshkin, "Stanovlenie sovetskoi metallurgii," in *Byli industrial'nye*, Moscow, 1973, pp. 190-195. Peshkin was a veteran journalist for the newspaper *Za industrializatsiiu* who worked closely with Ordzhonikidze.

of concrete conditions, but are formulated on the basis of what these conditions should be. And this is not the first year such a line has been followed. At the end of each year, it turns out that the plans have not been fulfilled. Someone catches hell, they give someone else a reprimand, they remove someone. And then in the following year they do the same thing, adopt unrealistic plans."

When Ordzhonikidze questioned this specialist in detail, the latter brought out a notebook where he had calculated what he considered the realistic possibilities of southern metallurgical plants. Tochinsky was summoned back to Moscow to attend a meeting on November 9, 1931. It turned out to be a session of the Central Committee's Commission for Ferrous Metallurgy, which was preparing the 1932 targets for the iron and steel industry. Tochinsky was introduced to the Politburo members Rudzutak and Voroshilov, who, with Ordzhonikidze, were members of this Commission.

Ordzhonikidze opened the meeting by declaring that "the plan for 1932 will be built on a realistic base. He put the accent on the word 'realistic.' As the basis for his report were the figures which Ordzhonikidze had jotted down in what earlier conversation with Tochinsky."[15]

While no direct corroboration of this encounter has been found, the targets for ferrous metallurgy in 1932 were, in fact, trimmed down.[16] Another source indicates that Stalin and Ordzhonikidze clashed over this area in 1931, although more precise details have not been revealed.[17] It is known, however, that the struggle over planning targets continued between 1932 and 1934, and extended to other areas, as the Stalinists projected ever higher goals for the Second Five-Year Plan.

While admitting that the quality of production deteriorated in the first two years of the Five-Year Plan, and that critical lags in output occurred in certain key areas, Stalin and Molotov continued to push for ever higher goals during 1931 and 1932. Stalin made this general approach to planning explicit a number of times, for example, in this statement of 1932: "The Five-Year Plan is accepted by us as a minimum. We will also have control figures which will expand the Five-Year Plan from year to year. We will also have counter plans which likewise will lead to a further expansion of the Five-Year Plan."[18] These remarks

[15] Ibid.

[16] *KPSS v rezoliutsiiakh*, pt. 3, pp. 140-141, 169-173; G. K. Ordzhonikidze, *Stat'i i rechi*, vol. 2, pp. 392-423.

[17] Roy Medvedev, *Let History Judge*, pp. 154-155, based on a manuscript memoir quoted by Medvedev.

[18] *Izvestiia*, Feb. 7, 1932; see also J. V. Stalin, *Voprosy Leninizma*, 11th ed., p. 349; *Piatnadtsatyi S"ezd VKP(b). Stenograficheskii otchet*, vol. 1, Moscow, 1961, p. 59.

were made at a time when Ordzhonikidze was sounding a very different note. In a speech a few days earlier, a report to the Seventeenth Party Congress, Ordzhonikidze displayed more concern for analyzing and correcting the faults in areas where lags were apparent than for setting ever higher goals for the quantity of production. In fact, where the Central Committee had set a goal of seventeen million tons of iron in 1933, Ordzhonikidze, in his closing remarks to this party Congress, spoke of thirteen million tons.[19]

The gap between industrial managers and production specialists on one side and Stalinist superindustrializers on the other became increasingly apparent in the years from 1931 to 1934. The lags between plan projection and fulfillment became especially apparent in such key areas as the iron and steel industry and electricity.[20] Gleb Krzhizhanovsky, one of a number of anti-Stalinists who worked under Ordzhonikidze after his dismissal as chairman of *Gosplan* in 1930, was in charge of fulfilling plans for the production of electricity. A graduate electrical engineer and long-time associate of Lenin, he warned Stalin and Molotov in 1931 that unrealistic figures made actual operational planning very difficult, advice they ignored.[21]

One can still ask why Stalin, Molotov, and others followed this strategy of projecting highly unrealistic targets. Up to a point, it may have been sound. They knew the tendency of managers and specialists to underestimate capacity, in order to receive plans that would be easier to fulfill. High expectations and strong enforcement by the authorities probably did have considerable effect in breaking the cake of custom—the lethargy of earlier work habits and the sleepy spirit of a still largely rural country. But even by 1931 it was evident that many plans in key areas were not being fulfilled.[22] Why, then, did Stalinists continue to call for even greater increases in such areas, rather than trimming plans until problems of fulfillment were solved? Part of the answer probably lies in what one recent historian has called the "revolutionary heroic" tradition in the party, which had been forged in the experiences of the revolutionary movement and civil war period, 1918 to 1921.[23] This tradition was summed up in Stalin's phrase of 1928, "There are no fortresses which Bolsheviks cannot storm." Probably as important was the usefulness of such high targets not only as a psychological device to stimulate maximum achievement, but also to control industrial management and the technical intelligentsia, and assert the primacy of

[19] *Pravda*, Feb. 2, 3, and 4, 1932.
[20] *Sotsialisticheskoe stroitel'stvo SSSR*, Moscow, 1936, pp. xxii-xxiii.
[21] Flakserman, p. 145.   [22] *XVI S"ezd*, pp. 300-329.
[23] Cohen, *Bukharin*, pp. 312-315.

Stalin's apparatus. Since plans were held to have the force of law, nonfulfillment was, in fact, a violation of law for which management and specialists could be held responsible.[24] It was, in essence, a club that could continually be held over such elements, lest economic successes go to their heads and be used to undermine the political *apparat*.

Ordzhonikidze succeeded in applying the brakes to the planning escalator during the Second Five-Year Plan, 1933 to 1937. His victory was a victory for the technical intelligentsia as well and was viewed as such. Ordzhonikidze followed party discipline and did not criticize high targets that had already been approved and, therefore, had the force of law behind them. When industrial managers asked for more time to fulfill goals, Ordzhonikidze's response was typically the following, "The dates given are law. We have no right to change them."[25] At the same time, however, he would do his best to assure adequate labor and supplies to fulfill high-priority targets. He also continued to analyze the problems caused by rapid tempos, and fought stubbornly for lower targets in the future.

In this struggle Ordzhonikidze had a considerable power base. As Commissar of Heavy Industry, he headed the most important sector of industry. This was the sector in which Stalin and the Central Committee vested their hopes for economic independence and national might, and to which the greatest proportion of capital investment was directed. Since 1930, Ordzhonikidze had also been a member of the Politburo, the inner circle of party leaders who formulated policy. A majority of this small group could still overrule Stalin. Ordzhonikidze had a strong ally in this body, an old friend from the civil war days, S. M. Kirov, who headed the Leningrad party organization.[26] Of the nine or ten members of the highest policy-making body in the party, in fact, Stalin probably could not rely consistently on the support of a majority in a showdown with Kirov and Ordzhonikidze during the early 1930s.

Until the transcripts of Politburo meetings in these years become

[24] *Piatnadtsatyi S"ezd*, vol. 1, Moscow, 1961, p. 59; A. F. Khavin, *U rulia industrii*, Moscow, 1968, p. 91.

[25] Khavin, p. 91.

[26] Ordzhonikidze and Kirov had been good friends for many years. Recent Soviet sources indicate that they corresponded frequently between 1926 and 1934 and spoke almost daily by phone. Stalin strongly disapproved of personal friendships among his associates, particularly those who had a reputation for independence, such as Kirov and Ordzhonikidze. Kirov had achieved a good deal of autonomy for the Leningrad party organization, and, in 1932, he defied Stalin during a severe shortage of foodstuffs, when he opened the granaries of Leningrad to hungry industrial workers. See S. Krasnikov, *Sergei Mironovich Kirov*, Moscow, 1964, pp. 136, 174-175, 194, 196; S. Sinelnikov, *Kirov*, Moscow, 1964, pp. 316, 321, 355, 360; Krasnikov, *S. M. Kirov v Leningrade*, Leningrad, 1966, pp. 17, 162-164, 191; Orlov, p. 253; Conquest, pp. 41-42.

available to researchers, we will not know the inside story of such conflicts. Even to a well-placed young party specialist, such as the engineer Kravchenko, the existence of such disputes was well-known. Writing in 1946, shortly after he elected to remain in the U.S. while working as a high official of the Soviet Lend Lease Commission in Washington, Kravchenko recalled Ordzhonikidze's allies in the Politburo. He noted that "Kossior, Rudzutak, Chubar, and Antipov usually supported him [Ordzhonikidze]—all four were later arrested and disappeared in the course of the purges."[27] His testimony on this score is corroborated by recent Soviet sources.[28]

In January 1933 the Central Committee reversed the 1932 directives on planning, which had emphasized continued high quantitative targets. The discussions that went on in this body and among Central Committee members in 1932 and 1933 on questions of planning are largely unknown. What probably strengthened Ordzhonikidze's drive for lower targets, however, was not only the information he received from such specialists as Tochinsky and Krzhizhanovsky, but the disastrous situation in the economy that became fully apparent during late 1932 and early 1933. As a result of forced collectivization, the harvest was down some twelve percent from the previous year,[29] and industrial production, instead of climbing to all-time highs, actually began to decline in certain key areas. For example, in the winter of 1932 and 1933, production of coal was down some six percent from the previous year; iron ore production declined four percent; pig iron, five percent; steel, eleven percent; and petroleum, some twenty-one percent. Of the key areas in heavy industry, only electric power showed a dramatic rise in output, up some twenty percent, but still below planned projections.[30] Most of the giant, new plants in which so much capital had been invested during the First Five-Year Plan were behind schedule and began to come into full production only around 1934. As a result, the Central Committee, in January 1933, scrapped the guidelines of the year before. They decided

[27] Kravchenko, p. 240.
[28] Kravchenko's account of Ordzhonikidze's allies in the Politburo is corroborated by the following Soviet studies: V. Z. Drobizhev and N. Dumiova, *V. Ya Chubar*, Moscow, 1963, p. 67; M. Pohrebinsky, *S. V. Kosior*, Kyiv, 1963; Anatolii I. Melchin, *Stanislav Kosior*, Moscow, 1964. For two accounts of Rudzutak's conflict with Stalin see German Trukans, *Ian Rudzutak*, Moscow, 1963, pp. 92-94; *Voprosy istorii*, no. 8, 1964, 38-39. Rudzutak had been appointed to oversee the development of the chemical industry and clashed bitterly with Stalin over the high goals the latter set in such areas as the production of synthetic rubber. Rudzutak also succeeded Ordzhonikidze as head of the Workers' and Peasants' Inspectorate after 1930. In 1934 Stalin maneuvered Rudzutak out of *Rabkrin*, reorganizing that institution to Rudzutak's great distress.
[29] Conquest, p. 22; Dana G. Dalrymple, "The Famine of 1932-1934," *Soviet Studies*, January 1964, 250-284.
[30] *Sotsialisticheskoe stroitel'stvo*, Moscow, 1936, pp. 79-81.

that the Second Five-Year Plan should concentrate not so much on new construction as on mastering and bringing into full production the plants already constructed but not yet operating at capacity. According to the resolutions of this plenum:

> From this, it follows that during the Second Five-Year Plan the chief role in the growth of industrial production will belong no longer to the old factories but to the new, whose technology still has to be mastered, a fact which brings in its wake a certain lessening in the tempo of growth of industrial production in comparison to the tempos of the First Five-Year Plan.
>
> From this arises the necessity of less rapid tempos of growth of industrial production in the period of the Second Five-Year Plan— at least for the first two or three years of this plan.[31]

The same plenum approved an annual target for the growth of overall industrial production in 1933 of sixteen and one-half percent. While still high, this was considerably lower than similar targets for 1931 and 1932, which were forty-two and thirty-six percent, respectively. The new emphasis on quality also raised the authority of the quality control apparatus in industry, where Ordzhonikidze placed in charge a recent Stalin critic and former leader of the moderate opposition, Bukharin.[32]

Ordzhonikidze pressed for lower targets at the Seventeenth Party Congress a year later and succeeded in scaling down some of the figures proposed by Molotov in this report on the Second Five-Year Plan. Despite the decision of the Central Committee the previous year that the average yearly growth of all industrial production in the Second Five-Year Plan would be targeted at thirteen to fourteen percent, Molotov proposed to the Seventeenth Congress a higher rate, a yearly average of nearly nineteen percent.[33]

[31] "Obedinennyi plenum TsK i TsKK VKP(b), 7-12, ianvaria 1933 g., Rezoliutsiia po dokladam tt. Stalina, Molotova, i Kuibysheva," *KPSS v rezoliutsiiakh*, pt. 3, p. 184.

[32] Shortly after this conference, the network of quality control laboratories that Bukharin headed was greatly expanded. In January 1933, Bukharin was elected chairman of the Council of Factory Laboratories, which included quality control bureaus in all industries, not just Heavy Industry where he worked. (See *Zavodskaia laboratoriia* for 1932 and 1933, especially, no. 3, 1932, 5-8; no. 7, 1933, 3-8; no. 9, 1933, 3-13. When I looked up this journal in the library of Moscow State University during the fall of 1973, I discovered that all of Bukharin's articles had been cut out and his name on the masthead and table of contents had been pasted over with strips of paper. Fortunately, more complete copies of this journal exist elsewhere.)

[33] *XVII S"ezd*, p. 354. Molotov and Kuibyshev gave the two reports on the Second Five-Year Plan, but only Molotov's provided overall targets for the growth of industrial production. Kuibyshev spoke in more detail about specific areas.

In an unusual move, Ordzhonikidze got up before the Congress and proposed a change in Molotov's figures. He suggested a lower overall rate for industrial production of sixteen and one-half percent yearly, a figure below the rate proposed by Molotov, but still above that suggested the previous year by the Central Committee.[34] This move indicates an unresolved conflict over planning between the moderates, led by Ordzhonikidze, and the Stalinists.

Despite Stalin's warning at the previous party Congress in 1930 that those who called for lower growth rates would be regarded as "enemies of socialism, agents of our class enemies,"[35] Ordzhonikidze adopted such a view in the course of attempting to fulfill high targets. His emphasis in the remarks made at the Seventeenth Party Congress in 1934 was hedged with a conciliatory tone, however. He agreed with Stalin on the general goals for investment and growth; growth should be concentrated especially in the area of machine building, he affirmed. Ordzhonikidze also agreed with Stalin on the need to concentrate more energy in the backward area of ferrous metallurgy, but he added a qualifying remark: "Some comrades" (whom he failed to name) would try to correct the situation here by proposing a goal of twenty-five to thirty million tons of pig iron in 1937 instead of the draft proposal presented to this Congress of eighteen million tons. Ordzhonikidze proposed an even lower goal, sixteen million tons. He also went on to propose lower goals for steel and electrical energy as well.[36] He summed up his approach in these words, "Comrades, we must see that the program we propose for ferrous metallurgy is fulfilled."[37] This statement is congruent with engineer Tochinsky's memoir discussed above, and reflects an attitude that Ordzhonikidze had apparently generalized to include other areas besides iron.

The changes proposed by Ordzhonikidze were submitted to a commission that included Stalin, Molotov, Kaganovich, Kuibyshev, Ordzhonikidze, Piatakov, Kirov, and most other leading party members. The commission incorporated the changes suggested by Ordzhonikidze, and the lower figures for industrial production were incorporated into the plan.[38] At the same time, the sums originally projected for capital investment in industry were left intact, giving industrial managers smaller goals to fulfill with the same capital. All in all, it seems that Ordzhonikidze and the industrial managers scored an impressive victory publicly. A prominent Soviet engineer and industrial manager, in his recent memoirs, confirms this point. The industrial managers and production

[34] Ibid., pp. 435-436.
[35] *XVI S"ezd*, p. 59.
[36] *XVII S"ezd*, pp. 435-436.
[37] Ibid.
[38] Ibid., pp. 648-650.

specialists viewed these decisions as a personal victory for Ordzhonikidze and themselves against some hotheads in the party who wanted to set much higher targets.[39] The stenographic report of the Congress indicates that even Molotov and Voroshilov, among Stalin's closest supporters, eventually expressed their approval of Ordzhonikidze's proposals, although no such remarks are recorded for Stalin.[40]

The discussions of the special commission have not been published, nor have the discussions of the Politburo and Central Committee sessions in this period. There is further evidence that Stalin was on the defensive at this time and was forced to compromise in order to preserve his position. One recent Soviet source claims that many of the delegates at the Seventeenth Party Congress wanted to remove Stalin as general secretary and transfer him to other party work. This source links Kirov's name to such an attempt.[41] In fact, at a Central Committee session held immediately after the Seventeenth Party Congress, Stalin apparently lost the title of general secretary, and was listed simply as a party secretary, one among several others.[42]

It appears, therefore, that Stalin was forced to compromise in the key area of planning. While Ordzhonikidze was conciliatory toward Stalin in other respects during public remarks at the Congress, he had made his point on the planning process. Neither he nor Kirov attempted to match Kuibyshev's effusive praise of Stalin's "genius" and the "brilliant foresight of our great leader." Kuibyshev, still head of the State Planning Commission (*Gosplan*) gave Stalin credit as the chief author of the unrevised Second Five-Year Plan.[43]

The conclusion suggested here is that Ordzhonikidze successfully challenged Stalin before a gathering that included the most important leaders of the Communist party. The result was more realistic goals for heavy industry, goals that came closer to fulfillment than those of the First Five-Year Plan and were overfulfilled in some areas. But there may have been another consequence of such independence on the part of important party members and industrial managers. Stalin was not one to forget a major challenge to his authority. In light of the above, the background and purposes served by the purges of 1936 to 1938 become somewhat clearer. A closer look at the evidence available, including the public statements of Stalin and Molotov in 1937, indicate

[39] V. Emelianov, "O vremeni, o tovarishchakh, o sebe; zapiski inzhenera," *Novyi mir*, nos. 1-2, 1967, 40.

[40] *XVII S"ezd*, p. 436.

[41] Krasnikov, *Kirov*, pp. 194-195. The possibility that this was so is corroborated independently by Bukharin's contemporary version (see Boris Nicolaevsky, *Power and the Soviet Elite*, New York, 1965, pp. 35ff.).

[42] *Pravda*, Feb. 11, 1934.   [43] *XVII S"ezd*, p. 413.

that the line followed by Ordzhonikidze and like-minded industrial managers was an important target of the purges.

Actually, several sources indicate that planning for the purges probably began as early as the spring of 1933, shortly after the so-called Riutin affair in the fall of 1932, and the Central Committee plenum of January 1933, which began to reverse the Stalinist line on planning.[44] Riutin, a former supporter of Bukharin and Rykov in the Moscow party organization in 1928, circulated a long manuscript in 1932 that called for removing Stalin and instituting a program of development similar to that of the earlier moderate opposition. Stalin apparently sought, but failed to obtain, the death penalty against Riutin. One of the few mentions of this affair in the Soviet press at the time can be found in a speech by Molotov, delivered to the trade union sections for the technical intelligentsia in November 1932. Molotov warned them that repression against the technical specialists could be resumed. They must be on guard, he noted, against "oppositionists like the Riutins." Molotov went on to warn that the attitude of the Soviet government toward specialists depended on the technical intelligentsia itself: "We will be severe to wreckers," he stressed, while those "honest non-party specialists will be helped."[45] His speech was the only one to sound this note at the Congress; the others reflected the Ordzhonikidze line on the need for improved quality of production work and technical education. Molotov's warning here was probably a fair reflection of Stalinist views, at a time when Stalin was furious at the party's reaction to the Riutin affair and was vulnerable because of the disastrous economic situation of 1932 and 1933. Molotov's words were followed by actions later that winter when a group of Soviet engineers and foreign specialists was arrested and charged with sabotage. They worked in the electrical industry under the general supervision of Ordzhonikidze and the anti-Stalinist, Krzhizhanovsky. The arrest and trial of the Metro-Vickers engineers, therefore, implied a slap at the leaders of industry for their lack of vigilance in uncovering such "sabotage." If the Metro-Vickers trial was an attempt to revive widespread terror against the engineers and to deflect attention from those responsible for the general political and economic situation during the terrible winter of 1932 and 1933, then it failed to develop in the manner of 1928 to 1931. Ordzhonikidze, judging from the newspaper published under his direction, tried, largely successfully, to keep this trial from signalling a new campaign of intimidation against the technical intelligentsia at large.[46] The Metro-Vickers trial was not accompanied by the widespread arrest of other technical

[44] *KPSS v rezoliutsiiakh*, pt. 3, p. 184.   [45] *Izvestiia*, Nov. 30, 1932.
[46] On the Metro-Vickers trial, see my dissertation, pp. 190-215.

specialists or adverse publicity against the technical intelligentsia as a group. It proved to be the last major Stalinist show trial that involved primarily members of the technostructure. The later trials of 1936 to 1938 focused on Bolsheviks and former oppositionists, including a number of prominent industrial managers under Ordzhonikidze. Engineers, as such, no longer figured as the major professional group singled out for such dubious attention.

How then did the purges of the later 1930s affect production specialists? To answer, we must first develop more background on the way the purges were planned and for what purposes they were carried out. According to a memoir in the Columbia University archive by a former high police official, which is consistent with the accounts of Nicolaevsky, Conquest, and Medvedev (although different in some details), preparations for the purges of the later 1930s began in association with the general party purge approved by the January 1933 Central Committee plenum.[47] This was to have been a conventional reexamination of party cards, similar to those of the 1920s, not the sweeping, bloody purge it became. Unknown to most, the staff set up for this purpose contained a large contingent of NKVD officers, and was under the general direction of Stalin's private *apparat*. The NKVD personnel began to gather dossiers not only on persons considered careerists, inefficient, or corrupt bureaucrats, minority nationalists, and so on, but also on former members of other parties and any one with a history of opposition to Stalin. Information gathered at this time was then passed on to the Commissions of Party and Soviet Control, which were set up after the Seventeenth Party Congress in early 1934, and served as a basis for the later purges. Yezhov, a Stalinist party official whose career was closely tied to that of Stalin's close supporter, L. M. Kaganovich, became head of the Commission of Party Control after March 1935, and he worked closely with a secret section of the NKVD set up to direct the operational side of the purges in May of 1935. This was headed by Major I. A. Serov. The NKVD officer who wrote this memoir worked under Serov and helped form groups to purge every major area of Soviet life. For example, NKVD purge groups were established for agriculture, every branch of industry, transport, communications, education, trade, the press, party cadres, etc. These groups finished their preparatory

---

[47] "Na sluzhbe u Stalina (Ispoved' chekista)," Columbia University Archive of Russian History and Culture. Written under a pseudonym, this is the memoir of a lieutenant colonel in the NKVD who defected in 1945. It is largely consistent with the account of the origins of the purges Bukharin related to Boris Nicolaevsky, who recorded it in "Letter of an Old Bolshevik," republished in *Power and the Soviet Elite*. See also pages 69-102 of that book for information about Stalin and Kirov.

work by October 1936, having listed those who were to be purged. Then these information-gathering groups were reorganized into operational sections for carrying out the purges on a territorial basis. According to the memoirist, all preparations for the massive acceleration of arrests, which had already begun after the murder of Kirov in December 1934, were ready by January 1937. Poskrebyshev, Stalin's private secretary, Malenkov, a young party official, Agranov, an NKVD officer, and Yezhov supervised most directly. (Yezhov had already been transferred from the party secretariat to become head of the NKVD by September 1936.) After purging the Red Army officer corps in May and June of 1937 to forestall army resistance, these operational groups were dispatched to local areas in the summer and fall of 1937, where they took over the actual purge process. They were instructed to arrest former oppositionists and persons considered responsible for poor administration, waste, deception of higher authorities, and nonfulfillment of plans, but their secret instructions ordered the purge of all possible future anti-Soviet elements. In practice, this often meant even those whose skeptical remarks about the Soviet regime had been recorded by the NKVD, and who had repeated anything considered an anti-Soviet joke or rumor.

To judge whether the purges were, in fact, as well-planned as this memoir contends, we must await further evidence. The categories of those to be purged and much of the timetable given are corroborated by what actually happened, however. Most interpretations, both Western and Soviet, agree that the purges of the later 1930s were designed by Stalin to destroy all real and potential opposition by attempting to atomize intermediary groups that might combine against him and his political machine. What previous interpretations have not done is to relate the purges more directly to a central thrust, aimed specifically at industrial managers and their allies both within and outside the Communist party, including many technical specialists. This was the group that had formed perhaps the most serious obstacle to Stalin's machine during the previous half decade.

According to one of Ordzhonikidze's Soviet biographers, Stalin and Ordzhonikidze had a violent quarrel in February 1937.[48] Although the biographer does not say so, this was only the culmination of a long struggle by Ordzhonikidze and like-minded industrial managers and specialists not only to influence plan formulation, but to oppose inter-

---

[48] I. Dubinskii-Mukhadze, Moscow, 1963, pp. 6-7. The second edition of this book, published in 1967, omits without explanation the account of the quarrel with Stalin. See also Medvedev, pages 193-196, for an account that includes extensive unpublished memoirs by Ordzhonikidze's associates and relatives.

ference in the production process from the Stalinist party and police apparatus. As Ordzhonikidze put it to Kravchenko when the young party engineer complained about party and police interference in his work at the production level, "You are only one of hundreds of leading engineers, Party members, who have made the same complaint in this office. As for your personal case, I promise that as long as I live and you continue to work honestly, no one will touch you. You have my word on that."[49] It was a promise immediately followed up, in Kravchenko's presence, by a long-distance call to the party secretary in this engineer's district. The party official was reprimanded for unnecessary interference in productive work. Harassment of Kravchenko ceased until Ordzhonikidze's death, according to this memoir, when it immediately resumed.

In February 1937, Ordzhonikidze was upset when the NKVD searched his own quarters. His brother had recently been arrested, and some of his top aides had been arrested and discredited (his chief assistant, Piatakov, for example, and the head of the chemical industry, Rataichak, both prominent Red Directors and former Trotsky supporters, who were convicted as spies and saboteurs in the show trial of January 1937).

In general, Ordzhonikidze had a reputation for hiring former party oppositionists and protecting technical specialists accused of wrecking. In his telephone conversation with Stalin, Ordzhonikidze demanded an end to interference in his work. According to this Soviet biography, Stalin answered that the NKVD was an organization that might search even his, Stalin's, quarters. A few hours later Ordzhonikidze was dead of a gunshot wound, self-inflicted, according to his Soviet biographer, although at the time the Soviet press stated that he had died of a heart ailment, from which he was known to suffer.[50] Ordzhonikidze's death cleared the way for an acceleration of the purges, approved by the Central Committee plenum of March 1937, and launched publicly by Stalin's and Molotov's speeches of March and April 1937.

In light of the above background, these two speeches take on added meaning, for they show the degree to which a successful industrial management, which challenged the political apparatus on important issues, was considered a threat by the Stalinists. In these speeches, the technical intelligentsia per se was no longer singled out as a central target, but rather their protectors, industrial managers who succumbed to a preoccupation with economic tasks and successes. The fact that the Second Five-Year Plan, with its slower tempos, was drawing to a largely

---

[49] Kravchenko, p. 197. For corroboration of Ordzhonikidze's attitude toward party officials and secret police, see Paramonov, *Puti*, pp. 207-208.

[50] Medvedev, pp. 193-196.

successful close in 1937, and targets for the Third Five-Year Plan were being formulated at this time did not help such industrial managers. It seems more than likely that a battle over the Third Five-Year Plan, scheduled to begin in 1938, was shaping up, and Stalin was determined to avoid a struggle similar to that over the Second Five-Year Plan. The actual instructions for creating the Third Five-Year Plan were issued in April 1937, shortly after Ordzhonikidze's death and the Central Committee plenum of March, which lowered the last barriers to the purges. The planning process took place during the height of the purges, the final plan being approved shortly after the end of the worst phase of terror, at the Eighteenth Party Congress in March 1939.[51]

The purges, of course, eliminated a wide spectrum of real and potential foes, from former anti-Stalin oppositionists to minority nationalists, but the speeches of Stalin and Molotov make it clear that industrial managers of the Ordzhonikidze stamp were a prime target, and differences over the planning process were a major reason.

As Stalin put it in his speech of March 3, 1937, "the mistake of some of our party comrades" was that they got carried away with economic work and the successes of the past several years: "They began to see in this work the beginning and end of everything," and they placed on the back burner such things as "the international position of the USSR, capitalist encirclement, strengthening the political work of the party, the struggle against wrecking."[52] Such people, Stalin warned, tended to exaggerate the importance of economic successes and had become overconfident. Some had even begun to doubt the need for the Communist party, once they had overfulfilled their plans. They had begun to think, "What strange people are sitting there in Moscow, in the Central Committee: They are thinking up all kinds of problems, talking about some kind of wrecking. They themselves don't sleep and they don't let anyone else sleep." Stalin stated that economic successes depended on the party's organizational and political work, and he criticized the view that a systematic fulfillment of economic plans made the search for wreckers moot. He considered this particularly short-sighted, "because wreckers remain and do most damage in time of war," an indication of the role the international situation played in his thinking, and the connection he attempted to make between the purges and internal opposition to his political *apparat*. Stalin also indicated that while wreckers still remained in Soviet society, they were different from those involved in the Shakhty and Industrial party affairs. In those cases, the wreckers

---

[51] *Istoriia SSSR s drevneishikh vremen do nashikh dnei*, vol. 9, Moscow, 1971, p. 318.

[52] *Za promyshlennye kadry*, no. 5, 1937, 9.

had been nonparty members whose wrecking had been possible because they were technically more literate than party members and could thereby deceive them. The new wreckers who were Stalin's main targets carried party cards and enjoyed "all the rights of members of the party." But these new wreckers were dispensable, Stalin indicated, thanks to the preparation of thousands of new red specialists in the intervening years:

> The present wreckers have no technical advantages by comparison with our people. On the contrary, our people are technically more prepared than the present wreckers, than the "Trotskyites." From the time of the Shakhty period to the present, tens of thousands of real, technically girded Bolshevik cadres have grown up.[53]

One is tempted to conclude from this that without the massive formation of a new technical intelligentsia, the Stalinist purges of the later 1930s could not have taken place in the way they did.

Molotov, as head of state, elaborated on these remarks and added a somewhat different stress. He emphasized three points: the education of cadres must improve with emphasis on both technical and political education; the selection of personnel must be made more carefully; management of the economy must improve.[54] He defended the Shakhty and Industrial party trials, and stressed their connection with the reorganization of higher technical education, particularly the recruitment of party members and industrial workers to technical schools. As a result of such policies, Molotov asserted, the Soviet Union now had a large percentage of loyal technical specialists who were from the "same flesh and blood as the industrial working class." At the same time, Molotov rebuked those officials who had let down their guard to concentrate on economic work: "We must increase watchfulness for the enemy." The "enemy's" methods had become more cunning, he asserted, and included as evidence the practice of underestimating the capacity of an industry when formulating plans, covering up such "anti-state activity by scientific and technical arguments." This statement is in striking contrast to the views of the technostructure and their allies in industrial management, who held that scientific and technical discussions should be freed from the suspicion of political disloyalty.

In the selection of subordinates, Molotov stressed the manager's duty to check constantly on the political loyalty of his staff. "There are those much too willing to forgive and forget, willing to employ them [former oppositionists] indiscriminately, saying that their work is essential." Both professional and political criteria should be used in the selection

[53] Ibid.   [54] *ZI*, April 20, 1937.

of new cadres, Molotov urged, but political considerations should be given first priority: "The lessons to be drawn are that politically reliable workers must be given promotion; and political reliability (even though the individual may be insufficiently trained) should be the main criterion."

Molotov devoted the final third of his speech to other criticisms of industrial managers. He was particularly harsh with those who ignored the party organizers and activists in their industries, using the slogan of "one-man management" as a shield to protect them from such interference in their work. "There are those who consider themselves free of control by public opinion of the masses and ordinary workers—they don't listen to the party activists. . . ." In this respect, he singled out for criticism a well-known industrial manager, Stepan Birman, head of a metallurgical complex in the south who, we know from other sources, had a history of conflict with party authorities and outside investigative bodies, dating back at least to 1929. Birman, according to Molotov, "is one-sided himself in that he puts all the blame on party workers and none on the managerial staff. . . . We're all for helping our managers, but on the other hand, we're not going to gloss over their faults (particularly after the discovery of all this wrecking . . .)."

Molotov went on to say that "some people contend that this talk of wrecking is much exaggerated and ask how we could achieve these great successes if there were wrecking; this [attitude] is a gross mistake." Molotov served notice that even the successful fulfillment of economic plans would not protect wreckers. As an example, he singled out Rataichak, just convicted with Piatakov: "Even though this head of the Main Chemical Directorate of the Commissariat of Heavy Industry overfulfilled his 1935 and 1936 plans, does this mean that Rataichak wasn't Rataichak, that wreckers aren't wreckers, that Trotskyites aren't Trotskyites? Of course not, wreckers have to survive, so they cannot be all that obvious."

Though the tortured logic of Molotov's speech is sometimes hard to follow, the main points come through clearly as an indictment of the Ordzhonikidze style of management, despite several words of praise for the recently deceased Commissar of Heavy Industry. According to Molotov, managers must take the party's leading role more seriously. They must not underestimate their capacity for production, must not use their successes in fulfilling specific economic plans as excuses for freeing themselves from criticism and political controls, must not defend persons unmasked by the political authorities as wreckers. New cadres must be promoted to replace such wreckers, as well as others who were simply unable to adapt themselves to the demands of a new situation. Professional preparation, including education, and political criteria should be used in selecting new cadres, but political reliability should be given first priority.

In the months that followed these two speeches, most of the prominent industrial managers associated with Ordzhonikidze were arrested. Others, such as Birman, cheated the NKVD by committing suicide.[55] Thousands of production specialists were also arrested. Graduate engineers who escaped arrest at this time often underwent a purgatory of suspicion and harassment. Kravchenko is a good example. The day after Ordzhonikidze's death, he received a telephone call from the local NKVD chief: "Your patron in Moscow is dead. Maybe we had better meet soon, have a 'little chat' about 'this and that.' "[56] Charges of wrecking against Kravchenko were soon revived, and he spent many months trying to document his contention that his purchase of unused foreign equipment did not constitute wrecking. He was eventually able to provide such proof, and was one of the fortunate production engineers who avoided arrest.

It appears that a large percentage of technical specialists who were arrested were later released and reinstated, often even promoted, in the years after 1937.[57] Some, we know, were shot or incarcerated for long terms, but many others returned to production work within a year or two after 1937, unlike almost all of the old-style industrial managers, who disappeared for good. The reasons for this are twofold: production suffered seriously in 1937 and 1938 as a result of the disruption caused by the purges, and people with technical backgrounds were essential to restore production, once the political aims of the purges had been accomplished. On the other hand, the old-style industrial managers, not production specialists per se, were a primary target of the purges, and the Stalinists had little use for people whose loyalty to them they questioned and whose knowledge of technology was often considered minimal.

Who replaced the old-style managers? There was no clearcut pat-

[55] Kravchenko, pp. 224-225; Medvedev, pp. 229-230; Vladimir Petrov, ed. *Soviet Historians and the German Invasion*, Columbia, S.C., 1968, pp. 116-122. A recent doctoral dissertation has attempted to assess the economic impact of these arrests: see Barbara G. Katz, "A Quantitative Evaluation of the Economic Impact of the Great Purges on the Soviet Union," University of Pennsylvania, 1974; see also *Industriia*, Nov. 16, Nov. 21, 1937; *Pravda*, Nov. 17, 1937. On Birman's earlier record, see chapter 5 of this study.

[56] Kravchenko, p. 237.

[57] *Inzhenernyi trud*, no. 2, 1938, 71ff.; see also the memoirs by P. K. Oshchepkov, and G. Ozerov, and the following Soviet studies, A. F. Khavin, "Razvitie tiazheloi promyshlennosti v tret'ei piatiletke 1938-iun'-1941 gg.," *Istoriia SSSR*, no. 1, 1959, 10-35; A. A. Kal'manson, "Bor'ba KPSS za razvitie tiazheloi promyshlennosti nakanune Velikoi Otechestvennoi Voiny (1938 g.-iun' 1941 goda)," 1962 diss. in the Lenin Library, Moscow, pp. 46ff.; *Komsomolskaia pravda*, Nov. 15, 1964, 4.

tern to suggest that production specialists with diplomas suddenly became the predominant element throughout all of Soviet industry, although they clearly made gains in some areas. This was especially true for young party specialists, mostly graduates of the years from 1930 to 1937, with working-class backgrounds and a clean political record. High party officials sometimes made explicit their preference for promoting people of this type.[58] The evidence overall is curiously mixed, however.

In some cases, men with little more technical background than Ordzhonikidze and the old-style managers moved in, but these men were closer to Stalin. After 1937, the Commissariat of Heavy Industry was broken down into more than a dozen separate commissariats, probably both to weaken its political influence and promote managerial efficiency as industry grew. The heads of these new commissariats were a mixed lot. Stalin's close associate, L. M. Kaganovich, headed one of them for a time, and apparently had a general supervisory role over industry within Stalin's *apparat*.[59] His brother became Commissar of the Aviation Industry.[60] By 1941, some of these new commissariats were headed by young graduate engineers, however, production specialists such as Mikhail Pervukhin as Commissar of Electric Power Stations, Kosygin as Commissar of the Textile Industry, Tevosian, head of the shipbuilding industry and later Commissar of the Iron and Steel industry, and so on.[61] For a less impressionistic picture, however, we must seek more comprehensive data.

What Soviet statistics and recently published Soviet archival documents show is that both graduate technical specialists and "practicals" benefited in the immediate wake of the purges. Graduate specialists soon rose to dominate industrial management at the higher levels in the most important sectors of heavy industry, while "practicals" dominated more in the lower and middle ranks at the production level, and particularly in light industry and food production, areas with lower overall priority. A look at some of these statistics is enlightening. Table 11.1 shows the educational level of managerial-engineering-technical positions in Soviet industry. This category includes all positions with supervisory or managerial functions that normally require some technical knowledge. It excludes purely technical positions in which no supervisory duties are involved. Persons in this category would range from foremen, shop

[58] See the speeches of A. A. Zhdanov, *Industriia*, March 21, 1939, and March 18, 1939; see also the report by Kaganovich to the Eighteenth Party Congress: *XVIII S"ezd, Stenograficheskii otchet*, Moscow, 1939.

[59] British Foreign Office Archives, N5458/42/38; *Bol'shevik*, no. 15-16, August 1940, 78; *Industriia*, June 30, 1939.

[60] *Pravda*, Oct. 30, 1937.

[61] See their biographies in *Bol'shaia sovetskaia entsiklopediia* and *Deputaty verkhovnogo soveta*.

TABLE 11.1. EDUCATIONAL BACKGROUND OF
ENGINEERING-TECHNICAL-MANAGERIAL PERSONNEL

Year	Higher Education	Specialized Secondary	Practicals	Total
1928	13.7[a]	10.5	75.8	100
1933	22.3	18.7	59.0	100
1936	18.4	24.1	57.5	100
1941	16.8	16.9	66.3	100

[a] All figures are percentages of the total group.

chiefs, chief engineers, and factory directors all the way up to heads of trusts and commissars of entire industries. All figures are given as percentages of the total group.[62]

Although these figures represent somewhat different samples from industry for different years, they suggest that "practicals" overall gained more, in a numerical sense, from the purges than did those with higher and specialized secondary education. They also show that during the period when Ordzhonikidze headed the most important sector of industry, 1931 to 1937, "practicals" were decreasing in number, a fact corroborated by a recent Soviet dissertation that indicates this was the result of deliberate policy by higher industrial authorities, and led to a considerable struggle within industry.[63] We shall have more to say about this struggle in the following chapter.

A different series of statistics gives a clearer idea of what happened to the technical intelligentsia overall. Table 11.2 gives the ratio of engineering-technical workers in industry, both with and without supervisory duties, per thousand production workers.[64]

This table shows that, over a ten-year period, engineers with and without diplomas made gains in Soviet industry, as a result of a large

TABLE 11.2. NUMBER OF ENGINEERING-TECHNICAL WORKERS
PER 1000 PRODUCTION WORKERS IN SOVIET INDUSTRY

Year	Higher Education	Secondary	Practicals	Total
1930	7.0	8.0	20.5	35.5
1936	13.0	17.0	40.5	70.5
1940	19.7	23.3	67.0	110.0

[62] De Witt, *Education and Professional Employment*, p. 501.
[63] Bashevoi dissertation, Lenin Library, Moscow, pp. 218-219.
[64] De Witt, *Soviet Professional Manpower*, pp. 249-250.

increase in the total number of engineering-technical workers per thousand production workers. The "practicals" increased more rapidly than did those with formal education, however, particularly during and after the purges.

Since these figures are aggregates for very large groups, the question of their distribution throughout industry still remains. Several Soviet archival documents, compiled by *Gosplan* in 1941 and recently published, give a breakdown by rank at the plant level (Table 11.3). All figures are percentages of the total number.[65]

TABLE 11.3. EDUCATIONAL LEVEL OF
MANAGERIAL-TECHNICAL PERSONNEL IN
SOVIET INDUSTRIAL PLANTS ON JANUARY 1, 1941

	Completed Higher Education	Incomplete Higher Education	Specialized Secondary Education	Practicals	Total
Plant directors	14.6 (12.2)[a]	3.0	5.9	76.5	100
Chief engineers & Technical directors	52.2 (49.0)	3.6	17.9	26.3	100
Plant *apparat* engineers	57.5 (49.6)	5.3	16.3	20.9	100
Shop heads	22.1 (20.3)	2.4	14.9	60.6	100
Assistant shop heads	31.5 (29.6)	2.6	18.8	47.1	100
Shop engineers	60.2 (53.7)	3.9	13.0	22.9	100
Foremen	3.0 (02.9)	0.7	7.5	88.8	100
Overall	18.4 (15.4)	2.7	18.7	60.2	100

[a] Figures in parentheses give the percentage having higher *technical* educations.

These figures in Table 11.3 show that while "practicals" overall held a majority of the engineering-technical and managerial positions at the plant level by the beginning of 1941, they were very unevenly distributed throughout the plant. They constituted an overwhelming proportion of foremen at the lower level, but they also held a surprisingly high percentage of the directorships of plants in 1941. (Directors with higher education increased from 13.6% in 1936 to a mere 14.6% in 1941.)[66] Those with higher *technical* education did not predominate at the plant level in *any* rank by 1941 except that of shop

[65] TsGANKh SSSR, f. 4372, op. 41, d. 33, ll. 10-19, 22-25; l. 54-g., published for the first time in *Industrializatsiia SSSR 1938-41*, pp. 269-276.

[66] Ibid., p. 276. Figures for 1936 are from V. Z. Drobizhev, *Glavnyi shtab sotsialisticheskoi promyshlennosti*, Moscow, 1966, p. 264.

engineer, usually a position with little or no supervisory responsibility. Unfortunately, no comparable breakdown for the period before the purges is available. We can conclude, however, that by 1941 at the plant level, "practicals" still held the numerical balance in managerial positions, except among chief engineers, *apparat* engineers, and assistant shop heads. The purges had not yet radically stacked the deck in favor of graduate specialists in managerial positions at the plant level. This outcome seems to conform to Molotov's promise to consider both professional and political criteria in promotions, but to weigh political reliability above that of professional training.

When we look at managerial positions above the plant level, however, in Trusts, Chief Directorates (*Glavki*), and Commissariats, particularly in branches of heavy industry, a different trend is already apparent by 1941. This second trend probably arose both from the functional necessity of assuring technically competent people at these levels,[67] as well as the desire of many graduate specialists to flee work close to production, because of the dangers and conflicts that will be made more explicit in the following chapter.

In a speech to the Eighteenth Party Congress in 1939, L. M. Kaganovich, reporting on the situation in heavy industry, noted that "over the period 1937-38 a huge renewal of administrative cadres has occurred. . . . Most of these promoted leaders are engineers, technicians."[68] The examples he gave were very selective, however, and he provided no detailed statistical breakdown. For example, he noted that among the heads of coal mining trusts, sixty-three percent were now engineers with higher education. Eighty-two to eighty-seven percent of the directors of defense and ferrous metallurgical plants also were said to have higher educations, figures well above the average of less than fifteen percent for all of Soviet industry in 1941.

An archival document recently published confirms this pattern for heavy industry. A 1939 survey of the Commissariat of Heavy Machine Building, one of the largest and most liberally supplied with graduate engineers and technicians, nonetheless indicated that only twenty-six percent of its technical staff had higher technical education, and over fifty percent were "practicals" without any formal technical education. But among the eight hundred fourteen most important managerial posts in this industry (the so-called *nomenklatura* positions, whose incumbents required party approval and who ranged from chief engineers of plants to heads of departments within the Commissariat itself), five hundred twenty-seven had been filled by people with higher technical

[67] This is made especially clear in the transcript of the Eighteenth Party Conference, held to discuss the problems of industry, in February 1941.

[68] *Industriia*, March 18, 1939.

education and one hundred eighty-seven by individuals with specialized secondary education. "An absolute majority of newly promoted managers have higher technical culture and long administrative experience in plants," this report concluded.[69]

That most of heavy industry was also better off in having educated specialists at the plant level can be seen from Table 11.4, which shows

TABLE 11.4. ENGINEERS AND TECHNICIANS WITH DIPLOMAS
WORKING AT THE PLANT LEVEL,
JANUARY 1, 1941[a]

	Engineers with Higher Education	Technicians with Specialized Secondary Education
All industry	15	16
Heavy machine building	31	26
Medium machine building	25	26
General machine building	25	26
Electric power stations	26	30
Electrical industry	47	28
Coal industry: plants	22	24
mines	5	7
Oil industry: refineries	28	19
drilling & pumping rigs	18	11
Ferrous metallurgy: plants	18	16
mines	10	11
Nonferrous metallurgy: plants	23	21
mines	12	14
Chemical industry	28	25
Construction materials	11	15
Lumber industry: mills	5	7
logging	2	6
Cellulose and paper	12	14
Textiles	6	11
Light industry	5	10
Food industry	8	12
Dairy industry	10	13
Fishing industry	7	12

[a] All figures are actual number of graduate technologists per 1000 production workers.

[69] "Iz spravki Narkomtiazhmasha SSSR v Tsentral'nyi Komitet VKP(b) o rabote s rukovodiashchimi kadrami," TsGANKh SSSR, f. 8243, op. 4, d. 544, ll. 1-3, 6-9, 11-13, in *Industrializatsiia SSSR 1938-41*, pp. 227-232.

the uneven distribution of graduate specialists among the various branches of industry.[70]

In 1939, Kaganovich summed up the results of the purges in industry with the following words, "As you see, comrades, the new people replaced those cadres who proved simply not to be adapted to a new period of leadership with a politically and culturally matured working class. . . . In selecting cadres, the Central Committee carried out, without deviation, the line given by Comrade Stalin. New people were selected on the basis of combining business-like qualities with political. . . . Now we have cadres who will fulfill any task of the party, the Central Committee, the Soviet government, any task of Comrade Stalin."[71]

In stating the *aims* of the purges in industry, nothing could be clearer than this statement. Yet when one begins to analyze the *results* of the purges, the clarity vanishes. Whereas one might expect from Kaganovich's statement that harmony and discipline would prevail after the purges, many of the same kinds of conflicts continued. In a sense, only the names of the persons involved had been changed. From the Stalinist viewpoint, there were, no doubt, some immediate gains. Clearly the power of industrial managers and specialists to influence planning *goals* had been diminished by the purges, at least for the short term. Heavy industry had been broken up into many parts, often administered by young and inexperienced people who owed their rapid rise to the Stalinists. The Third Five-Year Plan, which was formulated at the height of the purges and went into effect in 1938, soon became much more a Stalinist product, with a partial return to an emphasis on fast tempos, than the Second Five-Year Plan, which managers and production specialists had been able to influence to a greater extent.[72] As

[70] TsGANKh SSSR, f. 4372, op. 41, d. 311, l. 54-zh, 279.

[71] *Industriia*, March 18, 1939.

[72] See V. Molotov, *The Third Five Year Plan for the National Economic Development of the USSR*, Moscow, 1939; *XVIII S"ezd VKP*, Moscow, 1939, p. 19; A. Voznesensky, *Khoziastvennye itogi 1940 goda: plan razvitiia narodnogo khoziastva SSSR na 1941 god*, Moscow, pp. 8ff. The average annual tempo of growth for industry in the period 1938-1942 was projected at around fourteen percent, a somewhat lower percentage than that adopted for the Second Five-Year Plan in 1934. Considering, however, that the tempos approved in 1939 were on a much larger base than that of the earlier Five-Year Plan, and actual growth in ruble value was scheduled to be greater than that in the First and Second Five-Year Plans combined, we can see the degree to which the new plan was marked by the Stalinist emphasis on high "Bolshevik tempos" in planning, a point made explicit by Stalin in 1939. This emphasis, with the qualification that tempos must also be "realistic," however, indicates that Stalin had developed somewhat greater caution than he showed in the early 1930s. (See *XVIII S"ezd*, p. 24.) See also the article on wrecking in *Gosplan*, which indicates Stalinist dissatisfaction with "underestimators" in *Gosplan* and among industrial managers, who fought for lower targets: *Planovoe Khoziastvo*, nos. 5-6, 1937, 3-7. Recent Soviet sources show how ac-

Stalin phrased it in 1939, "We must assure higher tempos of growth for our industry to fulfill the Third Five-Year Plan."[73]

Yet evidence indicates that the purges had not resolved the inherent conflict in the Soviet system between the aims and interests of industrial managers and production specialists in planning and fulfilling industrial goals, and the aims and interests of the Stalinist political apparatus. Between 1938 and 1941 conflict was sharpest over the fulfillment rather than the formulation of goals, and here the role of the production specialists was especially crucial. If they had played an important, though subsidiary, role in formulating planning targets, production specialists were a key element and support of industrial managers in meeting such goals. For this reason, it is appropriate to turn our attention more specifically to relations at the production level, where most of the new 'red specialists' and industrial managers got their start.

Former Soviet technical specialists interviewed after World War II, by the Harvard Project on the Soviet Social System, generally agreed that cooperation between industrial managers and production specialists was fostered by the promotion of specialists with formal technical education into many of the more responsible posts in industrial management.[74] This process began under Ordzhonikidze during the early 1930s and continued after the purges. As one former chief engineer in heavy industry between 1927 and 1943 put it, "The relations between the chief engineer and the director became even better in the last years. Since he [the director] was an educated man, he was personally closer to me than he was to the workers. We could talk with him about other things besides work. Before, relations were less intimate. With the new director we could . . . discuss ideas and principles of work, and not only facts. This made our work more one of cooperation."[75] Another former specialist confirmed this when asked about the

<hr>

celerated the Third Five-Year Plan was, which they attribute to the approach of war, no doubt a major factor, but not the only one (see *Istoriia KPSS*, tom 5, Kniga pervaia, Moscow, 1970, pp. 16-45; *Istoriia SSSR*, no. 1, 1959, 10ff.).

[73] *XVIII S"ezd*, p. 64.

[74] These interviews are summarized in an unpublished study by Alexander Peskin, "Sociological Aspects of Soviet Industrial Management," Widener Library, Harvard, 1954. His conclusions are corroborated in several recent memoirs by major Soviet industrial managers and engineers in this period: see especially V. S. Emelianov, *O Vremeni, o tovarishchakh, o sebe*, Moscow, 1968, and *Na poroge voine*, Moscow, 1971; I. V. Paramonov, *Puti Proidennye*, Moscow, 1966, especially pp. 142-275, and *Uchit'sia upravliat', Mysli i opyt starogo khoziastvennika*, Moscow, 1967, 2nd ed., 1970; B. L. Vannikov, "Oboronnaia promyshlennost SSSR nakanune voiny (Iz zapisok narkoma)," *Voprosy istorii*, no. 1, 1969, 122-135.

[75] Harvard Project, Interview no. 400, B 2 Schedule, p. 4.

relations between the new type of manager and the chief engineer, who headed the entire technical staff of a plant: "They are better than they used to be, because the new type of manager is not afraid any more that the chief engineer will fool him. The old type of manager was somehow afraid of the chief engineer. He felt that the engineer was superior. He did not know about technology and he was afraid of being fooled."[76]

Several recent Soviet memoirs, one by the former Commissar of the Armaments Industry between 1938 and 1941, and another by an important specialist in the steel industry, confirm this and indicate the degree to which these newly promoted industrial managers from among the graduate specialists were willing to work for the common interests of managers and technical specialists, even in the immediate wake of the purges.[77]

Despite the party's continuing admonitions against "family groups" at the production level, the tendency of managers to form such cohesive groups with key production specialists (and often with their accountants and local party officials as well, when possible) continued after the purges.[78] One of the engineers interviewed reported the following typical situation:

A new director is appointed to a plant. He pulls strings to bring in his own chief engineer. The manager and the chief engineer have known each other, they have come together on other constructions, and they know and understand each other and can work together. But the manager does not know any other persons. So he says to the chief engineer: "You choose the other assistants." And thus a whole group comes to the new plant. Also you must remember that in recent years the director and the chief engineer may know each other from school days. True, they may not have taken the same course, but they may have been in the same school. Thus a much better understanding exists among them.[79]

None of this should be taken to indicate that industrial managers and specialists were able to re-create the power base Ordzhonikidze had built before 1937, at least certainly not before 1941. The Stalinist political *apparat* clearly had the ascendancy as a result of the purges. But there is every indication that the causes of the conflict had not been rooted out and would reassert themselves at the first opportunity. The

[76] Ibid., Interview no. 105, B 2 Schedule. See also Interview no. 485, B 2, pp. 4-7.

[77] See the Emelianov, Paramonov, and Vannikov memoirs cited above.

[78] See, for example, *Industriia*, Jan. 18, 1940, February 15, 1940, July 10, 1940; Harvard Project, Interview no. 64, p. 12.

[79] Harvard Project, Interview no. 105, B 2 Schedule. See also no. 64, p. 12.

Stalinists did not, and probably could not, root out tendencies that had led to conflicts with Ordzhonikidze and the purged managers. This is because such tendencies had their origins in work relations at the production level, shaped by the planning system, and these work relations could not change fundamentally as long as the same system of plan formulation and plan fulfillment existed. The purges did not change the industrial system itself, only much of the personnel. If anything, many of the personnel changes tended to increase the cohesiveness of managers and production specialists, particularly those who shared a common background in higher technical education and a similarity of outlook and interests in their work roles. These elements had learned during the first decade of the Stalinist planning system after 1928 that there were basically only two alternatives for survival: either band together and cooperate, or flee direct work in production. The evidence of considerable cohesiveness between elements of the technostructure and industrial management, however, should not be allowed to obscure the conflicts that still remained between graduate specialists and some elements of industrial management, as well as serious conflicts with other major groups at the production level: "practicals," industrial workers, party and police officials among the most important. Chapter 12 will examine such conflicts and their significance.

12

THE FLIGHT FROM PRODUCTION: CAUSES AND CONSEQUENCES

Our scientists and engineers will overtake and surpass Europe and America and will solve by their efforts problems of universal importance in technology and increase mankind's mastery over nature.

Ordzhonikidze[1]

There was a time when the industrialization of my country had been a challenge to stir young blood. . . . That creative impulse had been beaten out of me. Bold technical vision had been displaced by fear, caution, suspicion. . . . I was condemned to shoulder responsibilities in which there could be only danger but no joy.

Soviet production engineer, 1938[2]

The tendency for graduates of higher technical schools to avoid working directly in production was an old one in Russia, dating from well before the revolution and deeply rooted in the traditions of Russian engineering. I have already commented on the higher status and differing social origins of engineers employed in Tsarist ministries (chapter 1).[3] The so-called "Ministerial engineers" were the first formally educated technical specialists in Russia, drawn largely from the nobility in the beginning, to staff technical departments of the central government concerned with the military, civil engineering, mining, and transportation networks such as waterways and railroads. Their corporate tradition placed a high value on administrative and design work in offices, and they generally had looked down upon those engineers who

---

[1] G. K. Ordzhonikidze, *Stat'i i rechi*, vol. 2, Moscow, 1957, p. 668.

[2] Kravchenko, p. 297. For a similar view by a young production engineer at the same period, see the Harvard Project on the Soviet Social System, Interview no. 470, Widener Library, Harvard.

[3] See also the interesting discussion of career patterns of prerevolutionary engineers in Donald Webb Green, "Industrialization and the Engineering Ascendancy: A Comparative Study of American and Russian Engineering Elites 1870-1920," diss., University of California, Berkeley, 1972, pp. 234ff.

took line jobs, supervising workers or participating directly in production.

In some respects, the Soviet government worked hard to break down this psychology of the "white glove," as it was sometimes called, from the habit of prerevolutionary engineers who wore such gloves as a symbol of their separation from manual labor. The government tried to make production work more attractive to technical specialists, appealing both to their mercenary and their more idealistic sides. It reminded specialists of their duty to their country, and of the joys of building something new, "the pathos of construction," as such work was sometimes called. One reason given for recruiting more specialists from the working class was the hope that they would be attracted to remain in production. Production work generally paid much better after 1931, and good production engineers received apartments, even servants, the use of an automobile, sometimes a large house, and other privileges. The material benefits were at times so lavish that the proletarian father of one such specialist, newly promoted to chief engineer of a large plant, shook his head with disapproval at his son's style of living, which reminded him of a nobleman's under the old regime.[4] The analogy was not really apt, however, because such production specialists were scarcely a leisure class. On the one hand, the government rewarded them lavishly as long as they worked hard—frequently 12 to 16 hours a day—and were successful. On the other hand, the government was unable or unwilling, as the case may have been, to deal with a combination of severe conflicts, some of them the product of the planning system and others the result of cultural and educational differences at the production level, that reinforced the tendency of graduate specialists to flee production work. A diploma from a higher technical institute, which party and government leaders had hoped would eventually raise the quality of production work, became, ironically, what it had been so often under the Tsars: a ticket to work outside production—in administrative offices, as party officials, even as NKVD officers after 1938. As one young specialist put it, somewhat cynically, many young specialists were willing to work even for the secret police after the ordeal of production and the purges in industry: "The NKVD offered great possibility for intellectual development. Take, for example, a Soviet engineer. When can he go to the theatre? He has hardly any time. . . .

---

[4] Kravchenko, p. 200. See also John Scott's description of how the technical staff at Magnitogorsk lived. (Interview with Scott, an American who worked for a number of years in Soviet industry, taken by the U.S. State Department and dated February 8, 1938, State Department Decimal File, 861.651/17.) See also Scott's generally reliable memoir, *Behind the Urals*, New York, 1943.

But in the NKVD they don't work all day. They can read books, they can go to the theatre, this is an organization where people can develop themselves."[5]

We must analyze the nature of the conflicts at the production level and their consequences if we are to understand better the environment in which the technical intelligentsia worked during this period. This is also necessary for understanding the major change that began to occur in the composition of the Communist party and the background of its officials, as well as changes in the personnel of industry and government, including the NKVD.

Caused both by the dissatisfaction of production specialists and the desire of Stalinists to change the composition of the ruling elite by recruiting many young "red specialists," these changes eventually led to a partial integration of the technostructure and the Soviet power structure. Throughout this period we also see the persistence of strong conflicts between these two groups. Despite the recruitment of some of their members into higher levels of the party and government, technical specialists as a whole remained a middle element of Soviet society. This was particularly true for production specialists, who were caught between the ranks of party, police, and upper industrial management on one side and industrial workers on the other. Their lot was to be highly dissatisfied throughout this period, despite more optimistic prospects many had just prior to World War II. One obvious characteristic of all the memoirs of production specialists, whether by engineers who became emigrés or those who remained, is the degree to which conflict was endemic in their situation. Production work engendered a high degree of risk and dissatisfaction, and these conditions had major consequences. For some they served as a spur to internal emigration: a quest for a quiet corner in some office, laboratory, or educational institution where they could retreat into privatism and less dangerous work. For others, they created a desire to influence the power structure and change the balance at the production level in favor of the technical specialists, as we shall see below.

It is appropriate to begin with an analysis of the tension points between managers and graduate specialists, which arose in fulfilling plans, and then proceed to a discussion of the more sever conflicts with "practicals," industrial workers, and party and police officials. Though relations with industrial management grew closer, they were never free of conflict.

Those conflicts that did arise between technical specialists and man-

[5] Harvard Project, Interview no. 105, B 2 Schedule, pp. 42-43.

agers, however, were likely to involve several specific issues: quality control, innovations, fraudulent reporting of results, and scapegoating in particular. The difficulties of innovation will be dealt with in chapter 13. Quality control involved mostly those specialists assigned to the quality control sections of plants, not the chief engineers and other production specialists, who generally saw eye-to-eye with managers on this subject.

The declining quality of industrial goods became endemic with the adoption of the high goals of the First Five-Year Plan. Because both managers and specialists directly involved in production gave priority to achieving gross output figures, quality suffered accordingly. Several measures were devised to cope with this situation, which affected the work of technical specialists in differing ways. Committees of standardization were set up in every economic commissariat, and they were given power to prosecute those responsible for violating standards.[6] Legislation authorized and emphasized punishment for such violators, and the penalties were often severe. For systematic failure to observe standards in mass production, managers and specialists could be sentenced to prison or forced labor for one to five years, and even for more isolated instances where standards were ignored, penalties of one to two years forced labor were provided.[7] These penalties, however, seem to have been invoked only rarely—for example, in the case of a plant that produced tractors without motors.[8]

Punitive measures could have a dual effect on relations between specialists and managers. Where both groups were implicated, the psychology of partners in crime prevailed, that is, managers and specialists worked to cover up for each other. Yet, the fear of punishment could lead some managers to try to find a scapegoat, a phenomenon against which specialists tried to insure themselves, as we shall see below.

Although measures to improve quality naturally affected the work of technical specialists, another kind of effort affected them even more directly, viz., the considerable attention devoted to establishing quality control sections, or bureaus, within enterprises to catch defective goods before they left the plant. Technical specialists were generally placed in charge of these bureaus. Toward the end of 1929, the government decreed that every enterprise must establish a special quality control bureau no later than February 1930.[9] While this measure seems to have been carried out in most plants, the decree may have lost much of its

---

[6] *Sobranie zakonov*, 1930, Otdel I, art. 8; 1932, Otdel I.

[7] *Za industrializatsiiu* (*ZI*), Jan. 8, 1930; *Sobranie zakonov*, 1930, Otdel I, art. 9; *Sovetskaia iustitsiia*, no. 2, 1930, 31; no. 6, 1930, 21-23; no. 1, 1931, 14; no. 24, 1931, 29; no. 30, 1931, 13.

[8] *Predpriiatie*, no. 22, 1933, 1.   [9] *Sobranie zakonov*, Otdel I, 1930, art. 8.

force as a result of its sponsorship. It had been signed by Rykov, who had long opposed high output targets. Rykov was Stalin's opponent and was soon to be replaced as head of the government by Molotov. For Stalin and his *apparat* to have given strong public support at this time to such measures, which spoke of a sharp decline in quality, would have only given credence to the position of the moderate Right Opposition, who had earlier warned of such effects if inordinately high output targets were adopted. True, Stalin, a few years later, at the Seventeenth Party Congress, noted the continued existence of low quality production, but his public statements in these years are devoid of any analysis of its causes or strong backing for remedial measures. In general, he gave little emphasis to the problem, preferring to urge the fulfillment of the high quantitative targets adopted.

There is no evidence that the measure Rykov signed in 1929 to improve the quality of production was supported strongly by most party officials, industrial managers, or specialists directly involved in production. The available evidence points to the opposite conclusion. The work of these bureaus was hamstrung by several factors. The decree had provided that bonuses be withheld in plants that produced low quality goods, and that discounts in prices be given for such goods. Nevertheless, many managers continued to push for fulfillment of output plans first, even if that meant overruling the bureau for quality control and passing goods that fell below the standard of quality. In doing so, they apparently counted on escaping strong sanctions or penalties for their action. Until the early 1930s, the quality control bureaus remained subordinate to the director of the plant, but later they were made responsible to a higher industrial authority above the production level, a measure that allowed them some independence vis-à-vis plant managers but also increased the potential for conflict.[10]

Resistance to any overly zealous employees in quality control came from every level of production, where personnel had a material interest in meeting output targets. Therefore, the pressure on quality control specialists to cultivate the powers of oversight and apathy was great. When such personnel proved overzealous in the eyes of workers or the administration, they were ignored and even persecuted.[11] As one journal noted in 1933, "Frequently personnel of these organs suffer persecution solely from the fact that they have strongly protested against the output of low quality goods."[12]

[10] Ibid.; *XVI S"ezd*, p. 498.

[11] *ZI*, March 7, 1930; *Predpriiatie*, no. 7, 1932, 16; Harvard Project, Interview no. 384, B 2 Schedule, p. 16.

[12] *Predpriiatie*, no. 22, 1933, 1; no. 7, 1932, 8-9.

Quality control was often opposed by the rank-and-file production workers, who were generally paid on a piecework basis and were forced to fulfill high daily production norms. Workers objected that they were often unable to fulfill their norms and give quality production, too. According to several reports, they generally regarded the quality control workers as their personal enemies,[13] especially because workers could be fined for excessive waste in their production.[14] Since the quality control personnel were responsible for assigning the blame for such waste, they were unlikely to win any popularity contests among ordinary workers. Workers objected that they were frequently blamed for waste that was caused not by their workmanship, but by the poor quality of the materials they received.[15]

Complaints by workers threatened specialists less after 1931, due to the weakening of the trade unions and the tightening of labor discipline in industry; still, in this instance, workers often made common cause with managers and production specialists against the specialists in quality control.

The real solution to the problem of quality production lay in readjusting planned targets. There is some indirect evidence that the situation regarding quality may have improved during the Second Five-Year Plan. Qualitative indicators and their fulfillment still received little stress, compared to quantitative targets in this plan, but the pressure for speed—which led to carelessness and low quality—was eased somewhat by the lower output targets adopted.

As noted above, in January of 1933 the Central Committee decreed that quality of production was to be stressed in the Second Five-Year Plan in a way it had not been in the first.[16] This emphasis was attained at the Seventeenth Party Congress in 1934 through pressure by Ordzhonikidze and his supporters. Nonetheless, output targets remained high and pressure for speed in output was enhanced by the Stakhanovite movement, which began in 1935. While quality may have begun to improve gradually as output goals were made more realistic, and as the experience of workers, production specialists, and managers increased, contemporary Soviet sources document the continuance of conflicts with the quality controllers throughout this period.[17] Quality control

[13] *ZI*, June 4, 1930; *Industriia*, Jan. 3, 1939.
[14] *Deviatsatyi vsesoiuznyi s"ezd professional'nykh soiuzov SSR. Stenograficheskii otchet*, Moscow, 1933, p. 421.
[15] *Deviatsatyi vsesoiuznyi s"ezd*, p. 422.
[16] The law on contracts at this time also tightened provisions guaranteeing quality according to the official standards established by the government (see *Sobranie zakonov*, 1933, no. 73, art. 445).
[17] See *ZI*, Jan. 5, 1932, Jan. 17, 1937; *Industriia*, Feb. 3, 1940; *Zavodskaia laboratoriia*, no. 3, 1932, 5-8; nos. 8-9, 1932, 3-15; no. 4, 1933, 3-6; no. 6, 1933,

work was fraught with dangers for the technical specialists involved: they could lose their jobs, or worse, for overlooking low quality, yet the existence of quality control sections took the burden of responsibility from managers and production specialists, who at worst were generally only fined for substandard goods.

Most of the sources from this period agree that the "pressure-cooker" atmosphere created by the planning system also fostered a great deal of fraudulent reporting of results.[18] Managers generally tried to involve their specialists, as well as other members of their management team—accountants in particular—and local party and government authorities when possible. A wise specialist would spend much time writing insurance policies for himself, that is, writing reports showing that he had been ordered to do something illegal and placing them in his files. He could obtain additional "insurance" by reporting illegal activities to the press or the political police, in writing, so that later, should a manager or other authorities attempt to make him a scapegoat, he would have documentary evidence of his innocence. Of course, a specialist risked incurring the ire of industrial managers and other officials implicated in fraudulent reporting, as Kravchenko discovered early in his career as a chief engineer. Although pressured to cover up, he tried to avoid complicity in a fraudulent Stakhanovite record by reporting the fraud to higher authorities.[19] His superiors were furious with Kravchenko's self-protective measures, but, as he put it,

> It took months before these officials and factory colleagues forgot my "betrayal" and smiled at me again; but I did not regret my action. Whatever happened, my record was clear. In sober fact, nothing happened. Too many influential bureaucrats were involved in that piece of charlatanism.[20]

That the insecurity of production specialists made writing "insurance" common practice, is clear from a variety of sources. The Harvard Project came across a number of similar examples.[21] Some involved fraudulent reporting, others, industrial accidents. In both situations, a

---

3-7; no. 9, 1933, 3-13; no. 10, 1933, 4-6; no. 8, 1936, 900-921; no. 9, 1936, 259-540; nos. 4-6, 1937; nos. 1-3, 1939; no. 9, 1940; nos. 1-4, 1941; Harvard Interview Project, no. 384, no. 65, pp. 17-18.

[18] See, for example, *Predpriiatie*, nos. 5-6, 1934, 8; *ZI*, June 11, 1934, March 1, 1937, June 4, 1934; *Izvestiia*, Feb. 16, 1941; *Chernaia metallurgiia*, March 13, 1941; *Industriia*, March 11, 1940; Harvard Interview Project, no. 65, pp. 21-24; no. 202, pp. 15-16; no. 99, pp. 9-13; no. 251, pp. 2-3; no. 615, p. 6; no. 384, p. 3.

[19] Kravchenko, p. 300.   [20] Ibid., p. 302.

[21] See, for example, Harvard Interview Project, no. 70, p. 10; no. 396, p. 5; no. 26, pp. 13-14; no. 65, pp. 18-20.

production specialist who had not covered himself in writing could be in serious trouble. When the specialist and the director had a good working relationship, the director would usually support the specialist. This was especially true of directors who were themselves engineers and, therefore, held more responsibility for the technical side of the work. The greatest dangers lay with managers who were technically illiterate and tried to evade their responsibility. A case reported by the Harvard Project is indicative of this danger. The engineer reporting the case was head of a construction site for a giant steel mill in the Ukraine during the 1930s.

He received an order to build a concrete foundation at a temperature of −15 or −20 degrees centigrade. He knew that this was impossible, that the construction would be defective, and that it contradicted official norms. He tried to argue, and the engineers from the technical inspection commission supported his arguments. But his superior in line, the chief of the construction site, a Party member without technical education (although by regulation the post should have been filled by an engineer), threatened him at the point of a gun.[22]

The engineer, therefore, wrote a document for his files stating the circumstances of the case—his belief that the construction would be defective, and the fact that he was ordered to proceed. The following spring, when the thaws came, his prediction turned out to be true. The construction was defective and he was arrested, accused of "deep and hidden sabotage." After a three-month investigation, however, he was released.

In his opinion, two circumstances may have saved him. First, the document he had written, which showed that he had fought against the construction. Secondly, while the investigation was going on, another concrete wall split in two, though it had been built in the summer and by more experienced people than he.[23]

Because of the frequency of such incidents, most production specialists preferred to work with directors who were fellow engineers. The director with higher technical education shared more responsibility for the technical process and could defend it better. The relations of production specialists with this type of director "were like with a colleague. For instance, a certain technical process has to be changed. The chief engineer signs it and presents the plan to the director. The first type [with higher technical education] studies it and both put it into effect.

[22] Peskin, p. 145.   [23] Ibid., p. 146.

The second type [without higher technical education], on the other hand, does not sign it and leaves for somewhere when the job has to be done. He leaves instructions to the chief engineer to do it. The chief engineer then does it on his own risk. If there is failure the director says that it was done in his absence. The first type of director bears more responsibility for technical measures. He will argue for the correctness of the measure, he will try himself to find mistakes. The second only tries to keep clean."[24]

Relations with the uneducated sort of industrial manager were complicated by yet another factor, besides scapegoating: fear on the part of such managers that they would be displaced by the influx of new 'red specialists' in the 1930s. They had felt less insecurity with the old specialists, who had been tainted with the label "bourgeois," and with whom it had been possible to work out a clear division of labor that left the uneducated Red Directors relatively secure in their jobs, holding the upper hand in terms of political authority. The influx of new specialists, however, especially those who combined a working-class origin and party membership with higher technical knowledge, brought into the open a severe generational and intraclass struggle. This conflict became especially apparent in the early 1930s and continued throughout this period. It involved not only uneducated industrial managers, but a group with which such managers felt a close affinity: the "practicals" (*praktiki*), skilled workers who, due to the shortage of qualified specialists, were promoted to positions as engineers and technicians without the requisite education. In 1929, "practicals" accounted for forty-eight percent of all specialists, and, despite Ordzhonikidze's attempts after 1930 to reduce the size of this group, they actually grew in proportion during the later 1930s, as we saw in chapter 11, benefiting more from the purges numerically than did the educated group of specialists.

By 1941 "practicals" occupied more than sixty percent of all engineering-technical positions in Soviet industry. As they shared a keen sense of insecurity with the uneducated industral managers, it is not surprising that many industrial managers and "practicals" made common cause in holding back and even harassing young 'red specialists' who held engineering degrees.[25]

[24] Harvard Interview Project, no. 485, pp. 6-7.

[25] Young engineers frequently complained that, as a group, they were singled out for criticism of their work by plant newspapers, which were under the control of management. Various petty charges of work violations were brought against them and fines were levied. In one plant in 1930, for example, fully twenty-five percent of the young engineering-technical workers had been taken to court for such violations in the previous few months (*ZI*, March 22, 1930).

Young specialists complained frequently. They claimed that they were often placed on the extra board. They felt that they were not used up to their capacities, or in line with their training, and were given the most routine jobs in production where it was impossible to improve their qualifications. Some managers claimed that graduate engineers were not necessary, since they had a sufficient number of workers with practical experience and they preferred such men. When required by law and the large-scale growth of production to hire members of the younger group, some managers simply turned them into mechanics at the beginning or held them in reserve with various forms of busywork.[26]

Young specialists claimed that they received little help from the more experienced "practicals," who criticized them at every opportunity.[27] "In my work, the old specialists [in this case "practicals"] undermined my authority groundlessly. If I make a mistake, they ought to help me correct it rather than aggravate such a situation as I found in my factory."[28]

The younger group complained that the experienced "practicals" were often favored in promotions and pay increases—a practice that was forbidden by law.[29] They claimed that "practicals" received the more interesting work, while they were sometimes forced to work in routine jobs outside their own specialty. To a certain extent such complaints may simply have reflected the impatience of an ambitious group, eager to take command. To be sure, both the managers and the uneducated "practicals" had good reason to fear the younger group and obstruct their advancement whenever possible.

In 1928, in the wake of the Shakhty affair, the party passed resolutions urging the rapid promotion of young specialists into positions of responsibility. Shortly afterwards, the government abolished the prerogatives of seniority. Seniority was no longer sufficient grounds to hold a job against a better qualified competitor.[30] From that time forward, managers were required by law and the authority of the party to place young specialists with diplomas in positions occupied by "practicals." Only the severe shortage of specialists in this period of rapid growth— with the help and connivance of some managers—prevented many "practicals" from losing their jobs to younger, better educated men.

The party attempted to ease this changeover by providing opportunities for "practicals" to improve their qualifications through education. Correspondence courses, night schools, and some full-time stipends for study were made available to many "practicals," particularly the

26 *ZI*, April 6, 1930, 5; August 1, 1930, 4; March 3, 1933, 3.
27 *IT*, no. 10, 1931, 241-242.   28 *IT*, no. 2, 1930, 47.
29 *IT*, no. 2, 1930, 47; *ZI*, April 6, 1930, 5.
30 *Direktivy KPSS*, vol. 1, p. 847; *NR*, no. 9, 1929, 43.

younger ones.[31] Many felt too old for such education, however, and others resisted returning to the learner's bench probably out of pride and stubbornness. Whatever the reasons, the percentage of "practicals" who received and accepted such responsibilities was less than expected. A year and a half after the party had decreed that all "practicals" must return to school for retreading or lose their positions within three years, only some five to ten percent were actually enrolled in technical courses.[32] Eventually, however, as administrative pressure from above increased under Ordzhonikidze's aegis until 1937, many "practicals" were either forced to acquire the requisite education or were demoted to positions as skilled workers. Stalin's purges temporarily reversed their fortunes after 1937. This fact no doubt increased his base of support among a group that, as we have already seen, he had always courted, but it also increased the solidarity and sense of group cohesion among production specialists and managers who shared higher education in the face of hostility from "practicals" and uneducated managers.

Until late in 1930, many skilled workers were still promoted to the many new managerial posts created as industry grew.[33] In October of 1930, the Central Committee published a decree that prohibited further promotion of skilled workers directly from production to administration.[34] Many workers had been promoted to managerial posts during the general purge of Soviet institutions in 1929 and 1930, but the loss of so many skilled workers had a negative effect on production. After 1930, higher education was the chief route to promotion from the ranks of skilled workers to those of management, especially in heavy industry once Ordzhonikidze took charge. Although party membership and social background remained very important factors in advancement, the educational factor became primary. As a result, the qualifications of the managerial group began to improve.[35] Managers without a higher technical education felt the pressure of so many eager young competitors ready to fill their boots at the earliest opportunity, and their fears were realized in the statements of high industrial leaders. In 1933, for example, Ordzhonikidze made these remarks in a speech given wide circulation:

Without a doubt there is a certain conservatism in promoting young cadres, all the more so since there exists some jealousy, it

[31] *Kadry tiazheloi promyshlennosti v tsifrakh*, pp. 85-92.

[32] *IT*, no. 10, 1931, 242; *KPSS v rezoliutsiiakh*, pt. 2, pp. 632-642; *Bol'shevik*, no. 19-20, 1929.

[33] Drobizhev, *Istoriia SSSR*, p. 65; *Glavnyi shtab*, pp. 256-257; *ZI*, Jan. 28, 1930.

[34] *Istoriia SSSR s drevneishikh vremen*, vol. 8, pp. 509-512.

[35] Beilin (1935), pp. 219-220, 250; Drobizhev, *Glavnyi shtab*, pp. 261-264.

seems, among a portion of our older managers who have not kept up with the times. They reason this way: "you promote a young engineer and who knows, maybe he will replace me tomorrow." I can tell you a secret. He will, in fact, replace you. But all the better. The sooner we have engineers armed with a knowledge of technology in responsible posts in our plants, all the better it will be for our industry as well as our managers.[36]

It is not surprising, then, that many managers and "practicals" were hypercritical of the younger group. They were understandably not eager to aid in their own eventual downfall. They frequently criticized the younger group as incompetent and mercenary. One brigade of experienced workers investigating conditions in the Urals and the Ukraine reported, "Despite the fact that the majority of engineers and technicians are graduates of our higher technical schools, the quality of their preparation and their knowledge of production is extremely low, and this applies especially to graduates of recent years."[37] According to the director of one metallurgical plant, "These young specialists are useless; they don't know how to supervise the processes of production; they have no production experience; therefore, we cannot entrust them with a blast furnace or other work connected with the technical processes of production. It is possible to place them for two or three years as ordinary workers in order to acquire practical experience, and after this they can gradually be promoted to supervisory work. They play no role in the plant and cannot replace the old 'practicals' who know at a glance how to produce any quality of steel. If we place the young specialists as workers then the plant will be spared any particular harm."[38] While these remarks undoubtedly contained a certain truth, they also reflected a strong prejudice.

The attitude of some of the younger men aggravated matters. Many were imbued with great self-confidence because of their education and the knowledge that higher authorities often favored them even when local managers and "practicals" did not. The young specialists sometimes reacted with what was interpreted as arrogance and an unwarranted evaluation of their own skills and abilities. Foreign specialists, whom the younger Soviet specialists classed with the older specialists and managers, and hoped to replace as soon as possible, frequently reported this attitude. One American specialist observed in 1934:

Young Soviet engineers who have graduated in recent years from Soviet technical institutions, are thronging into Baku. These

[36] *ZI*, Jan. 22, 1933.   [37] *IT*, no. 16-17, 1930, 500.
[38] Ibid.; *ZI*, Jan. 11, 1930, 2; *IT*, 1930, no. 24, 724.

young men are over-confident and self-assured. They assume that they know more than the foreign engineers or the Soviet engineers of the old school. Through their party affiliations they frequently are in positions of greater influence than the older men. Upon these inexperienced engineers rests much of the blame for the present disorganization of the oil fields. They refuse to listen to the advice either of experienced engineers or of the drillers and mechanics, who, although not engineers, have worked for many years in the field and possess technical knowledge which could be of much value if utilized.[39]

While this condemnation of the younger group may have been too strong, it reflects an opinion of the younger "red specialists" that was widely shared by others in Soviet industry at the time.[40] As one older specialist, interviewed after World War II put it, the workers "had respect for the old engineers, but not for the 'Soviet' engineer. It often happened that a worker laughed at such a young engineer because the latter did not know how to do something. You explain to him that an engineer does not have to know everything. But the worker answers: 'What kind of an engineer is he? A Soviet engineer!' "[41] In part this reflects the prejudices of the old specialists toward the newer element of the technical intelligentsia, but it also shows the difficulties the younger specialist faced. This same specialist noted, however, that the new specialists "gradually acquired authority. Some acquired it fast, when the workers saw that they were competent. Sometimes the young engineer asked an old worker to teach him. But this did not happen often, they were ashamed."[42]

If the younger engineers and technicians were overbearing and too confident in the opinion of many older men in industry, their approach had a positive side. They were often more willing to take technical risks and—when given the opportunity—to introduce new methods of work and new forms of technology.[43]

Young Soviet specialists entered industry with the belief that they were the heirs apparent. It is not surprising, therefore, that they set out to prove themselves and seek their inheritance as soon as possible.

[39] Interview with August Tross, U.S. Embassy, Moscow, Nov. 3, 1934, in the State Department Decimal File, NA, 861.5017/771. Similar comments can be found in other interviews with American engineers in these years, for example, those reported with Gustaf A. Johnson in John P. Hurley, American Consul, Riga, Nov. 28, 1930 (861.5017/200), and that with Ellwood T. Riesing, reported in John E. Kehl to The Secretary of State, May 8, 1931, (861.5017/248).

[40] See, for example, *IT*, no. 1, 1932, 14-15.

[41] Harvard Interview Project, no. 384, p. 17.

[42] Ibid.   [43] *Inzhenernyi trud*, no. 1, 1932, 14-15.

Aided by the growth of industry and the purges of older men, many of them were to assume the highest managerial and technical posts in Soviet industry within a few years of their graduation.[44]

It is difficult to say in detail how sharp or widespread the generational and intraclass struggle was among managers and specialists in Soviet industry. The party leadership viewed it as a problem and the Soviet press devoted considerable space to specific examples, attempting to analyze the problem. If anything, it increased in the wake of the purges, due to the trends already noted. The industrial press noted the resistance among many at the production level to promoting young graduate engineers and complained, "There are still people to whom it has not yet sunk in that the higher the educational level of commanding cadres in production, the more successfully will our tasks be solved."[45] Another article from the same period, by the commissar of the iron and steel industry, noted, "The promotion of youth met resistance from a segment of the old managers who were falling behind in life."[46] The resistance is corroborated in the Harvard interviews. According to one graduate production engineer, "Usually new people are not liked. People think that one of their own should be promoted. . . . There are people who are native to the plant. They think: why a new man?"[47]

Young women engineers had a particularly difficult time in their relations with managers and production workers. Several reports in the industrial press indicate the resistance of men in some plants to accepting women engineers in supervisory positions. For example, Engineer Goldovskaia complained to the central newspaper *Za industrializatsiiu* of her harassment at the plant where she worked. Of six women engineers originally assigned to this plant, only one remained, she noted; an investigation by the editors of this paper bore out her charges of sexual bias. When she had trouble gaining the cooperation of the workers under her, who told her point blank that, "We don't consider you a boss," she got little help from plant managers. In fact, while on vacation, one manager told the chief mechanic, "She wants to be a boss in the plant, but she won't succeed in this."[48] She was eventually fired from this production job and offered one in research, a more typical position for women engineers in these years. After the investigation re-

[44] Ibid.

[45] *Industriia*, Feb. 1, 1940. See also Jan. 6, 1940, and June 30, 1939; *Vestnik inzhenerov*, no. 7, 1938, 398.

[46] *Industriia*, Feb. 18, 1940.

[47] Harvard Interview Project, no. 384, p. 22.

[48] *Industriia*, June 12, 1939. For other evidence of male opposition to women working at the production level, see *Industriia*, June 26, 1939, 3.

Fig. 3. Soviet political poster from the early 1930s urging women to study, work in industry, and take an active role in public life outside the home. The small caption reads: "The more widely we extend the network of day-care centers and public dining rooms, the more we will free millions of women for participation in socialist construction." The central figures are engaged in a technical design task. By 1941, forty percent of the students in higher technical education were women, and women constituted about fourteen percent of the engineers in Soviet industry. Many more women worked as technicians than as engineers.

ported above, the plant management was reprimanded, but there is no indication that this helped the situation of Engineer Goldovskaia or other women engineers in similar circumstances.

An archival document recently published indicates the degree to which women specialists who remained in production work by 1941 were still concentrated in the lower ranks and nonsupervisory positions. Although 14% of the graduate engineers in industry by this time were women, only 3.2% of the directors of factories, 3.9% of the chief engineers, and 7.6% of the shop heads were women. Most women at the production level held nonsupervisory positions: for example, 22.9% of the rank-and-file shop engineers, 35% of the shop technicians, and about 45% of the engineer-economists and shop planners were women.[49] The latter were often glorified clerical positions with little or no supervisory responsibility. Although women engineers received high posts in some plants, particularly in industries with high concentrations of women workers, as in light industry, by 1941 the typical woman production specialist had a long way to go for full acceptance.

If conflicts between industrial managers, "practicals," and graduate engineers continued throughout this period in the ways detailed above, conflict between production specialists and the industrial working class as a whole became less evident over the course of the first three Five-Year Plans. Nonetheless, the cultural gap between these two groups continued to make their relations uneasy. For one thing, millions of new workers who flocked into industry at this time were illiterate or barely literate. As one American observer put it, "The prevalence of illiteracy is indicated in the abundance of picture posters. At the exit of one of the divisions of the Electrozavod factory in Moscow, there is a battery of faucets and above them are pictures for the illiterate, and printed suggestions for the literate, of workmen washing off the grime after the day's work."[50] To accustom such workers to understanding an industrial process and the operation of complex machinery required enormous patience on the part of technical personnel, who bore the major responsibility for acculturating new workers to Soviet industry. It required an emphasis on teaching by example, at least until newly arrived workers acquired enough basic literacy to follow written directions. As this same American observer noted, "In some factories, for instance in the electrical factories, [many of] the workers are quite literate. On the other hand, the new industrial workers coming from

[49] TsGANKh, f. 4372, op. 41, d. 33, 1. 54-b, published for the first time in *Industrializatsiia SSSR 1938-1941*, p. 278.

[50] Elisha Friedman, *Russia in Transition*, New York, 1932, p. 173.

FIG. 4. A young technical specialist teaching a peasant woman the fundamentals of industrial work in the 1930s. (*Byli industrial'nye*, Moscow, 1973.)

the land are primitive. Some of them had never seen an electric light before coming to the city and are utterly without the tradition and feel for machinery. . . . The Russian workmen are acquiring the mechanical feel but are taking their lessons on some very expensive machinery, much like a novice learning to play on a Stradivarius."[51] He might have added that the resulting confusion was more than simply a strain on the nerves of overworked technical specialists, it added to the discordant environment that drove many a specialist out of production to some other, quieter line of work.

Ethnic conflict sometimes complicated the class relations of specialists with workers, especially in areas where there were large concentrations of workers from non-Russian groups. For example, at the start of the First Five-Year Plan, in 1928, only fourteen percent of the engineers and technicians in Ukrainian industry were Ukrainian, although the majority of workers were of that nationality.[52] This led to friction in the following years. Even minor incidents sometimes intensified into major conflicts. For example, in 1931 the journal of the Ukrainian engineers indicated the opposition to Ukrainianization, particularly the use of the Ukrainian language, that existed among some of the technical specialists. This journal noted that "some Russifying elements show great power chauvinism."[53]

At the giant Dnieper River Hydroelectric Project, where some sixty percent of the workers were Ukrainian and a high proportion of the technical specialists were Russian or Jewish, the local party committee tried to mediate ethnic tensions, supporting Ukrainianization until 1932, while at the same time calling "for a struggle against anti-semitism."[54]

A large number of Tatar workers at this site posed a particular problem, since the language barrier here was even greater. Lack of fluency in Russian or Ukrainian on their part, and Tatar on the part of their fellow workers, hindered communication and led to conflicts with managerial and technical personnel. Again the party intervened, trying to smooth relations by arranging for interpreters and establishing a special newspaper in Tatar to parallel the newspapers already published

[51] Ibid., p. 172.
[52] M. M. Polishchuk, "Borot'ba komunistichnoi partii ukraini za otvoreniia i vikhovaniia inzhenerno-tekhnichnikh kadriv 1928-1932 rr," diss. in Ukrainian, Kiev, 1971 (copy in the Lenin Library, Moscow), p. 202. See also *Bil'shovik Ukraini*, no. 11-12, 1937, 90.
[53] *Inzhenernyi rabotnik* (Kharkov), no. 5, May 1931, 67.
[54] PAZ obkoma KP Ukrainy, f. 1, op. 1, d. 473, ll. 128-193, cited in E. B. Kartsovnik, "Leninskii plan elektrifikatsii i bor'ba partii za sooruzhenie Dneprovskoi gidroelektrostantsii im. V. I. Lenina," diss. (in Russian), Kiev State University, 1964 (copy in Lenin Library, Moscow), p. 81.

at this construction site in Russian and Ukrainian.[55] In the Ukraine, one cause of tension abated when the percentage of Ukrainian engineers increased from fourteen percent in 1928 to some forty-five percent by 1933.[56] At the same time, Ukrainianization was ended as an official policy in 1932, taking some pressure off non-Ukrainian speaking specialists.

In Kazakhstan, similar tensions have been noted by a recent Soviet source. In 1933, 44.2 percent of the workers in the Kazakh coal industry, but only 15.7 percent of the technical intelligentsia were Kazakhs. Some leading managers opposed hiring Kazakhs, pointing to their lower labor productivity. At the same time, Kazakh nationalists advocated replacing Russian workers and specialists, and those of other nationalities, with Kazakh novices. Party authorities intervened with a resolution asserting that the preparation of cadres "from backward (*otstaly*) nationalities in no way replaces and must not weaken the task of preparing and promoting cadres from the proletarian elements of European nationalities living in Kazakhstan."[57]

Whether such measures were merely symbolic actions or whether they had a real effect in easing tensions is difficult to say. Certainly technical specialists had not been prepared by their formal educations to cope with such tensions and had to learn on the job, at times a painful experience. No doubt some ethnic tensions continued throughout the period, with concessions being made to non-Russian nationalities until the early 1930s, placing the high proportion of Russian and Russified specialists on the defensive. By the late 1930s, however, the atomsphere had changed, and Great Russian nationalism was no longer castigated but praised in the industrial press, a turn of events satisfying to many among the large proportion of Russian or Russified technologists.[58] Only the slow process of raising the proportion of non-Russian specialists could promise a gradual easing of tensions, along with greater understanding and experience of interaction among the various nationalities at the production level.

Despite these problems in their relations with workers, the high de-

[55] Ibid., p. 136, citing *Proletar Dniprobudu*, Oct. 30, 1931.

[56] *Narodne gospodarstvo Ukr. SSR*, Kiev, 1935, p. 485.

[57] N. Daulbaev, *Karagandinskii ugol'nyi bassein*, Alma-Ata, 1970, pp. 176-183, citing Partarkhiv Kazfiliala IML, f. 11, op. 1, ed. khr., 5767, ll. 99-101, and *Rezoliutsiia i postanovleniia V plenuma Kazkraikoma VKP(b)*, Alma-Ata, 1929, p. 74. For the party's attempts to cope with these tensions see Salim Khamzinovich Shakirov, "Dieiatel'nost' KPSS v oblasti razvitiia ekonomicheskogo i politicheskogo sotrudnichestva narodov SSSR v gody vtoroi piatiletki, 1933-1937," MGU, 1971, diss. in Lenin Library, Moscow.

[58] See *ZI*, Jan. 15, 1937.

315

gree of conflict over workers' control and the rights of technical specialists, which characterized the Russian revolution and continued throughout the 1920s, diminished greatly after 1931. The Communist party and the Soviet government sought to legitimize the role of the technical intelligentsia, partly by recruiting large numbers of new 'red specialists' from the industrial working class and partly, from 1935 on, by pointing to the technical intelligentsia as a model for the classless society of the future. Ironically, in an argument reminiscent of that used by Bukharin and elements of the old technical intelligentsia in the late 1920s (they had maintained that "managing-engineers" and "engineering-managers" were the vanguard of the future), Stalin declared in November 1935:

> Some people think that the elimination of the distinction between mental labor and manual labor can be achieved by means of a certain cultural and technical equalization of mental and manual workers by lowering the cultural and technical level of engineers and technicians, of mental workers, to the level of average skilled workers. That is absolutely incorrect. Only petty-bourgeois windbags can conceive communism in this way. In reality the elimination of the distinction between mental labor and manual labor can be brought about only by raising the cultural and technical level of the working class to the level of engineers and technical workers. . . . Only such a rise . . . can insure the high level of productivity of labor and the abundance of articles of consumption which are necessary in order to begin the transition from socialism to communism.[59]

The idea that the Soviet working class would eventually be raised to the level of the technical intelligentsia was adopted as party policy a month later, at the December 1935, Central Committee plenum.[60] It is hard to say who originated the idea, but Stalin developed it by expounding it publicly as a general principle for the transition to a "classless" society, which would be based on the model of the new Soviet intelligentsia, particularly the technical intelligentsia. The new policy was linked officially to the "technical minimum" examinations, first introduced for workers a few years earlier by heavy industry as a way of tying wages to formal tests of a worker's technical competence. It was also linked to the Stakhanovite movement, which began in the fall of

[59] I. V. Stalin, "Rech' na pervom vsesoiuznom soveshchanii stakhanovtsev," November 17, 1935, translated in Stalin, *Selected Writings*, Westport, Conn., 1970, pp. 368-369.
[60] *KPSS v rezoliutsiiakh*, Moscow, 1954, pt. 3, p. 271.

1935 under the sponsorship of Ordzhonikidze and the Commissariat of Heavy Industry.[61]

What Stalin did was to add his influence to the idea, shaping it to suit him, and making clear that there were several roads by which workers could raise themselves to the level of the technical intelligentsia. That is, they could do so not only through formal schooling, but, alternatively, through practical achievements in their work, which would lead to promotions and status as members of the new Soviet intelligentsia. As a Stalinist writer put it in 1939, paraphrasing Stalin's various public comments on the subject:

> This was a brilliant foresight, that socialist competition [in particular, the Stakhanovite movement] would in its development raise the cultural-technical level of the working class to the level of the intelligentsia. Cadres of the Soviet intelligentsia are being formed both from people prepared by the whole system of general and special education, as well as on the basis of the cultural, political, technical growth of workers and collective farmers in practical work and their promotion to leading government, economic, and social posts. . . . The Stakhanovite movement opened a new stage—the stage of preparing for the gradual transformation of the entire mass of toilers into intelligentsia.[62]

Whether this was, in fact, Stalin's "brilliant foresight" or someone else's idea originally, Stalin had the intelligence to see its significance, and the concept became embedded in Soviet thought, where it remains part of the official ideology on the transition to a Communist (classless) society. As evidence that this is happening, Soviet writers have pointed to the steady increase in the proportion of the Soviet population who are counted among the intelligentsia, the most rapid growth being among the technical intelligentsia.[63] The status of this idea as one of the

---

[61] In October 1932, Ordzhonikidze ordered "technical minimum" examinations for all workers in basic specialties of heavy industry, to certify their ranking and wage scales, a system extended to all workers from 1933 to 1937 (see *Soviet pri NKTP 15-19 iunia 1936. Stenograficheskii otchet*, Moscow, 1936; "G. K. Ordzhonikidze v glave sovetskoi promyshlennosti 1932-1937," diss. in Lenin Library, Moscow, p. 129).

[62] L. Al'ter, "Kulturno-tekhnicheskii pod'em trudiashchikhsia SSSR," *Planovoe khoziastvo*, no. 12, 1938, 29-33.

[63] See, for example, S. L. Seniavskii, *Izmeneniia v sotsial'noi strukture sovetskogo obshchestva 1938-1970*, Moscow, 1973, pp. 297-333, 373-400, 408-411; E. Arab-Ogli, *Nauchno-tekhnicheskaia revoliutsiia i obshchestvenny progress*, Moscow, 1969; Yu. Novgorodskii, *Tekhnicheskii progress i rabochie kadry*, Moscow, 1967; Medvedev, *On Socialist Democracy*, pp. 304-309; *Sovetskaia istoricheskaia entsiklopediia*, vol. 6, Moscow, 1965, pp. 11-119.

major social myths by which Soviet society is organized has been missed by most Western authors, and needs greater attention.

After 1935, Stalin and the Central Committee made the technical intelligentsia the particular model for all workers, and thereby legitimized its functions in a way that had not been true for many years following the Russian revolution. This ideological argument attempted to deal with class conflict between these two groups, the severity of which we have seen earlier in this study, by telling workers that their role was to study, work hard, and raise the level of their skills to that of specialists, not to oppose their authority.[64] Measures against specialist-baiting were strengthened and strikes, while not formally outlawed, became even less legitimate in the eyes of the authorities as a way of expressing conflict, since wages depended on norms fixed by experts and on the level of a worker's technical qualifications, checked by examinations, again administered by experts.[65] Norms, at the same time, were continually being pushed upward as a result of records, set by Stakhanovites, who in turn were supervised by members of the technical intelligentsia.[66]

Wages, therefore, were taken from the realm of collective bargaining, backed by the weapon of the strike, as was common in the West, and put in the care of the technical intelligentsia, who manned the "norm-setting" bureaus (buro normirovaniia) and directed the work of the industrial proletariat in production enterprises.[67] Class conflict was no longer viewed as normal, an inevitable expression of permanent differences between social groups. Rather, the promise made was of a gradual elimination of class differences and, thereby, the elimination of class conflict. While this promise was a basic ingredient of Marxism, the measures of the 1930s tried to give it a more explicit and concrete form. These changes help to underline a basic difference between

[64] On efforts in this direction see the NKTP journal, Za promyshlennye kadry, 1932-1937, and the Central Institute of Labor's journal, Organizatsiia truda, 1928-1938, as well as the following secondary sources: Marcel Anstett, La formation de la main-d'oeuvre qualifiée en Union Sovietique, Paris, 1958, pp. 107-179.

[65] Arvid Brodersen, The Soviet Worker, New York, 1966, pp. 59-92; Elisha Friedman, Russia in Transition, New York, 1932, p. 173.

[66] See Robert Conquest, Industrial Workers in the USSR, New York, 1967, pp. 44-94; Ivan Mikhailovich Samokhvalov, "Rukovodstvo partii massovym razvitiem sotsialisticheskogo sorevnovaniia v promyshlennosti v period 1936-41 gg.," diss. in Lenin Library, Moscow, 1965; Alexei Gastev, Organizatsiia truda v stakhanovskom dvizhenii, Moscow, 1936, and his article in Organizatsiia truda, no. 11, 1935, 6ff.; Kravchenko, pp. 187-191, 193-194, 217, 298-302; see also my dissertation, pp. 542-582.

[67] See the resolutions of the December 1935 Central Committee plenum KPSS v rezoliutsiiakh, Chast' III, Moscow, 1954, p. 271, and the 1937 speech by Stalin.

Soviet society and the situation in most Western societies, a difference, generally overlooked, that has major implications for social relationships.

Whether workers were convinced of the validity of such ideological promises is virtually impossible to answer for this period. We can say that the changing ideological climate and changes in the practical situation of production specialists vis-à-vis the industrial proletariat were interrelated, and made a significant difference for the work of both groups. The ideological change outlined above was preceded and accompanied by a series of tough measures to tighten labor discipline and give the upper hand to industrial management and the technical intelligentsia at the production level.

Beginning as early as 1931, when the terror against the old specialists ended and measures to strengthen the authority of the technical intelligentsia overall began, a law was introduced which allowed prison sentences for violations of labor discipline. In the same year, compulsory labor books, detailing the work record of each individual including violations of discipline, were introduced. In 1932, the death penalty was introduced for the theft of state property and the Labor Code was changed to allow superiors to transfer a worker without his consent.[68] The authority of administrative-technical personnel, undermined by the show trials of 1928 to 1931, was enhanced by such measures, at the expense of industrial democracy. In general, the approach in this area was very close to military discipline, and was reminiscent of the labor conscription measures of the civil war period.[69]

An American specialist with many years' experience in the Soviet oil industry described the situation in 1934:

> The difficulties with respect to labor discipline which existed several years ago in the Baku oil fields have been overcome in the sense that employees no longer endeavor to interfere with the operation of management in their place of work. For the most part, workmen now accept orders from their superiors without argument. I have never been surrounded by so cowed a group of men as the workers in the Baku oil fields. Oil workers do not have a voice even in determining the conditions under which they are employed. In case something goes wrong with machinery or with production one of them is usually selected as the scapegoat and discharged. A person discharged for cause must remain unem-

[68] Robert Conquest, *Industrial Workers in the USSR*, pp. 98-102.
[69] See Roger Pethybridge, *The Social Prelude to Stalinism*, London, 1974, pp. 38ff., 104ff.

ployed for six months since no trust is permitted to take him on until six months after the date of cessation of employment.[70]

Discharged workers were also likely to lose their bread ration cards and apartments, since these were assigned on the basis of their employment. The tables had been turned compared to the days when engineers and other technical personnel were the usual scapegoats when things went wrong.

The former situation returned for a time during the purges of 1936 to 1938, however, when disgruntled workers once again used the situation to their advantage, denouncing specialists or threatening to do so. In 1938 and 1939 the industrial press once again campaigned against specialist-baiting, citing a number of instances, including one in which a worker involved in a job dispute with his supervising engineer broke into the engineer's apartment and threatened to "annihilate him as a Trotskyite and spy." This dispute finally went to court and was settled in favor of the engineer.[71]

After the purges, the engineering-technical sections of the trade unions (ITS), which had kept a low profile during the purges, revived their role as defenders of production specialists in disputes with ordinary workers. The technical intelligentsia was the only group at the production level that maintained its own separate sections in the trade unions throughout this period. During the purges, some organizations of technical specialists even revived the call for a separate union of engineers.[72] Although this call was rejected, the ITSs once again performed their function of defending specialists, particularly against specialist-baiting by workers or managers.[73]

The existence of separate sections in the trade unions, though their power should not be exaggerated, did add to the prestige of production specialists, and, more importantly, provided them with an organization that promoted their self-consciousness as a separate group. At the same

[70] Interview with August Tross, quoted in a memorandum of the U.S. Embassy, Moscow, Nov. 3, 1934, State Department Decimal File, NA, 861.5017/771. Tross, an American citizen, spoke Russian fluently and had worked as an oil drilling superintendent in Baku from 1914 to 1919 and from 1928 to 1934. His view of the severe extent to which labor discipline was strengthened by 1934 is confirmed by Andrew Smith, an American Communist, who was working as a foreman in an electrical machine-building plant in Moscow (Smith, pp. 69, 211). As an indication of this tightening of labor discipline, official Soviet statistics show a sharp drop in unexcused absences from work after 1932 (*Sotsialisticheskoe stroitel'stvo SSSR*, 1936, p. 530).

[71] *Industriia*, August 2, 1939.

[72] *Vestnik inzhenerov*, no. 9, 1937, 518ff; no. 4, 1938, 194-197; no. 2, 1938, 1.

[73] Harvard Interview Project, no. 384, p. 15.

time these sections encouraged the technical intelligentsia to prove their loyalty to the Soviet system.

There was a variety of ways in which production specialists could do so, and these added to the pressures under which they operated in their relations with the industrial working class. For one thing, it was largely their responsibility to enforce the draconian labor laws of the late 1930s. These were designed to enforce labor discipline and improve productivity, but the technical specialists bore the brunt of the workers' resentment against such laws, including the use of books in which a worker's record, including violations of labor discipline, were recorded. (Workers referred to such books as "yellow tickets," a reference to the tickets prostitutes had been required to carry under the Tsarist regime.)[74] The new party leader in charge of heavy industry after 1937, Kaganovich, made examples of engineers who showed too much "liberalism" in their dealings with workers. For example, an engineer who did not dismiss miners with unexcused absences from work was himself fired and put on trial.[75] Engineers who had to deal with workers as human beings often tried to raise their pay in various ways or excuse them for absences by backdating leaves, sick days, etc. (Under the new labor laws after 1938, such workers could be tried and sentenced to prison or corrective labor, as thousands were in the years just prior to the German invasion.)[76]

Production specialists, therefore, found themselves ground between two stones, the punitive, production-oriented attitudes of higher management and political authorities, and the consumer-orientation and sullen resentment of many workers. In order to meet their quotas, specialists were not only forced into fraudulence as a way of life, they had to coax, cajole, and often force workers to produce. The better and more sensitive specialists found themselves taking on functions that the trade unions were supposed to shoulder, but did not or could not. When workers complained that they could not get enough through the regular supply system, specialists found themselves hunting food and fuel.[77] As one engineer expressed it, "I was concerned with labor problems, i.e. lunches on the construction site, living quarters, problems of liaison between the workers and the communal department of the Trust. I was also charged with the conduct of campaigns, for instance for loans. I

---

[74] Kravchenko, p. 312. For the 1938 law on the use of these labor books, see *Sobranie postanovlenii*, Dec. 31, 1938, Otdel I, no. 56, p. 725.

[75] *Industriia*, January 15, 1939.

[76] TsPA IML, f. 17, op. 2, d. 676, l. 45; TsGAOR, f. 8115, op. I, ed. khr. 239, l. 45, cited in Kal'manson diss., p. 142; see also *Planovoe khoziastvo*, no. 9, 1940, 21; *Mashinostroienie*, Feb. 15, 1939, 2; *Industriia*, May 29, 1940, 2.

[77] Harvard Interview Project, no. 65, p. 21.

had to make money advances to the workers, to supervise the distribution of special clothing. As chief of a section I was responsible for all this."[78]

That specialists were responsible for enforcing the work norms further complicated the relations of workers and technical personnel. After the adoption of the Taylor system during the 1920s, which included progressive rates for piecework, wages of industrial workers in the Soviet Union were not set by collective bargaining, but were established centrally, according to a worker's job rating and qualifications. Periodically, work norms were adjusted upward, due to some new output record by shock workers or Stakhanovites. Production specialists were under enormous pressure to organize Stakhanovite demonstrations, in which the best workers were given optimal conditions to perform at a new rate for a short period of time. These records were then used to readjust the work norms upward. The result was that average and below-average workers often could not earn a decent wage. It became common practice for production specialists to juggle the books in order to add to the wages of their workers. Despite the risks involved in such widespread illegalities the production specialists and higher management often closed their eyes to such practices. They did so because, in the words of one specialist, "if we did not do this, workers would be dissatisfied and leave the enterprise and then we could not fulfill the plan."[79] Workers would simply move on to a plant where better arrangements could be made, at least until the labor law of 1940, which tied workers to a particular enterprise.

The tightening of labor discipline during the 1930s was accompanied, after 1937, by the introduction of formal, hierarchical relations. "There were no open declarations and nothing was said at meetings or in newspapers. But privately we were told to behave differently."[80] Oral instructions encouraged a more rigid set of relations: "familiarity between superiors and subordinates" was discouraged; subordinates were not allowed to sit down when reporting to a superior; reports were to be short and given only after an appointment had been scheduled; when the director or chief engineer passed through a shop, the workers had to stand up to show their respect. Hierarchical relations were also encouraged outside work. "Hints were dropped that we should select our friends from among the personnel approximately equal in rank. The director called us to his office and gave us instructions in this respect; and we had to transmit these instructions to lower officials."[81] More

---

[78] Ibid., no. 202, B 2 Schedule, p. 7.   [79] Ibid., no. 65, p. 23.

[80] Ibid., no. 70, p. 17. This development paralleled the formalization of class relations throughout Soviet society in the wake of the purges.

[81] Ibid.

familiar relations among management, technical personnel, and workers, which had been a legacy of the revolution, were ended. As one engineer commented,

> For us bosses these new instructions were not so bad, that is from our personal interest. We thought that as older and experienced people we deserved this respect. But for the workers this was very disagreeable and you could feel this. From talks with foremen, with whom we had close relations, we learned that workers were very dissatisfied.[82]

Despite such resentment, the pressures on production specialists from below became more manageable by the end of the 1930s as their power over workers increased—though not without continued frictions and conflicts. The pressures from above never lessened, however, and were often extremely hard to bear. Knowing the tendency of specialists and managers to report underestimated capacity and overestimated results, and their penchant for independence, the political authorities attempted to surround them with an elaborate control system. As one Soviet production engineer put it, "The Soviet power needs a technical intelligentsia. But at the same time it is afraid of it. Because if people are educated they will become critical toward the Soviet regime. The Soviet power knows that the [technical] intelligentsia is ambivalent. Externally it is loyal to the regime, but internally it is critical. Therefore, in creating a technical intelligentsia, the Soviet regime must create an apparatus in order to hold this technical intelligentsia in check."[83]

The control apparatus that surrounded production specialists and managers in these years was composed of party, police (NKVD), and other state organs, whose duties were to verify the fulfillment of plans and decrees, and to try to assure the political loyalty of those in production. The result was an endemic tension between the organs of control and the organs of production. Technical specialists and industrial managers more often than not found themselves under enormous pressures, in conflict with party and police officials and organs of higher state control. The greatest potential for conflict existed with party and police officials, since they maintained a permanent presence in economic enterprises, unlike the organs of higher state control, which dispatched periodic commissions and inspectors (such as inspectors from the higher industrial administration, financial inspectors from the State Bank [*Gosbank*], etc.).[84] For that reason, the emphasis here will be on relations with the party apparatus and the political police. The trade unions

[82] Ibid., pp. 18-19.   [83] Ibid., no. 105.
[84] Peskin, pp. 14-43; Granick, *Management*, pp. 172-180, 189-202.

had such vastly diminished powers and were so firmly under the thumb of management after 1929 that we will not consider them separately here.

One Soviet specialist succinctly described the relationship between the production element and the control element: "The task of the NKVD is the following: If the plan is not fulfilled, then to discover the reasons, to investigate and to punish. The party punishes and favors. It may promote and demote a man. But the NKVD never favors, it only punishes."[85]

This oversimplifies the relationship, since the party had broader political functions in an enterprise, and the NKVD was also on the alert for political nonconformity, not just production mistakes, fraudulence, and nonfulfillment of plans. This source is correct, however, in asserting that the party's role at the production level was more open and active, and the NKVD's function was primarily to watch quietly, gather evidence, and intervene when something went wrong. One engineer said the police were always "sniffing about the plant," and the technical staff had to be on its toes. Relations between production specialists and party and police officials were strained throughout this period. As another Soviet engineer put it, "In production the engineer trembles all the time."[86]

The struggle between these groups was never resolved, and the Stalinist *apparat* probably intended it that way. Managers and specialists defended the principles of "one-man management" (*edinonachalie*) as formulated by Lenin, and interpreted this principle to mean an end to interference in their work by party, police, and trade union officials. They called for a clear definition of their rights and responsibilities. Party and police officials tended to interpret the principle differently. They viewed it as "one-man responsibility," that is, managerial and technical personnel were held responsible for results, but were not to be freed from outside controls and checks on their work. Managers and specialists remained without a clear definition of their rights and powers throughout these years. As one professional journal put it in 1929, engineers in shops "up till now have possessed responsibilities but no rights."[87] While their powers vis-à-vis workers were strengthened in subsequent years, their rights vis-à-vis the political authorities remained fuzzy in practice throughout this period. In his public statements, Stalin backed up the industrial managers and specialists, in principle, against undue interference in their operational decisions, but he made it clear

[85] Harvard Interview Project, no. 105, pp. 31-32.
[86] Kravchenko, p. 294; Harvard Interview Project, no. 384, pp. 8-9.
[87] *Predpriiatie*, no. 3, 1929, 26.

that party and other officials were needed at the factory level as a check on the work of managers and specialists. The fine line that separated such checking from interference, however, was never clearly drawn. Stalin was basically more interested in defining individual responsibility for work than in making clear the rights of managers and specialists, as his statements indicate.[88] Molotov, in a long speech during the purges of 1937, asserted, "we are for one-man management, but we must guard against pitfalls." He strongly criticized production personnel "who consider themselves free of control by public opinion of the masses and ordinary workers. . . ."[89] According to one of Stalin's closest supporters, Kaganovich, party and trade union organizations at the factory level were essential as a continued check on managers and specialists.[90] Such an attitude diluted the effect of decrees strengthening the hand of administrative and technical personnel. For example, it was an unwise manager or specialist who failed to consult party or police officials, particularly on personnel and disciplinary decisions. The managerial and technical personnel had high level decrees to strengthen their powers, but full-time party and police officials remained in every large factory and could do a great deal of mischief to uncooperative managers and specialists. The Soviet press after 1929 was filled with such instances, suggesting the continuance of this struggle.[91]

For example, party officials continued to interfere with managerial powers in the assignment and transfer of workers. In this respect, the authority of engineers, particularly at the shop level, was undermined. Party officials were also in the habit of commandeering men during working hours, often without permission or even the knowledge of their foremen and other managerial-technical personnel. In April 1930 the Central Committee once again decreed an end to such practices and affirmed, "It is necessary to overcome the interference by party and union organizations in the operational orders of the administrators. Directors and executives must be assured the right to independently appoint and transfer personnel."[92]

The disparity between decrees on paper and actual practice continued, however. As one management journal complained in 1932,

[88] *XVI S"ezd*, p. 89; Stalin, *Sochineniia*, vol. 13, pp. 60-62.
[89] *ZI*, April 20, 1937.
[90] *XVII S"ezd*, pp. 555, 561-562; Stalin, apparently as early as 1923, publicly favored having parallel authorities at the local level to provide a more accurate flow of information to the top (see Jerry F. Hough, *The Soviet Prefects*, Cambridge, Mass., 1969, p. 99).
[91] See, for example, *Predpriiatie*, no. 3, 1929, 15; no. 19-20, 1930, 3; no. 15, 1932, 1; no. 19, 1932, 9-10; *Pravda*, Dec. 7, 1929; *ZI* Jan. 18, 1930, 2; Feb. 15, 1930, 4; March 8, 1930, 5; June 8, 1930, 5; June 18, 1930, 4.
[92] *ZI*, April 12, 1930.

"Party cells and factory committees usurp the functions of managers, engineers, and foremen in factories. The chairmen of city and village governments, police officers and agents of the prosecutor's office right and left are carrying out management functions in plant sections, and when the administration objects, they are threatened with legal repression."[93]

Despite another decree by the government and Central Committee in March 1931, the party and even union committees continued to use working hours for their activities. "Union committees, party committees and city governments under all kinds of pretexts commandeer for protracted periods the very best production workers from plants not only without the permission of the administration but even without forewarning."[94] When managers and specialists objected, they were often either threatened with arrest, expulsion from the party, or both. The upshot was that relations with party officials tended to be formal and cool. Production specialists considered them nuisances and sometimes referred to the local party organizer behind his back as "our bishop," or to his face by the more formal "Comrade," rather than his first name, which was common among managers and technical personnel.[95] Directors and technical personnel generally attempted to deal with the situation by trying to make the party secretaries share responsibility for important production decisions.

On their part, at least until after the purges, party officials generally tried to avoid such responsibility for fear they would share the blame if something went wrong.[96] Nevertheless, party officials could also be very useful to a plant, by employing party channels to help with production problems, such as locating scarce supplies, and by using their authority to mobilize workers. Managers and technologists attempted to appeal to the "plant patriotism" of local party officials to gain their cooperation, and they often succeeded. As one specialist expressed it, "the Party secretary was loyal to the plant and even developed a certain plant patriotism. This is easy to explain. Various plants are competing among each other, and he is interested in a good performance for his plant."[97] Higher party officials were aware of this tendency and tried to deal with its effects in part by changing the party officials in a plant every two or three years, before their relations with the production staff became too "cosy."[98] Under Ordzhonikidze, local managerial and tech-

[93] *Predpriiatie*, no. 15, 1932, 1.   [94] Ibid.
[95] Harvard Interview Project, no. 384, p. 8.
[96] Ibid., pp. 24-25; no. 16, pp. 22-23; no. 70, p. 14.
[97] Ibid., no. 70, p. 15; no. 202, pp. 9-10.
[98] Ibid., no. 70, p. 12.

nical personnel gained considerable independence, although they never entirely escaped party interference and checking. Although occasionally, when a director was weak or lacked good connections, a local party official might overrule the plant director and his technical staff, this was more the exception than the rule during this period. Plant managers were generally members of the party and often members of the higher, provincial party bureau (*obkom*). They could also usually count on Ordzhonikidze's support in a major dispute with the party apparatus.[99] Party secretaries were often forced to court plant directors, waiting on them in the director's office, rather than the other way around. As one production specialist put it, "You could feel that 'a black cat' has run between the party men in economic posts and the party officials. I often visited the director, but I never saw the director and the Party organizer visiting each other. The director got torn away from the party and joined production."[100] This atmosphere helps to explain the particular vehemence with which the Stalinist *apparatchiki* attacked and purged those old Red Directors in the later 1930s who had become more "director" than "red."

Party officials attempted to deal with this situation in several ways. They remained powerful in their control over important posts in industry (the so-called *nomenklatura* positions, which usually included the posts of directors and chief engineers), and the local party secretary generally had to be consulted on appointments down to the level of foreman.[101] Party officials also tried to bring as many good engineers into party membership as possible, a process they hoped would subject the technical staff to more party control and would upgrade the technical knowledge of party cadres: "Suppose a man graduates from the institute. But he has not become a party member. From his first days in production he shows exceptional qualities: as a specialist, as a leader, as an organizer. He starts to advance. Now in this case the Party sees that this man will go very far. And they will say: 'It is useful to have this man in the Party, to have him with us.' And they start working on him. They talk to him, 'Look, you are a specialist. . . . Why aren't you in the party?' "[102] And eventually the ambitious man joined; otherwise

[99] Ibid., no. 105, pp. 30-31; no. 70, pp. 12-14; no. 403, pp. 2-5; no. 26, B 2 Schedule; Kravchenko, pp. 81-85, 196-197, 232, 239; V. Mezentsev, *Bardin*, Moscow, 1970, pp. 109-113.

[100] Harvard Interview Project, no. 384, p. 26. For some revealing comments about Ordzhonikidze's attitude toward party officials, see Paramonov, p. 208.

[101] Ibid., no. 485, p. 8; no. 70, p. 11.

[102] Ibid., no. 70, pp. 5-6. See also *Industriia*, Sept. 10, 1937, 3; Sept. 20, 1; June 14, 1940; July 31, 1940.

his career might be blocked at some point. These specialists became subject to party discipline and could be transferred by the party to help out in trouble spots anywhere in the U.S.S.R.[103]

At the same time, this process of influence could work both ways, for the technical intelligentsia in this manner gradually gained influence within the party. The second method the party apparatus used to gain influence within industry was to appoint special party organizers to large plans, organizers who reported directly to the Central Committee in Moscow (*Partorg TsK*). This practice apparently became widespread in the later 1930s, after the purges. These new *partorgs* were generally able to stand up to a powerful manager, but, to increase their authority, the party usually appointed engineers to these posts, people who could understand the process of production and not be easily hoodwinked by managers and their technical staff.[104] Again, it is difficult to say who gained most. To an extent the two groups were brought closer together, and the technical intelligentsia increased its influence and prestige in the process. We shall have more to say on this subject toward the end of the chapter.

The political police was a more formidable influence than the party apparatus at the production level. The technical intelligentsia faced a good deal of official interference by police officials in their work, and this could not be so easily countered. The secret police, who were perhaps closest to Stalin's personal *apparat* within the party, maintained special sections in every major plant and mine, conducting surveillance over managers and specialists, as well as other workers.[105] The detailed nature of this surveillance can be seen in many of the OGPU reports found in the archive of the Smolensk party organization. It is also an important theme in Soviet memoirs from this period and interviews with Soviet emigrés. The NKVD maintained permanent officials (in the *spetsotdels*) of every large plant, and developed networks of agents, particularly among clerical personnel and workers, to watch the technical and managerial staff, especially those in the important *nomenklatura* positions.[106] When directors and specialists became involved in dis-

[103] Ibid., no. 105, p. 14.

[104] Ibid., no. 470, pp. 5-6; no. 485, p. 8; no. 202, pp. 9-10.

[105] The existence of such special sections in factories was occasionally shown in Soviet organization charts at the time. See, for example, *Predpriiatie*, no. 19-20, 1930, 29. See also the comments on the activities of the police by a Soviet woman engineer, who worked in the mining industry during most of the 1930s. She was accustomed to regular phone calls late at night from the secret police seeking her opinions and information on activities at work. (Interview with Mrs. Rose Jermain, Feb. 13, 1970; copy in my possession.)

[106] Harvard Interview Project, no. 105, B 2, p. 11; no. 202, p. 12; no. 26, A Schedule, p. 8; no. 524, A Schedule, p. 16, B Schedule, p. 14.

putes with the NKVD, a production official with powerful party connections in Moscow could sometimes win a dispute with the police.[107]
Wise managers and specialists, particularly if they lacked powerful
connections, however, generally showed more deference to the NKVD
than they did to local party officials. Aware that they were being
watched, but unaware of what the NKVD knew or how it would react,
they dealt with the police cautiously and fiercely resented this interference. A nonparty specialist, especially one with something against
him in his record, had to be especially careful.[108] Even a plant director
would generally go to the chief of the *spetsotdel* in his plant, who was
subordinate to the Economic Department of the regional NKVD, for
advice before promoting a technical specialist. The chief of the *spetsotdel* would check his dossiers. If he found something, he would tell the
director, " 'I don't advise you to do that.' He won't say any more. But
that's enough."[109] The technical specialist would not be promoted.

Whenever something went wrong on the job, wise technical specialists
informed the police officials immediately, especially in the case of an
accident or an order that the specialist considered dangerous. If the
specialist could exonerate himself, an experienced NKVD officer might
say, "It's good you have come to me, because I would have found out
in half an hour anyhow."[110] Of course, NKVD officers were not always
so benevolent; during the purges they sometimes resorted to torturing
technical specialists, and they always conducted exhausting investigations
of any industrial accident or other suspicious circumstance that had
been reported to them.[111] The resentment of this police role comes
through strongly in most memoirs by Soviet production specialists,
whether published in the Soviet Union in the post-Stalin era or in the
West. Some major Soviet engineers, such as Emelianov, felt that the
security measures conducted by the NKVD in the 1930s were carried to
absurd lengths and hinted at the attitude production personnel sometimes held concerning such security. He related the anecdote of a mass
meeting held at his plant in 1935 where the director of plant security
warned against saboteurs and boasted of the measures taken by his

[107] Ibid., no. 105, p. 31; Kravchenko, pp. 181-185, 196-197, 232.
[108] Harvard Interview Project, no. 105, p. 16; see also no. 26, B 2 Schedule.
[109] Ibid., 24.   [110] Ibid., 33.
[111] Kravchenko, p. 294; interview with Mr. S. N. Baldwin, an American engineer employed in Soviet tractor plants between 1930 and 1938, U.S. State Dept.
Decimal File, 861.659-Tractors/24, dated Jan. 18, 1938; interview with John M.
Haber, American engineer employed in the Soviet oil industry from 1933 to 1938,
State Dept. Decimal File, 861.6363/348, Sept. 15, 1938; interview with T. W.
Jenkins, chief engineer in the Soviet Union for the United Engineering Co. of
Pittsburgh, Pa., dated Jan. 31, 1938, State Dept. Decimal File, 861.651/17; see
also Scott's book, *Behind the Urals*, pp. 187ff.

staff. The entire assembly broke up in laughter when a production worker spoke up, indicating that he had entered the plant for months with the picture of his grandmother attached to his security pass. Emelianov unfortunately tells us nothing about the fate of this joker.[112] In general, the NKVD showed little sense of humor. The relationship of production specialists with the NKVD was their single most trying experience. It was intended to be so, both to increase their efficiency on the job and to ensure their political conformity. For example, the chief of the *spetsotdel* might call a shop engineer into his office and tell him:

> "Your shop has been turning out defective production. You better do something about it. If you don't, you will lose my friendship." . . . If the engineer tries to justify himself, the chief of the spetsotdel will answer him. "Your justification will be in your actions, through your work." Now this man will do everything possible in order to correct the situation. He will work day and night, he will not leave the shop, he will establish a bed in the shop, he will have his lunch there, he will do everything in order to correct the situation.[113]

Such pressures on production specialists may have worked in individual instances to increase the efficiency of a notoriously inefficient economy, but much evidence, particularly from the later 1930s, shows them to have been counterproductive in an economic sense.[114] While such measures certainly worked to assure the outward loyalty of production specialists, the cumulative effect of all these pressures—high targets, police surveillance, troubled relations with workers, conflicts with party and state officials, heavy responsibilities with ill-defined rights—drove a large proportion of the technical intelligentsia, especially those with higher educational qualifications, who could more easily escape, to flee production work for less dangerous jobs in design bureaus, higher industrial administration, research, and teaching. Curiously enough, it also made many young specialists receptive to work as party and NKVD officials just at a time—in the later 1930s—when the party and police apparatuses decided to recruit large numbers of tech-

---

[112] Emelianov, *Novyi mir*, pp. 56-57.

[113] Harvard Interview Project, no. 105, p. 33.

[114] In addition to the sources in n. 111 above, see *Izvestiia*, April 29, 1937; *Pravda*, June 5, 1937; *Izvestiia*, June 9, 1937; and the dissertations by Katz and Kal'manson (the former, American; the latter, Soviet). See also British Foreign Office document, N5458/42/38, dated Nov. 5, 1937 (Public Record Office, London); and Medvedev, pp. 228-230; for some of the personnel trends during the purges see the recently published documents, TsGANKh SSSR, f. 8243, op. 4, 544, ll. 1-3, 6-9, 11-13, and TsGANKh SSSR, f. 4372, op. 41, d. 553, ll. 146-154, in *Industrializatsiia SSSR 1938-41*, pp. 227ff; 251ff.

nical specialists to replace cadres recently purged. The aftermath of the purges was marked by the penetration of engineers, in large numbers for the first time, into the ranks of both party and police apparatuses.

Several sources indicate that when Beria was appointed to replace Yezhov as head of the NKVD in late 1938, he began to recruit many technical specialists. Though a brutal man, Beria was himself a former engineering student who saw the need for greater technical expertise in the NKVD. During the purges, engineers were sometimes called in as technical consultants because the NKVD did not itself have the requisite expertise to conduct an interrogation that involved the details of engineering work.[115] As one former Soviet engineer noted, "When Beria took over, there was a purge in the ranks of the NKVD. A special commission was appointed. This was in 1938. And the commission decided that the NKVD must consist of competent people."[116] This change had an effect on the relations between the specialists and the political police. As another engineer, arrested during the purges, testified:

> In the beginning the NKVD men had little education, even the chiefs of the district and provincial NKVD. I saw this during my arrest. The NKVD man who interrogated me did not know anything about the production he was questioning me about. Very often he would resume the interrogation next day and admit freely that he had asked for information and now understood what I was telling. But already in the last years of my arrest, towards 1938, 1939, the situation changed, and I saw that people had become more competent. . . . A commission was appointed and it was decided that the NKVD people should know about the subject they were investigating. They began to draft people from production and also from higher schools into the NKVD.[117]

After his release, this engineer recalled meeting a district NKVD officer and being impressed. "He was an engineer, a competent man and an agreeable person"—a surprising comment from an emigré who had suffered at the hands of this organization.[118]

Just as the trials of engineers between 1928 and 1930 were accompanied by a large influx of technical specialists as party *members* for the first time, so the purges of 1936 to 1938 were followed by an influx of such specialists as party and police *officials* for the first time. We need to assess how this happened and how significant it was for the role of

[115] Kravchenko, pp. 288-293.
[116] Harvard Interview Project, no. 105, p. 36.
[117] Ibid., no. 70, p. 6.   [118] Ibid.

production specialists and, more generally, for the technical intelligentsia in Soviet society. While we have no overall figures for the proportion of technical specialists with higher education who came to occupy such posts by 1941, the speeches of high party officials, such as Zhdanov and Kaganovich, indicate it was the party's intention to upgrade its officials educationally, particularly with recent graduates from the years 1933 to 1938.[119] (This was the period when, as we know, major attempts were made to improve the quality of higher technical education and when large numbers of students had been recruited from the working class.) Zhdanov also indicated that the party rules were changed in 1939 to permit appointment as officials people who had only recently become members, a measure that aided the entry of young technical specialists into such work.[120] That these measures did bring a number of Soviet technical specialists into professional party work is corroborated by a spate of articles written by engineers serving as local party secretaries in the period between 1939 and 1941. It is also corroborated by evidence in a recent Soviet dissertation, which claims that, prior to 1939, party organizations had been preoccupied with agriculture and other political questions, and industry had suffered from relative neglect by professional party officials. In 1939, party rules were changed to reorganize local party bureaus and include a local professional party official for each branch of industry located in an area.[121] Engineers who were party members were frequently brought into such posts, as well as chairmanships of shop and factory party committees. In increasing numbers they also became heads of local party bureaus at the regional (*raikom*), city (*gorkom*), and provincial (*obkom*) levels.[122]

[119] For the Zhdanov speech, see *Industriia*, March 21, 1939; see also Kaganovich's report on industry to the Eighteenth Party Congress, *Industriia*, March 18, 1939.

[120] Ibid., *XVIII S"ezd VKP(b)*, Moscow, 1939, p. 49.

[121] Kal'manson diss., pp. 95-99; *Sovetskaia ukraina*, Dec. 8, 1940; *Industriia*, April 6, 1938, 3; April 21, 1938, 3; April 5, 1939, 2; June 20, 1938, 3.

[122] TsPA IML, f. 17, op. 22, ed. khr. 2237, l. 214, ed. khr. 2925, ll. 24-25, cited in Kal'manson diss., p. 272; see also pp. 90-95 of this dissertation. A number of biographies of Central Committee members between 1958 and 1965 reveal this pattern. After some experience as production engineers or agronomists, the Central Committee members below became party officials in most cases after 1937. See the biographies in *Deputaty verkhovnogo soveta*, Moscow, 1959, 1965 (those marked with an asterisk were also Politburo members either in the period from 1958 to 1965 or subsequently): N. V. Bannikov, L. I. Brezhnev,* I. S. Gustov, A. A. Goregliad, I. V. Kapitanov, I. P. Kazanets, S. D. Khitrov, A. P. Kirilenko,* V. K. Klimenko, A. V. Kovalenko, F. D. Kulakov,* V. V. Kuznetsov, I. V. Lavrenov, B. Mambetov, L. G. Mel'nikov, I. T. Novikov, G. S. Pavlov, G. P. Pavlov, D. S. Poliansky,* V. F. Promyslov, N. A. Shchelokov, P. E. Shelest,* S. A. Skachkov, T. I. Sokolov, A. P. Volkov, G. I. Voronov,* and V. P. Zhigalin. This list includes only those graduate production specialists who

What were the reasons for this trend? Beyond the general desire to increase the educational and cultural level of party officials in a society where a rising level of formal education was a general trend, some of the more specific reasons appeared in articles by engineers who served as party secretaries after the purges. One of the major reasons, of course, was to exert greater party control over production through people who understood the technical details. Yet, another common theme running through this period was the need to stem the flight of graduate specialists from production, to attract others back to such work, and to ease strained relations between production specialists and the political authorities. Obviously, material incentives, which had been considerable after 1931, had not been sufficient to keep competent technologists in production. Coercion, of course, could be, and was, used after 1938 to keep graduates in such work, but, along with these measures, others were needed. Engineer Khabarovsk, first secretary of a party *raikom* in Stalingrad, stated that measures must be taken to strengthen one-man management and to raise the authority of administrative and technical personnel: "Raikom committees of the party must direct work of primary party organs so that they do not duplicate the functions of managers, nor replace them."[123]

At the same time, the party was urged to take a more active interest in the technical line followed in enterprises, helping the production personnel while checking on them, criticizing them but not constantly replacing managerial-technical personnel, thus giving them a greater sense of job security. He noted that, as party secretary, he directed special attention to the local engineers, calling them to party headquarters for concrete talks about production, including the technical details. The engineers "acknowledge that they can discuss technical themes with the secretary of the party regional committee. This still further brought the engineers close to me."[124] How effective this really was in easing relations with production specialists and increasing party control over them cannot be judged from the present sources, of course, but these were certainly among the intentions of the party. The significance of this trend is that members of the technical intelligentsia were thrust into positions of prominence at the local level in party organizations, and were thus positioned for their eventual climb to dominance at

---

became party officials prior to the German invasion and later rose to the highest echelons of the ruling elite. The list could be expanded considerably if one were to add those who entered the party *apparat* in World War II, or prior to Stalin's death. Some of the above were only party organizers in factories by 1941, while others were already *raikom, gorkom,* or *obkom* first secretaries or higher ranking party officials.

[123] *Industriia*, April 5, 1939, 2.   [124] Ibid.

the top of the party over the next twenty to thirty years. Whether such party engineers remained good engineers is, of course, a different question. As Engineer Khabarovsk saw the problem in 1939:

> Have I fully utilized my knowledge as an engineer in my party work? I still cannot give a firm answer to this. . . . All my time is occupied, of course, with party-political work. . . . I have very little time remaining to perfect my education. And I must perfect it in two areas: widen my knowledge of Marxist-Leninist theory and develop myself as an engineer. Before me stands the danger of remaining on a lower level of technical qualifications. From the moment of my selection as the secretary of the *raikom*, speaking truthfully, I have not taken a technical book in my hand. How can I nonetheless widen my knowledge as an engineer? I have taken forceful measures with myself: I have agreed to read lectures in a local institute for raising the qualifications of managers. The problem of raising the knowledge of engineers working in party posts is a very real and serious one. I would like to ask all engineers who are working as secretaries of *raikom* and city committees of the Communist Party to respond to my remarks and discuss in the pages of this newspaper their work and methods of leadership, of budgeting their time, of combining party work with raising their own technical knowledge.[125]

Whether such intentions succeeded in their aims we cannot answer here, since the work of engineers as party officials in later years goes beyond the scope of this study. There is considerable evidence from a study of career patterns that many such engineers shifted back and forth in later years between professional party work and work as economic officials and technologists.[126]

Another marked trend can be seen in the Soviet press after 1938: criticizing those party organizations that took a negative attitude toward the technical intelligentsia. For example, in the fall of 1938 an article in *Industriia* blasted a local party committee and its head for neglecting and even allowing the persecution of the technical intelligentsia, blaming the technical intelligentsia for production problems in the local party newspaper: "Such behavior by the paper is not accidental. It reflects the line of the leaders of the party committee, who have shown an impermissible careless attitude to the specialists."[127] The article noted that over the past year, only one engineer had been brought into the party here and party members refused to sponsor others as party members, fearing that "nothing good will come of it." The local party secretary

---

[125] Ibid.
[126] See sources in n. 121 above.
[127] *Industriia*, Oct. 27, 1938.

was blamed for the situation: "Almost every day Comrade Kurakin visits the shops. But he is rarely seen talking with engineers, technicians, lab assistants. The conditions of work of the engineers, and technicians, their needs and requests do not interest the leaders of the party committee."[128] That such party officials were bucking official party policy after the purges is indicated by a series of articles in the central newspapers *Pravda* and *Industriia*, and by statistics on the influx of technical specialists into the party.[129] By 1937, forty-seven thousand party members had higher technical education, compared to only one hundred thirty-eight graduate engineers in 1928. Between 1939 and 1941, approximately seventy percent of the new party members enrolled came from the administrative and technical intelligentsia.[130]

The process of transforming the Communist party into a party with a white-collar majority and a heavy component from the technical intelligentsia was in full swing. There is, of course, no indication that such trends threatened the immediate dominance of Stalin's *apparat*. Quite the contrary. Most of these new technical specialists were young and inexperienced and had passed through an educational system that tried to condition them to political passivity. If anything, they owed a great deal to Stalin. His policies had thrust them into prominence, and they were not likely to challenge his dominance openly. Nonetheless, these trends also indicate a far greater integration of the new technostructure with the power structure than had existed previously. Such a development greatly increased the potential for mutual interaction between these two groups. Despite continued conflicts, the potential of the technical intelligentsia for exerting influence within the power structure was increased, just as the party's potential for influencing the technostructure increased.

By 1941, however, none of this seems to have solved the problem of the flight of graduate engineers from direct work in production. Despite the origins of the majority of the new specialists in the working class and peasantry, graduate specialists continued to use every opportunity to escape direct work in production and leave such work to less qualified *praktiki*. Their flight into party and police work promised greater prestige and power. Their flight into purely administrative positions in the economy, into research institutes, design bureaus, and education promised relief from the tyranny of fulfilling high production targets and the other pressures detailed in this chapter. Several recently published archival documents and many articles in the Soviet press from the period

---

[128] Ibid.

[129] For example, *Pravda*, Feb. 21, 1941; *Industriia*, Feb. 6, 1938; July 14 and July 31, 1940; Oct. 10, 1940, 3; Dec. 30, 1940, 2. See also the Kal'manson diss., p. 250, citing a party archival source, MPA, f. 4, op. 12, ed. khr. 7, l. 6-7.

[130] *Partiinoe stroitel'stvo*, no. 10, 1937, 24; nos. 11-12, 1940, 18-19.

indicate the persistence of the problem, corroborated by the reports of Soviet emigré engineers.[131] According to a survey conducted by *Gosplan*, which included some two hundred fourteen thousand of about two hundred ninety-one thousand graduate technologists in Soviet industry by early 1941, they were distributed as follows: only 31.8% worked directly in production, reflecting not an improvement but a significant decline over previous decades.[132] (In 1929, 54% of all specialists with completed higher education worked at the production level.)[133] The largest single proportion of graduate technologists in industry by 1941, 37.2%, were employed in purely administrative positions in plants, trusts, and People's Commissariats (Ministeries). Another 8.7% of such specialists were employed in design bureaus, and 8.3% worked in higher technical education. Only 7.8% were employed in industrial research institutes. (Where the remaining graduate specialists [6.2%] were employed is not shown in this study.)[134]

As one later Soviet emigré summed up his reasons for preferring work outside production, despite a lower income: outside production, one worked less. There was more time for self-development and for keeping up one's technical knowledge. (Production engineers frequently worked twelve to eighteen hours a day, much of it paperwork or dealing with the human problems, not the technical problems of production.) There was not so much responsibility outside production, nor the danger of being held accountable for nonfulfillment, accidents, or fraudulent reporting. Specialists outside production did not deal with workers, "we have no extra critic," as this engineer expressed it. The surveillance by the NKVD and pressure by the party were also less intensive.[135] In other words, the risks of production work were great, and the rewards were not commensurate in the judgment of an increasing proportion of such specialists. One young specialist who had entered production with great enthusiasm in 1936 quit two years later to become a journalist, after his work had been inspected twenty-nine times within a two-month period by various commissions and control groups.[136] As we shall see in the next section, however, some jobs outside production, such as those in research and development, also had their share of dangers and frustrations.

[131] See n. 114; also *Industriia*, March 10, 1937, 3; April 8, 1938, 3; Sept. 5, 1938, 3; May 6, 1939, 3; April 1, 1940, 2; Feb. 1, 1940, 1; March 20, 1940; March 15, 1940, 1; Jan. 26, 1940, 3; Jan. 6, 1940; Harvard Interview Project, no. 202, B 2, pp. 16-17; no. 384, pp. 2-3, 7; no. 26, B 2 Schedule.
[132] *Ratsionalizatsiia*, no. 13-14, 1930, 39-40.
[133] *Industriia*, March 20, 1940.
[134] *Industrializatsiia SSSR 1938-1941*, p. 270.
[135] Harvard Interview Project, no. 384, B 2, p. 7.
[136] Ibid., no. 470, pp. 1-10.

13

RESEARCH AND DEVELOPMENT: THE BARRIERS TO INNOVATION

The economic organizer, factory manager, engineer, inventor—these are not Russian types. . . . Machine industry is by its very nature "un-Russian" and will always be foreign to the Russian as something sinful, diabolical.

Oswald Spengler, 1922[1]

Only in a country building socialism, only under the leadership of the proletariat and its Communist Party can the technician and engineer develop their creative powers.

Soviet journal, 1935[2]

Our institute, with a staff of some 300 members, had a yearly output of maybe 40 new machines. Of these 40 machines only 2 were put into operation, the remaining 38 would land in file 13. For this reason we had a saying which went like this: "We are working for file 13."

Soviet engineer, 1930s[3]

Members of the technical intelligentsia who fled production for work in research and development found another set of problems in their new environment. While the conflicts and risks were somewhat different— their work was more removed from contact with the working class and from the pressures of fulfilling high quantitative targets—work in research and development had its own frustrations. Judging from contemporary accounts and memoirs, the greatest frustration was the difficulty of successfully introducing into production new inventions and processes worked out in research institutes and laboratories. The process of technological innovation required long lead times, and great patience and ingenuity on the part of researchers, for it met, at times,

[1] *Politische Schriften*, Munich, 1933, 99.
[2] *Front nauki i tekhniki*, no. 4, 1935, 30.
[3] Harvard Interview Project on the Soviet Social System, Interview no. 403, B 2 Schedule, p. 6.

with almost insuperable barriers. The situation was not as hopeless as portrayed by Spengler above, nor was it the result of the reasons he gave, but it fell far short of optimistic Soviet claims that only under socialism could the most rapid technological innovation be fostered, and science and industry brought closer together, claims contradicted by a mass of evidence from the Soviet press itself in these years.

Some of the barriers to innovation have been analyzed in recent studies that seek an explanation for the continuing low level of Soviet technological innovation in the 1960s and 1970s, despite the efforts of the government and party to increase that level. Looking for the historical roots of such problems in the conditions of the 1920s and 1930s, they have arrived at some interesting but incomplete conclusions.[4] No one has yet explored more systematically the sources for the period before World War II and attempted to synthesize from these sources, including case studies of technological innovation in this period, a more complete picture of the accomplishments and the failures of Soviet research and development (R & D) prior to World War II. This needs to be done not only because of later Soviet problems with technological innovation, which are receiving extensive treatment by scholars, but also to improve our understanding of the conditions, priorities, and expectations of the first three Five-Year Plans. In doing so, we can bring to bear what we have already learned here about the structure, education, and roles of the technical intelligentsia when analyzing the problems of Soviet research and development. This chapter will try to explain the barriers to successful innovation in terms of the social relations of the technostructure both internally and in its dealings with other major groups of Soviet society.

Despite rapid growth in the number of industrial research institutes, the number of research workers, and appropriations for such work during the early Five-Year Plans, the results—actual new inventions and processes introduced to industry—were considered disappointing. While Soviet figures should be used with caution, those below give some sense of the real growth in the R & D community. The proportion of

---

[4] See, for example, the article by Peter Solomon, "Technological Innovation and Soviet Industrialization," in Mark Field, ed., *The Social Consequences of Modernization in Socialist Countries*, Baltimore, 1976; Antony Sutton, *Western Technology and Soviet Economic Development 1930-1945*, Stanford, 1971; Joseph S. Berliner, "Bureaucratic Conservatism and Creativity in the Soviet Economy," in Fred W. Riggs, ed., *Frontiers of Development Administration*, Durham, N.C., 1970, pp. 586-629. Berliner is completing a book on the problems of technological innovation in the Soviet economy, which was unavailable to me at the time of writing. See also Manfred Balz, *Inventions and the Organization of Technical Progress in the Soviet Union*, Lexington, Mass., 1975.

graduate specialists employed in industrial research, for example, grew from some 2% of the total in 1930 to 7.8% by 1941.[5] In addition, 8.7% of the graduate specialists in industry by 1941 were employed in industrial design bureaus, giving a total proportion of 16.5% of the technical intelligentsia in industry who were occupied in some phase of the industrial research and development system by that time.[6] Even allowing for error or inaccuracy in these figures, they probably capture the general trend of growth in this sector of the economy. When one considers the large expansion in actual numbers of technical specialists by 1941, some idea of the Soviet R & D effort in numerical terms becomes apparent. A British scholar's recent study of Soviet appropriations also suggests that the proportion of national income committed to R & D increased from about 0.4% in 1928 and 1929 to 0.6% in 1935, a rise of about 50%. Though such appropriations failed to keep up with the percentage growth in R & D personnel, they probably represented a somewhat larger commitment of the national income to this sector in the U.S.S.R. than in the U.S. at the time, especially given the depression conditions in the West.[7]

Yet complaints by authoritative sources in 1928 and 1929 that research institutes were cut off from industry and that few new inventions or processes developed in these institutions were actually introduced were still common in the late 1930s.[8] A recent Western study concludes that only two examples of native technical innovations can be found in the Soviet Union prior to World War II—the development

[5] See Kuibyshev's report at the Sixteenth Party Congress, *XVI S"ezd*, p. 500; the figures for 1941 are in a recently published archival document, based on a survey of 214,236 specialists with higher education working under the auspices of all-union and union-republic industrial commissariats on January 1, 1941. This would include more than two-thirds of the graduate technical specialists employed in the Soviet economy by this time. (See Document no. 78, from the Central Statistical Administration of *Gosplan*, TsGANKh SSSR, f. 4372, op. 41, d. 33, ll. 10-19, 22-25, published in *Industrializatsiia SSSR 1938-1941*, p. 270.)

[6] Ibid., p. 270.

[7] Robert A. Lewis, "Some Aspects of the Research and Development Effort of the Soviet Union, 1924-35," in *Science Studies*, 2, 1972, 163-164.

[8] See, for example, O. Y. Shmidt, ed., *Nauchnye kadry i nauchno-issledovatel' skie uchrezhdeniia SSSR*, Moscow, 1930, pp. 5ff.; Aug. 7, 1928 government decree in *Resheniia partii i pravitel'stva po khoziastvennym voprosam*, vol. 1, Moscow, 1967, pp. 750-755; Kirillov, p. 313; V. D. Yesakov, *Sovetskaia nauka v gody pervoi piatiletki*, Moscow, 1971, pp. 82-93; *Industriia*, May 11, 1939, 2; April 1, 1939; Jan. 26, 1938, 2; July 27, 1939; July 6, 1939, 3; June 6, 1940, 1; June 11, 1940, 2; May 26, 1940, 1; June 26, 1940, 2; Feb. 12, 1939, 1; Feb. 26, 1939, 2; Nov. 29, 1939; Feb. 6, 1940, 3; Feb. 29, 1940, 2; June 17, 1940, 2; *Izobretatel'*, no. 8, 1935, 40; no. 9, 1935, 44; *Industriia*, June 9, 1937, 1; April 12, 1937, 1; March 12, April 8, April 12, 1937; *Front nauki i tekhniki*, no. 10, 1936, 100 ff; no. 4, 1935, 64.

of synthetic rubber and the more economical boiler developed by Professor Ramzin for steam power plants.[9] We should be cautious about accepting this conclusion at face value. Soviet sources would extend the list somewhat to include Kapitsa's invention of a cheap method for producing oxygen, the related development of oxygen steel making, the use of the turbodrill in the oil industry, the development of a method for producing synthetic acetic acid, the development of electric welding, underground gasification of coal, and others.[10] One should also remember that the foundations of Soviet rocketry and jet propulsion were laid during this period. Despite the underestimation of its value and the arrests of rocket designers during the purges, this early work, as well as the work of aircraft designers which will be explored further in the following chapter, made possible Soviet advances in these fields during and after World War II, although serious mistakes were made in the earlier period.[11]

The point here is not to engage in a polemic over the actual number of indigenous Soviet technological innovations prior to 1941. Whether their number was two, ten, or even several hundred, the fact remains that, given the thousands of specialists employed in R & D and the millions of rubles committed to it, the immediate return on this investment was small in terms of successful native technical innovations. One needs, of course, to distinguish between new inventions and processes and those actually introduced in the economy (the latter sense is the precise definition of a technical innovation).[12] The number of the

[9] Antony C. Sutton, *Western Technology and Soviet Economic Development 1930-1945*, Stanford, 1971, p. 329.

[10] See, for example, I. P. Bardin, ed., *Sovetskaia tekhnika za dvadtsat piat' let 1917-1942*, Moscow, 1945; *Industriia*, Feb. 6, 1940, 3; May 11, 1939, 2; Feb. 5, 1940, 2; I. I. Artobolevsky, *Ocherki po istorii tekhnik v SSSR*, Moscow, 1968; A. A. Armand, ed., *Nauchno-issledovatel'skie instituty NKTP*, Moscow, 1935; Robert W. Campbell, *Economics of Soviet Oil and Gas*, New York, 1968, pp. 101-120; Mykola Matiiko, *Evgen Oskarovich Paton*, Kiiv, 1961; A. D. Ul'yanova, *Evgen O. Paton 1870-1953*, Kiiv, 1965; Y. O. Paton, *Vospominaniia*, Moscow, 1958.

[11] See, for example, Yaroslav Golovanov, *Sergei Korolev, The Apprenticeship of a Space Pioneer*, Moscow, 1975; P. T. Astashenkov, *Glavnyi konstruktor*, Moscow, 1975; P. K. Oshchepkov, *Zhizn' i mechta*, p. 31.

[12] Peter Solomon has provided a good definition of technological innovation: "This term refers to the process through which scientific knowledge is translated into new products or processes which are then utilized in the productive process. Thus, innovation refers to more than either research or invention. Although both research and invention represent sources of new ideas, these ideas must then be translated into new products or processes; and this translation requires further 'development' activities, such as the designing, construction, and testing of models and the preparation of experimental production runs. Moreover, in our lexicon 'innovation' requires the production of genuinely *new* technologies; small modifications in existing technology, however profitable, will be termed 'adaptations,' rather than 'innovations.'" (op. cit., p. 2).

former was undoubtedly much larger than the latter. Even official Soviet figures for this period confirm as much: the number of technical innovations was small by comparison with the number of new inventions and processes worked out by researchers. While the Committee on Inventions and, later, *Gosplan*, annually registered thousands of new inventions (rising from about 5500 in 1929 and 1930 to 7000 in 1934, and declining to a total of 3902 during the period of the purges, from August 1936, to January 1939), Soviet data indicate that the proportion of these introduced into the economy was unsatisfactory, ranging between two and four percent of those registered between 1924 and 1934; like data are unavailable for the later 1930s, when industry was disrupted by the purges.[13] How accurate these figures are, and how original and significant the thousands of inventions registered, is open to dispute; but the point is that Soviet sources themselves show a nearly universal dissatisfaction with the R & D effort in this respect.

If the return on investment in R & D in terms of native technical innovations was disappointing in Soviet eyes, what specifically were the reasons for this? The overall industrial research effort in the Soviet Union at this time was conditioned by the needs and priorities of Soviet industrialization, and these involved certain basic antinomies, that is, contradictory tendencies that limited successful introduction of Soviet technical inventions and processes. As Peter Solomon has pointed out, successful innovation requires both the capacity for it and the demand. The Soviet Union in these years was creating an impressive capacity for R & D, but the demand for indigenous technical innovations was considerably less. The reasons for this limited demand, given below, differ in significant respects from those of other writers, particularly in points 2, 3, 4, 5, 6, and 8. The explanation developed here analyzes the environment of Soviet research and development and the problems with technological innovation in terms of the following major elements:

1) the tension between the need to borrow and adapt foreign technology as rapidly as possible, and the desire to compete with other countries in native technological creativity;

2) the lack of competition as an active stimulus to innovation, and countervailing pressures of the planning system that actively inhibited the adoption of innovations by industrial managers and and production specialists;

3) inhibitions created by the use of terror against some innovators and the resultant risks perceived for failure in a technological controversy or in taking responsibility for the introduction of a new invention or process;

[13] *Vestnik komiteta*, no. 3, 1931, 31-32; *Industriia*, April 1, 1939.

4) tensions created by the conflict between the professionalization of R & D and attempts on the part of the political structure to make the process of technological innovation a mass movement, stimulating technical creativity not only by the technical intelligentsia, but by the working class as well;

5) the relative abundance of unskilled manual labor and the relative scarcity of skilled workers and well educated specialists (particularly at the production level), who were adaptable to a high level of innovation;

6) the strong tradition of pure research in Russian science and the high status accorded to such work by comparison with technical innovation;

7) the organizational separation of research, development, and production;

8) the tendency on the part of R & D personnel to show less concern for economic criteria in producing new inventions and processes than for criteria of technical performance—a general reflection of the weak influence of economists as compared with that of engineers and applied scientists in research and development.

The direction of the Soviet research effort was shaped in large part by the priorities of the early Five-Year Plans, chief of which were the rapid growth of mining, metallurgy, and machine building—the so-called American option. During the 1920s a debate over whether the metallurgical and machine building branches, or energy production and the chemical industry should receive first priority in development was resolved in favor of the former groups, with electrification and the chemical industry receiving a somewhat lower priority. The "metal eaters" can be considered followers of the American model of industrialization; advocates of chemicalization and electrification preferred the more intensively science-based industries in which Germany had taken the lead. The "American option" was adopted in the early Five-Year Plans. Electrical energy production and the chemical industry, although certainly not ignored, received less emphasis as a result, despite the efforts of a group of Soviet applied scientists and engineers, including a number in the Marxist ideological organization for the technical intelligentsia (VARNITSO), who attempted to increase the attention given to electrification and chemicalization.[14]

---

[14] See the author's articles on the chemical and automotive industries in *Wirtschaft und Gesellschaft in industriezeitalter von 1750 bis zu Gegenwart*, vol. 3, Stuttgart, forthcoming; I. B. Reznik, *Ovladeem amerikanskoi tekhnikoi*, Moscow,

This choice was to have major consequences for Soviet R & D, since high growth rates in the metallurgical and machine building industries seemed to require less basic scientific research and certainly less original R & D than imitation and adaptation of foreign, especially American, technology. As Ordzhonikidze, who led an investigation of Soviet industrial research and development as head of the Workers' and Peasants' Inspectorate (*Rabkrin*) in 1928, put it succinctly in that year:

If indeed we hope to catch up with and surpass American industry, we must absorb those technical achievements which exist in America. Then indeed we would see not a 23% growth in production [the plan for 1927 and 1928], but twice that rate. How can this be done? We must invite foreign technical personnel, conclude technical aid agreements with them, and even more so, and first of all, send hundreds and thousands of our young engineers there, to learn how and what to do.[15]

Ordzhonikidze repeatedly stated the need to borrow Western technology as quickly as possible in these years, an attitude that reflected official policy and was also reflected in the statements of other political leaders, including Stalin.[16] This attitude was to have a strong effect on the work of specialists in Soviet R & D, as well as on production specialists.

Despite the emphasis on borrowed technology, considerable desire remained among an element of the technical intelligentsia and among some political leaders such as Bukharin (who headed industrial research after 1929) for the U.S.S.R. to play a role as innovator in world technology.[17] The U.S.S.R. by 1928 already had a considerable industrial research establishment, thanks to the initiative of technical specialists and Lenin's support of these initiatives after 1917. These research institutions were concentrated much more heavily in areas of chemicalization and energy-related concerns, including electrification, than they were in areas that received first priority in Soviet industrialization

---

1931; E. Domar, *Essays in the Theory of Economic Growth*, New York, 1957, pp. 223-261; Alec Nove, *An Economic History of the USSR*, pp. 119-135. See also Y. N. Flakserman, *Elektrifikatsiia-Baza sotsialisticheskogo stroitel'stva*, Moscow, 1930, pp. 9-36, and *Gleb Krzhizhanovskii*, pp. 111-112, 596-598; and the journal *Amerikanskaia tekhnika*.

[15] From Ordzhonikidze's speech of March 26, 1928, *Stat'i i rechi*, vol. 2, p. 121.

[16] See Kuibyshev's speech in *TPG*, March 7, 1928, 3; I. V. Stalin, *Works*, vol. 13, Moscow, 1955, pp. 140, 273; *KPSS v rezoliutsiiakh*, Moscow, 1954, vol. 2, pp. 493-500.

[17] See, for example, Bukharin's articles in *TPG*, Oct. 15, 1929, and *Pravda*, January 20, and Dec. 15, 1929.

after 1928. While a shift had occurred by 1932, R & D still remained out of balance with the priorities of industrialization.[18]

The dichotomy between the structure of R & D and the priorities of production remained strong at least until 1936, the last year for which we have statistical data, although more institutions in geology and mining, metallurgy and machine building were established.[19] The desire of an important element of the technical intelligentsia for its own R & D network, especially in areas on the cutting edge of world technology, clashed with the desire of the Bolsheviks for most rapid growth in older, more established areas of technology. As a group of chemical technologists put it to the government in early 1928, when criticizing the general plans for industrialization, "These plans for the most part mechanically borrow the routine and in most cases outmoded forms of foreign technology."[20] While the advocates of chemicalization and electrification did not succeed in changing the priorities of the plan, they did succeed in expanding the number of research institutions and research workers in their areas of concern by 1932 at a faster rate in some cases than for research in geology, mining, metallurgy, and machine building, thereby preserving the dominance of their own specialties in the R & D network.

This tension between two countervailing trends produced a research network that lacked strong ties to production. This was partly because R & D was slanted toward producing research in fields that received lesser priority in industrialization. Figures for new inventions approved during 1933 also support this conclusion. They show that mining, metallurgy, and machine building accounted for only 22.6% of all new inventions approved in that year, while chemical and electrical technology accounted for 26.5%[21]

Data of this kind have not been found for the later 1930s, so it is difficult to say with certainty if this situation changed significantly by 1941. What the sources do indicate is that, for the combination of reasons analyzed in this chapter, the inapplicability of indigenous tech-

[18] The sources for this are the following: TsGANKh, f. 3429, op. 61, ed. khr. 986, ll. 214-218, dated July 24, 1928, and published in *Organizatsiia sovetskoi nauki v 1926-1932 gg. Sbornik dokumentov*, Leningrad, 1974, pp. 271-274; O. Y. Shmidt, ed., *Nauchnye kadry i nauchno-issledovatel'skie uchrezhdeniia SSSR*, Moscow, 1930, pp. 5-88; TsPA IML, f. 85, op. 29, d. 26, l. 12 in V. D. Yesakov, *Sovetskaia nauka v gody pervoi piatiletki*, Moscow, 1971, p. 118.

[19] See, for example, the data in Armand, op. cit., concerning industrial research institutions in heavy industry as of 1936.

[20] *Pravda*, March 19, 1928; on the efforts to give greater priority to the chemical industry and electrification see V. S. Lel'chuk, "Deiatel'nost komiteta po khimizatsii narodnogo khoziastva SSSR, 1928-1934," *Istoriia SSSR*, no. 3, 1958, 201-203, and Flakserman, op. cit.

[21] *Vestnik komiteta po izobretatel'stvu*, nos. 3-4, 1934, 42.

nology to Soviet production remained an unsolved problem throughout this period. One of the major reasons, it seems likely, was the sectoral imbalance of production and the industrial research network, and the tension expressed in this imbalance between the policy of technological borrowing and the desire on the part of the research community for indigenous technical creativity, particularly in areas of lower priority for the production sector. Many of these researchers continued to pursue projects of fundamental interest to themselves, though less suited to the needs of industry and, therefore, less likely to find quick application there. In doing so, such researchers were required to cultivate a split personality, presenting themselves to industrial and political authorities as in tune with the needs of Soviet industrialization, which often meant performing technical first aid for the economy and devoting some time to adapting foreign technology to Soviet conditions, while at the same time pursuing their own interests.

On the one hand, a reform of the law on inventions in 1931 lauded the rejection of the principle of novelty and encouraged the widespread "plagiarism" and application of inventions already described in foreign literature.[22] On the other hand, research specialists seized what opportunities they could find to emphasize the need for native inventions. For example, expanding on a statement by Stalin on May 4, 1935 that "we have entered a new period" in which there would be a great need for people "capable of harnessing technology and advancing it,"[23] a prominent research specialist and member of VARNITSO wrote that "we must still borrow bourgeois technology but we must also develop our own,"[24] a call that found sympathetic echoes in the research community.[25]

The political leadership did not openly oppose indigenous innovations, but, in practice, it encouraged them strongly only in certain areas: the creation of substitutes for imported materials, for example, synthetics for costly imports such as rubber; and R & D in defense technology, where the difficulties and risks of borrowing were greater, although even here considerable borrowing took place.[26] Defense-re-

---

[22] *Sovetskaia gosudarstvo i revoliutsiia prava*, no. 4, April 1931, 111-120; see also Paramonov, *Puti*, p. 201 and the interview with W. C. Aitkenhead, by Prof. H. H. Fischer of Stanford, 1934-1936 (TS Russia, A 511), Hoover Institution Archive.

[23] Stalin, *Selected Works*, p. 363.   [24] *Front nauki i tekniki*, no. 7, 1935, 38.

[25] Ibid., no. 10, 1936, 100ff.; see also *Industriia*, March 5, 1937, 2.

[26] See the *Sovnarkom* decree of April 26, 1928 in *Direktivy KPSS i sovetskogo pravitel'stva po khoiastvennym voprosam*, vol. 1, pp. 815-816. See also the memoirs of Yakovlev and Emelianov, op. cit., as well as the following documents in the British Foreign Office Archives, Public Record Office, London, N5205/5205/38, dated Oct. 9, 1936, and N6142/38/38, dated December 9, 1936.

lated institutes, such as the Central Aviation Institute (TsAGI) were among the best equipped, and were held up as models, although even in defense research numerous problems, including neglect and wrong-headed interference by the political authorities, hindered the rapid application of research.[27] We shall have more to say about some of the problems of defense technology in chapter 14.

In practice, the government and political leadership saw the role of the Soviet R & D network in the following light: 1) It was to aid industry in raising the productivity of labor through mechanization, whether borrowed or indigenous, although, in practice, the authorities favored the application of proven methods from abroad. 2) It was to adapt these methods to Soviet materials, climate, and level of skill, simplifying them when necessary. 3) It was to free the U.S.S.R. from imports of foreign machinery and raw materials as quickly as possible, consistent with the emphasis after 1928 on autarchy, that is, economic self-sufficiency. Autarchy served at least two ends: promoting Stalin's claim that socialism could be built in a single country, and freeing the Soviet Union from a dangerous economic dependency on hostile nations, a dependency that had made Imperial Russia vulnerable during World War I and had nearly strangled the young Soviet Republic during the civil war. The lessons of the years from 1914 to 1921 were certainly strong in the minds of the power structure when they established priorities for the first Five-Year Plans, and the prestige of technical creativity held less attraction for them than developing the raw materials base and mechanical muscle with which the Soviet Union could hold its own against the capitalist nations. In the view of Soviet leaders, the United States had tipped the balance in World War I with its well developed machine industry and its high degree of material self-sufficiency. The leading role of mining, metallurgy, and machine building in the U.S. economy proved more attractive to the survival orientation of the Soviet power structure than the more science-intensive structure of industrial Germany, defeated and prostrate after World War I. While this may have been a misreading of where American industry was actually headed after World War I (electrification and chemicalization developed more rapidly in the U.S. between the two world wars), this was the

---

[27] See V. Chuvaev and K. Raigorodskii, *ITR v bor'be za izobretatel'stvo*, Moscow, 1932, pp. 1-8; *Za industrializatsiiu*, Dec. 18, 1931, 2. On TsAGI see James G. Crowther, *Soviet Science*, London, 1936, pp. 209ff., as well as the reports of visits to TsAGI by the British air attache, in the British Foreign Office Archives, Public Record Office, London, N1483/871/38, dated March 9, 1936, and N5456/41/38, dated Nov. 1, 1937; *Front nauki i tekhniki*, no. 12, 1933, 18-26; no. 10, 1937, 8-21; *ZI*, May 21, 1938, 1, 4; March 9, 1939, 3; March 15, 1939, 2; *Vestnik inzhenerov*, no. 10, 1937, 599-600.

reading given recent history by the Soviet power structure. Technological breakthroughs by the Soviet Union could come later, and for that reason original R & D, including work in electrification and chemicals, was not dismissed, but rather held in reserve for a more distant future.

Because of the shortages of fuel and other raw materials Russia experienced in World War I and the civil war, the government also stressed geological research in the tasks it expected the industrial research system to accomplish. Whereas in 1918, only some ten to eleven percent of the territory of the former Russian Empire had been surveyed geologically, by 1937 over forty-three percent of the U.S.S.R. had been explored for raw materials. As the government remained dissatisfied with these surveys and the degree to which they neglected the quality and accessibility for industrial use of the resources discovered, it wanted much effort devoted to such research.[28]

When one considers the above, some of the major reasons the U.S.S.R. produced few technological innovations in the period became clearer. Critics of Soviet technical innovations and of Soviet borrowing of most of its usable technology should keep these factors in mind. It is not surprising that a country late to industrialization should choose— given limited human and capital resources during this period—to assimilate first what is known abroad, as well as surveying its own natural resources, before embarking on a high level of technical creativity and indigenous innovation. What is surprising is not that borrowing was prevalent, but that such a large R & D community was established and that it struggled to be creative in light of all the counterpressures. That this occurred is no doubt a reflection of the pride and strong nationalism, even technical chauvinism of the Russian research community, stimulated by years of neglect under the Tsars when foreign industrialists and the Tsarist government itself largely ignored indigenous Russian inventors. This technological nationalism was partially released in the revolution of 1917, and was encouraged morally and materially by Lenin after 1917.

The accomplishments of Soviet R & D after 1928, then, need to be measured not so much in terms of native technological innovations successfully introduced before 1941 as in: its capacity for survival and growth, and its contribution to the industrialization effort in adapting foreign technology and surveying natural resources, while still struggling to create some original inventions and processes. What Soviet applied

---

[28] *Pervyi vsesoiuznyi gornyi nauchno-tekhnicheskii s"ezd. Trudy. April 14-27, 1926*, Moscow, 1927; *Industriia*, Feb. 3, 1938; April 2, 1938, 2; April 24, 1938, 1-2; Dec. 4, 1939; Feb. 15, 1940, 3; *Problemy sovetskoi geologii*, no. 1, 1938, 5-7; M. Lapidus, *Otkryvatel' podzemnykh tain*, Moscow, 1963, pp. 111ff.

scientists and engineers built in this period, with the support of the political leadership, was a growing infrastructure, representing a potential for future technical creativity. This said, we cannot ignore significant barriers to successful innovation that grew up at the same time, since they had a major effect on the work and psychology of the technical intelligentsia, with long-term carryover effects.

Given the general priorities of Soviet industrialization, what other aspects of the planning system affected Soviet industrial research in these years? While the government wanted both high quantitative targets for production and a high level of technical innovation, insisting that the two goals were complementary, in practice, industrial managers found them contradictory, and they adopted new technology only under the greatest pressure. They preferred to meet their quantitative targets with existing methods and greater inputs of labor when possible, rather than take the time and risk needed to master new technology; they paid lip service to technical innovation. Capital, required in large amounts for major innovations, was scarce, particularly in those areas of lesser priority where the research network was most productive. Hence there was a premium on fulfilling output plans with greater labor inputs rather than with technical innovations. Such "technical conservatism" and "antimechanizer" tendencies of managers and production specialists were continually decried in the press, but the problem was never solved during this period.[29]

Bureaus to supervise technical innovations and rationalization of production (*brizy*) were established at all levels of industry after 1928. Still the Soviet press was filled with complaints that the area was neglected by managers, who underestimated its importance and often put incompetent or unqualified personnel in these sections, and paid them comparatively low salaries.[30] After 1933, many *brizy* were abolished as ineffective. Production workers frequently resented their work and hindered them, even to the point of barring their representatives from entering shops.[31] Constant administrative pressure from above was necessary in many cases before responsible managers at the production level would give attention to innovation. As already discussed

[29] *Vestnik komiteta*, no. 4, 1936, 2; *Industriia*, January 20, 1937, 2; March 12, April 8, April 12, 1937; June 9, 1937, 1; February 12, 1939, 1; Sept. 11, 1939, 2; Feb. 29, 1940, 2; *Front nauki i tekhniki*, no. 10, 1936, 104; A. Khavin, *Shagi industrii*, p. 41; Paramonov, *Puti*, pp. 197, 214.

[30] See, e. g., *Predpriiatie*, no. 6, 1929, 21-23; *Ratsionalizatsiia proizvodstva*, no. 3, 1930, 11; no. 3, 1932, 3-4; 1933, no. 1, 1933, 32; *Vestnik komiteta*, no. 11, 1933, 1; *Predpriiatie*, no. 14, 1933, 6.

[31] *Predpriiatie*, no. 6, 1929, 22.

above, one reason for the unusually high production targets adopted in these years may have been to exert additional pressure on administrative-technical personnel to adopt new technology and more efficient methods of organization. Without such pressure, the reasoning may have run, many managers and specialists would continue in the familiar rut of established methods.

As it turned out, these high targets could also be used as an excuse by those in production to neglect innovations. Many complained they had no time for rationalization of production and especially invention, since they were forced to concentrate on the routine work of fulfilling high ouput plans.

After the elimination of *brizy* at the factory level in 1933 and 1934, many administrative-technical workers in production tried to shift the burden of involvement in this area to the trade unions and social organizations, such as the Society of Inventors,[32] rather than assuming it themselves as the government intended. Foremen and heads of shops frequently expressed attitudes such as this: "It is not our business to be involved with inventors."[33] As the director of one mine expressed it after the abolition of his special bureau for aiding inventions, "Things are easier for us now, there is less trouble. Let the Society [of Inventors] occupy itself with proposals. The bureaus for aiding inventions have been liquidated, and we must fulfill our plans."[34] In the better organized production shops and mines, factory laboratories existed and employed specialists interested in inventions who worked side by side with production personnel, aiding in the introduction of new methods and technology. Unfortunately, however, models of efficiency and imagination in this area were fewer than many research technologists would have preferred.[35]

As the Soviet physicist, Peter Kapitsa, complained in 1940, concerning the difficulty in implementing one of his inventions, "The whole point, in the view of the plant director, is to fulfill the plan and lower the cost of production. New tasks are incomprehensible and undefined. With them you can only slide into unpleasant consequences and there is no interest in doing so. The matter is risky and absolutely profitless."[36] After arguing many hours with this director, Kapitsa asked if

---

[32] *RP*, no. 9, 1933, 1.

[33] *Tekhnika*, Oct. 27, 1933.   [34] *VK*, no. 5-6, 1934, 2.

[35] In recent years, especially since 1959, the work of encouraging and implementing rationalization and invention has again been transferred from the shop level to special bureaus, subordinated administratively to the chief engineer or director of the enterprise (Richman, *Management Development*, p. 92).

[36] *Industriia*, Feb. 6, 1940, 3; see also Harvard Interview Project, no. 251, p. 6.

there was another suitable factory to build his invention and received a negative reply. Only after many months of dispute and administrative pressure from above were results forthcoming.[37]

The way output plans were written had other effects on innovation. On the one hand, as we have seen above, R & D personnel were instructed to develop inventions and processes that would conserve scarce materials. On the other hand, output plans were frequently expressed in gross weight, putting a premium on unnecessarily heavy products, as one inventor discovered to his sorrow. A professor of the Dnepropetrovsk Metallurgical Institute developed a device for automatically regulating the amount of steel poured in a particular process. It would have saved millions of rubles in scarce steel, but it was applied in only one instance. Other plants rejected it because the device would "ruin" plant output quotas, which were expressed in gross weight, not the size of the steel sheeting produced.[38] The professor's invention maximized the size while lessening the weight produced. In general, Soviet metal products and machinery were frequently heavier than they needed to be for similar reasons, certainly a disincentive for applying material-conserving innovations.[39]

Other difficulties impeded inventors in finding experimental facilities for testing and applying their innovations under factory conditions. Where experimental shops and factory labs existed to aid in such work, managers frequently overloaded them with routine tasks associated with fulfilling the production plan or checking the quality of output. Chief engineers were even known to turn such facilities into shops for repairing production equipment.[40]

Where incentive funds were available in plants for stimulating innovations, they were often unused, or misappropriated by managers and given to production specialists and workers as bonuses for fulfilling the output plan. When engineers and workers at the plant level came up with proposals of their own for technical innovations or rationalization of productive processes, managers not infrequently failed to reward them, or argued that the proposals came within the routine duties of such individuals and required no additional compensation.[41]

Young specialists, recent graduates from higher education, were apparently more willing to invent and try new methods than the older *praktiki*, but they were actively discouraged from such work, not only by the burdens of their other duties, but sometimes more directly by

[37] Ibid.
[38] Ibid., May 26, 1940, 1.   [39] Ibid., March 20, 1937, 2.
[40] Ibid., April 3, 1939, 3; January 17, 1940; January 3, 1939, 2.
[41] Chuvaev, pp. 6, 28; *Industriia*, July 27, 1939; Feb. 29, 1940, 2.

their supervisors. For example, the new head of a shop at a Moscow factory in 1939 was told by everyone from the technical director on down not to bother with innovations.[42] Whatever the merits of this particular case, it could be multiplied many times, and forms a pattern of active neglect of technical innovations by production personnel.

If the particular nature of the Soviet planning system shaped the negative attitudes of production personnel toward innovation, it also conditioned R & D personnel to neglect the implementation of their own innovations. Planning for industrial research institutions was introduced after 1928, but only in the most cursory and superficial way. Emphasis was put on paper results—completing a number of planned projects, submitting the results to industry, and perhaps publishing them, but not implementing them. If incentive pay existed at all in research institutions, it was generally for completing projects from a technical standpoint, not for the results, including savings, actually derived from their implentation in the economy. As Academician Kurnakov, a noted chemist, wrote in 1940, "Up till now many research workers consider that their business is laboratory research, not implementation—this is the job of industry."[43]

In 1936 Ordzhonikidze and Karl Bauman, head of the party's section for science and inventions, established in 1935 under the Central Committee, began to remedy defects in the planning system for R & D in heavy industry. After organizing a conference on this subject in 1936, Ordzhonikidze decreed important changes. He ordered that, by November 1, 1937, the heads of each Main Administration (*glavka*) in heavy industry must produce a plan for introducing inventions already prepared by industrial researchers. Funding would be made centrally through the Commissariat of Heavy Industry, assuring supplies of necessary material and equipment. All plants using the work of institutes were to give them twenty percent of the yearly economies realized from such innovations, in order to establish an incentive fund for R & D personnel.[44] Whether this plan would have improved the situation is a moot question, however. It was disrupted by the intervening purges and never effectively implemented.

Lest the discussion above give the impression that resistance to innovation was a purely Soviet problem, we should note that such resist-

[42] *Industriia*, Aug. 5, 1939, 3.

[43] Ibid., June 17, 1940, 2; see also March 9, 1937, 3; and the documents on planning industrial research in *Organizatsiia nauki, 1926-1932*, pp. 297-305; on the system of rewarding researchers, see the Harvard Interview Project, Group discussion no. 403, B 2 Schedule, p. 23.

[44] *Front nauki i tekhniki*, no. 10, 1936, 101ff.; see also *Izobretatel'*, no. 1, 1936, for speech by Karl Bauman.

ance has also been a prominent theme in the literature on inventions in the West. Western managers and production personnel have frequently feared and resisted technical innovations.[45] Still, the rate of such innovation has undeniably been higher in the West than in the U.S.S.R. What ingredient was missing in the Soviet case? Possibly not the only factor, the lack of both foreign and domestic competition for markets was a major element certainly missing in the Soviet case. Although the sources of innovation may be quite varied in the West, several major factors help to overcome managerial resistance: the fear of losing markets to foreign or domestic competitors, the hope of creating new markets, or carving out a larger share of an old market for a business firm.[46] Such competition was considered wasteful in the U.S.S.R. and was largely eliminated after 1928. Domestic firms in a particular branch of industry were given a monopoly position, and foreign imports of similar goods were strongly discouraged and increasingly eliminated during the 1930s.

Competition within plants and among plants for fulfilling production plans was encouraged, but generally not for the creation of new products or processes. Once managers and production specialists had a captive market for their production, one of the major stimuli for a high rate of innovation was eliminated. Whether the reader considers this good or bad, of course, depends on his point of view. Some may think that Western economies produce too many innovations, seeking to stimulate markets for useless or wasteful products. The point is that if one wishes a high level of innovation, not to mention higher quality, as Soviet leaders in this period contended they did, then competition among firms for markets is a major stimulant missing from the Soviet scene. This issue should be kept separate from the issue of capitalist ownership of the means of production, as has been recognized by market socialists in such countries as Yugoslavia and, more recently, Hungary, who have built into their system competition for markets between socialized firms.[47]

The value of competition in industrial research, if not in production, was recognized by some Soviet technologists, who tried to stem the tendency toward a monopoly position in Soviet R & D during this period. They pointed out that some of the most creative work was done when competition existed among research institutions, a view reinforced by

[45] David Allison, ed., *The R & D Game: Technical Men, Technical Managers and Research Productivity*, Cambridge, Mass., 1969, pp. 119-134.

[46] Ibid.

[47] See, for example, William F. Robinson, *Pattern of Reform in Hungary*, New York, 1973; Geza Lauter, *The Manager and Economic Reform in Hungary*, New York, 1972.

recent studies of inventions and scientific research in the West, which indicate that the more decentralized systems of research tend to be most creative.[48] In fact, some of the most productive results in Soviet industrial research were accomplished when competition existed between researchers, as in the invention of synthetic rubber in the late 1920s after a well-publicized contest conducted by the Supreme Economic Council.[49] The need for competing teams of aeronautical specialists was also acknowledged in later years by the man appointed head of R & D in this area just prior to World War II, A. S. Yakovlev. He recognized that some of the mistakes made in this industry during the 1930s derived from the monopoly position of a few design bureaus, a point that will be developed in chapter 14.

In general, however, the political leadership at this time, faced with the allocation of extremely scarce resources, preferred to eliminate what it viewed as "parallelism" and "wasteful duplication" in both R & D and production. Competition for markets was associated in their minds with capitalist ownership of the means of production, and had been replaced by centralized planning and allocation of resources, eliminating alternatives that might have better stimulated innovation. Administrative pressure and coercion, then, had to be substituted for market forces if significant technical advances were to be made and introduced. Such pressure tended to be focused by a centralized leadership on a few high priority areas at a time, mostly in defense and heavy industry. In other parts of the economy, inertia was given fuller rein.

The effects of terror on technical innovation are somewhat harder to gauge, since the topic was one that was less openly discussed in the contemporary Soviet press. Enough material did appear at the time, or has appeared subsequently in studies and memoirs however, to indicate that the risks of failure in developing and applying innovations were considered very high by technical specialists, inhibiting such work. As one production engineer, interviewed a decade later by the Harvard Project, put it, "You were afraid to introduce innovations and rationalization. We often thought that certain methods must be introduced. But usually we did not do it. If an experiment should fail we could be

[48] Joseph Ben-David, *The Scientist's Role in Society*, Englewood Cliffs, N.J., 1971; and John Jewkes, et al., *The Sources of Invention*, New York, 1969, pp. 169-228; J. Langrish, et al., *Wealth from Knowledge*, London, 1972, pp. 6-56; see also the following Soviet sources: *Industriia*, March 9, 1937, 3; Nov. 29, 1939; May 9, 1940, 2; June 17, 1940, 2.

[49] L. P. Brezhneva, "Deiatel'nost' Kommunisticheskoi Partii po sozdaniiu i razvitiiu sinteticheskogo kauchuka 1928-1937 gg.," Soviet diss., Lenin Library, Moscow, 1967, pp. 25ff.; Konstantin B. Piotrovskii, *Sergei Lebedev*, Moscow, 1960, pp. 125-151; S. P. Sergienko, *Akademik S. V. Lebedev*, Moscow, 1959, pp. 84-91.

charged with sabotage. This had a bad effect on the creative ability of many engineers."[50]

If this was true in production, for researchers the situation was a bit more complex, since they were expected to come up with new ideas. The greatest risk was not in developing new ideas per se, but in taking sole responsibility for approving or seeking to implement them, should they fail. A specialist who worked in a research institute during the 1930s described the effects of terror on the innovative process in his institute:

All these projects, inventions, additions and new ideas must be processed through a multitude of testing stages. It starts the moment when somebody conceives new ideas. First, the idea must be registered. Then the necessary statements are prepared and the file sent to the Suggestions Committee. There they enter the date received, acknowledge the suggestion, and since the Suggestions Committee is not in a position to make decisions of its own, it is referred to advisors for evaluation. These advisors, who are experts in different fields, work for various government agencies. This means that the suggestion has to be referred to the pertinent agency where it will be evaluated by the advisor. The advisor is troubled by the following thought: "This idea is brand new, and has never been tested. Maybe it is of no value to the government, and maybe it has been submitted by a saboteur who just wants us to waste a lot of valuable material. If I should approve this suggestion, then I may be sentenced as a saboteur. On the other hand, if it is a good suggestion, and I have disapproved it, and the inventor is ambitious enough to push it through despite my disapproval, then again I can be sentenced as a saboteur, for having killed a valuable improvement." Here is what he writes in his findings: . . . "the invention is no doubt interesting. However, since it is not confirmed by statements of a technical and economic nature, and no final blueprints as to its construction are attached, I am not in a position to draw final conclusions. I suggest that a special committee be established and that it be delegated the duty to evaluate this idea."[51]

Such buck-passing could delay the process of innovation by years. As the same witness noted, a decision would be made "only when there are so many people involved that in the case of a failure nobody would be able to trace the responsible ones."[52] In fact, if indications from the

[50] Interview no. 70, B 2 Schedule, p. 21.
[51] Group discussion no. 403, B 2 Schedule, pp. 4-5.
[52] Ibid.

Soviet press are any clue, the length of time from inception of a new technical idea to implementation was generally seven years or longer, at least in civilian areas.[53]

Such delays, as this chapter should make clear, were not solely attributable to the influence of terror, but even the scanty Soviet statistical sources on this subject suggest that terror had an inhibiting effect. For example, the number of new inventions by technical specialists registered with the State Committee on Inventions between 1929 and 1931 declined precipitously and only gradually grew once again, exceeding its 1928 and 1929 level, in 1935.[54] In other words, the drop in the number of applications for inventions accepted from this group was greatest in the years when their prestige and status was at its lowest ebb. Of course, this does not prove that the technical intelligentsia became less creative in these years, only that they registered fewer new inventions with the Committee on Inventions, but this in itself had an inhibiting effect, since the Committee was charged with publicizing such inventions and overseeing their wide application in industry, a process much more unlikely if specialists did not register their inventions with the Committee.[55]

Two different Soviet sources indicate a general drop in the number of new inventions registered during the period of the purges, between 1936 and 1938.[56] Neither source attributes the absolute decline in such registrations to the terror, but it is difficult to believe that such a trend in these two periods is purely coincidental. Some correlation between such purges and the decline in proposals for inventions is likely.

Besides such evidence, recent Soviet sources—both dissident and establishment views—indicate that the purges of 1936 to 1938 had a major effect on inventions and their application in the defense industry. It was in this area of technology that Stalin and the political leadership took the strongest interest in the late 1930s, to the point where Stalin actually tried out new weapons, crouching on the floor of his Kremlin office, for example, to test the feel of a new submachine gun and suggesting changes to the designer. Stalin, Beria, Kaganovich, Voroshilov, and others in the leadership actively participated in many commissions that made critical choices of defense technology, to the frequent exas-

[53] See the Soviet periodical sources cited in n. 8 above; Harvard Interview Project, Group discussion no. 403, p. 6.

[54] Data from *Vestnik komiteta*, no. 3, 1931, 31-32; no. 2, 1932, 31-33; nos. 3-4, 1934, 2, 41; no. 3, 1935, 1, 30; no. 3, 1936, 1, 18.

[55] *Sobranie zakonov*, Otdel I, 1931, no. 21, art. 181.

[56] See the article by P. Nikitin, head of the *Gosplan* section for registering new inventions, *Industriia*, April 1, 1939; and the graph in *Puti razvitiia tekhniki v SSSR*, Moscow, 1967, p. 175.

peration of key industrial managers and specialists. While such close attention by the political leadership could also help to cut red tape and obtain scarce resources more quickly, it sometimes led to disastrous consequences for members of the technostructure. As the Commissar of Armaments, Vannikov, put it, "A remark casually dropped by Stalin usually determined the outcome of a matter."[57] A number of inventors and designers in this industry were arrested in the years just prior to World War II, or had their work delayed, with serious consequences.[58] As Vannikov expressed it,

> The unjust arrests of a number of highly skilled specialists in industry and the central apparatus, their replacement by insufficiently experienced personnel seriously affected the rearmament of the Soviet Army. The frequent change of personnel engendered a lack of individual responsibility and diffidence; hampered the progress of scientific and technical work; and as a consequence of all this led to a decline in the quality of output.[59]

Specialists such as Emelianov, a metallurgical engineer, worked hard to outwit people in the political leadership whom they considered technically illiterate, trying to avoid serious mistakes in choices of technology. While Emelianov, a prominent member of the present Soviet technostructure, believed—contrary to Vannikov—that Stalin was capable of taking good technical advice and showed great ability to understand the details of a technical process, he also indicated that specialists frequently felt inhibited in Stalin's presence, afraid to contradict him, or to give him full information about a technological choice for fear of the consequences.[60]

If such fear in Stalin's presence was great, we must not be surprised to find it generalized throughout the technostructure. It was reinforced by the fate of some prominent Soviet inventors and some of the losers in technological controversies. We have already seen the fate of many old specialists who opposed the First Five-Year Plan on technical and

[57] B. L. Vannikov, "Iz zapisok narkoma vooruzheniia," *Voenno-istoricheskii zhurnal*, no. 2, 1962, 78-86, and his "Oboronnaia promyshlennost' SSSR nakanune voiny," in *Voprosy istorii*, no. 1, 1969, 122-135; see also Emelianov, op. cit., and Khavin, *Shagi industrii*, and his "Razvitie tiazheloi promyshlennosti v tretei piatiletke 1938-iun' 1941 gg.," *Istoriia SSSR*, no. 1, 1959, 10-34; Kal'manson diss., pp. 238ff.

[58] These included A. Tupolev, G. Langimak, L. Kurchevskii, V. Bekauri, V. Zaslavskii, I. Kleimenov, S. Korolev, Axel Berg, V. Glouchko, and others (see P. I. Yakir in *Le Monde*, March 16-17, 1969, 3; Roy Medvedev, *Let History Judge*, pp. 228-230).

[59] Vannikov, *Voenno-istoricheskii zhurnal*, 78ff.

[60] V. S. Emelianov, "O vremeni, o tovarishchakh, o sebe," *Novyi mir*, no. 2, 1967, 85-94.

economic grounds. Professor Ramzin, considered a particularly creative inventor, continued to work on his once-through boiler after his conviction in the Industrial party case. He was placed in a special prison design bureau, under Ordzhonikidze's protection, but he found responsible people in industry afraid to touch his invention until Ordzhonikidze pressured them into doing so.[61] Even so, seven years elapsed between the construction of Ramzin's first model in 1932 and its first timid application in industry. Ramzin himself was not rehabilitated until 1943, and his invention still had not found wide acceptance by that time.[62]

While we should be careful not to exaggerate examples of arrests of prominent specialists in R & D, since we have no comprehensive data on this subject, the arrests of losers in technological controversies were frequent enough to breed caution in innovators. For example, in the the area of mining technology, two prominent research specialists of the Kharkov Mining Institute promoted the "theory of concentration" during the mid-1930s. In their theory, borrowing some ideas from the West and including some of their own, they advocated closing down small mines and developing more mines of larger scale, in order to take full advantage of the application of mining machinery, central sources of electricity, mechanized processes of transport, and resources of skilled labor and competent specialists, who were especially scarce in the mining industry.[63] Mining only the largest and richest seams of coal, they believed, would rapidly increase production and labor productivity in the coal industry. Such changes, however, usually involved initial disruption of the productive process until workers and specialists mastered new techniques. A decline in coal production in the Donbass region during 1936 and early 1937 was blamed on the "theory of concentration," which had found wide application there. Stalin and Molotov condemned this theory in a major decree in April 1937, and its advocates were accused of wrecking.[64] Despite the attempts of Professor G. I. Goikhman and mining engineer I. D. Guberman of the Kharkov

[61] TsPA IML, f. 85, op. 29, ed. khr. 401, ll. 23-28, cited in R. G. Khromova, "G. K. Ordzhonikidze vo glave tiazheloi promyshlennosti, 1932-1937 gg.," Soviet diss., Lenin Library, Moscow, 1970.

[62] For the difficulties in applying this invention see *Industriia*, April 2, 1937, 2; April 11, 1937, 3; April 18, 1937, 2; July 4, 1937, 3; see also L. K. Ramzin, ed., *Priamotochnye kotly Ramzina*, Moscow, 1948, pp. 5-8; *Istoriia energeticheskoi tekhniki SSSR*, Moscow, 1957, vol. I, *Teplotekhnika*, pp. 218-241; for a Western reaction, see the articles in *Combustion*, July 1938, 35-36; *The Steam Engineer*, Sept. 1944, 358-364; July 1945, 292; Aug. 1945, 333.

[63] See *Ugol'*, Sept. 1936, 34-40; *Tekhnika gornogo dela i metallurgii*, Moscow, 1968, 84-88. On the scarcity of graduate engineers in mining see Chapter 11 and *Za Industrializatsiiu*, March 10, 1937, 3.

[64] *Industriia*, April 29, 1937, 1; May 5, 1937, 3; April 23, 1937, 3; May 23, 1937, 3.

Coal Research Institute (its leading proponents), to save a part of their theory while performing self-criticism (*samokritika*) in the press, they were soon arrested and disappeared during the purges.[65] Most of what they advocated was resumed in the post-Stalin era, and in recent years the techniques of concentration have been credited with large productivity increases in Soviet mining.[66] During the later 1930s, however, wrong-headed political intervention in this area inhibited the modernization of the coal industry. A similar fate befell a prominent group of aircraft designers between 1928 and 1931, and the aeronautical engineer Tupolev and his group in the late 1930s. Such aviation specialists were blamed for failures in their area, as we shall see in the next chapter, although many later reemerged in World War II and the postwar era among the most prominent and honored Soviet designers.

The situation of agricultural chemistry and the advocates of producing chemical fertilizers is a curiously mixed one. A controversy between two schools of soil scientists and agronomists—the Vil'iams school and that of Prianishnikov and Tulaikov—raged in the 1920s and 1930s.[67] Vil'iams advocated the use of a single system for assuring soil fertility throughout the Soviet Union, the so-called grasslands system (*travopol'ye*). The Prianishnikov-Tulaikov school claimed that this would not lead to the most abundant harvests and advocated, among other things, more reliance on chemical fertilizers, together with the use of machinery and other innovations in agricultural technique. Prianishnikov and Tuliakov opposed any single panacea, decreed from above, as the only viable system for Soviet agriculture. They promoted instead the use of different mixes of fertilizers, crop rotation, and mechanical working of the soil, after a careful study of local conditions by agrono-

[65] *Ugol'*, June 1937, 4-11.

[66] *Tekhnika gornogo dela*, 120, 210.

[67] The discussion is based on the following primary and secondary sources: *Sotsialisticheskaia rekonstruktsiia sel'skogo khoziastva*, no. 3, 1930; N. M. Tulaikov, ed., *Vsesoiuznyi institut zernovogo khoziastva*, Saratov, 1932; *Khimiia i khoziastvo*, no. 3, 1931, 3-60; no. 11-12, 1932, 38-49; *Bor'ba s zasukhoi. Vsesoiuznaia konferentsiia po bor'be szasukhoi*, Moscow, 1932; "Avtobiografiia i doklad N. M. Tulaikova," *Istoricheskii arkhiv*, no. 3, 1962, 100-119; N. M. Tulaikov, *Izbrannye proizvedeniia. Kritika travopolnoi sistemy*, Moscow, 1963; *Planovoe khoziastvo*, no. 7, 1937, 87-102; N. I. Vavilov in *Sotsialisticheskaia rekonstruktsiia sel'skogo khoziastva*, no. 5-6, 1931, 128-138; no. 3, 1931, 148-176; no. 6, 1937, 71ff.; no. 7, 1937, 20ff., 53ff., 80ff.; no. 9, 1937, 171ff.; no. 11-12, 1937, 205ff.; D. N. Prianishnikov, *Agrokhimiia v SSSR*, Moscow, 1931, 1940; *Izbrannye sochineniia*, vol. 1-4, Moscow, 1951-1954; 1963; *Moi vospominaniia*, Moscow, 1961; Arkhiv Akademii nauk SSSR, f. 632, op. 1, ed. khr. 326, ll. 1-12, ed. khr. 300, l. 1-2; ed. khr. 247, ll. 7-23, published for the first time in *D. N. Prianishnikov: Zhizn' i deiatel'nost'*, Moscow, 1972, pp. 189-211; O. Pisarzhevskii, *Prianishnikov*, Moscow, 1963; A. V. Peterburgskii, *D. N. Prianishnikov i ego shkola*, Moscow, 1962; I. and L. Krupenikovy, *Vil'iams*, Moscow, 1951; *Liudi russkoi nauki. Sel'skokhoziastvennye nauki*, pp. 795-814, 868-883; David Joravsky, *The Lysenko Affair*.

mists. Although adherents of the Vil'iams school disagreed among themselves on a precise definition of the grasslands system and how it should be developed, they vehemently opposed the rival school. Their claims won acceptance among the political leadership by the late 1930s. This was probably for several reasons: The Vil'iams school promised high productivity with less expenditure than that required by a more rapid expansion of the chemical fertilizer industry. The grasslands system also appeared to be a simpler, more universally applicable method, that could be centrally decreed by a highly centralized leadership. Moreover, Vil'iams, who had worked in greater harmony with the Tsarist regime than Prianishnikov, a political liberal, became a strong supporter of the Bolsheviks after 1917, and was one of the first soil scientists to join the Communist party in 1928. Prianishnikov's acceptance was slower, and he never joined the party. His pupil and, later, associate Tulaikov joined the party in 1930, but was associated with moderate, anti-Stalinist elements within the technostructure.

After a series of bitter exchanges in conferences and the technical press during the 1930s, the Vil'iams theory of grasslands achieved recognition in 1937 as the official theory for Soviet soil science.[68] Tulaikov and several of Prianishnikov's other students and followers were arrested and killed. Prianishnikov was deprived of major support and harassed in the press. Curiously enough, however, he was never arrested, and he continued to criticize publicly the grasslands system, advocating his own ideas. On the basis of available sources, it is difficult to understand why Tulaikov and Prianishnikov should suffer substantially different fates. Perhaps Prianishnikov was protected by his greater prominence as a member of the Academy of Sciences, his international reputation, and his forthrightness in defending his beliefs, but for the time being this must remain speculation.

The examples above far from exhaust the number of technological controversies involving innovators during the period of the first three Five-Year Plans. It is not surprising that there should have been such controversies in a rapidly industrializing society or that technological choices should have been made. Nor is it surprising that, given scarcer resources in the Soviet Union than the West, the tendency was to choose a single technology among various contenders and concentrate efforts on that choice.[69] Such choices appealed to Stalin's sense of order. He liked to pinpoint responsibility for important areas by designating single

[68] *Pravda*, June 30, 1937.

[69] In addition to the evidence for this in the other sources used in this chapter, see Robert W. Campbell, *The Economics of Soviet Oil and Gas*, pp. 101-120, and Khrushchev's testimony concerning Academician Paton's method for electric welding, which Stalin decreed for use throughout the U.S.S.R. (*Khrushchev Remembers*, pp. 118-122).

individuals as responsible for particular areas, sometimes creating in the process a series of "little Stalins" who aped his style and played a similar role in their own bailiwicks (the best known example, of course, was Lysenko). What is surprising is that some of the losers in technical controversies should have been treated so harshly, despite the inconsistent pattern of treatment. At least one Soviet source has attributed such intolerance to survivals of earlier religious traditions in which heresy hunting by the Russian Orthodox Church was widespread and backed up by the power of the state. This seems too pat an answer. The reason probably lies as much in the insecurity of the power structure and the technostructure in the early decades of Soviet rule. The power structure tended to choose for positions of responsibility those people whose records attested to political reliability, and the technostructure fought a series of fierce struggles over the allocation of scarce resources. To discredit one's rivals intellectually, and sometimes to eliminate them physically, was also to decrease the probability of having critics who would later watch, hawk-eyed, for failures in one's policies. Such failures on the part of technologists could lead to future withdrawal of appropriations by the government, the sole source of support for R & D in Soviet society. No one in a resource-starved society was eager for that to happen. While variety and competition in the Soviet research community were never entirely eliminated, the tendency of the 1930s was clearly in the direction of monopoly in many areas, and this led to fierce struggles, including charges of political disloyalty. Charges of sabotage by more unscrupulous members of the technostructure aided them in attempts to appeal to the Stalinists who claimed that wreckers were everywhere, requiring constant "vigilance" (*bditel'nost'*) to root them out. It is not surprising, therefore, that this atmosphere fostered great caution in developing and applying innovations. While the political atmosphere, including terror, was far from the only inhibition affecting the level of technical innovation, it was an important factor that cannot be discounted.

According to contemporary Soviet sources, the work of innovation was hampered by another set of conflicts. These involved the tension between the trend toward the professionalization of research and development and attempts on the part of the political structure to make the process of technological innovation a mass movement, stimulating technical creativity not only by the technical intelligentsia, but by the working class as well. In the West, of course, tension has also existed between individual, often self-taught inventors, and the trend toward professionalization of R & D in formal organizations usually staffed with graduates of higher education. Among Western economists and

360

students of the inventive process, there is no clear agreement that such a trend is the only one dictated by the needs of modern technology. Prominent theorists have continued to maintain that the sources of invention are varied and include the individual, even the self-taught inventor, as well as the small, less formal research group, and the large professional research organization. Although it is hard to conceive of large-scale new technology, whether weapons programs or otherwise, being developed by individuals, especially those without a scientific education, many significant inventions in the recent past have had their source among individual inventors, some of whom lacked formal higher education.[70]

The conflict between the individual inventor and the trend toward professionalization of R & D in formal organizations was complicated in the Soviet Union by an ideological commitment among those in power to fostering creativity among the working class, and by Stalin's personal bias toward the *praktiki*. In fact, the conflict between the *praktiki* and graduate specialists in production was paralleled in R & D by frequent conflicts between worker-inventors, striving to gain support and recognition for their work, and many graduate specialists who tended to think that such work belonged in special R & D organizations, staffed by certified personnel. In one well-publicized case from the mid-1930s, a worker-inventor named Sinitsyn was singled out for praise by Stalin. Sinitsyn had been doing work on cathode tubes that was considered promising, and the All-Union Electro-technical Institute had been asked to support his work. However, according to Sinitsyn, he was shunted aside there with the comment, "You see, he has no higher education and nothing further can be expected from him. For what he has already done we shall thank him, and further development of his invention should be transferred to some professor."[71] They refused him further money or support, although Coolidge, director of the General Electric Research Laboratories in the U.S., had supposedly been impressed by his work during a visit to the U.S.S.R. in 1934.[72]

Then one evening in 1936, according to a well-publicized report, a car summoned him to the Kremlin where he was met by Stalin, Molotov, Voroshilov, Kalinin, and others. "Seeing Stalin's eyes gazing attentively at me, I at once felt an unusually warm and straight-forward attitude toward me," Sinitsyn later rhapsodized. He explained his work and how the professional researchers at the institute were attempting to "stifle" it.

[70] See, for example, the case studies in Jewkes, pp. 79-103, 231-356.
[71] *Izobretatel'*, no. 11, 1936, 4; no. 12, 1935, 3.
[72] Ibid.

During the conversation Joseph Vissarionovich, rising suddenly, asked me if I didn't fear that he would spoil my relations with the director of the Institute. Seeing my amazement, he added, "But I will telephone him."

The telephone conversation with the Institute was brief: "Is this you, Rabinovich, director of the All-Union Electro-technical Institute? This is Stalin speaking. You have working at your institute an inventor, Sinitsyn. In my opinion, there is a great underestimation of his work, especially on the part of Comrade Prelkov, who heads up the section where he works. I think that from now on this attitude will change."

Brief, but to the point, Sinitsyn added.[73]

Whether such an interview occurred as described above is perhaps not as important as the message the story was meant to convey: Stalin and the political leadership were eager to appear as friends of the little man, including the worker-inventor and not just the graduate research specialist, a point reiterated by Stalin in a speech during 1938.[74] A great deal of time and energy was committed in the first Five-Year Plans to fostering a mass movement of worker-inventors, but evidence indicates that the results were most fruitful in stimulating rationalization proposals for small organizational changes and technical improvements, rather than major technical innovations from workers.[75] The work of the Sinitsyns in most cases came to little, and they eventually disappeared into oblivion.[76] One reason was that attempts to stimulate inventions from workers met a great deal of resistance on the part of graduate specialists, who considered such efforts a waste of time for the most part. This was especially so since they were often asked to evaluate these proposals, a task requiring time that graduate specialists preferred to devote to their own work. There were complaints that specialists tried to shirk such duties whenever possible, although it was usually difficult to do so without appearing politically disloyal. Few specialists dared to be as outspoken as one engineer who was pilloried by the press in 1931. He had requested additional pay for helping groups of workers who

---

[73] Ibid.   [74] See *Vysshaia shkola*, no. 5, 1935, 3-4.

[75] On rationalization proposals and inventions see *Ratsionalizatsiia promyshlennosti SSSR. Rabota komissii prezidiuma VSNKh SSSR*, Moscow, 1928; *Izobretatel'stvo i ratsionalizatsiia v SSSR*, Moscow, 1962; *Ratsionalizatsiia proizvodstva*, no. 3, 1932, 35; no. 1, 1933, 30-31; no. 6, 1933, 26; nos. 11-12, 1932, 15-16; *Predpriiatie*, no. 19, 1933, 14-15; *Vestnik komiteta*, no. 12, 1932, 2; some scattered reports on the results of rationalization and invention in individual trusts and factories have been published from the archives (see, for example, the documents in *Promyshlennost' i rabochii klass Ukrainskoi SSR*, pp. 313-314, 343-344, 538).

[76] Sinitsyn, for example, is not mentioned in any of the later Soviet histories of technology for this period or in later Soviet biographical sources.

were developing inventions and other improvements. He had done so, even though an earlier conference of the technical intelligentsia in his area had promised to help as one of their social duties. "Engineers are overburdened," he was quoted as saying, "and they cannot give away their free hours without pay."[77] The more usual response from engineers who felt this way, however, was simply to procrastinate, turning such questions over to a commission of experts, or giving their own help grudgingly.

John Littlepage, a highly respected American engineer who worked as chief engineer in the Soviet gold mining industry for ten years, was more outspoken than many Soviet engineers when describing the demands made upon his time by the proposals of amateur inventors:

> One small and unimportant example will serve to show as well as anything else how the busiest and best-trained engineers are bogged down in routine and pestered by political control. I refer to the perpetual nuisance of so-called inventors, crack-brained persons who are convinced they have made some amazing mechanical discovery, a type that seems to be more numerous in Russia than elsewhere. These people demand and usually get access to the chief engineer of an enterprise or trust, because underlings are afraid to take the responsibility of rejecting their contrivances, however obvious their uselessness may be.
>
> I worked as chief engineer not only in the main office but in some branch offices of the Gold Trust, and was bothered by a steady procession of these cranks. If they don't receive prompt and special attention, they rush around to some Communist politician and complain that the "bureaucrats" are neglecting them. The Communists, like all other politicians, always pose as the friend of the little people against the bureaucrats, and they can make an infernal amount of trouble for engineers or managers under a system where politicians control everything.
>
> To prevent their whole time being taken up with "inventors," Soviet chief engineers have worked out a stock subterfuge. When any contrivance is submitted, the chief immediately appoints a commission to look it over, even though he can see at a glance that it is useless. I knew about this trick, and when I was working in Moscow, used it to get rid of a particularly persistent "inventor." By naming a commission, I protected myself against accusations from the politicians that I was ignoring prospective geniuses.[78]

[77] *Inzhenernyi trud*, no. 8, 1931, 193.
[78] Littlepage and Bess, pp. 211-212. Littlepage worked for the Soviet Gold Trust between 1928 and 1937.

That Littlepage's attitude was shared by Soviet engineers is corroborated by other sources from this period.[79] Besides the duty of considering such proposals, technical specialists were frequently assigned special responsibilities for implementing various workers' proposals that had been judged useful.[80] This was also a time-consuming process, but again one that specialists could scarcely afford to ignore. Yet such loyalty tests took time away from possible creative work of their own. More than that, the movement for worker-inventors gave rise to a series of Rube Goldberg proposals. It also encouraged a group of real-life Ostap Benders (a fictional confidence man, Soviet style, who inhabited the popular novels of Ilf and Petrov in the 1920s and 1930s). The phenomenon of the "phoney inventor" aroused fears that a rash of well publicized cases where people used this movement to defraud the government would discredit the work of innovation in general. According to the industrial press in the 1930s, managers and specialists in production frequently cited such examples as an excuse for not paying more attention to technical innovations.

The experts in the Committee on Inventions mounted a campaign during the mid-1930s against self-styled inventors who lived an easy life collecting grants and awards for projects that were never implemented, or who lived off the largesse of the Society of Inventors, a group established in 1929 to aid the mass movement for invention.[81] No love was lost between this Society and graduate specialists in research institutions and the Committee on Inventions. As one member of the Society of Inventors reportedly expressed it to the applause of fellow members: "The employees of scientific-research organizations are often former pedagogues. A pedagogue is a person who preserves past human wisdom and very much fears everything new," claiming that such personnel dominating the research institutes held back the advance of new technology.[82]

The R & D establishment, for their part, attempted to discredit the Society of Inventors, claiming it was filled with charlatans of little knowledge or competence, whose inventions were never applied and whose existence hindered the work of real inventors and competent researchers. The head of the Committee on Inventions, G. Mel'nichan-

[79] See, for example, *Sovetskaia iustitsiia*, no. 14, 1931, 7-11; *Vestnik komiteta*, no. 12, 1932, 2.

[80] *Vestnik komiteta*, no. 8, 1933, 3-4; no. 11, 1933, 2; *Ratsionalizatsiia proizvodstva*, no. 6, 1933, 5.

[81] *Vestnik komiteta*, no. 2, 1932, 11; *Izobretatel'*, no. 4, 1935, 9; *Vestnik komiteta*, no. 4, 1936, 1-8. The Society of Inventors was a mass organization with 500,000 members in 1932 and 800,000 before its dissolution in 1938, most of them workers.

[82] *Vestnik komiteta*, no. 4, 1936, 6-7.

sky, wrote in 1935 that as a result of such abuses "many managers look on all inventors as charlatans." He cited a recent case in Leningrad. The defendant had only seven years of formal education and saw no need to enter higher technical education since he considered himself already a "scientist." Sentenced once in 1927 for fraudulent inventions in the electrical field, after his release he proposed to the Commissariat of Agriculture an invention for bombarding seeds with ultrahigh frequency waves as a means of stimulating large harvests. The officials there had given him 200,000 rubles and a laboratory of "electrical biology" in the All-Union Institute of Plant Growth. None of his ideas was ever applied; he rarely appeared for work, and eventually the NKVD began to investigate him, discovering that he spent a good deal of his time relaxing, wining and dining beautiful women in Leningrad.[83]

Such cases were not uncommon, according to the journal of the Committee on Inventions and the newspaper of heavy industry.[84] Industrial officials who controlled large funds for rewarding rationalization and invention proposals often paid premia to such charlatans just to get rid of them. This trait had given rise to a particular type of flim-flam man, the parasite "who attaches himself to a plant and terrorizes its administration to the point that he has entree everywhere and can make himself at home. They not only tolerate him but, strange to say, even fear him."[85]

Individually, they may have been "colorful characters," but such people had brought "great harm to the cause of invention, soiling and lowering the name of inventor" and they needed "to be exposed."[86] The Committee on Inventions proposed as a solution that individual inventors who were considered promising must be assigned to work in the established R & D system, under the supervision of competent people and "on tasks formulated by the party and government."[87] This, in fact, became the dominant trend by the end of the 1930s. Verbal encouragement of worker-inventors by the government never entirely disappeared, but, in practice, the tasks of technical innovation became more the province of professional R & D personnel.

Although the Committee on Inventions was abolished in 1936 (the government in a sense gave the chicken coop to the foxes by assigning the work of evaluating and supervising technical innovations solely to officials in the economic commissariats) the economic commissariats continued the campaign against "phoney inventors" and against the

[83] *Izobretatel'*, no. 4, 1935, 9.

[84] See, for example, *Vestnik komiteta*, no. 4, 1936, 2-4, and *Industriia*, Jan. 17, 1940.

[85] *Vestnik komiteta*, no. 4, 1936, 4.   [86] Ibid.

[87] Ibid.

Society of Inventors, which they saw as fostering charlatanism. The Society was attacked a number of times in 1937 and 1938, in articles claiming that its *apparat* had few proven inventors, and that it consumed a great deal of its budget providing for its staff and giving awards to non-inventors, building vacation resorts to be used by cronies of its chairman, and so on.[88] Its main function to some outsiders seemed to be tea drinking, giving out vacation vouchers, and providing theater tickets to its members. The campaign culminated in mid-1938 with the dissolution of the Society of Inventors.[89] The task of encouraging worker-inventors was turned over to local trade union organizations, which were generally under the thumbs of economic managers, and this proved to be a way of effectively burying the mass campaign for worker-inventors.

The route leading to work in Soviet research and development after 1938 was increasingly a single-lane road through higher education to a position in a formal R & D institution under the supervision of some branch of the government. The inhibiting effects of this single route on technical creativity need further evaluation, but, if the work of Jewkes, Langrish, and other Western students of inventiveness is any indication, then the cutting off of a variety of sources for invention, including opportunities for the eccentric, but nonetheless innovative individual, probably had a negative effect on Soviet R & D in these years. While the existence of charlatans may have galled professional researchers and given ammunition to industrial managers and production specialists who, for other reasons as well, wished to neglect innovation, perhaps the existence of occasional charlatans is one price an economy must pay if it wishes a high level of innovation. Such an economy needs to assure that the work of the technically imaginative individual, whether formally educated or not, is not stifled. While the movement for worker-inventors and the Society of Inventors had perhaps not guaranteed such results, the victory of Soviet industrial managers and graduate specialists, who had formally professionalized most inventive activities in government research institutions by the end of the 1930s, also did not prove itself by results, that is, by stimulating a noticeably higher level of technical creativity and innovations. It will be interesting to see if recent Chinese experiments in attempting to stimulate technical innovation among the general population will have greater success than the Soviet experience during the 1930s.[90]

[88] *Izobretatel'*, no. 9, 1936, 24; *Industriia*, April 18, 1937, 3; Feb. 16, 1938, 4; *Vestnik inzhenerov*, no. 12, 1937, 7, 3-8.

[89] *Vestnik inzhenerov*, no. 6, 1938, 284, 324-325; no. 9, 1938, 524-526, 576-577.

[90] On the conflict between the professional model of scientific-technical R & D and the mass movement model in Communist China, see Richard P. Suttmeier, *Research and Revolution*, Lexington, Mass., 1974, pp. 79-158.

Beyond the factors discussed above, the high percentage of *praktiki* at the production level, which has already been discussed in chapters 11 and 12, had a negative effect on innovation, according to Soviet sources. Young specialists complained that their suggestions and ideas for changes and improvements were simply ignored by the older "practicals," and the industrial press generally agreed with them. The attitude of the older group was expressed in words such as "you are going to teach us? We know what we are doing. I am in charge of rationalization. We have done everything necessary. I have more seniority than you."[91] The younger group charged that the "practicals" were set in their ways and inflexible. They often either dismissed a new idea or politely accepted a suggestion and then conveniently forgot to implement it.[92]

The importance of age and education should not be surprising, since older practicals and industrial managers who were not well versed in science and technology found it easier "to work in the same old way," as one Soviet source put it, rather than to adopt new methods.[93] Yet even young graduate specialists, both those who entered production and those who became researchers, were often weak in scientific theory and lacked a broad polytechnic background that would increase their flexibility in understanding new technology. Although the quality of higher technical education with respect to scientific theory and general technology improved after 1933, the encouragement of student self-initiative and creativity did not, as we have seen. This led to complaints that young graduate specialists were "lazy lovers of scientific titles," people who leaned on their possession of a higher degree but were not necessarily competent innovators.[94] While such comments should not be taken as a blanket condemnation of either *praktiki* or young graduate technologists, weaknesses in their scientific and technical knowledge undoubtedly did make it more attractive to rely on old methods that had been mastered, rather than risk innovations that their backgrounds had not prepared them to master rapidly. The education of younger specialists, as well as their lack of practical experience, made it less likely that this group would contribute to a growth in the number of inventions or their application during most of this period. These were years when they needed to acquire practical experience in established forms of technology and to increase their theoretical background by further reading and education.

Old traditions die hard, and one of the strongest traditions in Russian science had been the high prestige attached to basic research of a theo-

[91] *Predpriiatie*, no. 6, 22; see also the editorial in *Industriia*, June 30, 1939, 1.

[92] *Za industrializatsiiu*, Jan. 3, 1930, 5; *Inzhenernyi trud*, no. 2, 1930, 47; see also *Za industrializatsiiu*, June 19, 1930, 3.

[93] *Za industrializatsiiu*, June 9, 1937, 1.

[94] *Front nauki i tekhniki*, no. 4, 1935, 65.

retical nature, as contrasted with the work of the applied scientist and engineer. It was a tradition paralleling that in engineering, which assigned the "Ministerial" engineer and engineering professor a higher status than the production engineer. While there had been a counter-tradition in Russian science, going well back into the Imperial period, of scientists who advocated bringing the work of the scientist together with the practical needs of the economy and society (some of Russia's most outstanding scientists—Mendeleev, Dokuchaev, Vernadsky, Timiriazev, Sechenov, and others were influenced by this countertradition),[95] the prestige of the theoretical scientist, who worked mostly in his laboratory or office without immediate applications in mind and without close contact with the problems of material production, remained high. Despite all attempts to break down this status consciousness during the first Five-Year Plans and to give higher prestige to the work of applied scientists and industrial researchers and practitioners, evidence from this period indicates that such efforts were far from wholly successful.

The work of outstanding scientists who contributed to the economy—such as that of A. F. Ioffe, Peter Kapitsa, N. S. Kurnakov, A. I. Nekrassov, A. E. Fersman, and others—was widely published and honored.[96] In fact, as the computer study in the appendix shows, applied scientists were more highly honored than engineers in the Soviet Union, perhaps inadvertently reinforcing the higher social status accorded to the scientist in general.[97] Scientists such as Ioffe—who had first been trained as

[95] On this subject see, for example, Alexander Vucinich, *Science in Russian Culture, 1861-1917*, Stanford, 1970, especially pp. 12, 29, 102-103, 410-411, 486-487, 499, and the entries on the scientists listed above.

[96] See, for example, *Industriia*, June 17, 1940, 2; Feb. 6, 1940, 3; *Aleksandr E. Fersman*, Moscow, 1964; Oleg N. Pisarzhevskii, *A. N. Fersman, 1883-1945*, Moscow, 1959; James G. Crowther, *Soviet Science*, London, 1936; *A. I. Nekrasov Materialy K biobibliografia*, Moscow, 1950.

[97] See the computer tables in the appendix. The population at large rated the prestige of the scientist above that of the engineer, if the results of the questionnaire circulated after World War II by a Harvard sociologist among 2500 former Soviet citizens are accurate (see Peter Rossi, "Ratings of Selected Occupations in the USSR," unpublished manuscript in the Widener Library, Harvard, dated November 21, 1952). Rossi's ratings, however, do not distinguish between the research engineer and production engineer, but simply compare the occupation "engineer" with that of "scientific research worker" (*nauchnyi rabotnik*). His findings should be used with caution for the purposes of this study, an admonition reinforced by the fact that his questionnaire was taken a decade after the period covered by this study among former Soviet citizens, and could not be checked with a random sampling of responses from contemporary Soviet citizens who remained in the U.S.S.R. Nonetheless, that applied scientists involved in research received higher honors than engineers, as my computer study indicates, suggests that if Rossi's findings are accurate, both the general Soviet public and the government may have ascribed higher prestige to the scientist than the engineer.

an engineer before completing a doctorate in physics and heading the Leningrad Physical-Technical Institute—were tireless publicists for the unity of theory and practice and for the practical contributions of their institutes.[98] A Department of Technical Sciences was established in the Academy of Sciences in the 1930s and an engineer who had never published a scientific paper, I. P. Bardin, was selected to head this Department as a full member of the Academy. Upon election to the Academy in 1932, Bardin protested that he had never written a scientific treatise, but party officials pointed to one of the large blast furnaces he had constructed with the comment, "This was not only written down, but built. This is worth many scientific works."[99] While technologists such as Bardin were being brought into the country's most prestigious scientific institution, theoretical scientists were often placed in institutes under the industrial R & D network.

Yet evidence suggests that the status attributed to fundamental, theoretical research by many scientists and technologists remained higher than that of applied research, despite the efforts of the power structure and some of their scientific peers to change the situation during these years. In the mid- and late 1930s some engineers and applied scientists were still complaining that "pure" scientists would deny engineers who did experiments on industrial research "the title of 'scientist' (*uchenyi*)."[100] Research scientists sometimes indicated their status consciousness when they called for "raising engineers to the level of scientists" and declared that researchers without advanced scientific education and graduate degrees could not do really creative scientific work.[101]

One result was that those scientists who really preferred to be occupied with basic research and were less concerned with applications, developed something of a split personality. Under pressure from some of their peers and especially from the power structure to be "practical,"

[98] See the long bibliography of Ioffe's articles in *Abram F. Ioffe 1880-1960*, Moscow, 1960; and the biography by Monus S. Sominskii, *Abram Fedorovich Ioffe*, Moscow, 1964.

[99] V. Mezentsev, *Bardin*, Moscow, 1970, p. 114. On Bardin, see also my biographical entry in vol. 2 of the *Modern Encyclopedia of Russian and Soviet History*, Academic International Press, 1977.

[100] *Front nauki i tekhniki*, no. 7, 1935, 37.

[101] Ibid., no. 10, 1936; see the article in *Sovetskaia nauka*, no. 4, 1939, 145ff. These views echoed to some extent that of a leading engineering professor, Grinevetskii, before the revolution. Writing in 1915, he declared that industrial leadership should come from those specialists who had raised their qualifications by earning a second, scientific degree, in addition to their engineering degree. Academician Ioffe was a role model in this respect, since his first diploma was in electrical engineering and his doctorate in physics (see *Vestnik inzhenerov*, Feb. 1915, pp. 76-77).

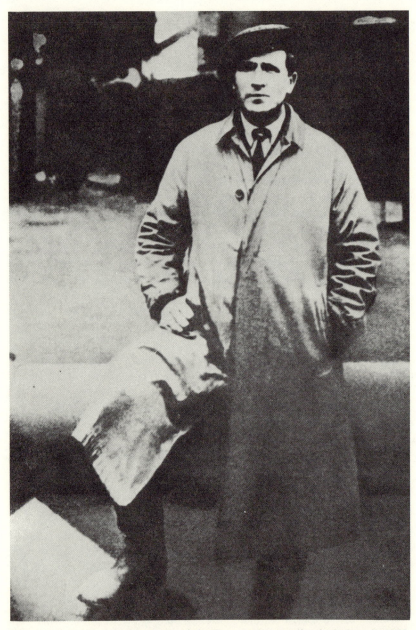

Fɪɢ. 5. Ivan Bardin, chief engineer of the Dneprovsky metallurgical plant, in 1929. He went on to become vice president of the U.S.S.R. Academy of Sciences, in charge of the technical sciences, and author of a widely read autobiography, *The Life of An Engineer*, first published in the late 1930s, and intended to encourage young people to enter the technical intelligentsia. Bardin provided an important link between the prerevolutionary and the postrevolutionary technostructures. (*Bardin* by V. Mezentsev, Moscow, 1970.)

they "began to relegate this 'practical work' to a particular section of the institute, a small and non-prestigious one; while the rest of the institute concentrated on 'real scientific work,' " as Peter Solomon has pointed out. "When scientists did visit factories, they sometimes betrayed their feelings about these chores. Their visits were described as 'episodic' and their attitudes toward plant technicians 'haughty.' According to factory personnel, the scientists 'came, gave instructions, and left.' "[102]

While Solomon does not elaborate on the prerevolutionary roots of this phenomenon, or point out that scientists were split on this issue, he is undoubtedly correct in seeing its negative effects on technical innovation. Scientists were often conditioned by the traditional status consciousness of their profession to value basic research more highly than applied, and this outlook was reinforced by the difficulties of applying their research in the economy both before and after the revolution. They found little incentive between 1928 and 1941 to do more than the minimum of applied research required to keep the government off their backs, particularly in view of the other factors in their environment that inhibited technical innovation. Such scientists were oriented more toward the frontiers of world science and a professional model of science that stressed interaction, praise, and criticism of colleagues involved in similar research, working autonomously from the control of the wider society.[103] They preferred to divert their time and resources as much as possible to their real scientific interests, which often had little relation to the immediate needs of Soviet industrialization. While it is difficult to say with any precision how strong this trend was among scientists in the R & D system, it undoubtedly added to the difficulties of effective technical innovation, and eventually led, in the post-Stalin era, to a greater separation of "pure" and applied research institutions in the Soviet Union.[104]

Technical innovation was further hindered by the lack, in most branches of the economy, of organizations responsible for all stages of the innovative process, from the examination of an idea to its development and introduction into mass production. With a few exceptions, the

---

[102] Solomon, p. 26, citing the speeches of R. L. Veller and A. A. Armand in *Zavodskaia laboratoriia*, no. 4, 1935, 127ff. and *Na fronte industrializatsii*, no. 24, 1930, 5-10; see also *Za industrializatsiiu*, Feb. 4, 1932, 3.

[103] On the conflict between the professional model of science and other models, see the excellent discussion in Suttmeier, pp. 79-118.

[104] On this subject, see Linda Lubrano, "Soviet Science Policy and the Scientific Establishment," *Survey*, Autumn 1971 and Winter 1972, and her "Policy-making in the USSR Academy of Sciences," *Journal of Contemporary History*, vol. 8, no. 4, 1973, 67-80, as well as Loren R. Graham, "Reorganization of the USSR Academy of Sciences," in P. H. Juviler, ed., *Soviet Policy-Making*, New York, 1967.

process was fragmented among separate organizations, some like the research institutes, responsible only for the original research of an idea and perhaps a prototype, separate design bureaus, responsible for the development of applicable models and processes, and finally, at the production level, factories that would convert models into mass production. While most of these institutions might be under the general supervision of an economic commissariat (such as Heavy Industry), they were separate administratively and, frequently, geographically. Evidence from contemporary Soviet sources indicates that such separation hindered the translation of ideas into production.

Some of the most important research centers were either outside the economic commissariats (as in the case of those under the Academy of Sciences) or were directly under the central administrative apparatus of each commissariat (in the case of *Vesenkha* and later Heavy Industry, whose Scientific-Technical Research Department supervised a number of the most important institutes). Most were under the Main Administrations (*glavki*) and Trusts of a commissariat, which supervised production in a particular branch of industry.[105] While individual factories might have a research laboratory, these laboratories rarely had the resources or the support of plant directors allowing them to undertake major innovations, as we have already seen above.

Thus the R & D system was really a series of fragmented pieces, something like a jigsaw puzzle, scattered among a group of people who rarely came together because they lived in different houses and saw themselves as basically incompatible. Research institutes complained that they were usually dependent on design bureaus and factories separate from them and uncooperative.[106] Design bureaus usually preferred the quickest and simplest means of implementation, and, as institute researchers charged, "blindly bow down before foreign 'authorities' and mechanically copy foreign technology. . . ."[107] The institutes considered most successful in innovation, both by contemporary Soviet and Western observers, were those with their own experimental shops and sometimes factories attached to them, such as the Central Aviation Institute

---

[105] On the organization of R & D, see the works cited by Yesakov, Schmidt, Armand, Lewis, and Solomon. See also the excellent discussion in Bruce Parrott's Ph.D. dissertation on Soviet technology, Chapter III (Faculty of Political Science, Columbia University, 1976).

[106] *Industriia*, July 6, 1939, 3.

[107] See, for example, *Industriia*, April 3, 1939, 3; March 12, 1937, 3; April 8, 1937, 3; January 17, 1940; Feb. 6, 1940, 3; April 11, 1937, 3; June 17, 1940, 2; see also *Vestnik metallopromyshlennosti*, no. 10, 1932, 8-20, and for the work of one of the largest design bureaus, in the metallurgical industry, see the history of *Gipromez* in *Sovetskaia metallurgiia*, no. 11, 1937, 32-51, and for a critique of design work in this industry, no. 7, 1937, 20ff.

(TsAGI).[108] These were exceptions, however, in areas of highest priority to the government.

After the rapid expansion of research institutions between 1928 and 1932, a retrenchment took place stressing a smaller number of more qualified institutes and personnel, with only gradual expansion in later years.[109] This trend after 1932 paralleled a similar emphasis in higher technical education and for many of the same reasons we have discussed in chapter 9, particularly the reemphasis on quality. However, in R & D this retrenchment had the effect of eliminating many branches of institutes that were closer to production, concentrating most research in large institutes located in the central cities, often far removed from the production base they were meant to serve. The well known chemist I. Shcherbakov noted in 1940:

> As practice has shown, the success of scientific endeavors decreased with the increased distance of the institute from the factory. Unfortunately outlying institutes are often devoid of the possibility of making their own decisions on projects. . . . It is naive to think that we can conduct the scientific business of the whole Union from one central base. . . . We must not consider advanced only the Moscow and Leningrad Institutes, but those which are most creative, which have given industry the highest quality work, which are closer to the factories. The problem is not one of creating institutes in all areas but of stopping the tendency to do away with the outlying institutes.[110]

American experience corroborates such comments on the need for close geographical or administrative ties between R & D and production if the level of innovation is to be high.[111] Yet the comments of Shcherbakov and like-minded people were in a sense voices crying in the wilderness. Little was done to correct the organizational deficiencies of Soviet R & D despite complaints of Soviet researchers and inventors from these years. Individual inventors who did not succumb to the temptations of quietude and the relative safety of nonapplied research in an institute found themselves facing a series of closed doors and other frustrations in their efforts to overcome organizational barriers. Bureaucratic divisions loomed up everywhere as a hindrance. As the Com-

[108] Crowther, *Soviet Science*, pp. 209-214; *Front nauki i tekhniki*, no. 4, 1932, 111-112. On TsAGI, see also chapter 14.

[109] For a discussion of this retrenchment, see *Za industrializatsiiu*, Feb. 13, 1931, 2; Feb. 16, 1931, 1; December 22, 1932; *Izvestiia*, January 25, 1932, 3; July 2, 1932, 3; Dec. 25, 1932, 3; Robert A. Lewis, op. cit., p. 162.

[110] *Industriia*, May 9, 1940, 2.

[111] See Morton in Allison, op. cit., pp. 225-226.

mittee on Inventions summed up the situation, "It often happens that an invention is recognized as useful and is slated for introduction, but the author finds himself spending years knocking at the doors of all sorts of bureaucrats and can obtain nothing unless some authoritative organization involves itself in the affair. . . ."[112]

A final barrier to successful innovation must be mentioned here. Applied scientists and engineers stressed technical criteria to the neglect of economic criteria in developing new inventions and processes. As Academician Kurnakov pointed out in 1940, researchers often worked out solutions "without a concern for economics. Sometimes [these solutions] proved more expensive than existing methods."[113] A good example would be the turbodrill in the oil industry, an innovation that began to be used in the later 1930s. An original Soviet invention that by the 1950s had largely replaced the American-style rotary drill in Soviet oil fields, it was touted by its developers and by L. M. Kaganovich at the Eighteenth Party Congress in 1939 as a device superior to any yet developed in the world's oil industry.[114] In some of its technical indices this may have been true. For example, it could drill deeper and faster than rotary bits, once set in position. The problem was that it took longer to set up for drilling and wore out faster than rotary drills. Beyond that, it necessitated a whole series of changes in auxiliary equipment and methods above ground, changes that managers frequently resisted.[115]

In his case study of this invention, Robert Campbell has concluded that it proved less economical over the long run than the rotary drill. Why, then, was it adopted? In this case, the answer would seem to be a combination of several factors: Soviet technical pride in a unique invention and political pressure by an important Politburo member like Kaganovich, who was impressed with its potential was one reason. Perhaps the major reason was the general neglect of economic factors by Soviet innovators. As Campbell has pointed out, "Designers were bemused by the 'engineering fallacy' of trying to maximize mechanical efficiency and neglected economic criteria."[116] This judgment is confirmed by Kurnakov's 1940 article concerning developments in another area, chemical technology. Kurnakov stressed that "a project completed under laboratory conditions must be technologically adapted to factory conditions and have an economical basis. Neglect of these necessary conditions has a strong effect on the introduction of scientific work, since managers customarily will not use them [innovations] on the

---

[112] *Vestnik komiteta*, no. 12, 1932, 5. [113] *Industriia*, June 17, 1940, 2.
[114] Ibid., Feb. 5, 1940, 2; Kaganovich speech in *XVIII S"ezd. Stenograficheskii otchet.*
[115] *Industriia*, Feb. 5, 1940, 2. [116] Campbell, op. cit., pp. 101-120.

pretext that they are not fully worked out."[117] Poorly versed in economics, cut off administratively from factory conditions, and lacking responsibility for the economic effects of their project, applied scientists and engineers frequently neglected the economic impact of innovations, an aspect of major concern to managers. It is not surprising that managers often preferred old methods, including the use of relatively cheap human labor, to more costly new machines and processes that experienced frequent breakdowns, shortages of spare parts, and the neglect of R & D personnel in adapting them economically to the needs of production.[118]

Despite attempts by some old specialists in the early years of the Soviet regime to increase the concrete economic knowledge of technologists, economics was generally neglected in higher technical education in these years, as we have seen in chapter 9. In addition, the training of large numbers of professional economists who might have helped staff of the R & D network also suffered relative neglect.[119] When these factors are added up, it is scarcely surprising to see a stress on technological criteria to the neglect of economics in Soviet R & D, further inhibiting the process of technical innovation.

Before concluding this chapter, a look at one extended case of major technological innovation in Soviet industry during these years seems appropriate. Perhaps the most highly publicized innovation, and one that led to the creation of an entirely new industry based upon indigenous Soviet technology, was the creation of synthetic rubber. There was no extensive foreign precedent for this. Foreign observers admit that the Soviet Union led the way in this area of world technology, spurred by defense needs and the desire for economic self-sufficiency. It will be instructive, therefore, to look briefly at both its successes and its difficulties as an important example of the process of Soviet innovation. Fortunately, there are extensive primary sources on this development and a good secondary literature based on hitherto unused party and industrial archives. These sources are remarkably frank in discussing the problems, as well as the partial successes of this new industry.

Dependent on imports of natural rubber, particularly from the British Empire, Russia, as well as Germany, before World War I began research on synthetic rubber, the necessity for which was greatly accelerated by the blockade suffered during the war. Some progress in

---

[117] *Industriia*, June 17, 1940, 2; see also April 8, 1937, 2.

[118] Ibid., Jan. 20, 1937, 2; Sept. 11, 1939, 2; Paramonov, p. 214.

[119] Seniavskii, pp. 297, 333; Prof. V. I. Obraztsov, *Opyt reorganizatsii uchebnoi postanovki v Moskovskom institute inzhenerov putei soobshchenii*, Moscow, 1924, pp. 5-6, 14-15; Chutkerashvili, pp. 125-128; *Kommunist*, no. 11, 1956, 60; Prokof'ev, op. cit., 210ff.

research, but not in actual production of a rubber substitute was registered in Russia during the war. Soon after the Brest-Litovsk treaty with Germany in 1918, a group of outstanding specialists working in this area—A. E. Favorsky, B. V. Byzov, I. I. Ostromyslenskii, S. V. Lebedev, and others—convened a conference under the sponsorship of *Vesenkha* to discuss the problems of synthetic rubber. Lenin and other Soviet leaders were particularly interested in such research, pointing to its military significance; still no major progress was made until the late 1920s.[120]

In 1926, the Scientific-Technical Section of *Vesenkha* sponsored a contest, with a prize of 100,000 rubles, for a successful natural rubber substitute. The conditions of the contest specified that the winner must use native materials to produce rubber, equal in quality to natural rubber and no costlier than the world price over the previous five years. Spurred on by the war scare of 1927 and the expected spurt in demand during the First Five-Year Plan, *Vesenkha* chose a winner early in 1928. Basically, there had been two finalists, both old specialists who had been working in this area since before the revolution—B. V. Byzov and S. V. Lebedev. Byzov used petroleum as his raw material, but Lebedev preferred ethyl alcohol produced from potatoes. His choice was dictated by several factors—the low Soviet production of oil from 1926 to 1928, the more complex apparatus and higher temperatures required for a petroleum-based process, the well-developed ethyl alcohol industry in Russia, and the relative abundance and low cost of potatoes. Lebedev's entry won, but was considered only partially successful in fulfilling the terms of the contest. Lebedev's material, SKB, was more expensive than natural rubber, and lacked some of its qualities.[121]

In 1929, the party's Central Committee declared complete freedom from imports of foreign rubber a goal, but decided to develop both natural rubber—looking for native vegetation that could be grown in Soviet plantations—and synthetic rubber.[122] Lebedev himself favored a continued search for synthetics with different characteristics for different purposes,[123] although this was not to occur in practice. The government put its primary emphasis and its largest investment into Lebedev's SKB, which was considered longer wearing than natural rubber but suffered from various weaknesses, such as low tensile strength and

[120] *Sinteticheskii kauchuk*, no. 1, 1932, 42; Brezhneva diss., p. 25; Piotrovskii, pp. 117ff.

[121] Piotrovskii, pp. 134ff.; V. S. Lel'chuk, *Sozdanie khimicheskoi promyshlennosti SSSR*, Moscow, 1964, pp. 290ff.

[122] Brezhneva, pp. 30ff.; Piotrovskii, p. 151; *Khimiia i khoziastvo*, no. 1, 101ff.; *Za industrializatsiiu*, March 5, 1937, 4; *Industriia*, Oct. 23, 1939, 3.

[123] A. E. Arbuzov, in *Akademik S. V. Lebedev*, Moscow, 1954, pp. 57-58.

brittleness in low temperatures. The latter quality was particularly disadvantageous for use in tires in that cold climate. Yet appropriations for research on uses of indigenous natural rubber and various alternative synthetics received much lower priority than the development and production of SKB, and even here high goals for production were paramount, to the virtual neglect of efforts to improve SKB's disadvantageous characteristics.

Lebedev himself was showered with hundreds of thousands of rubles to develop his product. He received the close attention of the party boss, Kirov, in his home base of Leningrad, and frequent visits from the heads of industry and economic planning, Kuibyshev and Ordzhonikidze. Called several times before the Politburo to report on progress, Lebedev had entree to the highest political authorities. A veritable cult grew up around this rather diffident man, who was a product of the old regime. The son of a Russian Orthodox priest, he had worked for capitalist firms before the revolution, and had also been a professor of chemistry in a Tsarist Military Academy. In 1931, Lebedev was awarded a Lenin Prize, 10,000 rubles, and soon afterwards a personal automobile. In 1932, he was chosen as a full member of the Academy of Sciences, along with a group of other outstanding technologists, all of them educated before the revolution and most of them with backgrounds from the bourgeoisie, the Tsarist bureaucracy, the nobility, or the clergy. More important to his work than praise and rewards, Lebedev was given the services of a group of talented chemists and engineers, and he was put in charge of building an experimental factory, a luxury afforded few Soviet innovators in these years. By 1931, the first Soviet plant for SKB was in production and two more were under construction. Government leaders argued whether to develop production in only three plants, or construct ten SKB factories, as Stalin wished.[124]

The major problems with SKB became apparent in the developmental stage. With a shortage of competent specialists and skilled workers, synthetic rubber development was plagued by a series of accidents, including explosions, which frightened away other potential specialists and workers. In a rush to produce SKB before an improved material had been developed and before the production process had been mastered, the plants producing it found their buyers—the managers and specialists of rubber products firms—refusing to use SKB, claiming it was an in-

[124] AGKKh, f. USK, d. 3, l. 36, 57, cited in Lel'chuk, p. 300. In 1931, Lebedev and his engineers considered Stalin's insistence on building ten plants instead of only three a "crime" (*prestuplenie*), and protested to Kirov that they would have to "build on a completely unprepared base, many problems were still unsolved . . ."; see also Lebedev's article in *Sinteticheskii kauchuk*, no. 4, 1933, 4-10.

ferior product; they continued to demand imports of natural rubber, which were cheaper and more usable. In 1934, this industry suffered a further setback when Lebedev himself died of typhus while on a trip to inspect a new SKB plant.[125]

By 1935, the situation in the synthetic rubber industry had reached crisis proportions; tons of the material piled up in warehouses. Ordzhonikidze summoned some seven conferences between 1931 and 1937 to deal with these problems. In 1935, after one such conference, he opened a contest to improve the quality and uses of SKB, but there were no winners. The conditions of the contest remained unfulfilled, indicating the lack of sufficient incentive for further improvements. Customers claimed that the quality of SKB was so uneven that a single batch might vary in consistency and technical quality. Not infrequently foreign objects, such as nails and dirt, were found in it. Managers preferred natural rubber, since the technology for its use was many decades old, and had already been mastered in the U.S.S.R., and its technical qualities were more consistent.[126] SKB was judged unsuitable for high quality tires and certain other products. The research institute for the rubber industry also preferred to work on uses of natural rubber, with which they were most familiar; the factory labs of SKB plants were burdened with routine tasks and lack of strong managerial support for more applied research.[127]

In 1937, the synthetic rubber industry was further disrupted by the purges. At least two of its leading engineers and managers, Osipov-Smit and Strezh, were arrested and killed, and the head of one of the principal factory labs in this industry, M. I. Farberov, was arrested. (He survived the camps and was rehabilitated in the 1950s, earning a doctorate in chemical technology and holding the chair in synthetic rubber at a Yaroslavl technical university.)[128] By late 1937 and 1938, the Soviet press was complaining that the quality of synthetic rubber had declined, and this complicated an already troubled rubber industry, including tire production.[129] Although the situation apparently improved somewhat

[125] Brezhneva, pp. 48-124, citing various party and government archival sources; Piotrovskii, p. 212; Lel'chuk, pp. 297-306.

[126] Brezhneva, pp. 176-190; *Za industrializatsiiu*, May 30, 1936; *Sinteticheskii kauchuk*, no. 2, 1934, 1-6; no. 2, 1936, 1-3; no. 5, 1936, 1-2; no. 7-8, 1936, 1-2; *Zhurnal rezinovoi promyshlennosti*, no. 3, 1936, 254.

[127] *Za industrializatsiiu*, July 27, 1932; Brezhneva, p. 175; *Industriia*, Jan. 3, 1939, 2; *Izvestiia*, May 17, 1932, 2.

[128] PAIaO, f. 273, op. 68, d. 405, l. 67; TsPA IML, f. 17, op. 21, d. 719, l. 208, cited in Brezhneva, pp. 144ff.; *Kauchuk i rezina*, no. 12, 1937, 29-34; no. 9, 1937, 79-81; no. 6, 1937, 3-7; no. 4, 1937, 103-106.

[129] *Pravda*, August 19 and 22, 1937; *Industriia*, June 8, 1939, 1; *Kauchuk i rezina*, no. 5, 1938, 1-9; no. 3, 1938, 87ff.; no. 6, 1938, 5-6; nos. 8-9, 1938, 3-5; no. 7, 1938, 4-10; no. 10, 1938, 3-8; *Industriia*, May 15, 1938, 2; see also British

just prior to World War II—usable tires were produced with equal proportions of synthetic and natural rubber—the Soviet Union did not produce a synthetic rubber equal in quality to the natural product until 1950, according to Soviet sources,[130] and even then, it was more costly. In the 1950s and 1960s, the U.S.S.R. imported some seventy percent of its rubber from Southeast Asia, reversing a trend from the late 1930s, when it was producing some ninety percent of its own rubber, mostly SKB and inferior grades of natural rubber from Soviet plantations.[131]

This fact indicates that the policy of autarchy was a partial economic and technical failure in this area. Although the capacity to produce a synthetic rubber helped during World War II, when supplies of natural rubber were disrupted, the Soviet Union was dissatisfied with both the quality and quantity of its own product. It received three synthetic rubber plants from the U.S. under Lend-Lease, and showed an intense interest in U.S. synthetic rubber research. Despite its late entry into the synthetic rubber industry, during World War II the U.S. produced differing varieties and qualities of synthetic rubbers that proved highly attractive to the U.S.S.R., which had put most of its eggs in a single basket.[132]

The major conclusion to be drawn from this is that, although the U.S.S.R. showed an impressive initial research effort, the development and production stages proved to be the principal weaknesses in carrying through successful innovation. A group of talented chemists and chemical engineers—mainly products of the old regime—worked with the strong support of the power structure to create a new product. This case suggests that without the support of some powerful interest within the state or party, the difficulties of the individual inventor were likely to be almost insurmountable. Even with such support, the difficulties were often hard to overcome. The case of synthetic rubber indicates that where the U.S.S.R. led the way in the early stages of a major innovation, it was eventually surpassed by other nations as it encountered serious problems in development and production, a conclusion that could be extended to include areas such as aeronautics, space exploration, and perhaps others in later years. Although the reasons for this deserve fuller treatment in a later work, we have suggested some of the major causes in this chapter.

To sum up the evidence of this chapter, probably the most important

---

Foreign Office Archives, April 15, 1939, 2035/2035/38, and *Khrushchev Remembers*, pp. 122-129.

[130] *Industriia*, June 26, 1940, 3; Piotrovskii, p. 221.
[131] *Industriia*, June 8, 1939, 1; October 23, 1939, 3.
[132] Sutton, vol. 3, Stanford, 1973, pp. 153-156.

causes for the problems of technological innovation were points 1, 2, 3, and 5 listed at the outset. These stand out more frequently in the sources used. Particularly important were the nature of the planning system, with its lack of competition for markets and demand for innovation; the effects of terror; and the shortage of skilled workers and technologists adequately educated for innovation. The other causes seem less important, but should not be dismissed. For example, recent experiments in the Soviet Union to end the separation of research, development, and production by creating unified R & D–production complexes, and to tie incentives for R & D personnel more clearly to the economic effectiveness of their proposals have not been significantly successful.[133] The problems would appear to be endemic to the entire system—the interrelated complex of causes discussed here, and not to a few isolated factors. Tinkering with only one or two parts of this complicated system has so far failed to stimulate a high level of indigenous technical innovation, except in some areas of military and heavy industrial technology where the most able technologists are concentrated. Here more internal competition has also been encouraged, and external competition with foreign powers has been unavoidable, as we shall see in the following chapter.

[133] Julian Cooper, "Research, Development and Innovation in the USSR," paper delivered at the Banff Conference of Slavists, 1974.

14

TECHNOLOGY AND LEGITIMACY:
SOVIET AVIATION AND STALINISM
IN THE 1930s

Between 1933 and 1938 the Soviet Union attempted to set a number of world records in aviation. The flood of books, articles, posters, films, postage stamps, and folk art commemorating these events has now nearly faded from the memory of all but a few collectors, yet the significance of this episode in the history of the 1930s goes well beyond its purely technical importance. The argument developed below views these events in a more general context and attempts to develop a novel interpretation of their significance. It focuses on the relationship between technology and social change in a developing society. The legitimizing function of technology in such a society has not received the attention it deserves from historians and social scientists. This chapter develops a case study that suggests some of the political uses technological achievements may have for the leaders of a country in transition to a more modern social structure. Specifically, it develops the following interpretation: During the 1930s Stalin and his associates used world records in aviation as a means of winning support for his regime at home and abroad, and of counterbalancing the effect of the purges. While this effort achieved some notable successes, it also detracted attention from the development of certain kinds of aviation necessary to Soviet defense and contributed significantly to the Soviet military disasters of 1941.

One of the more interesting questions debated by historians in recent years concerns the degree of Soviet preparedness at the time of the German attack in 1941. Did the Stalinist emphasis on heavy industry, and particularly the defense industry, make the U.S.S.R. as fully prepared as possible? That was the position argued by Stalin himself after World War II, and by defenders of Stalinism.[1] Were there, to the contrary, a number of serious weaknesses, for which Stalin and the supporters of his "cult of personality" could be blamed, most notably, of course, the disruption to industry and the Soviet defense position

---

[1] See Stalin's speech of February 1946, in I. V. Stalin, *Sochineniia*, tom 3 (16), Robert McNeal, ed., Hoover Institution, Stanford, 1967, pp. 1-22, as well as Soviet histories of this period prior to 1956. Although Isaac Deutscher hedges, his book (*Stalin: A Political Biography*, New York, 1966), comes closer to being a defense of Stalinism in this respect than most other Western studies.

brought about by the purges? This position was reflected in official Soviet historiography under Khrushchev and subsequently by dissenting Soviet historians and by most recent Western studies of the Stalin era.[2] This chapter does not try to deal definitively with that question, but focuses on the weakness of Soviet aviation. The official history of the Red Air Force, published by the U.S.S.R. Ministry of Defense during the Khrushchev era, admits its weakness at the beginning of the war with Germany, but does not offer an adequate explanation.[3] A. S. Yakovlev, a noted Soviet aeronautical engineer and chief of research and development in Soviet aviation (as deputy commissar of the aviation industry) at the beginning of the war, brings an insider's view to this question:

> By 1940, the basic might of the air force consisted of I-15 and I-16 fighters and TB-3 and SB bombers. These airplanes were obsolete and, as the experience in Spain had shown, they could not compare with German planes. There is no need to speak of still more antiquated airplanes, a large number of which were still in service.
>
> The rearmament of the air force began for all practical purposes in the first half of 1941. But as we have already stated, our misfortune consisted in the fact that at the time war broke out we still had too few new airplanes, and in the first days of the war our aviation suffered very heavy losses.[4]

Yakovlev offers an interesting, if inadequate, explanation for this situation. We will discuss the evidence for his answer below, as we attempt to deepen analysis of the question and to offer a more complete explanation by looking at how Stalin and his supporters used aviation technology in an effort to legitimize his regime.

[2] This position is argued by such dissenting Soviet historians as Roy Medvedev in *Let History Judge: The Origins and Consequences of Stalinism*, New York, 1971, and Aleksandr Nekrich in *June 22, 1941*. For a translation of the Nekrich book and the controversy surrounding it, see Vladimir Petrov, ed., *June 22, 1941: Soviet Historians and the German Invasion*. For the official Soviet position today, see *Istoriia SSSR s drevneishikh vremen do nashikh dnei*, Moscow, 1970, vol. 9, and *Istoriia KPSS*, Moscow, 1971, vol. 4, pt. 2. Recent Western studies include Adam Ulam, *Stalin: The Man and His Era*, New York, 1973, H. Montgomery Hyde, *Stalin*, New York, 1972, and Robert C. Tucker, ed., *Stalinism*, New York, 1976.

[3] For a translation of this book, see Ray Wagner, ed., *The Soviet Air Force in World War II: The Official History Originally Published by the Ministry of Defense of the U.S.S.R.*, New York, 1973.

[4] *Tsel' zhizni*, Moscow, 1966, pp. 243-249, translated in Seweryn Bialer, ed., *Stalin and His Generals: Soviet Military Memoirs of World War II*, New York, 1969, p. 207.

The problem of legitimacy was a major one for the Bolsheviks from the time of their revolution in 1917, for they could not really claim to represent a majority of the people. By the fall of 1917, it is true, they had won electoral majorities in several key Soviets, but they garnered only a quarter of the votes in the much more representative Constituent Assembly. They had come to power essentially by seizing the opportunity. It is not surprising, therefore, that many people regarded the Bolsheviks as usurpers. They could claim neither "divine right" nor a clear mandate from the people. They seized power in the name of the working class and their own allegedly superior understanding of the "scientific laws of history." Basically elitist in their approach to governing, they sought to legitimize their power in a way fundamentally new to political practice. They claimed legitimacy not only as the avant-garde of the industrial proletariat, but on the basis of their ability to transform nature and society.[5] Until they did so, however, this basis for their legitimacy was in doubt, and they had to rely on a high level of coercion against those elements who viewed their power as illegitimate.

In his climb to power during the 1920s, Stalin had the further problem of legitimizing his personal ascendancy within the Bolshevik regime. Partly by distorting the historical record, he emphasized his close relationship to Lenin and his loyalty to the Bolshevik party as one basis of his legitimacy. The cult of Lenin, after his death in 1924, was largely Stalin's creation, and historians and social scientists have often commented upon it as an important stage in Stalin's attempt to establish his personal legitimacy.

This was not the only form of legitimation Stalin used, of course. The shell, if not the substance, of popular legitimacy was reemphasized in the 1930s with the "Stalin Constitution" of 1936 and the widely publicized election campaigns to the Supreme Soviet during the late 1930s. Students of the Stalin era have commented frequently on these attempts to provide a facade of popular legitimacy to the regime. The form of legitimation that concerns us here, however, has not been carefully analyzed. A more implicit and subtle phenomenon, it is no less important as a key to understanding Stalinism and the development of Soviet communism. Technological legitimation was largely a form of political practice, not a self-conscious theory carefully articulated. It was not John Locke or Lenin writing, but Stalin acting. Its expression must be sought in the more scattered words and actions of Stalin, his closest associates, and the controlled Soviet media of the time. As Stalin

[5] See, for example, the 1919 Party Program and commentary on it in Nikolai Bukharin and Evgenii Preobrazhensky, *The ABC of Communism*, Ann Arbor, Mich., 1966.

and his associates moved from their underground past into the rapid modernization of the 1930s, they increasingly emphasized the "scientific" basis of their hegemony, and particularly their accomplishments in technology as evidence of their right to rule. Stalin built his power on his reputation as a "practical man," an activist and organizer in his struggle with the party's leading theoreticians, Trotsky and Bukharin.[6] It is not surprising, then, that achievements in technology would receive particular emphasis in these efforts at legitimation. Aviation was only one form of modern technology used in this way by the Stalinists. (Gigantic hydroelectric stations, canals, and metallurgical plants were others.) Aviation played a most prominent and dramatic role, however, at a critical time in the development of Stalinism; thus it is appropriate for a case study.

Although Soviet achievements in aviation had been touted as early as the 1920s, Stalin's strong personal interest in it dates at least from 1933. In that year, he praised the development of an aviation industry as one of the major accomplishments of the First Five-Year Plan (in many other respects the plan had been a disappointment to the leadership, and had fallen short of many targets). On April 28, 1933, at Stalin's initiative, the Soviet government designated a yearly festival, Aviation Day, to be celebrated every August 18. It became a major holiday in the new secular calendar of festivals that were occasions for ceremonial appearances by the leadership. With this new calendar the leadership was replacing the traditional calendar of Russian Orthodoxy by which the old regime had marked its yearly cycle of ceremonial appearances. By fall 1933, the Soviet Union had entered international competition for air records. Stalin's Foreign Commissar, commenting on the record set in a stratosphere balloon by the U.S. Navy, challenged the United States to compete with his country "for the conquest of the heights."[7] By January 1934, in time to impress the Seventeenth Party Congress, Soviet aviation authorities claimed a new world's record in height for a stratosphere balloon, though the feat had fatal consequences for the three balloonists.[8] Undeterred, Stalin by the mid-1930s had set Soviet aviators the task of mastering aviation technology by "flying farther than anyone, faster than anyone, and higher than anyone."[9]

[6] That Stalin still felt threatened by the ideas represented by these men seems evident from a study of the purges, and, in the case of Bukharin, the point has been well argued in the new biography of Stephen F. Cohen (*Bukharin and the Bolshevik Revolution*, New York, 1973).

[7] J. Gordon Vaeth in *U. S. Naval Institute Proceedings*, August 1963; *New York Times*, November 22, 1933. The Soviets claimed a new world's record on September 30, but it was not recognized by the International Aviation Federation (FAI), of which the U.S.S.R. was not a member.

[8] *New York Times*, February 1, 1934.   [9] *Grazhdanskaia aviatsiia*, Nov. 7, 1933.

It is not known, of course, whether this idea originated with Stalin. It may well have originated with elements of the technical intelligentsia who sought the government's favor. The engineers of the Central Aviation Institute (TsAGI), were especially active in these efforts, as were the designers and military men who were active in the civil defense organization (*Osoaviakhim*). We know that before 1933 the most prominent aviation designer of that era, A. N. Tupolev, who was head of TsAGI's design bureau and subsequently chief engineer of the aviation industry until 1938, was already constructing a plane for long-distance record flights.[10] What can be documented is the fact that Stalin coopted these efforts and closely associated his own name with them. Having noted the publicity potential of such efforts in the West, including Lindbergh's dramatic flight of 1927, the feats of Wiley Post, Amelia Earhart, and others, the U.S.S.R. gave massive publicity to the efforts of its own airmen. Aviation may have been singled out for special attention in this respect not only because of the progress the aviation industry had made in the First Five-Year Plan, but because Soviet leaders wished to prove that the U.S.S.R. could stand on its own feet (or better yet, fly with its own wings) in a field where German technical help had been so prominent before Hitler's takeover in 1933. How serious the loss of German cooperation in this field was after 1933 is difficult to say.[11] Aeronautics had strong native roots in Russia before World War I and produced a number of innovators, such as Zhukovsky, Chaplygin, and Tupolev, who remained in Russia after the revolution and made major contributions to aeronautical theory and practice (not to mention those who emigrated, de Seversky and Sikorsky for example, who had been associated with Zhukovsky and Tupolev at the Moscow Higher Technical School before the revolution).

The number of talented designers and the technical base in Soviet aviation was still small in 1933, and the loss of German contacts, not renewed until 1939, probably increased the need Stalin felt to prove

[10] The most comprehensive Soviet histories of aeronautical developments in the U.S.S.R. are P. D. Duz' *Istoriia vozdukhoplavaniia i aviatsii v SSSR*, Moscow, 1944, 1960, vols. 1-2; V. B. Shavrov, *Istoriia konstruktsii samoletov v SSSR*, and A. S. Yakovlev, *50 let sovetskogo samoletostroeniia*, Moscow, 1968. For the early activity of TsAGI, see James Crowther, *Soviet Science*, London, 1936, and articles in *Front nauki i tekhniki*, no. 12, 1933, 18-25; *SORENA*, no. 1, 1934, 105-109; *Grazhdanskaia aviatsiia*, no. 7, 1934, 13-19. On *Osoaviakhim*, see William Odom, *The Soviet Volunteers*, Princeton, 1973, and its journal, *Samolet*, 1933-1938.

[11] Documents concerning German aeronautical aid to the Soviet Union between 1925 and 1933 and its withdrawal after Hitler's accession to power can be found in Karl-Heinz Voelker, ed., *Dokumente und Dokumentarfotos zur Geschichte der Deutsche Luftwaffe Aus den Geheimakten des Reichswehrministeriums 1919-1933 und des Reichsluftfahrtministeriums 1933-1939*, Stuttgart, 1968, pp. 68-92.

independent Soviet capabilities both to his own people and to other nations. By 1938, Soviet spokesmen claimed to have set some sixty-two world records, including the longest, highest, and fastest flights, the first landing at the North Pole and the first flight between the Soviet Union and the United States by a polar route.[12] The validity of all these claims is not really as important as the political uses that were made of them. (Some were validated by observers of the International Aeronautical Federation in Paris; some were not.) Certain recurring themes and phrases can be noted in the propaganda about these flights.

The holders of these records were called "Stalin's falcons," and Stalin was prominently featured in Soviet publicity about their flights. While it was common all over the world to name airplanes and fliers after various birds, much of the publicity and phraseology of these efforts had a patriarchal, folklorelike quality to it that had especially rich connotations for a population still largely steeped in a traditional culture. The falcon, for example, is closely associated with princely powers in Russian folklore. Falconry was a royal privilege and sport from early times; and in Russian imagery, royalty were sometimes themselves portrayed as falcons. The Russian folk imagination had endowed some folklore heroes with the magical power to transform themselves into animals, and the bird was a favorite form for such changelings, as in the tales of Prince Volga Vseslavich.[13] Thus, the phrase "Stalin's falcons," which became a cliché, necessarily repeated in virtually every public reference to the feats of Soviet airmen after 1934, was abundant in associations with obedience to magical, princely powers. The patriarchal quality of this imagery comes through in the widely disseminated writings of Soviet air heroes at this time. For example, Chkalov, who was the first to reach the United States by a polar route from Moscow in June 1937, published an article entitled "Our Father" shortly after his flight. Referring to Stalin, he wrote:

> He is our father. The aviators of the Soviet Union call Soviet aviation, Stalinist aviation. He teaches us, nurtures us, warns us about risks like children who are close to his heart; he puts us on the right path, takes joy in our successes. We Soviet pilots feel his loving, attentive, fatherly eyes on us every day. He is our father. Proud parents find affectionate, heartfelt, encouraging words for each of their sons. Stalin has dubbed his aviators "falcons." He sends his falcons into flight and wherever they wander keeps track

[12] *Grazhdanskaia aviatsiia SSSR 1917-1967*, Moscow, 1967, p. 108.

[13] For translations of several of these tales, see Nora Chadwick, *Russian Heroic Poetry*, New York, 1967, pp. 33-52.

of them and when they return he presses them close to his loving heart.[14]

"Loving heart" is scarcely an expression most contemporary historians would use to describe the Stalin of these years, but perhaps that was exactly the point of such propaganda, to create a misleading and essentially false image of the man. In addition to the folklore quality already noted, a second recurrent theme of such propaganda was Stalin's affectionate concern for the lives and safety of Soviet aviators. In years when hundreds of thousands of Soviet citizens were disappearing into the forced labor camps and being executed by firing squads, the propaganda about Stalin's role in Soviet aviation reiterated the 'theme of his regard for human life.

Before each major record flight began, according to Soviet media, Stalin summoned the aviators and engineers involved to the Kremlin to go over their plans. He sometimes saw them off at the airport and generally was on hand to greet the successful upon their return. Again and again, Stalin is quoted on these occasions as telling the aviators, "Your lives are dearer than any machine," and expressing his concern for safety measures and against unnecessary risks.[15] In October 1938, at a Kremlin reception for three women aviators who had just set a new long-distance flying record, Stalin marked a general end to Soviet world record attempts during that period, by repeating a number of times the need for caution with the lives of aviators. The lives of Soviet flyers were so precious, he remarked, that from then on record flights would be allowed only in rare and extreme circumstances.[16] The possibility that other reasons may have existed for calling a general halt to such efforts will be discussed toward the close of this chapter.

A third recurring theme in the contemporary accounts of Soviet aviation records is to credit Stalin with much of the initiative and planning of such efforts. He is portrayed listening carefully to the ideas of Soviet aviators and aviation planners, tracing their routes, determining who will fly, and then giving the final permission. For example, the project to land a plane at the North Pole was supposedly the idea of aviators and scientists who approached the Commissar of Heavy Industry, Sergo Ordzhonikidze. Ordzhonikidze then put the proposal before Stalin, who

[14] *Letchik nashego vremeni*, Moscow, 1938, p. 315.

[15] *Pravda*, May 3, 1935; December 21, 1936; May 23, 1937; A. Y. Yegorov and V. P. Kliucharev, *Grazhdanskaia aviatsiia SSSR*, Moscow, 1937, pp. 98-99, 101; I. Karpov, *Aviatsiia strany sotsializma*, Leningrad, 1939, pp. 60-62; V. Chkalov, *Dva pereleta*, Moscow, 1938; G. F. Baidukov, *O Chkalove*, Moscow, 1939; Flora Leites, *Stalinskie sokoly*, Moscow, 1939.

[16] *Industriia*, October 28, 1938.

summoned a group of those concerned to the Kremlin in early 1937 and discussed their plans, tracing their route for them.

The polar flights and transpolar flights to the United States were the most widely publicized of these efforts, of which the first known attempts began in 1935. They are closely associated with the name of the Soviet scientist, Otto Y. Shmidt, a member of the Academy of Sciences, who, from 1932 to 1939, was head of the Administration for Northern Sea Routes, the government body charged with the development of the Soviet arctic. According to Shmidt, the widely publicized rescue by plane of the crew of the icebreaker *Cheliushkin* in 1934 made obvious the possibility that planes might also land at the North Pole. According to Shmidt's account, in 1935 he asked the well-known aviator M. V. Vodopianov to work up such a project. Vodopianov did so in the form of a novel, "A Pilot's Dream." (This subsequently became a popular Moscow play during 1937.)

Stalin summoned Shmidt and several aviators to the Kremlin on February 13, 1936, and told them how important transpolar and other record flights were, provided they were done with all due precaution. Exactly a year later, Shmidt was again summoned to the Kremlin to present a detailed plan. Stalin and the Politburo discussed his plan and gave written approval to the project, urging the utmost safety.[17] According to Shmidt, "Stalin here showed his great concern for people. . . ."

The purges at this time were moving into high gear. The planning for them had begun as early as the spring of 1933 with the appointment of a Purge Commission, but they gained momentum only after the murder of Kirov in December 1934. The major show trial of Kamenev and Zinoviev took place in August 1936, and that of Piatakov and others in Moscow, during early February 1937. As the arrests reached a crescendo in the middle of 1937, a series of spectacular air feats unfolded in the Soviet press. As already noted, the planning for a systematic race for air records began in the U.S.S.R. in the latter part of 1933. They gained momentum during 1935 and reached a high point in the fall of 1936 and through the summer of 1937. On May 22, 1937, the first airplane landed at the North Pole, which the Soviets claimed as Soviet territory in a barrage of publicity. The press dubbed the fliers "Bolshevik knights of culture and progress," and radio broadcasts were beamed daily from the Polar expedition to millions of Soviet citizens. The feat virtually monopolized Soviet media in a way similar to the dramatic launching of the first Soviet Sputnik and other space feats at a later time. The content of these radio broadcasts comes as no surprise.

[17] Yegorov, pp. 98-106.

Here is a typical message broadcast on May 24, at 1900 hours: "We gathered under an open sky but we didn't feel the cold, wrapped as we are in the glowing words pulsating with the concern of the great Stalin, feeling the warm breath of our beloved Motherland listening to us."[18] A few days later the successful crew was greeted by a smiling Stalin and decorated with the highest Soviet awards.

A few weeks later, on June 20, Soviet flyers completed the first successful nonstop flight from Moscow to the United States via a polar route, and the media were again filled with the accounts. More than a week before, on June 11, the newspapers had announced that the cream of the Red Army officer corps had been arrested and executed as traitors. As the *New York Times* correspondent wrote, Soviet morale had been badly shaken by the purges but was bolstered by the polar flight to the United States, "a legitimate reason for pride in national accomplishment."[19] Soviet editorials stressed that only a socialist state could organize such feats. The commander of the expedition, in an interview with a Western correspondent, indicated that Stalin had summoned them to the Kremlin on May 25, 1937, and given permission for the flight. "Our flight is primarily of a political-economic nature," he stressed.[20] Another member of his crew, speaking at the Overseas Press Club in New York after the flight, declared, "Don't believe all the fairy tales you hear about our country, but instead believe such feats as these."[21]

A second, and a third transpolar flight were planned for the summer of 1937. On June 10, the day before the executions of Red Army leaders were publicly announced, Stalin summoned another air crew to the Kremlin, to approve the second flight. On July 15, 1937, Gromov, the commander of this plane, set a new world's nonstop record, flying from Moscow to San Jacinto, near San Diego. On August 12, 1937, a third crew met with Stalin and departed the following day for North America. The last message from that plane was broadcast as it crossed the North Pole, after which it disappeared without a trace. The extensive search for this crew occupied many Western papers for weeks, but was largely underplayed by the Soviet press.

Was there a connection between these sensational flights and the purges? Coincidence, of course, does not prove correlation, and the answer must at present be somewhat speculative. It is based largely on

18 Ibid., p. 89.

19 *New York Times*, June 27, 1937, IV; for corroboration of this from Soviet sources see *Priroda*, no. 6, 1937, 17-23; no. 10, 5-9; no. 12, 59-64; no. 3, 1938, 3-7; no. 4, 3-4.

20 Ibid., June 20, 1937, 25; June 21, 1937, 3.

21 Ibid., June 29, 1937, 14.

how Soviet media handled the two series of events. On the basis of such evidence it would be folly to assert that the sole purpose of these flights was to divert attention from the purges. In all probability, they served several purposes, judging by the way publicity about them was handled at home and abroad. One purpose may have been to impress other nations with the coming of age of the Soviet Union in a technological sense and, perhaps, to mask the actual weaknesses of Soviet economic development. If so, however, they were not entirely successful. Their possible foreign economic and military intent was mentioned by Soviet and Western sources at the time, who pointed out, for example, that the polar flights attempted to demonstrate, among other things, the feasibility of an air link with North America using transpolar routes. (Such a link may have had particular significance to Soviet leaders, since at this time they were developing a connection with American aviation companies to replace the German connection lost after Hitler's rise to power.) However, because of the dangers involved and the loss of the third plane in August 1937, these flights remained impractical until the 1950s. During World War II, the Soviets ferried hundreds of American planes and other lend-lease supplies on short runs across the Bering Sea from Alaska or by sea via Murmansk and the Persian Gulf. Some sources at the time also noted the possible military significance of these flights for the development of long-range bomber operations. But again the flights failed to impress foreign military experts. The plane that completed these first flights, Western sources noted, was a rather slow, one-engine machine ill-adapted for bombing missions.

The way these flights were interpreted for Soviet citizens by the controlled press is what concerns us most here. It was the political significance of these flights domestically that was emphasized in media directed at the Soviet population itself. The record flights came at an opportune time for the regime, and they captured much of the attention of the media at a time of internal upheaval caused by the purges. In interpreting these accomplishments the domestic Soviet press attempted to spark the imagination of the public concerning the unlimited possibilities of technology. The planning of the record flights may have been only coincidental with the purges, but the opportunity they presented was exploited fully by the leadership. Acclaim for "Stalin's falcons" and for Stalin himself was aroused at a time when the victims of the purges were most in need of public sympathy and critical scrutiny of the charges brought against them. Hundreds of thousands of so-called "enemies of the people" were being quietly rounded up and carted off in these months with comparatively little or no official publicity. To use a metaphor, it was a time of falcons and ravens, "raven" being the

Soviet slang term for the unmarked black vans of the NKVD that transported political prisoners to their fate. In 1937, the falcons received far greater attention in official media. Analyzing the content of the Soviet press at this time would show how the media accentuated the positive, with far more emphasis on accomplishments in technology —especially aviation—than on the purges. One can be excused for interpreting the way these air spectaculars were used by the regime at home as a means of diverting attention from the abuses of the regime. Whether they were planned primarily for this purpose or simply came at a convenient time is another matter. The answer to that question cannot be documented at the present time.

When the more prominent victims of the purges were mentioned in public, it was with disgust and the sharpest epithets, sometimes contrasted with praise for Soviet air heroes. The latter became prime exhibits of the "new Soviet men" whom the authorities wished to create. When Shmidt and others of his expedition returned from the North Pole on June 26, 1937, Stalin personally welcomed them at the airport. According to the *New York Times* correspondent present at this occasion, Shmidt gave Stalin credit as the real originator and organizer of the polar conquest. As movie cameras captured the scene for a mass audience, Soviet leaders praised the airmen in speeches that bristled with references to "traitors," whose deeds were excoriated and contrasted sharply with those of "Stalin's falcons."[22]

The manufactured excitement of aviation achievements effectively contributed to concealing the real workings of the Stalinist regime from many in the Soviet Union and abroad. Just as "divine right" monarchs, including some of the bloodiest, were once portrayed by their own propagandists as floating above the earth, surrounded by saints and angels, and perhaps even ringed by a halo of their own, so Soviet citizens became familiar at this time with photographs and posters of Stalin and his intimates, with a symbolic backdrop of Soviet planes flying over the Kremlin towers, surrounded by such aviation heroes as Chkalov, Baidukov, Vodopianov, Papanin, and others. Radio, films, the press and countless speeches reiterated the symbolic link between the Stalinist regime and aviation. The result was the creation of a modern myth that, to be believed, had to be repeated in countless and sometimes rather fantastic forms. L. M. Kaganovich, a Politburo member and a major promoter of this myth, wrote in September 1936:

Observing Comrade Stalin's daily work in the area of aviation, his concern for its human cadres, we can say without any trace of ex-

[22] Ibid., June 26, 1937, 7; *Izvestiia*, June 25, 1937.

Fig. 6. "Defending the U.S.S.R.," peasant art by Pavel Bazhenov, 1935, a painter from the village of Palekh. The figure in the foreground is a frontier guard, posed against a background of the symbols of the Soviet Union's new technology. The large airplane at the top, among the largest in the world at the time, bears the name "Joseph Stalin" on its wings. For centuries before the revolutions of 1917, the peasant artists of Palekh, north of Moscow, had painted icons for members of the Russian Orthodox Church. After the revolutions, under the patronage of Maxim Gorky, they turned to contemporary themes and scenes from folklore. (*Palekh—A Village of Artists*, Moscow, n.d.)

aggeration that the founder and creator of our Soviet aviation, both its material part and its cadres, is our teacher and leader Comrade Stalin.[23]

Again in October 1938, Kaganovich is quoted: "Aviation is the highest expression of our achievements. Our aviation is a child of Stalinist industrialization; flyers are our proud falcons, raised lovingly and with care by Stalin."[24]

Official Soviet holidays became suffused with shows of aviation technology. The twentieth anniversary of the October Revolution in 1937 gave special emphasis to air records as symbolic of the regime's attainments in numerous scientific and technical fields; massive flights of aircraft became traditional on this holiday.[25] The annual Aviation Day on August 18 became even more of a public holiday for the celebration of aeronautical ingenuity and its symbolic link with Stalinism. In 1937, for example, nearly a million people streamed out to Tushino Air Field near Moscow, coming by bus, train, lorry, and even by foot. As Stalin and the Politburo watched, a stratosphere balloon slowly raised a huge canvas image of Stalin above the crowd. Dozens of planes then flew overhead, changing formations to spell out the words L-e-n-i-n, S-t-a-l-i-n, U-S-S-R, and then the image of a five-pointed star.[26] With such dramatic displays of human organization and power over nature, one might say that the Soviet modernizers attempted to erase from the minds of their people the religious symbols of political legitimacy used by the previous regime, implanting a different justification for political power. The analogy to the religious calendar and the ceremonial appearances of the Tsar on important religious holidays is apparent. The revolutionary and technological celebrations such as Aviation Day, Navy Day, May Day, the anniversary of the October Revolution and many others became to a modernizing regime what the older religious holidays were to a traditional one.

Such was the myth of Stalinist aviation and some of its manifestations. What were some of the realities in these years? We should not be surprised to find that they were much different from the myth. Although there was an element of truth to it, the myth concealed the numerous false starts, failures, accidents, and weaknesses of Soviet aviation. We are far from knowing the whole story of the development of Soviet aviation in these years; much of the necessary documentary material is still unavailable. Still, we can gain some fascinating insights from the available material.

[23] *Pravda*, September 20, 1936.
[25] *Pravda*, November 7, 1937.
[24] *Industriia*, October 28, 1938.
[26] *Industriia*, August 20, 1937.

What we find is evidence that the achievement of world aviation records cost dearly in military unpreparedness, and the continuation of these efforts sparked controversy in the Soviet press. Immediately following the first successful transpolar flight from Moscow to the United States in June 1937, an interesting series of articles began to appear. On June 21, for example, A. N. Tupolev, the dean of Soviet airplane designers and the designer of the one-engine ANT-25, which completed the successful flight, made a surprising admission. He noted that the ANT-25 was five years old and already outdated by contemporary aviation standards, especially by its slow speed. In making such a frank admission, however, he called for the creation of new and better machines for record flights: "If Comrades Chkalov, Baidukov and Beliakov —experienced, brave fliers—safely completed their flight and chalked up yet another great aviation victory for the land of the Soviets in an old plane like the ANT-25, then think what still greater victories our proud falcons will win in new machines."[27]

A few weeks later, I. Stoman, a colleague of Tupolev at the Central Aviation Institute and the engineer directly in charge of the ANT-25, supported Tupolev's sentiments and plans for constructing a new plane for long-distance records.[28] Again on July 26, Tupolev wrote that among the three goals set for Soviet aviation—the struggle for distance, speed, and height—distance was the most important. He noted first of all that civil aviation would be able to compete with other forms of transportation only when the problems of long-distance flying were solved. Secondly, he noted the importance of long-distance flying for the development of heavy bombers.[29]

On August 18, 1937, two articles took issue with the position expressed by Tupolev and Stoman. Although they did not directly attack these men by name or denigrate the feats of Stalin's record-breaking "falcons," the difference in position is striking. The first article was by an aeronautical engineer named G. Bertosh. He pointed out the urgent need for a flexible one-engine military plane that could serve as a scout, a fighter, or a light bomber. Such a plane would fly at low altitudes, and be fast and highly maneuverable. He indicated that such multipurpose planes already existed abroad and that their usefulness had been demonstrated by the experience of the German, Italian, and Japanese aggressors in Spain and East Asia.[30]

On the same page, the head of the Red Air Force, General Jan Alksnis, made the point even more directly. He began with the usual

[27] *Industriia*, June 21, 1937.
[28] Ibid., July 12, 1937.
[29] Ibid., July 26, 1937.
[30] Ibid., August 18, 1937.

tribute to the achievements of Soviet aviation, "we know our aviation is strong, as evidenced by the record flights. . . . But the tense international situation demands from us an even greater strengthening of the defense capability of the Soviet Union, first of all its army-air force." In contrast to Tupolev's position, he maintained that speed was of primary importance: "*He who has the highest speed can beat the enemy in the air.*" (Underlined in the original.) Tupolev had emphasized that distance was the first priority. Alksnis went on to say that the Red Air Force was on the level of contemporary world aviation, but that it must strive for greater speed, distance, height, and cargo-carrying ability. The greatest of these, he stressed, was "*speed, speed, and still more speed.*"[31] Furthermore, aircraft design should concentrate on the use of fire-resistant materials, instrument flying, and easy maneuverability. Development of such features rested first and foremost with the construction engineers, the technical people, he stressed. The indirect criticism of an emphasis on designing for spectacular achievements by air heroes comes through clearly: "Finally, we must occupy ourselves seriously with the problem of maneuvering the aircraft. The constructor who creates and equips the plane must be oriented not toward phenomenally gifted flyers but toward rank-and-file pilots."[32] He called for doubling, even tripling, the number of Soviet airmen as quickly as possible. The article ended with an expression of confidence that all these things would be achieved under the leadership of Stalin.

The articles by Bertosh and Alksnis were in all probability sparked by two events of July 1937. During the spring, German aviation had been taking the offensive in Spain, and by the Battle of Brunette in July, it was clearly gaining control of the Spanish skies for Franco.[33] What gave the Germans aerial superiority in Spain was a combination of factors: superior aerial tactics and the training of her pilots, combined with an increasing technical edge as new models, especially fighters and dive bombers, were tried out in Spain. The Soviets sent far more fighters to the Spanish Loyalists than Hitler sent through his Condor Legion

[31] Ibid.   [32] Ibid.

[33] Kilmarx, *History of Soviet Airpower*, New York, 1962, pp. 143-147; Asher Lee, *The Soviet Air Force*, New York, 1962, pp. 32-42; *New York Times*, June 22, 1937; July 27, 1937. Accounts by Soviet air force personnel who participated on the loyalist side can be found in Boris N. Smirnov, *Ispanskii veter: zapiski letchika*, Moscow, 1963, pp. 139-143, and Generals M. N. Yakushin and G. M. Prokof'ev, *Pod znamenem ispanskoi respubliki*, Moscow, 1965, pp. 483-540. An account by a Franco pilot is Jose Larios, *Combat Over Spain*, New York, 1966, especially pp. 120-155. The chief of the Spanish Republic Air Force, Ignacio Hidalgo de Cisneros, discusses Soviet aid and his meetings with Stalin and Voroshilov during 1938 in his *Memorias*, Paris, 1964, vol. 2, pp. 355-474.

to aid Franco, but quality made the difference. Stalin sent an estimated five hundred fifty Soviet I-15 biplane fighters and four hundred seventy-five monoplane I-16 fighters by sea and then hundreds more overland through France, as fascist submarines began to tighten their blockade of Republican Spain in the spring and summer of 1937.[34] This compared with an average strength of rarely over one hundred planes for the Condor Legion, of which about half were fast fighters.[35] The supply of Soviet planes and aviation experts was, in fact, not cut off until Stalin withdrew them in the summer or fall of 1938. By then the latest German fighters, the Messerschmitt 109E, ruled supreme, and continued Soviet participation in the air war became increasingly futile and dangerous to Soviet military prestige.

What had happened to bring about this situation? The memoirs of A. S. Yakovlev, the Soviet designer, are worth quoting in this connection:

In 1936, at the beginning of the Civil War in Spain, the I-15 and I-16 met with the Messerschmitts for the first time. These were the first ME-109V fighters with a Junkers UMO-210 610 hp. engines and a top speed of 470 km/hr.

In terms of speed, our fighters were not inferior to the Messerschmitts—the armaments of both fighters were roughly similar —7.6 mm machine guns, but ours were more maneuverable, and they really gave it to the "Messers."

The leaders of our aviation were very happy with this. An air of placidity developed, and no one was in a hurry to modernize Soviet

[34] British Foreign Office Archives, Public Record Office, London, W3987/1245/41; W7480/83/41; W4382/83/41; W9248/83/41; W16269/29/41; W9363/83/41; W6200/83/41; W3734/83/41; David T. Cattell *Communism and the Spanish Civil War*, New York, 1965, pp. 73-79; Herbert Malloy Mason, Jr., *Rise of the Luftwaffe*, New York, 1973, pp. 236-237.

[35] Karl-Heinz Voelker, *Die Deutsche Luftwaffe 1933-1939*, Stuttgart, 1967, pp. 149-154. The records of the Condor Legion are in Luftwaffengruppen kommando 3 Nr. 7179/38, Dokumentenzentrale des Militaergeschichtlichen Forschungsamtes, Freiburg. According to another source, the total number of foreign military planes supplied to the two sides was roughly equal over the entire period of the civil war. The Franco forces received around twelve hundred planes, mostly German and Italian, while the loyalists also had around twelve hundred planes, mostly Russian and French. Technically, the best aircraft on each side were German and Russian, respectively. Contrary to the accounts of many loyalists and some Soviet participants, this source concludes that the Republic did not lose primarily because of a lack of armaments, including aircraft, caused by the fascist blockade and Western nonintervention. The flow of Soviet arms to the Republicans was ample, despite these difficulties. "In the last analysis, the Republic did not lose because it could not get enough foreign arms." Robert H. Whealey, "Foreign Intervention in the Spanish Civil War," in Raymond Carr, ed. *The Republic and the Civil War in Spain*, New York, 1971, p. 233.

fighter aircraft. At the same time, the Hitlerites were working fever-
ishly, learning from the results of the first aerial battles in the skies
over Spain.[36]

The Germans quickly improved the speed and armaments of their
aircraft, and developed tactics to counter the advantage the I-16 had
in turning ratios. The growing German advantage in aviation was becoming clear in Spain by July 1937. The superiority of German fighters
in speed was also demonstrated for all to see at the Zurich International
Air Meet on July 26, 1937, when a German pilot swept the honors for
speed in an exhibition model of the ME-109.[37]

How did Stalin, who had staked so much of his prestige on the accomplishments of Soviet aviation, and who had apparently centralized
so much of the decision-making power over aviation in his own hands,[38]
react to these events? We can't be sure how soon he learned the true
state of affairs in Spain. It is possible that subordinates tried to conceal
the extent of Soviet weakness, fearing the response of someone who was
so quick to lop off heads, especially during the purge years of 1937 and
1938. By late 1937 or early 1938, however, as the war turned increasingly against the Spanish Republicans, he was certainly aware of the
situation and he reacted, first of all, with a search for scapegoats.

A. N. Tupolev, the designer most closely associated with long-distance record attempts, was arrested. The new plane for long-distance
records that he had proposed building in June 1937 was never built.
Instead, sometime in the winter of 1938 and 1939, he and his design
bureau began work on the TU-2 light bomber in a special prison camp
set up for that purpose, a design bureau similar to that described by
Solzhenitsyn in the novel *The First Circle*.[39] Even the head of the Red
Air Force, Alksnis, who had dared to sound a public warning in August
1937 about the need for faster military planes was purged. Not as

---

[36] *Tsel' zhizni*, pp. 173-183, translated in Bialer, p. 169.

[37] *New York Times*, July 26, 1937.

[38] An interesting testimonial regarding the personal control Stalin exercised over
aviation can be found in the memoir of A. D. Charomskii, an engineer in charge
of constructing experimental aviation motors. In the early 1930s, a dispute arose
over control of an experimental factory that the automobile industry was attempting to take away from aviation. "The question could only be decided by I. V.
Stalin, and Stalin was in Sochi." So Charomskii was required to fly to the Black
Sea resort to receive Stalin's personal decision giving control of the factory to
aviation. (*Byli industrial'nye: Ocherki i vospominaniia*, Moscow, 1973, p. 116.)

[39] For an interesting account of this prison design bureau, see the memoir of
G. A. Ozerov, which circulated as a *samizdat* manuscript in the Soviet Union,
and was recently published in West Germany (*Tupolevskaia sharaga*, Frankfurt,
1971). He dates the origin of this particular project to the time period cited
(p. 63).

lucky as Tupolev, he was shot on July 29, 1938.[40] According to Yakovlev,

> Stalin reacted very painfully to our failures in Spain. His dissatisfaction and wrath were directed against those who quite recently had been considered heroes and who had been showered with richly deserved honors. . . .[41]

According to another recent memoir by a Soviet aeronautical engineer of that time, G. A. Ozerov, a large proportion of the experienced technical personnel in the aviation industry were arrested in late 1937 and 1938. These included Tupolev, with whom Ozerov worked closely both in and out of prison and Col. Kharlamov, the head of the Central Aviation Institute (TsAGI), with which Tupolev was associated. Ozerov names nearly a hundred arrested engineers, including some who were members of the Academy of Sciences, and estimates that between four hundred fifty and five hundred engineers from the Commissariat of Aviation Industry were arrested at this time. Of these, fifty to seventy were executed, and a hundred or so were lost in the hard labor camps. The remainder, about three hundred, wasted long months in prison cells before their idleness was ended by the NKVD, and they were put back to work in prison design bureaus set up in late 1938 and 1939, to produce new airplanes.[42] The aviation industry was seriously disrupted, and, while the damage wrought by the purges was eventually patched, the months of idleness and disorganization that accompanied this process contributed heavily to the disasters of 1941.

The search for scapegoats is not surprising, given what we now know of Stalin's style and personality. What is surprising, however, is the lack of speed with which the leadership moved to create a fleet of military aircraft that could hold its own with those of fascist powers, particularly designed for air defense and support of the army in the field.

This is not to say that the Stalinist leadership neglected the air force. Quite the contrary. If anything, its control and supervision were too minute. In 1936, the leadership began to step up its military preparedness in general. The overall Soviet defense budget, according to Soviet and Western sources, increased by some eighty percent; and in November of that year, defense industries, including the aviation industry, were taken away from the Commissariat of Heavy Industry as a result of military dissatisfaction with civilian managers. They were grouped under

[40] Medvedev, *Let History Judge*, pp. 211, 405; *Bol'shaia Sovetskaia Entsiklopediia*, Moscow, 1970, vol. I, "Alksnis, Y. I."
[41] *Tsel' zhizni*, pp. 173-183; Bialer, p. 168.
[42] Ozerov, p. 29.

the newly formed Commissariat of the Defense Industry, which was subordinate to the Commissariat of Defense.[43] In January 1937, the Army Air Force was upgraded and its commander became a Deputy Commissar of Defense. 1937 saw an increase in technical aid contracts between Soviet military authorities and Western, particularly American, aircraft companies. As Loy Henderson, at the U.S. Embassy in Moscow, suggested in a memorandum to the Secretary of State, dated May 24, 1937 (the time of all the North Pole excitement):

Despite the fact that Soviet pilots, in Soviet-made planes have established a number of world records, it would appear that the military authorities at least are not satisfied with the development of Soviet aviation and, therefore, have decided to modernize their air fleet through technical assistance contracts with companies such as those enumerated above. [Douglas, Consolidated, Vultee, et al.][44]

Western aviation experts and diplomats noted the Soviet weakness of design in aviation engines and military airframes as early as 1936 and mid-1937. Soviet bombers were clumsy and vulnerable to attack, and Soviet fighters were not up to the latest foreign standards in speed and maneuverability, according to a report from the British air attaché in Moscow, dated June 1937.[45] This was, in fact, a period of technological revolution in world aviation; the Soviet Union did not initiate it and was slow to respond to it.

The U.S.S.R. had the largest air force in the world at this time, and this fact, plus all the publicity concerning Soviet air records, seems to have created inertia and prevented Stalin and other responsible leaders from carrying out a basic change of aviation policy until 1939. This is supported in the memoirs of Yakovlev:

The influence of the Douhet doctrine on certain of our aviation leaders in the 1930s was expressed in the overestimation of bomber aircraft and the clear underestimation of other types of aircraft. The airplanes steadily became larger and larger. For a long time heavy bombers were produced in large series, gladdening the hearts of those who saw in the large machines the basic and decisive striking arm of our air force.

[43] British Foreign Office Archives, N3420/47/38; *Pravda*, August 19 and 22, 1937.
[44] State Dept. Decimal File, National Archives, Washington, D.C., 711.00111 Lic. Consolidated Aircraft Corp. 1/61.
[45] Report of the Air Attaché, March 9, 1936, British Foreign Office, N1483/871/38, and Annual Report for 1936, June 16, 1937, N506/506/38.

To be sure, the gigantic machines made a great impression at parades and attested to the growing potential of the Soviet aviation industry and the accomplishments of Soviet aviation technology. From the military point of view, however, experience has shown that they were ineffectual. The negative side of the gigantomania and even of the records of that time was that they created an atmosphere of complacency and a false notion that aviation could safeguard the frontiers.[46]

Yakovlev notes that the kind of planes often used for setting Soviet air records did not necessarily have military value. "There was an air of confidence that both our sports aircraft *and* our military aircraft were the best in the world. The true state of affairs became known during the events in Spain."[47]

This criticism may have been motivated in part by a quarrel among Soviet aircraft designers, the feeling on the part of a younger designer like Yakovlev that he had been held back by the emphasis and support given the well-established Tupolev and other older designers before 1938.[48] The experience of World War II in the Soviet Union largely validated Yakovlev's viewpoint here. As others have observed, however, such a mistaken emphasis was not unique to Stalin and the Soviet Union. Most of the Western powers in the 1930s, following the strategic theories of the Italian general, Douhet, overestimated the importance of heavy bombers in destroying the morale and industrial fabric of a hostile power, and underestimated the need for tactical aircraft to support an army in the field and provide air defense for their own cities and military installations. Only the Germans and Japanese in the later 1930s, followed tardily by the British, began to build a more balanced air force, with emphasis on lighter and speedier aircraft—fighters and dive bombers, for example.

The Soviets lagged behind in this respect and were reluctant to change. "We must beat the enemy in his lair," was a favorite phrase of the Stalinist leadership at this time, giving their imprimatur to heavy bombers. As late as March 1939, one of Stalin's closest cronies, Voroshilov, the Commissar of Defense, indicated in his report to the Eighteenth Party Congress, that the doctrines of Douhet were still overwhelmingly influential. "As if it were an accomplishment, the People's Commissar of Defense reported to the Congress that the production of light bombers, assault planes, and reconnaissance aircraft had been cut

[46] *Tsel' zhizni*, pp. 243-249; Bialer, p. 207.
[47] Ibid., 173-183; Bialer, p. 167.
[48] Evidence for such rivalry can be found in Ozerov, p. 59, as well as in Yakovlev's own memoir.

two-fold in favor of heavy bombers."[49] The critical difference between the Soviet Union and these other countries was the political style of the Stalinist leadership and the overcentralization of decision-making powers, which existed in aviation as well as other segments of Soviet society. This made it difficult and dangerous for those military specialists and technical experts who saw the need for change to make their influence felt with Stalin and his immediate entourage, which included old civil war political commissars like Voroshilov. Voroshilov and Stalin seemed at this time to prefer horse-cavalry officers like Marshal Budenny to military modernizers like Marshal Tukachevsky and Jan Alksnis. Restricted by the norms of party discipline and intimidated by the purges, officers with unorthodox ideas were unable to change the basic direction of Soviet policy. Only Stalin and his closest associates were able to do this; and they seem to have been captives of inertia in the crucial period between 1937 and 1939. First lashing out at his military and technical specialists for the debacle in Spain, Stalin brought about a fundamental change in policy rather reluctantly.[50]

[49] Yakovlev, pp. 173-183; Bialer, p. 171. The relevant passages in Voroshilov's speech can be found in *XVIII S"ezd VKP(b). Stenograficheskii otchet*, Moscow, 1939, p. 195.

[50] As late as the winter of 1938 and 1939, according to Ozerov, Stalin, acting through the NKVD chief Beria, asked Tupolev to begin work on a new four-engine heavy bomber. Tupolev, though a prisoner of the NKVD, protested that a good heavy bomber already existed and that a new two-engine light bomber ought to be built. Stalin agreed to postpone the new heavy bomber and let Tupolev first work on the TU-2 light bomber (Ozerov, p. 65).

By the middle of 1939, the Red Air Force had begun to correct deficiencies revealed in Spain, according to a recent Soviet article. It had come out well in border clashes with the Japanese Air Force above Khalkin Gol in Mongolia. Installing more powerful engines on the I-16 fighters to increase their speed, introducing a new experimental fast fighter, the I-153, using air-to-air rockets for the first time, and improving their tactical formations, the Soviets overcame initial setbacks and, by August 1939, had gained control of the skies over Mongolia from the Japanese. According to this source, between May and September 1939, the Japanese lost 642 military aircraft to 207 Soviet planes lost. The Soviets brought in their best planes and air aces and had numerical superiority in the major clashes. As Marshal Zhukov, who was in charge of overall Soviet military operations at Khalkin Gol expressed it in his memoirs, "At the beginning of the campaign, the Japanese Air Force beat ours. Their planes were superior to our machines until we received an improved version of the 'Chaika' (I-153) and the I-16. When a group of pilots, headed by Y. V. Smushkevich, all of them Heroes of the Soviet Union, arrived, our air superiority was unquestionable." (*The Memoirs of Marshal Zhukov*, New York, 1971, p. 169.)

The article noted above, based on hitherto uncited Soviet military archives, is by M. V. Novikov. ("V nebe Khalkin-Gola," *Voprosy istorii*, no. 3, 1974, 201-204.)

According to Prof. Alvin D. Coox of California State University, however, this contradicts classified Japanese military records that he used and interviews with surviving Japanese pilots who were at Khalkin Gol. According to these sources,

During 1937 and most of 1938, the press continued to feature talk of new record attempts, despite the warnings of some military aviation experts of the need to concentrate on military aviation for defense, and despite the purge of designers associated with previous records. A non-stop, around-the-world flight was talked of, and in January 1938, M. V. Vodopianov, a flyer whose novel *A Pilot's Dream* had set the stage for the North Pole landing, published a lead article in *Pravda*, the central party newspaper. Entitled "A New Year's Dream," this article proposed a landing at the South Pole, supported by the new Soviet icebreaker, the *Joseph Stalin*, then being constructed. When Soviet landings had been accomplished at the South Pole as well as the North Pole, Vodopianov bubbled, "The world will rotate on a Bolshevik axis."[51] The prominence given record flights and the talk of further such exploits well into 1938[52] leads one to conclude that their political usefulness to the regime was still given priority over an exclusive concern with military aviation, particularly a program focused on fighters and light bombers that could support the Red Army in the field. Only in October 1938, as already noted, did Stalin publicly indicate a deemphasis of attempts at spectacular records, citing his concern for the lives and safety of the pilots. By then, the obsolescence of much of Soviet military aviation was widely known, and Stalin had withdrawn his air force from Spain. The purges were tapering off with the removal of the NKVD chief Yezhov. The country began to settle down to the hard

---

the Soviets improved their performance in the air toward the end of the summer for the reasons given above, but never gained air superiority, even though the Japanese continued to use their old T-95 fighters and did not bring in their best air aces from China. The Japanese, in fact, considered Khalkin Gol a "major victory for them in the air but a disaster on the ground." The Japanese did not think highly of the technical quality of Soviet aviation, noting problems with aircraft engines, a common observation of other foreign military observers in this period. Classified Japanese military records showed a loss of 149 Japanese aircraft from beginning to end of the incident, while they counted 1252 Soviet planes destroyed. Which version are we to believe? While the Soviets repelled the Japanese at Khalkin Gol, it seems likely, given their earlier experience in Spain and their later problems in the air during 1941, that their claims to overwhelming victory against the Japanese Air Force at Khalkin Gol are exaggerated. The fact that 96% of Soviet air losses in this incident were attributed to Japanese fighters is consistent with the other information in this article concerning the weakness of Soviet tactical aviation at this time. As Prof. Coox has put it, "I used to think that the Japanese claims were absurd, but the more I examined Japanese records and the more I interviewed surviving Japanese combat pilots, fighter and bomber, the more I became convinced that, even allowing for some exaggeration and some duplication, the Japanese won the war in the air in 1939." (Letter to the author, August 4, 1974.)

[51] *Pravda*, January 1, 1938.
[52] See, for example, *Izvestiia*, July 30, 1938.

task of repairing the damage done by the purges and increasing its military preparedness.

Only one air record attempt was recorded for 1939. The projects for an around-the-world flight, and a landing at the South Pole slipped into oblivion at this time. Only between 1939 and 1941 did the Soviet government begin to shift its policy in military aviation and turn to younger designers in its efforts to catch up.[53]

Yakovlev, who designed the most successful Soviet fighters of World War II (half the Soviet fighters built between 1941 and 1945 were Yaks) received little high-level support until then. The most lavish support had gone to designers like Tupolev and Polikarpov, designer of the I-15 and I-16 fighters, in the Central Aviation Institute and the Zhukhovsky Air Academy, respectively, a symptom of the overcentralization in research and development and the lack of internal checks and balances fostered by Stalinism. Yakovlev felt strongly that this situation was another cause of the lag in Soviet aviation:

> Another error consisted in the fact that up to the end of the 1930s, there were only two major design bureaus in our country— one for bombers and the other for fighters and each of them monopolized its special field.

> To be sure, there were also several small design groups at the time, but most of them had no substantial influence on the development of Soviet aviation. For the entire decade preceding the war, it was chiefly the airplanes of A. N. Tupolev and N. N. Polikarpov that were mass produced for the armed forces. Despite all the outstanding merits of these designers, the existence of only two design bureaus for a country like the USSR was a serious miscalculation.[54]

The younger Yakovlev had to make do with the workers and equipment of an old bed factory for his design bureau and experimental factory until the later 1930s, and was employed designing small sports aircraft for aviation clubs. The same was true for another major team of young designers, Mikoyan and Gurevich, creators of the MiG series of fighters. Lavish public attention and rewards came to these designers only in 1939 and 1940. On April 27, 1939, after the successful design of a new fighter in the record time of a few months, Yakovlev was summoned to the Kremlin. Stalin and Voroshilov presented him with the Order of Lenin, a new ZIS limousine and 100,000 rubles.[55] When the first of the new Stalin prizes was announced on March 15, 1941, ten of

---

[53] *Tsel' zhizni*, pp. 173-183; Bialer, p. 171.
[54] Ibid.　　　　　　　　　　[55] *Tsel' zhizni*.

the twenty top prizes for new inventions went to designers of military aircraft and aircraft armaments.[56]

If not too little, much of this activity came too late to be of much help in the early months of the war with Germany. Most of these newer aircraft were only being tested in 1940 and 1941. While military aircraft of Soviet design eventually proved themselves against the Luftwaffe in the later years of the war, Soviet air defenses on June 22, 1941, were woefully inadequate. Only about one hundred of the new Yak-1, the only Soviet fighter that could hold its own adequately against German fighters at the beginning of the war, were in position in the Western border districts.[57] Official Soviet figures indicate that some seventy-eight hundred planes were lost in the first three and a half months following June 22, 1941, two thousand in the first two days. The German Air Force had only about two thousand combat aircraft on the Eastern Front at the beginning of the war, compared to ten thousand Soviet military planes. For the Soviet Union, the overemphasis on heavy bombers proved a disaster. "During the first and second days of the war, the Soviet Command committed the bulk of its bomber force to massive ineffectual strikes, during which it was virtually destroyed. Field Marshal von Kesselring, Commander of the German Second Air Army, describes the Luftwaffe's encounter with those bombers, which were flying in tactically impossible formations without fighter escort as 'infanticide.' "[58]

The error of the 1930s was eventually corrected, and the priorities in aviation were completely reversed. During the remainder of World War II, only seventy-nine heavy bombers were produced by Soviet factories. The overwhelming emphasis was on fighters, light bombers, and other tactical aircraft. By 1943, the Soviets had regained control of their own airspace, but at an incalculable cost in human lives and a razor-thin escape from total defeat.

What can one conclude from all this? Yakovlev's explanation, connecting Soviet mistakes with the emphasis on strategic bombers, with complacency bred by spectacular air records of little military significance, with a lack of competing design bureaus makes sense, but is incomplete. What Yakovlev fails to do is to connect these phenomena directly with Stalin and his form of rule. He puts the responsibility on unnamed "air experts" and "would-be tacticians" without being more specific or deepening his analysis. That he does not place the responsibility squarely on Stalin's shoulders is not surprising, given the sensitivities of Soviet censorship at the time his memoirs were published and

[56] *Izvestiia*, March 15, 1941.   [57] *The Soviet Air Force*, pp. 1-16.
[58] Albert von Kesselring, *A Soldier's Record*, New York, 1954, p. 90.

the fact that Yakovlev owed his own rapid rise after 1938 to Stalin's patronage. He became Stalin's favorite designer during World War II and was himself virtual dictator of aeronautical R and D during this period, arousing the resentment and jealousy of many other engineers who considered him Stalin's lackey.[59]

A more adequate explanation must be sought in the intimate connection between Stalinism and certain kinds of technology, especially those projects of a proportion calculated to make the biggest publicity splash. In summing up, then, the findings of this study support the following interpretation: Soviet stress in the 1930s on the Douhet doctrine of strategic offense, which emphasized the role of heavy bombers in modern warfare, was not the only reason for Soviet aviation's unpreparedness in 1941. The need for political legitimacy and security led Stalin, in the period from 1933 to 1938, to stress a series of aviation stunts that had little relevance to the needs of Soviet defense and crippled Soviet military aviation unnecessarily in the early years of World War II. The particular way in which aviation technology was used by the Stalinists to emphasize the legitimacy of their regime was ultimately of less real use to the Soviet Union than a greater and earlier emphasis on air defense capabilities would have been.[60]

Stalin, of course, did not originate the spectacular air shows and world record competitions; they were already part of an international aeronautical culture in the 1920s, well before he made wide use of them. Stalin and his supporters did give their own political twist to these events in the unique conditions of Soviet Society during the 1930s. Stalin's own name and reputation were more closely associated with the practice of technological legitimation than any other major leader during this period, and aviation was one of the most spectacular forms this practice took. Although the results were often impressive at the time, and may have created a temporary euphoria useful to Stalin in achieving his political purposes during the purges, the results also involved great risks and were sometimes as quickly dissipated as the balloons with Stalin's picture that floated above Moscow on Aviation Day. World

[59] "Among the workers of the aviation industry Yakovlev was not liked, since they considered, not without foundation, that being an advisor of Himself [*Samogo*, Ozerov's ironic term for Stalin] involved certain compromises of moral principles on the part of Yakovlev." (Ozerov, p. 54.)

[60] Not only was the development of fighter aircraft and light tactical bombers neglected, the promising Soviet program in radar technology was seriously disrupted. (See the memoir by the chief engineer of the radar program in the 1930s, P. K. Oshchepkov, *Zhizn' i mechta*, Moscow, 1965; and the excellent analysis of the Soviet program in this area by John Erickson, "Radio-location and the air defence problem: The design and development of Soviet radar, 1934-40," in *Science Studies* 2, 1972, 241-268.)

aviation records, as the Soviets soon discovered, were very dangerous to undertake and easily shattered. A number of Soviet flyers were lost in such attempts. As early as November 13, 1938, the Soviets had already lost to a British bomber the nonstop distance record set in 1937.[61] An attempt to set a new nonstop distance record by flying from Moscow to New York in time for the New York World's Fair ended ingloriously on April 29, 1939. The Soviet test pilot, General Kokkinaki, and a colleague crashed on a remote island in New Brunswick, Canada, and were brought to the World's Fair in an American rescue plane.[62] While their flight was an impressive one, the finale was not the one the Soviet leadership desired. That event ended the Soviet effort to capture world aviation records prior to World War II. One can see a precedent in these earlier attempts for the space race and the political uses made of it by both the Soviet Union and the United States following the launching of the first Soviet sputnik in October 1957, in time for the fortieth anniversary of the Bolshevik Revolution. Technological legitimation is clearly a game suited for two or more players. The achievements in such politically motivated games have sometimes been real, but so have the costs in the diversion of resources and attention from other, sometimes more vital areas.

[61] *New York Times*, November 13, 1938.
[62] Ibid., April 29, 1939.

CONCLUSIONS

I would be among the first to declare that the long run purpose of all empirical research is the construction of sound theories—which are no more than verifiable generalizations about the world we live in. But, this said . . . I believe there is more to be learned about the actual mechanisms, the dynamics of social change, from the careful reading of a single [empirical] study . . . each account complete with penetrating study of the nature of social roles and norms in their relation to change—than in all the theories of change, at least as presently constituted in the social sciences, put together.
Robert Nisbet[1]

No man knows the revolution he makes.
Friedrich Engels[2]

One of the central questions for understanding the Soviet Union concerns the way in which Soviet society in its early years reestablished sufficient cohesion to engage in normal social life, including material production and distribution. After a period of severe social conflict—seven years of world war, revolution, and civil war—in which the fabric of Imperial Russian society was torn apart, and material production in both agriculture and industry fell to a small fraction of its previous level, Soviet society after 1921 faced the difficult task of recreating a sense of social cooperation to ensure its survival and growth.

The majority of historians until recently have been so fascinated by the revolution itself, its leaders, and its various manifestations that its aftermath and many of its long-term social consequences have been neglected. Yet wars and revolutions are rarer in human history than the time consumed by processes in which a society organizes itself for material production and distribution, and for the normal social relations in which people work, play, and try to ensure the continuity of themselves, their culture, and their society. Questions connected with some of the latter activities are the ones that concern us most here. The time has come to pose, with greater incisiveness, questions concerning the

---

[1] *Social Change*, New York, 1972, pp. vi-vii.
[2] Friedrich Engels, *Collected Works*, Moscow, 1954, Volume III.

aftermath of the Russian revolution and the kind of society that emerged from the rubble of the revolutionary years. The technical intelligentsia is a crucial group for understanding many facets of this process because it occupied a middle position in Soviet society during these years. While largely subordinated to the power structure, it was at the same time charged with directing the work of an increasing proportion of the population, and it had the specialized technological knowledge without which industrialization could not have proceeded. A study of the technostructure is well suited not only for gaining some answers to the central question posed above, but also for yielding some theoretical insights concerning the relationship between technology and society.

In the years after 1917, particularly 1928, Soviet society faced a series of choices: in foreign policy, in political structure and leadership, in broad economic policy, in questions of social welfare, and in choices of technology, with implications for all of the above. It is on the latter area where we need to focus in order to draw a major conclusion from this study.

As indicated in chapter 13, most of the technology adopted by the Soviet Union in the years covered by this study was Western in origin, although the degree of adaptation and the number of original inventions by Soviet technologists may have been somewhat greater than previously thought. The Soviet Union continued the prerevolutionary practice of wide technological borrowing from the West, and Western technology predominated in most areas of the economy. Despite a mass campaign for inventiveness, the original inventions that resulted met almost insuperable barriers to effective adoption. Widespread adaptations of Western technology to fit Soviet conditions did not change the basically Western nature of most Soviet technology. Yet the evidence of this study also indicates that the social relations connected with the use of such technology were in key respects quite different from those in the West. A major implication of this is that similarities in technology adopted by industrial societies do not necessarily determine the kind of social relations that may emerge. Quite the contrary. Differing cultural traditions, ideological climate, and social structure at the time of adoption are crucial factors. A rigid technological determinism seems contradicted by the evidence of this study.

The Soviet Union, no doubt, had to industrialize in order to survive as an independent nation. I would not dispute the arguments of Theodore von Laue and others on that score.[3] At the same time, the decision to industrialize, borrowing most of its early technology from the West, did not lead to the same kind of social relations in the organization of

[3] See, for example, von Laue's *Why Lenin? Why Stalin?*, Philadelphia, 1971.

work based on such technology. The central issue is the alternative form of social organization that was adopted in the Soviet Union and why. Most of the preceding study has focused on the nature of some of these social relations, and does not require repeating here. But perhaps the most dramatic example of difference can be found in the way social conflicts involving the technical intelligentsia were handled in this period, and particularly the novel way in which Soviet society dealt with class conflict beginning in the mid-1930s.

Immediately following the Bolshevik Revolution of 1917, the Soviet technostructure—particularly those members with formal higher education—found themselves more isolated and vulnerable than in the previous years. Largely urban, mostly drawn from families of the small middle and upper classes of Imperial Russian society, generally nationalistic, and believers in hierarchy (though one of talents rather than of birth), these technical specialists were immersed in a sea of peasants and working class people whose energies and hostilities had been released in the revolutionary process. They found themselves not infrequently the targets of specialist-baiting, their authority and ability to direct the work of those whom they had traditionally supervised, undermined. Like the Communist party itself, the technostructure was a small minority of the population facing the problem of how once again to organize its work effectively. Like the Communist party, it faced a crisis of legitimacy: how could it gain authority in the eyes of the Soviet population in order to exert powers that would enable technical specialists to carry out their tasks?

Although as early as 1918, these two small minorities—the Communist party and the technostructure—began to develop a working relationship, it was a fragile one, often marked by tension, suspicion, and mutual hostility. Most likely two major factors kept the alliance from breaking apart entirely: the mutual need to survive in an atmosphere of great insecurity, and the overlapping of certain values, particularly Promethean values in which both groups shared the belief that mankind could consciously increase the forces of production and manipulate nature to improve the material standard of life. The forces of mutual attraction proved stronger than the forces of mutual repulsion, as represented by differing ideas concerning the value of private enterprise, of professional autonomy, of political forms such as democracy, socialism or liberalism, and of the proper way to industrialize (differences that, it should be realized, existed also within the technostructure). The alliance survived the most troubled times, including the years from 1928 to 1931. After 1931, the crisis of legitimacy faced by both groups was resolved in a unique way. The Communist party and Stalin in particular used, along with other forms of legitimation, technological achievements designed and carried out under the supervision of the technical intelligentsia, to help legitimize the party's and Stalin's own claims to power. At the same time, especially after 1931, the Communist party increasingly used its power to raise the authority and status of the technical intelligentsia, legitimizing its powers over the working class.

This series of measures was accompanied by an ideological innovation with far-reaching implications. Stalin and the Central Committee in 1935 put forward the view that the new technical intelligentsia would be a model for the development of a Communist (classless) society in the U.S.S.R., in which the working class would eventually be raised to the level of the technical intelligentsia. Stalin put his own stamp on this idea by insisting that the new technical intelligentsia would be composed of two streams: one composed of those with practical experience, but not necessarily possessed of formal education, who would earn positions as technical specialists by their achievements in production, and the other composed of those who passed through the formal educational system. This view—together with tough new measures on labor discipline—was intended to increase social cohesion and moderate class conflict between workers and technical specialists. Ironically, instead of the hoped for convergence this attitude insured, in practice, that the conflict between *praktiki* and those with formal technical education continued throughout this period, despite increasing efforts by the party to conciliate such intraclass conflict. While there is evidence that other forms of conflict, including ethnic and sex role conflict, which the authorities tried at times to mitigate, played some role in relations between the technostructure and the working class—as well as between some elements within the technostructure—these conflicts do not show up as major themes in the historical sources of the period. Interclass and intraclass conflict was a major theme, although it was rarely labeled such in the historical sources. The evidence of such conflict is abundant; and the party and government gave major attention to some of its manifestations, such as specialist-baiting, and disputes over wages and working conditions.

At least from the mid-1930s on, class conflict was no longer viewed as normal or acceptable in Soviet society. The U.S.S.R. was proclaimed a nation of nonantagonistic classes, no matter how much evidence to the contrary there may have been. Workers were told that their role was to study, work hard, and raise the level of their skills to that of the technical intelligentsia, not to oppose their authority. The path to a classless (Communist) society was to be through massive upward mobility, through the upgrading of industrial skills and general cultural levels, supervised in large part by the technical intelligentsia in factory schools, apprenticeship programs, and other forms of on-the-job training. Although the training received may have been similar, the ideological climate in which it was carried out was radically unlike that in Western industrial societies.

In the West, the dominant view was that, given the complex division of labor, social differences were inevitable, and the attempt was made to mitigate, rather than abolish class conflict by channeling it away from revolutionary and violent manifestations into collective bargaining.[4] Workers generally had the right to strike, at least as a last resort, in negotiating wages and working conditions, with collective bargaining the preferred way of moderating economic class conflicts. Soviet society in the 1930s developed a very different set of social relations in this area, although not without some grass-roots opposition and alienation— the degree and consequences of which are hard to gauge. Wages were largely turned over to technical experts and industrial managers to set and regulate, thus eliminating collective bargaining over wages and the right to strike. Taylorist methods of "scientific management," preferred by Lenin but not fully instituted in the 1920s, became the chief means by which wages for the working class were set after 1931. The technical intelligentsia staffed the bureaus (*buro normirovaniia*) and provided the experts who set them, within the general guidelines of the party and within the general wage funds appropriated by the government and administered by industrial management.[5]

Just as the powers of production specialists vis-à-vis workers were strengthened both legally and ideologically, so the authority of teachers over the work of students was strengthened, and research work was increasingly professionalized, shutting out to a greater extent the worker-inventors whom technical specialists often regarded as a plague. Although interference from party, police, and, to a lesser extent, trade union officials never ceased during this period in the major work en-

[4] See, for example, Ralf Dahrendorf, *Class and Class Conflict in Industrial Society*, Stanford, 1959.

[5] On Taylorism, see the article by K. E. Bailes, "Alexei Gastev and The Controversy over Taylorism in Early Soviet Society," (*Soviet Studies*, July 1977). On Soviet wage policy and socialist competition, see Abram Bergson, *The Structure of Soviet Wages*, Cambridge, 1944; *KPSS v rezoliutsiiakh*, Moscow, 1954, vol. 3, p. 144; Stalin, *Problems of Leninism*, Moscow, 1953, p. 674; Isaac Deutscher, *Soviet Trade Unions*, London, 1950, pp. 100-116; Robert Conquest, *Industrial Workers in the USSR*, New York, 1967, pp. 44-94; Ivan Mikhailovich Samokhvalov, "Rukovodstvo partii massovym razvitiem sotsialisticheskogo sorevnovaniia v promyshlennosti v period 1936-41," Soviet diss., 1965, in Lenin Library, Moscow.

vironments of the technical intelligentsia, interference from rank-and-file workers and students diminished to a large extent, as hierarchical relations became more fixed.

Given this trade-off between the technostructure and the power structure, together with the importance of industrialization to the regime's survival, as well as the dramatic increase in the numbers of technical specialists—many of them drawn from working class backgrounds—it should not be surprising to find their numbers in the Communist party increasing rapidly in the 1930s. They began as rank-and-file members, but, in the wake of the purges of the later 1930s, they increasingly became party officials at the provincial levels and important government officials and economic managers. If the technical intelligentsia was to be the model for the transition to a classless society, it was logical that its members should gradually merge into the power structure at higher levels. This was particularly true for younger members who had the right political tickets: i.e., working class backgrounds and Communist party membership unblemished by a record of anti-Stalin opposition. By 1941 the technostructure was becoming the vanguard of the future in Stalin's Russia, although the process may not have been entirely clear to contemporaries. What was left unresolved was the relative importance of formal higher technical education, which was a cohesive force among those who had it, but often a divisive one between those who had it and those who lacked it. Stalinist biases in this area toward the *praktiki* had not yet given those with diplomas a decided advantage, although they appeared to be gaining ground as managers in some key segments of industry, and to have penetrated the ranks of party officialdom in sizable numbers for the first time after 1937.

Had the technostructure as a whole become part of the ruling class by 1941? If "ruling class" is defined, not as Marx defined it, in terms of the private legal ownership of the means of production, but in terms of effective control over society, can the technostructure be said to have gained such effective control by 1941? The evidence of this study does not support such a conclusion. Yet members of the technostructure did enjoy increasing access to power after 1937 by comparison with representatives from the other two major social classes of Soviet society, the peasantry and the industrial working class. Members of these classes could still achieve social mobility, but, increasingly, that meant joining the technical intelligentsia, in effect changing their class.

In political organization, the role of the technical intelligentsia during this period was distinct and became progressively more important. This group had shifted from a position of considerable tension with those in power in the early years of this study, to a position of increasing integration and cooperation, while at the same time it changed in social composition and role and grew enormously in size. Its relationship to political power was a complex one throughout this period, however. It would be a distortion to say that all elements of the technical intelligentsia were in harmony with the ruling elite by the beginning of World War II. The shift from conflict to increasing cooperation and integration must be understood in relative terms. The ruling elite of Stalinist society was being drawn increasingly from the technical intelligentsia by the end of this period, but the technostructure was far from a unified group, and only part of it, not necessarily the most competent, gained access to the higher circles of the Stalinist elite, which directly controlled the means of production. Stalin and his closest associates still preferred to keep technical specialists in positions of subordination to themselves. Stalinist wills continued to be the final arbiters of all important policy decisions at the end of this period. Elements of the technostructure, though, had influence and some power, even though it was far from clear that they could come to power in their own right, particularly those with formal higher education.

By the beginning of World War II, the most that can be said is that the basis of recruitment for leading roles in the Communist party had shifted preponderantly from the working class and from the revolutionary and cultural strata of the intelligentsia to the stratum of the technical intelligentsia. Stalinism, both as a way of governing and as a social system, included—following in this respect Lenin's precedent—a concern for technology and technological choices that grew stronger with the introduction of the Five-Year Plans. Particularly with the purges and the prelude to World War II, Stalin and his associates became more concerned to recruit younger technical specialists—whose loyalty they hoped would be more certain, given the way in which they were recruited and educated—into the more powerful echelons of Soviet society. They put increasing stress on technical backgrounds as a major criterion—albeit not the only one—for promotion into policy-making and high executive positions.

Although elements of the technical intelligentsia did not escape the purges—far from it—as a group, their status and access to power increased in the aftermath of these events. Yet we should keep in mind that there were major differences in access to power among the elements that comprised the technical intelligentsia. Certain elements were more likely to be recruited into administrative and party roles, and others to remain involved primarily in technical roles. My computer analysis, using biographical data from approximately eleven hundred members of the technical intelligentsia who were active in the years of this study, and who were singled out for recognition between 1958 and 1965, suggests what some of the criteria for power may have been. (For the computer tables and methodology on which these conclusions are based, see the appendix.)

To sum up the brief statistical comparison made in the appendix, Soviet citizens with a background in the technical intelligentsia, who eventually rose to high positions in the power structure during the post-Stalin era, differed considerably from those who became prominent largely in technical positions. Although higher technical education was almost a sine qua non for membership in either group (indicating the degree to which the *praktiki*, who were still prominent at the production level, and worker-inventors had been cut out from major recognition in these two elites by 1958 to 1965), in other respects the politicians tended to be closer in age, more proletarian in social background, and more provincial in education than those who remained technologists. The politicians were trained mostly during the first three Five-Year Plans, in areas reflecting the priorities of the 1928 to 1941 era, especially metallurgy and mechanical engineering. They were largely Slavic (with Russians overrepresented), and contained a significant sprinkling of Armenians and Georgians, but almost no Jews. Turks were underrepresented by comparison with the general population, and women even more so. As expected, they were mostly party members, a majority of whom joined before 1941 (with a large influx, nearly a third, immediately after the purges and before the German invasion). Their career patterns also showed a primary orientation toward combining production experience, which usually came early in a politician's career, with a later climb up the ladder of party or government administration, unlike most of the technologists. Few of the politicians had any direct experience in research and development, or as teachers in higher technical education, while the technologists had heavy concentration in both career areas (Table A.8).

As interesting as such conclusions based on statistics are, they can provide only some of the parameters of a group—in this case, two elites that should be considered unrepresentative of the technical intelligentsia as a whole before 1941. They should be taken primarily for what they indicate concerning criteria associated with later success and public recognition among members of the Soviet technostructure, and differences between those who entered the power structure and those who became prominent in technical roles. They may also raise important questions for further research, and in that spirit they are cited here. (The reader interested in a fuller discussion of this statistical comparison should turn to the appendix.)

The discussion so far leaves unanswered the question of how *active* a role the technical intelligentsia played in the development of Soviet society between 1917 and 1941. Were its members simply the executors of others' decisions, the passive recipients of orders and of both punishments and rewards? Or were they involved in a continual interaction with the power structure and the rest of society, initiating and debating plans and projects among themselves and with the power structure, and exerting influence in a number of ways? The evidence of this study suggests that the latter view is closer to the truth. While it might seem excessive at first glance to argue that the Communist party and the technical intelligentsia were the two most important group influences in the development of Soviet society during the first generation of its existence, this view may not be so far off the mark. While the Communist party, and particularly its leadership, was the final arbiter of policy decisions and the major organizer of social change in this period, in fact it relied far more heavily than often realized on the plans and projects, advice, executive ability, and knowledge of the technostructure, particularly its core group, the graduate technologists.

The Bolsheviks took power with two major sets of goals: egalitarian goals linked with their concepts of socialism and Communism, and the goal of further industrialization—raising the level of productive forces. The egalitarian goals were postponed in order to create what was viewed as the long-term means to the final end of an egalitarian (classless) society, namely industrialization. Whether this choice was a historical necessity, as Stalinists argued, or involved a mistaken overemphasis on inequality, as Mao and his followers have argued more recently, will be left for the reader to decide.[6] The point is that, given this choice, the Bolsheviks had no blueprint for industrialization and no direct experience in organizing it. Those who supplied them were the technical specialists. It is no exaggeration to state that most of the major projects of the period between 1917 and 1941, and many of the techniques of planning, were already being worked out by the technical intelligentsia in its offices, laboratories, and professional congresses in the period before 1917 and during the 1920s.[7] Whether one looks at the prehistory

[6] See, for example, *On the Question of Stalin*, Peking, 1963.

[7] This point is made by Leon Smolinski in "Grinevetskii and Soviet Industrialization," *Survey*, April 1968, 111-115, and strongly corroborated in such primary and secondary sources as the following: Ministerstvo putei soobscheniia, *Trudy XI S"ezda russkikh deiateli po vodianym putiam*, St. Petersburg, 1909; *Trudy XII S"ezda* (of the same group), St. Petersburg, 1910; N. P. Puzyrevskii, *Mysli ob ustroistve vodnykh putei soobshcheniia*, St. Petersburg, 1906; *Trudy I vserossiiskogo eletrotekhnicheskogo s"ezda*, St. Petersburg, 1900; *Trudy VIII vserossiiskogo elektrotekhnicheskogo s"ezda (1912)*, Moscow, 1920; G. O. Levit, *Istoriia energeticheskikh obshchestv SSSR*, Moscow, 1957, pp. 12-23; *Trudy GOELRO. Doku-*

of the GOELRO Plan for electrification, the creation of a second metallurgical base in the East (the Urals-Kuzbass combine), giant hydroelectric projects such as Volkhovstroi ·and Dneprostroi, canal projects such as the Volga-Don, the creation of an automotive and aviation industry, the use of chemical fertilizers in agriculture, the material balances system in planning, or the adoption of Taylorist methods for the organization of industrial work, we find not only precedents for them in the prerevolutionary history of the Russian technostructure, but often detailed projects and debates in their professional journals and congresses.

It is no accident, as the popular Russian expression goes, that Lenin called the plans of the technical intelligentsia embodied in the GOELRO project, "our second party program." As early as December 22, 1920, while creating the State Planning Commission (*Gosplan*), and insisting that it be staffed with several hundred non-Bolshevik technologists, the large majority of them hostile to Bolshevik ideology, Lenin wrote:

> In my view this is the second program of the party. We have the [1919] party program. This is the political program. . . . It must be supplemented by a second party program, a plan of work for the creation of our economy and bringing it up to the level of contemporary technology.[8]

Lenin not only permitted the prerevolutionary congresses of technical specialists in various branches of technology to be revived after 1920, he insisted that, where appropriate, *Gosplan* projects be submitted to these congresses for wide debate and correction.[9] While one should not underestimate the role of economists, excluded from this study yet important in *Gosplan* during the 1920s and 1930s, it seems safe to say that

---

menty i materialy, Moscow, 1960, vol. I; V. I. Grinevetskii, *Poslevoennye perspektivy russkoi promyshlennosti*, 2nd ed., Moscow, 1922; F. Ya. Nesteruk, *Razvitie gidroenergetiki SSSR*, Moscow, 1963; Akademiia nauk SSSR, *Stroitel' pervykh gidroelektrostantsii v SSSR. Akademik Genrikh Osipovich Graftio 1869-1949*, Moscow, 1953; V. V. Prokof'ev, op. cit., pp. 22ff.; *Ocherki istorii tekhniki v Rossii (1861-1917)*, Moscow, 1973. See also the following Soviet dissertations: N. G. Fillipov, "Russkoe tekhnicheskoe obshchestvo 1866-1905gg.," Moscow, 1965; V. M. Potemkin, "KPSS v bor'be za stroitel'stvo i osvoenie Kuznetskogo metallurgicheskogo kombinata, 1929-1932," MGU, 1955; V. K. Korol'kov, "Bor'ba KPSS za sozdanie i osvoenie magnitogorskogo metalkombinata im. I. V. Stalina, 1929-1933 gg.," Leningrad, 1955; E. V. Kartsovnik, "Leninskii plan elektrifikatsii i bor'ba partii za sooruzhenie Dneprovskoi gidroelektrostantsii im. V. I. Lenina," Kiev State University, 1964. Copies of these dissertations are in the Lenin Library, Moscow.

[8] *Trudy GOELRO*, vol. I, p. 595.

[9] *Energetika narodnogo khoziastva v plane GOELRO*, Moscow, 1966, p. 6.

most of the projects chosen for development in the 1920s and the first Five-Year Plans were selected from among those initiated by the technical intelligentsia, although the degree of modification by party officials and economists deserves closer study, a task at present difficult due to lack of access to Soviet archives.

The same generalization would hold for the creation of a network of industrial research institutes after 1918. These projects were initiated by technical specialists and approved by the party. The party and Bolshevik government put their stamp on them mainly by the degree of selectivity they showed in those approved, the financing they dispensed, the work they assigned to these institutes, and the final authority they had over the personnel employed in industrial research. The situation in this area, however, was genuinely the result of an interaction between the technostructure and the power structure. As it would be rash to argue that the two groups were equal partners, it would be equally rash to portray the technical intelligentsia as purely passive and without considerable influence over the results.[10]

The same arguments could be made in the areas of higher technical education and work at the production level, based on the evidence of this study. Although varying over the time span of this study, the technical intelligentsia had considerable influence as well as some powers over conditions in all these areas. They clearly remained junior partners throughout this period of industrialization; and trials, like those of the Shakhty and Industrial party engineers, together with other measures described in this study, were intended to keep them subordinate to the Stalinist power structure. Nonetheless, one can conclude that these two groups proved indispensable to each other. The specialists provided the technical knowledge, and the Communist party supplied the link, largely missing before the revolution, between the masses of the population and the plans and projects of the technostructure. That is, the Communist party supplied the machinery of organization—the combination of force with material and moral incentives—to realize more rapidly much of what the technical intelligentsia had only dreamed before the revolution. Whatever one may think of the value of such rapid industrialization and the methods employed—many of them brutal and also, perhaps, not the most efficient, certainly not the most

---

[10] The major failing of Jeremy Azrael's pioneering and very useful study, *Managerial Power and Soviet Politics*, in my opinion, is that he does not distinguish adequately between the technical specialists and industrial managers, or delineate sufficiently their complex relationship; nor does he show the degree to which the technical intelligentsia was an active force in shaping Soviet development policies in the 1920s and 1930s.

humane—one needs to understand the nature of the partial symbiosis achieved between these two groups. Its historical consequences have been profound.

The questions above have dealt mainly with the external relations of the technical intelligentsia: its dealings with other groups in Soviet society. How cohesive was this group? Was the technical intelligentsia a consciously unified interest group in its own right, or is it better understood in terms of a variety of competing subgroups, serving broader, more heterogeneous bureaucratic groups, such as the economic commissariats, the party bureaucracy, the military, etc. From the evidence presented, it can be understood best as both, that is, sometimes consciously unified across bureaucratic lines and professional specialties to defend certain broad interests, and also often in conflict among its subgroups over specific political and professional issues. There were, for example, broad areas of agreement over the need for certain kinds of working conditions, including security from specialist-baiting and more clearly defined powers and responsibilities in their work environments, together with a rising social status. But there were also frequent conflicts among bureaucratic and professional interest groups within the technostructure concerning the adoption of particular types of technology, the role of professional organizations, the political role of the technical intelligentsia vis-à-vis the government and Communist party, the form and content of higher technical education, the organization of research, and introduction of inventions, etc. The conflict between *praktiki* and diplomaed specialists has already been given detailed treatment.

This said, it nonetheless seems justified to view this group first as a whole, rather than initially devoting a monograph or series of books to its various subgroups in isolation. This is especially true because the power structure viewed the technical intelligentsia as a significant group in itself that required separate treatment and, in many respects, a common approach. Members of the technostructure also frequently viewed themselves this way. The term *tekhnicheskaia intelligentsia* entered the Soviet vocabulary in these years because it was often needed to describe a key element of Soviet society. With the present macrocosmic view as a basis, it will be useful for future studies to concentrate in more depth on individual subgroups of the technical intelligentsia and their interaction, particularly when they conflicted over differing goals or conceptions of their role.

The macrocosmic approach leads to another important question for this study. By comparison with the prerevolutionary period—the characterization given here of the Russian technostructure preceding the 1917 revolutions—what did technical specialists gain and what did they lose in the generation after 1917? Not only did they gradually gain the upper hand over the working class, they no longer had significant opposition to their roles from those grounded in a religious view of nature, as for example, with Russian Orthodoxy in important respects, and Islam among many of the Asiatic peoples of the U.S.S.R. Nor was there a significant conservation movement that could oppose their projects effectively on scientific grounds. Although such a movement had arisen in the Tsarist period, after 1928 the tiny conservation society that still existed had only a handful of members, mostly biologists and students with no significant governmental, monetary, or moral support. In its public statements, this society paid obeisance to industrialization and sought only to prevent the most blatant ravaging of natural resources, such as forests and wild animals.[11] A significant conservation mentality began to develop only in the late Stalin era and more notably after the 1950s.[12] Even less evident by 1941 were any public doubts of the engineer's prominence in Soviet society, such as those later expressed by Pasternak in lines such as these: "Does a canal justify human sacrifices? He is godless, your engineer, and what power he acquired!"[13]

Despite friction with both the working class and the power structure, the technical intelligentsia gained far more material and moral support for carrying out its projects than it had had during the late Imperial period. In terms of resources allocated to capital investment in industrialization and to higher technical education—although formal education had a lower priority than many teachers in this area would have liked—the technostructure benefitted enormously, although not all its subgroups benefitted equally. Advocates of chemicalization, electrifica-

---

[11] *Front nauki i tekhniki*, no. 12, 1933, 77-79; no. 6, 1938, 63-82; *Priroda i sotsialisticheskoe khoziastvo. Sbornik*, no. 6, Moscow, 1933, pp. 185-188; no. 7, Moscow, 1935; no. 8, Chast' 2, Moscow, 1941, pp. 482-484; *Okhrana prirody. Sbornik zakonodatel'nykh aktov*, Moscow, 1961, pp. 4-9; *Trudy pervogo vsesoiuznogo s"ezda po okhrane prirody v SSSR*, Moscow, 1935; *Trudy pervogo vserossiiskogo s"ezda po okhrane prirody*, Moscow, 1930; *Ocherki po istorii lesnykh obshchestv dorevoliutsionnoi Rossii*, Moscow, 1962.

[12] See my forthcoming article, "Conservation in Russia and the USSR," in *The Modern Encyclopedia of Russian and Soviet History*, Academic International Press, 1977; V. M. Blinov, *Okhrana prirody*, Moscow, 1971; *Okhrana prirody i zapovednoe delo v SSSR za 50 let*, Moscow, 1967.

[13] These two lines are from Pasternak's Russian translation of Goethe's *Faust*, written after World War Two and first published in 1953. It appears to be a deliberate mistranslation of the German original, in keeping with Pasternak's views on nature and mankind but not with the literal meaning of Goethe's lines. The lines in the second edition, which appeared in 1955, are closer to the German. For background on Pasternak's translation, see Vladimir Markov, "An Unnoticed Aspect of Pasternak's Translations," *Slavic Review*, October 1961, 503-508. My thanks to Prof. Guy de Mallac, who is completing a biographical and critical study of Pasternak, for bringing this to my attention.

tion, and the automobile, for example, felt slighted by comparison with the emphasis on mining, metallurgy, and heavy machine building. Conflicts over locational decisions (as in the Urals-Kuzbass decision), and between adherents of large hydroelectric projects versus steam power technology, between the advocates of the Douhet doctrine with its emphasis on strategic bombers and the proponents of tactical aviation, between adherents of the "theory of concentration" in mining and its opponents, etc. were resolved in favor of one or another of these subgroups of the technostructure.

That technological choices had to be, and were, made is not surprising, but the fate of the losers, by contrast with both Western and pre-revolutionary Russian practices is surprising, as it tended at times to be much bitterer than the fate of those who lost similar controversies in the late Imperial period. Widespread arrests, imprisonment, or execution of the losers in a technological debate would have been unthinkable under Nicholas II. The worst fate would have been a loss of prestige, perhaps the loss of a job, and of other financial support. Under Stalin it was no longer unthinkable for a loss in a technical debate to be followed by accusations of wrecking and arrests, particularly widespread in the period from 1928 to 1931 and after 1937. While the phenomenon characteristic of Lysenkoism in biology was commoner in technology than we have known before, it should not be exaggerated. Loss in a technological debate was not inevitably followed by arrest and a purge of the losers, even after 1928. We really cannot at this point, with the evidence available, explain why this happened at some times and not at others. Clearly, this is an area where our knowledge is still fragmentary.

What we can say is that such repression had long-range effects on Soviet inventiveness, as well as on the spirit in which debates concerning technological issues were carried out, lending at times a note of hysteria to such debate. While the technostructure had suffered before the revolution from neglect by the power structure, during the Stalin era it suffered at times from too much malevolent concern. Suspicions of "sabotage" and political phrase-mongering came to hover often over debates concerning technological choices. This had an inhibiting effect on technological innovation, and it served to sharpen the battle lines between divergent groups of technologists competing for the allocation of scarce resources. One can trace at least some of the most serious problems of the Soviet economy, including lags in agricultural output, lags in automation of industrial processes and the use of computers, to the negative atmosphere created by the political authorities during the 1930s. (The discrediting of agronomists who advocated the chemicalization of agriculture and the disruption to the Soviet radar program caused by the purges are cases in point. The intimate connection between radar technology and the development of computerization in the West has been detailed recently by Prof. Charles Susskind of Berkeley.)[14] While other technological choices made before 1941 may have been wise ones, the political atmosphere and manner in which losers in technological controversies were sometimes treated had long-term negative effects that should not be overlooked in any analysis of the current Soviet economy. In general, the combination of autarchical policies and the spy mania of these years made ties with Western science and technology more tenuous than before 1917, and this became a source of grievance on the part of the more innovation-minded specialists, particularly some of those in research and development. At the same time, the greater isolation of the late 1930s helped to nurture an already strong sense of nationalism among the technical intelligentsia and a greater confidence among many Soviet specialists in their own abilities, particularly when it was difficult for most to make first-hand comparisons with Western economies. The rudest shocks for most came in World War II and the post-Stalin era, when contacts with the advanced industrial countries once again increased.[15]

The increase in size and geographical distribution of the technical intelligentsia between 1917 and 1941 was probably a factor lessening its overall cohesion somewhat by comparison with the prerevolutionary period. Although graduate technologists in particular still tended to concentrate in the large metropolitan centers and in central government offices, in design bureaus, and in education, rather than working directly in production—thus continuing a prerevolutionary pattern—the enormous increase in the size of this group and its partial dispersion meant that the power structure could pick and choose among individual technologists more than in the past. This, in turn, meant less contact and less security among its individual members. The fate of professional organizations among the technical intelligentsia is indicative of this trend. By 1941, although a national union organization of engineers and technicians still existed, together with a large number of "scientific-technical societies" for different branches of technology, they were relatively ineffectual as power centers for the technical intelligentsia. No

[14] See Charles Susskind, *Understanding Technology*, Baltimore, 1973, pp. 40-58; and his forthcoming book, *The Birth of the Golden Cockerel: A History of the Development of Radar*.

[15] The harmful effects to Soviet science and technology of isolation from the West has been a major theme in the works of Sakharov and the Medvedev brothers (see especially *Sakharov Speaks*, New York, 1973; *My Country and the World*, New York, 1975; Zhores Medvedev, *The Medvedev Papers*, London, 1971).

longer restricted to diplomaed specialists, these organizations had been opened up to a mass membership, including workers in many cases, and brought under tighter supervision by the party, government, and central trade union organization. They were no longer the organizing centers and lobbies for graduate specialists that the Russian Technical Society, Polytechnic Society, Technological Society, All-Russian Association of Engineers, and various branch societies had been before the Bolshevik revolution, although to a certain extent the Marxist ideological organization for specialists (VARNITSO) played this role on some issues. Professional autonomy, both in education and in their professional societies, which had loomed so large an issue for the liberally minded engineers and applied scientists who dominated the Russian technostructure before the Soviet period, was virtually lost between 1917 and 1941. The technical intelligentsia was forced to find other channels of influence. This they achieved partially through industrial managers and party members, first largely through surrogates who were not themselves technologists during the 1920s, and after 1931 and the purges of 1936 to 1938, partially through their own members who rose in the party and government hierarchies.

The forms for expressing the organized interests of the technostructure changed, but the drive to exert influence on policies affecting their work did not. Given the evidence of this study, it is impossible to believe that important groups of the technostructure ever became completely inert or paralyzed under Stalin's cobra gaze. Both conflict and cooperation characterized their relations among themselves, as well as with the Stalinist power structure. This entire period is characterized by a tug of war between forces of conflict and attempts to create bonds of cooperation both within the technostructure, and between it and the power structure.

The technostructure not only persisted, it grew in size, status, and material privileges. Even allowing for some exaggeration in Soviet figures, there can be little doubt that the technostructure was the fastest growing sector of the intelligentsia, that its growth produced a profound change in the nature of the intelligentsia, and that the technostructure became the preponderant segment of the Soviet intelligentsia, both in numbers and influnce. It also proved to be one of the groups in Soviet society to show the greatest continuity with its prerevolutionary past by 1941, both in terms of actual personnel as well as in traditions and patterns of behavior. While professional autonomy in the prerevolutionary sense was lost, a far larger proportion of the "old specialists" was still around in 1941 than of other prerevolutionary elites. The Tsarist power structure—the landowning nobility and Imperial family—

had disappeared, the clergy had been decimated, even the revolutionary elites, including most of the old Bolsheviks, were dead or in exile, with the exception of a small coterie around Stalin. Although the old techno-structure was immersed in a mass of new red specialists, who composed at least ninety percent of this group by 1941, and even though some of the old specialists had disappeared into the "gulag archipelago" or had gone into exile, as a group the "old specialists" still dominated the professorial ranks of higher technical education, where they could exert a major influence on the attitudes of new specialists. They were also dominant in the network of industrial research institutes and the Academy of Sciences, and were not infrequently consultants or administrators in the economy by 1941. While many still remained outside the party before World War II, they were surrounded by honors, high status, and concern by the authorities, which served somewhat to balance the surveillance and controls over their work.

Not surprisingly in view of this continuity, many if not all prerevolutionary patterns of behavior reemerged among the technical intelligentsia during these years, including hierarchical relations in industry and education not unlike those before the revolution. Major differences existed in the political atmosphere, of course, with the technical intelligentsia no longer free to participate actively in opposition parties, with a stronger apparatus of repression than had existed in the late Imperial period, and with their energies channeled much more directly into goals decided centrally, although frequently with their input.

Besides a stronger atmosphere of repression, perhaps the major difference between pre- and postrevolutionary periods was the existence of the central planning system. The planning system molded the social relations of this group in a way that had never been true before the revolution. The irony is that while articulate members of the technical intelligentsia had favored comprehensive economic planning, and had played a major role in setting up that system in the 1920s, in later years they sometimes found themselves at odds with the particular goals adopted, especially with the primary emphasis on high quantitative targets, as well as the enormous demand for paperwork and accounting of results that this system imposed on them in all their major work environments—education, research and development, and, particularly, production. The technostructure as a group was not necessarily inimical to economic planning. What it wanted was planning in which its technical expertise figured prominently, and in which goals would be realistic, backed up by materials, manpower, and organization to make them achievable. Frequent lapses in these areas remained a major grievance by 1941.

Judging from their experience in World War I and before the revolution, technical specialists tended to favor a strong central government that planned and carried out economic growth. Nor were they necessarily friends of private enterprise, the profit system, or a consumption-oriented economy. This is not to imply that they were necessarily friends of dictatorship, or of single-party socialism, Soviet style. While they may have disagreed among themselves on the particular blend of public and private enterprise, consumption and investment, the role of labor, consumers, management, and technical experts in setting and carrying out the goals of a strong central government, the technostructure needs to be distinguished from the bourgeoisie in the sense that the latter is a group primarily interested in private ownership of the means of production and the pursuit of profits and consumption. The technical intelligentsia could more easily fit into the framework of the Soviet system because, in mentality and function, they were largely distinct from the bourgeoisie and closer to some of the values and goals of the Bolsheviks, including economic planning and a priority on production and growth, rather than private consumption per se. It is not surprising, therefore, that they should adapt to the Soviet system and show a high degree of continuity with prerevolutionary personnel and patterns of behavior. What is surprising is that they should survive with less change in personnel and mentality than the Communist party, that the old Bolsheviks should be virtually destroyed and replaced in increasing numbers by members of the technical intelligentsia. This might lead one to conclude that the means—industrialization—came permanently to replace the end—egalitarianism—as it was originally expressed in the Bolshevik revolution. Stalinists, of course, argued that this was not the case and that the ultimate goals remained. Those who replaced the old Bolsheviks, they claimed, were both Communists and more competent in technology than those who were replaced. Yet during this period and subsequently, industrialization and inequality have prevailed. We should be wary, however, in concluding that this path is permanently dictated by the nature of modern technology. One of the strongest indications of this study is that technology does not predetermine social relations, but only creates a certain range of alternatives toward one of which a variety of other factors—cultural, social structural, and historical—predispose a society at a particular point in its development.

The future may hold other alternatives, not necessarily the same combination of ideological promises, material incentives, repression, and hierarchical relations that were chosen during the Stalinist era in conditions of poverty, insecurity, sharp cultural and social divisions, a low level of modern technical skills, and memories of war and revolution. While such factors are overcome and changed only slowly, a new situation emerges when cultural and technical levels change, and when a stronger sense of internal and international security develops. Then the old social relations may once again be called into question, particularly if the ideological promises, hierarchical relations, and level of repression no longer seem functional to an increasing proportion of the population. Soviet society is held together by a variety of glues, but if one or several of them come unstuck, that society may once again face a crisis of legitimacy as it did in the period studied here. The dissent of the 1960s and early 1970s was to some extent a glimmer of that, and it was no accident that some members of the technical intelligentsia, such as Sakharov, a nuclear weapons specialist, and General Grigorenko, a cybernetics expert, as well as others less known, have played an important role in such dissent. At the same time, the mass of the technical intelligentsia have remained publicly silent. It is by no means certain that a majority of them share many of the criticisms voiced by Sakharov and other applied scientists and engineers. Some of these criticisms had their origins in frustrations with work in the Soviet economy, especially in research and development, which attracted some of the best educated and most talented members of the technostructure starting with the period analyzed here. Such dissent later broadened to include wider social issues, as in the case of Sakharov.

The roots of the paradox with which we began this study—the fact that a majority of the ruling elite of Soviet society, as well as many dissenters, have a technical background—are to be found in the ambivalence felt by the technical intelligentsia towards the power structure, beginning in the first generation after the Bolshevik Revolution. Yet the balance up to the present has been struck in favor of a peaceful evolution of the Soviet system, with most technologists working quietly within, rather than becoming open dissenters. The Soviet system has given the technical intelligentsia a great deal, even while it has brought frustrations and taken away values and other trends favored by elements of the technostructure. There seems no reason why this ambivalence, and the paradox to which it has given rise, may not continue for the foreseeable future without a majority of the technical intelligentsia becoming a radical force for social change outside the established system, particularly in view of its intimate connections with the power structure.

It is not appropriate here to speculate at length on the future of the Soviet system, but one comment seems in order. To date, upward social mobility—the increasing numbers of the Soviet population who have entered the intelligentsia and particularly the technical intelligentsia

—has given some credence to the ideological claim that this is the path toward a classless (Communist) society.[16] If, some time in the future, however, such mobility should cease, if material privileges, access to education and to power become more hereditary, then Soviet society may once again face a sharpened crisis of legitimacy, with the chance of increased and more open class conflict. This is certainly not the only possible source of future change—the international environment among other factors has been a crucial source—but it is one worth considering. In such an event, one of several things seems likely: a long-term continuance of the contradiction between ideology and social reality, a situation not uncommon in history, despite the conflicts it creates; an eventual ideological change, justifying permanent inequalities, together with continued repression; or experimentation with more democratic forms of social relations, giving increased reality to claims that higher cultural-technical levels can lead to greater material equality and more democratic access to power. Which of these, or other alternatives, will be chosen, only the future can tell. The choice, however, will have major implications for the long-term historical role of the Soviet technical intelligentsia, and for the interpretation given to the events analyzed in this study.

[16] See, for example, S. L. Seniavskii, *Izmeneniia v sotsial'noi strukture sovetskogo obshchestva 1938-1970*, Moscow, 1973, pp. 297-333, 373-400, 408-411.

GLOSSARY OF TERMS AND ABBREVIATIONS

AGKKh	State Archive of the Chemical Industry
BSE	*Large Soviet Encyclopedia*
CC	Central Committee of the CPSU
Cheka	Soviet secret police, 1917 to 1921
CPSU	Communist party of the Soviet Union
d. (delo)	item, unit in an archival collection
ed. khr.	storage unit of an archival group or record group
f. (fond)	archival or record group
Glavprofobr	Chief Administration of Professional Education, *Narkompros*
gorkom	city committee of the CPSU
Gosplan	State Planning Commission, under the *Sovnarkom*
GPU	Soviet secret police, 1920s
IMFLS, IML	Institute of Marxism-Leninism
IT	*Engineering Labor*, journal of VMBIT
ITR	engineering-technical workers
ITS	engineering-technical sections of the trade unions
Komsomol	Young Communists
KS	*Red Students*, journal of the Proletarian Students' Union
1., ll.	*list* or plural, *listy*, folio, leaf, sheet in an archival collection
MPA	Moscow Party Archive
MTU, MVTU	Moscow Higher Technical School (university)
Narkompros	People's Commissariat of Education (Enlightenment)
NKTP	People's Commissariat of Heavy Industry
NKVD	People's Commissariat of Internal Affairs (after 1934, these initials replaced others to designate the secret police)
nomenklatura	the system of designating key jobs throughout the government and economy, the candidates for which were supplied by, or had to be approved by, the party's secretariat in Moscow. A key source of patronage controlled by the central party *apparat*

427

NR	*Scientific Worker*, the journal of the Union of Scientific Workers
obkom	provincial (*oblast'*) party committee
OGPU	Soviet secret police from late 1920s until 1934
op. (opis')	inventory, or shelf list of an archival fond
Partorg TsK	Party organizer for a large factory, directly appointed by the Central Committee secretariat in Moscow
PAIaO	Party Archive of Iaroslavl' Province (*oblast'*)
PAIIP	Party Archive, Institute of Party History, Ukrainian CP
Politburo	highest policy-making body of the CPSU
praktiki	persons holding engineering or technical posts on the basis of experience, rather than formal education
raikom	regional (*raion*) party committee, a smaller unit within an *oblast'* or province (see *obkom*)
Rabkrin	Workers' and Peasants' Inspectorate, the central governmental body charged with verifying the fulfillment of governmental policies
RP	*Rationalization of Production*, journal published by *Rabkrin*
RTO	Russian Technical Society, 1866 to 1929
SGRP	Soviet journal, *Soviet Government and Law*, published by Law Institute of the U.S.S.R. Academy of Sciences
SKB	synthetic rubber, Type B, the invention of S. V. Lebedev
Sovnarkom	Council of People's Commissars, the government cabinet
spetsotdel	special section run by the secret police in a Soviet institution, such as a factory, school, or research institute
SI	*Soviet Justice*, a journal of the Commissariat of Justice
STO	Council for Labor and Defense, the government's economic cabinet
TPG	daily newspaper of the Supreme Economic Council (*Vesenkha*), until 1930
TsAGI	Central Aviation Institute
TsGANKh	Central State Archive of the National Economy

TsGAOR	Central State Archive of the October Revolution
TsPA	Central Party Archive
VAI	All-Union Association of Engineers, 1921 to 1929
VARNITSO	All-Union Association of Workers of Science and Technology Building Socialism
VI	*Engineers' Herald*, journal of VSI and VAI
VK	journal of the Committee of Inventions under *Gosplan*
VK VTO	journal of the Committee for Higher Technical Education
VMBIT	All-Union Intersectional Bureau of Engineers and Technicians, the national trade union organization for the technical intelligentsia from 1921 to 1941
VSI	All-Russian Union of Engineers, 1917 to 1919
VSNKh, *Vesenkha*	Supreme Economic Council, administering large-scale Soviet industry from 1918 to 1931
vtuzy	higher technical schools (universities)
vuz	higher educational institution
ZI	*For Industrialization*, daily newspaper of VSNKh and NKTP, 1929 to 1937
ZPK	*For Proletarian Cadres*, journal of NKTP, Chief Administration for Higher Technical Education

APPENDIX

Computer Study of
the Soviet Technical Intelligentsia

The cases for this computer study fell into two subgroups, with only minimal overlap. The first subgroup (245 cases) includes those members of the technostructure who had been active by 1941, and who were elected to the Supreme Soviet between 1958 and 1965. This group included all members of the Politburo and Central Committee with a background from the technical intelligentsia in these later years. The second subgroup was much more numerous (790 cases), and included all those members of the technical intelligentsia active between 1917 and 1941, who were later singled out for recognition by the publishers of the *Large Soviet Encyclopedia* and the Institute for the History of Science and Technology of the Academy of Sciences. They were singled out (in a two-volume reference work published in 1958 and 1959) for their contributions to Soviet technology.

Neither group, therefore, can be taken as typical of the technical intelligentsia as a whole during the period covered by this study. Rather, they represent elites within an elite: members of the technostructure who began their careers before the Nazi invasion, and who were most successful in winning recognition within a decade or so of Stalin's death. Yet these two subgroups differ significantly. Group 1, those who became officials and politicians, including most of the current Soviet leadership, shared certain traits to a much higher degree than those who remained primarily in technical roles and made their mark in the latter area. For example, Group 1 (who will be called politicians) form a tighter age cohort than Group 2 (hereafter called technologists). Of the politicians, 73.4% were born within a fifteen-year period (1900-1914), and 97.1% were born within a twenty-three year period (1898-1920). By contrast, the technologists were largely an older group and showed a much wider age span; 66% were born between 1843 and 1899, and only 33.2% in the years between 1900 and 1914 (or 38.2% between 1898 and 1920). (See Table A.1.)

The politicians also show a much higher proportion of persons who claimed a worker or peasant origin: 49.8% versus 2.4% of the technologists (Table A.2); 89.9% of the technologists' biographies listed no social origin, leading one to conclude they were probably from non-

TABLE A.1.

Date	Technologists			Politicians	
of Birth	Number	Percent		Number	Percent
No data	1	0.1		1	0.4
1843-1899	521	66.0	(1892-1898) 6		2.5
1900-1914	262	33.2		180	73.4
1915-1920	6	0.7		58	23.7
Total	790	100.0		245	100.0

TABLE A.2.

	Technologists		Politicians	
Social Origins	Number	Percent	Number	Percent
No data	710	89.9	89	36.3
Worker	9	1.1	64	26.1
Peasant	10	1.2	58	23.7
Intelligentsia	37	4.7	14	5.7
(Technical)	(20)	(2.5)	(1)	(0.4)
Clergy	4	0.5	—	—
Nobility	4	0.5	—	—
Civil service or military	10	1.3	20	8.2
Merchant or white collar	6	0.8	—	—
Total	790	100.0	245	100.0

peasant or worker stock. (The Soviet compilers of these reference works had no reason to omit origins in the working class or the peasantry; they would tend, if anything, to exaggerate this figure. They could have reasons to omit nonproletarian origins, however, for so crucial a stratum as the technical intelligentsia.) Data on ethnic origins are available only for the politicians, and show a higher percentage of Russians (60.4%), Slavs including Russians (80%), and Caucasians (Armenians and Georgians, 6.2%) than their percentage of the general population (Table A.3). They also show a much lower representation of Turkic peoples (8.4%) and Jews (0.8%). This despite the fact that Jews, at least, composed between 14% and 17% of the students in higher technical education during the early Five-Year Plans, when most

TABLE A.3.

Ethnic Origins	Technologists		Politicians	
	Number	Percent	Number	Percent
No data	790	100.0	1	0.4
Russian			148	60.4
Ukrainian			45	18.4
Belorussian			3	1.2
Armenian			7	2.9
Georgian			8	3.3
Jewish			2	0.8
Kirghiz			1	0.4
Azeri			6	2.4
Uzbek			3	1.2
Kazakh			6	2.4
Tatar			2	0.8
Bashkir			1	0.4
Avar			1	0.4
Tadzhik			1	0.4
Latvian			2	0.8
Lithuanian			1	0.4
Estonian			2	0.8
Other			4	1.6
Total	790	100.0	245	100.0

of the politicians were educated. Women were even more seriously underrepresented in both groups, but especially among the technologists (1.1%). They composed only 2% of the politicians, although by 1940 they made up some 40% of the students in higher technical education and 14% of the graduate engineers in industry.

All the politicians included in this study had higher education, but dates of graduation were available for only 52.2%. All those for whom data were available received their higher technical educations after the revolution, and 88.2% of them received their degrees between 1929 and 1941 (Table A.4). Among the technologists 43.4% earned their diplomas between 1866 and 1917; 25.2% between 1918 and 1928, and only 22.6% between 1929 and 1941. The technologists also proved to be a more metropolitan group in their educations (Table A.5). 73.7% received their degrees from an institute in Moscow (33.5%), Leningrad (35.2%), or Kiev (5%). In contrast, only 42% of the politicians re-

TABLE A.4.

Date Higher Education Completed	Technologists		Politicians	
	Number	Percent	Number	Percent
No data	67	8.5	117	47.8
1866-1917	343	43.4	0	0.0
1918-1928	199	25.2	3	1.2
1929-1941	179	22.6	113	46.1
1942-1949	2	0.2	12	4.9
Total	790	100.0	245	100.0

TABLE A.5.

Site of Higher Education	Technologists		Politicians	
	Number	Percent	Number	Percent
No data	52	6.6	3	1.2
Moscow	265	33.5	63	25.7
Leningrad	278	35.2	32	13.1
Kiev	39	5.0	8	3.2
Provincial	144	18.2	139	56.8
W. Europe	12	1.5	0	0.0
Total	790	100.0	245	100.0

ceived such degrees, and 56.8% of them were educated in provincial institutions outside Moscow, Leningrad, or Kiev. In the specialties for which they were trained, these two groups also show significant differences (Table A.6). Those with scientific rather than technical specialties form a much higher proportion of the technologists than the politicians. Among the politicians, metallurgists and mechanical engineers are a more prominent proportion of the group, as one might expect given the priorities of Soviet industrialization discussed in chapter 13.

Also as expected, the politicians showed a much higher proportion of party members (95.1%) than the technologists (35.9%). Among the politicians, 9% joined the CPSU before 1928; 52.6% joined between 1928 and 1941 (35.5% joined between 1939 and 1941 in the wake of the purges); 26.5% joined during World War II, and only 6.8% joined after World War II (Table A.7). Of the technologists, 4.8% joined before 1928, 12.4% joined between 1928 and 1941, 9.7% joined in

TABLE A.6.

Specialties	Technologists		Politicians	
	Number	*Percent*	*Number*	*Percent*
Applied scientist[a]	173	21.9	5	2.0
Geodesist	6	0.8	0	0.0
Geologist	101	12.8	5	2.0
Metallurgist	53	6.7	23	9.5
Mechanical engineer	159	20.1	90	36.7
Electrical engineer	69	8.7	8	3.3
Chemical engineer	22	2.8	4	1.6
Petroleum engineer	9	1.1	12	4.9
Mining engineer	22	2.8	5	2.0
Construction engineer	60	7.6	20	8.2
Forestry specialist	7	0.9	2	0.8
Agricultural specialist[b]	109	13.8	69	28.2
Unknown	—	—	2	0.8
Total	790	100.0	245	100.0

[a] Includes chemists, physicists, biologists, and mathematicians.
[b] Includes agronomists, veterinarians, plant specialists, etc.

TABLE A.7.

Party Membership	Technologists		Politicians	
	Number	*Percent*	*Number*	*Percent*
Nonmember	506	64.1	12	4.9
Before 1928	38	4.8	22	9.0
1928-1941	98	12.4	129	52.6
1942-1945	76	9.7	65	26.5
1946-1959	71	8.9	17	7.0
Unknown date	1	0.1	—	—
Total	790	100.0	245	100.0

World War II, and 8.9% joined between 1946 and 1957. Their average age at joining was much higher than that of the politicians. Among the technologists, the specialties with the lowest party membership were the more science-based specialties (chemical and electrical engineering in particular); and a large proportion of applied scientists and the more science-based specialists joined the CPSU only after 1941 (Table A.8).

In career patterns (Table A.9), the politicians showed a much higher

TABLE A.8. TECHNOLOGISTS: CROSS-TABULATION
OF SPECIALTY BY PARTY MEMBERSHIP[a]

Specialty	Non-members	Joined CP Before 1928	Joined CP 1928-1931	Joined CP 1932-1941	Joined CP 1942-1959	Row Total
Applied	120	4	4	16	35	179
scientists	67.0	2.2	2.2	8.9	19.6	22.7
	23.7	10.3	25.0	19.5	23.8	
	15.2	.5	.5	2.0	4.4	
Metallurgists	38	6	1	1	7	53
	71.7	11.3	1.9	1.9	13.2	6.7
	7.5	15.4	6.2	1.2	4.8	
	4.8	.8	.1	.1	.9	
Geologists	70	6	1	10	14	101
	69.3	5.9	1.0	9.9	13.9	12.8
	13.8	15.4	6.2	12.2	9.5	
	8.9	.8	.1	1.3	1.8	
Mechanical	99	7	2	18	33	159
engineers	62.3	4.4	1.3	11.3	20.8	20.1
	19.6	17.9	12.5	22.0	22.4	
	12.5	.9	.3	2.3	4.2	
Electrical	52	2	0	7	8	69
engineers	75.4	2.9	.0	10.1	11.6	8.7
	10.3	5.1	.0	8.5	5.4	
	6.6	.3	.0	.9	1.0	
Chemical	25	1	0	2	3	31
engineers	80.6	3.2	.0	6.5	9.7	3.9
	4.9	2.6	.0	2.4	2.0	
	3.2	.1	.0	.3	.4	
Mining	13	2	0	3	4	22
engineers	59.1	9.1	.0	13.6	18.2	2.8
	2.6	5.1	.0	3.7	2.7	
	1.6	.3	.0	.4	.5	

[a] Reading from top to bottom in each column, the figures show number, row percentage, column percentage, and total percentage.

TABLE A.8. (*Cont.*)

Specialty	Non-members	Joined CP Before 1928	Joined CP 1928-1931	Joined CP 1932-1941	Joined CP 1942-1959	Row Total
Construction	32	3	1	8	16	60
engineers	53.3	5.0	1.7	13.3	26.7	7.6
	6.3	7.7	6.2	9.8	10.9	
	4.1	.4	.1	1.0	2.0	
Foresters and	13	1	2	7	9	32
plant	40.6	3.1	6.2	21.9	28.1	4.1
specialists	2.6	2.6	12.5	8.5	6.1	
	1.6	.1	.3	.9	1.1	
Agronomists and	44	7	5	10	18	84
veterinarians	52.4	8.3	6.0	11.9	21.4	10.6
	8.7	17.9	31.3	12.2	12.2	
	5.6	.9	.6	1.3	2.3	
Column total	506	39	16	82	147	790
	64.1	4.9	2.0	10.4	18.6	100.0

TABLE A.9.

Career Patterns[a]	Technologists		Politicians	
	Number	Percent	Number	Percent
Teacher	263	33.3	1	0.4
Teacher-lower administrator	167	21.1	0	0.0
Teacher-middle administrator	12	1.5	0	0.0
Teacher-high party or government official	18	2.3	1	0.4
Researcher	57	7.2	1	0.4
Researcher-lower administrator	53	6.7	4	1.6

[a] Each category represents, in abbreviated form, a particular mix of career experience. For example, those tabulated under "teacher" spent their entire careers in this area, while a "teacher-middle administrator" had some mixture of teaching and administrative experience in the teaching area, but never rose above the middle administrative level (e.g., director of a higher educational institute).

TABLE A.9. (*Cont.*)

Career Patterns[a]	Technologists		Politicians	
	Number	Percent	Number	Percent
Researcher-middle administrator	4	0.5	0	0.0
Researcher-high party or government official	13	1.6	3	1.2
Production engineer	2	0.3	0	0.0
Prod. eng.-lower administrator	10	1.3	27	11.0
Prod. eng.-middle administrator	1	0.1	6	2.4
Prod. eng.-high party or government official	14	1.8	154	62.9
Prod. eng.-teacher	82	10.4	1	0.4
Prod. eng.-teacher-lower administrator	38	4.8	5	2.0
Prod. eng.-teacher-middle admin.	4	0.5	1	0.4
Prod. eng.-teacher-high party or government official	7	0.9	11	4.5
Prod. eng.-researcher	17	2.2	0	0.0
Prod. eng.-researcher-lower administrator	15	1.9	4	1.6
Prod. eng.-researcher-middle admin.	6	0.8	2	0.8
Prod. eng.-researcher-high party or government official	4	0.5	11	4.5
Worker-inventor	3	0.4	0	0.0
Party official since graduation	0	0.0	12	4.9
Unknown	0	0.0	1	0.4
Total	790	100.0	245	100.0

proportion of members with some production experience (90.5%) and a much lower proportion with some research or teaching experience (18.2%). Only 25.5% of the technologists had any production experience listed in their biographies, while 96.3% had some research or teaching experience. In fact, the majority of this group spent most of their careers as researchers, teachers, or both. The highest professional mobility (in terms of the administrative responsibility attached to their jobs) was enjoyed, of course, by the politicians. Table A.10 shows that

TABLE A.10.

Professional Mobility	Technologists		Politicians	
	Number	Percent	Number	Percent
No administrative experience	424	53.7	3	1.2
Lower-level admin.	283	35.8	40	16.3
Middle-level admin.	27	3.4	9	3.7
High gov't or party official	56	7.1	192	78.4
(Politburo or CC)	(2)	(0.3)	(128)	(52.2)
Unknown	—	—	1	0.4
Total	790	100.0	245	100.0

82.1% of this group reached the level of provincial party secretary (*obkom* secretary), government minister, or higher. Only 3 of these 245 cases had no administrative experience. Most of the technologists, however, never rose above middle-level administrative posts (92.9%), and 53.9% had no significant administrative experience, remaining either teachers, researchers, or rank-and-file production specialists throughout their careers. During the period from 1917 to 1941, however, these two subgroups were closer in terms of professional mobility (Table A.11). Of the politicians, by 1941 38.4% were still rank-and-file, and 45.3% were lower administrative personnel; 6.9% had achieved middle-level administrative position by 1941, and only 9% had major administrative responsibilities as important party or government officials by that time. None were yet Central Committee or Politburo members, although among the technologists one member, Krzhizhanovsky, belonged to the Central Committee.

While the technologists had less power, in terms of the positions they came to occupy by the late 1950s, they proved to be the more honored group in terms of state awards and election to the various Academies

Table A.11.

Professional Mobility, 1917-1941	Technologists		Politicians	
	Number	Percent	Number	Percent
No administrative experience	551	69.7	94	38.4
Lower-level admin.	219	27.8	111	45.3
Middle-level admin.	16	2.0	17	6.9
High gov't or party official	4	0.5	22	9.0
(Central Committee)	(1)	(0.1)	(0)	(0.0)
Unknown	0	—	1	0.4
Total	790	100.0	245	100.0

of Sciences. Table A.12 shows that 66.5% of the politicians had few or no such honors recorded in their biographies, while only 50.8% of the technologists fell in a similar range. On the other end of the scale, 14.4% of the technologists showed very high honors, while only 7.8% of the politicians belonged to a similar range (Table A.11). This suggests a somewhat negative correlation between power and status in terms of such honors in Soviet society.

Tables A.1-A.12 were constructed on the basis of information in two Soviet reference works: *Biograficheskii slovar' deiatelei nauki i tekhniki*, Moscow, 2 vols., 1958 and 1959 (for the technologists), and *Deputaty soveta soiuza i soveta natsional'nostei*, Moscow, 1959, 1965 (for the politicians). All biographies of engineers and applied scientists who began their careers prior to the German invasion of 1941 and were active during the first three Five-Year Plans were selected and coded. The coding was then double-checked for accuracy and the information was fed into a Sigma 7 computer, programmed with the Statistical Package for the Social Sciences. The criterion used for selecting engineers was either a diploma in engineering or a clear indication that some of an individual's career was spent in a technical post in the economy. (As it turned out, most of the engineers listed in these two sources had obtained higher technical education.) The criteria for selecting applied scientists were the following: that the individual had either worked in a technical post involved with material production in the period from 1917 to 1941, or that the majority of an individual's research and teaching in this period was directly concerned with applying scientific knowledge to material production in Soviet society. Scientists (including

TABLE A.12.

Weighted Honors Index[a]	Technologists		Politicians	
	Number	*Percent*	*Number*	*Percent*
0-9	401	50.8	163	66.5
10-19	275	34.8	63	25.7
20-38	114	14.4	19	7.8
Totals	790	100.0	245	100.0

[a] Honors:

U.S.S.R. Academy of Sciences, full member	= 10;
U.S.S.R. Academy of Sciences, corresponding member	= 9;
Stalin or Lenin Prize	= 8 (+ 1 for each additional such prize);
Deputy of Supreme Soviet	= 7 (+ 1 for each additional time elected);
Soviet Medal (Hero of Socialist Labor, etc.)	= 6 (+ 1 for each additional);
Provincial Academy of Sciences, full member	= 5;
Provincial Academy of Sciences, corresponding member	= 4; and
Honored Worker of Science and Technology	= 3.

mathematicians and geologists) whose work seemed primarily theoretical and uninvolved with direct application, and who occupied no posts either as consultants to the economy or directly in material production during this period were not included. When in doubt on this question, a biography was excluded.

SELECTED BIBLIOGRAPHY

Only primary sources and selected secondary sources are listed here. Readers should see the footnotes for complete citations of the sources used in this study.

1. PRIMARY SOURCES

A. Unpublished Documents, Interviews, and Memoirs

Ivanov, Nikolai. "Higher Technical Training in the USSR." Memoir in the Archive of Russian History and Culture, Columbia University.

Jermain, Mrs. George (Rose). Taped interview, Feb. 13, 1970, with a former Soviet mining engineer. In possession of the author.

British Foreign Office Archives. Russian Correspondence, 1928-1941. Public Record Office, London.

Everhard, E. P. Diary and letters of an American engineer in Russia. Copies in possession of the author. Used with permission of the owner, Mrs. Rose Congleton.

The Harvard Project on the Soviet Social System. Widener Library, Harvard University. Interviews with World War II Soviet refugees, completed 1949-1951, by the Russian Research Center at Harvard.

Hoover Institution Archive, Stanford. H. H. Fischer Collection. Interviews with American engineers who worked in the U.S.S.R., completed 1934-1936.

Hoover Institution Archive, Stanford. Boris Nicolaevsky Collection.

Lee, Gilbert Henry. Letters to daughter, Elizabeth Lee, 1931-1932. Copies in possession of the author. Used with permission of the owner, Mrs. Elizabeth (Lee) Robson.

Samygin, M. M. "Prompartiia," n.d. Memoir in Archive of Russian History and Culture, Columbia University.

Smolensk Party Archive 1917-1941. The National Archives, Washington, D.C. Available on microfilm.

State Department Decimal File. 1928-1941. The National Archives, Washington, D.C.

Trotsky Archive, Houghton Library, Harvard University.

Valentinov, N. V. (Volkov). "Vospominaniia." Archive of Russian History and Culture, Columbia University.

Vernadskaia, Nina. "Vospominaniia." Hoover Institution Archive, Stanford.

BIBLIOGRAPHY

"Na sluzhbe u Stalina (Ispoved' chekista)." Memoir of a Lt. Colonel in the NKVD, written under a pseudonym after 1945. Archive of Russian History and Culture, Columbia University.

B. Periodicals

Institutional affiliations of these journals and holdings in American libraries can be found in *Fifty Years of Soviet Periodicals*, two volumes, Washington, 1968. Full runs for some can be found only in the Lenin Library, Moscow.

Bil'shovik Ukraini
Biulleten VK VTO
Bol'shevik
Chernaia metallurgiia
Front nauki i tekhniki
Grazhdanskaia aviatsiia
Inprecor
Inzhenernyi rabotnik
Inzhenernyi trud
Izvestiia
Izvestiia MTU
Izvestiia teplotekhnicheskogo institua
Izvestiia TsK
Kauchuk i rezina
Khimiia i khoziastvo
Komsomolskaia pravda
Mashinostroienie
Nashi dostizheniia
New York Times
Krasnoe studenchestvo
Leningradskaia Pravda
Narodnoe prosveshchenie
Nauchnyi rabotnik
Organizatsiia truda
Partiinoe stroitel'stvo
Planovoe khoziastvo
Petrogradskaia Pravda
Pod znamenem marksizma
Politicheskii dnevnik
Pravda
Predpriiatie
Proletarii na uchebe
Priroda

Problemy sovestskoi geologii
Puti industrializatsii
Rabochaia Moskva
Ratsionalizatsiia proizvodstva
Revoliutsiia i kul'tura
Revoliutsiia i natsional'nost'
Russkoe slovo
Samolet
Severnaia kommuna
Sinteticheskii kauchuk
SORENA
Sotsialisticheskaia rekonstruktsiia sel'skogo khoziastva
Sotsialisticheskii vestnik
Sovetskaia metallurgiia
Sovetskaia nauka
Sovetskaia ukraina
Sovetskoe gosudarstvo i revoliutsiia prava
Tekhnicheskoe obrazovanie
Tsement
Ugol'
Vestnik inzhenerov
Vestnik komiteta po izobretatel' stvu
Sovetskaia iustitsiia
Vestnik metallopromyshlennosti
Vestnik standardizatsii
Vysshaia shkola
Za industrializatsiiu
Za promyshlennye kadry
Zavodskaia laboratoriia
Zhurnal rezinovoi promyshlennosti

C. Other Primary Sources

Armand, A. A., ed. *Nauchno-issledovatel'skie instituty NKTP*. Moscow, 1935.

"Avtobiografiia i doklad N. M. Tulaikova." *Istoricheskii arkhiv*, No. 3, 1962, 100-119.

Baidukov, G. F. *O Chkalove*. Moscow, 1939.

Bardin, I. P. *Zhizn' inzhenera*. Moscow, 1938.

Beilin, A. E. *Podgotovka kadrov v SSSR za 15 let*. Leningrad, 1932.

―――. *Kadry spetsialistov SSSR. Ikh formirovanie i rost*. Moscow, 1935.

Bernatskii, M. V., ed. *K Kharakteristike sovremennogo studenchestva*. St. Petersburg, 1911.

Bialer, Seweryn, ed. *Stalin and His Generals: Soviet Military Memoirs of World War II*. New York, 1969.

Biulleteni moskovskogo oblastnogo biuro i moskovskogo otdeleniia vserossiiskogo soiuza inzhenerov, 1918.

Blok, A. *Obzor nauchno-izdatel'skoi deiatel'nosti KEPS, 1915-1920*. Petrograd, 1920.

Bor'ba zasukhoi. Vsesoiuznaia konferentsiia po bor'be s zasukhoi. Moscow, 1932.

Budanow, J. *Technical Institutes in the USSR*. Research Project on the U.S.S.R., No. 26, 1952. (Copy in the Archive of Russian History and Culture, Columbia University.)

Bukharin, Nikolai. *Socialist Reconstruction and the Struggle for Technique*. Moscow, 1932.

Burrell, George A. *An American Engineer Looks at Russia*. Boston, 1932.

Byli industrial'nye. Ocherki i vospominaniia. Moscow, 1973.

Chuvaev, V. and K. Raigorodskii. *ITR v bor'be za izobretatel'stvo*. Moscow, 1932.

Crowther, James G. *Soviet Science*. London, 1936.

Deviatsatyi vsesoiuznii s"ezd professional'nykh soiuzov SSSR. Stenograficheskii otchet. Moscow, 1933.

Direktivy KPSS i Sovetskogo pravitel'stva po khoziastvennym voprosam. Vols. 1 and 2, *1917-1941*. Moscow, 1957.

"Dokumenty F. E. Dzherzhinskogo po khoziastvennym voprosam 1922-1926 gg." *Istoricheskii arkhiv*, No. 2, 1960.

Dzerzhinskii, F. E. *Izbrannye proizvedeniia v dvukh tomakh*. Moscow, 1957.

Emelianov, V. S. *O vremeni, o tovarishchakh, o sebe*. Moscow, 1968.

―――. *Na poroge voine*. Moscow, 1971.

Energetika narodnogo khoziastva v plane GOELRO. Moscow, 1966.

Everhard, E. P. "Kuznetsk." *Blast Furnace and Steel Plant.* Vol. 20, No. 12, December, 1932.

Freyn, H. J. "The Life and Work of American Engineers in Soviet Russia." *Engineers and Engineering,* June 1931.

Friedman, Elisha. *Russia in Transition.* New York, 1932.

Friese, H. G. "Student Life in a Soviet University." In George Kline, ed., *Soviet Education.* New York, 1957.

Gastev, Alexei. *Organizatsiia truda v stakhanovskom dvizhenii.* Moscow, 1936.

Gor'kii i nauka. Stat'i, rechi, pis'ma, vospominaniia. Moscow, 1964.

Grinevetskii, V. Poslevoiennye perspektivy russkoi promyshlennosti. 2nd ed. Moscow, 1922.

Hilger, Gustav and A. G. Meyer. *Incompatible Allies.* New York, 1953.

Ipatieff, V. N. *Life of a Chemist.* Stanford, 1946.

Iz istorii VChK 1917-1921 gg. Sbornik dokumentov. Moscow, 1958.

Kadry tiazheloi promyshlennosti v tsifrakh. Moscow, 1936.

Khodorovskii, I. I., ed. *Kakogo inzhenera dolzhny gotovit' nashi vtuzy: Otzyvy deiateli promyshlennosti, nauki, i tekhniki.* Moscow, 1928.

KPSS v rezoliutsiiakh i resheniiakh. Vol. 5. Moscow, 1971.

Kratkii obzor deiatel'nosti postoiannoi kommissii po izuchenniiu estestvennykh proizvoditel'nykh sil. Petrograd, 1919.

Kravchenko, V. *I Chose Freedom.* New York, 1946.

Krylenko, N. V. *Za piat' let. 1918-1922. Obvinitel'nye rechi.* Moscow, 1923.

Krylov, A. N. *Moi vospominaniia.* Moscow, 1945.

Industrializatsiia SSSR 1938-1941. Moscow, 1973.

Kuibyshev, V. V. *Izbrannye proizvedeniia.* Moscow, 1958.

Kul'turnoe stroitel'stvo SSSR 1928-1938. Moscow, 1940.

Kul'turnoe stroitel'stvo v SSSR 1930-1934. Moscow, 1935.

Larsons, M. J. *An Expert in the Service of the Soviets.* London, 1929.

Lenin, V. I. *Polnoe sobranie sochineniia.* 5th ed. Vols. 1-55.

V. I. Lenin i Akademiia nauk. Sbornik dokumentov. Moscow, 1969.

Lenin and Stalin on Labour. Moscow, 1940.

Littlepage, John D. and Demaree Bess. *In Search of Soviet Gold.* New York, 1938.

"A. V. Lunacharskii." *Literaturnoe nasledstvo.* Vol. 74. p. 29. Moscow, 1965.

Lyons, Eugene. *Assignment in Utopia.* London, 1938.

Mandel'shtam, Nadezhda. *Hope Against Hope: A Memoir.* New York, 1970.

Molotov, V. *The Third Five-Year Plan for the National Economic Development of the USSR.* Moscow, 1939.

Moskva v tsifrakh. Moscow, 1934.

Narodne gospodarstvo UKr. SSR. Kiev, 1935.

Narodnoe khoziastvo SSSR: Statisticheskii spravochnik. Moscow, 1932.

Natsional'naia politika VKP(b) v tsifrakh. Moscow, 1930.

Obraztsov, V. I. *Opyt reorganizatsii uchebnoi postanovki v Moskovskom institute inzhenerov putei soobshchenii.* Moscow, 1924.

Okhrana prirody. Sbornik zakonodatel'nykh aktov. Moscow, 1961.

Ordzhonikidze, G. K. *Izbrannye stat'i i rechi, 1911-1937.* Moscow, 1939.

Ordzhonikidze, Z. G. *Put' bol'shevika; stranitsy iz vospominanii o Sergo Ordzhonikidze.* Moscow, 1938, 1945, 1956.

Organizatsiia sovetskoi nauk v 1926-1932 gg. Moscow, 1974.

Organizatsiia nauki v pervye gody Sovetskoi vlasti, 1917-1929. Sbornik dokumentov. Leningrad, 1968.

Orlov, Alexander. *The Secret History of Stalin's Crimes.* London, 1954.

Oshchepkov, P. K. *Zhizn' i mechta.* Moscow, 1965.

Ozerov, G. A. *Tupolevskaia sharaga.* Frankfurt, 1971.

Paramonov, I. V. *Puti proidennye.* Moscow, 1966.

―――. *Uchit'sia upravliat': Mysli i opyt starogo khoziastvennika.* Moscow, 1967, 1970.

Paton, E. O. *Vospominaniia.* Moscow, 1958.

Pavlov, M. A. *Vospominaniia metallurga.* Moscow, 1945.

Pervaia vsesoiuznaia konferentsiia rabotnikov sotsialisticheskoi promyshlennosti: Stengraficheskii otchet. Moscow, 1931.

Pervyi vsesoiuznyi gornyi nauchno-tekhnicheskii s"ezd. Trudy. April 14-27, 1926. Moscow, 1927.

Petrovskii, D., ed. *Kadry tiazheloi promyshlennosti v tsifrakh.* Moscow, 1936.

V Vsesoiuznyi s"ezd inzhenerov i tekhnikov. 25 noiabria-1 dekabria 1932 goda. Moscow, 1933.

Podgotovka kadrov v SSSR. 1927-1931 gg. Moscow, 1933.

Prianishnikov, D. N. *Agrokhimiia v SSSR.* Moscow, 1931, 1940.

―――. *Izbrannye sochineniia.* Vols. 1-4. Moscow, 1951-1954, 1963.

―――. *Moi vospominaniia.* Moscow, 1961.

D. N. Prianishnikov: Zhizn' i deiatel'nost'. Moscow, 1972.

Priroda i sotsialisticheskoe khoziastvo. Sbornik. No. 6. Moscow, 1933. No. 7. Moscow, 1935. No. 8. Chast' II. Moscow, 1941.

Proekt razvitiia MTU v shkolu politekhnicheskogo tipa. Moscow, 1915.

Programmy priemnykh ispytanii vuzy, vtuzy, universitety i tekhnikumy. Narkompros RSFSR. Moscow, 1932.

Protess 'prompartii' (25 noiabr-7 dekabria 1930 g.). Stenogramma sudebnogo protsessa i materialy, priobshchennye k delu. Moscow, 1931.

Puzyrevskii, N. P. *Mysli ob ustroistve vodnykh putei soobshcheniia.* St. Petersburg, 1906.

Rabchinskii, I. *O sisteme Teilora.* Moscow, 1921.

Rabota nauchno-tekhnicheskikh uchrezhdenii Respubliki, 1918-1919 gg. Moscow, 1919.

Reswick, William. *I Dreamt Revolution.* Chicago, 1952.

Reznik, I. B. *Ovladeem amerikanskoi tekhnikoi.* Moscow, 1931.

Rezoliutsiia III vsesoiuznogo s"ezda proletarskogo studenchestva. Moscow, 1929.

Rukeyser, Walter Arnold. *Working for the Soviets: An American Engineer in Russia.* London, 1932.

Ryss, M. B. i V. A. Smelev. *Problema kadrov spetsialistov v promyshlennosti.* Moscow, 1930.

Scott, John. *Behind the Urals.* Boston, 1942.

The Second Five-Year Plan 1933-1937. Moscow, 1936.

XVII Konferentsiia VKP(b). Stenograficheskii otchet. Moscow, 1932.

XVII S"ezd VPK(b). Stenograficheskii otchet. Moscow, 1934.

Shestnadtsataia konferentsiia VKP(b). Stenograficheskii otchet. Moscow, 1962.

XVI S"ezd VKP(b). Stenograficheskii otchet. Moscow, 1931.

Shein, S. D. *Sud nad ekonomicheskoi kontr-revoliutsiie v Donbasse.* Moscow, 1928.

Shmidt, O. Y., ed. *Nauchnye kadry i nauchno-issledovatel'skie uchrezhdeniia SSSR.* Moscow, 1930.

V. A. Smelev. *Voprosy podgotovki inzhenerno-tekhnicheskikh kadrov.* Moscow, 1931.

Smith, Andrew and Maria. *I was a Soviet Worker.* London, 1937.

Sobranie zakonov i rasporiazhenii, 1938-1941.

Socialist Construction in the USSR. Moscow, 1936.

Sostav rukovodiashchikh rabotnikov i spetsialistov Soiuza SSSR. Moscow, 1936.

Sotsialisticheskoe stroitel'stvo SSSR. Moscow, 1934.

Sotsialisticheskoe stroitel'stvo SSSR 1933-38. Moscow, 1939.

Soviet pri NKTP 15-19 iunia 1936. Stenograficheskii otchet. Moscow, 1936.

Spravochnik dlia postupaiushikh v vuzy i vtuzy. Moscow, 1940.

Stalin, I. V. *Collected Works.* 13 vols. Moscow, 1952-1954.

———. *Sochineniia.* 13 vols. Moscow, 1946.

———. *Sochineniia.* Vol. 1 (14), 1934-1940, edited by Robert H. McNeal, Stanford, 1967.

———. *Voprosy Leninizma.* Moscow, 1926.

Stenograficheskii otchet I Vsesoiuznoi konferentsii VARNITSO, 26-28 April 1928. Moscow, 1928.

Studenchestvo v tsifrakh. St. Petersburg, 1909.

Tekhnologicheskii institut, Sto let 1828-1928. Leningrad, 1928.

Terpigorev, A. M. *Vospominaniia gornogo inzhenera.* Moscow, 1956.

Timoshenko, Sergei. *As I Remember.* Princeton, 1968.

Tipovye uchebno-proizvodstvennye plany industrialnykh-tekhnicheskikh vuzov. Moscow, 1931.

III Vsesoiuznyi s"ezd nauchnykh rabotnikov. Sputnik delegata s"ezda. Moscow, 1929.

Trud v SSSR. Moscow, 1934, 1936.

Trudy GOELRO. Dokumenty i materialy. Moscow, 1960.

Trudy XI S"ezda russkikh deiatelei po vodianym putiam. St. Petersburg, 1909.

Trudy I vserossiiskogo elektrotekhnicheskogo s"ezda. St. Petersburg, 1900.

Trudy pervogo vserossiiskogo s"ezda po okhrane prirody. Moscow, 1930.

Trudy pervogo vsesoiuznogo s"ezda po okhrane prirody v SSSR. Moscow, 1935.

Tulaikov, N. M. *Izbrannye proizvedeniia. Kritika travopolnoi sistemy.* Moscow, 1963.

Tulaikov, N. M., ed. *Vsesoiuznyi institut zernovogo khoziastva.* Saratov, 1932.

Vannikov, B. L. "Iz zapisok narkom vooruzheniia," *Voenno-istoricheskii zhurnal*, No. 2, 1962, 78-86.

―――. "Oboronnaia promyshlennost' SSSR nakanune voiny (Iz zapisok narkoma)," *Voprosy istorii*, No. 1, 1969, 122-135.

Vernadsky, Vladimir. *O blizhaishikh zadachakh KEPS.* Petrograd, 1917.

Vernadsky, Vladimir. "Ob izuchenii estestvennykh proizvoditel'nykh sil Rossii," *Izvestiia Akademii nauk*, 6th ser. Vol. 9, No. 8, 1915.

―――. "The First Year of the Ukrainian Academy of Sciences," *The Annals of the Ukrainian Academy of Arts and Sciences in the U.S.*, vol. 11, Nos. 1-2, 3-31.

Voelker, Karl-Heinz, ed. *Dokumente und Dokumentarfotos zur Geschichte der Deutsche Luftwaffe Aus den Geheimakten des Reichswehrministeriums 1919-1933 und des Reichsluftfahrtministeriums 1933-1939.* Stuttgart, 1968.

XVIII S"ezd KPSS. Stenograficheskii otchet. Moscow, 1939.

Voznesenskii, A. *Khoziastvennye itogi 1940 goda: plan razvitiia narodnogo khoziastva SSSR na 1941 god.* Moscow, 1941.

Vserossiiskii soiuz inzhenerov. *Otchet' zaniatiiakh 2-oi moskovskoi oblastnoi konferentsii, 18-21 oktiabria, 1918 g.* Moscow, 1918.

VKP(b) v tsifrakh. Vypusk 8. Moscow, 1928.

Wrecking Activities at Power Stations in the Soviet Union. English translation of the transcript of the Metro-Vickers trial. Moscow, 1933.

Yakovlev, A. S. *Tsel' zhizni.* Moscow, 1966.

Yegorov, A. Y. and V. P. Kliucharev. *Grazhdanskaia aviatsiia SSSR.* Moscow, 1937.

Zaniatiia I-go moskovskogo oblastnogo delegatskogo s"ezda VSI, 4-6 ianvaria 1918 g. Moscow, 1918.

2. SECONDARY SOURCES

A. Dissertations and Papers (Soviet and American)

Akopov, M. A. "Partiinaia i gosudarstvennaia deiatel'nost' S. I. Kirova, 1926-1934 gg." Lenin Library, Moscow, 1967.

Bailes, Kendall E. "Stalin and Revolution from Above: The Formation of the Soviet Technical Intelligentsia 1928-1934." Ph.D. dissertation, Columbia University, 1971.

Bashevoi, Vladimir Filippovich. "Deiatel'nost' KP/b/Ukr. v oblasti podgotovki kadrov proizvodstvenno-tekhnicheskoi intelligentsii v period vtoroi piatiletki 1933-1937." Leningrad, 1966, in the Lenin Library, Moscow.

Brezhneva, L. P. "Deiatel'nost' Kommunisticheskoi Partii po sozdaniiu i razvitiiu sinteticheskogo kauchuka 1928-1937 gg." Lenin Library, Moscow, 1967.

Cooper, Julian. "Research, Development and Innovation in the USSR." Paper delivered at the International Congress of Slavists, Banff, Canada, September 1974.

Feldmesser, Robert A. "Aspects of Social Mobility in the Soviet Union." Ph.D. dissertation, Harvard University, 1955.

Filippov, N. G. "Russkoe tekhnicheskoe obshchestvo, 1866-1905." Lenin Library, Moscow, 1965.

Graham, Loren R. "The Formation of Soviet Research Institutes." Paper presented at the International Congress of Slavists, Banff, Canada, September, 1974.

Green, Donald Webb. "Industrialization and the Engineering Ascendancy: A Comparative Study of American and Russian Engineering Elites 1870-1920." Ph.D. dissertation, University of California, Berkeley, 1972.

Kal'manson, A. A. "Bor'ba KPSS za razvitie tiazheloi promyshlennosti nakanune Velikoi Otechestvennoi Voiny (1938- g.- iun' 1941 goda)." Lenin Library, Moscow, 1962.

Kardash, A. I. "Organizatsiia nauchno-tekhnicheskikh obshchestv v SSSR 1921-1929." Lenin Library, Moscow, 1968.

Kartsovnik, E. B. "Leninskii plan elektrifikatsii i bor'ba partii za sooruzhenie Dneprovskoi gidroelektrostantsii im. V. I. Lenina." Kiev State University, 1963, in the Lenin Library, Moscow.

Khromova, R. G. "G. K. Ordzhonikidze vo glave tiazheloi promyshlennosti 1932-1937 gg." Lenin Library, Moscow, 1970.

Klishin, S. F. "Moskovskaia partiinaia organizatsiia v bor'be za podgotovku inzhenerno-tekhnicheskikh kadrov 1928-1937 gg." Lenin Library, Moscow, 1967.

Koroleva, N. A. "Opyt KPSS po perevospitaniiu staroi i podgotovke novoi intelligentsii." Lenin Library, Moscow, 1968.

Kruglova, Zoia S. "Studencheskoe dvizhenie v period novogo Revoliutsionnogo pod'ema, 1910-1914." Lenin Library, Moscow, 1965.

Ocharkov, A. I. "Bor'ba KPSS za sozdaniiu inzhenerno-tekhnicheskikh kadrov tiazheloi promyshlennosti 1928-1933 gg." Lenin Library, Moscow, 1965.

Peskin, Alexander. "Sociological Aspects of Soviet Industrial Management." Unpublished study based on Harvard Interview Project, Widener Library, Harvard, 1954.

Polishchuk, M. M. "Borot'ba komunistichnoi partii Ukraini za otvoreniia i vikhovaniia inzhenerno-tekhnichnikh kadriv 1928-1932 rr." (in Ukrainian), Kiev, 1971, Lenin Library, Moscow.

Potemkin, V. M. "Bor'ba KPSS za sozdanie i osvoenie Magnitogorskogo metalkombinata im. I. V. Staline, 1929-1933 gg." Leningrad, 1955, in Lenin Library, Moscow.

Rossi, Peter. "Ratings of Selected Occupations in the USSR." Manuscript in the Harvard Project on the Soviet Social System, Widener Library, Harvard, November 1952.

Samokhvalov, Ivan Mikhailovich. "Rukovodstvo partii massovym razvitiem sotsialisticheskogo sorevnovaniia v promyshlennosti v period 1936-41 gg." Lenin Library, Moscow, 1965.

Shakirov, Salim Khamzinovich. "Deiatel'nost' KPSS v oblasti razvitiia ekonomicheskogo i politicheskogo sotrudnichestva narodov SSSR v gody vtoroi piatiletki 1933-1937." Moscow State University, 1971, in Lenin Library, Moscow.

Smirnova, T. M. "Reforma vysshei shkoly RSFSR 1917 g.-okt. 1922 g." Lenin Library, Moscow, 1968.

Swanson, James Martin. "The Bolshevization of Scientific Societies in the Soviet Union: An Historical Analysis of the Character, Function and Legal Position of Scientific and Scientific-Technical Societies in the USSR, 1929-1936." Indiana, 1968.

Vovk, V. E. "Deiatel'nost' KPSS po podgotovke rukovodiashchikh khoziastvennykh i inzhenerno-tekhnicheskikh kadrov dlia promyshlennosti v gody sozdaniia fundamenta sotsialisticheskoi ekonomiki 1926-1932 gg." Lenin Library, Moscow, 1970.

Wutke, Eugene Roger. "Technology: It Failed To Save the Nation." Ph.D. dissertation, University of Missouri, 1964.

Yakovlev, V. P. "Politika russkogo samoderzhaviia v universitetskom voprose 1905-1911 gg." Lenin Library, Moscow.

B. Books and Articles

Allison, David, ed. *The R & D game: Technical Men, Technical Managers and Research Productivity.* Cambridge, Mass., 1969.

Andreiuk, G. P. "Vydvizhenstvo i ego rol' v formirovanii intelligentsii (1921-1932 gg.)." *Iz istorii sovetskoi intelligentsii.* Moscow, 1966.

Anstett, Marcel. *La formation de la main-d'oeuvre qualifiee en Union Sovietique,* Paris, 1958.

Artobolevskii, I. I. *Ocherki po istorii tekhnik v SSSR.* Moscow, 1968.

Astashenkov, P. T. *Glavnyi konstruktor.* Moscow, 1975.

Avtorkhanov, Abdurakhman. *Stalin and the Soviet Communist Party: A Study in the Technology of Power.* New York, 1959.

Azrael, Jeremy R. *Managerial Power & Soviet Politics.* Cambridge, Mass., 1966.

Azumanian, Ashot. *Taina bulata.* Moscow, 1967.

Bailes, K. E. "The Politics of Technology." *American Historical Review,* April 1974.

————. "Revolution, Work and Culture: The Controversy Over Scientific Management in the Soviet Union, 1920-1924." *Soviet Studies,* July 1977.

————. "Technology and Legitimacy: Soviet Aviation and Stalinism in the 1930s." *Technology and Culture,* January 1976.

Balz, Manfred. *Inventions and the Organization of Technical Progress in the Soviet Union.* Lexington, Mass., 1975.

Bardin, I. P., ed. *Sovetskaia tekhnika za dvadtsat' piat' let 1917-1942.* Moscow, 1945.

Bastrakova, M. S. *Stanovlenie Sovetskoi sistemy organizatsii nauki, 1917-1922.* Moscow, 1973.

Ben-David, Joseph. *The Scientist's Role In Society.* Englewood Cliffs, N.J., 1971.

Bergson, Abram. *The Structure of Soviet Wages.* Cambridge, Mass., 1944.

Beriozov, P. I. *Valerian Vladimirovich Kuibyshev 1888-1935.* Moscow, 1958.

Berliner, Joseph S. "Bureaucratic Conservatism and Creativity in the Soviet Economy." In Fred W. Riggs, ed. *Frontiers of Development Administration*. Durham, N.C., 1970.

————. *Factory and Manager in the U.S.S.R.* Cambridge, Mass., 1957.

Biograficheskii slovar' deiatelei estestvoznaniia i tekhniki. 2 vols. Moscow, 1958-1959.

Blackwell, William. *The Beginning of Russian Industrialization*. Princeton, 1968.

Blinov, V. M. *Okhrana prirody*. Moscow, 1971.

Bol'shaia Sovetskaia entsiklopediia. Vol. 9, 1951.

Brodskii, L. I. "Ideino-politicheskoe vospitanie tekhnicheskikh spetsialistov dorevoliutsionnoi shkoly v gody pervoi piatiletki." *Trudy Leningradskogo politekhnicheskogo instituta, Obshchestvennye nauki*, No. 261.

Brusnikin, E. M. "Iz istorii bor'by KP za vuzovskuiu intelligentsiiu v 1917-1922 gg." *Voprosy istorii KPSS*, No. 8, 1972.

Campbell, Robert W. *The Economics of Soviet Oil and Gas*. New York, 1968.

Carr, E. H. *Socialism in One Country*. Baltimore, 1970.

———— and R. W. Davies. *Foundations of a Planned Economy*. 2 vols. London, 1969.

Chapman, Janet. *Real Wages in Russia Since 1928*. Cambridge, Mass., 1963.

Chen, Theodore Hsi-en. *The Maoist Education Revolution*. New York, 1974.

Chutkerashvili, E. V. *Razvitie vysshego obrazovaniia v SSSR*. Moscow, 1961.

Cohen, Stephen F. *Bukharin and the Bolshevik Revolution*. New York, 1973.

Conquest, Robert. *The Great Terror*. New York, 1968.

————, ed. *Industrial Workers in the U.S.S.R.* New York, 1967.

Dahrendorf, Ralf. *Class and Class Conflict in Industrial Society*. Stanford, 1959.

Dalrymple, Dana G. "The Famine of 1932-1934." *Soviet Studies*, January 1964, pp. 256-284.

Daniels, Robert Vincent. *The Conscience of the Revolution*. New York, Clarion ed., 1969.

Daulbaev, N. *Karagandinskii ugol'nyi bassein*. Alma-Ata, 1970.

Deputaty soveta soiuza i soveta natsional'nosti. Moscow, 1959, 1965.

Dewar, Margaret. *Labor Policy in the U.S.S.R., 1917-1928*. London, 1956.

De Witt, Nicholas. *Education and Professional Employment in the USSR*. Washington, 1961.

———. *Soviet Professional Manpower*. Washington, 1955.

Dodge, Norton D. *Women in the Soviet Economy*. Baltimore, 1966.

Drobizhev, V. Z. "Rol' rabochego klassa SSSR v formirovanii komandnykh kadrov sotsialisticheskoi promyshlennosti (1917-1936 gg.)." *Istoriia SSSR*, No. 4, 1961.

———. "Sovershenstvovanie upravleniia promyshlennosti v gody pervoi piatletki." *Voprosy istorii*, No. 6, 1966, pp. 9-23.

——— and N. Dumoiva. *V.Ya Chubar*. Moscow, 1963.

Dubinski-Mukhadze, I. M. *Ordzhonikidze*. Moscow, 1963.

Duz', P. D. *Istoriia vozdukhoplavaniia i aviatsii v SSSR*. 2 vols. Moscow, 1944, 1960.

Dyck, Harvey. *Weimar Germany & Soviet Russia*. London, 1966.

Erikson, John. "Radio-Location and the Air Defense Problem: The Design and Development of Soviet Radar, 1934-40." *Science Studies* 2 (1972), 241-268.

Erlich, Alexander. *The Soviet Industrialization Debate (1924-1928)*. Cambridge, Mass., 1960.

Erman, L. K. *Intelligentsiia v pervoi russkoi revoliutsii*. Moscow, 1966.

Fainsod, Merle. *Smolensk Under Soviet Rule*. New York, Vintage ed., 1963.

Fazin, Zinovii I. *Tovarishch Sergo*. Moscow, 1970.

Fediukin, S. A. *Privlechenie burzhuaznoi tekhnicheskoi intelligentsii k sotialisticheskomu stroitel'stvu v SSSR*. Moscow, 1960.

———. *Sovetskaia vlast' i burzhuaznye spetsialisty*. Moscow, 1965.

———. *Velikii oktiabr' i intelligentsiia*. Moscow, 1972.

Fischer, George. *The Soviet System and Modern Society*. New York, 1968.

Fitzpatrick, Sheila. *The Commissariat of Englightenment*. Cambridge, Mass., 1970.

———. "Cultural Revolution in Russia 1928-1932." *Journal of Contempoary History*, January 1974, 33-52.

Flakserman, Iu. N. *Gleb Maksimilianovich Krzhizhanovskii*. Moscow, 1964.

Gehlen, Michael P. and Michael McBride. "The Soviet Central Committee." *American Political Science Review*. December 1968.

Genkina, E. B. "Deiatel'nost Gosplana v 1921-1925 gg. i bor'ba s burzhuaznoi ideologiei po voprosam planirovaniia." *Istoriia SSSR*, No. 6, 1961.

Glavatskii, M. E. "Sovetskaia istoricheskaia literature o formirovanii proizvodstvenno-tekhnicheskoi intelligentsii (1956-1964)." *Kul'turnaia revoliutsiia v SSSR. 1917-1965*.

Golinkov, D. L. *Krushenie antisovetskogo podpol'ia v SSSR*. Moscow, 1975.

Golovanov, Yaroslav. *Sergei Korolev, The Apprenticeship of a Space Pioneer*. Moscow, 1975.

Granick, David. *Management of the Industrial Firm in the U.S.S.R.* New York, 1954.

———. *The Red Executive*. Garden City, 1960.

Grazhdanskaia aviatsiia SSSR 1917-1967. Moscow, 1967.

Grigoriants, A. K. *Formirovanie i razvitie tekhnicheskoi intelligentsii Armenii (1920-1965)*. Erevan, 1966.

Gumilevskii, L. I. *Russkie inzhenery*. Moscow, 1953.

Gvishiani, D. M., ed. *Nauchno-tekhnicheskaia revoliutsiia i izmenenie struktury nauchnykh kadrov SSSR*. Moscow, 1973.

Hans, Nicholas. *History of Russian Educational Policy (1701-1917)*. London, 1931.

Abram F. Ioffe 1880-1960. Moscow, 1960.

Istoriia energeticheskoi tekhniki SSSR. Vol. 1. *Teplotekhnika*. Moscow, 1957.

Jewkes, John et al. *The Sources of Invention*. New York, 1969.

Joravsky, David. *The Lysenko Affair*. Cambridge, Mass., 1970.

Khavin, A. F. "Kapitany sovetskoi industrii 1926-1940 godu." *Voprosy Istorii*, No. 5, 1966, pp. 3-14.

———. "Razvitie tiazheloi promyshlennosti v tret'ei piatiletke 1938-iun' 1941 gg." *Istoriia SSSR*, No. 1, 1959, pp. 10-35.

———. *U rulia industrii*. Moscow, 1968.

Kirillov, V. S. and A. Ya. Sverdlov. *Grigorii Konstantinovich Ordzhonikidze (Sergo). Biografiia*. Moscow, 1962.

Konchalovsky, D. P. "Sovetskie vuzy i studenchestvo." *Novyi zhurnal*, No. 90.

Korol, A. G. *Soviet Education for Science and Technology*. Cambridge, Mass., 1957.

Kostiuk, Hryhory. *Stalinist Rule in the Ukraine*. New York, 1960.

Kozlov, V. V. *Ocherki istorii khimicheskikh obshchestv SSSR*. Moscow, 1968.

Krasnikov, S. *S. M. Kirov v Leningrade*. Leningrad, 1966.

Krasnikov, S. *Sergei Mironovich Kirov*. Moscow, 1964.

Krupenikovy, I. and L. *Vil'iams*. Moscow, 1951.

G. M. Krzhizhanovskii, Zhizn' in deiatel'nost'. Moscow, 1974 .

Kuibysheva, G. V., O. A. Lezhava, N. V. Nelidov, and A. F. Khavin. *Valerian Vladimirovich Kuibyshev: Biografiia*. Moscow, 1966.

Langrish, J. et al. *Wealth From Knowledge*. London, 1972.

Lapidus, M. *Otkryvatel' podzemnykh tain*. Moscow, 1963.

Leikina-Svirskaia, V. P. *Intelligentsiia v Rossii v vtoroi polovine XIX veka*. Moscow, 1971.

Lel'chuk, V. S. *Sozdanie khimicheskoi promyshlennosti SSSR. Iz istorii sotsialisticheskoi industrializatsii*. Moscow, 1964.

Levit, G. O. *Istoriia energeticheskikh obshchestv SSSR*. Moscow, 1957.

Lewis, Robert A. "Some Aspects of the Research and Development Effort of the Soviet Union, 1924-35." *Science Studies* 2, 1972, 153-179.

Liudy russkoi nauki. Vols. 1-5. Moscow, 1961-1964.

Loewy, A. G. *Die Weltgeschichte ist das Weltgericht: Bucharin: Vision des Kommunismus*. Vienna, 1969.

Lutchenko, A. I. "Rukovodstvo KPSS formirovaniem kadrov tekhnicheskoi intelligentsii (1926-1933 gg.)." *Voprosy istorii KPSS*, No. 2, 1966.

Lyashnikov, I. *Podgotovka spetsialistov promyshlennosti SSSR*. Moscow, 1954.

McClelland, James C. "Bolshevik Approaches to Higher Education." *Slavic Review*, December 1971, 818-831.

McKay, John P. *Pioneers for Profit: Foreign Entrepreneurship and Russian Industrialization 1885-1913*. Chicago, 1970.

Matiiko, Mykola. *Evgen Oskarovich Paton*. Kyiv, 1961.

Medvedev, Roy A. *Let History Judge: The Origins and Consequences of Stalinism*. New York, 1971.

Medvedev, Zhores. *The Medvedev Papers*. London, 1972.

Melchin, Anatolii I. *Stanislav Kosior*. Moscow, 1964.

Mezentsev, V. *Bardin*. Moscow, 1970.

Morozov, L. F. and V. P. Portnov. *Organy partiino-gosudarstvennogo kontrolia (1923-1934)*. Moscow, 1964.

Morozov, L. F. *Reshaiushchii etap bor'by s nepmanskoi burzhuaziei (Iz istorii likvidatsii kapitalisticheskikh elementov goroda 1926-1929 gg.)*. Moscow, 1960.

Nesteruk, F. Ya. *Razvitie gidro-energetiki SSSR*. Moscow, 1963.

Novgorotsev, Paul J. *Russian Schools and Universities in the World War*. New Haven, 1929.

Novikov, M. V. "V nebe Khalkin-Gola." *Voprosy istorii*, No. 3, 1974, 201-204.

Ocherki istorii tekhniki v Rossii 1861-1917. Moscow, 1973.

Ocherki po istorii lesnykh obshchestv dorevoliutsionnoi Rossii. Moscow, 1962.

Ozerov, L. S. "Iz opyta raboty partii po organizatsii zavodov-vtuzov." *Voprosy istorii KPSS*, No. 6, 1961.

Peterburgskii, A. V. *D. N. Prianishnikov i ego shkola*. Moscow, 1962.

Piotrovskii, Konstantin B. *Sergei Lebedev*. Moscow, 1960.

Pisarzhevskii, O. *Prianishnikov*. Moscow, 1963.

——. *Stranitsy zhizni bol'shevika-uchenogo*. Moscow, 1960.

Pohrebinskii, M. *S. V. Kosior*. [In Ukrainian.] Kyiv, 1963.

Poliakova, E. I. "N. P. Gorbunov." *Istoriia SSSR*, No. 5, 1968.

Prokof'ev, V. I. *Moskovskoe vysshee tekhnicheskoe uchilishche*. Moscow, 1955.

Prominent Personalities in the USSR. Metuchen, N.J., 1968.

Puti razvitiia tekhniki v SSSR. Moscow, 1967.

Rozentretter, V. A. *A. M. Terpigorev*. Moscow, 1965.

Sakharov, Andrei. *Progress, Coexistence and Intellectual Freedom*. New York, 1968.

Schmookler, Jacob. *Invention and Economic Growth*. Cambridge, Mass., 1966.

Seniavskii, S. L. *Izmeneniia v sotsial'noi strukture sovetskogo obshchestva 1938-1970*. Moscow, 1973.

Sergienko, S. P. *Akademik S. V. Lebedev*. Moscow, 1959.

Sharapov, N. P. "Ob uchastii inostrannykh rabochikh i spetsialistov v sotialisticheskom stroitel'stve na Urale (1930-1934 gg.)." *Voprosy istorii KPSS*, No. 3, 1966.

Shavrov, V. B. *Istoriia konstruktsii samoletov v SSSR*.

Shendrik, L. K. *Podgotovka khoziastvennykh i inzhenerno-tekhnicheskikh kadrov iz rabochikh v 1918-1932 gg. Sbornik statei*. Moscow, 1958.

Sinetskii, A. *Professorsko-prepodavatel'skie kadry vysshei shkoly SSSR*. Moscow, 1950.

Smolinski, Leon. "Grinivetskii and Soviet Industrialization." *Survey*, April 1968.

Solomon, Peter. "Technological Innovation and Soviet Industrialization." In Mark Field, ed. *The Social Consequences of Modernization in Socialist Countries*. Baltimore, 1976.

Solzhenitsyn, Alexander. *The Gulag Archipelago*. Vol. 1. New York, paperback, 1973.

——. *The Gulag Archipelago*. Vol. 2. New York, paperback, 1974.

Sominskii, Monus S. *Abram Fedorovich Ioffe*. Moscow, 1964.

SSSR i zarubezhnye strany. Moscow, 1970.

Suttemeier, Richard P. *Research and Revolution*. Lexington, Mass., 1974.

Sutton, Antony C. *Western Technology and Soviet Economic Development, 1917 to 1930*. Stanford, 1968.

——. *Western Technology and Soviet Economic Development 1930-1945*. Stanford, 1971.

Tekhnika gornogo dela i metallurgii. Moscow, 1968.

Timoshenko, Stephen P. "The Development of Engineering Education in Russia." *Russian Review*, July 1956.

Trukans, German. *Ian Rudzutak.* Moscow, 1963.

Ul'yanova, A. D. *Evgen O. Paton 1870-1953.* Kyiv, 1965.

Ulianovskaia, V. A. *Formirovanie nauchnoi intelligentsii v SSSR, 1917-1937 gg.* Moscow, 1966.

Vernadskii, George V. "Bratstvo 'Priutino.' " *Novyi zhurnal*, Kniga 97, New York, 1969, pp. 228-231.

Vucinich, Alexander. *Science in Russian Culture.* Vol. 2. Stanford, 1973.

Vysshee obrazovanie v SSSR. Moscow, 1961.

Wickenden, William E. *A Comparative Study of Engineering Education in the United States and in Europe.* Bulletin No. 16. Society for the Promotion of Engineering Education. New York, 1929.

Yakovlev, A. S. *50 let sovetskogo samoletostroeniia.* Moscow, 1968.

Yesakov, V. D. *Sovetskaia nauka v gody pervoi piatiletki.* Moscow, 1971.

Zak, L. M. "Sozdanie i deiatel'nost' 'VARNITSO' v 1927-1932 gg." *Istoriia SSSR*, No. 6, 1958.

―――. " 'VARNITSO' v gody vtoroi piatiletki." *Trudy Moskovskogo gosudarstvennogo istoriko-arkhivnogo instituta*, Vol. 14, 1960.

INDEX*

Academy of Sciences, USSR, 24, 25, 40, 41, 49, 53, 56, 102, 234, 359, 369, 372, 377, 388, 398, 423
Administration for Northern Sea Routes, 388
Agranov, 282
Alksnis, Jan, 394, 395, 397, 401
All Russian Association of Engineers (VAI), 59, 63, 102, 103, 104, 105, 106, 110, 113, 120, 422
All-Russian Union of Engineers (VSI), 19, 20, 21, 22, 23, 24, 42, 45, 46, 58
All-Union Electro-technical Institute, 361, 362
All-Union Institute of Plant Growth, 365
All-Union Textile Syndicate, 96
anarchists, 24, 47
Anti-Bolshevik, 20, 45, 47, 48
anti-intellectualism, 24, 52, 73, 176
anti-semitism, 314
applied research and development, 56
Armenian Communist party, 135
Armenians, 203, 205, 206, 208, 210, 213, 414
Army Air Force, 399
artillery specialists, 40
auditors, 194, 195
Aviation Day, 384, 393, 394, 405
Avtorkhanov, Abdurakhnan, 74, 75, 77
Azeri, 203, 205

Baidukov, 391, 394
Bakh, A. N., 139
Bardin, I. P., 369
Bashkin, 93
Bastrakova, M. S., 40
Bauman, Karl, 351
Bauman Institute, 235
Beliakov, 394
Bender, Ostap, 364
Beria, L. P., 331, 355
Bertosh, G., 394, 395
Birman, S. P., 123, 124, 125, 126, 286, 287
Bogdanov, A. A., 116
Bogdanov, P. A.., 23

Bolshevik Revolution, 25, 37, 48, 105, 127, 406, 409, 422, 424, 425
Bolsheviks, 20, 21, 23, 24, 25, 29, 36, 44, 45, 46, 47, 48, 49, 53, 54, 55, 56, 59, 63, 73, 88, 91, 101, 102, 103, 110, 127, 148, 152, 160, 185, 225, 228, 257, 272, 274, 281, 344, 359, 383, 415, 423, 424. *See also* Communist party
"bourgeois nationalism," 241
"bourgeois specialists," 50, 51, 86, 88, 98, 104, 113, 119, 155
Brest-Litovsk treaty, 376
Brezhnev, Leonid, 6
brizy (rationalization bureaus), 348, 349
Bubnov, Aleksandr, 72
Bukharin, N. I., 73, 82, 83, 84, 106, 109, 110, 114, 115, 141, 142, 149, 154, 161, 163, 171, 175, 181, 197, 234, 271, 277, 280, 316, 343, 384
Bukharin-Rykov opposition, 271
Bureau of Mines, 25
Byzov, B. V., 376

Campbell, Robert, 374
capitalism, 52, 54, 155
capitalists, 54, 91, 119, 125
Carr, E. H., and Davies, R. W., *Foundations of a Planned Economy*, 5
Carroll, Lewis, 69
Caucasians, 203, 212, 214
Central Aviation Institute (TsAGI), 56, 346, 372, 385, 398, 403
Central Council of Trade Unions, 135
Central Executive Committee, 203
centralization, 217, 218, 226, 260
Central Labor Institute, 50
Central Trade Unions' Council, 59, 79, 173
Central War Industry Committee, 49
"Change of Landmarks" movement (*smenovekhodstvo*), 72, 73
Chaplygin, S. A., 385
charlatanism, 366
charlatans, 365, 366

* My thanks to Jeannine Vance for compiling this index.

459

STUDIES OF THE RUSSIAN INSTITUTE

ABRAM BERGSON, *Soviet National Income in 1937* (1953).

ERNEST J. SIMMONS, JR., ed., *Through the Glass of Soviet Literature: Views of Russian Society* (1953).

THAD PAUL ALTON, *Polish Postwar Economy* (1954).

DAVID GRANICK, *Management of the Industrial Firm in the USSR: A Study in Soviet Economic Planning* (1954).

ALLEN S. WHITING, *Soviet Policies in China, 1917-1924* (1954).

GEORGE S. N. LUCKYJ, *Literary Politics in the Soviet Ukraine, 1917-1934* (1956).

MICHAEL BORO PETROVICH, *The Emergence of Russian Panslavism, 1856-1870* (1956).

THOMAS TAYLOR HAMMOND, *Lenin on Trade Unions and Revolution, 1893-1917* (1956).

DAVID MARSHALL LANG, *The Last Years of the Georgian Monarchy, 1658-1832* (1957).

JAMES WILLIAM MORLEY, *The Japanese Thrust into Siberia, 1918* (1957).

ALEXANDER G. PARK, *Bolshevism in Turkestan, 1917-1927* (1957).

HERBERT MARCUSE, *Soviet Marxism: A Critical Analysis* (1958).

CHARLES B. MCLANE, *Soviet Policy and the Chinese Communists, 1931-1946* (1958).

OLIVER H. RADKEY, *The Agrarian Foes of Bolshevism: Promise and Defeat of the Russian Socialist Revolutionaries, February to October, 1917* (1958).

RALPH TALCOTT FISHER, JR., *Pattern for Soviet Youth: A Study of the Congresses of the Komsomol, 1918-1954* (1959).

ALFRED ERICH SENN, *The Emergence of Modern Lithuania* (1959).

ELLIOT R. GOODMAN, *The Soviet Design for a World State* (1960).

JOHN N. HAZARD, *Settling Disputes in Soviet Society: The Formative Years of Legal Institutions* (1960).

DAVID JORAVSKY, *Soviet Marxism and Natural Science, 1917-1932* (1961).

MAURICE FRIEDBERG, *Russian Classics in Soviet Jackets* (1962).

ALFRED J. RIEBER, *Stalin and the French Communist Party, 1941-1947* (1962).

THEODORE K. VON LAUE, *Sergei Witte and the Industrialization of Russia* (1962).

JOHN A. ARMSTRONG, *Ukrainian Nationalism* (1963).

OLIVER H. RADKEY, *The Sickle under the Hammer: The Russian Socialist Revolutionaries in the Early Months of Soviet Rule* (1963).

KERMIT E. MCKENZIE, *Comintern and World Revolution, 1928-1943: The Shaping of Doctrine* (1964).

HARVEY L. DYCK, *Weimar Germany and Soviet Russia, 1926-1933: A Study in Diplomatic Instability* (1966).

(Above titles published by Columbia University Press.)

HAROLD J. NOAH, *Financing Soviet Schools* (Teachers College, 1966).

JOHN M. THOMPSON, *Russia, Bolshevism, and the Versailles Peace* (Princeton, 1966).

PAUL AVRICH, *The Russian Anarchists* (Princeton, 1967).

LOREN R. GRAHAM, *The Soviet Academy of Sciences and the Communist Party, 1927-1932* (Princeton, 1967).

ROBERT A. MAGUIRE, *Red Virgin Soil: Soviet Literature in the 1920's* (Princeton, 1968).

T. H. RIGBY, *Communist Party Membership in the U.S.S.R., 1917-1967* (Princeton, 1968).

RICHARD T. DE GEORGE, *Soviet Ethics and Morality* (University of Michigan, 1969).

JONATHAN FRANKEL, *Vladimir Akimov on the Dilemmas of Russian Marxism, 1895-1903* (Cambridge, 1969).

WILLIAM ZIMMERMAN, *Soviet Perspectives on International Relations, 1956-1967* (Princeton, 1969).

PAUL AVRICH, *Kronstadt, 1921* (Princeton, 1970).

EZRA MENDELSOHN, *Class Struggle in the Pale: The Formative Years of the Jewish Workers' Movement in Tsarist Russia* (Cambridge, 1970).

EDWARD J. BROWN, *The Proletarian Episode in Russian Literature* (Columbia, 1971).

PATRICIA K. GRIMSTED, *Archives and Manuscript Repositories in the USSR: Moscow and Leningrad* (Princeton, 1972).

RONALD G. SUNY, *The Baku Commune, 1917-1918* (Princeton, 1972).

EDWARD J. BROWN, *Mayakovsky: A Poet in the Revolution* (Princeton, 1973).

MILTON EHRE, *Oblomov and his Creator: The Life and Art of Ivan Goncharov* (Princeton, 1973).

HENRY KRISCH, *German Politics under Soviet Occupation* (Columbia, 1974).

HENRY W. MORTON and RUDOLF L. TÖKÉS, eds., *Soviet Politics and Society in the 1970's* (Free Press, 1974).

WILLIAM G. ROSENBERG, *Liberals in the Russian Revolution* (Princeton, 1974).

RICHARD G. ROBBINS, JR., *Famine in Russia, 1891-1892* (Columbia, 1975).

VERA DUNHAM, *In Stalin's Time: Middleclass Values in Soviet Fiction* (Cambridge, 1976).

WALTER SABLINSKY, *The Road to Bloody Sunday* (Princeton, 1976).

WILLIAM MILLS TODD III, *The Familiar Letter as a Literary Genre in the Age of Pushkin* (Princeton, 1976).

ELIZABETH VALKENIER, *Russian Realist Art. The State and Society: The Peredvizhniki and Their Tradition* (Ardis, 1977).

SUSAN SOLOMON, *The Soviet Agrarian Debate* (Westview, 1978).

SHEILA FITZPATRICK, ed., *Cultural Revolution in Russia, 1928-1931* (Indiana, 1978).

PETER SOLOMON, *Soviet Criminologists and Criminal Policy: Specialists in Policy-Making* (Columbia, 1978).

LIBRARY OF CONGRESS CATALOGING
IN PUBLICATION DATA

Bailes, Kendall E.
    Technology and society under Lenin and Stalin.

    (Studies of the Russian Institute, Columbia University)
    Bibliography: p.
    Includes index.
    1. Technology—Social aspects—Russia.   2. Tech-
nologists—Russia.   3. Elite (Social sciences)—Russia.
4. Russia—Social conditions—1917-   I. Title.
II. Series: Columbia University. Russian Institute.
Studies.
T26.R9B315   323.3.   78-1451
ISBN 0-691-05265-4
ISBN 0-691-10063-2 pbk.